THE
ESSENTIALS
OF
FINANCIAL
ANALYSIS

D1616061

THE

ESSENTIALS

OF

FINANCIAL

ANALYSIS

SAMUEL C. WEAVER, Ph.D.

New York   Chicago   San Francisco   Lisbon   London
Madrid   Mexico City   Milan   New Delhi   San Juan
Seoul   Singapore   Sydney   Toronto

1 2 3 4 5 6 7 8 9 0 DOC/DOC 1 6 5 4 3 2 1

ISBN   978-0-07-176836-8
MHID   0-07-176836-X

e-ISBN   978-0-07-176837-5
e-MHID   0-07-176837-8

This publication is designed to provide accurate and authoritative information in regard to the subject matter covered. It is sold with the understanding that neither the author nor the publisher is engaged in rendering legal, accounting, or other professional service. If legal advice or other expert assistance is required, the services of a competent professional person should be sought.

> —*From a declaration of principles jointly adopted by a Committee of the American Bar Association and a Committee of Publishers.*

McGraw-Hill products are available at special quantity discounts to use as premiums and sales promotions or for use in corporate training programs. To contact a representative, please e-mail us at bulksales@mcgraw-hill.com.

This book is printed on acid-free paper.

This is dedicated to the treasure of my life:
Kerry Diane Weaver.

And to our wonderful blessings:
Derek, Andrea, and Trey;
Justin, Jen, Sebastien, and Madeleine; and
Kristine, John, Jenna, and Christian.

CONTENTS

PREFACE

This text is the outgrowth of a never-ending passion for my chosen vocation, corporate finance. Finance is a discipline that moves business domestically and internationally. The material in this text is essential for anyone who is already or wants to be involved in business, no matter what your professional training or functional area. We all need to know how to use finance to communicate. We all need to know how to structure financial analysis to make the best business decisions. It is as important to the entrepreneur as it is to a department head and to the chief executive officer of a Fortune 500 company. However, the implications of finance do not stop "at the end of the day." Many of the financial principles are directly applicable to personal life as well.

This text embodies academic training through a Ph.D. level, a 20-year career of hands-on applications, and 25 years of teaching MBA and undergraduate students as well as executives in numerous professional training programs. Many of my former students now lead successful organizations. As a result of conducting extensive executive education workshops, I bring to this work a focused professional tone that is augmented with years of real-world experience and consulting applications. Finally, personal research and consulting ensures a book that is true to the latest theoretical and applied research with relevant and timely examples.

I thank my colleagues at the Perella Department of Finance, College of Business and Economics, Lehigh University, for direct and indirect contributions to this text. I also thank the students in my graduate and undergraduate classes and participants at my professional workshops for their input into this text.

A big thank you goes to Mary Glenn, Associate Publisher, and Morgan Ertel, Associate Editor, McGraw-Hill Professional, and their wonderful team including Devanand Madhukar, Director, Paradigm Data Services (P) Ltd.

Despite diligent efforts, there will always be opportunities to improve this book. I accept responsibility for any errors and welcome any suggestions from readers.

I truly hope that *The Essentials of Financial Analysis* will help you as you navigate the many financial challenges and opportunities you face in today's business world. I know that throughout this book there are helpful and useful approaches to addressing those opportunities. I also wish you success as you adapt and apply these concepts throughout your career.

Samuel C. Weaver

PART ONE

ACCOUNTING AND FINANCE FUNDAMENTALS

THE ROLE AND FUNCTIONS OF ACCOUNTING AND FINANCE

Corporate finance is a middle ground between economics and accounting. Corporate finance is based on theoretical economic concepts applied to the "hard" numbers developed by accountants. Finance uses accounting information to analyze economic events. In a phrase, finance is applied economics. While accounting is the language of business, finance is its literature. Financial analysis provides a systematic approach to making business decisions.

Finance is not an end in and of itself. It is a tool used to monitor, evaluate, and communicate the results of business decisions. Finance is a tool used to assess past events as well as anticipate the consequences of future decisions. It is a tool that is well suited for the board room and the production-shop floor, the executive suite and the distribution center, and corporate and divisional staff offices to a distant sales office. Improving financial performance is the responsibility of every member of the organization, either directly or indirectly.

FINANCE IS EVERYONE'S JOB

In order to take on a general management role or become the head of a business unit or functional unit, every manager must have a working knowledge of finance. He or she must be adaptive in improving day-to-day operations and enhancing the value of the organization. Managers must know how to make strategic investment decisions as well as operational decisions that use the many tools introduced and illustrated in this book.

Large corporations have specific staff to handle financial analysis and to help managers make business decisions. In many organizations, diverse cross-functional project teams are formed to tackle specific assignments. These teams may include members from operations such as sales, marketing, production, and logistics and staff areas such as human resources, engineering, research and development, and legal. These teams often will include a finance professional to help lead and guide the group's efforts toward financially sound decisions. It is important for each functional area to better understand the role of finance and for finance to understand the role of the other functional areas as well as the company's business model, its supply chain, and its strategic direction.

In smaller organizations, it is even more important for functional areas to understand finance and financial implications because often there is no dedicated financial analysis staff to assume responsibility.

Both the nonfinancial professional and the financial professional must be able to understand and clearly communicate financial results and objectives. In a way, all managers are financial managers because everyone has an impact on the bottom line and affects the value of the organization. Whatever your position, you need to know about the following necessary topics to be a more effective member of any business team:

- Reading, understanding, and using financial statements
- Analyzing financial statements to determine the financial health of a company and its competitors, suppliers, and customers
- Managing the supply chain
- Planning the financial direction in support of the organization's mission, goals, and objectives
- Investing in the business through new products, new facilities, and cost-saving equipment
- Financing business growth through various techniques
- Determining the intrinsic value of the organization and how to enhance that value
- Growing the business via acquisitions

Many members of an organization have bonuses and other compensation tied to achieving certain specific financial goals as well as the organization's common financial objectives. It is important to understand the drivers for attaining those goals as well as the other areas that are affected.

For example, sales and marketing often share an objective centered on top-line (sales) growth. This objective can be achieved easily with price reductions, advertising, or promotions (such as a buy-one-get-one-free offer) and so on. Of course, all those "solutions" have income and cash-flow effects that may have a negative impact on the financial health of the organization. By extending the objectives for the sales and marketing group to include sales and income targets, the situation is partially resolved. However, sales and marketing will quickly learn about extended dating on accounts receivables. That is, instead of 30 days for a customer to pay its bills, customers are given 60 or more days to pay. While there are only minimal indirect income statement effects (i.e., additional interest expense or lost interest income), the balance-sheet implications and additional investment in working capital add pressure to financing availability and even may result in less business reinvestment in other areas.

Engineering, production, logistics, and research may want to manufacture products using the latest equipment with the fastest capabilities in a world class manufacturing facility. However, the financial implications must be understood.

That is, does this investment provide an adequate rate of return? What are other business ramifications? Financing limitations may be imposed, balance sheets may be weakened, and business risk may increase substantially. Perhaps a less expensive alternative would provide maximum shareholder value without having a discernible impact on the quality of the product. Capital investment analysis determines the value-enhancement attributes of any capital project, whereas financial strategic planning anticipates the financial impact and assists in ranking alternative approaches.

Business is a series of managed conflicts. Marketing and sales want to sell an infinite variety of products, whereas production would like to produce one product. The conflicts can be resolved through financial information and its valuation impact. It is the systematic and common approach that leads to resolving these tensions successfully. Finance provides a common focus on goal attainment and value enhancement.

Real-world examples and discussions about familiar business topics provide comforting links to finance and business. For example, some engineers and other professionals are familiar with capital budgeting from the technical (or equipment) side but do not understand the financial aspects of the process. Through this book, that gap will be closed, and the professional will appreciate the financial rationale for capital investment analysis.

FINANCE IN THE ORGANIZATIONAL STRUCTURE OF THE FIRM

The nature of finance activities can be explained within the framework of where finance fits in the organizational structure of the firm.

An Overview

Figure 1-1 provides a picture of a general organization structure. The *board of directors* represents the shareholders. The *chairperson of the board* therefore has major responsibilities on behalf of the shareholders. The *chief executive officer* (CEO) is the highest-ranking company employee. The CEO is involved with the strategic direction of the organization. As shown in Figure 1-1, some corporations have a *chief operating officer* (COO). The COO is responsible for the day-to-day operations because the divisions and their presidents report directly to the COO.

One of the top executives is the *vice president of finance* or *chief financial officer* (CFO), who is responsible for the formulation and implementation of major financial policies. The title maybe enhanced by the title of *senior* or *executive vice president*. The CFO interacts with other members of the senior management team, operating managers and professionals, external analysts, and

FIGURE   1-1

Typical corporate organization chart.

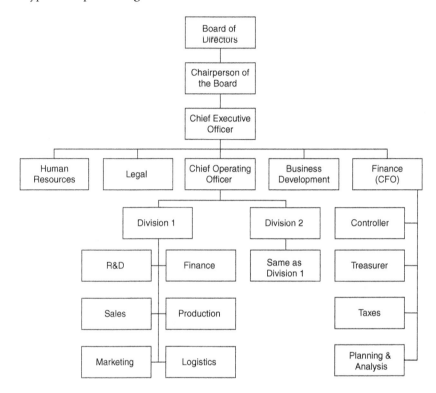

a large number of other external constituencies. The CFO communicates the financial results and future implications of alternative policies and decisions.

All important episodes in the life of a corporation have major financial implications: adding a new product line or dropping an old one, expanding or adding a plant, broadening the geographic sales of a product, selling additional new securities, entering into leasing arrangements, and paying dividends and making share repurchases. These decisions have a lasting effect on long-run profitability and therefore require top-management consideration. Hence the finance function typically is close to the top in the organizational structure of the firm.

Most of the finance functions are performed by the controller and the treasurer. Other functions, such as the tax department and financial planning and analysis, also, may report to the CFO. In some cases, internal audit also may report directly to the CFO, board, chairperson, or CEO.

The *controller's* function includes accounting, reporting, and control. The controller's core function is the recording and reporting of financial information. This typically includes the preparation of financial statements and budgets. In fact, the controller is often referred to as the *chief accounting officer* (CAO) of the firm. As depicted in the organizational chart (Figure 1-1), the corporate controller's office serves more of a consolidating role, where each division's financials are combined and consolidated with corporate items and then reported to the public.

Figure 1-1 also shows that each division has its own *vice president of finance*, who reports directly to the president of that division with "dotted" lines to the CFO. The division vice president is responsible for day-to-day transactions processing as well as advising the division's sales, marketing, production, and logistics functions.

In "flatter" organizations without a divisional structure, the corporate controller also may be responsible for operational accounting functions such as accounts receivable, accounts payable, and payroll. This also may be the case if a divisionally structured organization considers such operational accounting functions as part of "shared services" for the entire organization.

The *treasurer* reports on the daily cash and working-capital position of the firm, formulates cash budgets, and generally reports on cash flows and cash conservation. The treasurer handles the acquisition and custody of funds. As a part of this role, the treasurer usually maintains the firm's relationships with commercial banks and investment bankers. The treasurer is also usually responsible for credit management, insurance, and pension-fund management.

Some large firms include another corporate officer—the *corporate secretary* —whose activities are related to the finance function. The corporate secretary is responsible for record keeping in connection with the instruments of ownership and borrowing activities of the firm (e.g., stocks and bonds). The corporate secretary may have a legal training because the duties of that officer also may encompass legal affairs and recording the minutes of top-level committee meetings.

In addition to individual financial officers, larger enterprises use *finance committees*. Ideally, a committee assembles persons of different backgrounds and abilities to formulate policies and decisions. Financing decisions require a wide scope of knowledge and balanced judgments. For example, to obtain outside funds is a major decision. A difference of 0.25 or 0.50 percent in interest rates may represent a large amount of money in absolute terms. When a firm borrows $600 million, an interest-rate difference of 0.50 percent amounts to $3 million per year. Therefore, the judgments of senior managers with finance backgrounds are valuable in arriving at decisions with bankers on the timing and terms of a loan. Also, the finance committee, working closely with the board of directors, characteristically has major responsibility for administering the capital and operating budgets.

In larger firms, in addition to the general finance committee, there may be subcommittees. A *capital appropriations committee* is responsible primarily for capital budgeting and expenditures. A *budget committee* develops and approves operating budgets, both short and long term. A *pension committee* invests the funds involved in employee pension plans. A *salary and profit-sharing committee* is responsible for salary administration as well as the classification and compensation of top-level executives. This committee seeks to set up a system of rewards and penalties that will provide the proper incentives to make the planning and control system of the firm work effectively.

RESPONSIBILITIES OF FINANCIAL MANAGERS

The number one responsibility of financial managers is to interact with all other parts of the organization to help improve operating performance in all areas of the company. By interacting with all activities in a team effort, as well as understanding the firm's strategies, financial officers develop the skills of overall business leadership. Therefore, the number one responsibility of financial managers is to bring their expertise to strategic and operating decisions.

Partnership with Operations

Through continued interaction with all managers, financial managers increase their understanding of operating requirements, manufacturing capabilities, and marketing challenges. Through this understanding, financial managers can look for opportunities to streamline their organization's operations. They also can lend analytical support to these other areas to determine the financial implications of new policy choices before they are recommended. For example, what are the financial implications of a buy-one-get-one-free product promotion? Should we hedge a commodity purchase? Should we extend credits terms from 30 to 45 days? The financial professional must be knowledgeable and available to council operating managers on a day-to-day basis.

Investment Decisions

The first function of financial managers, therefore, is to bring their expertise to all the decision areas of the firm. A second important function is to take major responsibility for capital budgeting decisions. A successful firm is usually a growing firm, which requires the support of increased investments. Financial managers participate in establishing sales growth goals and evaluating alternative investments to support such growth. Finance helps to decide on the specific investments to be made and the alternative sources and forms of funds for financing those investments. Decision variables include internal versus external funds, debt versus owners' funds, and long-term versus short-term financing.

Financing Sources, Forms, and Methods

The financial manager links the firm to the money and capital markets in which funds are raised and in which the firm's securities are sold and traded. Financing changes throughout the firm's life cycle. At the earliest stages, funds come from owners and their relatives and friends. As the firm grows, it may receive funds from "angels." *Angels* are wealthy individuals with experience in the industry related to the new firm. They invest seed money and also help the founder to test and refine his or her business model, recommend experienced managers, and develop business operations. As the firm grows, *venture capitalists* also may provide additional funds.

As a startup firm develops a track record, it may be able to go public by issuing securities in financial markets. Investment banking firms may contract to bring out an initial public offering (IPO). Once a firm has gone public, a wide array of debt and equity forms becomes available.

Business Ethics

Financial executives contribute to a firm's ethical reputation. Business ethics is the conduct and behavior of a firm's management toward its stockholders, employees, customers, the community, and all stakeholders. Business ethics is measured by a firm's behavior in all aspects of its dealings with others.

The case for ethical behavior is based on widely accepted codes of conduct. Without integrity, a person cannot be healthy psychologically. If people cannot be trusted, the social system cannot function effectively. In addition, though, a reputation for ethical behavior and fairness to all stakeholders is a source of considerable organizational value. A reputation for integrity enables a firm to attract employees who believe in and behave according to ethical principles. Customers will respond favorably to business firms that treat them honestly. Such behavior contributes to the health of the community where the firm operates.

Firms should have codes of ethical behavior in writing and conduct training programs to make clear to employees the standards that the firms seek to achieve. Johnson & Johnson is a shining example of an organization that lives by its very public moral compass, its *credo*. Hershey captures its values in a code of ethical business conduct. This is an area in which the firm's board of directors and top management must provide leadership. They must demonstrate by their actions as well as by communications their strong commitment to ethical conduct. The company's promotion and compensation systems should reward ethical behavior and punish conduct that impairs the firm's reputation for integrity.

The behavior of top executives of a firm establishes the firm's reputation. If the behavior of the firm is not consistently ethical, other stakeholders—workers, consumers, suppliers, and so on—will begin to question every action and decision of the firm. For example, the bonds and common stock of a firm with a flawed, uncertain reputation will be viewed with suspicion by the market. The securities will be sold at lower prices, which means that the returns to investors will have to be higher to take into account that the issuing firm may be selling a "lemon"—trying to put something over on investors.

Thus a strong case can be made that financial executives and the firm should establish a reputation for unquestioned ethical behavior. The reputation of the firm is a valuable asset.

Extending Ethical Behavior to All Stakeholders

One of the major responsibilities of senior management is to carefully balance the interests of stakeholders. A *stakeholder* is anyone who has any interest in the firm. The following constitute stakeholders:

- Customers
- Consumers

- Suppliers
- Employees
- Unions
- Management
- Government (all levels)
- Local community
- Banks
- Other debt holders
- Stockholders

This list distinguishes Hershey's customers (e.g., Walmart, Kroger, CVS, etc.) from consumers (you and me), identifies worker stakeholders, as well as the broader community, and financial stakeholders (e.g., banks, bondholders, and stockholders).

As I said earlier, business is a careful balance. It is up to senior management to balance opposing views. Raise your prices too high, and sales will fall. Underpay your employees, and talent will leave, and the remaining employees will become uncommitted. Use inferior (and lower-priced) ingredients, and quality, along with sales, profits, and cash flow, will fall.

With a solid ethical reputation and unquestionable ethics, management carefully balances the interests of all stakeholders. In this way, shareholder value will be maximized.

GOALS OF THE FIRM

The number one objective, as discussed below, is to maximize the value of the firm.

Finance and Firm Value

A fundamental question in the study of finance is whether financial executives can increase the value of a firm. Economic and financial theorists begin with models of an idealized world of no taxes, no transactions costs of issuing debt or equity securities, the managers of firms and its outside investors all having the same information about the firm's future cash flows, no costs of financial distress, and no costs of resolving conflicts of interest among different stakeholders of the firm. In such a world, financial decisions do not matter.

The pure, idealized models of finance are useful in that they stress the importance of investment opportunities, current and future, on the value of the firm. In the actual world, however, taxes, bankruptcy costs, transactions costs, and the information content of cash flows and dividend or share-repurchase policies cause financial policies to have an influence on the value of the firm. Also of great importance is the role of finance in developing information flows and appropriate financial analysis so that a firm can evaluate the effectiveness of alternative strategies, policies, decisions, operations, and outcomes. The objective is to create an information flow to provide rapid feedback as a basis for the revision of strategies and decisions to enlarge the growth opportunities of firms and to improve their performance.

Thus there are important ways in which financial executives can contribute to the improved performance of a firm and therefore increase its value. This is the central theme of this book, and I shall return to it repeatedly as I discuss how financial concepts can contribute to increasing the value of a firm and the returns to its stakeholders, as well as to society as a whole.

Value Maximization

Within the preceding framework, the *goal of management is to maximize the value of the firm* (for the benefit of stockholders), subject to the constraints of responsibilities to other stakeholders, consumers, employers, suppliers, communities, and governments. *Value maximization* is broader than *profit maximization*. Maximizing value takes the time value of money into account. First, funds that are received this year have more value than funds that may be received 10 years from now. Second, value maximization considers the riskiness of the income stream. For example, the rate of return required on an investment starting a new business is in the range of 25 to 35 percent but 7 to 10 percent in established firms. Third, the "quality" and timing of expected future cash flows may vary. Profit figures can vary widely depending on the accounting rules and conventions used.

Thus value maximization is broader and more general than profit maximization and is the unifying concept used throughout this book. Value maximization provides criteria for pricing the use of resources such as capital investments in plant and machinery. If limited resources are not allocated by efficiency criteria, production will be inefficient. Value maximization provides a solution to these kinds of problems.

The Risk/Return Tradeoff

Financial decisions affect the level of a firm's stock price by influencing the cash-flow stream and the riskiness of the firm. Risk and return jointly determine the value of the firm.

The firm first must assess the international and national macroeconomic environments. Changing political and cultural factors also must be projected. The primary policy decision is made in choosing the product markets in which the firm operates. Profitability and risk are influenced further by decisions relating to the size of the firm, its growth rate, the types and methods of production and marketing, the extent to which debt is employed, the firm's liquidity position, and dividend and share-repurchase policies. An increase in the cash position reduces risk, but since cash is not an earning asset, converting other assets to cash also reduces profitability. Similarly, the use of additional debt raises the rate of return on the stockholders' equity, but more debt means more risk. The financial manager seeks to strike a balance between risk and profitability that will maximize stockholder wealth. Most financial decisions involve *risk/return tradeoffs.*

ORGANIZATION OF THIS BOOK

The aim of this book is to explain the procedures, practices, and policies used every day in accounting and finance. The emphasis is on financial analysis of business decisions. Ultimately, these decisions will increase the value of the firm.

The central function of finance is to interact with other managers to continuously improve the performance of the organization so that value grows. Finance participates in the evaluation of alternative strategies and policies. It is equally important for the professional to be able to interact with the financial manager by understanding and speaking the same language. The subjects of this book are useful for all professionals, managers, and executives seeking to understand how financial analysis can be applied in day-to-day activities that will improve an organization's performance and enhance shareholder value.

This text provides a clear, practical approach to corporate finance. The book follows a "matter of fact" style when presenting and discussing the material. After the foundation is built, the material is amplified with appropriate considerations and real-world applications.

The book is organized into five major sections:

Part	Topics	Chapters
1	Accounting and finance fundamentals	1, 2, 3, 4
2	Financial planning and control	5, 6
3	Capital analysis and corporate investment decisions	7, 8, 9, 10
4	Long-term financing strategies	11, 12, 13
5	Finance and corporate strategies	14, 15

Concept applications (or end-of-chapter problems) and their solutions are found on this book's Web site, which is: http://www.mhprofessional.com/essentialsoffinancialanalysis.

Financial Calculators and Excel

Financial calculators, such as the Hewlett Packard 10BII+ or the Texas Instruments BAII+, are introduced in chapter 7. These inexpensive tools are very useful for time value of money applications such as capital investment analysis, financing decisions, and valuation. These calculators are discussed and illustrated within the appropriate chapters and facilitate the application of many of the concepts in this book.

Excel (or other spreadsheet software) is also an indispensable tool. As you read about and review a number of financial models presented in this book, it will become clear how essential Excel is for financial analysis. A number of more common Excel functions are covered throughout the book including chapter 14, that details a significant Excel feature known as "Data Tables". This tool is useful for insightful financial and managerial analysis.

THE HERSHEY COMPANY

Presentation of simple models, equations, and concepts can be very dry and boring. Presentations of fictitious companies using contrived situations leave the professional skeptical about how things work in the real world. The illustrations in this book are consistently applied to the actual financial results of The Hershey Company. While Hershey is the primary focus, other companies are also used throughout the discussion.

Hershey is "the leading North American manufacturer of quality chocolate and non-chocolate confectionery and chocolate-related grocery products. The company also is a leader in the gum and mint category" (Hershey Web site: www.hersheys.com). Its sales approached $5.7 billion in 2010, with 85 percent of those sales coming from the United States. Hershey was founded in 1893 by Milton S. Hershey, and its headquarters continue to be located in Hershey, Pennsylvania. The company's Web site proudly discusses Mr. Hershey's legacy and the history of The Hershey Company.

The Hershey Company (NYSE: HSY) will be my illustrative example because Hershey's products are simple to understand. Many of us grew up understanding the company's products very well. The company's supply-chain business model (i.e., sales, marketing, production, and distribution) is straight-forward. The following link demonstrates the production process through a company video: www.hersheys.com/discover/tour_video.asp. This video shows significant capital investments. Hershey's financial record is stellar, with solid profitability and a strong balance sheet. In addition, its Web site (Hersheys.com) provides a wealth of financial information, including annual and quarterly reports, Securities and Exchange Commission (SEC) filings, audio versions of earnings release conference calls, and complete investment analyst presenta-tions. Some investment analyst presentations last approximately three hours. The Web site includes the presentation slides and the audio of the presentation. Finally, Hershey's ethical reputation is unsurpassed for quality and fair treatment of all its stakeholders, which ties in well with the overriding theme of this text. With all this in mind, my applications can focus on the financial aspects rather than explaining a unique business situation.

Hershey's practices, procedures, and issues are common throughout most organizations. You, too, hopefully will identify with an organizational issue discussed in this text.

The food industry provides a valuable background for comparative financial performance with a real-world presentation and feel. Other companies supplement the Hershey and food-industry illustrations where appropriate, such as Apple, Dell, Heinz, Hewlett-Packard, and Walmart. The restaurant chain, P. F. Chang's China Bistro is featured as well. The company's investor relations Web page (www.pfcb.com/) provides unsurpassed detailed information.

SUMMARY

The chapters of this book logically develop the financial concepts necessary for financial analysis. Along the way, there is an analysis and valuation of The Hershey Company (Figure 1-2).

F I G U R E   1-2

Hershey Illustrated Chapters.

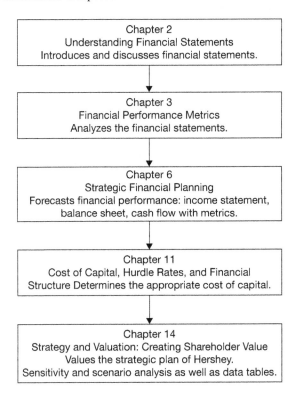

There are numerous specific examples throughout the text. However, these three specific examples capture the distinctive essence of this book:

Financial statement analysis. After reviewing Hershey's financial statements in Chapter 2, Chapter 3 begins with a 2010 food-industry common size, annual growth, and compound annual growth rate analysis which is illustrated using graphs. Hershey is compared with a self-constructed food-processing industry. A single-company 2008 through 2010 analysis follows for Hershey. After that, Hershey and Heinz are compared for 2008 and 2010 using financial performance metrics (or financial ratios). The metrics are presented matter-of-factly and discussed. Ultimately, the DuPont analysis approach to metrics is introduced as a method for systematically beginning any financial statement analysis.

Strategic financial planning. Chapter 6 integrates strategy assessment into financial planning. Based on analysis from Chapter 3, I develop a realistic (albeit hypothetical) strategic financial plan. This approach incorporates projected growth rates, margins, turnovers, capital investment, financing considerations, and so on. The final analysis includes a projected income statement, balance sheet, cash-flow statement, and forecasted financial performance metrics. Sensitivity and scenario analysis completes the evaluation.

Valuation. After discussing capital investment evaluation (Chapters 9 and 10) and the cost of capital (Chapter 11), Chapter 14 revisits the strategic financial plan, focuses on operating cash flows (excluding financing cash flows), estimates a cost of capital and residual value, and values Hershey based on the projections made as part of the plan in Chapter 6. The valuation is supplemented with Excel data-table analysis.

Readers are encouraged to download financial reports from the Hershey or P. F. Chang Web site. In addition, readers also should apply this analysis to other companies in which they are interested, whether they are companies in which readers invest or companies for which readers work (or hope to work). The practical applications of finance should be part of your reading.

UNDERSTANDING FINANCIAL STATEMENTS

Financial statements report the historical performance of a company and provide a basis for assessing the firm's achievements. Along with general national and international economic business conditions and a strategic assessment of the company, financial statements provide a foundation for projecting the firm's future performance. Financial statements in the United States are guided by *Generally Accepted Accounting Principles*, commonly called *U.S. GAAP*. For public corporations, financial statements are publicly disclosed annually through an annual report and a 10K statement (a Securities and Exchange Commission [SEC] requirement) and quarterly through a more concise quarterly report and 10Q statement. In some cases, a company incorporates its annual report directly into its 10K statement and thus reduces the administrative duplication of work and expense of preparing two separate documents.

A firm's management team would not be able to manage the business successfully with only annual or quarterly financial information. Therefore, beyond the external reporting requirements, within firms, financial statements are prepared on a monthly basis to assist management. In some cases, key components of the financial statements (such as product sales and product costs) are available on a daily basis.

The Internal Revenue Service (IRS) and foreign governments (in the case of multinationals) have their own very specific guidelines for reporting financial data. *International Financial Reporting Standards* are an attempt at convergence of the world's individual countries' GAAP or one set of accounting rules throughout the world.

This chapter describes the basic financial statements, develops key accounting concepts that underlie the financial statements, demonstrates the interrelationships among the statements, and provides an overview of essential financial data that are contained in the notes accompanying financial statements. The 2010 financial statements of The Hershey Company will be the primary example throughout this chapter. However, the discussion will be augmented with the 2010 financial statements from other companies.

ROLE OF FINANCIAL STATEMENTS

We walk into a room where a friend is watching a sporting event. Whether its baseball, football, hockey, basketball, or whatever, our first questions usually are "Who's playing?" and "What's the score?" Financial statements provide an important measure of a firm's score. Although the firm is not meeting a competitor in a sporting event at a stadium, the firm is continuously meeting its competition head-on in the marketing arena in a battle for its customers' dollars and in the investing arena in a battle for investors' capital.

The "score" is one measure of a team's performance. The score does not capture all other dimensions of the team's performance, such as the batting averages, number of first downs, shots on goal, and so on. These types of box-score measures present additional attributes for evaluating a team's performance and individual contributions to the team's success. Although assessing the performance of a firm is more complicated because there is no simple "score," financial statements provide the scorecard for judging a company's performance.

This company assessment is extended to evaluating the performance of the management team. Management's compensation is often based on the financial information provided by financial statements. Financial statements also form the foundation on which valuation of the firm is based. The objective for a management team is to *maximize the value of the firm*. By maximizing (or enhancing) the value of the firm, the management team increases its "score."

Valuation is a central theme to this book. Understanding financial statements is one of the key factors for evaluating the performance of a firm. Chapter 3 builds on the principles developed in this chapter.

A complete description of a firm's financial activities during a year consists of three basic financial statements.

1. An *income statement* shows the activities as measured by revenues (or sales) less expenses of the firm throughout the period.

2. A *balance sheet* provides a snapshot of what the firm owns and what the firm owes at a specific moment in time.

3. A *statement of cash flows* presents the underlying transactions that cause the cash balance to change between periods of time.

There is a fourth statement, *consolidated statement of stockholders' equity*, that will be discussed briefly along with the material included in accompanying notes to the financial statements. The management's discussion and analysis (MD&A), the CEO's letter to shareholders, and many other inclusions in an annual report provide valuable supplementary information for assessing a firm.

Figure 2-1 presents an overview of the timing of the primary financial statements. Balance sheets are struck at a moment in time at the end of a specific period, whereas income statements and cash flow statements measure performance throughout a period of time. In this example, two year-end balance sheets are prepared as of December 31, 2009, and December 31, 2010, and are accompanied by quarterly balance sheets prepared at the end of each quarter. The income

FIGURE 2-1

Timing of primary financial statements.

and cash flow statements measure the activities throughout each period by quarter and then for the year 2010.

INCOME STATEMENT

The income statement records revenues and expenses to derive income over a specific period of time.

$$\text{Income} = \text{revenue} - \text{expenses} \qquad (2.1)$$

Table 2-1 presents the Hershey 2008 to 2010 income statements as reported in its 2010 annual report (and the 10K). Some companies refer to this as a *profit and loss (P&L) statement*.

TABLE 2-1

The Hershey Company Consolidated Statements of Income
($ millions, except per-share amounts)

	For the years ended 12/31:		
	2010	**2009**	**2008**
Net sales	$ 5,671.0	$ 5,298.7	$ 5,132.8
Costs and expenses			
Cost of sales	3,255.8	3,245.5	3,375.1
Selling, marketing, and administrative	1,426.5	1,208.7	1,073.0
Business realignment and asset impairment, net	83.4	82.9	94.8
Total costs and expense	4,765.7	4,537.1	4,542.9
Income before interest and income taxes	905.3	761.6	589.9
Interest expense, net	96.4	90.5	97.9
Income before income taxes	808.9	671.1	492.0
Provision for income taxes	299.1	235.1	180.6
Net income	$ 509.8	$ 436.0	$ 311.4
Earnings per share, basic	$ 2.29	$ 1.97	$ 1.41
Earnings per share, diluted	$ 2.21	$ 1.90	$ 1.36

The Hershey Company

The Hershey Company (stock symbol is HSY) is the largest producer of quality chocolate in North America and a global leader in chocolate and sugar confections. It is primarily a domestic company, with less than 10 percent of its sales coming from outside the United States and even a significantly smaller portion from outside North America. Hershey's financial statements are relatively straightforward and will be used throughout this book for illustrative purposes. Selected financial data from other companies will be used when appropriate.

Net Sales

The income statement begins with the revenue or net sales of the firm. In 2010, Hershey had $5,671.0 million in net sales. This represents a tremendous amount of peanut butter cups, kisses, Hershey bars, and so on sold in 2010. The term *net sales* indicates that gross sales have been reduced for returned products, discounts taken for prompt payment of invoices, allowances for damaged products, and trade promotions or price reductions. The 2010 net sales were $372.3 million higher than in 2009, or 7.0 percent higher.

The income statement is silent about what drove the revenue growth: new products, line extensions, expansion into new geographic markets, enhanced distribution channels, price increase, volume increase, foreign currency changes, acquisitions, and so on. Further explanation must be found elsewhere in the annual report, in the MD&A, or in the CEO's letter. The 2010 net sales growth for Hershey was primarily the result of a sales volume increase (4.0 percent) for domestic core business and new products, price increases accounted for over 2.0 percent growth, and exchange-rate changes contributed about 1 percent sales growth.

Expenses

Costs and expenses include at least two lines of distinction: (1) cost of sales (also called *cost of goods sold*) and (2) selling, marketing, and administrative. The cost of sales captures the manufacturing expenses for the products sold. The cost of sales includes raw materials (i.e., cocoa beans, milk, sugar, etc.), direct labor of the people producing the product, and factory overhead. The factory overhead includes direct and indirect overhead expenses such as electricity, property taxes, insurance, maintenance, and depreciation expense for the plant and production equipment. Also included in overhead are the salaries, employee benefits, and employment taxes of production supervisors and general plant management. The depreciation expense item deserves some special attention.

U.S. GAAP accounting is prepared using accrual-based accounting, which is in sharp contrast to cash-based accounting. This is what drives the distinction between the income statement and statement of cash flow. Let's say that three years ago a piece of manufacturing equipment was purchased for $10,000 with an expected life of 10 years. A cash-based system would recognize the $10,000 purchase as an equipment expense in the year the purchase was made (three years ago), and consequently, there would be no expense in the current year. An accrual-based accounting system (i.e., U.S. GAAP) recognizes that there was cash outflow to buy the equipment three years ago. However, under accrual-based accounting, the expense comes from the productivity consumption over the life of the asset. In this case, $1,000 ($10,000/10 years) per year would be recognized as depreciation expense in the current year and annually over the 10-year life of the equipment.

If the depreciating equipment was used primarily for or related to the manufacture of product, the $1,000 depreciation expense would be included in cost of sales. If the depreciation was associated with corporate headquarters or a regional sales office, that expense would be included in selling, marketing, and administrative. In the case of Hershey, the depreciation expense is not specifically identified on the income statement. However, a supplemental summary reveals a 2010 depreciation expense of $169.7 million. It is silent on the split between cost of sales and selling, marketing, and administrative expense. The majority of the depreciation would be found in the cost of sales given Hershey's business model and investment in manufacturing equipment.

Selling, marketing, and administrative (SM&A) expenses include (1) selling expenses, such as salespersons' salaries, bonuses, benefits, employment taxes, automobiles, office expenses, broker fees if the product is sold by a third party, and so on, (2) marketing expenses, including consumer promotions, cents-off coupons, advertising, marketing research, salaries, and so on, and (3) administrative expenses, outlays for corporate and divisional staffs, executive compensation, training, consulting fees, research and development, and so on. SM&A expenses are sometimes referred to as *general and administrative (G&A) expense, operating expense*, or similar type of label.

Extraordinary Items

Companies incur expenses for or benefits from *one-time, nonrecurring gains or losses* that are listed separately on the income statement. Examples of these one-time events include:

- *Business realignment (or restructuring charges:* An accumulation of anticipated expenses associated with closing a plant, division, or other business segment, as well as the expenses incurred for a workforce reduction.
- *Asset impairment:* A decrease in the value of a purchased asset, as explained below.
- *Discontinued operations:* Current-period income or loss from a business that has been identified to be discontinued through a shutdown or divestiture.
- *Gains (or losses) from the disposal of businesses:* A business unit, product line, or individual product was sold resulting in a gain (or loss).
- *Extraordinary gains (losses):* As the name implies.

These nonrecurring items may need to be adjusted to get a more accurate portrayal of the company's normal business activities.

As illustrated on Hershey's income statement, there is a series of one-time expense items that are identified separately, namely, business realignment and asset impairments, net. The 2010 business realignment and asset impairment charge ($83.4 million) was the result of two major expenses incurred for a workforce reduction owing to a plant rationalization of $33.2 million and an asset impairment of $44.7 million for Godrej Hershey as well as $5.5 million other similar expenses. The plant rationalization was the effect of a major capital initiative to build a new Hershey, PA, chocolate plant that is more efficient and reduces head count by 600 employees. Their severance expenses are included in this realignment charge. The goodwill impairment was attributable to Hershey's entry into India via Godrej Hershey. During 2010, it was recognized that the expectations of growth and profitability would not materialize, and Hershey took an extraordinary charge to reduce its goodwill in the division.

Business realignment and assets impairment, net, appeared every year attributed to unique and nonrecurring annual expenses. In 2009, the primary items included a plant closure expense and pension settlement losses. In 2008, there were more items accounting for $94.8 million, with the largest attributed to plant closures and the trademark impairment for the Mauna Loa brand.

To explain impairments a bit more, in 2004, Hershey consummated the acquisition of Mauna Loa, a Hawaiian company that produced and marketed primarily macadamia nuts. In 2004, Hershey paid $127.8 million for the company and received assets worth let's say (the exact amounts have not been reported, and these amounts are illustrative) $80.0 million and liabilities of $25.0 million for a total of net assets received of $55.0 million. The difference (between the price paid and the net assets acquired of $72.8 million) is considered goodwill or intangibles resulting from business acquisitions. In 2008, and in accordance with U.S. GAAP, the assumptions underlying the valuation at the time of the Mauna Loa acquisition were revisited, resulting in a lower value owing to reduced expectations for future sales and cash flows compared with the valuation on the acquisition date. If Hershey would have known in 2004 what it knew in 2008, the company would have paid $45.7 million less, or $82.1 million. In 2008, goodwill was reduced, and a one-time asset impairment charge was expensed.

Measures of Income

The next line, income before interest and income taxes, or earnings before interest and taxes (EBIT), represents sales less total cost of sales, G&A expenses, and extraordinary items. Many firms also refer to this as *operating income* (OI). However, from a technical perspective, operating income does not include the effects of one-time extraordinary items. Of course, if a company does not have any extraordinary expenses, then operating income and EBIT are one and the same.

A variation on EBIT that has grown increasingly popular with the investment community is a measure called *earnings before interest, taxes, depreciation, and amortization* (EBITDA). While EBITDA is not a U.S. GAAP measure, it is easy to compute by adding depreciation and amortization (similar to depreciation of an intangible asset) back to EBIT. In Hershey's case for 2010, Hershey's EBIT was $905.3 million, and adding back $167.9 million for depreciation and $29.2 million for amortization, which also was included in the "Total cost and expenses," results in an EBITDA of $1,102.4 million. The depreciation and amortization values were reported in the cash flow statement and footnotes. EBITDA represents a quasi-measure of the gross amount of cash generated by the business's operations.

Interest expense, net, includes gross interest expense less interest income. Gross interest expense includes the cost of borrowing funds via long-term debt as part of the permanent capital structure of a firm and short-term debt for working capital needs. Interest income represents the interest "earnings" on cash balances and marketable securities such as bank certificates of deposit (CDs), Treasury bills, commercial paper, and so on.

Income (earnings) before income taxes (EBT) or, simply, pretax income results from subtracting interest expense from EBIT. The provision for income taxes is the combined amounts that are owed to the U.S., state, local, and foreign governments based on the pretax income. Subtracting taxes from EBT results in net income, as shown on Table 2-1.

Net income is the infamous "bottom line" and represents the amount left over from sales after all the expenses have been considered and taxes paid. When net income is divided by the average annual number of shares outstanding, basic net income per share (or earnings per share [EPS]) results. EPS, diluted, or, simply, diluted EPS is an accounting practice wherein all company-based outstanding options on Hershey stock are assumed to be converted into "new" shares of Hershey's common stock. This process provides a conservative view on the potential number of shares outstanding and a resulting conservative EPS value. In 2010, Hershey reported EPS, basic, of $2.29 and EPS, diluted, of $2.21. This indicated that Hershey's executive option compensation program cost approximately $0.08 per share.

Normalized income, or pro-forma income, is a non–U.S. GAAP measure of income that attempts to portray the net income (after taxes) excluding extraordinary items such as after-tax restructuring charges or after-tax asset impairment. The after-tax effects from any extraordinary gains or losses that result from the sale of an asset, from a divestiture, or from discontinuing a business are reversed to arrive at normalized income.

We already discussed Hershey' restructuring and asset impairment expenses earlier to arrive at the net income. Now we want to reverse the effects, as detailed in the footnotes and shown in Table 2-2.

Normalized income allows us to see how the underlying business is performing. While 2009 was a solid year, normalized income allows us to appreciate the improvement in the business without distortions owing to one-time expenses. The year 2008 is also shown in a more consistent light using normalized income,

TABLE 2-2

Hershey's Normalized Income
($ millions)

	2010	2009	2008
Net income	$ 509.8	$436.0	$311.4
Extraordinary charges pretax			
As reported separately	83.4	82.9	94.8
Part of cost of goods sold	13.7	10.1	77.8
Part of SM&A	1.5	6.1	8.1
Tax effects	(20.7)	(38.3)	(61.6)
Normalized income	$ 587.7	$496.8	$430.5

and only business operations affected the performance differences. In this case, a clearer picture of Hershey's improving operations is seen. Often it is necessary to read the footnotes to understand the presented charges properly on an after-tax basis.

Income Statements of Other Companies

It is helpful to look at the income statements of other companies to see slightly different formats that management finds more useful in presenting and discussing their financial results. Remember, the basic design is revenue (or sales) less cost of goods sold and operating expenses to arrive at operating income (OI) or earnings before interest and taxes (EBIT). From EBIT, interest expense and taxes are removed to derive net income. Along the way, one-time events are also identified and considered.

Walmart

Notice the 2010 income statement for Walmart, the world's largest retail organization (Table 2-3). The 2010 income statement actually ended on January 31, 2011, so it sometimes may be referred to as the *2011 income statement*. The values are listed in millions of dollars, which says that Walmart's 2011 sales were $419.0 billion (with a *b*), with an additional $2.9 billion in membership fees and other income. Their 2011 income statement is straightforward, with only one minor extraordinary item—income (loss) from discontinued operations, net of tax. However, instead reporting net interest or provision for income taxes (income tax expense), Walmart provides additional details about both expenses right on the income statement rather than only in the footnotes.

The company indicates that of its over $2.0 billion in interest expense, $1.9 billion came from its debt and another $0.3 billion was embedded in leases, whereas interest income offset over $0.2 billion of the expense. The company also separates its tax expense into current ($6,703 million immediately payable) and deferred ($876 million) taxes (see Chapter 4) for a total tax expense of $7,579 million.

TABLE 2-3

Walmart Consolidated Statements of Income
($ millions)

| | For the years ended 1/31: | | |
	2011	2010	2009
Revenue			
Net sales	$ 418,952	$ 405,132	$ 401,087
Membership and other income	2,897	2,953	3,167
Total revenue	421,849	408,085	404,254
Costs and expenses			
Cost of sales	315,287	304,444	303,941
Operating, selling, general, and administrative	81,020	79,639	77,546
Operating income	25,542	24,002	22,767
Interest, debt	1,928	1,787	1,896
Interest, capital leases	277	278	288
Interest income	(201)	(181)	(284)
Interest, net	2,004	1,884	1,900
Income from continuing operations before income taxes	23,538	22,118	20,867
Provision for income taxes, current	6,703	7,643	6,564
Provision for income taxes, deferred	876	(487)	569
Income from continuing operations	15,959	14,962	13,734
Income (loss) from discontinued operations, net of tax	1,034	(79)	146
Consolidated net income	16,993	14,883	13,880
Less consolidated net income attributable to noncontrolling interest	(604)	(513)	(499)
Consolidated net income attributable to Walmart	$ 16,389	$ 14,370	$ 13,381

One final item of note: As part of its business activities, Walmart enters into joint ventures, or arrangements where it owns more than 50 percent of a business but not the full amount. The results of these businesses are added (consolidated) into Walmart's sales, cost of sales, and so on as if Walmart wholly owned the business. At the end of the income statement, the portion of the income that belongs to the minority business partners is subtracted from Walmart's results on the line "Consolidated net income attributable to noncontrolling interest" (shown in Table 2-3). If Walmart (or any company) owns 20 to 50 percent of a joint venture, it recognizes its share of the venture's income as investment income, which is often included in other income. Finally, if Walmart owns less than 20 percent of a joint venture, it simply recognizes the dividends it receives from the venture as income.

P. F. Chang's China Bistro, Inc.

P. F. Chang's China Bistro, Inc. (stock symbol PFCB), owns and operates two restaurants in the Asian niche: P. F. Chang's China Bistro, which is a full-service upscale casual dining concept, and Pei Wei Asian Diner, which is a quick casual concept. Over the past three years, the company's sales grew modestly, but its net income experienced strong growth, as shown in Table 2-4.

A few items to point out: (1) The company's fiscal (financial) year "floats" by a few days and ends on the Sunday closest to December 31, (2) PFCB (and a number of restaurant companies) reveal more expense detail than just the cost of goods

TABLE 2-4

P. F. Chang's China Bistro, Inc., Consolidated Statements of Income
($ millions, except per-share amounts)

	January 2, 2011	January 3, 2010	December 28, 2008
Revenues	$ 1,242.8	$ 1,228.2	$ 1,198.1
Operating costs and expenses			
Cost of sales	324.8	326.4	325.6
Labor	410.0	401.6	396.9
Operating	208.3	203.9	199.0
Occupancy	73.7	70.6	69.8
General and administrative	81.9	82.8	77.5
Depreciation and amortization	77.5	74.4	68.7
Preopening expense	2.0	3.9	8.5
Partner investment expense	(0.4)	(0.6)	(0.4)
Total costs and expense	1,177.8	1,163.0	1,145.6
Income from operations	65.0	65.2	52.5
Interest and other income (expense), net	(0.5)	(1.6)	(3.4)
Income from continuing operations before taxes	64.5	63.6	49.1
Provision for income taxes	(17.2)	(18.5)	(12.1)
Income from continuing operations, net of taxes	47.3	45.1	37.0
Income (loss) from discontinued operations, net of taxes	-	(0.5)	(7.6)
Net income	47.3	44.6	29.4
Less net income attributable to noncontrolling interests	0.7	1.4	2.0
Net income attributable to PFCB	$ 46.6	$ 43.2	$ 27.4
Earnings per share, basic	$ 2.05	$ 1.88	$ 1.15
Earnings per share, diluted	$ 2.02	$ 1.85	$ 1.14

TABLE 2-5

PFCB's Normalized Income
($ millions)

	2010	2009	2008
Net income attributable to PFCB	$46.6	$43.2	$27.4
(Income) or loss from discontinued operations, net of tax	—	0.5	7.6
Normalized income	$46.6	$43.7	$35.0

sold and general and administrative (as used by PFCB, cost of sales represents just the cost of the food [raw material]), and (3) partner investment expense is unique to the PFCB ownership structure of individual units. The recognition of this expense was eliminated in April 2010 when the partnership model was altered. Also, PFCB had discontinued operations that represented the closure of 10 Pei Wei restaurants in 2008 and the related unwinding of related leases and severance pay in subsequent years. Also in 2008, the company closed a third restaurant concept, Taneko Japanese Tavern, which was developed in 2006. Finally, PFCB has noncontrolling partners that are "paid" their appropriate portion of income to arrive at PFCB's net income.

The normalized income for PFCB is estimated as shown in Table 2-5.

Once again, normalized income provides a more realistic view of the continuing ongoing operations of PFCB.

The Walt Disney Company

The Walt Disney Company provides an excellent example of a *consolidating income statement* in Figure 2-2. Disney is a diversified worldwide entertainment company with operations in five business segments: Media Networks, Parks and Resorts, Studio Entertainment, Consumer Products, and Interactive Media. Within Disney, each segment has its own income statement leading to operating income. Supporting each segment is a number of different income statements prepared for deeper levels of management control.

For example, Parks and Resorts is comprised of Walt Disney World Resort in Florida and Disneyland in California, along with the Disney Vacation Club, Disney Cruise Line, and Disney Adventures and portions of Disney International parks and resorts. Each property at Disney World (4 major theme parks, 17 hotels and resorts, and a shopping area known as Downtown Disney) has its own income statement, which consolidates to the Disney World Parks and Resorts income statement. And underlying each theme park and each resort is an even more detailed level of income statement by each theme area within the parks, each restaurant, and each shop.

By providing selected financial information to the most nuclear level of the organization, all employees can understand their contributions to the overall success of the organization.

The Walt Disney Company 2010 consolidated income statements.
($ millions)

	Media Networks	Parks & Resorts	Studio Entertainment	Consumer Products	Interactive Media
Revenues	$ 17,162	$ 10,761	$ 6,701	$ 2,678	$ 761
Operating expenses	(9,961)	(6,787)	(3,469)	(1,236)	(581)
Selling and administrative	(2,285)	(1,517)	(2,450)	(687)	(371)
Depreciation	(222)	(1,139)	(89)	(78)	(43)
Equity in the income of investees	438	-	-	-	-
Operating income	$ 5,132	$ 1,318	$ 693	$ 677	$ (234)

Consolidated	
Total operating income	$ 7,586
Corporate and shared expenses	(420)
Restructuring and impairment	(270)
Interest expense	(409)
Other income	140
Income before income taxes	6,627
Income taxes	(2,314)
Net income	4,313
Net income to noncontrolling	(350)
Net income to Disney	$ 3,963

BALANCE SHEET

Balance sheets capture the financial position of a firm at a point in time. Hershey is a calendar fiscal year-end company, which means that its financial year coincides with the calendar. It begins on January 1 and ends on December 31. Table 2-6 presents the Hershey balance sheet for 2009 and 2010. Only two years of presentation are required for the balance sheet, whereas three years of data are presented on the other financial statements. For our discussion purposes only, in Table 2-6, alongside the Hershey balance sheet is a column that calculates the change (increase or decrease) from 2009 to 2010 for each line of the balance sheet.

A balance sheet is founded on double-entry accounting and its identity equation:

$$\text{Assets} = \text{liabilities} + \text{equity} \qquad (2.2)$$

TABLE 2-6

Hershey Foods Corporation Consolidated Balance Sheet
($ millions)

| | For the years ended 12/31: | | |
	2010	2009	Change*
Current assets:			
Cash and cash equivalents	$ 884.6	$ 253.6	$ 631.0
Accounts receivable, trade	390.1	410.4	(20.3)
Inventories	533.6	519.7	13.9
Other current assets	196.9	201.7	(4.8)
Total current assets	2,005.2	1,385.4	619.8
Property, plant and equipment, net	1,437.7	1,404.8	32.9
Goodwill (intangibles resulting from acquisitions)	524.1	571.6	(47.5)
Other assets	305.7	313.2	(7.5)
Total assets	$ 4,272.7	$ 3,675.0	$ 597.7
Current liabilities:			
Accounts payable	$ 410.6	$ 287.9	$ 122.7
Accrued liabilities	602.7	583.4	19.3
Short-term debt	24.1	24.1	-
Current portion of long-term debt	261.4	15.2	246.2
Total current liabilities	1,298.8	910.6	388.2
Long-term debt	1,541.8	1,502.8	39.0
Other long-term liabilities	494.5	501.3	(6.8)
Total liabilities	3,335.1	2,914.7	420.4
Total stockholders' equity	937.6	760.3	177.3
Total liabilities and stockholders' equity	$ 4,272.7	$ 3,675.0	$ 597.7

*Note: The change column is not part of the actual balance sheet. It is provided here for later reference.

Assets and liabilities are further classified as current or long term according to how quickly they will be converted to cash (assets) or be paid off (liabilities). In general, assets with less than a year (or an operating cycle) until they are converted into cash are considered current assets, and liabilities with less than a year (or an operating cycle) until they need to be paid are considered current liabilities. Equation (2.2) can be expanded to reflect this added distinction:

$$\text{Current assets} + \text{long-term assets} = \text{current liabilities} + \text{long-term liabilities} + \text{equity} \tag{2.3}$$

Equity is also referred to as the *book value* of the firm. By accounting conventions, many of the underlying values are based on historical costs. The common balance sheet accounts are reviewed below specifically for Hershey. Keep in mind that these captions pertain to any company.

Cash and Cash Equivalents

The $884.6 million in cash and cash equivalents on Hershey's 2010 balance sheet represents additional accumulation of cash from Hershey's strong operating cash flow and a $350 million debt issuance in December 2010. These cash funds go beyond the amounts needed to run the day-to-day operations of the firm. The cash equivalents (sometimes referred to as *marketable securities*) include temporary investment of "excess" (beyond immediate needs) cash in interest-income-producing investments, which can be converted into cash with relatively small risk of a decline in their stated values. Examples of such investments include time deposits with banks, money-market accounts, and other highly liquid instruments with less than three-month maturities.

Accounts Receivable

Accounts receivable, trade, or simply accounts receivable reflect sales made to customers for which Hershey has not yet received payment. Accounts receivable represent the amount that customers owe to Hershey at any point in time.

Inventory

Inventories represent the dollar amount of raw material (e.g., cocoa beans, sugar, milk, packaging material, etc.), goods-in-process, and finished goods (at the cost of production) that Hershey has on hand. The footnotes to the financial statements detail the major components of Hershey's inventories and are summarized in Table 2.7.

There are a few alternatives available for valuing inventory. The two most common alternatives are first-in, first-out (FIFO) and last-in, first-out (LIFO). FIFO records inventory as the first units in are the first units out. For

TABLE 2-7

Hershey's Inventory Composition
($ millions)

	2010	2009
Raw material	$ 209.0	$ 246.5
Goods-in-process	73.1	84.0
Finished goods	404.7	376.6
Inventories at FIFO	686.8	707.1
Less: Adjustments to LIFO	(153.2)	(187.4)
Total inventories	$ 533.6	$ 519.7

example, the first candy bars made are the first candy bars sold. While this is the actual inventory management practice, for "accounting" purposes, Hershey uses the LIFO inventory method. In an inflationary environment, LIFO recognizes more expensive production costs sooner, but this approach implies that the last candy bars made are the first ones sold. Consequently, Hershey's inventory is reported $153.2 million lower than the actual cost of the specific inventory on hand (LIFO adjustment). Yes, Hershey's internal accounting records imply that the company has 50-year-old candy bars in the distribution centers!

Other Current Assets

The remaining current assets (returning to Table 2-6) include $55.8 million for current deferred income taxes (which will be discussed in Chapter 4), as well as prepaid expenses and other current assets, which include a variety of assets used for certain commodity and Treasury hedging. Notice that these other current assets approximated $200 million in both 2010 and 2009.

Property, Plant, and Equipment, Net

Property, plant, and equipment, net—also known as *net PP&E*—is a long-term asset and summarizes the company's investment in land, building, equipment, and fixtures net of accumulated depreciation (see Table 2-8). As discussed on the income statement, depreciation expense represents an estimate of the annual consumption of a fixed asset's value. Accumulated depreciation is the accumulation of all the depreciation expense since the asset was first purchased. Further detail is provided in the accompanying notes of the annual report.

TABLE 2-8

Hershey's Net PP&E Composition
($ millions)

	2010	2000
Land	$ 71.1	$ 70.4
Building	843.1	807.2
Equipment and fixtures	2,410.6	2,365.3
Total PP&E, gross	3,324.8	3, 242.9
Less: Accumulated depreciation	(1,887.1)	(1,838.1)
PP&E, net	$1,437.7	$1,404.8

PP&E, gross, is recorded at the original purchase price. Market value, replacement value, and current cost are not considered. However, economic value is considered only if the specific asset is "impaired" and no longer worth the depreciated value of the asset. For example, one of the major chains built a first-class hotel in the 1980s at a cost of over $400 million. The investment was made and the hotel built to service the Denver airport, with the underlying assumptions of more than 90 percent occupancy and rooms at an average rate of $250 per night. Unfortunately for the hotel, Denver moved its airport in 1995. Occupancy rates dropped well below 50 percent, with room rates averaging well below $100 per night. This asset was "impaired" as its economic value fell. It no longer was worth the depreciated value. Thus an impairment charge would have been recognized on the income statement because the asset value would have been "written down" on the balance sheet. Of course, conservatism plays a role, and if the hotel would have had windfall gains, accounting does not allow for the recognition of a gain and the write-up of the hotel. This has some interesting consequences.

An 80-acre tract of land that was purchased before 1900 and currently holds Hershey's major production facilities and divisional offices is still carried at its historical cost of $1 million instead of an appreciated value.

Another illustration: In the process of making milk chocolate, the chocolate paste needs to be "conched" for an extended period of time. (*Conching* is equivalent to blending and mixing.) The machines used in this process are called *conches*. The conches at Hershey are still functional, cost-effective, and efficient after 85 years of operation. Although there is significant economic value, these conches are recorded on the books at their original purchase price less their accumulated depreciation. These conches are currently on the books at a zero dollar value. In fact, these conches were fully depreciated (or written off) before any of Hershey's senior management team was born! However, there is remaining economic value in this equipment, but owing to the nature of accounting for PP&E, only historical cost less accumulated depreciation is recorded.

Intangibles Resulting from Business Acquisitions

Intangibles resulting from business acquisitions, which are also referred to as *goodwill*, represent the extra amount paid for an acquisition beyond the acquired assets. The Mauna Loa acquisition discussed earlier created $72.8 million of goodwill in 2004. This was added to all the previous goodwill from other acquisitions. More is said about goodwill in Chapter 15.

Other Assets

This final category on Hershey's assets is a catchall reporting category called *other assets*. As presented in Table 2-6, other assets also include other intangibles, primarily trademarks and patents obtained through business acquisitions. Trademarks are held with no amortization, and patents are amortized (similar to depreciated) over their legal lives of approximately 17 years. The other long-term assets include capitalized software, long-term business investments, and long-term deferred tax assets. In summary, Hershey reports $4,272.7 million in assets at book value. Their replacement value could be higher, as we discussed about inventories and plant, property, and equipment, net. Next we will consider the liabilities—current and long term.

Current liabilities usually are comprised of two types of short-term liabilities: (1) operating liabilities such as payables and accruals, and (2) financing liabilities such as short-term borrowings.

Payables and Accruals

Hershey presents separate lines for accounts payable and accrued liabilities. Other common payables include taxes payable and wages payable. Both accounts payable and accrued liabilities represent the amounts owed to suppliers for purchases of goods and services. The distinguishing characteristic hinges on whether an invoice was received or not. Accounts payable have been billed by the supplier, whereas for accrued liabilities, charges for services or products have been incurred but have not yet been billed. In some cases, some suppliers may have agreements in place that make the formal billing process unnecessary. In Hershey's case, some major commodity suppliers have this arrangement.

Short-Term Debt

Short-term debt represents interest-bearing loans. On the Hershey balance sheet, short-term borrowings are captured as short-term debt. Other common short-term debt balance sheet line items are short-term bank borrowing and notes payable. The current portion of long-term debt is exactly that, long-term debt that will mature within the next year. From the long-term debt schedule in Table 2-9, you can see that Hershey needs to pay off a $250 million note in 2011. Thus this long-term debt instrument is reclassified as current portion of long-term debt.

T A B L E   2-9

Hershey's Financial Debt Composition
($ millions)

Instrument	Rate	2010	2009
Notes			
Due 2011	5.30%	$ 250.0	$ 250.0
Due 2012	6.95%	92.5	150.0
Due 2013	5.00%	250.0	250.0
Due 2015	4.85%	250.0	250.0
Due 2016	5.45%	250.0	250.0
Due 2020	4.125%	350.0	—
Debenture			
Due 2021	8.80%	100.0	100.0
Due 2027	7.20%	250.0	250.0
Other obligations		10.7	18.0
Total long-term debt		1,803.2	1,518.0
Less: Current portion		261.4	15.2
Long-term portion		$ 1,541.8	$ 1,502.8

Long-Term Liabilities

Commonly, long-term liabilities include the two liabilities on Hershey's balance sheet. Long-term debt is interest-bearing debt that Hershey issued directly to lenders through notes and debentures. *Notes* is the term applied to borrowing with less than a 10-year maturity. *Debentures* are unsecured borrowings that may have a longer than 10-year maturity date. As detailed in a Hershey footnote, long-term debt includes everything listed in Table 2-9. In 2010, $350 million in new debt was issued with a rate of 4.125 percent and maturity in 2020.

Other long-term liabilities is another catchall presentation line detailed in the footnotes. However, the largest items in other long-term liabilities are pension liabilities ($61.3 million for 2010 and $50.7 million for 2009) and postretirement benefits other than pension (PBOP; in 2010, this was $278.0 million, and in 2009, it was $293.3 million). PBOP is similar to a pension liability except that it is related to nonpension benefits such as retiree's medical premiums.

Stockholders' Equity

Although condensed in Table 2-6, the stockholders' equity section includes four distinct sections, as shown in Table 2-10.

Once again, the current market value of the equity is not reflected in stockholder's equity. Simply put, stockholders' equity represents (1) the original

TABLE 2-10

Stockholders' Equity Composition

Balance Sheet Item	Comment
1. Preferred stock Common stock Class B common stock Additional paid-in capital	In combination, these accounts represent the proceeds received when stock was originally issued.
2. Retained earnings	The accumulated net income retained (not paid as a dividend) in the corporation since inception.
3. Treasury stock	A reduction that reflects amounts paid when Hershey bought back its shares from shareholders.
4. Accumulated other	Miscellaneous impacts that are assigned directly to equity.

proceeds from the company selling shares *plus* (2) the accumulated earnings that were not paid out in the form of dividends *less* (3) the repurchased amount of shares at the existing market prices at the time of repurchase and (4) other.

The next section introduces the cash flow statement and develops a link between the three financial statements.

ANALYSIS OF CASH FLOWS

The income statement presents revenue, expenses, and income over a period of time. It is based on accrual accounting and does not detail cash flow over time. The balance sheet represents the financial picture of the firm at a point in time—what it owns and what it owes. The balance sheet includes the cash balances from one period to the next and consequently the change or total amount of cash flow for the period. From the balance sheet in Table 2-6, Hershey's cash balance increased by $631.0 million. This represents a tremendous cash flow for 2010. However, there are no details as to where the cash came from and where it went.

In order to answer the question of where the cash came from and where it went, we need to review the cash flow statement or, more formally, *the consolidated statement of cash flows*. This statement is organized by where the cash flows came from (a source of cash) or where the cash went (a use of cash):

- Cash from operations
- Cash (used for) investments
- Cash from (used for) financing

In general, the cash from operations section begins with net income and adds back any noncash expense (such as depreciation). This is followed by cash flow implications of changes in operating assets (e.g., accounts receivable, inventory, etc.) or operating liabilities (e.g., payables, accruals, etc.).

Many cash flow statements today have been complicated by today's accounting requirements. This is also the case with Hershey's. Therefore, before we look at Hershey's actual cash flow statement, let's examine a hypothetical cash flow statement (Table 2-11).

Table 2-11 provides a complete set of financial statements for a hypothetical company. The income statement is straightforward and does not include any extraordinary items. As you can see, sales are $1,000, leading to gross income, operating income, and net income of $370, $170, and $90, respectively. The 2010 balance sheet includes total assets of $900 primarily net, plant property, and equipment of $525, inventory of $115, and so on. You'll also notice that this firm has marketable securities (highly liquid short-term investments such as commercial paper, CDs, etc.). The firm also has cash of $50 in 2010, or an increase of $15. But where did it come from?

The cash flow statement begins by presenting the impact of the income statement and then categorizes each change in the balance sheet item as operating, investing, or financing cash and denotes whether the change is a source (or use).

In this case, cash flow from (or used for) operations begins with net income and then reverses all "noncash" expenses or income items. From this example, net income is $90 after deducting $50 of depreciation expense. But depreciation expense is a noncash expense. The company never writes out a check for depreciation the same way it does a pay "check." So we need to reverse its effects and add back the depreciation to determine the appropriate cash flows. This is where any noncash extraordinary charges (such as restructuring, asset impairment, etc.) would be reversed (added back) on an after-tax basis or any noncash extraordinary benefits would be reversed (subtracted out) on an after-tax basis.

After adjusting the income statement items to move closer to a cash basis, the cash flow statement then considers the cash flows derived from (or used for) operating balance sheet items. From this example, accounts receivable and inventory increased by $20 and $15, respectively. We invested our cash into these two other balance sheet items. We bought $15 more inventory, and we financed $20 more of our customers' purchases. In other words, we *used* our cash to buy more inventory and to support our customers' purchases! On the other hand, other current assets decreased by $10. Whatever they represent, we sold off $10 worth of them, and consequently, this change in other current assets provided a source of cash to the firm. For liabilities, the $8 increase in accounts payable shows that we had increased supplier financing (a source), whereas the $5 decrease in accrued liabilities indicates that we "paid off" that amount (a use).

To summarizes the cash flow implications of changes in the balance sheet, see Table 2-12.

This source or use matrix applies to all balance sheet lines. A decrease (increase) in an asset (liability) produces a source of cash while an increase (decrease) in an asset (liability) results in a use of cash. The cash flow from

Simplified Cash Flow Statement Illustration

($ millions)

Income Statement

Items	2010
Sales	$ 1,000
Cost of goods sold*	580
Depreciation	50
Gross income	370
Operating expenses:	
Selling	45
Marketing	85
Administrative	70
Operating income	170
Interest expense	20
Pretax income	150
Tax provision	60
Net income	$ 90

Balance Sheet

Items	2010	2009	Change
Cash & equivalents	$ 50	$ 35	$ 15
Marketable securities	75	50	25
Accounts receivable	95	75	20
Inventory	115	100	15
Other current assets	25	35	(10)
Total current assets	360	295	65
Net, PP&E	525	493	32
Other assets	15	12	3
Total assets	$ 900	$ 800	$ 100
Accounts payable	$ 70	$ 62	$ 8
Accrued liabilities	50	55	(5)
Short-term debt	63	78	(15)
Other current liab.	12	10	2
Total current liab.	195	205	(10)
Long-term debt	445	382	63
Other long-term liab.	22	18	4
Stockholders' equity	238	195	43
Total liabilities and stockholders' equity	$ 900	$ 800	$ 100

Cash Flow Statement

Items	2010
Net income	$ 90
Depreciation	50
Change in:	
Accounts receivable	(20)
Inventory	(15)
Other current assets	10
Other assets	(3)
Accounts payable	8
Accrued liabilities	(5)
Other current liab.	2
Other long-term liab.	4
Cash flow, operations	121
Capital expenditures	(82)
Sale of mkt securities	175
Purchase of mkt sec.	(200)
Cash flow – investing	(107)
Repayment of ST debt	(15)
Issuance of LT debt	63
Dividends paid	(12)
Share repurchase	(35)
Cash flow, financing	1
Total cash flow	$ 15

*Cost of goods sold excludes depreciation expense.

T A B L E   2-12

Cash Flow Implications of Balance Sheet Changes

	Asset Change	Liability Change
Source of cash	Decrease	Increase
Use of cash	Increase	Decrease

operations shows how much cash was generated during the normal course of business operations!

As far as cash flows from (or used for) investing activities is concerned, the major line item is for capital expenditures, which can go by names such as *additions to plant, property, and equipment* or *payments for property and equipment* or a variety of other captions. Capital expenditures represent long-term investments in the firm and a use of cash. As noted in this example, sometimes companies also will indicate the total amount of cash received when their short-term investments mature, offset by the reinvestment when they purchase additional marketable securities.

Other common captions in the investing section include *source of cash from selling equipment, use of cash for acquisitions, source of cash from divestitures*, and so on.

The final cash flow section is cash provided by (or used for) financing. Usually this section includes three subsections representing the impact of cash flow on debt, equity, and any other financing-related transaction. In the example in Table 2-11, the repayment for short-term debt represents a use of cash, whereas the issuance of long-term debt represents a source. For the equity, dividends paid and share repurchases are uses of cash. If this company would have issued equity, that would be reflected as a source of cash.

In total, in this example, total cash flow was $15 and is reflected as an increase in the cash & equivalents balance. Once again, in this simple model, the changes in the balance sheet accounts are directly traceable to the cash flow statement, with three exceptions that require some additional explanation to see their multiple links to the balance sheet, as shown on Table 2-13.

The $25 increase in marketable securities (a use of cash) reflects the $175 sale of marketable securities offset by $200 purchases of additional market securities. Net, plant property, and equipment showed a $32 increase in Table 2-11 or a use of $32 of cash. This included $82 spent for capital equipment offset by $50 of depreciation. If any equipment would have been sold, the sale would have reduced the value of the net, PP&E while being reflected as a source of cash. Finally, the source of $43 or the increase in stockholders' equity was the result of net income ($90) reduced by $12 for dividends and $35 for the repurchase of shares.

TABLE 2-13

Simplified Cash Flow Statement Illustration: Additional Balance Sheet
Relationships
($ millions)

Balance Sheet Accounts	Cash-Flow Statement Lines	Amount	Source or Use
Marketable securities (mkt sec)			
	+ Sale of mkt sec	$ 175	Source
	− Purchase of mkt sec	200	Use
	Increase in marketable securities	$ 25	Net use
Net, plant, property, and equipment			
	+ Capital expenditures	$ 82	Use
	− Depreciation	50	Source
	− Sale of net, PP&E	−	Source
	Increase in net, PP&E	$ 32	Net use
Stockholders' equity			
	+ Net income	$ 90	Source
	− Dividends	12	Use
	− Share repurchases	35	Use
	+ Share issuance	−	Source
	Increase in stockholders' equity	$ 43	Net source

While Table 2-11 was a hypothetical illustration, it did demonstrate
the clear links between the income statement, balance sheet, and cash flow
statement. The actual Hershey, Walmart, P. F. Chang's, and Disney cash flow
statements are complicated, and the logic, as demonstrated in Table 2-11, is
obscured owing to restructuring charges, asset impairments, business closings,
divestitures, acquisitions, foreign currency impact, stock-based compensation,
and so on. However, the common items as presented in Table 2-11 remain in
place.

Table 2-14 summarizes Hershey's actual 2010 statement of consolidated
cash flow without trying to reconcile the schedule to the income statement or balance sheet. During 2010, Hershey generated $901.4 million of cash through its
business operations, invested $199.3 million back into the business, and used a
net of $71.1 million for financing. Actually, the financing section included a use
of $283.4 million and $169.1 million for dividends and share repurchase, respectively, offset by additional debt (primarily long term) of $277.7 and other items
of $103.7 million.

T A B L E   2-14

Consolidated Cash Flow Statement—The Hershey Company
($ millions)

	2010	2009	2008
Cash flow from (used by) operations			
Net income	$ 509.8	$ 436.0	$ 311.4
Adjustments to reconcile income to cash			
Depreciation and amortization	197.1	182.4	249.5
Stock-based compensation expense, net of tax	30.7	30.4	22.2
Deferred income taxes	(18.7)	(40.6)	(17.1)
Business realignment, net of taxes	77.9	60.8	119.1
Contributions to pension plans	(6.1)	(54.4)	(32.7)
Change in balance sheet items net of acquisitions and divestitures			
Accounts receivable, trade	20.3	46.6	31.7
Inventories	(13.9)	74.0	7.7
Accounts payable	90.5	37.2	26.4
Other assets and liabilities	13.8	293.3	(198.6)
Net cash provided from operating activities	901.4	1,065.7	519.6
Cash flow from (used by) investing			
Capital expenditures	(179.5)	(126.3)	(262.7)
Capitalized software additions	(22.0)	(19.2)	(20.3)
Proceeds from sale of equipment	2.2	10.4	82.8
Business acquisitions	–	(15.2)	–
Divestitures	–	–	2.0
Net cash (used by) investing activities	(199.3)	(150.3)	(198.2)
Cash flow from (used by) financing			
Net change in short-term borrowing	1.1	(458.0)	(371.4)
Net long-term debt borrowing (repayment)	276.6	(8.3)	242.8
Dividends	(283.4)	(263.4)	(262.9)
Share repurchases	(169.1)	(9.3)	(60.4)
Exercise of stock options, net of taxes	93.5	32.8	38.4
Miscellaneous other stockholders' equity	10.2	7.3	–
Net cash used by financing activities	(71.1)	(698.9)	(413.5)
Increase (decrease) in cash	$ 631.0	$ 216.5	$ (92.1)

CONSOLIDATED STATEMENT OF STOCKHOLDERS' EQUITY

There is a "fourth" financial statement that details the accumulation of stockholders' equity over the past three years, *consolidated statement of stockholders' equity.* The statement provides the financial detail concerning the amount of preferred and common stock outstanding, including the stock's par value (the amount at which the stock was originally recorded on the books—common values are $1 or $0.01 per share) and paid-in excess capital (the amount actually paid for the share of stock over and above the par value at the time of issuance). This statement also presents the detail concerning retained earnings (net income retained in the business and not paid out as dividends) and treasury stock (stock that has been repurchased from stockholders). It also details various amounts for noncontrolling interests, such as the income or return of capital distributed to them or subsequent investment by the noncontrolling interests. Finally, the fourth statement reflects "comprehensive income," which basically reflects nonrealized gains and losses. The major categories include such items as the foreign-currency impact on foreign capital investments, pension and postretirement benefit costs, and market-value adjustments for securities, derivatives, foreign currency, and other hedges.

RESTATEMENT OF FINANCIAL REPORTS

Companies may restate prior years' results for a variety of reasons. Sometimes it's related to a new accounting pronouncement, and sometimes it's related to how the company reported historically within an existing guideline, and other times it is related to the operations of the corporation.

As mentioned earlier, in 2008 P. F. Chang's China Bistro closed 10 Pei Wei restaurants and a third restaurant concept, Taneko Japanese Tavern. The financials results of these closures are reflected as discontinued operations in the 2008 annual report. Table 2-15 compares the year 2007 to 2004 as originally reported in the five-year summary of the 2007 annual report and the same period from the 2008 annual report. The originally reported (2007 annual report) level of sales was $1,092.7 million. However, after the closures, PFCB isolated all sales generated by the closed units and "restated" sales as only $1,084.2 million, or $8.5 million less sales than originally reported in 2007. Although restated sales were lower, restated income (operating or from continuing operations) actually was higher. The closed units were incurring losses and were closed.

ADDITIONAL REPORTING REQUIREMENTS

For businesses with substantial (defined as 10 percent or more) portions of their business in more than one line or with a substantial (10 percent or more) portion of their business outside the United States, additional reporting is required for each significant line of business or geographic region:

- Net sales
- Operating income
- Identifiable assets
- Capital expenditures
- Depreciation and amortization expense

TABLE 2-15

P.F. Chang's China Bistro, Inc. Consolidated Statements of Income
($ millions)

	Fiscal Years				
	2008	2007	2006	2005	2004
Sales					
2008 annual report	$ 1,198.1	$ 1,084.2	$ 932.1	$ 806.8	$ 706.4
2007 annual report	n/a	1,092.7	936.9	809.2	706.9
Difference	n/a	$ (8.5)	$ (4.8)	$ (2.4)	$ (0.5)
Operating income					
2008 annual report	$ 52.5	$ 53.3	$ 55.7	$ 61.4	$ 46.4
2007 annual report	n/a	51.1	54.7	61.1	46.2
Difference	n/a	$ 2.2	$ 1.0	$ 0.3	$ 0.2
Income from continuing operations					
2008 annual report	$ 35.0	$ 36.6	$ 34.8	$ 37.9	$ 26.2
2007 annual report	n/a	35.2	34.2	37.8	26.1
Difference	n/a	$ 1.4	$ 0.6	$ 0.1	$ 0.1

Since Hershey is primarily a domestic, single-line-of-business company, it does not report this supplemental information. However, as we saw in Figure 2-2, Disney is a well-diversified company that goes above and beyond requirements. Figure 2-2 provided operating income statements for all five of Disney's areas. Table 2-16 provides additional data by business segment and Table 2-17 by geographic location.

Despite the limited data, insights can be gleaned about the Disney business. Disney has continued to invest in all its business segments through all its regions of operations.

NOTES TO FINANCIAL STATEMENTS

In addition to the three primary financial statements discussed earlier, a company is required to report additional information that is detailed in the *notes to financial statements*. Usually, within the first note, the firm clarifies its accounting policies, which generally includes discussing its inventory, depreciation, and amortization policies; additional expense detail such as advertising and promotion expense and research and development expense; and other accounting issues, such as treatment of foreign currency and financial instruments.

Additional notes discuss the firm's acquisitions and divestitures, capital stock position, short- and long-term debt, lease commitments, income taxes, hedging activities using derivatives, retirement plans, postretirement benefits other than pensions, incentive plans, quarterly information, and so on. These notes discuss the company's activities and/or policies related to each of the topics. A fair

T A B L E   2-16

Product Line Segment Information—Disney
($ millions)

	Net Revenue			Segment Operating Income		
	2010	2009	2008	2010	2009	2008
Media networks	$ 17,162	$ 16,209	$ 15,857	$ 5,132	$ 4,765	$ 4,981
Parks and resorts	10,761	10,667	11,504	1,318	1,418	1,897
Studio entertainment	6,701	6,136	7,348	693	175	1,086
Consumer products	2,678	2,425	2,415	677	609	778
Interactive media	761	712	719	(234)	(295)	(258)
Total segments	38,063	36,149	37,843	7,586	6,672	8,484
Corporate	–	–	–	–	–	–
Total consolidated	$ 38,063	$ 36,149	$ 37,843	$ 7,586	$ 6,672	$ 8,484

	Capital Expenditures			Depreciation Expense		
	2010	2009	2008	2010	2009	2008
Media networks	$ 224	$ 294	$ 338	$ 213	$ 197	$ 179
Parks and resorts	1,533	1,182	933	1,139	1,148	1,145
Studio entertainment	102	135	126	56	50	41
Consumer products	97	46	51	33	29	18
Interactive media	17	21	40	19	28	21
Total segments	1,973	1,678	1,488	1,460	1,452	1,404
Corporate	137	75	90	142	128	123
Total consolidated	$ 2,110	$ 1,753	$ 1,578	$ 1,602	$ 1,580	$ 1,527

	Amortization of Intangible Assets			Identifiable Assets		
	2010	2009	2008	2010	2009	2008
Media networks	$ 9	$ 9	$ 9	$ 27,112	$ 26,936	$ 26,786
Parks and resorts	–	–	–	17,529	16,945	16,916
Studio entertainment	33	10	9	12,742	11,104	11,123
Consumer products	45	10	11	4,786	1,486	1,601
Interactive media	24	22	26	1,756	988	987
Total segments	111	51	55	63,925	57,459	57,413
Corporate	–	–	–	5,281	5,658	5,084
Total consolidated	$ 111	$ 51	$ 55	$ 69,206	$ 63,117	$ 62,497

number of these notes have been approved by the American Medical Association as a cure for insomnia. They are long and arduous. While Table 2-18 lists the footnotes (by number) for the four companies we discussed in this chapter, their details are beyond our scope.

TABLE 2-17

Geographic Information—Disney
($ millions)

	Net Revenue			Segment Operating Income		
	2010	2009	2008	2010	2009	2008
United States and Canada	$ 28,279	$ 27,508	$ 28,506	$ 5,474	$ 4,923	$ 6,500
Europe	6,550	6,012	6,805	1,275	1,158	1,423
Asia Pacific	2,320	1,860	1,811	620	430	386
Latin America and other	914	769	721	217	161	175
Total consolidated	$ 38,063	$ 36,149	$ 37,843	$ 7,586	$ 6,672	$ 8,484

	Long-Lived Assets		
	2010	2009	2008
United States and Canada	$ 47,766	$ 43,570	$ 43,521
Europe	5,090	3,708	3,923
Asia Pacific	1,828	1,805	1,786
Latin America and other	237	188	189
Total consolidated	$ 54,921	$ 49,271	$ 49,419

Finally, a *comparison of five-year cumulative total return* (stock price) and a *summary of key financial data* also are provided in the annual report. The cumulative stock price comparison uses index values to illustrate an investment in the company's stock compared with a broad stock market index (such as the Standard & Poor's [S&P] 500 Index) and an industry benchmark. For example, a $100 investment made five years ago would be worth how much at the end of the latest fiscal year? For Hershey, the answer was $98 (the stock lost value), while both the S&P 500 Index and S&P Food Index were at $112 and $144, respectively.

The summary presents 5 to 11 years' worth of key financial data for the firm, thus providing a greater historical picture, as well as a fuller appreciation of underlying trends. The data are taken from the income statement, balance sheet, cash flow statement, and even selected critical pieces of data from the footnotes as management deems important. The summary may include "key" financial metrics (see Chapter 3) in addition to the financial data.

FINANCIAL REPORTING

With the advent of many financial reporting issues since 2000, as well as the outright fraud, new, sweeping legislation was enacted—the Sarbanes-Oxley Act of 2002.

TABLE 2-18

2010 Annual Report Review: Notes to the Financial Statements

	Information Found in Footnote Number:			
	Hershey	Walmart	P. F. Chang's	Disney
1. Summary of significant accounting policies	1	1, 16	1	2, 3
2. Acquisitions and divestitures	2	9	2	4
3. Business realignment and impairment charges	3	15	n/a	18
4. Noncontrolling interest in subsidiaries	4	n/a	16	6, 7
5. Commitments and contingencies	5	12	18	15
6. Derivative instruments and hedging activities	6	6	n/a	17
7. Financial instruments	7	n/a	n/a	
8. Fair-value accounting	8	5	10	16
9. Comprehensive income	9	7	n/a	n/a
10. Interest expense	10	n/a	n/a	n/a
11. Short-term debt	11	} 4	8	} 9
12. Long-term debt	12		9, 11	
13. Income taxes	13	8	17	10
14. Pension and postretirement benefit plans	14	13	14, 15	11
15. Savings plans	15	n/a	n/a	n/a
16. Capital stock and net income per share	16	3	n/a	12
17. Stock compensation plans	17	10	13	13
18. Supplemental balance sheet information	18	2	3, 4, 5, 6, 7, 12	14
19. Segment information	19	14	19	1
20. Quarterly data	20	17	20	19
Non-Hershey financial footnotes				
Legal proceedings		11		
Partnership structure			16	
Subsequent events			21	
Supplemental income statement information				5, 8

Sarbanes-Oxley is the most important legislation in this area since the Securities Act of 1933. Its primary impacts include the following:

- It establishes the Public Company Accounting Oversight Board, which is a nongovernmental panel to deal with violations.
- It strengthen auditors:
  - Auditors report to the audit committee of the company's board of directors.
  - The audit committee will be comprised of independent board members and not management of the company and contain at least one financial expert.
  - It is now unlawful to coerce or influence auditors.
- Auditors of the company no longer can provide other services, such as consulting, to the company.
- It establishes an *internal control report* as part of the annual report.
- It requires the CEO and CFO to sign responsibility statements for the financial statements.
- It requires disclosure of transactions between management and principal stockholders.
- It prohibits personal loans between the company and executives.

The act reaches widely to ensure public company accounting reform and investor protection. Stockholders receive consolidated financial information from annual reports and quarterly reports as well as SEC filings. The SEC requires that all publicly held corporations submit a standardized annual report called a *10K*, which usually contains more information than the annual report. Firms are required to send the 10K to all stockholders who request it. In addition, there is a quarterly filing called the *10Q*. The SEC further requires that whenever a corporation wishes to issue securities to the public, it must file a registration statement that discloses the current financial data as well as such items as the purpose for issuing the securities. Most corporations simply post their financial reports on their company's Internet site under "Investor Relations."

Tax agencies at the federal, state, local, and international levels receive their appropriate filings. As discussed briefly earlier and explained more fully in Chapter 4, tax reporting differs from U.S. GAAP accounting. Tax accounting in general is more "cash oriented" rather than "accrual oriented."

From time to time, additional "audiences" may require financial statements. These audiences include:

- Debt holders, debt rating agencies, and banks
- Suppliers
- Investment analysts
- Employees or potential employees

- Labor unions
- Business partners (i.e., joint-venture partners)

Each of these additional audiences will focus on the publicly reported consolidated financial statements and SEC filings.

Internal Financial Reporting

Internal personnel focus on consolidated reports and financial reports that "drill" deeper into the organization. With major enterprise resource planning tools such as SAP or Oracle, data are stored in a data warehouse using multiple classification dimensions at granular levels of recordkeeping. The data can be used routinely for regular monthly reporting or accessed for special project requests and reviews.

Four areas of internal reporting focus include divisional financial statements, cost accounting reports, annual budgets, and financial plans. Divisional financial statements provide the same financial information as consolidated financial statements and should be prepared in parallel with the organizational structure of the firm. In some companies, these divisional statements are "drilled" deeper to product lines, products, sales regions, plants, production lines, and administrative cost centers or areas such as the CFO's office. Each level may have its own full or abbreviated set of financial statements. Often an abbreviated set of financials focuses on the income statement or specific lines on an income statement. For example, reporting of administrative cost centers would involve detailed expense items such as salaries, travel, training, and so on by each administrative management area, such as finance, law, human resources, and so on, that total to the related administrative expense on an income statement.

While monthly internal reports may be the norm, some departments such as sales may receive daily sales reports by product and/or by region. A leading international pharmaceutical corporation has an internal financial system that provides daily information (with a one-day delay) on the sales and gross profit (sales less cost of goods sold) of any of its hundreds of products from its many worldwide regions and in total worldwide.

External reporting requirements or external benchmarking and analysis are often oriented as this year versus last year, where two historical periods are compared. Budgets are seldom (actually, more like never) shared outside the organization. However, a dynamic internal management style compares performance versus expectations as reflected in annual budgets and plans and updated routinely through a series of "outlooks." A distinction is made between planning (a broader, less-detailed, longer-term direction and target-setting process) and annual budgets, which provide a day-to-day detailed operational focus that ties to the plan. Most companies compare this year's financial statements with budgeted financial statements. Budgets embody the financial objectives and aspirations of the firm. Budgets already have been benchmarked to historical performance, so now current performance need only be compared with the budget. Some companies recast their budget throughout the year (say, at the end of the second quarter) as an "outlook" for the year. Of course, the outlook contains more recent information based on six months of actual performance and six months of estimates using current market conditions and expectations.

At their worst, financial plans and budgets are control tools used to keep managers in line. At their best, financial plans and budgets are wonderful management tools that:

- Facilitate communications throughout an organization
- Engage all members of the organization if implemented as a participatory exercise
- Establish a common goal and set of objectives to attain that goal
- Identify performance shortfalls from aspiration levels of performance and facilitate addressing those shortfalls without the "heat of the battle" immediately pressing
- Prioritize competing strategies
- Determine compensation targets
- Provide a barometer to gauge the progress and effectiveness of implementation

For more information, see Chapter 6. In general, plans remain as internal standards of performance. On occasion, some annual reports discuss general objectives of the firm, such as "double-digit growth" in sales or income as well as profitability standards as return on assets, return on equity, and margins (see Chapter 3).

International Financial Reporting Standards

Currently, U.S. GAAP accounting standards are going through an unprecedented review as part of the convergence of the world's accounting systems into one common approach throughout all countries. This commonality could lead to enhance comparability between the results of companies that are based in different countries. The "new approach" is labeled as *International Financing Reporting Standards* (IFRS) and is led by the International Accounting Standards Board. IFRS would replace U.S. GAAP. While discussions are ongoing, the impact could range from the way specific items are recorded (such as the elimination of the LIFO inventory accounting approach) to greatly revised presentation of financial statements.

SUMMARY

This chapter provided an overview of the three primary financial statements of the firm: income statement, balance sheet, and cash flow statement. The Hershey Company was used throughout as an illustrative example. Along the way, though, the financial statements of Walmart, P. F. Chang's China Bistro, and Walt Disney Company were interjected to provide additional depth to specific topics. While income statements garner a great deal of attention, the analyst and businessperson also should be aware of the information found on the balance sheet and cash flow statements as well as in the financial footnotes of a corporation.

Numerous specifics were reviewed, including reconciliation of the cash flow statement (prepared to demonstrate the interrelationship of the three financial statements), the "fourth" financial statement (or the consolidated statement of stockholders' equity), different measures of income, restated financial statements, comprehensive income, and the information contained in the financial footnotes. Finally, internal reporting options and international reporting requirements were discussed.

FINANCIAL PERFORMANCE METRICS

It is important to know a company's financial data in absolute terms, but it may be even more important to examine those data on a relative basis compared with (1) the company's past years of performance, (2) specific individual competitors, (3) an industry average, and (4) aspirations of the firm's management team. It is critical that the firm identifies its financial strengths and weakness. The strengths must be understood if they are to be used to proper advantage, and the weaknesses must be recognized if corrective actions are to be taken.

For example, how profitable is the company? Are inventories adequate to support the projected level of sales? Does the firm have too heavy an investment in accounts receivable, and does this condition reflect a lax collection policy? For efficient operations, does the firm have too much or too little invested in plant and equipment? How financially strong are the company's customers and suppliers?

Financial performance metrics provide a relative basis for comparing a company with itself over time or with a company versus competitors within its industry. Metrics provide a comparative basis for evaluating suppliers and customers and can be used for historical analysis as well as projected performance. Financial performance metrics also know no international boundaries and are useful in assessing company performance throughout the world. It often has been said that accounting and financial statements are the languages of business, as in Chapter 2. Extending this further, financial analysis using financial performance metrics provides the "literature" of business.

The world is becoming more dynamic and subject to rapid changes. It is not enough to analyze historical operating performance. Financial analysis also must include consideration of strategic and economic developments for the firm's long-run success. Financial managers and general senior managers are demanding evaluative standards by which they can rapidly measure the firm's performance and chart an appropriate course. Operational managers also are seeking performance metrics that can aid them in running the business on a day-by-day or week-by-week basis. These metrics should provide actionable feedback immediately to improve the operations of the firm.

Management's intense interest in financial performance metrics has risen dramatically as more and more annual and long-term incentive compensation is tied to attaining acceptable levels of performance, as measured by financial performance metrics. Many of these financial performance metrics provide the link from strategic plans to operations as *key performance indicators* (KPIs) in what many call the company's internal scorecard or dashboard.

The firm's external traditional stakeholders, stockholders, and creditors now also include employees, unions, consumers, customers, social and environmental interest groups, suppliers, the government, and regulatory interests. Each of these constituencies has a particular interest in the firm's performance and judges the success or failure of the firm using a variety of performance metrics.

Different groups and analysts use a variety of financial metrics for analysis. There is no one list of metrics that can be applied universally to all situations. The metrics provided in this chapter are intended to be suggestive only. For some situations, even more elaborate financial ratios may be useful, and for other decisions, only a few ratios are sufficient. There is no one set of metrics that needs to be used all the time, only those ratios for the decision at hand.

A number, such as 5, is neither good nor bad. It needs to be placed in a context. It needs to be compared with a similarly measured value for another time period or against another organization. From decade to decade and within an industry, minimal acceptable levels of strength change, and in the case of some ratios, there are no established minimally acceptable levels.

There are potentially thousands of ratios and metrics to discuss. Many of these ratios have several permutations or slight variations. Take one number and divide it by another number, and you've created a ratio. Whether the resulting ratio makes any sense and whether you can use that number for business decision making is another question. The numbers are not an end in themselves. They are aids to stimulate questions, further investigation, and generate additional analysis with the ultimate goal of better economic analysis for improved managerial decisions.

Financial analysis is a combination of science and art. This chapter seeks to cover the science part; the art comes with experience—from many hours of "number crunching" and use of numbers to make decisions on the firing line. Good finance managers are made, not born.

This chapter develops an analytical foundation by reviewing traditional financial analysis and financial performance metrics. At the same time, this chapter illustrates competitive financial analysis and its managerial implications. Rest assured that this chapter does not review thousands or even hundreds of ratios but rather focuses on the *major* categories of ratios and the fundamental ratios within each category.

COMPARATIVE BASIS STANDARDS

Just as in Chapter 2, The Hershey Company will be the central company in this analysis. Hershey's financial statements were discussed in Chapter 2.

Financial ratio performance standards come from a number of sources:

- Company historical performance
- Performance established as a target or objective within a plan
- Single or multiple competitors
- Industry averages and standards
- Best-demonstrated-practices companies

Historical performance establishes a baseline of performance on which an organization can build and improve. If a specific metric receives particular focus, that objective may be elevated to a strategic objective. More will be said about this in Chapter 6. Another source of performance standards is through competitive benchmarking with other companies in the firm's industry group. Finally, certain key companies may have been identified as having the best demonstrated practices. They usually have the optimal financial performance metrics and represent a superior way of conducting a certain aspect of business.

In this chapter, the first financial performance metrics compare the sales and growth of Hershey with the general food industry. Other financial performance metrics are introduced by comparing The Hershey Company against itself over a three-year period (2008 versus 2010) and with the 2008 and 2010 performance of H. J. Heinz, Inc. Finally, the food-processing industry is once again used to present the DuPont ratio analysis process and its related analysis.

Industry data are available from a wide variety of sources and can be used to obtain standards for evaluating the ratios that are calculated for an individual company. Listed below are many specialized producers of industry data, both private and governmental sources:

- *Dun & Bradstreet (D&B).* D&B provides ratios calculated for a large number of industries. The data give industry norms (common-size financial statements[1]) and numerous ratios, with the median, lower, and upper quartiles, for over 800 lines of business.

- *Risk Management Association (RMA; formerly known as Robert Morris Associates).* Another group of useful financial ratios can be found in the annual *Statement Studies*, compiled and published by RMA through the cooperation of the National Association of Bank Loan Officers. Average common-size[1] balance sheet and income statement data and 17 ratios are calculated for about 400 industries. Multiple-year data are presented for four size categories and the total industry.

- *Quarterly Financial Report for Manufacturing Corporations.* The Bureau of the Census in the U.S. Department of Commerce publishes quarterly financial data on manufacturing companies. The data include an analysis by industry groups and by asset size and financial statements in a common-size[1] format.

---

[1] Common-size statements express all line items as a percent of sales (in the case of a common-size income statement) or as a percent of total assets (in the case of a common-size balance sheet).

- *Trade associations and professional societies.* Trade associations and professional societies often will compile data related to a specific industry or a particular function (e.g., treasury management functions).

- *Financial services.* Specialist firms that compile and publish financial data, such as Value Line, Standard & Poor's, and Moody's, develop industry composites. Brokerage firms such as Merrill Lynch, UBS, Morgan Stanley Smith Barney, Fidelity, Vanguard, E*Trade, and so on periodically publish industry studies.

- *Financial press.* Financial periodicals such as *BusinessWeek, Forbes, Fortune*, and so on publish quarterly or annual studies that center on financial performance metrics with companies grouped by industry.

However, a problem that may be encountered is that many diverse firms may be included in the industry category. The general industry data may be fine for a quick comparison, but most companies, investment analysts, and professionals construct their own industry groups. With the considerable diversification by firms that exists today, selected firms may be more comparable than industry groupings. This was the case at Hershey. The corporation wanted to compare itself with major, branded food-processing companies. Companies were selected that, in general, were larger than Hershey (a group that Hershey was aspiring to be like, which is also called an *aspirant group*) or companies that compete more directly in the broader snack food industry, even though they may be smaller.

Figure 3-1 captures a comparative industry group of branded food companies that are appropriate in the analysis of Hershey. There are notably some companies that are not included in this industry group. M & M Mars (formerly Masterfoods) is not included in this industry group because Mars is a private organization and not required to disclose its financial information publicly. Nestle and Unilever also are not included because both are foreign companies and are subject to different accounting practices and different reporting requirements.

Although Tootsie Roll is less than one-tenth Hershey's size, Tootsie Roll is included in this branded food-processing industry because it is the only other publicly traded confectionery company in the United States.

Figure 3-1 also demonstrates a graphing technique (bar chart) to illustrate the 2010 sales of the companies in this industry group. Clearly, Kraft, is the largest domestic food company by a wide margin, with 2010 sales of $49,207 million after the acquisition of Cadbury in early 2010. On this absolute basis, it is no contest because sales at Kraft is more than 232 percent larger (or 3.32 times larger) than its next-closest competitor (General Mills) and 8.68 times larger than the sales at Hershey. In fact, Kraft's 2010 net income of $4,114 million is almost eight times larger than the $517 million of Tootsie Roll sales.

FIGURE   3-1

2010 Net Sales.
($ millions)

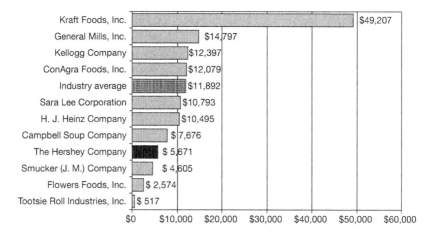

FIGURE   3-2

Annual growth in net sales, 2010.

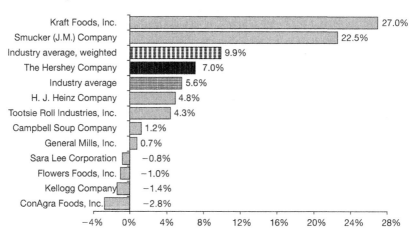

Figure 3-2 presents the 2010 annual growth in net sales and our first relative comparison metric, *annual growth*. This relative metric compares the performance of all 11 companies without letting size influence the result. It's commonly acknowledged that an ant is one of the strongest animals. However, that is relative to its body weight! In a similar fashion, the performance metrics that we will look at generally are *relative* metrics where size is not a determining factor.

In 2010, Hershey finished the year with growth that ranked third out of this industry group and sandwiched (no pun intended) between both industry averages. Once again, Kraft Foods was leading the way owing primarily to the early 2010 acquisition of Cadbury, which added $9,023 million of sales to 2010, or 23.3 percent, while organic growth (from the 2009 existing business) accounted for 3.7 percent of Kraft's 2010 growth (from the Kraft 2010 Annual Report, page 27).[2] Even for the Smucker Company, the annualization of the 2009 Folgers acquisition increased sales by over 24 percent. Thus, without the acquisition, the Smucker Company's organic business declined in 2009.

There is a story behind every number. Throughout this chapter and when employing financial performance metrics, it is important to understand the company's business and recent events within the company. The financial results of these events are captured on the financial statements and are reflected through the performance metrics.

You also will notice on Figure 3-2 that there are two industry averages. The *industry average* is simply an average of all the growth rates, that is, the average of Kraft's 27.0 percent annual growth, Smucker's 22.5 percent, and Hershey's 7.0 percent, all the way through ConAgra Foods' (e.g., Healthy Choice, Chef Boyardee, Hunts, and many other fine brands) contraction of 2.8 percent. The growth of all companies is treated the same, and an overall industry average is created. The second industry average is the *weighted industry average*, which first sums the 2010 and 2009 sales for all 11 companies and then computes the annual growth rate on these totals. Consequently, Kraft has its growth weighted the most (32.5 percent), whereas Tootsie Roll has its growth weighted the least at 0.4 percent.

Figure 3-3 presents the *compound annual growth rate* (CAGR) over a four-year time period from 2006 to 2010. This topic is discussed much more thoroughly in Chapter 7. For our purposes here, the four-year sales CAGR is calculated as:

$$(FV/PV)^{(1/n)} - 1 \tag{3.1}$$

Specifically, $(sales_{2010}/sales_{2006})^{(1/4)} - 1$, or $(\$5,671.0/\$4,946.7)^{(0.25)} - 1 = 3.5$ percent (the figures are in millions of dollars). In this example, n is four years (i.e., $2010 - 2006$). This provides a longer-term perspective on the growth of the food-processing industry.

Over this period, and thanks to the previously mentioned acquisition, the Smucker Company led all industry members with a 20.9 percent compound annual growth rate. In 2006, Smucker's sales were $2,154.7 million, but through a series of acquisitions, the company's sales grew to be $4,605.3 million. This would be the same as growing the $2,154.7 million at 20.9 percent for 2007 and then growing that at 20.9 percent for 2008, 2009, and 2010 to arrive at $4,605.3

---

[2] Company's annual reports (or 10Ks) will be considered the source of all data in this chapter unless specifically stated otherwise.

FIGURE 3-3

Net Sales, compound annual growth rate, 2006–2010.

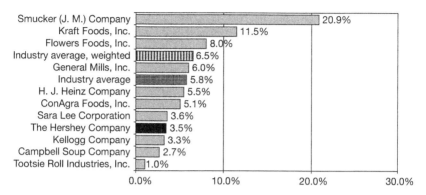

million. Over this period, Hershey's growth had been modest while trailing both industry averages.

Again, two industry averages are presented in Figure 3-3. This industry group will be revisited in the DuPont analysis section.

BASIC FINANCIAL STATEMENT ANALYSIS

Basic financial statement analysis begins by examining income statements and balance sheets on a relative basis, including:

- Analyzing the annual growth rate of each line item, which was started earlier

- Representing line items on an income statement as a percent of sales, line items on a balance sheet as a percent of total assets, and line items on the statement of cash flows as a percent of sales (common-size statement)

- Indexing each line item as a percentage of the first year, 2008 (common base year)

This type of analysis is done at the most fundamental level. After discussing the specific calculations, a review of Hershey will be conducted. Table 3-1 analyzes Hershey's income statement. Panel *A* provides the actual information, which also was included in Chapter 2.

In Table 3-1, annual growth (panel *B*) is calculated as:

$$2010 \text{ Annual growth in net sales} = \frac{2010 \text{ net sales}}{2009 \text{ net sales}} - 1 = \frac{\$5,671.0}{\$5,298.7} - 1 = 7.0\% \quad (3.2)$$

TABLE 3-1

Income Statement Analysis

The Hershey Company, 2008, 2009, and 2010
($ millions)

	A. Income Statement			B. Annual Growth			C. % of Net Sales			D. Index Value		
	2008	2009	2010	2009	2010	CAGR*	2008	2009	2010	2008	2009	2010
Net sales	$5,132.8	$5,298.7	$5,671.0	3.2%	7.0%	5.1%	100.0%	100.0%	100.0%	100.0	103.2	110.5
Costs and expenses												
Cost of sales	3,375.1	3,245.5	3,255.8	−3.8%	0.3%	−1.8%	65.8%	61.3%	57.4%	100.0	96.2	96.5
Selling, marketing, and admin	1,073.0	1,208.7	1,426.5	12.6%	18.0%	15.3%	20.9%	22.7%	25.1%	100.0	112.6	132.9
Business realign and asset impair	94.8	82.9	83.4	−12.6%	0.6%	−6.2%	1.8%	1.6%	1.5%	100.0	87.4	88.0
Total costs and expenses	4,542.9	4,537.1	4,765.7	−0.1%	5.0%	2.4%	88.5%	85.6%	84.0%	100.0	99.9	104.9
Income before interest and taxes	589.9	761.6	905.3	29.1%	18.9%	23.9%	11.5%	14.4%	16.0%	100.0	129.1	153.5
Interest expense, net	97.9	90.5	96.4	−7.6%	6.5%	−0.8%	1.9%	1.7%	1.7%	100.0	92.4	98.5
Income before income taxes	492.0	671.1	808.9	36.4%	20.5%	28.2%	9.6%	12.7%	14.3%	100.0	136.4	164.4
Provision for income taxes	180.6	235.1	299.1	30.2%	27.2%	28.7%	3.5%	4.5%	5.3%	100.0	130.2	165.6
Net income	$ 311.4	$ 436.0	$ 509.8	40.0%	16.9%	28.0%	6.1%	8.2%	9.0%	100.0	140.0	163.7

*CAGR: compound annual growth rate from 2008 to 2010.

The compound annual growth rate (CAGR) from 2008 to 2010 (also in panel B) is calculated as before:

$$2010 \text{ CAGR} = \left(\frac{2010 \text{ net sales}}{2008 \text{ net sales}}\right)^{(1/n)} - 1 = \left(\frac{\$5,671.0}{\$5,132.8}\right)^{0.5} - 1 = 5.1\% \quad (3.3)$$

Hershey's 2010 improved annual growth, of course, is reflected in this two-year compound annual growth rate. The percent of net sales (panel C) is calculated as each line item on the income statement divided by net sales ($ millions):

$$2010 \text{ Cost of sales as a percent of net sales} = \frac{\text{cost of sales}}{\text{net sales}} = \frac{\$3,255.8}{\$5,671.0} = 57.4\% \quad (3.4)$$

This is referred to as the *common-size analysis*.

Finally, the index value (panel D) is calculated as:

$$2010 \text{ Index value of net sales} = \frac{2010 \text{ net sales}}{2008 \text{ net sales}} \times 100 = \frac{\$5,671.0}{\$5,132.8} \times 100 = 110.5 \quad (3.5)$$

The index value shows the accumulated growth from the base year. This is also referred to as *common base-year analysis*.

From Table 3-1, the three years presented (2008–2010) were a period of modest (but increasing) sales growth declining to flat cost of goods sold and double-digit growth in selling, marketing, and administrative expenses. All this led to dramatic growth in all measures of income for Hershey: Operating income (or income before interest and taxes) increased 23.9 percent over the two-year period (CAGR), pretax income (or income before income taxes) was up 28.2 percent as a 2008–2010 CAGR, and net income increased by 28.0 percent CAGR over the same time period.

Panel C provides additional pieces of the performance story as a percent of sales and based on a common size of sales set at 100 percent. Cost of goods sold decreased dramatically between 2008 and 2010 and dropped by 8.4 percentage points. This can be due to a reduction in the cost of raw materials, weight reductions, price increases, and product mix (lower-cost items are sold in place of high-cost items). As a business manager, you are faced with choices on how to "spend" the production windfall represented by the reduction in the cost of goods sold. Do you take it to the bottom line, or do you spend it elsewhere in the business? Hershey's management team decided to do both! Selling, marketing, and administrative (SMA) expenses grew steadily as a percent of sales (4.2 percentage points of sales increase) because about half the reduction in production cost was reinvested in the business through business building efforts centered on direct brand expenses for higher levels of advertising, promotions, and so on. In fact, over this two-year period (2008–2010), Hershey's annual advertising expense increased by $230.0 million. Despite this added direct brand expense, all measures of income (as a percent of sales) also expanded.

The final panel (panel *D*) shows an index value where the first year of the analysis was set to 100.0 for all line items. Notice that sales and all income measures expanded, as did SMA and, of course, income taxes, whereas the cost of sales, business realignment and asset impairment, and interest expense fell.

This type of simple financial analysis can be centered on one company or applied to every member of the food-processing industry. By expanding the view, appropriate comparisons can be made. This analysis also can be applied to balance sheets and statements of cash flows. Finally, this analysis could be extended over a 5- or 10-year period to better envision underlying trends.

FINANCIAL RATIO ANALYSIS

The basic financial statement analysis just presented—growth analysis, common-size statement analysis, and common base-year or indexed statements—is the most fundamental of all analytical assessments. Although the components of the basic financial statement analysis are appropriate for comparisons between companies, the analysis was illustrated earlier as a way of examining a company versus itself over time.

Table 3-2 provides summary financial information. Specifically, data are provided for a comparative analysis of the past three years for Hershey (2008 versus 2010) and Heinz.[3]

In an analysis of the absolute financial data, the comparison of selected financial data limits the analysis: Generally, Hershey is half the size of Heinz. However, the next section compares and contrasts Hershey on a relative basis using financial performance metrics.

Financial Metrics and Ratios

Financial ratio analysis includes five broad groupings of ratios:

1. *Profitability.* How profitable is the company? These metrics measure management's overall ability to generate profits in relation to its sales or investment.

2. *Activity.* How effective is the company in managing its assets? These metrics measure the efficacious of the company's use of its resources.

3. *Leverage.* How is the company financed? These metrics measure the extent to which the firm's assets have been financed by debt.

4. *Liquidity.* How liquid is the company? These metrics measure the firm's ability to meet its maturing short-term obligations.

5. *Market.* How does the company's performance "translate" in the stock market? These metrics measure the firm's relationship to the broader stock market.

---

[3] H. J. Heinz Company is a major, branded food-processing company that serves consumers, food-service, and institutional customers worldwide.

TABLE 3-2

Selected Financial Data
($ millions, except per share)

	Hershey		Heinz	
	2008	2010	2008	2010
Sales	$ 5,132.8	$ 5,671.0	$ 10,070.8	$ 10,495.0
Cost of goods sold	3,375.1	3,255.8	6,390.1	6,700.7
Administrative costs	1,073.0	1,426.5	2,111.7	2,235.1
Operating income	589.9	905.3	1,541.1	1,541.0
Interest expense, net	97.9	96.4	323.3	250.5
Pretax income	492.0	808.9	1,217.8	1,290.5
Income taxes	180.6	299.1	372.9	358.5
Net income	311.4	509.8	844.9	864.9
EBITDA	839.4	1,102.4	1,857.9	1,862.1
Earnings per share, diluted	1.36	2.21	2.63	2.71
Normalized income	430.5	587.7	844.9	914.5
Cash & equivalents	37.1	884.6	617.7	483.3
Accounts receivable	455.2	390.1	1,161.5	1,045.3
Inventory	592.5	533.6	1,378.2	1,249.1
Current assets	1,344.9	2,005.2	3,325.6	3,051.1
Net, plant, prop, & equipment	1,458.9	1,437.7	2,104.7	2,091.8
Total assets	3,634.7	4,272.7	10,565.0	10,075.7
Current liabilities	1,270.2	1,298.8	2,670.1	2,175.4
Total liabilities	3,284.8	3,335.1	8,677.2	8,127.2
Stockholders' equity	349.9	937.6	1,887.8	1,948.5
Short-term debt	483.1	24.1	124.3	43.9
Current portion LTD	18.4	261.4	328.4	15.2
Long-term debt	1,506.0	1,541.8	4,730.9	4,559.2
Interest-bearing debt (IBD)	2,007.5	1,827.3	5,183.6	4,618.3
Beginning of year stock price	39.40	36.01	46.61	33.99
Year-end stock price	34.74	47.32	47.03	45.76
Shares outstanding	227.0	227.0	311.5	317.7
Dividends per share	1.19	1.28	1.52	1.68

In addition, basic financial statement analysis includes two additional categories of financial ratios:

1. *Growth.* How has the company been growing? These metrics include annual growth rates and compound annual growth rates over extended time periods (see above) of key income statement and balance sheet line items and measure the firm's ability to maintain its economic position in the growth of the economy and industry.

2. *Cost management.* What are the underlying cost trends relative to other measures? These metrics include measuring expenses as a percent of each sales dollar, as in the common-size income statement in Table 3-1.

Within each of these categories are numerous individual performance metrics. The most common of the metrics are discussed below.

Profitability Metrics

Profitability ratios measure management's overall efficiency at generating *profits*. One common set of profitability ratios examines some measure of income as a percent of sales, whereas another group of metrics focuses on income in relation to some measure of investment, as captured by the balance sheet.

We will begin by working our way down an income statement and consider first the gross margin (Table 3-3).

Gross margin develops a profitability relationship between gross income and sales, where:

$$\text{Gross income} = \text{sales} - \text{cost of goods sold} \qquad (3.6)$$

Gross income represents the inherent profitability of making a product. Cost of goods sold encompasses total cost of production—raw materials, direct labor, plant overhead, manufacturing depreciation, and so on. After absorbing the costs of making the product, how profitable is the company?

$$\text{Hershey's 2010 gross margin} = \frac{\text{sales} - \text{cost of good sold}}{\text{sales}}$$

$$= \frac{(\$5,671.0 - \$3,255.8)}{\$5,671.0} = 42.59\% \qquad (3.7)$$

In 2010, Hershey' made almost 42.6 cents for every dollar of sales after considering the cost of producing its products. From previous years, Hershey improved its gross margins significantly, whereas the gross margin at Heinz fell.

Operating margin is calculated as:

$$\text{Hershey's 2010 operating margin} = \frac{\text{operating income}}{\text{sales}} = \frac{\$905.3}{\$5,671.0} = 15.96\% \qquad (3.8)$$

For every dollar of sales, Hershey generated about 16 cents of operating income or earnings before interest and tax (EBIT). This represents the profitability of the corporation before considering financing costs (interest) and income taxes. As a result, often an operating margin is used as a performance metric to monitor the success of a division, business unit, or even product line. For Hershey, again, this metric increased sharply from 2008 and is measurably stronger than Heinz.

The difference between operating income (EBIT) and pretax income is interest expense. In Table 3-2, Hershey's 2010 operating income (\$905.3 million) less interest expense (\$96.4 million) equals a pretax income of \$808.9 million.

TABLE 3-3

Profitability Performance Metrics

	Hershey		Heinz	
Financial Performance Metric	**2008**	**2010**	**2008**	**2010**
Gross margin	34.24%	42.59%	36.55%	36.15%
Operating margin	11.49%	15.96%	15.30%	14.68%
Pretax margin	9.59%	14.26%	12.09%	12.30%
Net margin	6.07%	8.99%	8.39%	8.24%
EBITDA margin	16.35%	19.44%	18.45%	17.74%
Normalized income margin	8.39%	10.36%	8.39%	8.71%
Return on assets	8.57%	11.93%	8.00%	8.58%
Return on net assets	10.87%	15.64%	10.12%	10.87%
Return on financial capital	13.21%	18.44%	11.95%	13.17%
Return on equity	89.00%	54.37%	44.76%	44.39%

Financial Performance Metric	**Calculation and Strength***	
Gross margin	(Sales – cost of goods sold)/sales	+
Operating margin	Operating income/sales	+
Pretax margin	Pretax income/sales	+
Net margin	Net income/sales	+
EBITDA margin	EBITDA/sales	+
Normalized income margin	Normalized income/sales	+
Return on assets	Net income/assets	+
Return on net assets	Net income/predetermined investment base**	+
Return on financial capital	Net income/(IBD + equity)	+
Return on equity	Net income/equity	+

* A calculation designated with a "+" ("-") indicates that an increase (decrease) in this metric is a strength.
**In this case, the *predetermined investment* base is defined as total assets less non-interest-bearing current liabilities.

Similarly, the difference between the operating margin and pretax margin represents interest expense as a percent of sales, or in this case, 1.70 cents of every sales dollar go to pay interest expense.

Pretax margin reveals how profitable the firm is before considering the effects of income taxes. It is calculated as:

$$\text{Hershey's 2010 pretax margin} = \frac{\text{pretax income}}{\text{sales}} = \frac{\$808.9}{\$5,671.0} = 14.26\% \quad (3.9)$$

In 2010, Hershey had a pretax margin of 14.26 percent, which again increased sharply from 2008. In both years, Hershey remained more profitable

TABLE 3-4

Effective Tax Rate Comparison
($ millions)

	Horohoy Effective Tax Rate		Heinz Effective Tax Rate	
	2008	2010	2008	2010
Income tax provision	$ 180.6	$ 299.1	$ 372.9	$ 358.5
Pre-tax income	492.0	808.9	1,217.8	1,290.5
Effective tax rate	36.7%	37.0%	30.6%	27.8%

than Heinz. The difference between Hershey's pretax margin (14.26 percent) and net margin (8.99 percent) is 5.27 cents (14.26 percent − 8.99 percent), or 5.27 percent of every dollar of Hershey's sales went to pay income taxes. Using this relationship or simply income taxes, as noted in Table 3-2, provides a related measure, the *effective tax rate*. The effective tax rate is calculated as:

$$\text{Hershey's 2010 effective tax rate} = \frac{\text{income taxes}}{\text{pretax income}} = \frac{\$299.1}{\$808.9} = 37.0\% \quad (3.10)$$

Thirty-seven percent of Hershey's pretax income was recognized as a tax expense for 2010. Over this time period and compared with Heinz, Hershey's effective tax rate increased (Table 3-4).

More will be said about corporate income taxes in Chapter 4. Suffice it to say, at this point, that Hershey is at a large disadvantage in terms of the effective tax rate owing to the geographic nature of both companies: Hershey, domestic, and Heinz, international.

Net income margin or, simply, *net margin* is one of the most frequently cited metrics. This measure is also called the *return on sales*. Senior management often sets targets and objectives that include the net margin. Often a senior manager's bonus is tied directly or indirectly to the net margin. Simply, the net margin reflects the number of pennies of income for every dollar of sales:

$$\text{Hershey's 2010 net income margin} = \frac{\text{net income}}{\text{sales}} = \frac{\$509.8}{\$5,671.0} = 8.99\% \quad (3.11)$$

For every dollar of sales, Hershey generated 8.99 cents of net income, that is, income after paying all its production costs, operating expenses, interest, and taxes. Hershey's net margin improved significantly by 2.92 percent (percentage points) from its 2008 level (6.07 percent) in part as a result of implementing operating efficiencies, including a reduction in the cost of raw materials, product weight reductions, price increases, and product mix (lower-cost items sold in place of higher-cost items).

TABLE   3-5

Profitability Analysis: Income Statement (% of sales)

	Hershey		Heinz	
	2008	2010	2008	2010
Sales	100.00%	100.00%	100.00%	100.00%
Cost of goods sold	65.76%	57.41%	63.45%	63.85%
Gross margin	**34.24%**	**42.59%**	**36.55%**	**36.15%**
Selling, general administrative	20.90%	25.16%	20.97%	21.30%
Other expenses	1.85%	1.47%	0.28%	0.17%
Operating margin	**11.49%**	**15.96%**	**15.30%**	**14.68%**
Interest expense	1.90%	1.70%	3.21%	2.38%
Pretax margin	**9.59%**	**14.26%**	**12.09%**	**12.30%**
Income tax provision	3.52%	5.27%	3.70%	3.42%
Other expense, net	0.00%	0.00%	0.00%	0.64%
Net margin	**6.07%**	**8.99%**	**8.39%**	**8.24%**
EBITDA margin	16.35%	19.44%	18.45%	17.74%
Normalized margin	8.39%	10.36%	8.39%	8.71%

Table 3-5 summarizes. The profitability measures discussed so far are highlighted.

For Hershey with 2010 sales of $5,671.0 million, a 0.1 percent improvement in the net margin enhances Hershey's profitability by almost $5.7 million. Extending this further, the 2.92 percent net margin improvement resulted in an additional $165.6 million of income! It is easy to see why management teams pay attention to the net margin.

Generally, the higher the net margin (or any profitability metric), the better is the underlying performance of the company. There are two ways to improve your net margin. One way is to reduce expenses; the other way is to increase prices. However, as mentioned earlier, anything taken to an extreme can become a weakness. Kellogg was the perennial leader of the food industry with net margins approaching 10 percent in the late 1980s when the industry average was approximately 5 percent. Also, in the late 1980s and early 1990s, Kellogg was the number one cereal company with the largest market share. In the early 1990s, Kellogg went through a series of price increases that boosted its net margin to over 11.0 percent. Of course, as consumers, we were all less than thrilled to pay $4 and $5 for a box of cereal.

Companies that produced generic and store-brand cereals seized the opportunity with lower-priced substitutes. We, as consumers, learned that we could eat cereal that didn't come in a box but rather came in a cellophane bag or that came from a store-brand box. Competition heated up. Kellogg's price increase was broken, and its total sales began to fall. Prices fell, and heavy expenses were incurred for store coupons, promotions, and advertising. Kellogg's sales declined, its number one market share eroded, and its net margins shrank. The company's strict adherence to raising prices for a higher net margin eventually cost the company in the long term. All ratios must be balanced carefully and the industry dynamics understood to better signal when a strength could become a weakness.

As discussed in Chapter 2, earnings before interest, taxes, depreciation, and amortization (EBITDA, a quasi-operating cash-flow metric) and normalized income also can be thought of as a percent of sales. Once again, the higher the value is generally, the stronger the company.

In summary, when comparing Hershey with itself over the last three years (similar to the basic analysis), it is apparent that Hershey has improved in every measure. Broadening the analysis to include Heinz, it can be seen that Hershey trailed Heinz in all profitability measures (as a percent of sales) in 2008 with the lone exception of normalized income, in which the companies were tied. Between 2008 and 2010, Heinz slipped in almost all measures, and Hershey overtook it in all measures of income as a percent of sales. Of course, we used financial analysis to identify the situation; now is when the difficult work begins to understand what drove the shift in performance and how to drive additional profitability.

Return on Investment
This next series of profitability metrics looks at the amount of profitability for every dollar of investment. These measures are broadly referred to as *return on investment* (ROI) or *accounting returns on investment*. In these cases, profitability and investment definitions vary with the particular focus of the analysis.

Assets represent the total investment made by the corporation on behalf of its stockholders. As discussed in Chapter 2, accounting values do not represent current values, fair market values, or even replacement value of assets. In fact, a portion of the balance sheet captures only historical costs of the assets. Or balance sheet values also may capture "impaired" values but never "windfall" values! Still other asset values go unacknowledged, such as the value of intellectual property, strong brands, technology, and highly knowledgeable employees. Despite these frailties, a balance sheet does reasonably capture and represent assets on a consistently measured basis among organizations.

Referencing Table 3-3 again, *return on assets* (ROA) measures the return (income) for every dollar of assets:

$$\text{Hershey's 2010 return on assets} = \frac{\text{net income}}{\text{total assets}} = \frac{\$509.8}{\$4,272.7} = 11.93\% \quad (3.12)$$

In 2010, Hershey generated 11.93 cents on every dollar of assets, which was substantially higher than its ROA for 2008. Hershey's 2010 profitability superiority to Heinz once again is evidenced because Hershey's ROA is 3.35 percentage points higher than the ROA of Heinz!

Many companies establish internal profitability metrics. Hershey called its metric *return on net assets* (RONA). Many companies have a similarly defined metric that goes by different acronyms and names:

- Return on net assets (RONA)
- Operating return on net assets (ORONA)
- Return on net investment (RONI)
- Return on invested capital (ROIC)
- Return on capital invested (ROCI)
- Return on gross employed capital (ROGEC)

While these measures may have slight variations in the definition of the denominator, we will use a fairly common variety of net asset definition for our discussion:

$$\text{Net assets} = \text{total assets} - \text{non-interest-bearing current liabilities} \quad (3.13)$$

In Hershey's 2010 case, non-interest-bearing current liabilities totaled $1,013.3 million: $410.6 million in accounts payable and $602.7 million in accrued liabilities. Net assets were: Net assets = $4,272.7 − $1,013.3 = $3,259.4. Said differently, net assets represent financial capital (i.e., equity, long-term debt, short-term debt, and current portion of long-term debt) and long-term operating liabilities, such as deferred taxes and other long-term liabilities. The return on net assets represents the return on total assets less spontaneous current operating liabilities:

$$\text{Hershey's 2010 return on net assets} = \frac{\text{net income}}{\text{net assets}} = \frac{\$509.8}{\$3,259.4} = 15.64\% \quad (3.14)$$

Again, as seen with the return on assets, Hershey's 2010 RONA was significantly more than what it was in 2008 and now leads Heinz by an even larger amount.

Narrowing the investment base a bit more, provides *return on capital* (ROC), where capital is the book value of financial capital (interest-bearing debt *plus* equity). Remember, interest-bearing debt (IBD) is equal to short-term debt, bank borrowings, notes payable, current portion of long-term debt, and long-term debt:

$$\text{Hershey's 2010 return on captial} = \frac{\text{net income}}{\text{financial capital}} = \frac{\$509.8}{\$2,764.9} = 18.44\% \quad (3.15)$$

For every dollar of financial capital (debt and equity) that Hershey employed, it generated 18.44 cents of income. Using this metric and continuing prior trends, Hershey already was stronger than Heinz in 2008 and grew even stronger by 2010. Heinz also improved over this period.

Return on equity (ROE) is the final profitability metric and has the narrowest definition of a capital base used in the return metrics. Return on equity for Hershey in 2010 was 54.37 percent:

$$\text{Hershey's 2010 return on equity} = \frac{\text{net income}}{\text{equity}} = \frac{\$509.8}{\$937.6} = 54.37\% \quad (3.16)$$

For every dollar of total stockholders' equity (original investment and retained earnings offset by share repurchases), Hershey generated 54.37 cents of income after paying all production costs, operating expenses, interest expense, and income taxes. In 2008, Hershey's stockholders' equity was abnormally low owing to share repurchases and resulted in an ROE of almost 90%. In both years, Hershey outpaced Heinz by a substantial amount.

Permutations of RONA

When calculating any return on investment metrics as discussed earlier, the analyst is faced with a choice of numerous ways to "adjust" either the numerator (income) or denominator (investment base). As presented earlier, net income was used consistently as the numerator, and the year-end balance sheet values were used according to the return metric (e.g., assets for ROA, equity for ROE, etc.).

Table 3-6 outlines general considerations encountered with a variety of these alternative or nontraditional, nongeneric ROI measures:

- *Income consideration.* Is income a standard traditional measure of income or an adjusted measure of income that includes or excludes specific items such as interest, taxes, extraordinary items (e.g.,

T A B L E   3-6

Permutations of ROI

Income Consideration	Investment Base
Traditional	Traditional
Net income	Total assets
Operating income	Financial capital
Adjustments	"Net" assets
Interest	Equity
Taxes	Inclusions/exclusions
Depreciation	Any balance sheet line
Amortization & others	
Extraordinary items	**Basis**
Acquisition impact	Book
	Market
Time Frame	
Period	**Balance Sheet Period(s)**
Quarter	End of the period
Year-to-date	Beginning of the period
Rolling year	Begin/end average
	4-Qtr rolling average
Application Level	5-Qtr rolling average
Corporate	8-Qtr rolling average
Division	Other rolling average
Business unit	

restructuring charges, asset impairments, etc.), and the first-year impact of acquisitions on a pretax or posttax basis? In Chapter 2, we discussed "normalized" income, or income without the impact of extraordinary one-time charges.

- *Time frame.* For what period of time is the income measured: a month, a quarter, year to date, or rolling year? Rolling year (or rolling period) includes the last 12 months or 4 quarters of "income" and changes with every passing month or quarter.

- *Application level and responsibility.* What level of the organization is under review, and what level of responsibility is under the control of the management team under review? For example, many business unit or divisional management teams are reviewed and compared based on operating income because the managers do not have tax or borrowing responsibility, whereas corporate management teams usually are held responsible for all decisions and therefore consider net income.

- *Investment base.* Often multiple ROIs are used at different levels of the organization and for different purposes. What distinguishes the investment base are the specific inclusions or exclusions that may be applied. Usually, this is aligned with the appropriate level and responsibility for the assets and liabilities under the direct control of the management team's authority. Just as with income considerations, the focus on the investment base may change depending on the specific level under review.

- *Basis.* Most financial performance metrics including ROI reflect the book values as presented on the balance sheet. On occasion, the market value of equity may be substituted for the book value of equity.

- *Balance sheet periods.* Throughout this chapter, all balance sheet values used in calculations are as of the end of the year. Other approaches include beginning of the year (or period) balance sheet values, a two-point average of the beginning and end of the period values, or a multiple-period rolling average.

Continuing with this last point, using year-end balances to calculate ROI, this is a very conservative posture and assumes that management generated income throughout the year on newly invested capital. Usually, using year-end values results in the lowest ROI values. A more aggressive posture uses the beginning balance (e.g., end of the last fiscal year) of investment. This is the same as suggesting that all annual investment in the corporation occurs at the end of the year and therefore is not available throughout the year to generate any income. Another approach averages the two, the beginning and ending investment (i.e., balance sheet) values. By doing this, management is more realistically charged with earning a return as investment is made in the organization.

Unless there is some pressing business rationale or significant shifts in the business, the use of balance sheet values at year end or the beginning of the year or their average will have minimal impact on telling the long-term story that underlies the analysis. Yes, there will be different exact, specific numbers, but the underlying trends will be consistent. For simplistic illustration, year-end balance sheet values are used is this section and throughout this chapter.

Different approaches in practice:

1. Hershey's return on net assets (RONA) was calculated as described earlier: Net income/(total assets − nondebt current liabilities). However, instead of using the end of the year's balance sheet values, Hershey used a five-quarter rolling average. This is to say, the balance sheet values were the average of the quarterly values on December 31, 2009, April 4, 2010, July 4, 2010, October 3, 2010, and December 31, 2010. In Hershey's opinion, this was the fairest representation of the investment base.

2. Kellogg also provides insight into what it considers one of its key performance indicators (KPI), return on invested capital (ROIC). It calculates ROIC as

$$\frac{\text{Operating income} + \text{amortization} - \text{income taxes}}{\substack{\text{Average of beginning and ending annual balances of (total equity} + \\ \text{interest-bearing debt} + \text{deferred taxes} + \text{accumulated amortization)}}} \quad (3.17)$$

Kellogg begins with operating income (or earnings before interest and taxes) of $1,990 million and enhances it by amortization of intangibles ($22 million in 2010), which was a recognized expense on its income statement. Thus the company is reversing a noncash accounting charge and increasing operating income. Then it subtracts taxes to arrive at the numerator. Another way of looking at the numerator is by starting with net income and adding back after-tax interest expense and after-tax amortization expense. The numerator begins much as return on capital, but deferred taxes and accumulated amortization are added back to the investment base.

3. Finally, a common permutation of return on assets (ROA) also adjusts the impact of interest from the numerator:

$$\frac{\text{Net income} + (1 - \text{tax rate}) \times \text{interest expense}}{\text{Total assets}} \quad (3.18)$$

Some argue that since interest is a return on capital and total assets are comprised of debt and equity, the explicit cost of the debt after tax should not be considered in the numerator. This is the underlying premise for Kellogg's ROIC calculation.

4. Other approaches use a *free cash-flow* measure that is often defined as cash flow from operations less capital expenditures and dividends instead of any measure of income.

5. Still a few others use a residual income approach that was rekindled in the mid–1990s as *economic value added* (EVA). Effectively,

EVA is a dollarized RONA that begins with normalized income but then imposes non–U.S. GAAP accounting treatments such as capitalizing, subsequently amortizing expenses such as advertising, research and development, training, and so on while dividing by a capital base that may be similar to a net assets base except that it has been further adjusted for the accumulation of these non–U.S. GAAP accounting treatments. Simultaneously, EVA compares this RONA (or as the consulting firm of Stern Stewart calls it, ROIC) with the cost of capital (see Chapter 11) and dollarizes that difference.

In the final analysis, there are many permutations of ROI metrics used in practice. It is very important to understand exactly the calculation if you are comparing two separate entities or an entity with itself over time. Consistency is the key to better understanding and a better analysis of one company versus another or one company versus itself over time.

Activity Metrics

Activity ratios measure how effectively a company is using its resources (Table 3-7). Throughout this section, income statement and balance sheet line items will be used for comparison. In all cases, year-end balance sheet values are used.

The total asset turnover ratio gives the broadest and most strategically focused activity measure. Additional activity metrics target specific areas of management for closer, day-to-day scrutiny.

Total asset turnover is defined as sales divided by total assets:

$$\text{Hershey's 2010 total asset turnover} = \frac{\text{sales}}{\text{total assets}} = \frac{\$5,671.0}{\$4,272.7} = 1.327 \quad (3.19)$$

For every dollar of assets, Hershey generates $1.327 in sales. For every dollar of assets that society has entrusted to the managers at Hershey, $1.327 worth of sales is generated. Over time, this metric has slipped for Hershey from 2008 (1.412) and its recent peak of 1.442 in 2009. This is a negative signal that underperforming assets have been added to Hershey's balance sheet.

Often this is due to a new plant or other facility coming online and not yet reaching its full potential. This is evidenced by a large increase in net, plant, property, and equipment (PP&E). However, in this specific case, net PP&E actually declined from $1,458.9 million in 2008 to $1,437.7 million in 2010. From an operations perspective, a buildup of inventory or receivables also will drive the total asset turnover lower. We will examine receivables and inventory separately. A strategic impact could be due to a large acquisition and reflected in a dramatic increase in "intangibles resulting from business acquisitions (or goodwill)." But none of these usual suspects are causing the drop in Hershey's total asset turnover.

However, an unlikely suspect and the root of this decline is cash. Cash and equivalents had the single largest asset expansion between 2008 and 2010,

TABLE 3-7

Activity Performance Metrics

	Hershey		Heinz	
	2008	2010	2008	2010
Total asset turnover	1.412	1.327	0.953	1.042
Fixed asset turnover	3.518	3.944	4.785	5.017
Current asset turnover	3.816	2.828	3.028	3.440
Accounts receivable turnover	11.276	14.537	8.671	10.040
Average collection period	32.37	25.11	42.10	36.35
Inventory turnover	5.696	6.102	4.637	5.364
Inventory days outstanding	64.08	59.82	78.72	68.04
Financial Performance Metric	**Calculation and Strength***			
Total asset turnover	Sales/total assets			+
Fixed asset turnover	Sales/net plant, property, & equipment			+
Current asset turnover	Sales/current assets			+
Accounts receivable turnover	Sales/accounts receivable			+
Average collection period	365 days/accounts receivable turnover			−
Inventory turnover	Cost of goods sold/inventory			+
Inventory days outstanding	365 days/inventory turnover			−

* A calculation designated with a "+" ("−") indicates that an increase (decrease) in this metric is a strength.

with an increase of almost $850 million. Cash is an underperforming asset in the low-interest-rate environment of 2010 and certainly does not earn the return provided by productively employed assets at Hershey. It is difficult to think of too much cash as a negative, but from this viewpoint, it absolutely is detrimental!

On the other hand, Heinz saw improvement in its total asset turnover, but at a significantly lower level than Hershey. In 2010, Hershey generated 28.5 cents more sales per dollar of assets than did Heinz. The difference may be an indication that Hershey has a superior sales force, or it may be the result of more efficient production facilities, or it simply may be the result of factors such as asset mix, product mix, or other factors that are not directly related to management efficiency. The total asset turnover alerts management to overall efficiency differences. The other activity ratios make the analysis more operational by identifying key areas for management's attention.

Fixed asset turnover, or the rate of fixed asset utilization, is critical because investments in plant and equipment are both large and of long duration. A mistake in fixed asset investments (i.e., net, plant, property, and equipment) may be reversed, but the consequences are likely to be long-lasting. To focus on plant and equipment investment, the fixed asset turnover centers on net, plant, property, and equipment and is determined as follows:

$$\text{Hershey's 2010 fixed asset turnover} = \frac{\text{sales}}{\text{NPP\&E}} = \frac{\$5,671.0}{\$1,437.7} = 3.944 \quad (3.20)$$

For every dollar of net, plant, property and equipment (NPP&E), Hershey generated over $3.94 worth of sales. Hershey's performance showed improvement over this time span. However, when compared with Heinz, Hershey trails both years. Heinz generates over $1.07 more ($5.017 versus $3.944) in sales for every dollar invested in net, plant, property, and equipment.

Although this metric points to stronger managerial performance at Heinz, this difference could be due to a number of reasons, such as (1) the age of the plants, (2) the number of different products produced at one location, (3) the physical production plant's configuration, (4) the total number of units produced, (5) the product's shelf life, (6) the mix of products sold, and (7) the amount of outsourcing.

Older facilities presumably are operationally less efficient but are represented on the books in depreciated dollar amounts based on their original purchase price. Newer facilities tend to be more efficient, cost more, and are underutilized initially. Consequently, the NPP&E balance is higher with newer equipment. The number of products produced at one facility affects the plant utilization rate. Production facilities are much more efficient when producing one product. With outsourced production, generally, the supplier who is building the product owns the equipment. Therefore, the assets are not reflected in the outsourcing company's NPP&E. All these aspects affect this metric.

Unfortunately, we are not able to analyze the plants of Hershey or Heinz more specifically owing to a lack of available *public* plant-specific data. However, the managerial objectives remain clear for Hershey: Generate more sales and/or reduce the investment in net, plant, property, and equipment. Continuous improvement objectives can be implemented at each manufacturing facility within Hershey.

Once again, permutations of fixed asset turnover are possible. The most common one is to use all noncurrent assets in the denominator. This version may lose operational focus. The current assets turnover simply uses total current assets divided into sales:

$$\text{Hershey's 2010 current asset turnover} = \frac{\text{sales}}{\text{current assets}} = \frac{\$5,671.0}{\$2,005.2} = 2.828 \quad (3.21)$$

For every dollar of current assets, Hershey generates over $2.82 in sales, which is a sharp decline of almost $1.00 from 2008. Notice that Heinz improved (increased) from 2008 to 2010 and now outpaces Hershey.

To better understand what is driving this reduction, it is often necessary to examine the activity of the two largest operating current assets—accounts receivable and inventory—and their own activity ratios.

Accounts receivable turnover is calculated similarly to the other turnovers:

Hershey's 2010 accounts receivable turnover =

$$\frac{\text{credit sales}}{\text{accounts receivable}} = \frac{\$5,671.0}{\$390.1} = 14.537 \qquad (3.22)$$

The assumption is that all of Hershey's sales are made on credit, which is legitimate for most businesses. Additionally, even in a business that is mostly cash, there is generally no distinction made in an annual report between cash sales and credit sales. This measure suggests that over 14.5 times a year, Hershey collects all its accounts receivables from its customers. This performance is better than the 2008 performance, when the receivables were collected 11.276 times a year, and is measurably stronger than the 2010 accounts receivable turnover for Heinz of 10.040.

Very closely related to the accounts receivable turnover ratio is another activity ratio called the *average collection period*. The average collection period measures the length of time that it takes to collect from a customer. It is calculated by dividing 365 days in a year by the accounts receivable turnover:

Hershey's 2010 average collection period =

$$\frac{365}{\text{accounts receivable turnover}} = \frac{365}{14.537} = 25.11 \qquad (3.23)$$

In 2010, Hershey took 25.11 days to collect from its customers. This is over a week sooner than in 2008, and a lower value indicates strength! Once again, Heinz also has improved but trails the performance of Hershey in 2010 by over 11 days.

Usual credit terms are "2/10 net 30," which means that if you pay in the first 10 days, you get a 2 percent discount. If you don't pay in the first 10 days, the entire amount (no discounts) is payable in 30 days. Under these circumstances, an average collection period of 30 days or less is a standard of excellence. On the surface, Hershey's 2010 performance is impressive, but it also raises a concern. Is Hershey's accounts receivable policy too tight? Is Hershey losing sales by restricting only its best customers to being able to purchase on credit? Once again, a directionally strong metric may become a weakness if it is taken to extremes.

The final activity ratio examined in this section is the *inventory turnover ratio*. Inventory turnover is calculated using the cost of goods sold instead of sales to eliminate the "profit" component and more accurately reflect this metric because inventory is carried at production cost, not the anticipated selling price:

$$\text{Hershey's 2010 inventory turnover} = \frac{\text{cost of goods sold}}{\text{inventory}} = \frac{\$3,255.8}{\$533.6} = 6.102 \qquad (3.24)$$

In 2010, Hershey sold off its entire inventory 6.102 times in the year. That is, it cleaned out its warehouses, sold everything off the shelves 6.102 times in 2010. This ratio has shown steady improvement at Hershey because it became an important operational objective over this time period. In 2008, the inventory "turned" only 5.696 times. In 1999, Hershey installed a new computer system (an enterprise resource planning [ERP] system by SAP) that enabled the streamlining of its inventory management practices, resulting in improved inventory turns. In 1999, Hershey's inventory turnover was only 3.910 turns. If Hershey would have maintained the same inventory turnover as in 1999, the 2010 inventory would have been $832.7 million ($3,255.8/3.910 times). Hershey would have had almost $300 million more invested in inventory than it actually had if focus would not have been drawn to inventory management, and enhanced management techniques would not have been enabled by an ERP installation.

A variation of the inventory turnover is to measure the number of days of inventory on hand. This is accomplished by dividing 365 days in the year by the number of turnovers per year:

$$\text{Hershey's 2010 inventory days outstanding} = \frac{365}{\text{inventory turnover}} = \frac{365}{6.102} = 59.82 \quad (3.25)$$

Every 59.82 days, Hershey sells off its entire inventory, which is about a four-day improvement over its 2008 performance and over a week better than the 2010 performance of Heinz. Once again, the fewer days outstanding represent stronger performance.

This metric can be applied at a lower level within a firm. It can be applied by business units and by isolating inventory into raw materials, goods in process, and finished goods. Standards of performance can be established for these individual inventory components and across business units or even production facilities. Internal best demonstrated practices can be shared throughout the organization.

Activity ratios provide an overview of how effectively a company is using its assets. The activity ratios addressed in this section provide a review of the major metrics in this category. Again, this is not an exhaustive list. Turnovers can be calculated by taking any balance sheet item and dividing it into sales or cost of goods sold. Any turnover can be presented as days outstanding by dividing 365 days in a year by the turnover value. The activity ratio discussion provided an analytical framework that can be used to build other turnovers or days outstanding as specific business needs dictate.

Leverage Metrics

Decisions about the use of debt must balance hoped-for higher operating returns against the increased financial risk of the consequences firms face when they are unable to meet interest payments or maturing obligations. The use of debt has a number of implications for a firm:

- Creditors look at equity, or owner-supplied funds, as a cushion or base for the use of debt. If owners provide only a small proportion of total financing, the risks of the enterprise are borne mainly by its creditors.
- By raising funds through debt, the owners gain the benefits of increased capital while maintaining control of the firm.

- The use of debt with a fixed interest rate magnifies both the gains and losses to the owners.

- The use of debt with a fixed interest cost and a specified maturity increases the risk that the firm may not be able to meet its obligations.

Leverage metrics measure the extent to which a firm is financed by debt. The first group of leverage metrics uses the accounting balance sheet identity relationship:

$$\text{Assets} = \text{liabilities} + \text{stockholders' equity} \qquad (3.26)$$

This group of leverage metrics uses total liabilities (including accounts payable, accrued liabilities, deferred taxes, other long-term liabilities, and interest-bearing debt) synonymously with the word *debt*. Another group of leverage ratios centers on balance sheet relationships but defines debt only as interest-bearing debt. The third group of leverage metrics concentrates on income statement relationships and the ability of the firm to pay its interest expense (Table 3-8).

Debt to equity uses the term *debt* referring to total liabilities. It is calculated as:

$$\text{Hershey's 2010 debt-to-equity ratio} = \frac{\text{debt (or liabilities)}}{\text{stockholders' equity}} = \frac{\$3,335.1}{\$937.6} = 3.557 \qquad (3.27)$$

For every dollar of stockholders' equity, Hershey supports $3.557 worth of liabilities. A higher debt-to-equity ratio indicates that the firm is using more total liabilities to finance its assets. From a banker's point of view, the higher the debt-to-equity ratio, the weaker a company is because it is more risky. Said differently, a low debt-to-equity ratio indicates that the firm is committing a large portion of equity in financing the business. Therefore, a firm with a low debt-to-equity ratio is less risky and consequently stronger than a firm with a higher ratio. In 2008, a dollar of Hershey's equity supported $9.388 in debt. Hershey is currently in a significantly stronger position.

Heinz also has improved its performance but supports $4.171 debt (liabilities) for every $1 of its equity in 2010. From a banker's perspective, this is a demonstrated strength of Hershey versus Heinz in 2010. Later in this chapter, I point out that under the right circumstances and with a specific point of reference, debt actually can be a performance-enhancing addition to the balance sheet and a firm's overall performance!

This analysis can be extended by examining current liabilities, long-term liabilities, or any liability in relation to equity (i.e., divided by equity).

Financial leverage is closely aligned with the debt-to-equity ratio. Financial leverage measures the extent to which the shareholders' equity investment is magnified by the use of total debt (or liabilities) in financing the firm's total assets. Financial leverage illustrates the number of dollars of assets for every one dollar of stockholders' equity:

$$\text{Hershey's 2010 financial leverage} = \frac{\text{assets}}{\text{stockholders' equity}} = \frac{\$4,272.7}{\$937.6} = 4.557 \qquad (3.28)$$

TABLE 3-8

Leverage Performance Metrics

Financial Performance Metric	Hershey		Heinz	
	2008	2010	2008	2010
Debt to equity	9.388	3.557	4.596	4.171
Current debt to equity	3.630	1.385	1.414	1.116
Long-term debt to equity	5.758	2.172	3.182	3.055
Financial leverage	10.388	4.557	5.596	5.171
Capitalization ratio	85.16%	66.09%	73.30%	70.33%
Long-term capitalization ratio	81.15%	62.18%	71.48%	70.06%
Interest coverage	6.026	9.391	4.767	6.152

Financial Performance Metric	Calculation and Strength*	
Debt to equity	Liabilities/equity	−
Current debt to equity	Current liabilities/equity	−
Long-term debt to equity	Long-term liabilities/equity	−
Financial leverage	Assets/equity	−
Capitalization ratio	IBD/(IBD + equity)	−
Long-term capitalization ratio	Long-term debt/(long-term debt + equity)	−
Interest coverage	Earnings before interest and tax/interest expense	+
Where IBD = interest-bearing debt both short and long term.		

* A calculation designated with a "+" ("−") indicates that an increase (decrease) in this metric is a strength.

At Hershey, every dollar of stockholders' equity supported $4.557 of assets. Once again, the 2010 performance of Hershey is slightly lower (better) than that of Heinz (5.171) in 2010.

The financial leverage also can be determined by adding 1 to the debt-to-equity ratio:

$$\text{Hershey's 2010 financial leverage} = 1 + \frac{\text{debt (or liabilities)}}{\text{stockholders' equity}} = 1 + \frac{\$3,335.1}{\$937.6} = 4.557 \quad (3.29)$$

As an algebraic note, remember the old high school algebra "trick" that one can equal any number divided by itself (identity property). In the preceding equation, let 1 be equity/equity. This allows the combination of terms (equity + debt), which based on the accounting identity equals total assets:

$$1 + \frac{\text{debt}}{\text{equity}} = \frac{\text{equity}}{\text{equity}} + \frac{\text{debt}}{\text{equity}} = \frac{(\text{equity} + \text{debt})}{\text{equity}} = \frac{\text{assets}}{\text{equity}} \quad (3.30)$$

The accounting identity equation also captures this relationship:

$$\text{Assets} = \text{liabilities} + \text{stockholders' equity} \qquad (3.31)$$
$$\$4.557 = \$3.557 + \$1.000$$

Additional leverage metrics can be constructed from this relationship.

These metrics look at what percentages of the assets are financed with liabilities and what percentage are financed with stockholders' equity:

$$\text{Hershey's 2010 debt-to-asset ratio} = \frac{\text{liabilities}}{\text{assets}} = \frac{\$3,335.1}{\$4,272.7} = 78.06\% \qquad (3.32)$$

$$\text{Hershey's 2010 equity-to-asset ratio} = \frac{\text{stockholders' equity}}{\text{assets}} = \frac{\$937.6}{\$4,272.7} = 21.94\% \quad (3.33)$$

These ratios must total 100 percent. Slightly over 78 percent of Hershey's assets are financed with debt and 22 percent with equity.

From the basic accounting identity relationship, we constructed two ratios and noted some additional variations:

- Debt to equity
  - Current liabilities to equity
  - Long-term liabilities to equity
- Financial leverage (or assets to equity)
- Other
  - Debt to assets
  - Equity to assets

The underlying relationships, trends, and comparisons portrayed by these ratios don't change. In fact, these metrics provide redundant information. In all cases, Hershey is now less leveraged than in 2008 and uses less debt (or more equity) in financing than Heinz with one noted exception—current debt to equity. What is different among these metrics is their focus. How comfortable is your company's management team in discussing leverage in relation to percent of assets versus percent of equity? This should determine how the analysis is presented.

Balance sheet line items such as accounts payable, accrued liabilities, and long-term liabilities including deferred taxes stem from the operations of the business. These liabilities sometimes are referred to as *spontaneous operating liabilities*. The second group of leverage metrics centers exclusively on financial liabilities and interest-bearing debt. Financial liabilities include all interest-bearing debt, which is to say, all short-term debt, bank borrowings (loans), notes payable, current portion of long-term debt, and long-term debt. Total financial capital consists of interest-bearing debt and stockholders' equity. The next two leverage metrics examine financial capital on a relative basis.

The *capitalization ratio* calculates the percentage that the interest-bearing debt represents of the total capital pool:

$$\text{Hershey's 2010 capitalization ratio} = \frac{\text{interest-bearing debt}}{(\text{interest-bearing debt} + \text{equity})}$$

$$= \frac{\$1,827.3}{\$2,764.9} = 66.09\% \tag{3.34}$$

Hershey has raised over 66 percent of its financial capital using interest-bearing debt. Again, this is significantly lower than two years earlier (85.16 percent) and even slightly lower than for Heinz in 2010. The managerial value of the capitalization ratio is that we are more focused on true capital structure and do not include any operating liabilities such as accounts payable, accrued liabilities, deferred taxes, pension liabilities, and so on. As with all the metrics at this stage of our discussion, the values of the interest-bearing debt and equity are based on book values as found in the company's annual report. In Chapter 11, I introduce a similar type of metric using the market value of the debt and equity.

Variations of the capitalization ratio differ in what is considered in the numerator. Are bank borrowings (loans), short-term debt, notes payable, and the current portion of long-term debt part of the permanent financial capital structure of the firm, or are they just another form of operating liabilities? If those interest-bearing debt items are merely operating liabilities, should they be excluded from the capitalization ratio? The answer lies in the motives of the corporation. Many companies have incorporated a long-term financing strategy of "rolling over" short-term debt. With the financial flexibility provided by swaps and other instruments and the relatively calm debt markets (prior to 2008), many firms saved millions of dollars annually by taking advantage of lower short-term interest rates and financing a portion of their permanent assets with short-term borrowings. In these cases, it is clear that short-term borrowings are part of the permanent financial structure and should be included as interest-bearing debt in the capitalization ratio.

Other companies within other industries could argue that all short-term financing supports temporary working capital needs. They may choose to exclude short-term borrowings for purposes of the capitalization ratio and narrow the metric to:

$$\text{Hershey's 2010 long-term capitalization ratio} = \frac{\text{long-term debt}}{(\text{long-term debt} + \text{equity})}$$

$$= \frac{\$1,541.8}{\$2,479.4} = 62.18\% \tag{3.35}$$

This more narrowly focused metric centers on long-term debt as a percent of a similarly narrowed definition of capital. In this example, 62.18 percent of Hershey's capital pool (excluding short-term borrowings) comes from long-term debt. In 2008, Hershey derived 81.15 percent of its long-term capital from long-term interest-bearing debt. In 2010, Heinz is somewhat more levered (70.06 percent) than Hershey because it uses more long-term debt in its capital structure.

Notice in Table 3-8 that the difference between the capitalization ratio and the long-term capitalization ratio shows the extent to which each company used short-term interest-bearing debt. Both variations of the capitalization ratio are appropriate depending on the circumstances. It appears that the food industry incorporates short-term borrowings into its permanent capital structures. Consequently, the former version of the capitalization ratio (including short-term borrowings) would be more appropriate for the food industry.

The final type of leverage metric, *interest coverage,* centers on the income statement and examines how many times the interest could be paid off with operating income:

$$\text{Hershey's 2010 interest coverage} = \frac{\text{EBIT}}{\text{interest expense}} = \frac{\$905.3}{\$96.4} = 9.391 \quad (3.36)$$

EBIT represents earnings before interest and taxes or operating income. Simply put, for every dollar that Hershey owes for interest expense, Hershey earns $9.391 in operating income that could be used to pay the interest. From a banker's perspective, the higher this ratio, the stronger the company.

In summary, there are three different types of leverage metrics:

1. Total liabilities (or assets) versus equity
2. Interest-bearing debt as a percent of the financial capital
3. The ability to pay any required debt-service costs (i.e., interest)

These measures are similar to the leverage measures used when you buy a $500,000 home with the help of a $400,000 mortgage and your own $100,000 cash down payment. The mortgage company wants to be assured that you have some equity invested in the home (usually about 20 percent). Therefore, in other words, a debt-to-equity ratio of 4.0 ($400,000/$100,000) or less is required. The mortgage company also wants to be sure that you have the financial wherewithal to pay off the mortgage. This is measured by comparing the mortgage amount versus all your other financial assets. In a way, this is similar to a capitalization ratio. And finally, the mortgage company wants to check out your income (last year's tax returns, last number of pay stubs, etc.) to be sure that you have the appropriate level of income to support making the monthly mortgage payments.

With the financial crisis of 2008, many of these commonsense leverage requirements were waived. People were allowed to borrow up to 100 percent of the purchase price of their homes, prices inflated, and then there was a disruption in the income stream as unemployment rose. While this is an oversimplification, it was a "perfect storm" situation that devastated the world economies.

Finally, the picture portrayed in this section on leverage shows Hershey and Heinz as leveraged companies. This is absolutely true, but both companies have the ongoing means to pay interest and to pay off their debt. While we addressed leverage from a banker's perspective, that is, one where leverage is negative, we will see below how leverage can be used to enhance the returns of an organization. Once again, there is duplicity behind the connotation of *leverage*.

The next set of financial ratios centers on liquidity.

Liquidity Metrics

Liquidity ratios measure a firm's ability to pay off its maturing short-term obligations. The broadest view of liquidity is captured in the *current ratio* (Table 3-9).

The *current ratio* is calculated as current assets divided by current liabilities. Current assets include cash and marketable securities, accounts receivable, inventory, and any other line items that comprise current assets. Current assets are categories that will be converted to cash in the coming accounting cycle or fiscal year. Current liabilities include accounts payable, accrued liabilities, other payables and accruals, short-term debt, and the current portion long-term debt. Current liabilities represent items that must be paid in the coming accounting cycle or fiscal year. Thus the current ratio is calculated by taking current liabilities or obligations that need to be paid in the coming year and dividing that into current assets or items that the company will convert into cash in the coming year. Said differently, the current ratio shows that for every dollar you owe in the coming year, you have x dollars to pay it off. For Hershey for 2010 ($ millions):

$$\text{Hershey's 2010 current ratio} = \frac{\text{current assets}}{\text{current liabilities}} = \frac{\$2,005.2}{\$1,298.8} = 1.544 \quad (3.37)$$

TABLE 3-9

Liquidity Performance Metrics

	Hershey		Heinz	
	2008	2010	2008	2010
Current ratio	1.059	1.544	1.245	1.403
Net working capital ($ millions)	$ 74.7	$ 706.4	$ 655.5	$ 875.7
Quick ratio	0.592	1.133	0.729	0.828
Cash ratio	0.029	0.681	0.231	0.222

Financial Performance Metric	Calculation and Strength*	
Current ratio	Current assets/current liabilities	+
Net working capital	Current assets − current liabilities	+
Quick ratio	(Current assets − inventories)/current liabilities	+
Cash ratio	Cash/current liabilities	+

* A calculation designated with a "+" ("−") indicates that an increase (decrease) in this metric is a strength.

For every dollar that Hershey owes over the coming year, it has over $1.54 with which to pay it off. As late as the mid–1980s, a strong current ratio had a value greater than 2.00. However, in the past 25 years, companies have altered their current asset structure with such processes as "just-in-time" inventory management, more aggressive management of accounts receivable, and a limiting of cash and cash equivalents. In addition, with the increased efficiencies of interest-rate swaps, many companies have been taking advantage of lower short-term interest rates because they have made a strategy of "rolling over" short-term borrowing as a part of their permanent capital structure. Consequently, companies have systematically shed current assets while purposefully increasing their current liabilities, thus lowering the current ratio standard to between 1.00 and 1.50.

Ratios, including the current ratio, tend to have performance standards related to the industry. Restaurants or fast-food chains have a current ratio standard that is less than 1! Their current liabilities exceed their current assets. Think about P. F. Chang's China Bistro, Inc. (PFCB), and the components of its current assets and current liabilities. On the current asset side, PFCB does have cash but no accounts receivable because it considers credit-card sales to be cash equivalents because the company receives payment from the credit-card companies in two to four days. As far as inventory is concerned, again think about PFCB's business. It has no finished goods inventory or goods in process. It only has a fresh raw materials inventory with limited shelf life. On the liability side, PFCB has all the normal liabilities, such as accounts payable, construction payable, accrued liabilities, unearned revenues (outstanding gift cards), and the current portion of long-term debt. Thus PFCB has all the normal liabilities but a thinner level of current assets. Consequently, its current ratio is 0.934 in 2010 and was 0.717 in 2008! For the restaurant industry, a current ratio approaching 1.00 would be a strong performance standard.

Nonetheless, the higher the current ratio, the stronger is the firm's performance. Again, anything taken to an extreme actually could show signs of an underlying weakness. For example, a current ratio of 8.00 could show:

- Hoarding of cash
- Noncollection of receivables
- Inventory buildup
- Inefficient use of "free" financing from suppliers
- Limited short-term borrowings

Just as with all metrics, industry, competitor, and self-comparisons are instrumental in determining performance strengths and weaknesses. Table 3-9 compares the 2008 and 2010 performance of The Hershey Company along with a contrast with Heinz. For the food industry, a current ratio of approximately 1.50 shows strength. Hershey's performance has improved since 2008. While Heinz improved more slowly in that two-year time span, Hershey is stronger than Heinz with regard to the current ratio.

A related metric, although not a comparative metric because it is expressed in absolute, not relative, terms, is net *working capital*. Net working capital is simply current assets (CA) less current liabilities (CL) and represents the amount left over after a firm pays off all its immediate liabilities. For Hershey in 2010, working capital was $706.4 million:

$$\text{Hershey's 2010 net working capital} = \text{CA} - \text{CL}$$
$$= \$2,005.2 - \$1,298.8 \qquad (3.38)$$
$$= \$706.4$$

This net working capital (current assets less than current liabilities) is consistent with a current ratio of greater than 1.00.

The *quick ratio*, or *acid-test ratio*, is similar to the current ratio except inventories are eliminated from the current assets. Why do companies go bankrupt? There are many responses to this question, but in the end it often boils down to no one wanting the company's product. There are some companies that make a highly desirable product and are successful despite inadequate managerial processes and leadership. There are other organizations with great management teams but a product that no one wants. These companies are doomed to failure.

The quick ratio eliminates inventory from current assets. That is, what if you could not realize any value for your finished goods, your goods in process, or even your raw materials? The quick ratio for Hershey in 2010 was:

$$\text{Hershey's 2010 quick ratio} = \frac{(\text{current assets} - \text{inventory})}{\text{current liabilities}}$$
$$= \frac{(\$2,005.2 - \$533.6)}{\$1,298.8} = 1.133 \qquad (3.39)$$

For every dollar that Hershey owes over the coming year, it has $1.133 to pay it off in current assets excluding inventories. Similar to the current ratio and also owing to the impact of debt, Hershey's quick ratio has risen dramatically, and both years show strength compared with Heinz.

Another way of stating the quick ratio is to examine the remaining current assets that are used in the numerator. For every dollar that Hershey owes over the coming year, it has $1.133 in cash and cash equivalents, accounts receivable, and other current assets to pay off its current liabilities. But what if the accounts receivable are noncollectible or partially noncollectible, what if deferred tax assets are not realizable, and what if prepaid expenses and other assets could not be readily (or fully) converted to cash? Permutations of an "adjusted" quick ratio abound for any specific situation.

The *cash ratio* is the most restrictive liquidity ratio and assumes that only cash and cash equivalents are available to pay off current liabilities. The cash ratio is calculated as:

$$\text{Hershey's 2010 cash ratio} = \frac{\text{cash and equivalents}}{\text{current liabilities}} = \frac{\$884.6}{\$1,298.8} = 0.681 \quad (3.40)$$

The term *equivalents* includes short-term investments in such things as a savings account, money-market account, certificate of deposit, U.S. Treasury bills, and so on. Equivalents include any short-term, highly marketable security.

For every dollar Hershey owes within the next year, at the end of 2010, Hershey has 68 cents in cash (and cash equivalents) with which to pay its obligations. This metric has improved significantly over 2008 (2.9 cents) and surpasses Heinz' cash ratio of 22.2 cents for every dollar of current liabilities.

In summary, the liquidity performance metrics show that Hershey has improved dramatically in all measures and outpaces Heinz in all measures except for the absolute value of net working capital.

Market-Related Metrics

The market-related metrics incorporate current stock prices into the performance metrics (Table 3-10).

Market capitalization is the current value of a company's equity based on the stock market at any point in time. In 2010, Hershey had 227.0 million shares outstanding. Based on a year-end stock price of $47.32, Hershey had a market capitalization (or simply, a market cap) of $10.7 billion:

$$
\begin{aligned}
\text{Hershey's 2010 market capitalization} \\
= \text{market price per share} \times \text{shares outstanding} \\
= \$47.32 \times 227.0 \\
= \$10{,}741.6 \text{ million} \qquad\qquad (3.41)
\end{aligned}
$$

The market capitalization (or current market value) of Hershey has grown significantly over the past two years. Since the market capitalization is an "absolute" measure, there are few relevant direct comparisons that can be made except to say "larger or smaller." Relative measures such as growth rates or the market-related metrics discussed below allow comparisons of a firm's stock market–based performance. Hershey's market capitalization has grown by 16.71 percent (CAGR) since 2008 versus the "flat" performance at Heinz.

Price/earnings ratios compare the market price per share with earnings per share. This widely used measure is simply called the *P/E ratio* (or *P/E multiple*) and is often reported within a stock listing in a daily business newspaper such as the *Wall Street Journal*. This metric is calculated as:

$$
\begin{aligned}
\text{Hershey's 2010 price/earnings ratio} &= \frac{\text{market price per share}}{\text{earnings per share}} \\
&= \frac{\$47.32}{\$2.21} = 21.41 \qquad\qquad (3.42)
\end{aligned}
$$

Broadly interpreted, the P/E ratio indicates that for every $1 of Hershey's earnings, the stock market (or actually an investor) is willing to pay $21.41. This is less than it was in 2008 but notably higher than Heinz (16.89). The stock market is valuing a dollar of Hershey earnings more highly than a dollar of Heinz earnings.

TABLE 3-10

Market Performance Metrics

	Hershey		Heinz	
	2008	2010	2008	2010
Market capitalization ($ millions)	$ 7,886.0	$ 10,741.6	$ 14,649.8	$ 14,538.0
Price/earnings	25.54	21.41	17.88	16.89
Price/sales	1.54	1.89	1.45	1.39
Price/EBITDA	9.39	9.74	7.89	7.81
Market to book	22.54	11.46	7.76	7.46
Shareholder returns	−8.81%	34.96%	4.16%	39.57%
Dividend yield	3.02%	3.55%	3.26%	4.94%
Current dividend yield	3.43%	2.70%	3.23%	3.67%
Dividend payout	87.50%	57.92%	57.79%	61.99%

Financial Performance Metric	Calculation and Strength*	
Market capitalization	Stock price per share × shares outstanding	+
Price/earnings	Stock price per share/earnings per share	
	or market capitalization/net income**	+
Price/sales	Market capitalization/sales	+
Price/EBITDA	Market capitalization/EBITDA	+
Market to book	Market value/book value	+
Shareholder returns	(Cap apprec + dividends)/beginning stock price	+
Dividend yield	Dividend per share/beginning stock price	+
Current dividend yield	Dividend per share/ending stock price	+
Dividend payout	Dividend per share/earnings per share	?

* A calculation designated with a "+" ("−") indicates that an increase (decrease) in this metric is a strength.
** Using MC/NI provides slightly different results due to "diluted" EPS used in this calculation.

A simple variation of this exact definition is to use earnings per share, basic, instead of earnings per share, diluted. In this case, Hershey's P/E would have been 20.66 ($47.32 per share/$2.29). Another alternative calculation uses market capitalization (or stock price times shares outstanding) divided by net income (or earnings per share times shares outstanding). Using this approach, Hershey's 2010 P/E ratio is 21.07 ($10,741.6 million/$509.8 million). Given all the possible variations, once again, consistency in the calculation approach is the key.

P/E ratios reflect many, sometimes offsetting influences that make their interpretations difficult. Often the higher the expected growth rate of the firm, the higher the price/earnings ratio is. All else being the same, an investor is willing to pay more for every dollar of earnings assuming that the dollar will grow faster.

Price/sales and price/EBITDA have the same fundamental calculation and interpretation as the P/E ratio:

$$\text{Hershey's 2010 price/sales ratio} = \frac{\text{market capitalization}}{\text{sales}} = \frac{\$10,741.6}{\$5,671.0} = 1.89 \qquad (3.43)$$

$$\text{Hershey's 2010 price/EBITDA ratio} = \frac{\text{market capitalization}}{\text{EBITDA}} = 9.74 \qquad (3.44)$$

Compared with Heinz using either of these two relative metrics, Hershey is more valuable than Heinz.

The *market-to-book ratio* measures the value that financial markets attach to the management and organization of the firm as a going concern. As noted on Table 3-10, the ratio is calculated as:

$$\text{Hershey's 2010 market-to-book ratio} = \frac{\text{market capitalization}}{\text{stockholders' equity}}$$

$$= \frac{\$10,741.6}{\$937.6} = 11.46 \qquad (3.45)$$

Hershey's market value of equity is over $10.7 billion. The historical "book value" of stockholders' equity is a less meaningful value owing to its historical nature, as we discussed in Chapter 2. Book value is also reduced by share-repurchase programs, which both Hershey and Heinz have in place.

The market-to-book ratio suggests that for every dollar of Hershey's net book value (or stockholders' equity), the market is willing to pay $11.46. Since the balance sheet does not capture the value of brands, the U.S. sales force and distribution system, intellectual property, proprietary processes, knowledge workers, and so on, some people argue that the market-to-book ratio reflects the relative value of these intangibles. This point is seen dramatically in extremely high market-to-book ratios for "new economy" companies.

Shareholder returns have become the key to much financial and investment analysis. The theme of enhancing shareholder value is the subject of many books/articles and is highlighted in the annual reports of many individual companies. The shareholder return measures what shareholders actually earn over a period of time. This is a widely used measure in making comparisons between the market returns among a wide range of financial instruments.

Shareholder return (also called *holding-period return*) is defined as the sum of capital appreciation and dividends over a period of time. The period of time can be monthly, quarterly, annually, or a number of years. The shareholder return for Hershey for 2010 was:

$$\text{Hershey's 2010 shareholder return} = \frac{2010 \text{ capital appreciation} + 2010 \text{ dividends}}{\text{stock price on } 12/31/09}$$

$$= \frac{(\$47.32 - \$36.01) + \$1.28}{\$36.01}$$

$$= \frac{\$11.31 + \$1.28}{\$36.01} = 34.96\% \qquad (3.46)$$

In 2010, Hershey stock provided a solid capital gain of 31.41 percent ($11.31/$36.01) to its stockholders. In other words, if you bought the stock on December 31, 2009, you would have paid $36.01 for that share. At year end (whether you sell your share or not), the value of that share increased $11.31 to $47.32. In addition, the stockholder received a dividend of $1.28 throughout 2010, which represents a dividend yield of 3.55 percent ($1.28/$36.01). The capital appreciation plus the dividend yield provided a total shareholder return of 34.96 percent.

This was significantly better than the 2008 shareholder return, when Hershey's stockholders lost 8.81 percent. Notice that in both 2008 and 2010 Hershey's shareholder return fell short of the return earned by investors in Heinz stock.

Dividend yield represents the dividend received over a period of time compared with the initial price of the stock. In the preceding example,

$$\text{Hershey's 2010 dividend yield} = \frac{2010 \text{ dividends}}{\text{stock price on } 12/31/09} = \frac{\$1.28}{\$36.01} = 3.55\% \qquad (3.47)$$

Dividend yield measures the return from the company that a stockholder earns or is paid directly by that company. In this case, it measures the return over the entire year.

An important variation is the *current dividend yield*, which represents the dividend yield at today's stock price. This metric is often reported in the financial press along with stock price quotes. It measures the return directly from a company (i.e., the dividend) for a new stockholder buying the share of stock at the daily quoted stock price. In our case, we are using the current dividend yield for someone who purchased Hershey's stock on December 31, 2010, but this could be generalized for any particular day or moment through the day as stock prices fluctuate:

$$\text{Hershey's 2010 current dividend yield} = \frac{2010 \text{ dividends}}{\text{stock price on } 12/31/10}$$

$$= \frac{\$1.28}{\$47.32} = 2.70\% \qquad (3.48)$$

In this case, the current dividend yield measures the annualized dividend return to shareholders at a moment in time.

Finally, the dividend payout ratio is calculated as:

$$\text{Hershey's 2010 dividend payout} = \frac{2010 \text{ dividends per share}}{2010 \text{ earnings per share}}$$

$$= \frac{\$1.28}{\$2.21} = 57.92\% \qquad (3.49)$$

Hershey dividends almost 58 percent of every dollar of income to its stock-holders. Of course, there are many permutations of this metric, too. In this example, the dividend was calculated based on diluted earnings per share (EPS). A more common approach may use basic EPS. Likewise, an alternative calculation is total dividends divided by net income (or even normalized income). In this analysis using the approach employed here, Heinz had a more stable payout policy. In general, for all market metrics, higher values indicate a stronger performance.

OTHER RATIOS AND METRICS

Two other types of ratios are important for the business professional—growth metrics and cost-management metrics. Annual growth rates and compound annual growth rates over an extended period of time were illustrated in the basic financial statement analysis section. Growth can be calculated on any income statement (Table 3-1) or balance sheet line. Five- and 10-year growth rates provide a long-term barometer of a firm's health and its ability to conduct business. Chapter 7 discusses the tools to calculate a compound annual growth rate (CAGR) in much more depth.

Cost-management ratios take many forms. In the basic financial statement analysis (Table 3-1) and profitability analysis (Table 3-5), we looked at costs as a percent of sales. Cost management stresses that lower costs (as a percent of sales) are a sign of strength. Again, balance is key. Everything must be considered including the product's positioning and the company's product strategy. A low-cost, undifferentiated product manufacturer (i.e., a commodity business) seeks the lowest-cost inputs, whereas a high-value-added, differentiated product manufacturer strives to purchase high-quality raw materials for the least amount of money.

Take the case of a vehicle seat in the auto industry. A seat serves the same purpose regardless of the quality that underlies its materials and construction. At the low end, there are (1) cloth seats, then (2) leather seats, then (3) automatic leather seats, then (4) heated automatic leather seats, and then (5) heated automatic leather seats with air conditioning until you reach the ultimate, and (6) heated automatic leather seats with air conditioning and massage. Obviously, the cloth seat is considerably less expensive than the heated automatic leather seat with air conditioning and massage. If Mercedes-Benz wished to manage its costs, cloth seats would be installed in all new vehicles. However, the customer purchasing a $100,000-plus Mercedes would be nothing short of disappointed if the vehicle had only cloth seats. After such disappointment, sales would decline. Again, any application of the metrics taken to an extreme can turn that positive position into a negative if not fully considered in the context of the business.

Examining specific, individual expenses as a percent of sales creates additional cost-management measures. That is, some expenses, such as research and development (R&D), advertising, and depreciation, are reported in the footnotes or supplemental schedules of annual reports. Each of these expenses can be calculated as a percent of sales (e.g., R&D expense/sales) for a historical period and compared with other firms in the industry.

Furthermore, by using non-publicly reported internal numbers, all the organization's business units and functional areas can be viewed as a percent of sales tracked over years of experience compared with other areas or business units, and appropriate ongoing expenditure targets can be set.

Finally, other relative cost-management ratios can be calculated based on other statistics. One of the most common of these ratios is sales per employee. Some people consider the year-to-year change in this ratio as a measure of employee productivity.

In summary, while there is a wide array of potential metrics, the ones discussed in this chapter provide a framework for understanding virtually any financial performance metric.

DUPONT RATIO ANALYSIS

With so many numbers and so many ratios, where do we begin our diagnosis of a company's fiscal health? *DuPont ratio analysis* is a systematic approach to financial analysis that was developed by analysts at E. I. Du Pont de Nemours & Company. It does not add to our "bag" of analytical metrics, but it does help us to organize the metrics to tell a clear and concise story.

A System of Metrics

DuPont analysis uses metrics that were introduced earlier in this chapter. The first part of the analysis examines the return on assets as a function of profitability and turnover. Profitability is measured using net margin, whereas turnover is measured using total asset turnover:

$$\text{Return on assets} = \text{net margin} \times \text{asset turnover} \qquad (3.50)$$

$$\frac{\text{Net income}}{\text{Assets}} = \frac{\text{net income}}{\text{sales}} \times \frac{\text{sales}}{\text{total assets}} \qquad (3.51)$$

The algebra is trivial! Sales *cancel each other out*, and we're left with net income divided by total assets or the return on assets. Next, we can take the return on assets and multiply it by financial leverage:

$$\text{Return on equity} = \text{return on assets} \times \text{financial leverage} \qquad (3.52)$$

$$\frac{\text{Net income}}{\text{Equity}} = \frac{\text{net income}}{\text{total assets}} \times \frac{\text{total assets}}{\text{equity}} \qquad (3.53)$$

Once again, the algebra is trivial! Total assets *cancel each other out*, and we're left with net income divided by equity or the return on equity. Yes, we could have calculated the return on assets or return on equity directly. However, by isolating the individual operating components, we can address strengths and weaknesses in the firm. These strengths and weaknesses ultimately are manifested in the return on equity. For example, Table 3-11 compares the performance of Hershey and Heinz, as before.

First, comparing Hershey with Heinz in 2008, Heinz was more profitable and generated over 2 cents more than Hershey did from every sales dollar. However, Hershey's operators used their asset base more effectively to generate significantly more sales out of every dollar of assets, and consequently, return on assets was better for Hershey. When we discussed leverage before, we did it from a banker's perspective, where more leverage (more debt) was considered a negative position. DuPont analysis shows how having more debt actually can be a good business decision because the already solid 2008 return on assets (ROA) is magnified 10.388 times for a return on equity of 89.00 percent and more than double the 2008 figure for Heinz!

By 2010, Hershey improved its profitability, although turnovers fell. Recall from the previous discussion that turnover fell because of the rapid buildup of cash. Nevertheless, ROA improved significantly at Hershey. The profitability of Heinz slipped a little bit, but turnovers improved, and Heinz improved its ROA! Both companies became more conservative with leverage, and Hershey became even less leveraged than Heinz by 2010. However, Hershey's return on equity (ROE) was still better than that of Heinz by almost 10 percentage points.

TABLE 3-11

Performance Metrics

		Hershey		Heinz	
		2008	2010	2008	2010
Net margin	NI/sales	6.07%	8.99%	8.39%	8.24%
×					
Total asset turnover	Sales/total assets	1.412	1.327	0.953	1.042
=					
Return on assets	Net income/total assets	8.57%	11.93%	8.00%	8.58%
×					
Financial leverage	Total assets/equity	10.388	4.557	5.596	5.171
=					
Return on equity	Net income/equity	89.00%	54.37%	44.76%	44.39%

DuPont analysis strengthens our understanding of what drives a business. For example, for every dollar in assets in 2010, Hershey generated $1.327 in sales. Those sales were profitable at the rate of 8.99 cents for every sales dollar or 11.93 cents for the $1.327 in sales. In total, that $1 of assets generated $1.327 in sales, which generated 11.93 cents of income. Looking at Heinz, for every $1 of assets, Heinz generated only $1.042 in sales, which generated profit at the rate of 8.24 cents for every sales dollar or 8.58 cents of income for every dollar of assets.

In addition, Hershey chose to finance its assets a bit more conservatively, so $1 in equity supported $4.557 in assets, which generated sales at the rate of $1.327 (per $1 of asset), or $6.05 ($4.557 × $1.327) of sales were generated from $1 in equity. Those sales generated income at the rate of 8.99 cents for every dollar of sales or 54.37 cents for every dollar of equity. Heinz generated $5.39 ($5.171 × $1.042) of sales with its $1 of equity, which provided income of 44.39 cents for every dollar of equity.

To summarize the point of leverage, in 2008, Heinz was more profitable than Hershey, but through better asset utilization and more leverage, Hershey more than doubled the Heinz ROE. In this case and with a shareholder's perspective, leverage is a welcomed business risk that enhances a stockholder's return. Earlier I said that low measures of financial leverage were strength from a banker's perspective. In this case and many others, the equity holders view leverage in a favorable light. However, leverage is a double-edged tool that accents losses as well!

One final point: DuPont analysis is also an effective tool that can be used to examine industries, businesses within an industry, or even divisions or business units. Think once again about the restaurant industry. At the one extreme is a fine-dining restaurant with a very pricey, limited menu and lavish decor, with the dining experience taking well over an hour. At the other end is the typical American-style of take-out Chinese restaurant with a menu of 200 (or more) reasonably-priced items all prepared in 10 minutes. The fine-dining restaurant earns large margins but has slower turnover, whereas the take-out restaurant has thin margins but fast turnover.

P. F. Chang's China Bistro has both types of restaurants. The company's full-service Bistro restaurants feature "a blend of high-quality, Chinese-inspired cuisine and attentive service in a high-energy contemporary bistro setting that offers intensely flavored, highly memorable culinary creations prepared from fresh ingredients, including premium herbs and spices imported directly from China." Their second, more casual restaurant is Pei Wei Asian Diner. Pei Wei "offers a menu of fresh, high-quality Asian cuisine and provides a comfortable, quick, and casual dine-in experience as well as the flexibility, speed, and convenience of take-away service."

Table 3-12 uses DuPont analysis to compare and contrast the results of both business units. This analysis excludes corporate expenses, taxes, and all leverage consideration because that is not part of the operating management's responsibility. While both business units have strong operating return on assets, the path to get there is uniquely different, as conjectured earlier! Bistros have an excellent margin with good turnover, whereas Pei Wei has a reasonable margin and excellent turnover. How does your business "go to business"?

One final restaurant note: Even the fine-dining restaurants have implemented customer-management systems that time how long you are at your table

TABLE 3-12

P. F. Chang's China Bistro, Inc., Operating Segment Analysis

		Bistro		Pei Wei	
		2009	2010	2009	2010
Operating margin	Operating income / sales	13.36%	12.60%	9.22%	9.51%
×					
Total asset turnover	Sales / total assets	1.770	1.802	2.780	3.177
=					
Operating ROA	Operating income / total assets	23.64%	22.70%	25.62%	30.23%
Segment information ($ millions)					
Segment revenue		$ 925.3	$ 929.4	$ 302.7	$ 310.1
Segment profit (or operating income)		123.6	117.1	27.9	29.5
Segment assets		522.9	515.9	108.9	97.6

and look to turn that same table a few times per night to maximize their turnover and their return on assets.

DuPont analysis also can be expanded to include a prefix, the tax impact of the firm:

$$\text{Net margin} = \text{pretax margin} \times (1 - \text{tax rate}) \qquad (3.54)$$

$$\frac{\text{Net income}}{\text{Sales}} = \frac{\text{pretax income}}{\text{sales}} \times \left(1 - \frac{\text{tax expense}}{\text{pretax income}}\right) \qquad (3.55)$$

In this case, using a high school algebra trick, the 1 can be rewritten as pretax income (PTI) divided by itself. Then, within the brackets, the terms can be combined:

$$\frac{\text{PTI}}{\text{Sales}} \times \left[\left(\frac{\text{PTI}}{\text{PTI}}\right) - \left(\frac{\text{tax expense}}{\text{PTI}}\right)\right] \qquad (3.56)$$

$$\frac{\text{PTI}}{\text{Sales}} \times \frac{(\text{PTI} - \text{income taxes})}{\text{PTI}} = \frac{\text{net income}}{\text{sales}} \qquad (3.57)$$

Pretax income less income taxes is the same thing as net income, and the PTIs cancel out. By adding this prefix to the DuPont analysis, we can focus on the impact of income taxes.

Up to this point, we have generally compared Hershey with itself and with Heinz. Table 3-13 provides a 2010 DuPont analysis for the members of the food-processing industry. The last lines provide industry averages, which may or may not be useful depending on the specific metric under consideration. The averages and companies are the same ones that we discussed at the beginning of this chapter.

TABLE 3-13

2010 DuPont Analysis

	Pretax Margin*	After-Tax Retention	Net Margin	Asset Turnover	Return on Assets	Financial Leverage	Return on Equity
The Hershey Company	14.26%	63.02%	8.99%	1.327	11.93%	4.557	54.37%
Campbell Soup Company	16.18%	67.95%	11.00%	0.975	10.72%	4.451	47.74%
ConAgra Foods, Inc.	9.02%	66.60%	6.01%	1.029	6.18%	2.381	14.73%
Flowers Foods, Inc.	8.17%	65.16%	5.33%	1.942	10.34%	1.666	17.23%
General Mills, Inc.	15.91%	65.01%	10.34%	0.837	8.66%	3.130	27.10%
H. J. Heinz Company	11.42%	72.15%	8.24%	1.042	8.58%	5.171	44.39%
Kellogg Company	14.13%	71.18%	10.06%	1.046	10.53%	5.500	57.89%
Kraft Foods, Inc.	13.10%	63.82%	8.36%	0.516	4.32%	2.651	11.45%
Sara Lee Corporation	10.91%	42.99%	4.69%	1.221	5.73%	5.832	33.40%
Smucker (J. M.) Company	15.87%	67.62%	10.73%	0.577	6.20%	1.497	9.28%
Tootsie Roll Industries, Inc.	14.33%	72.47%	10.38%	0.601	6.24%	1.286	8.03%
Industry average, weighted	13.06%	64.55%	8.43%	0.736	6.20%	2.884	17.89%
Industry average	13.03%	65.27%	8.56%	1.010	8.13%	3.466	29.60%

*Note: All pretax margins have been adjusted to reflect the pretax amounts of gains (losses) or discontinued operations.

The first column on Table 3-13 is the pretax margin. Notice that some adjustments need to be made to categorize discontinued operations and gains (losses) at pretax values with applicable taxes combined with reported income taxes. Originally, these items were reported net of taxes. As your eyes wander up and down that column, notice that Hershey's performance is fifth behind. The simple industry average of all the pretax margins is 13.03 percent with a slightly higher weighted average margin.

After-tax retention is calculated as 1 − tax rate. The larger this value, the more the company retains after paying income taxes. Excluding the Sara Lee Corporation, values in this column range from a low of 63.02 percent (Hershey) to a high of 72.47 percent (Tootsie Roll), which indicates almost a 10 percentage point difference between the high and low tax rates. Hershey is primarily a domestic company and as such is subject to the higher tax rates of the United States. International income earned by the other companies is afforded lower tax rates than a primarily domestic company. The net margin has Campbell Soup Company leading the group with a margin of 11.00 percent on every dollar of sales. However, Campbell stumbles on asset turnover (seventh overall), and its ROA falls behind the industry leader, Hershey.

The industry's philosophy on debt is extremely varied. At the one extreme are Tootsie Roll, Smucker, and Flowers Foods with little to no interest-bearing debt in their capital structure. At the other extreme are companies such as Sara Lee, Kellogg, and Heinz, which are extremely leveraged. Hershey's ROE ranks second in this industry study. Kellogg, with a more aggressive leverage philosophy, is the number one in ROE.

Tootsie Roll begins with an impressive pretax margin and net margin but quickly loses ground owing to its asset utilization and its financial structure. Costs and expenses seem well managed, but it does not appear that Tootsie Roll's management is driving all the business aspects (asset utilization and leverage). As a result, the ROE falls to last place.

From a strategic perspective, DuPont analysis highlights areas where a management team may want to explore further and determine specific areas to improve. For example, if turnover is an issue highlighted by the DuPont analysis, then management needs to understand what component of the balance sheet is causing the stumble in performance vis-à-vis the industry or the company's historical performance.

DuPont analysis is an effective tool for observing and analyzing a company's strengths and weaknesses, as well as the actions of competitors. However, metrics that are left in the board room are of minimal benefit in today's fast-pace business environment. DuPont analysis can be driven from the board room to the shop floor. Everyone can contribute to the success of the organization.

The messages can be clearly stated for all managers and employees:

- Generate sales and sales growth through production of consistent, quality products, effective marketing campaigns, a dedicated, well-trained sales force, and successful new product introductions.

- Minimize production costs by effectively purchasing raw materials, minimizing down time, minimizing waste and rework, and reducing overhead expenses.
- Minimize selling, general, and administrative expenses by effectively purchasing all supplies, investing in effective marketing campaigns, and holding the line on all spending.
- Limit the investment in working capital by collecting receivables more quickly, managing inventories, developing effective supplier and customer relations to optimize the supply chain throughput, and extending payables where possible.
- Minimize the investment in fixed capital by productively employing idled equipment and investing in projects with returns that exceed the cost of capital.
- Review the capital structure of the firm and take corrective action to optimize the amount of leverage employed. This primarily affects the corporate treasurer's office.

Operational and financial metrics can be employed to capture performance targets for the organization and in an individual's annual performance objectives.

SUMMARY

Financial performance analysis starts with the fundamental financial statements of the firm: income statements, balance sheets, and cash-flow statements. Unlike the absolute dollar comparison of financial statements, financial performance metrics provide relative comparisons of financial performance. There are potentially thousands of different financial performance metrics. Each has its own specific calculation. Alter one item slightly to better fit your situation, and you have created another financial performance metric or at least a permutation of one. While the term *return on investment* is common, there is no one definition of ROI, only a general construct based on some measure of assets or equity, as discussed in this chapter.

In this chapter, a common-size and common-base-year approach was introduced first, followed by a presentation of the seven primary categories of financial ratios:

- Profitability
- Activity
- Leverage
- Liquidity
- Market
- Growth
- Cost management

To be useful, metrics must be related to some standards. One approach is to use the firm's own historical patterns, which involves comparing its metrics for a number of years to determine whether performance is improving or deteriorating. A second approach is to make comparisons with other firms in the same industry or with best-demonstrated-practices firms. Sometimes industry composite data supplied from outside sources will be useful. Other times it is necessary to select more directly comparable firms to get added clarity. Finally, in some cases, a company can compare its performance internally by divisions or business units.

Basic financial statement analysis and DuPont ratio analysis were introduced as a systematic approach to structuring a financial analysis. Subsequent analysis is required to enrich the evaluation. This chapter provided examples of subsequent analysis and evaluation by comparing members of the food-processing industry, specifically Hershey and Heinz.

THE IMPACT OF INCOME TAXES ON FINANCIAL ANALYSIS

Business organizations are faced with a variety of taxes from multiple governmental levels. At the local level, there are real estate taxes and income taxes. At the state level, there are employment taxes paid for the benefit of employees and state income taxes. Finally, at the national level, there are additional employment taxes, excise taxes, and federal income taxes. This chapter focuses on a few key U.S. federal income tax provisions that find their way into many business decisions. While the federal tax system is voluminous, and tax attorneys and tax accountants spend years studying the tax code, learning its implications, and practicing its content, we are going to focus on a few concepts that are important to financial analysis. Complex rules of taxation cannot be treated in a book of this type. Therefore, always seek professional tax advice for very specific and specialized tax situations.

With a tax rate of 35 percent on "large" corporations (those with pretax incomes of more than $18,333,333), the federal government is often called the most important shareholder in the U.S. economy. While this is not literally true because the government does not own corporate shares in the strict sense of the word, the government receives a significant percentage of business profits in the form of taxes.

With such a large percentage of business income going to the government, it is not surprising that taxes play an important role in financial decisions. To incorporate or to conduct business as a partnership or proprietorship, to lease or buy, to issue common stock or debt, to make or not to make a particular investment, to merge or not to merge—all these decisions are influenced by tax factors.

With ratification of the Sixteenth Amendment in 1913, Congress was given the authority to impose a federal income tax. While significant changes and refinements were made to the tax laws, the Tax Reform Act of 1986 was one of the most far-reaching revisions with its much-publicized goals of simplification and fairness. Tax laws are changing constantly in response to different political and public-policy goals and economic circumstances, as we have seen since the financial collapse.

Despite major overhauls and minor modifications, most tax issues that are important for financial decision making remain basically unchanged. In fact, there is a great deal of legislative and judicial precedent that "grandfathers" many tax structures. This provides consistency for decision makers.

RECENT COLLECTIONS

The enormity of the U.S. Internal Revenue Service (IRS) is overwhelming. In 2010, the IRS collected $1,877.8 billion (or $1.88 trillion or $1,877,800,000,000).

As you can see in Table 4-1, $814.0 billion (43.35 percent of the total) was collected through individual income taxes. Actually, there was a total of $1,176.0 billion collected from individuals. However, that amount was offset by $362.0 billion in tax overpayment refunds and tax credits for the American Recovery and Reinvestment Act (ARRA) of 2009, including the three major programs—Making Work Pay Tax Credit, American Opportunity Tax Credit, and First-Time Homebuyer Credit. This resulted in the net collections reported in Table 4-1. With the continued economic improvement in 2010, corporate income taxes exhibited the highest annual growth (37.84 percent). With a broader-term perspective in mind, employment taxes (i.e., Federal Insurance Contributions Act [FICA], which is commonly called the Social Security Tax, unemployment insurance, and the railroad retirement fund) were the fastest-growing component from either 1980 (6.39 percent compound annual growth rate [CAGR]) or 1990 (4.12 percent). Employment taxes include both those paid by individuals and those paid by corporations. The other taxes include estate taxes ($16.1 billion), gift taxes ($2.7 billion),

T A B L E   4-1

IRS Net Collections, 2010
($ billions)

	Tax Amount	Growth			% of Total
		Annual	CAGR* from 1980	CAGR* from 1990	
Income taxes					
Individual	$814.0	−4.68%	4.11%	2.86%	43.35%
Corporation	179.6	37.84%	3.47%	3.34%	9.56%
Total	993.6	0.94%	3.99%	2.94%	52.91%
Employment taxes	820.0	−4.07%	6.39%	4.12%	43.67%
Other taxes	64.2	−6.46%	2.49%	2.85%	3.42%
Total	$1,877.8	−1.57%	4.76%	3.42%	100.00%

*Compound annual growth rate

FIGURE 4-1

Net federal collections.
($ billions)

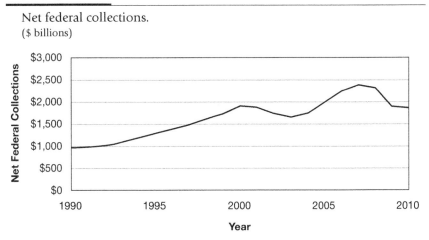

and excise taxes ($45.4 billion). In 2010, a historic point, as seen in Table 4-1, was reached. For the first time, net collections from employment taxes were the largest single source of revenue for the federal government.

Figure 4-1 shows the total net collections since 1990. Through the 1990s, net collections rose steadily (7.08 percent CAGR 1990–2000) until the Internet dot-com bubble burst. Once again, collections started to increase from 2003 to 2007 (9.78 percent CAGR). After falling the past two years, net collections may have started to level off in 2010.

DETERMINING CORPORATE TAXES
FROM TAXABLE INCOME

Before considering the numerous tax issues, it is important to understand how taxes are actually calculated once taxable income is determined. The Tax Reform Act of 1986 (effective July 1, 1987) reduced the corporate tax rate structure significantly. Immediately prior to that date, the highest corporate tax rate was 46 percent. After the Tax Reform Act (TRA) the highest corporate tax rate fell to 34 percent, which created a large windfall for any full taxpayer such as Hershey. In 1993, the highest tax rate was raised to 35 percent, which is still significantly lower than pre-TRA 1986 highest tax rate of 46 percent.

Table 4-2 presents the complete corporate tax rates for corporate taxable income. If a corporation had income of $110,000 in 2010, its tax would be calculated as follows:

- The first $50,000 of income would be taxed at 15 percent: $7,500, or $50,000(0.15).

- The next $25,000 of income would be taxed at 25 percent: $6,250, or $25,000(0.25).

T A B L E   4-2

Marginal and Average Corporate Tax Rates

Taxable Corporate Income (1)	Marginal Tax Rate (2)	Incremental Taxes Paid* (3)	Total Taxes Paid* (4)	Average Tax Rate* (5)
Up to $50,000	15.00%	$7,500	$7,500	15.00%
$50,001 to $75,000	25.00%	6,250	13,750	18.33%
$75,001 to $100,000	34.00%	8,500	22,250	22.25%
$100,001 to $335,000	39.00%	91,650	113,900	34.00%
$335,001 to $10,000,000	34.00%	3,286,100	3,400,000	34.00%
$10,000,001 to $15,000,000	35.00%	1,750,000	5,150,000	34.33%
$15,000,001 to $18,333,333	38.00%	1,266,667	6,416,667	35.00%
Over $18,333,333	35.00%	28,583,333	35,000,000	35.00%**

*Columns (3), (4), and (5) are based on upper limit of income range.
**The last line of the table, columns (3), (4), and (5), assumes a taxable income of $100 million.

- The next $25,000 of income would be taxed at 34 percent: $8,500, or $25,000(0.34).
- The remaining $10,000 would be taxed at 39 percent: $3,900, or $10,000(0.39).

Summing these incremental tax amount yields a total tax of $26,150 on the $110,000 of taxable income. The corporation's average tax rate is 23.77 percent ($26,150/$110,000). If that same corporation had $100,000 of taxable income in 2010, its tax would have been $22,250. In this example, the 2010 incremental $10,000 increase in taxable income caused the tax amount to increase by $3,900. Said differently, this extra $10,000 caused the corporation to move to a higher tax bracket, but notice that it is only this incremental $10,000 that gets taxed in the higher tax bracket. The original $100,000 is taxed at the same rate, and the remaining $10,000 is taxed at an incremental tax rate of 39 percent! However, if the top tax rate is only 35 percent, why is this corporation being taxed at 39 percent? To see the answer, let's look at another example.

If a second corporation had income of $500,000 in 2010, the corporation's tax on the $500,000 of taxable income is computed as shown in Table 4-3.

The corporation's tax is $170,000 for this $500,000 of taxable income. Thus the corporation's average tax rate is 34 percent (or $170,000/$500,000). The purpose of the higher tax rate bracket (39 percent) between $100,001 and $335,000 is to offset the benefits of low tax rates on low levels of corporate taxable income for high-income corporations. This higher tax rate—39 percent—includes a 5 percent tax surcharge. For any corporation with taxable income greater than $335,000 (or said to be fully subject to the surtax),

TABLE   4-3

Corporate Income Tax on $500,000

Incremental Taxable Income	Incremental Tax Rate	Incremental Tax Amount
$ 50,000	15 percent	$ 7,500
25,000	25 percent	6,250
25,000	34 percent	8,500
235,000	39 percent	91,650
165,000	34 percent	56,100
$ 500,000		$ 170,000

the marginal and average tax rates are the same, 34 percent, as illustrated in Table 4-2 and Figure 4-2, panel A. The effect of this surcharge is that all income is taxed at the 34 percent rate between $335,000 and $10.0 million. In our example, if the first $100,000 were taxed at a 34 percent tax rate, the corporation would be required to pay $34,000 in taxes. However, the corporation pays only $22,250 on its first $100,000 of income. In effect, this is an $11,750 tax savings provided to small corporations. This is in line with the progressive nature of the U.S. tax system (more income gets taxed at higher rates).

However, as a corporation makes significantly more than $100,000, the tax code minimizes and eventually erases this tax savings. Notice that this surcharge of 5 percent provides additional taxes of $11,750 on the incremental $235,000 of taxable income. Consequently, all benefits from the lower tax brackets are erased.

The same logic is applied to the 3 percent surcharge (38 percent tax rate) applied between $15.0 million and $18.3 million. At $10.0 million, the corporate tax rate becomes 35 percent and remains there until $15.0 million. A 3 percent surcharge kicks in between $15.0 million and $18,333,333, and the corporation "pays back" the $100,000 of tax savings at 34 percent (instead of 35 percent) for taxable income on its first $10.0 million, erasing all benefits of all lower tax brackets. Above $18,333,333, marginal and average tax rates are 35 percent.

ESSENTIAL ASPECTS OF THE CORPORATE INCOME TAX

The following discussion provides a brief summary of the key aspects of the tax laws and regulations that will affect the financial decision maker. These aspects will be used throughout the remaining chapters of this book and commonly will cover many tax issues encountered by financial managers. However, this chapter is not intended to substitute for the need to use tax accountants and tax attorneys on real-life matters of complexity.

F I G U R E   4-2

Marginal and average corporate tax rates.

Panel A: Taxable Income: $0 to $500,000

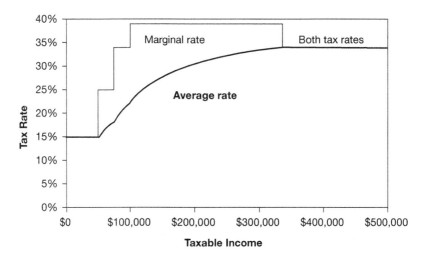

Panel B: Taxable Income: $500,000 to $20,000,000+

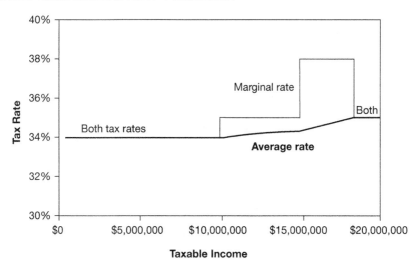

On the surface, the concept of the corporate income tax is quite simple and direct: Accumulate total sales (and other income) and subtract total expenses to arrive at taxable income. Multiply the taxable income by the tax rates to determine the amount of taxes to be paid by the corporation. However simple the concept, the actual application requires a closer examination of sales, other income, and expenses.

Corporate Income

Corporate taxable income consists of two general kinds of income: (1) ordinary income or income from the normal due course of business, along with dividends, interest, rents, and royalties, and (2) profits from the sale of capital assets (capital gains and losses). This income definition is very similar to the income definition in Chapter 2 with some noted exceptions or notable differences, as discussed below.

Dividend Income

Various percentages of dividends received by one corporation from another are exempt from taxation. If a corporation owns up to 20 percent of the stock of another, 70 percent of the dividends received may be excluded from taxable income. If the corporation owns at least 20 percent but less than 80 percent of another corporation, it may exclude 80 percent of dividends received. If the corporation owns 80 percent or more of the stock of another firm, it can file a consolidated tax return. In this latter situation, there are no dividends as far as the IRS is concerned, so there is obviously no tax on fund transfers between the two entities.

Many treasurers, especially in these days of minimal short-term interest rates, buy shares in large, high-dividend-yielding companies with very little stock price volatility (or risk). Since they own far less than 20 percent, 70 percent of the dividend income will be excluded from taxation. Thus what may have started out to be a 5.00 percent dividend yield (compared with interest of 0.25 percent on short-term money-market accounts) receives a second benefit that only 1.50 percent of that total dividend yield is taxed. Even in a 35 percent tax bracket, this leaves 0.975 percent after taxes for a total after-tax yield of 4.475 percent.

Another example: Corporation H owns 40 percent of the stock of Corporation J and receives $100,000 in dividends from that corporation. It pays taxes only on $20,000 of the $100,000. Assuming that Corporation H is in the 35 percent tax bracket, the tax is $7,000, or 7.00 percent of the dividends received. The reason for this reduced tax is that subjecting intercorporate dividends to the full corporate tax rate would be triple taxation. First, Corporation J would pay its regular taxes. Then Corporation H would pay a second tax on the dividends received from Corporation J. Finally, Corporation H's stockholders would be subject to taxes on their individual dividend income. The dividend exclusion reduces the multiple-taxation effect of corporate income.

Interest, Rent, Royalties, and Other Income

Interest, rent, royalties, and other income are considered ordinary income and subject to income taxes. Other income consists of usually insignificant amounts and serves as a catchall for such items as partnership income and recovery of a previous year's bad-debt expense.

Corporate Capital Gains and Losses

Corporate taxable income consists of two kinds of profits from the sale of capital assets (capital gains and losses) and all other income (ordinary income). *Capital assets* (e.g., buildings or security investments) are defined as assets not bought or sold in the ordinary course of a firm's business. Gains and losses on the sale of capital assets, while technically defined as capital gains and losses, can be taxed at ordinary rates or preferential capital gains rates. Gains or losses from the sale of capital assets employed in businesses operations (usually part of net, plant, property, and equipment) are taxed at ordinary rates, whereas gains or losses from the sale of financial security holdings are taxed at preferential rates. Tax laws also distinguish between *long-* and *short-term* capital gains based on the length of time the asset is held (currently one year).

For example, five years ago you purchased a manufacturing piece of equipment for $950,000 and incurred $50,000 of installation charges. Over the five years, you had depreciation totaling $776,900 (see below) and consequently a tax basis of $223,100. You now can sell the piece of equipment for $500,000. Table 4-4 presents a summary of this concept.

These circumstances result in a long-term capital gain (technically speaking). However, this gain is taxed at ordinary rates because the asset was used in the normal course of business.

While the exact handling of capital gains is beyond the scope of this chapter, suffice it to say that the sale of most business equipment and buildings generates a capital gain or loss that is taxed at ordinary tax rates. In this simple example, over this five-year period, depreciation was considered an expense that reduced the corporation's ordinary income and income taxes (at a 35 percent tax rate). The gain effectively comes about because there was "too much" depreciation ascribed to the asset in terms of fair market value. This "excess" depreciation provided an added tax-deductible expense that saved the company taxes at a rate of 35 percent, or $96,915 ($276,900 × 0.35). To recover this "extra" tax benefit that the corporation enjoyed, the gain is taxed at ordinary rates (35 percent) to fully recover the tax advantage provided by the depreciation. This process is known as *depreciation recapture*. If the gain were taxed at the favorable capital gains tax rate of 15 percent, the tax on the gain would be only $41,535, and the corporation's depreciation-driven tax savings would not be fully recovered by the IRS.

T A B L E   4-4

Capital Gain Illustration

Cost of equipment	$ 950,000
Add: Installation	50,000
Depreciable basis	1,000,000
Less: Accumulated depreciation	776,900
Tax basis	$ 223,100
Sale price	$ 500,000
Less: Tax basis	223,100
Capital gain (loss)	$ 276,900

For our purposes, we assume throughout this text that corporate capital gains are subject to ordinary tax rates. This is typically the case for any depreciable asset or any short-term gain resulting from temporary holdings of marketable securities bought and sold on the open exchange.

Most long-term capital gains derived from the sale of a financial asset such as a share of stock is taxed at the capital gain preferential rate of 15 percent. For example, if the same capital gain of $276,900 occurred as a result of the sale of a long-term stock holding, then that gain would be subject to a 15 percent tax rate and $41,535 of taxes. If the stock were held for less than a year, ordinary rates would apply.

Corporate Deductions

The corporate deductions are listed below.

Deductibility of Interest and Dividend Payments

Interest payments made by a corporation are a deductible expense to the firm, but dividends paid on its common stock are not. If a firm raises $1 million (through debt) and contracts to pay the suppliers of this money 5 percent, or $50,000, a year, the $50,000 is deductible. If the $1 million is raised by selling stock and the $50,000 is paid as dividends, the dividend payment is not tax deductible. This differential treatment of dividends and interest payments has an important effect on the methods by which firms raise capital.

Net Operating Losses Carryover

To help "smooth out" a difficult year when a firm may incur business losses, the tax code has provisions to recover taxes previously paid over the past two years when the company had income and special provisions to offset future taxable income by these net operating losses (NOLs). The allowable carryback period for a NOL is 2 years, and NOLs can be carried forward 20 years. Consequently, firms with NOLs have a 22-year period in which to recoup taxes paid on past profits or absorb losses against future profits. In all cases, once the NOL is offset by income, the tax preference goes away.

To illustrate, let's say that KJD Computers made $300 million, $400 million, and $500 million before taxes in 2007, 2008, and 2009, respectively. However, in 2010, it suffered a $2,000 million operating loss (see Table 4-5, panel A). Reported income KJD Computers could use the carryback feature to recover the taxes it paid in 2008. Since $1,600 million of losses remain ($2,000 million 2010 loss offset by $400 million of 2008 income), the taxes paid in 2009 also could be recovered. As seen in panel B of the table, KJD recovers $315 million of previously paid taxes in 2010 as a result of carrybacks. The remaining $1,100 million of loss (panel C) will be carried forward to reduce taxable income to zero in 2011 (thus saving $245 million of tax expense in 2011). In 2012, $400 million of NOL remains and is used to cut the 2012 income in half and saves another $140 million in taxes.

For 2010, the carryback period was extended back five years in certain circumstances for smaller businesses. There are restrictions as well; for example, the

TABLE   4-5

Illustration of Net Operating Losses
($ millions)

A. Reported income	2007	2008	2009	2010
Taxable income	$ 300.0	$ 400.0	$ 500.0	$ (2,000.0)
Income taxes (35%)	(105.0)	(140.0)	(175.0)	
Net income	$ 195.0	$ 260.0	$ 325.0	
B. Carryback	**2007**	**2008**	**2009**	**2010**
Taxable income	$ 300.0	$ 400.0	$ 500.0	$ (2,000.0)
Income taxes (35%)	(105.0)	(140.0)	(175.0)	315.0
Net income	$ 195.0	$ 260.0	$ 325.0	$ (1,685.0)
C. Carry forward	**2010**	**2011**	**2012**	**2013**
Original taxable income	$ (2,000.0)	$ 700.0	$ 800.0	$ 1,000.0
Less: Carry forward	-	(700.0)	(400.0)	-
Taxable income	(2,000.0)	-	400.0	1,000.0
Income taxes (35%)	315.0	-	(140.0)	(350.0)
Net income	$ (1,685.0)	$ 700.0	$ 260.0	$ 650.0

acquisition of a NOL company generally results in the inability to use the NOLs on behalf of the acquiring company. Also, NOL carryovers also figure prominently in the calculation of the Alternative Minimum Tax. Once again, these special circumstances are too complex for this brief summary.

Depreciation
Depreciation refers to allocating the cost of an asset over its life. Suppose that a business firm buys a piece of equipment that costs $500,000, and the equipment is expected to last five years. The equipment will increase profits (earnings before interest, taxes, depreciation, and amortization [EBITDA]) to $1,000,000 per year. Without the concept of depreciation, the entire cost of the equipment would be a business expense against the first year's income alone; this is equivalent to depreciating the asset over one year. The pattern of accounting net income would be as indicated in Table 4-6 (we assume that interest expense is zero to focus on depreciation).

The primary assumption of depreciation is that because the equipment contributes revenues over the entire five-year period, its cost should be allocated over the same period. If we accept this assumption, then the immediate write-off illustrated understates net income for year 1 and overstates net income for years 2 through 5. Now assume that the firm uses straight-line depreciation so that one-fifth of the cost of the equipment is allocated against each year's EBITDA, as illustrated in Table 4-7.

TABLE 4-6

Case 1: Immediately Expensed

	Year 1	Years 2–5
EBITDA	$1,000,000	$1,000,000
Depreciation	500,000	—
Pretax income	500,000	1,000,000
Taxes (34 percent)	170,000	340,000
Net income	$ 330,000	$ 660,000

TABLE 4-7

Case 2: Straight-Line Depreciation

	Years 1–5
EBITDA	$1,000,000
Depreciation	100,000
Pretax income	900,000
Taxes (34 percent)	306,000
Net income	$ 594,000

TABLE 4-8

Case 2: Straight-Line Depreciation and Annual Cash Flow

Annual Cash Flow	Year 1	Years 2–5
Net income	$ 594,000	$ 594,000
Add: Depreciation	100,000	100,000
Less: Investment	(500,000)	—
Cash flow	$ 194,000	$ 694,000

Accounting net income is the same for each of the five years.

Depreciation and Cash Flows

I have illustrated the effect of depreciation on accounting earnings. However, depreciation is a special kind of tax-deductible expense in that it is *not* a cash outlay. Whether we consider depreciation or not, the only cash outflow in the preceding example occurs at the start of year 1 when the equipment is purchased. For case 1, therefore, cash flows and accounting net income are the same, but for case 2, the noncash nature of depreciation expense causes cash flows to be different from accounting income, as seen in Table 4-8.

TABLE 4-9

Present Value Comparison of Depreciation Methods

	Case 1: Immediate Write-Off			Case 2: 5-Year Depreciation		
Year	Net Income	Cash Flow	Present Value (PV) of Cash Flow	Net Income	Cash Flow	PV of Cash Flow
1	$ 330,000	$ 330,000	$ 300,000	$ 594,000	$ 194,000	$ 176,364
2	660,000	660,000	545,455	594,000	694,000	573,554
3	660,000	660,000	495,868	594,000	694,000	521,412
4	660,000	660,000	450,789	594,000	694,000	474,011
5	660,000	660,000	409,808	594,000	694,000	430,919
	$2,970,000	$2,970,000	$2,201,919	$2,970,000	$2,970,000	$2,176,261

Because depreciation is noncash expense, it is added back to net income to determine cash flows. Cash flows also must be adjusted in year 1 to reflect the cash outlay that took place when the equipment was purchased (Table 4-9).

The five-year total of net income and cash flow for both cases is $2,970,000. So what is the point (and "big deal") about depreciation? The only effect is on the *timing of cash flows*. Assuming a 10 percent discount rate, we calculate the present value of the cash flows for both cases using the following equation to "discount" the cash flows:

$$\text{Future value}/(1 + \text{discount rate})^{(\text{number of years})} = \text{present value (PV)} \quad (4.1)$$

Thus the present value of the first year's cash flow for case 1 is $330,000/(1.10)^1 = \$300,000$. And for the second year's cash flow for case 1, the present value is $\$660,000/(1.10)^2 = \$660,000/(1.2100) = \$545,455$. As another example and for case 2, straight-line depreciation, the present value of the year 5 cash flow is calculated as $\$694,000/(1.10)^5 = \$694,000/(1.61051) = \$430,919$. Chapter 7 provides for a more detailed discussion of present value.

Clearly, the higher value is attained with the immediate write-off of the asset. In this example, the only difference between the two cases is when the tax benefit for the depreciation is received. The immediate write-off results in a $25,658 advantage. Firms prefer to write off assets as they are purchased rather than depreciating them over their useful lives. This is not permitted, however, by either accounting conventions (U.S. Generally Accepted Accounting Principles [GAAP]) or tax laws. Given that assets must be depreciated, firms generally will want to depreciate them as quickly as possible.

Section 179 Benefit for Small Companies
The federal tax code has a provision, Section 179, that allows the immediate expensing of up to $500,000 of "capital" expenditures in the year that the purchase was made if the company meets certain guidelines.

Accelerated Depreciation

There are two ways for a firm to write off assets more quickly. One is to shorten the period over which the asset is depreciated. The other is to use an accelerated depreciation method (such as the 150 percent declining-balance method or the double-declining-balance method). U.S. tax laws permit firms to do both using a procedure known as the *Modified Accelerated Cost Recovery System* (MACRS, pronounced "makers").

Anyone who has ever purchased a new car has experienced the concepts that underlie accelerated depreciation. In that first year of use, the value of the new car drops more dramatically than in the car's tenth year! Likewise, the value of a brand-new computer drops more rapidly when it is a few months old than when it is five years old! Accelerated depreciation systematically incorporates this feature when estimating depreciation.

Under MACRS, there is no need to estimate the expected useful economic life of an asset. Instead, assets are categorized into several classes, each with its own *class life* and *recovery period* over which the asset is to be depreciated. The asset classes and types of property included in each are listed in Table 4-10. Notice that most industrial manufacturing equipment is included as seven-year property. Yes, industrial equipment used to make steel is different from equipment to make chocolate and is different from equipment used to make computer chips. However, rather than complicate the application of MACRS, generally, all industrial equipment is considered to have the same seven-year tax life.

These statutory lives are usually shorter than the economic lives of the assets; furthermore, MACRS allows an accelerated depreciation method, specifically, 200 percent (or double-declining-balance) depreciation for most classes of assets. (Also, 15- and 20-year assets are depreciated using the 150 percent declining-balance

T A B L E   4-10

Recovery Periods for MACRS

Class	Type of Property
3-year	Short-lived property, such as over-the-road tractor units, race horses over two years old, and other horses over 12 years old
5-year	Cars and trucks, computers and peripherals, calculators, copiers and typewriters, and specific items used in research
7-year	Office furniture and fixtures, plus any asset not designated to be in another class; most industrial equipment
10-year	Vessels, barges, tugs, and similar equipment related to water transportation and single-purpose agricultural structures
15-year	Roads, shrubbery, wharves, and sewage treatment plants
20-year	Farm buildings, sewer pipe, and other long-lived equipment
27.5-year*	Residential rental real property
31.5-year*	Nonresidential real property

*Depreciated using the straight-line method.

TABLE 4-11

Recovery Allowance Percentages under MACRS
(half-year convention)

| Year | Class Life | | | |
	3-Year	5-Year	7-Year	10-Year
1	33.33%	20.00%	14.29%	10.00%
2	44.45%	32.00%	24.49%	18.00%
3	14.81%	19.20%	17.49%	14.40%
4	7.41%	11.52%	12.49%	11.52%
5		11.52%	8.93%	9.22%
6		5.76%	8.93%	7.37%
7			8.93%	6.55%
8			4.45%	6.55%
9				6.56%
10				6.55%
11				3.28%
Total	100.00%	100.00%	100.00%	100.00%

Source: IRS Publication 946 (2010), p.75.

method, and real property must be depreciated over 27.5 or 31.5 years using the straight-line method.) The effect of MACRS is to accelerate depreciation, increasing the depreciation tax shelter and thus increasing cash flows earlier and value.

The percentages are applied to the total cost of the asset, including the asset itself, the transportation, and the installation, without consideration of salvage value. MACRS incorporates a half-year convention for the initial and final years. The half-year convention assumes that, on average, capital is spent midyear of the first year (Table 4-11).

In Table 4-12, panel A computes the MACRS depreciation and remaining tax book value for a $1 million asset with a seven-year MACRS life. Notice that the asset is fully written off after eight years, considering the half-year convention in the first and last years. In panel B, we reduce the earnings before depreciation by this MACRS depreciation amount to calculate taxable income less the tax payment (at 34 percent because the taxable income is between $5 million and $10 million) to derive the company's net income according to the IRS. More will be said about this when deferred taxes are discussed.

Accelerated Depreciation, Present Value, and the Impact on Capital Investment
Just as we saw when we considered the case of immediately expensing an asset versus depreciating that same asset over five years, accelerated depreciation (such as MACRS) results in lower tax payments in the early years when compared with straight-line depreciation and thus greater cash flow in earlier years. Consequently,

TABLE 4-12

MACRS Depreciation
($1,000,000 Asset, 7-Year MACRS)

Panel A: Depreciation and Tax Book Values

Year	Rate	Opening Balance	Depreciation	Ending Balance
1	14.29%	$ 1,000,000	$ 142,900	$ 857,100
2	24.49%	857,100	244,900	612,200
3	17.49%	612,200	174,900	437,300
4	12.49%	437,300	124,900	312,400
5	8.93%	312,400	89,300	223,100
6	8.93%	223,100	89,300	133,800
7	8.93%	133,800	89,300	44,500
8	4.45%	44,500	44,500	–
9	0.00%	–	–	–
10	0.00%	–	–	–
Total	100.00%	n/a	$ 1,000,000	n/a

Panel B: Pretax Income, Provision for Taxes, and Reported Net Income

Year	EBIT before Depreciation	Depreciation	Taxable Income	Income Tax Payment	IRS Net Income
1	$ 10,000,000	$ 142,900	$ 9,857,100	$ 3,351,414	$ 6,505,686
2	10,000,000	244,900	9,755,100	3,316,734	6,438,366
3	10,000,000	174,900	9,825,100	3,340,534	6,484,566
4	10,000,000	124,900	9,875,100	3,357,534	6,517,566
5	10,000,000	89,300	9,910,700	3,369,638	6,541,062
6	10,000,000	89,300	9,910,700	3,369,638	6,541,062
7	10,000,000	89,300	9,910,700	3,369,638	6,541,062
8	10,000,000	44,500	9,955,500	3,384,870	6,570,630
9	10,000,000	–	10,000,000	3,400,000	6,600,000
10	10,000,000	–	10,000,000	3,400,000	6,600,000
Total	$ 100,000,000	$ 1,000,000	$ 99,000,000	$ 33,660,000	$ 65,340,000

capital investment aided by MACRS depreciation is of higher value than the same investment limited by straight-line depreciation. While the total cash flows over the life of the project do not change, the timing of the cash flows does change. The project (and the depreciation approach) that delivers the cash flow more quickly is the more valuable project.

Tax Credits

Tax credits are deductions from the tax bill itself rather than deductions from taxable income and thus are potentially very valuable. Today, there are only two minor tax credits detailed on Form 1120 for corporations—credit for tax paid on undistributed capital gains (in special cases of a real estate investment trust) and credit for federal tax on fuels. In the past, one of the major tax credits that remains in the tax code, but at a 0 percent rate, was the Investment Tax Credit (ITC) Program.

Under the ITC Program, business firms could deduct from their income tax liability a specified percentage (often as high as 10 percent) of the dollar amount of new investment in each of certain categories of capital assets. Tax credits, like tax rates and depreciation methods, are subject to congressional changes reflecting public policy and economic considerations. The Tax Reform Act of 1986 reduced the credit to 0 percent, which effectively eliminated the investment tax credit on capital assets. However, the credit remains in the legislation and could be reinstated simply by changing the 0 percent credit rate.

Tax credits also have been used to stimulate other socially desirable ends, such as those for investment in targeted jobs (employers may deduct a percentage of first-year wages paid to "disadvantaged" individuals), disabled access, small-employer pension plan startup costs, incremental research and development, alternative sources of business energy (including solar, geothermal, and ocean thermal), and low-income housing.

Payment of Tax in Installments

Firms must estimate their taxable income for the current year and, if reporting on a calendar-year basis, pay one-fourth of the estimated tax on April 15, June 15, September 15, and December 15 of that year. The estimated taxes must be identical to those of the previous year or at least 90 percent of actual tax liability for the current year, or the firm will be subject to penalties. Any differences between estimated and actual taxes are payable by March 15 of the following year. For example, if a firm expected to earn taxable income of $1 million in 2011 with a tax obligation of $340,000, then it must file an estimated income statement and pay $76,500 ($340,000 × 90 percent divided by 4) on the 15th of April, June, September, and December of 2011. By March 15, 2012, it must file a final income statement and pay any shortfall (or receive a refund for overages) between estimated and actual taxes.

DEFERRED TAXES

Deferred taxes are taxes that a company owes (liability) to the IRS that will be payable in the future or taxes that a company "prepays" (asset) to the IRS. Deferred taxes result from accounting differences between U.S. GAAP accounting and tax accounting. By the third (or certainly the fourth) session of any television crime show, there is at least one episode about the unscrupulous businessperson who always seems to keep a second set of books in his or her lower right-hand desk drawer. In reality, every company maintains two sets of books: (1) U.S. GAAP–based books or books for public reporting, and (2) IRS or tax books. Most of the accounting regulations are the same between the sets of books. However, with regard to depreciation and the book value of an asset, firms are allowed by law to keep two sets of books—one for reporting to investors and one for taxes.

To illustrate, accelerated depreciation increases cash flows (over straight-line depreciation) while reducing accounting net income. Most firms use accelerated depreciation for tax purposes but straight-line depreciation (with its higher reported net income) for stockholder reporting purposes. The use of straight-line depreciation minimizes the negative effect on accounting net income and is said to "normalize" or "stabilize" reported income, especially when the total of asset purchases are inconsistent from year to year.

Effects of Depreciation on Taxes and Net Income

Panel A of Table 4-13 shows the U.S. GAAP "book" balances and depreciation on a $1 million piece of manufacturing equipment using straight-line depreciation over its economic life, which is assumed to be 10 years, with no assumed salvage value. Each year, $100,000 is expensed, and thus the book balance of the asset is reduced by $100,000 per year until it has a zero value ("fully written off") at the end of year 10.

In Table 4-13, panel B begins with income or earnings before interest, taxes, and depreciation, similar to Table 4-12. Assuming that interest expense is zero, we can focus on the effects of depreciation. Panel B continues with depreciation, pretax income, provision for taxes (as reported in an annual report), and reported net income. You see that reported pretax income is $9.9 million each year, taxes (or more formally, provision for income tax) is $3.366 million each year and results in reported annual net income of $6.534 million. The income is "smoothed," and the same amount is reported each year.

Comparing Tables 4-12 and 4-13, you will notice that the totals are identical after 10 years—earnings before interest, taxes, and depreciation, depreciation, taxable income, tax payment, and net income. The only difference is the annual timing and dollar amount of the depreciation expense. As a result of these timing differences, the firm reports to the IRS $244,900 of depreciation expense, taxable income of $9,755,100, taxes paid of $3,316,734, and net income as reported to the IRS of $6,438,366 in the second year. Table 4-14 summarizes the second year from a tax-reporting perspective and an annual report (or book) perspective.

As noted, more commonly, the corporation uses straight-line depreciation for annual stockholder reporting (annual report). It reports $100,000 in depreciation, with pretax income of $9,900,000 and $3,366,000 as a provision for taxes (even though its actual tax bill is only $3,316,734), and a net income of $6,534,000. The difference of $49,266 ($3,366,000 − $3,316,734) in reported versus paid taxes represents *deferred taxes*—that is, the firm has been able to

TABLE 4-13

Straight-Line Depreciation
($1,000,000 Asset, 10-Year Life)

Panel A: Depreciation and Book Values

Year	Opening Balance	Depreciation	Ending Balance
1	$ 1,000,000	$ 100,000	$ 900,000
2	900,000	100,000	800,000
3	800,000	100,000	700,000
4	700,000	100,000	600,000
5	600,000	100,000	500,000
6	500,000	100,000	400,000
7	400,000	100,000	300,000
8	300,000	100,000	200,000
9	200,000	100,000	100,000
10	100,000	100,000	–
Total	n/a	$ 1,000,000	n/a

Panel B: Pretax Income, Provision for Taxes, and Reported Net Income

Year	EBIT before Depreciation	Depreciation	Pre-Tax Income	Provision for Income Tax	Reported Net Income
1	$ 10,000,000	$ 100,000	$ 9,900,000	$ 3,366,000	$ 6,534,000
2	10,000,000	100,000	9,900,000	3,366,000	6,534,000
3	10,000,000	100,000	9,900,000	3,366,000	6,534,000
4	10,000,000	100,000	9,900,000	3,366,000	6,534,000
5	10,000,000	100,000	9,900,000	3,366,000	6,534,000
6	10,000,000	100,000	9,900,000	3,366,000	6,534,000
7	10,000,000	100,000	9,900,000	3,366,000	6,534,000
8	10,000,000	100,000	9,900,000	3,366,000	6,534,000
9	10,000,000	100,000	9,900,000	3,366,000	6,534,000
10	10,000,000	100,000	9,900,000	3,366,000	6,534,000
Total	$100,000,000	$ 1,000,000	$ 99,000,000	$33,660,000	$ 65,340,000

defer paying these taxes until a later date because it used an accelerated depreciation method for calculating taxable income.

This effect continues throughout the 10-year life of this project. Table 4-15 summarizes the ninth year from a book (annual report) perspective and a tax-reporting perspective.

T A B L E   4-14

IRS and U.S. GAAP Reporting Comparison

Year 2			
Tax-Reporting Purposes (Table 4-12)		**Annual Report Purposes (Table 4-13)**	
EBITD	$ 10,000,000	EBITD	$ 10,000,000
Depreciation	244,900	Depreciation	100,000
Taxable income	9,755,100	Pretax income	9,900,000
Tax payment	3,316,734	Provision for tax	3,366,000
IRS net income	$ 6,438,366	Annual report net income	$ 6,534,000

T A B L E   4-15

IRS and U.S. GAAP Reporting Comparison

Year 9			
Tax-Reporting Purposes (Table 4-12)		**Annual Report Purposes (Table 4-13)**	
EBITD	$ 10,000,000	EBITD	$ 10,000,000
Depreciation	—	Depreciation	100,000
Taxable income	10,000,000	Pretax income	9,900,000
Tax payment	3,400,000	Provision for tax	3,366,000
IRS net income	$ 6,600,000	Annual report net income	$ 6,534,000

By year 9, the asset is fully depreciated for tax purposes, but for annual report purposes, the depreciation continues. In this year, the corporation reports a provision for income taxes of $3,366,000 (the same as every year). However, in the ninth year, the corporation writes a check to the government for $3,400,000. The extra $34,000 is reflected as a reduction in deferred taxes.

Deferred Taxes on the Balance Sheet

The cumulative deferred taxes just calculated are reported on the balance sheet under an account titled "Deferred taxes." In this example, deferred taxes constitute a long-term liability—in effect, they represent an interest-free loan from the federal government. Table 4-16 reflects the account balance over our 10-year period. By the end of year 4, the account balance reaches its peak and then is whittled to a zero balance at the end of 10 years.

However, for growing firms, assets and their depreciation are growing over time, so the total deferred taxes account is never reduced to zero. In this case, the total deferred tax account is likely to grow while the deferred taxes for specific individual older assets decline to zero.

T A B L E   4-16

Deferred Tax Balance

($1,000,000 Asset, 10-Year Straight-Line and 7-Year MACRS)

Year	Table 4-13* Provision for Income Taxes	Table 4-12** Income Tax Payment	Annual Amount Deferred	Deferred Tax Liability Balance
1	$ 3,366,000	$ 3,351,414	$ 14,586	$ 14,586
2	3,366,000	3,316,734	49,266	63,852
3	3,366,000	3,340,534	25,466	89,318
4	3,366,000	3,357,534	8,466	97,784
5	3,366,000	3,369,638	(3,638)	94,146
6	3,366,000	3,369,638	(3,638)	90,508
7	3,366,000	3,369,638	(3,638)	86,870
8	3,366,000	3,384,870	(18,870)	68,000
9	3,366,000	3,400,000	(34,000)	34,000
10	3,366,000	3,400,000	(34,000)	–

*Table 4-13: What you report on your income statement.
**Table 4-12: What you actually pay to the IRS, or "current taxes."

Deferred Tax Assets

There are a few accounting differences between tax (IRS) accounting and U.S. GAAP accounting. The most pronounced is the difference in depreciation, as discussed earlier. That difference gives rise to long-term deferred tax liability.

However, some differences cause deferred tax assets. For example, say that a firm currently is offering a special one-time two-year warranty when a customer purchases its product. The firm estimates that over a two-year period it is likely to spend a total of $100,000 in warranty repairs. Table 4-17 presents the reported income for this two-year period using U.S. GAAP rules.

U.S. GAAP recognizes the warranty expense when the sale (and warranty commitment) is made. The IRS only allows a tax payer to deduct actual warranty expense, not projected expense. Consequently, the following is reported to the IRS, assuming that the warranty actually does cost a total of $100,000 but incurred over the two-year period, as illustrated in Table 4-18.

In this example, the corporation reports a year 1 provision for income taxes of $3,366,000 and actually paid $3,386,000 to the federal government. The difference ($20,000) is considered a deferred tax asset and is reported in the current asset portion of the balance sheet. In other words, the company actually paid the IRS more than what was reported on the company's income statement. This "overpayment" is considered a deferred tax asset, and because it is now short term (one year) in nature, it is a current deferred tax asset and similar to a prepaid expense.

TABLE   4-17

U.S. GAAP Handling of Warranty Expense

	Year 1*	Year 2*
Income before warranty expense	$10,000	$10,000
Warranty expense	100	—
Pretax income	9,900	10,000
Provision for income taxes (34 percent)	3,366	3,400
Reported net income	$ 6,534	$ 6,600

* All dollar amounts are in thousands.

TABLE   4-18

IRS Handling of Warranty Expense

	Year 1*	Year 2*
Income before warranty expense	$10,000	$10,000
Warranty expense	40	60
Pretax income	9,960	9,940
Income tax payment (34 percent)	3,386	3,380
Reported net income	$ 6,574	$ 6,560

* All dollar amounts are in thousands.

In the second year, the corporation reports a provision for income taxes of $3,400,000 but actually pays $3,380,000 in federal income taxes. In this case, the check written to the IRS is $20,000 less than the provision reported on the company's second-year income statement. The deferred tax asset is decreased by $20,000 to a net balance of zero after this two-year period.

In general, there are a few expenses (such as this warranty expense) that U.S. GAAP says must be handled in one way, whereas for tax purposes, the expenses are handled in another way. We will look at the reality when we review the reported tax footnotes of Hershey, P. F. Chang's, Disney, and Walmart.

DIVIDENDS PAID TO STOCKHOLDERS

Dividends are not an expense, and therefore, for corporate income tax purposes, dividends are not a tax deductible "expense." They do not get considered in deriving pretax income or taxes or net income. Dividends are a return of capital to a stockholder. They are a corporate payment from after-tax net income. However, from your stockholders' perspective, dividends are a taxable-income event, and individuals must pay tax on dividends.

From a personal perspective, dividends are taxed separately from other income and at rates much lower than ordinary income. In 2010, the tax rate on dividends was 15 percent for any single tax filer with $34,000 or more of taxable income or $68,000 or more for any married filing jointly tax filers. If your taxable income was below those income levels, your tax rate was 0 percent. Thus, effectively, dividends are a tax-free event for any lower-income personal tax filer.

For individuals with lower income and who own dividend-paying stock, there is no double taxation on dividends. A corporation makes pretax income, pays taxes, and pays dividends to the low-income stockholder who pays no taxes. The individual's portion of corporate pretax income was taxed fully at the corporate level and at 35 percent in most cases.

However, if you are an individual who makes more than those income limits, your dividends are taxed at a maximum 15% tax rate! This gives rise to double taxation of dividends, as shown in Table 4-19.

For example, Corporation A earns $1 billion before taxes and is subject to a 35 percent tax rate. Corporation A dividended all its income to its stockholder, Individual A, who had to report all the dividend income as income subject to a 15 percent tax rate, or $97.5 million in additional taxes. In this example, the only real income that was created was the $1,000 million from Corporation A. However, in total, there were $447.5 million of taxes paid (or a 44.75 percent tax rate)!

If Individual A would have been another corporation (Corporation B) with dividend exclusions of 70 percent (if it owned less than 20 percent of the company) or 80 percent (if it owned more than 20 percent of the company), double taxation still would occur. Let's say that Corporation B has more than $18,333,333 in taxable income and therefore is in the 35 percent tax bracket. With a $650 million dividend and 70 percent dividend exclusion, Corporation B would pay $68.25 million, or an effective tax rate of 10.5 percent. With 80 percent dividend exclusion, Corporation B would pay $45.5 million, or an effective tax rate of 7.0 percent ($45.5/$650).

If Corporation B paid dividends to its shareholders, "triple taxation" would occur.

TABLE   4-19

Double Taxation of Dividends

Corporation A*		Individual A*	
Pretax income	$1,000.0	Dividend income	$ 650.0
Taxes (35 percent)	350.0	Taxes (15 percent)	97.5
Net income	$ 650.0	After-tax income	$ 552.5
Dividends	$ 650.0		

* All dollar amounts are in millions.

CORPORATE TAX FOOTNOTE ANALYSIS

Publicly traded companies include an interesting and related tax footnote in their annual report or 10K. The footnote decomposes the corporation's effective tax rate, separates the tax provision into current taxes and deferred taxes, and details the components that gave rise to the balances in deferred tax assets and liabilities. We consider the companies discussed in Chapter 2—Hershey, P. F. Chang's, Disney, and Walmart.

Table 4-20 starts with the federal statutory tax rate of 35.0 percent for all four companies and adjusts it for state income taxes paid, net of the federal tax impact. Since state income taxes are deductible for corporations at the federal level, every 1 percent of state tax costs the company 0.65 percent [or the 1 percent state tax rate times (1 − the 35 percent federal tax rate)]. Also having an impact on the effective tax rate are international taxes. P. F. Chang's and Disney did not report the tax-rate impact separately owing to their international operations, whereas Walmart reported a 5 percent reduction in its effective tax rate owing to its international operations. As mentioned before, Hershey is primarily a domestic company with its largest international business found in Canada. Canada is an even higher tax jurisdiction! "Other" makes up the final adjustment. P. F. Chang's earned a 10.7 percent effective tax-rate reduction via the FICA tip credit. This is an annually recurring tax-rate reduction for P. F. Chang's. Of the four diversified companies, Hershey is the only one with a higher effective tax rate than the statutory 35 percent rate.

Table 4-21 shows the dollar amount of current and deferred taxes that total the tax provision for income taxes, as presented on the income statement. Walmart routinely presents the tax provision as current and deferred within its income statement. Notice that three of the four companies actually paid more in income taxes than reported in their income statements.

T A B L E 4-20

Effective Tax Rates, 2010

Item	Hershey	PF Chang's	Disney	Walmart
Federal statutory rate	35.0%	35.0%	35.0%	35.0%
State income taxes*	2.8%	5.3%	2.6%	2.0%
International	0.4%	**	**	−5.0%
Other	−1.2%	−13.4%	−2.7%	0.4%
Total	37.0%	26.9%	34.9%	32.4%

*State income tax rates are net of the federal tax savings.
**International taxes were not identified separately and are included in "Other."
For P. F. Chang's, the other category include a −10.7 percent reduction owing to the "FICA tip credit."

TABLE 4-21

Current and Deferred Taxes, 2010
($ millions)

Item	Hershey	PF Chang's	Disney	Walmart
Current*	$ 317.7	$ 21.6	$ 2,198.0	$ 7,643.0
Deferred	(18.7)	(4.5)	116.0	(504.0)
Tax provision**	$ 299.0	$ 17.1	$ 2,314.0	$ 7,139.0
Percent of tax provision:				
Current*	106.3%	126.3%	95.0%	107.1%
Deferred	−6.3%	−26.3%	5.0%	−7.1%
Tax provision**	100.0%	100.0%	100.0%	100.0%

*The current taxes relate to what is actually paid to the government.
**Tax provision is also called *tax expense* and is what is reported on the income statement.

TABLE 4-22

Deferred Tax Assets and Liabilities, 2010
($ millions)

Item	Hershey	P. F. Chang's	Disney	Walmart
Deferred tax assets				
Stock-based compensation	$ 72.5	$ 15.7	$ 379.0	$ 267.0
Carry-forwards	54.6	2.3	375.0	2,713.0
Postretirement benefits	115.1	**	**	**
Other accrued expenses	120.3	22.5	2,270.0	3,141.0
Other	(52.3)	0.6	439.0	(1,416.0)
Total	$ 310.2	$ 41.1	$ 3,463.0	$ 4,705.0
Deferred tax liabilities				
Depreciation	$ 145.4	$ 35.7	$ 4,510.0	$ 4,015.0
Inventory	25.7	0.0	**	1,120.0
Other	61.9	0.0	566.0	609.0
Total	$ 233.0	$ 35.7	$ 5,076.0	$ 5,744.0
Net, deferred tax asset (liability)	$ 77.2	$ 5.4	$ (1,613.0)	$ (1,039.0)

**Not separately identified.

Finally, Table 4-22 identifies the causes of the deferred tax assets and liabilities. Depreciation, as described earlier, is the largest accounting difference
(between U.S. GAAP and IRS accounting) that gave rise to deferred tax liabilities for all four companies, whereas, for deferred tax assets, other accrued
expenses constitute the largest category. Additionally, all four companies realized

a deferred tax asset for stock-based compensation and carry-forwards such as NOLs. Once again, the deferred tax asset happened because U.S. GAAP forced the company to realize an expense that the IRS would not accept until the expense actually was paid.

SUMMARY

This chapter provides some basic background on the tax environment within which business firms operate. The massive size of the taxes collected by the federal government is mind boggling, as is the volatility of the past decade owing to general underlying economic conditions.

For corporations, the tax rate begins at 15 percent on income below $50,000, moves to 25 percent on income between $50,000 and $75,000, then 34 percent above $75,000, then to $10 million, and then 35 percent above $10 million. Surcharges at certain income levels have been introduced into the corporate tax structure to derive an average corporate tax rate of 34 percent below $10 million and 35 percent for income above $18,333,333. Estimated taxes are paid in quarterly installments during the year in which the income is earned; when the returns are filed, the actual tax liability results either in additional payments or a refund. Any operating loss incurred by the corporation can be carried back two years and forward 20 years against income in those years.

Between 70 and 80 percent of the dividends received by a corporation owning stock in another firm may be excluded from the receiving firm's taxable income. Dividends paid are not a tax-deductible expense. Regardless of its profitability, a corporation does not have to pay dividends if it needs funds for expansion or other legitimate business purposes. Interest paid is a tax-deductible expense; interest received is taxable as ordinary income.

Depreciation is a special kind of tax-deductible business expense in that it does not represent a cash expenditure but reduces pretax income and consequently lowers tax payments. Tax authorities allow a specified accelerated depreciation method under the Modified Accelerated Cost Recovery System (MACRS); the effect is to reduce taxable income and the cash outflow for taxes in the early years of asset ownership. However, firms may use alternative methods that increase reported net income for purposes of reporting to shareholders. These accounting differences between U.S. GAAP (reported) and IRS (tax) methodology give rise to recognition of timing differences and result in deferred taxes. This chapter ends with a review of the required financial reporting corporate tax footnote.

The information presented here on the tax system is not designed to make a tax expert of the reader. It merely provides a few essentials for recognizing the tax aspects of business financial problems and for developing an awareness of the kinds of situations that should be dealt with by tax specialists. These basics, however, are referred to frequently throughout this text because income taxes are often an important factor in business financial decisions.

TWO

FINANCIAL PLANNING
AND CONTROL

SHORT-TERM FINANCIAL MANAGEMENT AND SUPPLY CHAIN FINANCE

In broad terms, this chapter reviews three short-term areas of financial management: (1) short-term operating performance, (2) working capital management or supply-chain finance, and (3) short-term financing. Breakeven analysis and leverage analysis are necessary to better understand the impact of how the organization "goes to business" in the short term. Both are useful in making operating decisions on a day-to-day basis. They are at the foundation of business decisions, even though tools and techniques are introduced in later chapters that will blur the effectiveness of these short-term tools. In later chapters I discuss a more in-depth and longer-term approach to strategic financial planning (Chapter 6) and investment analysis (Chapters 9 and 10).

I have already touched on aspects of working capital (i.e., current assets less current liabilities) management. Chapter 2 introduced and discussed common current accounts such as cash, cash equivalents (or marketable securities), accounts receivable, inventory, accounts payable, and accrued liabilities. Chapter 3 introduced activity metrics centered on accounts receivable and inventory turnover or days outstanding. These measures are effective metrics used to judge the management of those specific accounts at a "20,000-foot level." I will also discuss methods of forecasting working capital in a strategic financial plan (Chapter 6), as well as anticipate its effects in capital investment analysis (Chapter 10).

Working capital represents the investment of hundreds of billions of dollars throughout corporate America and a critical component of most individual company's balance sheets requiring focused management attention. Proper working capital management often plays a critical role in sustainability of many smaller organizations as well as some large organizations.

It is beyond the scope of this text to delve into the specifics of working capital management and the management of each major type of current asset and current liabilities from an operational perspective. Often organizations have specific departments involved in the day-to-day management of working capital. Each division or strategic business unit may have its own accounts receivable, accounts payable, and inventory departments. Goals and objectives can be established for the organization but implemented at a local level to better align with the practices of the industry or the local country. Responsibility for inventory management is often dispersed through many departments within a strategic business unit. Often there are separate managers for each stage of inventory, raw materials, goods in process, and finished goods. As inventory moves through production, each manufacturing facility could have an inventory manager, and there may be several finished-goods managers assigned to manage the different finished products.

The tools established in this chapter will assist management in target setting and establishing objectives at a corporate or divisional level, but it's up to the operating managers to implement the established direction.

BREAKEVEN ANALYSIS

Breakeven analysis is an approach used to determine the unit level of sales that will cover all fixed and variable expenses. It is the point where a product or project just "breaks even" without generating any profit or incurring any losses. It is often too detail-oriented to be useful at a corporate level. Benchmarking with other competitors (similar to Chapter 3) is not possible because the required information is not publicly available in annual reports or from other sources.

However, breakeven analysis is a useful concept and tool to help a business understand the implications of how it "goes to business" or even if it *should* go to business. After reading an article about retiring early, a friend of mine purchased four vending machines for $10,000, or $2,500 each. The vending machines were the type that sold tasty heated (and reheated and reheated . . .) individual cans of soup, pasta, and so on. Each can sold, on average, for $1.50 and was purchased from a local grocery store for $1.20 per can (including the placement-site floor rental of $0.20 per can). The machines had a fixed cost that included depreciation of $1,250 per year (eight-year life with straight-line depreciation). In addition, the business incurred a weekly expense of $25 for gasoline as my friend drove to restock and collect his sales proceeds every week. The expenditure for gasoline occurred weekly regardless the level of food sales. This resulted in $1,300 of additional fixed expense.

How many cans of food did my friend need to sell in a year to break even? Breakeven analysis addresses this very issue by calculating the breakeven point (BEP):

$$BEP = \frac{\text{fixed cost}}{\text{contribution income}}$$
$$= \frac{(\text{depreciation} + \text{other fixed costs})}{(\text{sales price} - \text{variable cost})} \qquad (5.1)$$

Sales price and variable costs are on a per-unit basis (per can in this example): ($1,250 + $1,300)/($1.50 − $1.20) = $2,550/$0.30 = 8,500 units. In order to just break even, my friend needed to sell 8,500 cans each year. This was a nauseating prospect (for more than one reason). However, since this was for four vending machines, it was only 2,125 cans per machine, although it is still somewhat nauseating to think about eating that many cans of heated and reheated individual servings. On a weekly basis, though, each machine needed to sell about 41 units, or roughly 8 cans a day (assuming five-day weeks) or 6 cans a day (assuming seven-day weeks).

On a college campus, in a place of business, in a shopping area, or anywhere there is a lot of foot traffic, it is conceivable that you would sell the required number of cans to break even and even do better than just breaking even. Of course, all those potential spots were already taken by very large, full-service vending machine companies. My friend was only able to place his machines in back-alley automobile garages. Thus he had to hope that the three to six employees that worked in such places, along with the people dropping off or picking up their cars, were extremely hungry! Needless to say, my friend's venture failed miserably, and it wasn't until after that fact that we sat down to this type of analysis.

In this one case, without the more sophisticated concepts developed in later chapters, my friend could have framed this dismal outlook and perhaps decided that this was not the retirement vehicle of his dreams. Or he could have considered other ways to "go to business," such as higher prices, lower variable costs, and reduced fixed cost, along with the most impactful business adjustment, continuing to work on the location of alternative machine placement sites.

We also could have continued on to refine breakeven analysis to look at a *cash breakeven point* (CBEP). Depreciation is a fixed expense, but it is a noncash expense. Therefore, if the definition of BEP is refined as in Eq. (5.2), then only cash fixed expenses are used:

$$CBEP = \frac{\text{cash fixed cost}}{\text{contribution income}}$$
$$= \frac{\text{cash fixed cost}}{(\text{sales price} - \text{variable cost})} \qquad (5.2)$$

To determine CBEP, my friend would have performed the following calculation: $1,300/($1.50 − $1.20) = $1,300/$0.30 = 4,333 units. Once again,

FIGURE 5-1

Breakeven analysis.

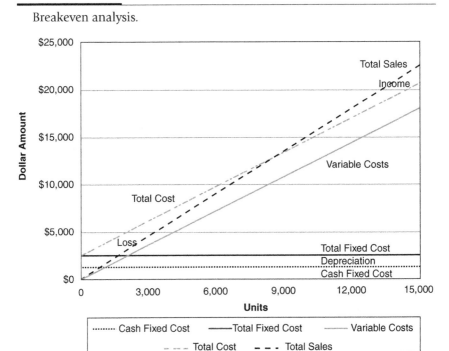

this is for four vending machines or for 21 cans per week (4.2 cans per day) for each vending machine for the business to be cash-neutral—not generate cash but not consume cash either. Figure 5-1 shows income statement results at various levels of units sold. Notice that at 8,500 units sold, my friend breaks even—no income or no loss. Also at 8,500 units, however, the business is generating $1,250 in cash.

Further refinement of the BEP could have captured the inclusion of a desired $600 of income or cash generation (note that for this discussion I am referring to this value as cash income), as in Eq. (5.3):

$$\begin{aligned} \text{CBEPI} &= \frac{(\text{cash fixed cost} + \text{cash income})}{\text{contribution income}} \\ &= \frac{(\text{cash fixed cost} + \text{cash income})}{(\text{sales price} - \text{variable cost})} \end{aligned} \quad (5.3)$$

To determine the CBEP with cash income (CBEPI), my friend would have performed the following calculation: ($1,300 + $600)/($1.50 − $1.20) = $1,900/$0.30 = 6,333 units. As such, in order to generate $600 in cash (or income), my friend would have needed to sell 2,000 units more in total, or almost 10 more cans of food per week from each machine:

TABLE 5-1

Various BEP Summaries

		Required to Break Even	
	Reference	Units	Sales $
Breakeven point (BEP)	Eq. (5.1)	8,500	$12,750
Cash breakeven point (CBEP)	Eq. (5.2)	4,333	6,500
CBEP with cash income (CBEPI)	Eq. (5.3)	6,333	9,500
Cash income to generate $600	Eq. (5.4)	2,000	3,000

$$\text{Units necessary to generate \$600 cash income} = \frac{\$600}{(\$1.50 - \$1.20)} = \frac{\$600}{\$0.30} = 2,000 \quad (5.4)$$

Most operations people such as my friend prefer to speak in terms of the number of units necessary to break even. However, for a sales organization, it may be more interesting to speak in terms of total sales dollars. Since the average selling price was $1.50 per unit, take whatever number of units, and multiply that by $1.50 to reveal the sales level that matches those number of units.

In summary, there are multiple BEPs that could be considered. Table 5-1 summarizes my BEP analysis, the required number of unit sales, and the total dollars of sales assuming an average sales price of $1.50.

The perspective of the decision maker is very important—income or cash, breakeven or cash income generation. Unfortunately for my friend, any perspective in this specific case told the dismal story of his vending machine venture.

BUSINESS LEVERAGE

Business leverage is a related concept to breakeven analysis. It is another short-term financial management tool that adds perspective on how a company "goes to business." Business leverage uses a similar breakdown as breakeven analysis—variable costs and fixed costs.

The concept of business leverage has three distinct dimensions:

- *Operating leverage (OL).* A percentage change in sales results in an OL percentage change in operating income or earnings before interest and tax.

- *Financial leverage (FL).* A percentage change in operating income (earnings before interest and taxes) results in an FL percentage change in pretax tax income (and with a constant tax rate, net income as well). This is a very different definition of financial leverage than encountered in Chapter 3. In that chapter, financial leverage was defined as total assets divided by equity.

- *Combined leverage (CL).* A percentage change in sales results in a CL percentage change in pretax income (and with a constant tax rate, net income as well).

In this case, the percentage change in sales is assumed to be the percentage change in number of units sold (i.e., no price increases). While there are alternative ways to calculate the business leverage metric, the simplest and most straightforward approaches are list below:

Operating leverage (OL):

$$OL = \frac{\text{contribution income}}{\text{operating income}} = \frac{(\text{sales} - \text{variable cost})}{(\text{sales} - \text{variable cost} - \text{fixed cost})} \quad (5.5)$$

Financial leverage (FL):

$$FL = \frac{\text{operating income}}{\text{pretax income}} = \frac{(\text{sales} - \text{variable cost} - \text{fixed cost})}{(\text{sales} - \text{variable cost} - \text{fixed cost} - \text{interest})} \quad (5.6)$$

Combined leverage (CL):

$$CL = \frac{\text{contribution income}}{\text{pretax income}} = \frac{(\text{sales} - \text{variable cost})}{(\text{sales} - \text{variable cost} - \text{fixed cost} - \text{interest})} \quad (5.7)$$

CL as product of OL × FL:

$$CL = OL \times FL \frac{\text{contribution income}}{\text{operating income}} \times \frac{\text{operating income}}{\text{pretax income}} = \frac{\text{contribution income}}{\text{pretax income}} \quad (5.8)$$

While the calculations of business leverage are straightforward, the concept and business implications are not easy to visualize in just these equations. In this case, Table 5-2 illustrates the concept of business leverage using two hypothetical companies.

Company A is a firm that has a conservative perspective of investing in technology but a more aggressive view about borrowing money. Company A could be a company led by finance professionals who are comfortable with financial markets but less so in the capital equipment market. Company B is a company that has a more aggressive view on operations and invests more heavily in technology while financing operations with less reliance on debt. Company B could be led by engineers who appreciate the potential of the latest equipment while being more conservative toward borrowing.

Comparing the base scenarios, the operating tradeoffs are clear even though the $10,000 in sales for either company generates $2,000 of operating income for both companies. The path to get there is quite different. Company A uses variable costs (e.g., raw materials, labor, etc.) to a significantly greater extent than Company B. Company B uses new equipment and technology that can reduce variable costs but results in significantly higher depreciation and other fixed costs. Company A has an operating leverage of only 2.00, whereas Company B's operating leverage is 4.00.

TABLE 5-2

Business Leverage Illustration: Business Growth

	Base Scenarios				10% Growth in Sales			
	A. FL Emphasis		B. OL Emphasis		A. FL Emphasis		B. OL Emphasis	
	Per Unit	Total	Per Unit	Total	Total	Growth	Total	Growth
Units sold		1,000		1,000	1,100	10.0%	1,100	10.0%
Sales	$ 10	$ 10,000	$ 10	$ 10,000	$ 11,000	10.0%	$ 11,000	10.0%
Variable cost	6	6,000	2	2,000	6,600		2,200	
Contribution Income (CI)		4,000		8,000	4,400		8,800	
Fixed cost		2,000		6,000	2,000		6,000	
Operating income (OI)		2,000		2,000	2,400	20.0%	2,800	40.0%
Interest		1,333		667	1,333		667	
Pretax income (PTI)		667		$ 1,333	1,067	60.0%	2,133	60.0%
Income taxes (40%)		267		533	427		853	
Net income (NI)		$ 400		$ 800	$ 640	60.0%	$ 1,280	60.0%
Operating leverage = CI/OI		2.00		4.00				
Financial leverage = OI/PTI		3.00		1.50				
Combined leverage = CI/PTI		6.00		6.00				

Table 5-2 demonstrates what happens to both companies if sales grow by 10 percent. Company B's operating income leaps to $2,800, or a 40 percent increase, whereas Company A's operating income rises to $2,400, or a 20 percent increase. Operating leverage (OL) indicates that for a 10 percent increase in sales, operating income (OI) goes up by 10 percent times the operating leverage:

- For Company A, a 10 percent increase in sales led to 2 times 10 percent or a 20 percent increase in operating income.
- For Company B, a 10 percent increase in sales led to 4 times 10 percent or a 40 percent increase in operating income.

Operating leverage enhances and magnifies operating income. Continuing with Table 5-2, for every 1 percent growth in operating income, pretax income expands by a factor represented by financial leverage. Company A has financial leverage of 3.00 times. Thus a 20 percent increase in operating income results in a 60 percent increase in pretax income (3.00 × 20 percent) and, ultimately, a 60 percent increase in net income assuming a constant tax rate (percentage of pretax income). With a financial leverage factor for Company B of 1.50, notice that a 40 percent increase in operating income drives pretax and net income up 60 percent (1.50 × 40 percent).

TABLE 5-3

Business Leverage Illustration: Business Decline

	Base Scenarios				10% Decrease in Sales			
	A. FL Emphasis		B. OL Emphasis		A. FL Emphasis		B. OL Emphasis	
	Per Unit	Total	Per Unit	Total	Total	Growth	Total	Growth
Units sold		1,000		1,000	900	−10.0%	900	−10.0%
Sales	$10	$10,000	$10	$10,000	$9,000	−10.0%	$9,000	−10.0%
Variable cost	6	6,000	2	2,000	5,400		1,800	
Contribution income (CI)		4,000		8,000	3,600		7,200	
Fixed cost		2,000		6,000	2,000		6,000	
Operating income (OI)		2,000		2,000	1,600	−20.0%	1,200	−40.0%
Interest		1,333		667	1,333		667	
Pretax income (PTI)		667		$ 1,333	267	−60.0%	533	−60.0%
Income taxes (40%)		267		533	107		213	
Net income (NI)		$ 400		$ 800	$ 160	−60.0%	$ 320	−60.0%
Operating leverage = CI/OI		2.00		4.00				
Financial leverage = OI/PTI		3.00		1.50				
Combined leverage = CI/PTI		6.00		6.00				

Combined leverage for both companies is the same at 6.00. A 10 percent increase in sales results in a 60 percent increase in pretax income. While both companies wind up at the same point, how they get there is by different business approaches.

If you believe that your market always will expand, invest in the most efficient equipment possible to reduce your variable costs, and leverage the company with a heavy component of debt. In our case, if Company B would have used as much debt as Company A, the combined leverage would have been 12.00. Thus a 10 percent change in sales would have resulted in a 120 percent change in pretax (or net) income! If it were this easy, why wouldn't everyone just leverage their firms as high as possible? The thing about leverage is that it is a double-edged sword. Table 5-3 shows what happens with a 10 percent decline in sales. For both companies, pretax income drops by 60 percent!

Longer-term views on breakeven analysis and leverage are also considered in Chapters 6, 9, and 10, which are about strategic planning and capital investment decisions. Chapter 11 also discusses financial leverage.

OVERVIEW OF WORKING CAPITAL MANAGEMENT

In Chapter 3, I introduced a number of performance measures used to judge the effective use of working capital. These metrics are appropriate as an overview of the firm's ability to manage its working capital positions. This chapter focuses narrowly on the operating working capital components of accounts receivable, inventory, and accounts payable, which are found the supply chains of most organizations.

Table 5-4 presents the operating working capital balances along with sales and cost of goods sold for Dell Computer (2009 and 2010) and 2010 values for Hewlett-Packard (HP) and Apple, Inc.[1] The table also presents turnovers and days outstanding, which are calculated just as in Chapter 3.

The Firm's Operating and Cash Cycles

Using the days outstanding information from Table 5-4, in 2010, Dell had 9.48 days of sales invested in inventory, which was slightly weaker but similar to the

TABLE 5-4

Computer Industry: Operating and Cash Cycles
($ millions)

| | | Dell Computer | | HP | Apple |
	Calculation	2009	2010	2010	2010
Sales (S)		$ 52,902	$ 61,494	$ 126,033	$ 65,225
Cost of goods sold (COGS)		43,641	50,098	95,787	39,541
Accounts receivable (AR)		5,837	6,493	18,481	5,510
Inventory (IN)		1,051	1,301	6,466	1,051
Accounts payable (AP)		11,373	11,293	14,365	12,015
Turnovers					
Accounts receivable turnover	S/AR	9.06	9.47	6.82	11.84
Inventory turnover	COGS/IN	41.52	38.51	14.81	37.62
Accounts payable turnover	COGS/AP	3.84	4.44	6.67	3.29
Days outstanding:					
(1) Accounts receivable	365/AR turn	40.27	38.54	53.52	30.83
(2) Inventory	365/IN turn	8.79	9.48	24.64	9.70
Operating cycle	(1) + (2)	49.06	48.02	78.16	40.53
(3) Accounts payable	365/AP turn	95.12	82.28	54.74	110.91
Cash cycle	(1) + (2) − (3)	(46.06)	(34.26)	23.42	(70.38)

[1] Dell is one of the acknowledged corporate leaders in supply-chain management. Hewlett-Packard and Apple provide contrasting results.

number of days outstanding in inventory in 2009 (8.79 days). One of Dell's most successful business methods involves building its products on demand once a customer places an order. When an order is placed, Dell orders and receives raw materials and component parts, assembles the final product, and ships it directly to the customer. This process took approximately 9.50 days, on average, in 2010. Over the past few years, Dell has been selling more of its products through traditional retail outlets, which added days to the inventory process but also provided substantial growth. On the other hand, Hewlett-Packard generally does not build to order. Its products are assembled, held, and sold. The company's business model required over two weeks longer (24.64 days compared with 9.48 days) to "manage" its inventory and resulted in more days of sales invested in inventory. Apple approximated Dell's performance in inventory days outstanding.

When the final product is shipped, an account receivable is created. On average, in 2010, Dell collected its accounts receivables every 38.54 days. This is almost two days faster than in 2009. Hewlett-Packard, however, took almost two weeks longer to collect its receivables than Dell in 2010. Apple had an even stronger collection policy and collected its receivables over a week sooner than Dell.

Combining the inventory and receivable days outstanding results in the *operating cycle*, or the length of time that it takes from when the raw materials are received until cash is collected from the customer. Thus in 2010 the operating cycle for Dell was slightly over one and a half months (48.02 days) and approximately one day shorter than in 2009! Hewlett-Packard's operating cycle was over two and a half months (78.16 days), and Apple's was almost eight days shorter than Dell on the strength of its accounts receivable collections.

The cash cycle takes the operating cycle one step further by reducing it to the number of days that the firm takes until it pays its suppliers for the inventory. Accounts payable days outstanding is calculated as 365 days divided by accounts payable turnover. Accounts payable turnover is calculated as cost of goods sold divided by accounts payable. More broadly, the cash cycle reflects how long it takes for a firm to recoup its investment of a dollar in the operations of the firm. Figure 5-2 illustrates the cash cycle for Hewlett-Packard.

As we saw before, Hewlett-Packard had an operating cycle of 78.16 days but received 54.74 days of supplier financing until it paid its suppliers. This resulted in a cash cycle of less than one month. Thus Hewlett-Packard has 23.42 days of its cash tied up in its working capital. The cash cycle is the time that it takes the company to recoup its dollar of cash outflow from its normal business transactions. On average, the actual cash outflow occurred on day 54.74, and collections happened on day 78.16, resulting in over three weeks that the company's cash is exposed and invested in the business.

Dell and Apple (Table 5-4) provide a stark contrast with their nonconventional cash cycle. As discussed earlier, Dell's operating cycle is an impressive 48.02 days. Furthermore, in 2010, Dell significantly took over two and a half months (82.28 days) to pay its suppliers and financed its day-to-day operations with its suppliers' funds. An amazing feat in any industry! However, Apple is even

FIGURE   5-2

Hewlett-Packard:Operating and cash cycles, 2010.

Operating cycle
(78.16 days)

| Inventory days outstanding 24.64 days | Accounts receivable collection (53.52 days) |

Cash cycle (23.42 days)

54.74 days

| Days to pay accounts payable (54.74 days) |

more aggressive in this area and takes over three and a half months to pay its suppliers! This results in a negative cash cycle that is well over two months for Apple! Both Dell and Apple accomplish this performance with their extraordinary inventory-management/production processes, credit extension and collection policies, and supplier payment and relationship procedures.

One final view on both Dell's and Apple's cash cycles is in order. If you bought a computer from Dell in 2010, a month (34.26 days) before you placed the order, Dell collected the cash for your sale! While the mechanics of this statement makes no sense, this is what a negative cash cycle suggests!

Dell is extraordinary! If Dell stayed at its current size (sales of $61.5 billion and COGS of $50.1 billion) but relaxed its supply-chain processes to the point that its days outstanding were the same as Hewlett-Packard's days outstanding, Dell would need to invest an additional $8.4 billion in the business (working capital) without accounting for the extra production or distribution facilities, the added personnel, and so on, necessary to manage the significantly larger investment (Table 5-5). When compared with Hewlett-Packard, Dell would have an additional $2.5 billion invested in accounts receivable. This was estimated using the number

TABLE   5-5

Dell's Operating Investment at Hewlett-Packard Days Outstanding

2010	Days of Investment			Dell Investment ($ Millions)		
	Dell	HP	More (less)	Actual	At HP Days	More (less)
Days outstanding:						
(1) Accounts receivable	38.54	53.52	14.98	$ 6,493 $	9,017 $	2,524
(2) Inventory	9.48	24.64	15.16	1,301	3,381	2,080
Operating cycle	48.02	78.16				
Gross operating working capital investment				7,794	12,398	4,604
(3) Accounts payable	82.28	54.74	27.54	11,293	7,513	3,780
Cash cycle	(34.26)	23.42				
Net operating working capital investment				$(3,499) $	4,885 $	8,384

of days Hewlett-Packard has in accounts receivable (53.52 days, or an increase of 14.98 days) and the size (daily sales) of Dell ($168.5 million). This same procedure was repeated with inventory and accounts payable using costs of goods sold ($137.3 million per day) instead of sales. This resulted in increased investment in inventory of $2.1 billion with additional funding requirements of $3.8 billion to augment for an accounts payable (free supplier financing) shortfall. If Dell did not elevate the supply chain and short-term financial management as a strategic initiative, Dell would have required an additional investment of $8.4 billion in working capital! That is, $8.4 billion less for capital expenditures, acquisitions, business growth, share repurchases, and so on—or $8.4 billion more borrowing! Effective working capital management is just that important!

In a similar fashion, if Hewlett-Packard could adopt the same practices, policies, and procedures as Dell, it could withdraw $16.4 billion in operating working capital owing to its larger size. While it is not possible for Hewlett-Packard to implement Dell's business approaches immediately, Hewlett-Packard has clear signals that it can manage these investments better.

Therefore, compared with Hewlett-Packard in 2010, Dell's management team has done a wonderful job managing its supply chain. Compared with Dell's performance in 2009, though, the cash cycle for Dell increased owing to faster payment of suppliers. Maybe this was a necessary and strategic move to keep some of its suppliers afloat during the financial crisis; regardless, Dell invested $1,566 million more in its supply chain than it would have with the approaches used in 2009.

T A B L E   5-6

Dell's Operating Investment Comparisons, 2010
($ millions)

	Savings (Shortfall) versus Target of:		
	HP 2010	Dell 2009	Apple 2010
Accounts receivable	$ 2,524	$ 291	$ (1,299)
Inventory	2,080	(95)	30
	4,604	196	(1,269)
Accounts payable	3,780	(1,762)	(3,929)
Total savings (shortfall)	$ 8,384	$ (1,566)	$ (5,198)

While Dell is exemplary, if Dell were as efficient and effective as Apple's supply-chain management team in 2010, Dell would have been able to reduce its working capital and realize improvement of almost $5.2 billion primarily from its customer collections process as well as its supplier payment process.

CASH AND MARKETABLE SECURITIES

This section discusses effective management of cash and marketable securities. It begins by forecasting cash and then discusses appropriate short-term financial investments in marketable securities as well as short-term financing sources.

Cash Budgets

Chapter 2 introduced the concept of the cash-flow statement as a link between the balance sheet and the income statement. The cash-flow statement had three different sections: cash from (used for) operations, cash from (used for) investing, and cash from (used for) financing purposes.

In this section I introduce another cash-flow analysis called the *cash budget*. The cash budget is a day-to-day operational tool that considers anticipated cash receipts and cash disbursements. Will the company have excess cash above its day-to-day operating needs that can be invested in marketable securities? Or will the company be in a cash shortfall position and require short-term funds to see it through from one month (or even one week) to the next?

The cash budget is a projection or forecast of future cash receipts and cash disbursements over some time interval. It enables the financial executive to determine whether and when additional financing will be required and provides lead time for taking the actions necessary to provide for future financing. The cash budget also supplies information on whether and when the firm may have positive, sustainable cash inflows available for a number of alternative uses.

The cash budget is similar to a personal budget. From time to time, you may prepare a personal monthly budget, or you may have solid personal discipline and use software tools such as Quicken or Money to help you track, manage, and plan your personal cash needs. A personal budget lists all the anticipated receipts, such as the paycheck or dividend/interest income receipts. It also includes all monthly recurring disbursements, such as grocery bills, payments to credit cards, home mortgages, car loans, and so on, and any nonrecurring monthly payments for real estate taxes, annual life insurance payment, and so on. A personal budget lists anticipated cash receipts against cash disbursements. If it's anticipated to be a good month, you will have excess cash at the end. If it is a month of heavy cash outflow, you may need to borrow on a personal line of credit or transfer money from a savings account.

Within major corporations, the controller's office is responsible for preparing accurate financial statements that are bound by U.S. Generally Accepted Accounting Principles (GAAP). This includes the cash-flow statement that we examined in Chapter 2. This cash-flow statement conforms to all U.S. GAAP standards and is called the *indirect approach*, in the sense that it results from the income statement and the balance sheet.

It is the treasurer's office, more specifically, an assistant treasurer or cash manager, that is responsible for preparing a cash budget, which is prepared directly from the organization's anticipated cash receipts and cash disbursements.

Hence this type of cash budget is referred to as a *direct cash-flow statement*. In the end, the indirect and direct cash-flow statements must yield the same result, that is, the cash generated (used) over a specific time period.

Overview of Cash Budgets

The cash budget illustrated in the figures that follow considers the amount of cash flow for the next six months. It anticipates the amount of cash collected from accounts receivable and other sources as well as all cash disbursements for raw materials, labor, wages, and so on. The result shows the cash manager the amount of cash that will be available for investment if there is excess cash generated in any given month, or the cash budget will highlight any cash shortfall that needs to be accommodated from the company's line of credit or other sources.

In practice, the financial manager will create more detailed cash budgets on a weekly or even daily basis. Daily cash budgets consider the heavier daily cash collections at the beginning of the week and the anticipated accounts payable disbursements made at the end of the week, along with specific timing for payroll, dividends, loan payments, and so on.

To facilitate this discussion, there are three separate parts to the cash budget: cash receipts (Table 5-7), cash disbursements (Table 5-8), and net cash flow, including balances for cash and short-term debt (Table 5-9).

Cash Receipts

Sales forecasts for product lines and in total are critical to every firm. The sales forecast drives the anticipated cash receipts.

Table 5-7 presents a schedule of sales and cash collections. The organization sells on a 30-day basis (i.e.,customers have 30 days to pay). From accounts receivable experience, the firm estimates that, on average, 10 percent of the sales are collected in the month of the sale, 60 percent in the month following the sale, and 30 percent during the second month following the sale.

Row 1 in Table 5-7 presents the sales forecast. Row 2 sets forth collections made in the month of sale or 10 percent of January's projected sales. Row 3 lists the collections for sales from the prior month. In this example, 60 percent of December's sales are collected in January. In row 4, the collections during the second month after sales would be 30 percent, or $300 (30 percent of November's actual sales of $1,000). Since there were no other collections in January, total collections for January would be $1,320. The process repeats itself for each month.

The full amount of January's $1,200 sales is collected over three months: $120 in January, $720 in February, and $360 in March. If "bad debts" typically averaged 2 percent of sales, then the third month (March) could be adjusted to show only 28 percent of January's sales.

TABLE 5-7

Sales and Cash Collections

	November	December	January	February	March	April	May	June	July
1. Sales	$ 1,000	$ 1,500	$ 1,200	$ 800	$ 1,400	$1,800	$ 2,000	$1,600	
Accounts receivable collection:									
Collections based on sales from:									
2. Current month 10.0%			120	80	140	180	200	160	
3. Prior month 60.0%			900	720	480	840	1,080	1,200	
4. Two months ago 30.0%			300	450	360	240	420	540	
5. Total collections from receivables			1,320	1,250	980	1,260	1,700	1,900	
Other collections									
6. Dividends received				105				50	
7. Sale of idle equipment									
8. Long-term debt issuance				100					
9. Total collections (Sum of lines 2 to 8)			$ 1,320	$ 1,455	$ 980	$1,260	$ 1,700	$1,950	

139

Other Cash Receipts

Continuing with Table 5-7, a company can have cash receipts from sources other than just sales and the business operations of the firm. Usually, however, these other cash receipts do not occur every month (dividends received $50), can be one-time events ($105 sale of a piece of equipment), or can arise from financing ($100 issuance of long-term debt). A partial list of such cash receipts includes:

- Royalty receipts
- Interest and dividends received
- Sale of idle equipment
- Sale of an operation or discontinued business
- Sale or maturing of a long-term investment
- Issuance of debt, short or long term
- Issuance of equity, preferred or common

As such, most receipts are generated as a function of the business of the organization.

Cash Disbursements

Table 5-8 shows the schedule of cash disbursements. Notice that the cash disbursement schedule is comprised of monthly, recurring, business-driven expenditures and other periodic disbursements that recur on a quarterly or semiannual basis, as well as nonrecurring expenditures.

Monthly Recurring Disbursements

Similar to the cash-receipt schedule, Table 5-8 starts with the sales forecast. Purchases of raw materials have to be made in anticipation of sales. Based on the firm's experience, raw materials purchases represent about 60 percent of next month's sales, on average. We assume further that purchases are paid for in the month after the purchase. Taking the row 2 figures and shifting them forward one month gives us the cash outflows for payment of raw materials purchases shown in row 3.

In January, marketing anticipates $1,200 of sales. In order to have enough finished goods available to satisfy this projected sales level, the company purchases raw materials and completes the production in the month before the anticipated sale. Consequently, the company purchases $720 ($1,200 × 60 percent) of raw materials in December (line 2 of Table 5-8). Assuming payment terms of "net 30 days," the December raw materials purchases are paid in January, as shown on line 3. Line 3 begins the disbursements. So the process continues for each month.

To convert the raw materials into final product, the company hires production employees. Owing to the seasonality of the business, the company pays overtime to its full-time production team and augments the workforce with part-time

TABLE 5-8

Purchases and Cash Disbursements

	November	December	January	February	March	April	May	June	July
1. Sales			$ 1,200	$ 800	$ 1,400	$ 1,800	$ 2,000	$ 1,600	$ 1,000
2. Raw materials purchase 60.0% of sales$_{(t+1)}$		720	480	840	1,080	1,200	960	600	
3. Raw materials payment			720	480	840	1,080	1,200	960	
4. Production wages 35.0% of raw mat. purchase$_{(t)}$			168	294	378	420	336	210	
5. Administrative salaries			80	80	80	80	80	80	
6. Other operating expenses			25	25	25	25	25	25	
7. Income tax disbursement					50	100		100	
8. Capital expenditure payment					95		70		
9. Purchase of business line					375				
10. Dividend payment			35			35			
11. Debt repayment				450					
12. Total disbursements (Sum of lines 3 to 11)			$ 1,028	$ 1,329	$ 1,843	$ 1,740	$ 1,711	$ 1,375	

personnel on a flexible work schedule and temporary laborers. The direct labor costs are 35 percent of this month's raw materials purchases. We also assume that wages and other expenses are paid during the month they are incurred. Hence row 4 represents cash outlays for production wages and is 35 percent of purchases made this month.

Continuing the January illustration in Table 5-8, February's sales are anticipated to be $800, which requires the support of a $480 purchase of raw materials in January. These raw materials are converted to finished product at a direct labor cost of $168 (35 percent of $480), which is paid to the production workers at the end of January.

Administrative salaries (row 5) and other operating expenses (row 6) remain fairly constant over this six-month period. These expenses are more or less fixed by their very nature and are not a function of seasonal sales patterns. On the other hand, long-term company trends certainly would influence both cash disbursements and expenses. Lines 7 through 11 of Table 5-8 present five other common disbursements encountered by many organizations. Line 12 totals all the monthly disbursements.

Disbursements versus Expenses

The following three points must be remembered when comparing expenses with disbursements:

1. Not all cash disbursements are expenses.

2. Not all expenses are cash disbursements.

3. Expenses and cash disbursements can be different dollar amounts.

These three points are discussed in greater detail below.

Not All Disbursements Are Expenses

The first five disbursements in Table 5-8 are related to the various expenses incurred by the firm. The last five line items, however, are not considered "expenses," even though they represent cash outflows. The payments for capital equipment and the purchase of an acquisition or line of business are reinvestments into the business and are reflected solely on the balance sheet with no immediate income statement impact. Likewise, dividend payments and debt repayments are financing transactions and represent adjustments in the capital structure of the firm.

Not All Expenses Are Cash Disbursements

When computing the company's gross income (sales less cost of goods sold [COGS]), COGS includes expenditures for raw materials, direct labor, and depreciation. There is no cash flow related to depreciation because it is a noncash expense. The indirect cash-flow statement, which is compiled from the income statement and balance sheet, as we did in Chapter 2, began with net income and added back the noncash expense. The direct cash-flow statement, however, does not begin with net income. It includes only cash flows! Consequently, there is no need to add back depreciation, much as a personal budget generally never includes depreciation on a car or computer.

Expenses and Cash Disbursements Can Be Different Dollar Amounts
Some recognized expenses may have a portion that requires a cash payment and another portion that is deferred or accrued and involves no cash payment at the time of the expense. U.S. GAAP requires warranties to be considered immediately as an expense, even though actual cash expenditures on the warranties will take place at a later time when the claims take place. Insurance payments may be made once every six months (or year). Such payments are an actual cash-flow drain when they occur, but U.S. GAAP requires the monthly expense to represent one-sixth (or one-twelfth) of the actual payment. As we saw in Chapter 4, income tax payments differ from the U.S. GAAP "provision for income taxes." The cash budget considers only the actual cash payments for income taxes, as illustrated on line 7 of Table 5-8. The final section completes our discussion of the cash budget. Table 5-9 brings together the monthly cash collections and disbursements.

Net Cash Flow and Cash Requirements

Lines 1 and 2 of Table 5-9 summarize the results of the preceding two tables. The difference between total cash receipts and total cash expenditures is the net cash flow shown on line 3.

T A B L E   5-9

Net Cash Flow and Account Balances

	January	February	March	April	May	June
1. Total collections	$ 1,320	$ 1,455	$ 980	$1,260	$1,700	$ 1,950
2. Total disbursements	1,028	1,329	1,843	1,740	1,711	1,375
3. Net cash flow	$ 292	$ 126	$ (863)	$ (480)	$ (11)	$ 575
Account Balances						
4. Beginning balance, cash	$ 465	$ 757	$ 883	$ 50	$ 50	$ 50
5. + Net cash flow	292	126	(863)	(480)	(11)	575
6. Preliminary balance of cash	757	883	20	(430)	39	625
7. Required short-term borrowing	–	–	30	480	11	–
8. Payment of short-term borrowing	–	–	–	–	–	(521)
9. Ending balance, cash	$ 757	$ 883	$ 50	$ 50	$ 50	$ 104
10. Ending balance, short-term debt	$ –	$ –	$ 30	$ 510	$ 521	$ –

For January, the company is anticipating collections of $1,320 while paying out $1,028, for a net cash flow of $292. This amount of cash flow increases the beginning balance of cash (which is also the December ending balance of cash of $465) to a January ending balance of $757. The January ending balance becomes the beginning cash balance for February, which is augmented by February's cash flow of $126. This leaves a February ending balance of $883.

For March, expenditures exceed collections by $863, which for the first time in this example creates a preliminary balance of cash (line 6) of only $20. Assuming that the company is required to have a $50 balance in cash at all times by its bank, the company has a $30 shortcoming. The company must arrange short-term borrowing to the tune of $30 for the month of March (line 7). At the end of March, the company has a cash balance of $50 (line 9) and a short-term debt balance of $30 (line 10).

The month of April has a cash shortfall of $480, which requires additional short-term borrowing. Thus the month of April ends with a cash balance of $50 and short-term borrowings of $510 ($30 opening balance plus $480 of additional borrowing in April). During May, negative net cash flows linger, and the company must borrow $11 more in May. May ends with a $50 cash balance and a $521 short-term debt balance. In June, positive net cash flows return because collections ($1,950) exceed disbursements ($1,375) by $575. The cash flow is used immediately to pay off the short-term debt balance ($510) while maintaining the required $50 cash balance. The company ends June with a cash balance of $104. As presented, the analysis did not include the impact of interest income earned on cash balances or interest expense paid on borrowings. The analysis easily could be expanded to include those impacts. We concentrated on strictly an operating cash budget.

The cash budget facilitates banking relationships. The treasurer of this company could anticipate in December that the company would have a cash shortfall in March lasting for three months. In December, borrowing alternatives could be evaluated and the best alternative arranged. If the shortfall appears to be nontemporary, the treasurer could evaluate intermediate- or long-term financing alternatives and begin making arrangements for such financing.

Reasons for Holding Cash

Cash and marketable securities are discussed together because marketable securities can be converted quickly into cash with only small transactions costs, so they are often regarded as a form of backup cash. When I refer to cash (currency holdings), I am using cash in the broad sense, including cash equivalents— demand deposits (checking accounts) and money-market accounts.

Because returns from marketable securities generally are lower returns than returns from operations, I am not an advocate of cash management practices that hoard cash. I believe that large cash balances should be paid to stockholders if the company has no alternative business investments. But who can argue with success: Microsoft holds $36.8 billion in cash (and equivalents and short-term investments), or almost 43 percent of its total assets and almost two years of net income!

Businesses and individuals have four primary motives for holding cash and cash backup in the form of marketable securities: (1) the transactions motive, (2) the precautionary motive, (3) to meet future needs, and (4) to satisfy compensating balance requirements. Each company assesses its cash requirements to satisfy these criteria:

1. *Transactions motive.* The principal motive for holding cash is to enable the firm to conduct its ordinary business—making purchases and sales.

2. *Precautionary motive.* The precautionary motive for holding safety stocks of cash relates primarily to the predictability of cash inflows and outflows.

3. *Future needs.* The firm's cash and marketable securities accounts may rise to rather sizable levels on a temporary basis as funds are accumulated to meet specific future needs. Many technology and pharmaceutical firms hold significant amounts of cash and marketable securities to fund research and development, acquisitions, and so on. Cash and marketable securities also represent a "war chest" or pool of funds from which a firm may draw quickly to meet a short-term opportunity, including acquisitions. This is sometimes referred to as the *speculative motive* for holding cash.

4. *Compensating balance requirements.* Business firms (just like personal accounts) pay for commercial banking services in part by direct fees and sometimes in part by maintaining compensating balances at the bank. Compensating balances represent the minimum level that a firm agrees to maintain in its "checking" account with the bank or to satisfy any other covenant that requires a minimum cash balance.

The decisions with regard to holding cash and marketable securities require careful analysis in order to balance the rationales just noted with lower business returns.

Marketable Securities

Marketable securities are relatively short-term, highly liquid, and highly secure (limited risk) financial assets. The most common types of marketable securities are (1) offered by commercial banks and financial institutions in the form of negotiable certificates of deposit (CDs) and money-market accounts, (2) short-term debt instruments from the federal government (Treasury bills), federal agencies, and local municipal or state governments, and (3) commercial paper from highly creditworthy corporations. Most organizations will have a marketable securities portfolio containing securities from a number of sources as they evaluate and diversify their risk/return tradeoffs.

When evaluating an investment in marketable securities, you must consider the underlying financial risk, interest-rate risk, purchasing-power risk, the liquidity or marketability of the security, and the taxability of its returns.

- *Financial risk.* The greater the degree to which the price and returns of a security fluctuate, the greater is the financial risk—the risk of default. While U.S. government securities do not carry the risk of default (because the federal government can always print money), securities issued by state and local governments, financial institutions, and other corporations are considered to be subject to some degree of default risk.

- *Interest-rate risk.* Changes in the general level of interest rates will cause the prices of securities to fluctuate. The shorter the maturity of a debt instrument, the smaller is the size of the fluctuations in its price.

- *Purchasing-power risk.* Changes in general price levels will affect the purchasing power of both the principal and the income from investments in securities. Once again, short-term securities are less affected by inflationary considerations.

- *Liquidity risk.* The potential decline from a security's quoted market price when the security is sold is its liquidity or marketability risk. Liquidity risk is related to the breadth or thinness of the market for a security. The types of securities mentioned earlier have very deep and liquid markets.

- *Taxability.* The tax position of a firm's marketable securities portfolio is influenced by the overall tax position of the firm. Securities from municipalities and state governments are generally exempt from federal taxation. Thus, when constructing a portfolio of marketable securities, the treasurer must consider all returns on an after-tax basis.

In addition to the number of traditional choices for marketable securities, a number of new and engineered instruments also are available. The financial manager must maintain contact with developments in the money market. Your specific choice of marketable securities must be based on the objective of short-term investing—preserving capital and providing liquidity, not just adding a few basis points!

The choice of marketable securities also should match the timing determined by the monthly cash budget and more refined daily/weekly cash budget. The underlying forecasts are the key to effective cash management models.

ACCOUNTS RECEIVABLE MANAGEMENT POLICIES AND PRACTICES

While every organization has an accounts receivable function, most employees will not spend any portion of their careers in the accounts receivable department. However, professionals working in marketing, sales, treasury, and other financial areas may be involved with establishing the company's accounts receivable poli-cies and practices. A careful operational (and even strategic) balance must be struck. Force your customers to pay for everything immediately, and sales will fall. Extend credit to all customers, and sales will flourish, but bad debt expense will grow and income and cash flow will lag.

Accounts receivable management consists of three interrelated phases. The first phase is establishing credit terms based on industry standards and broad eco-nomic forces as well as specific company creditworthiness. Within this phase is the need to analyze and decide to whom credit will be granted, how much will be extended, and under what terms and conditions. The second phase of accounts receivable management relates to the monitoring and tracking of customer payments and outstanding receivable balances. The third and final phase is the collection process. My emphasis here will be on the first phase—establishing credit terms.

Credit Background and Assessment

Credit terms specify the period for which credit is extended and the discount, if any, for early payment. For example, if a firm has credit terms of "2/10, net 30," then a 2 percent discount from the stated sales price is granted if payment is made within 10 days, and the entire amount is due 30 days from the invoice date if the discount is not taken. These are very common credit terms. If the terms are stated "net 60," this indicates that no discount is offered and that the bill is due and payable 60 days after the invoice date.

On a macro level, there are five aspects of credit terms in which industry circumstances and practices play an important role. Also, the economic nature of the industry and the product outlines the credit policy. For example, commodi-ties-based industries with low (high) sales turnover are sold on relatively long (short) credit terms. Grocery stores require immediate payment, whereas jewelry and furniture retailers may extend credit for six months or longer.

Additionally, the seller's operational position, financial strength, and size all play a general role in establishing credit terms. While larger and sounder firms could justify the longer terms to smaller customers, often the expense of the added administrative burden dictates selling to smaller clients through a network of wholesalers or brokers. The buyer's operational position also may play a role, but this soon becomes a micro-level issue (discussed below).

Finally, credit-period terms and available cash discounts may be a common practice in an industry. To remain competitive, a company may need to conform with the general industry practices. Lengthening the credit period stimulates sales, but there is a cost to tying up funds in receivables. For example, if a firm changes its terms from net 30 to net 60, the average receivables for the year may rise from $8 million to $20 million. Part of the increase is simply due to doubling the receivables period (from $8 million to $16 million), part may be due to a larger volume of sales, which is the underlying intent of the change, but an addi-tional portion may be due to the addition of bad debts, customers taking longer than 60 days to pay, and other unintended negative impacts that increase the receivables balance. The optimal credit period is determined by the point where marginal profits on increased sales are offset by the costs of carrying the higher amounts of accounts receivable.

Additionally, in many industries, variations in credit terms can be used as a sales promotion device, especially when the industry has excess capacity. In some cases, some management teams use extended credit terms as a sales stimulus. A customer who normally would buy products in January (or the first month of the new fiscal year) under standard terms of 2/10, net 30, could be induced to buy those products in December (the last month of the current fiscal year) by extending terms for 30 days to 2/40, net 60. Not only could this policy endanger sound credit management, it also could endanger sound business management because the current fiscal year becomes effectively a 13-month year and next year becomes an 11-month year unless the practice continues every year. This type of practice can be spotted easily because the company's fourth-quarter accounts receivable spike.

From the general and macro level to the specific company and micro level, the next section discusses credit analysis for a specific company.

Credit Analysis

Credit analysis seeks to determine who will receive credit and under what conditions. Two aspects of the process should be distinguished: the new customer versus continuing accounts. The second is much less difficult because experience provides considerable information. Credit analysis obviously is a tougher problem for new customers. Two main approaches are taken.

One is to determine how the prospective customer has behaved with other suppliers. This kind of information can be obtained at a price from specialized financial information agencies such as the National Association of Credit Management (NACM) and credit-reporting agencies such as Dun & Bradstreet (D&B).

In addition, the firm will perform its own analysis to make its own independent decision. When trade credit is involved, the firm is both selling goods and extending credit. The two activities are intertwined. How the customer behaves may depend in part on how the sales organization has been treating the customer. The collections policies and practices of the seller may adversely affect the selling efforts of the firm's sales organization. The seller may decide not to rely completely on the experience of other selling firms. There may be an opportunity to develop a new customer relationship. Often the micro assessment of extending trade credit to potential customers comes down to the firm's established and systematic approach of determining creditworthiness. The "five C's" approach to receivables assessment blends qualitative and quantitative assessment—character, capacity, capital, collateral, and conditions.

First, *character* has to do with the probability that a customer will try to honor his or her obligations. What is the "general word on the streets"? What did you hear from a local NACM chapter meeting or the annual conference? What has been the experience of other companies? What does a D&B report or the Better Business Bureau indicate? Who is in the leadership of the organization, and what has been his or her track record? What is his or her character?

Capacity provides an objective judgment of the customer's ability to pay by assessing the potential customer's financial statement analysis from audited sources (preferred) or income tax returns. What are the levels of sales, income, cash, current assets, total assets, accounts payable, accrued liabilities, current liabilities, cash flow from operations, and so on? Using the financial performance metrics of Chapter 3, analyze the potential customer's liquidity (i.e., current ratio, quick ratio, and cash ratio), profitability (i.e., margins, expense analysis, returns on assets, and return on equity), effectiveness (i.e., operating and cash cycles), and leverage (i.e., debt-to-equity ratio, capitalization ratio, and equity multiplier). In addition, the credit department may have some of its own metrics that are deemed critical and are centered on short-term balance sheet analysis, such as accounts payable as a percent of sales, accounts payable as a percent of cash and marketable securities, cash flow as a percent of sales, long- and short-term debt due over the next three years, other financial obligations due over the next three years, and so on. Of course, owing to the nature of accrued liabilities, many of these metrics should be extended to include accruals wherever accounts payable are listed, that is, accounts payable and accrued liabilities as a percent of cash and marketable securities. Capacity also may involve site visits of potential customers first to be sure that the customer is viably established at the location indicated and also to assess the condition of physical property (well maintained to poor condition in need of a major renovation).

Capital, the third C, is generally a deeper review of the short- and long-term financial capital (debt and equity) position of the firm. Particular emphasis is given to tangible assets and net worth, as well as working capital. *Collateral* is represented by assets the customer offers as a pledge for security of the credit extension. This is more specific by industry and highly dependent on the asset the company sells. In this example, collateral is disregarded. *Conditions* of the firm have to do with the impact of general economic trends on the firm or special developments in certain areas of the economy that may affect the customer's ability to meet the obligation.

After analyzing the potential customer's credit information, the seller systematically evaluates the data, ultimately leading to a weighted *credit score* in quantitative terms. Table 5-10 illustrates such a scoring based on the five C's and a D&B report. As you can see, there is a total possible score of 400 points. Each C has an underlying subset of criteria that may earn the potential customer up to the noted point values (e.g., 40 points for character). The heaviest weight is 260 points for capacity. The higher the total score, the more credit is extended.

TABLE 5-10

Systematic Credit Rating Score

	Possible Points
Five C's assessment	
Character (very strong, strong, average, weak)	40
Capacity (size – $ millions)	
Customer size	30
Liquidity	40
Profitability	40
Leverage	40
Cash flow	40
Effectiveness	40
Short-term balance sheet analysis	30
Capital (size – $ millions)	
Analysis of tangible debt and equity	40
Collateral	n/a
Conditions (very favorable, favorable, average, weak)	20
Total five C's assessment	360
Dun & Bradstreet report (very strong, strong, average, weak)	40
Total credit score	400

TABLE 5-11

Credit Extension Policy

Credit Score	340–400	280–340	Below 280
Terms	2/10, net 30	2/10, net 30	Cash only
Account limits	$500,000	$200,000	$0
Review period	Every two years	Annually	Customer request

Based on years of experience with the credit scores of other customers, a seller may set up risk categories, as shown in Table 5-11.

The strongest customers (credit scores of 340 or more) will see terms of 2/10, net 30, and have an account limit of $500,000. Also, their account will be reviewed every two years or as conditions warrant. With a credit score of 280 to 340, only credit of $200,000 is extended with annual reviews. Finally, the third category must pay cash for any purchase. This category of customer can request a credit reevaluation when his or her profile becomes stronger.

After a company establishes a credit history with your firm, it is easier to monitor its payment pattern and judge its five C's assessment. However, attention still must be paid so as to avoid any unpleasant surprises brought about by specific issues within your customer or the customer's industry.

Invoice Accuracy

One of the major issues in accounts receivable management that has emerged in the past few years is related to the quality of invoices. In the simplest example, a customer purchased and received $100,000 worth of product, an invoice was issued for $100,000, and payment was made for $100,000 (or $98,000 for payment within the discount period). The transaction was simple and straightforward—but far from many experiences today.

Shipping and billing errors do occur. Partial orders are shipped, and products that were not ordered are shipped and invoiced. Broken or malfunctioning products may be received by the customer. Seasonal products may have arrived late in the season and be unwanted in part or in total. Customers may misunderstand pricing and promotional incentives offered by the company and may take the discount well after the discount period.

Some customers are very strict about receiving their orders. They specify the day and even the hour they expect a shipment. If a shipment is not received at that time, the customer "bills" the seller through a deduction to the invoice. At the BMW plant in South Carolina, if a supplier misses a deliver slot and the plant runs out of a part, that supplier is "charged" $10,000 for every minute the production line is shut down.

All these circumstances give rise to discrepancies. Successful management and timely resolution of these discrepancies are critical components of the credit manager's responsibilities and directly affect the bottom line and cash flow of every company.

INVENTORY MANAGEMENT

Manufacturing firms generally have three kinds of inventories: (1) raw materials, (2) work in process, and (3) finished goods. The level of raw materials inventories is influenced by anticipated production, seasonality of production, reliability of sources of supply, and the efficiency of scheduling purchases and production operations. Work-in-process inventory is strongly influenced by the length of the production period, which is the time between placing raw materials in production and completing the finished product.

The level of finished goods inventory is a matter of coordinating production and sales. Realistic sales forecasts and accompanying production schedules are critical to success. Understate the sales forecast and production schedule, and shortages of the finished good may occur, leading to missed sales opportunities and "stockout" costs. A sales forecast that is too ambitious results in unsold finished goods inventory.

My primary focus in this section is control of investment in inventories. Most firms consolidate raw materials purchasing responsibilities at some level (e.g., division, subsidiary, or corporate) to enhanced purchasing decisions, maximize quantity discounts, provide more consistent raw materials, and reduce investment. For example, in the case of Hershey, there was a central department that had overall purchasing responsibilities, and specific individuals were assigned responsibility for each of Hershey's three critical raw materials (i.e., milk, cocoa, and sugar), whereas other members of that group had purchasing responsibility for all the other ingredients and packaging materials.

Beyond purchasing, the inventory management process was decentralized. Production facilities had responsibility for the actual physical handling of the raw materials. This extended to goods in process, where plant management and divisional manufacturing shouldered the responsibility of effective handling and processing goods in process. Finished product inventory continued to be the responsibility of manufacturing and distribution center management. At the distribution center, products once again were viewed on a consolidated basis to optimize distribution to customers.

While each business unit and organization needs to streamline its own inventory management processes, my focus will be on a central view and analysis of inventory. Any procedure that can reduce the investment required to support a given sales volume will have a beneficial effect on the firm's rate of return and hence on the value of the firm, as we saw at the start of this chapter when the inventory position of Dell Computer was discussed.

In addition to the capital employed, when there is too much investment in inventory, the firm incurs additional carrying costs such as additional storage, insurance, obsolescence, and so on (Table 5-12). Counterbalancing the argument for too low an inventory level are the cost of placing orders and the cost of a stockout (lost sales). It is a careful balance of all costs and the proper level of inventory investment that will enhance the value of the firm.

TABLE 5-12

Costs Associated with Inventories

Carrying Costs	Ordering Costs	Stockout Costs
1. Storage	1. Cost of placing an order	1. Loss of sales
2. Insurance	2. Production set up costs	2. Loss of customer goodwill
3. "Shrinkage" or security	3. Shipping and handling costs	3. Disruption of production schedules
4. Property taxes	4. Quantity discounts lost	
5. Depreciation		
6. Obsolescence		
7. Cost of capital		

Controlling Investments in Inventories

From an operational perspective, the major determinants of investment in inventory are (1) level of sales, (2) length and technical nature of the production processes (including the availability and complexity of raw materials), and (3) durability versus perishability (the style factors) in the end product. Considering retailers, it's no surprise that the some of the lowest number of inventory days outstanding are found in restaurants and food stores. Quality meats, fruits, and vegetables are determined in part by freshness and can be kept on hand only for limited periods. Inventories in general merchandise stores, department stores, and specialty stores are held significantly longer owing to the nonperishability of the stock. For Walmart and other mass merchandisers, customer loyalty is low, and customers will purchase the good where it is available. Thus the potential cost of stockouts leads to the company holding more inventory. However, for the past 20 years, Walmart has transformed and expanded its reach as the largest grocery store in the United States. This transition reduced the total number of inventory days outstanding because a larger proportion of Walmart's sales came through its grocery business. At the other end of the retail spectrum are jewelry stores. For example, Tiffany & Company had 442 days (14.5 months) outstanding in inventory. While jewelry is nonperishable, it is also a highly profitable product. Part of the added "cost" of running a successful jewelry store is carrying enough varied inventory to satisfy customers' demands. If the product is not in the store, Tiffany's ultimately could lose the sale to a competitor.

To balance all the operational influences as well as the financial considerations, many companies have implemented enterprise resource planning (ERP) systems such as SAP, Oracle, Baan, and PeopleSoft that enable them generally to focus on working capital and inventory management specifically. These innovative technology tools are fully integrated, all-encompassing computer systems that span all processes within an organization while combining financial reporting as a natural process of the work flow. The major business processes center around the supply side (i.e., production planning, procurement, and manufacturing) and the demand side (i.e., new product introduction, sales, marketing, and logistics) with strong infrastructure support in the areas of accounting, finance, and human resources.

Often the implementation of an ERP system requires reengineering of the organization or at least reengineering of some of the major processes. With the use of an ERP system, important developments affecting the fundamental philosophy of inventory management and value-chain management methods have taken place. Production methods have experienced fundamental changes. The assembly lines with long production runs for a given product have been yielding to an emphasis on flexible manufacturing systems. More intense competition to produce better products, coupled with consumer desires for increased variety and product change, also has contributed to the need for flexible manufacturing systems. Financial management of inventories has had to join in the performance reappraisal and streamlining to improve the firm's competitive position.

Relationships have been forged between suppliers and customers to wring the costs out of the value chain. More information is exchanged between customers and suppliers with greater frequency and facilitated by ERP systems. Many manufacturing firms share production schedules with suppliers and customers. On the inbound side, raw materials suppliers know when they must deliver the required amount of raw materials. On the outbound customer side, a manufacturing firm will deliver optimal quantities of inventory at the right time to help minimize the investment in inventory both for itself and for its customers. Enhanced technology (i.e., the Internet, ERP systems, etc.) facilitate such reengineering.

I emphasize that what is involved is an entire philosophical approach to manufacturing processes rather than inventory management alone. Changes in inventory methods could not have been made without rethinking the entire approach to manufacturing methods. In turn, these new approaches to manufacturing processes, including inventory planning and control methods, require a change in practices and attitudes of workers and plant supervisors. Fundamental changes in the approach to human resource management therefore also are involved. Much new learning in management systems is required. Here is another example of my basic approach to managerial finance. Models are useful tools. But much more important is the broader philosophical approach to management systems. Financial management must be integrated with the broader aspects of operating management as well as with the broader framework of the firm's strategic planning.

SHORT-TERM FINANCING

This section discusses the use of short-term financing for both permanent and temporary financing. I begin with a discussion of the *matching principle*, where financing sources are paired with the type of asset that is being financed. I discuss common short-term borrowing sources, understanding the advantages and disadvantages of each source, and calculating the cost of such financing, and I end with a discussion of secured short-term financing.

Figure 5-3 presents a greatly simplified view of a firm's assets. It shows a firm that is growing over time in terms of both fixed assets and current assets. But current assets are further detailed to reveal permanent current assets and temporary current assets.

The phrase *permanent current assets* seems like a contradiction in terms because *current assets* imply an asset that is converted to cash within one year. My use of the term *permanent* represents a permanent level of current assets. For example, if a company holds 30 days of inventory on hand at any one point, the specific inventory items are manufactured, stored, and sold; manufactured, stored, and sold; and so on. The specific inventory itself is constantly being sold and replenished. However, the firm continually has 30 days of inventory on hand.

FIGURE 5-3

Assets held over time.

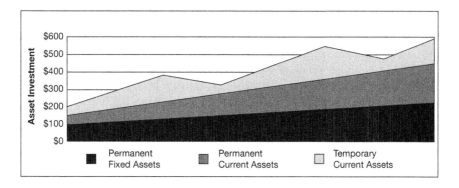

The inventory investment amount is not changing. Likewise, individual accounts receivable are collected, but the continuous operations of the firm will result in rising investments in receivables. As sales increase, the investment in receivables and inventories must grow proportionately. A steadily rising level of sales over the years will result in permanent increases in current assets.

Seasonal patterns exist for many businesses, and business cycles cause asset requirements to fluctuate. Temporary seasonal fluctuations in sales would be followed (or preceded) by similar fluctuations in current asset requirements. Figure 5-3 illustrates this phenomenon. There exists a level of permanent fixed assets that is required by the business to produce product and house employees. This grows over time and in support of sales. The middle layer represents permanent current asset investment. Finally, the top portion of the figure represents the seasonal aspects of working capital.

The question that needs to be addressed is how to finance the asset base. That is, how much of the financing should be long term and how much should be short term? In this case, long-term financing includes long-term debt and stockholders' equity. In general, many companies attempt to match the type of financing with the type of asset, which is known as the *matching principle*. There is no right or wrong answer. It is a matter of company policy, industry practice, and the current economic climate. The subject of long-term financing is discussed in Chapters 11 and 12. This section reviews short-term financing options.

There are four common types of short-term financing available to most corporations: trade credit and credit from commercial banks in the forms of short-term loans, lines of credit, and specific asset financing. Large, highly creditworthy corporations also can go directly to the debt market by issuing commercial paper.

Trade Credit

In the ordinary course of events, a firm buys its supplies and materials on credit from other firms, recording the liability as accounts payable. Accounts payable, or *trade credit*, is the largest single category of short-term credit, representing over 31 percent of current liabilities for nonfinancial corporations. This percentage is somewhat larger for small firms.

Trade credit is a spontaneous source of financing in that it arises from ordinary business transactions. This is the opposite side of an accounts receivable. This is a source of financing that your suppliers provide to you.

Trade credit, a customary part of doing business in most industries, is convenient and informal. A firm that does not qualify for credit from a financial institution may receive trade credit because previous experience has familiarized the seller with the creditworthiness of the customer. Trade credit is usually thought of as "free financing" because there is no explicit interest expense associated with trade credit. However, foregoing a discount is an opportunity cost of trade credit. With terms of "2/10, net 30," when you don't pay within the first 10 days, you forego the 2 percent discount. The question to ask is what is the cost of foregoing this discount?

To determine this cost as a percentage, for a one-time skipped discount, we simplistically calculate

$$\text{Cost of not taking a discount} = \text{stated rate per period} \times \text{number of periods per year} \quad (5.9)$$

where:

$$\text{Stated rate per period} = \frac{\text{discount\%}}{(1 - \text{discount\%})} = \frac{0.02}{(1 - 0.02)} = \frac{0.02}{0.98} = 0.0204 \quad \text{or} \quad 2.04\%$$

$$\text{Number of periods per year} = \frac{365 \text{ days}}{(\text{due date} - \text{discount period})} = \frac{365}{(30 - 10)} = \frac{365}{20} = 18.25$$

For the period of 20 days, which is the number of days between the discount period and the due date, the cost to borrow is 2.04 percent per period. However, there are 18.25 twenty-day periods in the year. Consequently, the annualized cost of foregoing this discount is 37.23 percent: Cost of not taking a discount = 0.0204 × 18.25 = 37.23 percent. Thus, if the customer were able to borrow from another source at less than 37.23 percent, he or she should do so to take advantage of the available discount.

The annualized cost is better represented as the effective annual rate of interest. Please see Chapter 7 for more on this.

$$\text{EAR} = (1 + \text{stated rate per period})^{\text{number of periods per year}} - 1 \quad (5.10)$$

If the company can borrow funds at less than 44.56 percent [arrived at via EAR $= (1 + 0.0204)^{18.25} - 1 = 1.0204^{18.25} = 44.56$ percent], it should arrange such financing because it is less expensive. While trade credit is "free" financing, the cost of missing discounts is high. Other financing sources should be established so that discounts are not missed.

This is also true in your personal life. Real estate taxes often offer a 2% discount if paid before a specific date. If not paid by that date, then 60 days later the entire amount is due. The simple cost of foregoing the discount on real estate taxes is 12.40 percent (2.04% the period cost of foregoing the discount times 6.08 sixty day periods in a year) and effective cost of 13.06 percent $((1+ 0.0204)^{6.08}-1)$. If you can borrow money at less than 12.40 percent (APR) or 13.06 percent (EAR), then you should borrow the money to take the discount.

Short-Term Financing by Commercial Banks

Commercial bank borrowing, which appears on the balance sheet as notes payable, bank borrowings, or short-term debt, is also significantly important as a source of short-term financing. Banks occupy a pivotal position in the short- and intermediate-term money markets. Banks provide nonspontaneous funds. As a firm's financing needs increase, it requests additional funds from banks. If the request is denied, often the alternative is to slow down the rate of growth or to cut back operations. Banks provide noncollateralized short-term loans as well as collateralized loans (loans with specific current operating assets backing them) for a specified period of time.

A line of credit is the most common loan between a bank and an organization and typically is noncollateralized. It is an agreement between the bank and the borrower concerning the maximum loan balance the bank will allow the borrower. For example, a bank loan officer may indicate to a company's treasurer that the bank regards the firm as "good" for up to $250,000 for the forthcoming year. Subsequently, over the course of the year, the treasurer may borrow up to that amount. For this flexibility, the borrower may be required to pay 0.25 percent to 0.50 percent per annum for the unused line of credit as well as interest on the portion that is borrowed.

Loans from commercial banks vary in cost, with the effective rate depending on the characteristics of the firm and the level of interest rates in the economy. If the firm can qualify as a prime risk because of its size and financial strength, the rate of interest will be at the *prime* interest rate. The *prime rate* is a bank-set interest rate that is higher than the discount rate charged by Federal Reserve banks to commercial banks. On the other hand, a small firm with below-average financial metrics (similar to the five C's used in receivables management) may be required to provide collateral security and to pay an effective rate of interest of 2 to 3 (or more) percentage points above the prime rate.

Determining the effective, or true, rate of interest on a loan depends on the stated rate of interest and the lender's method of charging interest. Table 5-13 shows the three common ways to calculate interest.

T A B L E 5-13

Costs of Commercial Bank Loans

Type of Interest	General Calculation	Cost for $50,000 Loan	Comments
1. Regular	$\dfrac{\text{Interest rate}}{\text{Borrowed amount}}$	$\dfrac{\$5,000}{\$50,000} = 10.0\%$	Straight 10% loan. No compensating balance or dicounting.
2. Compensating balance	$\dfrac{\text{Interest rate}}{(1 - \text{Compensating balance})}$	$\dfrac{0.10}{(1-0.20)} = 12.5\%$	10% loan with 20% compensating balance
3. Discounted loan	$\dfrac{\text{Interest rate}}{(1 - \text{Interest rate})}$	$\dfrac{0.10}{(1-0.10)} = 11.1\%$	Discounted 10% loan

If the interest is paid at the maturity of the loan, the stated rate of interest is the effective rate of interest. In the Table 5-13 example for a regular 10 percent loan, the cost is 10 percent:

$$\text{``Regular'' loan} = \frac{\text{interest}}{\text{borrowed amount}} = \frac{\$5,000}{\$50,000} = 10\% \qquad (5.11)$$

If this same 10 percent loan had a 20 percent compensating-balance requirement, the effective interest rate would be 12.5 percent. To obtain $50,000, you would be required to borrow $62,500:

$$\text{Amount to borrow} = \frac{\text{required amount}}{(1 - \text{compensating balance})} = \frac{\$50,000}{(1 - 0.20)}$$
$$= \frac{\$50,000}{0.80} = \$62,500 \qquad (5.12)$$

So the company borrows $62,500, keeps $12,500 (or 20 percent) on hand at the bank as a compensating balance, and walks away with $50,000, but it pays 10 percent interest on the full amount (or $6,250) for an effective cost of 12.5 percent ($6,250/$50,000). If the same 10 percent loan were discounted, the bank would deduct the interest in advance (discount the loan), and the effective rate of interest would be 11.1 percent. To obtain $50,000 from a 10 percent discounted loan, the company would need to borrow $55,555.55, keep $5,555.55 at the bank as a prepayment of the loan's interest, walk away with the needed $50,000, and pay 11.1 percent ($5,555.55/$50,000.00) for the funds.

Secured Short-Term Financing

Given a choice, it is ordinarily better to borrow on an unsecured basis because the administrative costs of secured loans are often high. However, a potential borrower's credit rating may not be sufficiently strong to justify an unsecured loan. If the loan can be secured by some form of collateral to be claimed by the lender in the event of default, then the lender may extend credit to an otherwise unacceptable firm. Similarly, a firm that can borrow on an unsecured basis may elect to use security if it finds that this will induce lenders to quote a lower interest rate.

Accounts receivable financing involves either the assigning of receivables or the selling of receivables (factoring). Assigning (or pledging) or discounting of accounts receivable is characterized by the fact that the lender not only has a lien on the receivables but also has recourse to the borrower (seller of the goods); if the person or firm that bought the goods does not pay, the selling firm must take the loss. In other words, the risk of default on the accounts receivable pledged remains with the borrower.

Factoring, or selling accounts receivable, involves the purchase of accounts receivable by the lender without recourse to the borrower (seller of the goods). The buyer of the goods is notified of the transfer and makes payment directly to the lender. Since the factoring firm assumes the risk of default on bad accounts, it must do the credit checking. Accordingly, factors provide not only money but also a credit department for the borrower.

If a firm is a relatively good credit risk, the mere existence of the inventory may be a sufficient basis for receiving an unsecured loan. If the firm is a relatively poor risk, the lending institution may insist on security, which often takes the form of a blanket lien (or general lien) against all inventory. Alternatively, trust receipts, field warehouse financing, or collateral certificates can be used to secure loans using specific assets such as an auto dealer borrowing against and pledging specific automobiles in inventory.

Short-Term Financing Using Commercial Paper

Commercial paper (CP) consists of unsecured promissory notes issued by only the largest, most creditworthy firms to finance short-term credit needs. CP has become an increasingly important source of short-term financing for many types of corporations, including utilities, finance companies, insurance companies, bank holding companies, and manufacturing companies. It is often sold directly to investors, including business corporations, commercial banks, insurance companies, and state and local government units.

Maturities of CP generally vary from one day to one year, with an average of about five months. The rates on prime CP vary, but they are tied to short-term rates generally 0.05 to 0.25 percent above the Treasury bill rate.

SUMMARY

This chapter covered numerous topics related to short-term financial management and working capital management or supply-chain finance. The chapter began with a look at how the company "goes to business" using breakeven analysis and business leverage. While there may be long-term strategic implications of both, business is conducted on a day-to-day operational level, where these tools are also useful.

The operating cycle shows how long it takes for a firm to turn inventory into collected cash. The cash cycle shows how many days it takes the company to recover its cash after paying for the inventory. Both are effective tools to understand, manage, and assess a firm's working capital policy.

Effective cash management begins with a detailed cash budget. Monthly, weekly, and even daily cash budgets are prepared routinely by the treasurer's office within a large corporation. These budgets are fully integrated with the operations of the firm and anticipate cash receipts and cash disbursements. Excess cash can be invested in marketable securities and any short-term borrowing needs identified well before they arise.

In establishing a credit policy, a firm formulates its credit standards and its credit terms. Credit standards that are too strict will lose sales; credit standards that are too relaxed will result in excessive bad-debt losses. To determine optimal credit standards, the firm relates the marginal costs of credit to the marginal profits on the increased sales. Credit analyses and the evaluations of prospective customers typically include assessment of the five C's, with an analysis of the potential customer's financial performance metrics as well as outside credit reports.

Inventories—raw materials, work in process, and finished goods—are necessary in most businesses. New systems for controlling the level of inventories have been designed, and enterprise resource planning (ERP) software has enabled many of the advances in this area. In addition, ERP systems and the Internet facilitate closer "just-in-time" inventory relationships with suppliers and customers via the sharing of materials requirements for both inbound and outbound areas.

Many organizations try to "match" the maturity of their assets with their approach to financing. Permanent fixed assets typically are financed with long-term financing in the form of debt or equity, whereas temporary current assets that arise owing to seasonality generally are financed with short-term financing. Short-term credit is debt originally scheduled for repayment within one year. The three major sources of short-term credit are trade credit among firms, loans from commercial banks, and commercial paper. Trade credit (accounts payable) is a spontaneous source of financing in that it arises from ordinary business transactions and is the largest single category of short-term credit.

STRATEGIC FINANCIAL PLANNING

It is not enough for a firm to perform well in the current quarter. The firm always must be looking ahead. It must engage in long-range planning as well as operate effectively in the present. This is especially true as markets become increasingly international in scope and the economies of the world become increasingly inter-linked. As a consequence, more variables affect the national economy and industries within it. The resulting increased turbulence in the economic and political environments make it necessary for business firms to engage in long-range planning.

As mentioned in Chapter 1, corporate finance does not exist as an end in itself. Much like a computer is a tool that is used to complete an analysis or write a report, corporate finance is a tool that helps business people to maximize the value of the firm. In this chapter, I will develop another important value-adding dimension of corporate finance—the strategic financial plan.

This chapter first provides a brief managerial overview of strategic planning, introduces the concept of supporting that plan with simple financial models to approximate the results of planned activities, and then develops a fully interactive and supportive financial model that includes integrated financial statements—income statement, balance sheet, and cash-flow statement with financial performance metric analysis. I use a hypothetical strategic financial plan illustration for both The Hershey Company, and P. F. Chang's China Bistro, Inc.

OVERVIEW OF STRATEGIC PLANNING

Strategic planning provides an organization with an opportunity for self-examination. It is an important time when senior management can step away from "fighting the fires" of running a business and reflect on the organization itself. Strategic planning is a never-ending process that develops basic business objectives and establishes (or reconfirms) business direction. The organization must come to grips with answers to a basic set of thought- and discussion-provoking questions:

- What do we (the organization) want to do?
- Where do we want to do it?
- When do we want to do it?

- Who is going to do it?
- What resources do we require?

The strategic planning process:

- Facilitates communication among the senior executives of an organization
- Sets a business direction
- Prioritizes opportunities and requirements
- Establishes business performance standards and objectives

However, the strategic plan must be a living, actionable tool. Strategy is planning for the future of the enterprise. Although the emphasis of strategy is on the long view, to be implemented properly, strategy also takes into account shorter-term decisions and actions. Strategy is not static. Individual strategies, plans, or policies may be used in a set of formal procedures. Strategy is a way of thinking that requires diverse inputs. In these continuing interactive processes, financial management is key. There are numerous elements, approaches, and frameworks that structure and support the strategic planning process.

Approaches to Strategy

While diverse approaches to strategic planning are observed, there is no "one size fits all." It is important that every management team develop its own formal procedures.

Proven Techniques

Numerous techniques are used by many corporations and consulting firms to initiate strategic-level discussions about the organization. One self-assessment technique, *Porter's five forces*, which refers to Michael Porter's model, can be applied to each strategic business unit and/or the company as a whole. This model includes five economic dimensions. Management develops characteristics for each dimension and, after considerable discussion, rates the priority of that dimension as low, medium, or high. The dimensions are:

- Threat of new entrants
- Threat of substitution
- Bargaining power of suppliers
- Bargaining power of buyers
- Rivalry among competitors

There are numerous variations on this approach in practice. Another assessment tool is *strengths, weaknesses, opportunities, and threats (SWOT) analysis*. This technique requires some soul searching on the part of management, as do all these tools (Table 6-1). This approach uses a self-examination process to identify

T A B L E   6-1

Background on the SWOT Analysis Approach to Planning

		Internal Factors	
		Strengths List 4 to 8	**Weaknesses List 4 to 8**
External factors	Opportunities List 4 to 8	Create strategies using strengths to capitalize on opportunities.	Create strategies to improve weaknesses and capitalize on opportunities.
	Threats List 4 to 8	Create strategies using strengths to minimize threats.	Create strategies to reduce weaknesses and minimize threats.

the corporation's strengths and weaknesses and then expands to consider the external opportunities and threats that are anticipated in the industry's future. When four to eight (or more) strengths have been identified, the management team also identifies four to eight (or more) weaknesses of the corporation. The discussion moves on to consider and list four to eight (or more) external opportunities as well as four to eight (or more) external threats. This identification process may take a half day or even a full day of brainstorming and free thought. It also is a very fluid process with no clear-cut answers.

The final step of SWOT analysis addresses each "window" of this two-by-two matrix and the cross-junctions of all the internal and external perspectives. The management team collectively generates ideas that lead to strategies and address:

- Strengths to capitalize on opportunities
- Ways to overcome weaknesses to also capitalize on opportunities
- Strengths that will reduce or eliminate threats
- Ways to reduce weaknesses to minimize threats

Another popular technique that has been used successfully to generate discussion and debate in the initial phase of strategic planning is the Boston Consulting Group (BCG) *growth-share matrix*, which is a two-by-two matrix. The process examines individual business units or products on the dimension of relative comparative position within an industry (based on that unit's market share compared with competitors) and on the general growth of the industry (based on annual sales growth). Often, a third dimension is added to this two-dimensional space by letting a circle represent each business unit with the size of that circle signifying sales volume in millions of dollars. You can add a fourth dimension to the graph by adding a wisp to each circle to indicate the movement of that business unit (circle) from the prior year.

A similar window diagram is found with the General Electric *strategic analysis matrix*. In this case, a three-by-three matrix is generated using two dimensions with three tiers each. Once again, the process is founded on examining business units or products within a corporation. For the first dimension, each unit is assessed a grade of strong, average, or weak based on the unit's strength and competitive position. The second dimension rates the unit's industry attractiveness on a scale of high, medium, or low. The first part of the exercise requires management to define competitive position and industry attractiveness; the second part places each business unit on the matrix. Similar to the BCG exercise, a third dimension is often introduced with a pie chart that shows the business unit sales as a slice of total industry sales.

Many techniques are offered by a vast group of consultants. Each approach goes beyond the walls of the corporation, examines the competitive economic climate, and is designed to stimulate open conversation around the business units.

FINANCIAL PLANNING AND CONTROL PROCESSES

Financial planning and control processes are closely tied to strategic planning. Figure 6-1 begins with external factors that describe the industry, domestic macro-economic factors, and international economic factors. These external factors are blended with senior management's self-assessment through the techniques presented

FIGURE   6-1

Essential elements in the strategic plan.

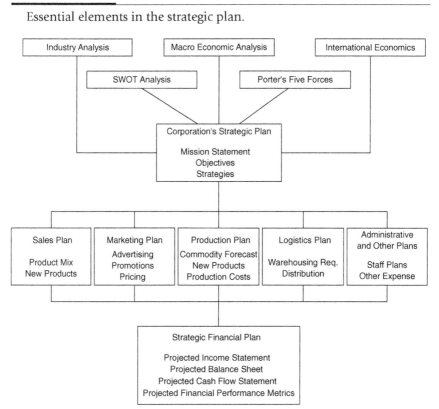

earlier to develop the enterprise's mission statement, objectives, and strategies. In the framework of mission and objectives, business strategies are formulated.

Financial planning turns the qualitative assessment into a quantifiable plan that sets performance standards for the future. Financial planning is distinguished from budgeting in that planning is more strategic, of longer duration, and less detailed than a budget. Budgets usually have a one-year duration and are extremely explicit, including specific tactical details.

The financial plans are comprised of separate but interlinked plans. Each organization must decide how detailed the strategic plan needs to be. Hershey prepared divisional strategic financial plans that incorporate sales and production costs at the strategic business unit (SBU) level. This is in sharp contrast to the detailed annual budget that would prepare sales forecasts (by customer by region) and very detailed cost of goods sold estimates (by plant by cost component) for each of its 1,500+ stock-keeping units (SKUs).

At this point, financial management has key responsibilities to perform, particularly in the areas of financial planning and control. Financial planning and control involve the use of projections based on standards and the development of a feedback and adjustment process to improve performance. This financial planning and control process involves forecasts and the use of several types of supporting plans. Supporting plans are developed for every significant area of the firm's activities, as shown by Figure 6-1.

Key decisions involve the choice of products and markets. These decisions result in a product-mix strategy complete with a schedule of new product introductions and aging-product rationalizations (or eliminations). The sales plan also must be married to the marketing plan. Sales and marketing must work closely together as they consider the marketing expenditures and emphasis in support of a particular product. This, in turn, provides a basis for long-range sales forecasts. Sales forecasts are the basis for modeling all the other activities of the firm.

The production plan first analyzes the use of materials, parts, labor, and facilities. The production plan also reviews and incorporates costs of key specialty ingredients, commodities hedging positions, labor union contract impacts, and so on. Manufacturing then completes the production plan by integrating the sales plan from sales and marketing. Any shortfalls can be identified and reconciled well in advance. Supporting the production plan, each of its major elements is likely to have its own plan (or supporting schedules)—a materials plan, a hedged commodity schedule, a personnel plan, and a facilities plan.

The facilities plan identifies any opportunities or shortfalls in production capacity or new plant requirements. Since strategic planning has a long-term focus, new production lines and even new plants can be anticipated and addressed in a timely manner. This facilities plan provides the basis for the capital expenditures plan.

Likewise, logistics works with the sales and production plan to identify any changes in distribution or warehousing capacity requirements. Any shortfalls can be identified and addressed. Shortfalls in warehousing capacity can give rise to building additional warehousing space (if the shortfall appears to be permanent) or renting warehouse space (if the shortfall appears temporary).

Administrative plans can be developed at a cost-center level or for the functional area. For instance, the senior vice president and chief financial officer may be comfortable projecting area growth matching the rate of inflation (say 2.0 to 3.0 percent) without feeling the need to have each cost center prepare a strategic plan and cost-center-level projections. Once again, annual budgets should be prepared for the lowest organizational unit, such as a cost center, to assist the manager of that unit in making day-to-day decisions. For a strategic plan, however, cost-center detailed budget-level projections provide a false sense of accuracy and in general provide little or no value. Only when a specific functional area's plan is prepared does it provide a general sense of that area's spending to an appropriate level of detail.

Other administrative budgets are developed to cover miscellaneous administrative and executive requirements. Finally, corporate (or divisional) finance may be aware of some additional expenses that are not covered anywhere else. Interest is an example of this type of additional expense.

The results of projecting all these elements of cost are reflected in the projected (also called *pro forma*) income statement. Anticipated sales give rise to consideration of the various types of investments in working capital that are needed to produce and sell the products. These working capital investments and the facilities/production requirements identified in the facilities plan, together with the beginning balance sheet, provide the necessary data for developing the assets side of the balance sheet.

Assets must be financed, so a cash-flow analysis is needed. The cash plan integrates the income statement projections with the projected investments in both fixed and working capital. The cash plan incorporates projected dividend payments and required debt repayment. It also reflects any planned share repurchases. The projected cash-flow statement is useful in identifying any additional cash funding needs. A positive net cash flow indicates that the firm has sufficient financing. However, if an increase in the volume of operations, for example, leads to a negative cash flow, additional financing is required. The longer the lead-time in arranging for the required financing, the greater is the opportunity for assessing optimal sources of capital, developing required documentation, and working out arrangements with chosen financing sources.

Financial planning control seeks to improve profitability, avoid cash squeezes, and improve the performance of individual divisions of a company. These responsibilities involve the topics covered in this chapter.

Planning is a continuous process. The strategic review and strategic financial plan usually start early in a fiscal year. The first year of the strategic plan becomes the preliminary, targeted financial performance for the following year's budget. After consideration of many tactical alternatives by division senior management and other operations managers, priorities are established and detailed budgets are developed. The budget (compared with the strategic plan) is prepared in far more detail, at SKU, plant, sales office, and cost-center levels. Literally tens of millions of detailed assumptions are made in the annual budgeting process. The budgeting process often starts as early as six months before the next year.

Figure 6-2 presents a diagram of the complete planning cycle. Of course, developing the plan and the budget is the easy part. The hard part is implementing all strategies successfully and surpassing the objectives. This critical component—implementation—can never be overlooked. Supportive feedback systems complete the planning process, provide variance analysis, assess performance success or failure, and facilitate adjustments for incorporation during the next planning cycle.

The remainder of this chapter develops the concept behind a comprehensive strategic financial planning model, creates a detailed projected income statement for P. F. Chang's China Bistro, Inc., and develops a complete strategic (albeit hypothetical) plan for The Hershey Company.

Strategic Planning Structure

An overall approach must be decided on early in the strategic planning process. A tone must be set by the chief executive officer (CEO). Will the strategic planning process be a top-down approach or a bottom-up approach or even a combination of the two? How much collaboration will take place in setting the firm's future direction?

F I G U R E   6-2

From strategies to action—operationalizing strategic plans.

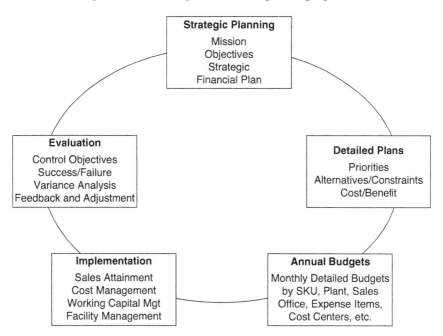

The process for many corporations is a collaborative effort that begins as a bottom-up approach. Divisional plans are accumulated, corporate expenses are added, and projected corporate consolidated financial statements are prepared. The consolidated plan performance is compared with prior stated corporate objectives as well as the CEO's expectations. Often at a strategic planning conference, corporate and division senior managers discuss the overall direction of the organization and address any shortfall in projected performance. Management-designed strategies attempt to eliminate performance gaps. This process is classified as a collaborative bottom-up initial approach that is driven to an overall corporate (top-down) level of financial performance.

At what level in the organization should the strategic plan be built? Every company has its own complex organizational structure. For many organizations, this includes the overall corporate level with numerous divisions reporting to the corporate level. Each division has its own number of SBUs comprised of numerous products. Each product has a number of SKUs. For Hershey, an SKU represented a product variation such as different sizes of products, different bag weights, or different seasonal wraps. In total, Hershey had over 1,500+ SKUs. The strategic plan was prepared at the corporate and division levels with some discussion of SBUs as the situation warranted. Only on rare occasions would a strategic plan include product- or SKU-specific discussion.

BASIC FINANCIAL FORECASTS

As a prelude to the comprehensive financial model, this section will cover three basic models (referred to as the *triplets*). Each model includes a simplified set of financial statements, hardly a useful tool, but they are illustrative of what's to come.

Simple Financial Planning Model

Table 6-2 contains three separate strategic financial planning models. All three are independent of each other, quite simplistic, and will be covered in turn. All three start with the same year 0 results and forecast the plan for year 1 given a different set of assumptions. The financial statements include a three-line income statement, a six-line balance sheet, and a five-line cash-flow statement. Please notice that there are two balance sheets, a preliminary one and a final one. Year 1 assumptions are listed in the middle column of each panel.

While this section is quite mechanical, it does illustrate the modeling concept. The first panel of the table (panel A) projects next year's performance assuming no growth in other assets or in liabilities. It starts with 10 percent sales growth and an expense ratio that stays the same (as a percent of sales—90 percent), just like year 0. The first pass of the balance sheet includes only the simple values that we know. Specifically, we know that other assets and liabilities will remain constant from year 0, but we need more information (from the cash-flow statement) to project the year 1 cash balance, and we need to know the dividend amount as well as net income to forecast stockholders' equity. Therefore,

TABLE 6-2

Simple Strategic Financial Plan

	A. No Growth Other Assets/Liabilities			B. 10% Growth Other Assets/Liabilities			C. Variety of Assumptions		
	Year 0	Assumption	Year 1	Year 0	Assumption	Year 1	Year 0	Assumption	Year 1
Income statement									
Sales	$ 1,000	10% Growth	$ 1,100	$ 1,000	10% Growth	$ 1,100	$ 1,000	10% Decline	$ 900
Expenses	900	Same % of sales	990	900	Same % of sales	990	900	88% of sales	792
Net income (NI)	$ 100		$ 110	$ 100		$ 110	$ 100		$ 108
Preliminary balance sheet: First pass, incomplete									
Cash	$ 200		$ –	$ 200		$ –	$ 200		$ –
Other assets	800	0% Growth	800	800	10% Growth	880	800	5% Decline	760
Total assets	$ 1,000		$ 800	$ 1,000		$ 880	$ 1,000		$ 760
Liabilities	$ 600	0% Growth	600	$ 600	10% Growth	660	$ 600	5% Increase	630
Equity	400		–	400		–	400		–
Total liab & equity	$ 1,000		$ 600	$ 1,000		$ 660	$ 1,000		$ 630
Cash-flow statement									
Net income	$ 100		$ 110	$ 100		$ 110	$ 100		$ 108
Cash S (U) O assets	(20)		–	(20)		(80)	(20)		40
Dividends (Div)	(40)	40% Payout	(44)	(40)	40% Payout	(44)	(40)	Assume $45	(45)
Cash S (U) liabilities	15		–	15		60	15		30
Change in cash	$ 55		$ 66	$ 55		$ 46	$ 55		$ 133
Final balance sheet									
Cash	$ 200	Beg bal + Δ in cash	266	$ 200	Beg bal + Δ in cash	246	$ 200	Beg bal + Δ in cash	333
Other assets	800	0% Growth	800	800	10% Growth	880	800	5% Decline	760
Total assets	$ 1,000		$ 1,066	$ 1,000		$ 1,126	$ 1,000		$ 1,093
Liabilities	$ 600	0% Growth	600	$ 600	10% Growth	660	$ 600	5% Increase	630
Equity	400	Beg bal + NI – Div.	466	400	Beg bal + NI – Div.	466	400	Beg bal + NI – Div.	463
Total liab & equity	$ 1,000		$ 1,066	$ 1,000		$ 1,126	$ 1,000		$ 1,093

in the preliminary balance sheet, all we see is other that assets remain at $800 and liabilities at $600. The cash-flow statement (as in Chapter 2) begins with net income, considers any operating sources or uses that result from changes in assets or liabilities, and also forecasts a use of cash to pay dividends. With net income in panel A equal to $110, dividends of $44, and no changes to assets or liabilities, the year 1 cash flow is $66.

Finalizing the balance sheet, the beginning balance of cash ($200) plus the change in cash ($66) equals the year 1 cash balance ($266) for total assets of $1,066. Recall from Chapter 2 that this year's balance of stockholders' equity is equal to the beginning balance ($400) increased by net income ($110) and reduced by dividends ($44) for a projected value of $466. This first accounting identity is captured in Eq (6.1).

$$\text{Equity}_t = \text{equity}_{(t-1)} + \text{net income}_t - \text{dividends}_t \qquad (6.1)$$

Although it was not the case here, equity$_t$ also would have been increased (decreased) for any stock issuance (or repurchases). You'll notice that the final balance sheet balances without any plugs, and you have just completed your first (extremely simple) financial statement projection.

Continuing on to panel B of Table 6-2, we assume the same 10 percent growth rate in sales and that expenses remain at 90 percent of sales. However, we assume that both other assets and liabilities increase by 10 percent. Once again, other assets and liabilities ($880 and $660, respectively) are entered in the preliminary balance sheet. The cash flow follows with net income and dividends as in panel A. However, this time the change in other assets is included as an $80 use of cash—we bought $80 more of assets—and the change in liabilities is captured as a $60 source of financing. The resulting change in cash was $46 in panel B. Completing the final balance sheet: Cash was $246 (the beginning balance plus the change in cash), and stockholder's equity remained $466 just as in panel A (beginning balance plus net income less dividends). Once again, the model "worked," and the balance sheet balanced!

Finally, the third triplet has varying assumptions, as listed in panel C of Table 6-2. Starting with a sales decline of 10 percent, sales dropped to $900. In this environment of a declining top line, though, costs are managed to 88 percent of sales and result in net income of $108. On the preliminary balance sheet, clearly other assets (e.g., receivables, inventory, and net, plant, property, and equipment) declined by 5 percent, or $40, whereas liabilities grew by 5 percent, or $30.

The resulting cash-flow statement begins with net income of $108 and includes a dividend of $45 as a stated amount. The change in other assets is reflected as a $40 source (remember from Chapter 2 that a reduction in an asset is a source), and the increase in liabilities is a source of $30. This results in a cash-flow amount of $133. Moving on to the final balance sheet in panel C, cash is now projected to be $333 ($200 beginning balance increased by the change in cash of $133). Stockholders' equity is $463 (the beginning balance of $400 increased by net income of $108 less dividend of $45). For the third time, the model "worked," and the balance sheet balanced without any plugs to make it balance!

From a comparison of all three, it should be clear that assumptions do not matter for the model to work and the balance sheet to balance. In practice, assumptions are what drive the planning process, and the mechanical model is secondary. For our purposes, though, the model is the learning outcome, and assumptions are secondary. However, as I apply and develop the modeling concept more, reasonable assumptions will play a role.

Financial Projection Worksheet

Table 6-3 expands on the triplets presented in Table 6-2. While each financial statement is more developed and different forecasting methodologies are employed, the mechanical approach remains the same.

T A B L E   6-3

Projection Worksheet: Preliminary Balance Sheet

	2011	Projection Assumptions	2012 Plan
Income statement			
Sales	$ 5,000	20% increase	$ 6,000
Cost of goods sold (ex. dep)	3,350	Same % of sales as in 2011	4,020
Depreciation (dep)	150	Increase by $30	180
General and administrative	650	16% of sales	960
Operating income	850		840
Net interest expense	75	Given	40
Pretax income	775		800
Taxes	325	40% tax rate	320
Net income	$ 450		$ 480
Preliminary balance sheet			
Cash	$ 867		$ –
Accounts receivable	700	Same turnover as in 2011	840
Inventory	195	36.5 days outstanding	402
Current assets	1,762		–
Net, plant, property, and equip	2,800		–
Other assets	235	Decrease by $15	220
Total assets	$ 4,797		$ –
Accounts payable	$ 280	10% of COGS (ex. dep)	$ 402
Accrued liabilities	110	Decrease by $35	75
Short-term debt	300		–
Other current liabilities	55	Increase by $10	65
Current liabilities	745		–
Long-term debt	800	Increase by $100	900
Stockholders' equity	3,252		–
Total liabilities and equity	$ 4,797		$ –

(Continued)

TABLE 6-3

Projection Worksheet: Preliminary Balance Sheet *(Continued)*

	2011	Projection Assumptions	2012 Plan
Cash-flow statement		Sources (Uses)	
Net income	$ 450	From income statement	$ 480
Depreciation	150	From income statement	180
Change in accounts receivable	(234)	From preliminary balance sheet	(140)
Change in inventory	189	From preliminary balance sheet	(207)
Change in other assets	(11)	From preliminary balance sheet	15
Change in accounts payable	273	From preliminary balance sheet	122
Change in accrued liabilities	(56)	From preliminary balance sheet	(35)
Change in other current liabilities	68	From preliminary balance sheet	10
Cash flow from operations	829		
Capital expenditures	(425)	Estimate – assumption	(550)
Change in short-term debt	50	Estimate – assumption	(150)
Change in long-term debt	50	From preliminary balance sheet	100
Dividends	(175)	40% dividend payout assumption	(192)
Cash from (used for) financing	(75)		(242)
Change in cash	$ 329		

First, we look at the income statement, where sales are expected to increase by 20 percent and the cost of goods sold excluding depreciation is forecast to remain at 67 percent of sales. We are told that depreciation will increase by $30 to $180. General and administrative (G&A) expenses are expected to increase to 16 percent of sales from the 2011 level of 13 percent owing primarily to increased direct brand expense, such as advertising, coupons, and promotions. All these assumptions provide operating income or earnings before interest and taxes (EBIT) of $840. With interest expense projected at $40, along with a 40 percent tax rate, the pretax income is $800, and net income is $480.

Continuing with Table 6-3, the preliminary balance sheet includes values derived from assumptions in conjunction with the income statement or stated dollar-amount assumptions. For example, accounts receivable are estimated based on the 2011 accounts receivable turnover of 7.1429 ($5000/$700) divided into the 2012 project sales level of $6,000 for a 2012 project accounts receivable balance of $840. Likewise, inventory is projected as 36.5 days of inventory outstanding. Of course (and remembering Chapters 3 and 5), inventory turnover or days outstanding are based on cost of goods sold. The 2012 projection of cost of goods sold excluding depreciation is $4,020, or $11.0137 of inventory per day ($4,020/365), or $402 of inventory for the expected 36.5 days outstanding. Notice also that 36.5 days is one-tenth of a year, and the inventory balance would be one-tenth the cost of goods sold. Finally, accounts payable are estimated as 10 percent of the cost of goods sold excluding depreciation, or, once again, $402. The other line items projected on the preliminary balance sheet are determined by increases or decreases from the prior year. However, after completing the preliminary balance sheet, there remain four blank-line items excluding the totals and subtotals.

Before completing the balance sheet, we need to complete the cash-flow statement for what we learned from the income statement and preliminary balance sheet, as well as three items estimated directly on the cash-flow statement (i.e., capital expenditures, short-term debt repayment, and dividends). Net income and depreciation come straight from the income statement. Remember, as discussed in Chapter 2, that depreciation is added back because while it legitimately is an expense (and was subtracted from income); it is a noncash expense and must be added back into get a true picture of cash flow. The next few items come from the balance sheet.

The integrative nature of the balance sheet and cash-flow statement is quite clear. Accounts receivable are forecast to increase by $140. We used our cash to finance our customer's purchases. Likewise, inventory is estimated to increase by $207 in 2012. We are planning to use our cash to buy more inventory. But notice that other assets decrease by $15. Somewhat tongue in cheek, I am not even sure what other assets are, but whatever they are, we sold $15 of them and got cash for that sale. On the liability side, accounts payable are expected to increase by $122. This indicates that suppliers are offering us increased free financing, and thus this is a source of cash, just as "other current liabilities" provide a source of cash. Finally, we are using our cash to pay off some accrued liabilities. Table 6-4 summarizes the cash-flow implications of changes in the balance sheet.

A decrease (increase) in an asset (liability) produces a *source* of cash, whereas an increase (decrease) in an asset (liability) results in a *use* of cash.

From the cash-flow statement, we learn the following:

- Capital expenditures are anticipated as $550 in 2012. We are using our cash to buy more plant, property, and equipment, and so on.
- A total of $150 of short-term debt is being paid off, a use of cash.
- Dividends are estimated as 40 percent of net income, or, in our case, $192. We are using our cash to pay dividends.

TABLE 6-4

Cash Flow Implications of Balance Sheet Changes

	Asset Change	Liability Change
Source of cash	Decrease	Increase
Use of cash	Increase	Decrease

Considering all the cash-flow items, the change in cash is a reduction of ($367), or $425 from operations offset by a use of ($550) for capital expenditures and a use of ($242) for financing.

Table 6-5 completes the balance sheet for what we learned on the cash-flow statement. The balance sheet has four new lines completed as well as the totals and subtotals. The other 2012 values come directly from the preliminary balance sheet. Cash and stockholders' equity are projected as we did before in the triplets.

Another accounting identity is required to complete the 2012 net, plant, property, and equipment (NPPE), as shown in Eq. (6.2):

$$\text{NPPE}_t = \text{NPPE}_{(t-1)} + \text{capital expenditures}_t - \text{depreciation}_t \qquad (6.2)$$

To project the 2012 net, plant, property, and equipment, we begin with the 2011 balance and add 2012 capital expenditures while subtracting 2012 depreciation. Capital expenditures are a use of cash. However, here we are not adding a negative use of cash. We are adding capital expenditures (or said differently, their absolute value). Thus the 2012 NPPE balance is $3,170 (or $2,800 + $550 − $180).

Completing the final balance sheet line item, the beginning balance of short-term debt ($300) plus the change in short-term debt (an assumption from the cash-flow statement) of a $150 payment equals the 2012 short-term debt

T A B L E   6-5

Projection Worksheet: Final Balance Sheet

	2011	Projection Assumptions	2012 Plan
Final balance sheet			
Cash	$ 867	2011 Balance +Δ cash	$ 500
Accounts receivable	700		840
Inventory	195		402
Current assets	1,762		1,742
Net, plant, property, and equip	2,800	2011 Bal + cap exp – dep	3,170
Other assets	235		220
Total assets	$ 4,797		$ 5,132
Accounts payable	$ 280		$ 402
Accrued liabilities	110		75
Short-term debt	300	2011 Balance +Δ short-term debt	150
Other current liabilities	55		65
Current liabilities	745		692
Long-term debt	800		900
Stockholders' equity	3,252	2011 Bal + net inc – dividends	3,540
Total liabilities and equity	$ 4,797		$ 5,132

balance of $150. Once again, the mechanics work and, for the projection work-sheet, total assets equal total liabilities and stockholders' equity.

This background provides a general overview of the methodology and techniques further developed in this chapter. The next section digs more deeply into actual applications in practice.

Forecasting the Income Statement

While the complete set of financial statements (i.e., income statement, balance sheet, and cash-flow statement), along with financial performance metrics, is a comprehensive corporate management approach, many divisional or business-unit managers are more concerned with forecasting the income statement than either of the other two financial statements. This section offers two different looks at two different processes before moving on to look at a complete strategic financial plan for Hershey.

Strategic financial plans come in all shapes and sizes in practice. Table 6-6 is just such an example that a solid medium-sized company used in its planning. While the model is simplistic, it is effective for the firm and its state of strategic financial planning.

The four projected years are presented on Table 6-6 along with the 2011 income statement. You'll notice that internally the business started with gross sales of $210 million, but owing to product returns, sales discounts taken, or promotional activities, its net sales are $200 million. Returns, discounts, and allowances were 5 percent of net sales. The business had gross income (contribution profit) of $104.3 million, or 52.15 percent. Brand support (i.e., advertising, coupons, training, etc.) amounted to $37.5 million, or 18.75 percent, leaving direct contribution (or income from the product sales less any specific product expenses). After departmental expenses, operating income was $27.2 million, or 13.60 percent of sales.

The company was setting some long-range direction based on a key target of 3 percent sales growth and maintenance of all expenses (or income) margins. As a result, net sales grew by a compound annual growth rate (CAGR) of 3 percent to $225.1 million, and the operating margin was maintained at 13.60 percent to yield $30.6 million of project operating income by 2015. Management saw this as minimal performance or a base performance level.

Table 6-7 shows the 2015 income statement results for two other operating scenarios. The differences are a result of different growth and margin assumptions. The base-case results are as determined in Table 6-6 and are offered for comparison.

The enhanced case shows improved results to $38.9 million of operating income by 2015 compared with a base case of $30.6 million. While the enhanced case is predicated on 5 percent net sales growth, with a reduction in returns, discounts, and allowances (RD&As) from 5 percent of net sales in 2011 to 2 percent of net sales in 2015, gross sales would need to expand by only 4.59 percent. The enhanced case also reduces a number of expenses as a percent of sales: cost of

TABLE 6-6

Base Income Statement Projection

$ millions	Actual		Assumption	Plan					
	2011	% of Net Sales		2012	2013	2014	2015	% of Net Sales	4-Year CAGR
Gross sales	$ 210.0	105.00%		$ 216.3	$ 222.8	$ 229.5	$ 236.4	105.00%	3.00%
RD&As*	10.0	5.00%	5.00%**	10.3	10.6	10.9	11.3	5.00%	3.00%
Net sales	200.0	100.00%	3.00%^{G}	206.0	212.2	218.6	225.1	100.00%	3.00%
Cost of goods sold	84.0	42.00%	42.00%**	86.5	89.1	91.8	94.5	42.00%	3.00%
Distribution cost	11.7	5.85%	5.85%**	12.1	12.4	12.8	13.2	5.85%	3.00%
Gross contribution	104.3	52.15%		107.4	110.7	114.0	117.4	52.15%	3.00%
Brand support	37.5	18.75%	18.75%**	38.6	39.8	41.0	42.2	18.75%	3.00%
Direct contribution	66.8	33.40%		68.8	70.9	73.0	75.2	33.40%	3.00%
Departmental expenses	39.6	19.80%	19.80%**	40.8	42.0	43.3	44.6	19.80%	3.00%
Operating income	$ 27.2	13.60%		$ 28.0	$ 28.9	$ 29.7	$ 30.6	13.60%	3.00%

*Returns, discounts, and allowances.

** = % of net sales.

G = growth.

TABLE 6-7

Scenario Comparison

$ millions	Actual 2011	% of Net Sales	Base Case 2015	Enhanced Case 2015	Enhanced + Price Inc 2015
Gross sales	$ 210.0	105.00%	$ 236.4	$ 248.0	$ 257.5
RD&As*	10.0	5.00%	11.3	4.9	5.0
Net sales	200.0	100.00%	225.1	243.1	252.5
Cost of goods sold	84.0	42.00%	94.5	97.2	97.2
Distribution cost	11.7	5.85%	13.2	12.2	12.2
Gross contribution	104.3	52.15%	117.4	133.7	143.1
Brand support	37.5	18.75%	42.2	51.1	51.1
Direct contribution	66.8	33.40%	75.2	82.7	92.0
Departmental expenses	39.6	19.80%	44.6	43.8	43.8
Operating income	$ 27.2	13.60%	$ 30.6	$ 38.9	$ 48.3
Net sales growth rate, all four years			3.00%	5.00%	6.00%
Operating Margin – % of Net Sales			13.60%	16.00%	19.13%
Operating Income CAGR (2011 – 2015)			3.00%	9.36%	15.43%

*Returns, discounts, and allowances.

goods sold (2.00 percent), distribution (0.85 percent), and department expenses (1.80 percent). However, brand support would increase from 18.75 percent of sales to 21.00 percent because a large portion of the cost savings would be reinvested in the business to drive the top-line (sales) growth. A side note, while a 1.80 percent (as a percent of sales) reduction in departmental expenses sounds oppressive, total departmental expenses increased by $4.2 million, or 2.53 percent, from 2011 to 2015.

If sales grew by 5 percent while margins stayed constant (13.60 percent), operating income would have grown to $33.1 million. If, on the other hand, the margins improved to 16 percent while sales grew at only 3 percent, operating income would be $36.0 million. However, combined, the two enhancements produce the $38.9 million of operating income discussed earlier.

Before leaving this simplistic model, it is worthwhile considering the final scenario that incorporates the same profile developed in the enhanced scenario and adds to it a 1 percent price increase. In this case, sales are growing by 6 percent (the 5 percent enhanced growth plus 1 percent price increase) and result in 2015 net sales of $252.5 million. Here's the point of a price increase: Expenses stay the same! The costs in the enhanced scenario with a price increase reflect exactly the same expenses as the enhanced case, but operating income now reaches $48.3 million, a margin of 19.13 percent with a CAGR of 15.43 percent.

The bottom-line strategic financial planning (and management) is adaptable to fit the needs of many audiences at many different levels.

Analyzing and Forecasting
P. F. Chang's China Bistro, Inc.

As stated earlier, the sales forecast is the most important assumption for any strategic financial plan. P. F. Chang's China Bistro, Inc. (PFCB), provides an annual report that is a treasure chest full of information about the company's latest fiscal year and details about its two distinct Asian restaurant brands, Bistro and Pei Wei. PFCB provides some of the most unique data not available from many (or any) other companies. This disclosure parallels the internal data used by a company to manage its business. All of this detail allows an investment analyst (or any outsider) to decompose the PFCB consolidated information in an attempt to gain a better perspective on the company's consolidated business.

Table 6-8 analyzes the most recent history for PFCB by its business units (brands). An appropriate historical analysis of the company's 2010 annual report allows us to project its business results. Also refer to chapters two and three.

To begin, section A of Table 6-8 examines sales per unit. PFCB provides 2008 to 2010 sales detail by each year that restaurants were first opened from 2002 to 2010 and for units opened before 2002. In addition, PFCB lists the total number of units opened and the newly opened stores for each year (2002 to 2010) and in total before 2002. The first piece of information from section A shows us that sales for a Bistro are approximately $4.6 million (all units including newly opened) to $4.8 million (opened before 2008—mature units) per store, whereas sales per restaurant at Pei Wei are at about $1.8 million to $1.9 million. Second, using 2009 as an example, you'll see that sales per newly opened unit approximately double in the second year (2010). This is due to the timing of opening a new unit—from a partial year to a full year—or annualization of sales. Third, as best illustrated by looking at average sales per unit opened before 2008, Bistro sales per unit declined in 2009 by almost 4.5 percent. In 2010, Bistro's contraction continued but at a slower rate. This is reflecting the economic conditions and general restaurant industry slowdown. On the other hand, Pei Wei's sales per unit expanded by 2.17 percent in 2009 and were approximately flat in 2010. This sales information (sales per unit, annualization, and per unit sales growth) will be included in our projections.

Section B of Table 6-8 isolates the cost as a percent of sales, historical trends broken out by restaurant brand by line item. This provides significantly more detail than just cost of sales and general and administrative expense. Notice that Bistros are 3 to 5 percent (as a percent of sales) more profitable than Pei Wei.

TABLE 6-8

P. F. Chang's Historical Analysis
($ 000s)

	Bistro			Pei Wei		
	2008	**2009**	**2010**	**2008**	**2009**	**2010**
A. Average sales per unit ($000s)						
Opened before 2008	$ 5,106.8	$ 4,879.4	$ 4,759.1	$ 1,865.1	$ 1,905.7	$ 1,899.0
Opened during 2008	2,433.5	4,286.4	4,030.5	1,129.2	1,633.6	1,639.4
Opened during 2009	–	1,644.0	4,271.3	–	925.6	1,703.1
Opened during 2010	–	–	1,995.5	–	–	1,347.5
Total all units	$ 4,575.8	$ 4,603.4	$ 4,623.0	$ 1,655.7	$ 1,801.7	$ 1,845.7
New units	17	8	4	25	7	2
Sales growth, opened before 2008	n/a	–4.45%	–2.47%	n/a	2.18%	–0.35%
B. General expense analysis, % of sales						
Revenue	100.00%	100.00%	100.00%	100.00%	100.00%	100.00%
Cost of sales	27.17%	26.46%	26.01%	27.22%	26.96%	26.75%
Labor	32.82%	32.50%	33.16%	34.13%	33.30%	32.84%
Operating	16.21%	16.31%	16.47%	17.93%	17.50%	17.80%
Occupancy	5.51%	5.42%	5.65%	6.88%	6.75%	6.84%
Depreciation and amortization	5.55%	5.89%	6.07%	5.82%	5.98%	6.11%
Total restaurant expense	87.26%	86.58%	87.36%	91.98%	90.49%	90.34%
Preopening expense	0.62%	0.31%	0.16%	1.00%	0.36%	0.16%
Restaurant-level operating income	12.12%	13.11%	12.48%	7.02%	9.15%	9.50%

(Continued)

TABLE 6-8

P. F. Chang's Historical Analysis (*Continued*)
($ 000s)

	Bistro			Pei Wei		
	2008	**2009**	**2010**	**2008**	**2009**	**2010**
C. Preopening expense analysis						
Preopening expense ($000s)	$ 5,677.0	$ 2,835.0	$ 1,467.0	$ 2,780.0	$ 1,084.0	$ 509.0
New units opened	17	8	4	25	7	2
Average preopening expense per unit	$ 333.9	$ 354.4	$ 366.8	$ 111.2	$ 154.9	$ 254.5
Management guidance (per unit)			$ 350–$400			$140–$160
D. Capital expenditures ($000s)						
New stores	$48,165.0	$19,633.0	$11,440.0	$17,262.0	$ 5,059.0	$ 2,604.0
Refurbishing and other	17,381.0	16,547.0	14,476.0	1,920.0	5,878.0	5,783.0
Total capital expenditures	$65,546.0	$36,180.0	$25,916.0	$19,182.0	$10,937.0	$ 8,387.0
Average capital per new store	$ 2,833.2	$ 2,454.1	$ 2,860.0	$ 690.5	$ 722.7	$ 1,302.0
Management guidance			$2.5–$2.9 mm			$750–$850
Number of new stores in 2011			6 to 8			n/a

Section C incorporates additional information provided in the PCFB 2010 annual report, an analysis of preopening expense. Using the total annual expense and the number of new restaurants opened, we can estimate an average preopening expense per new unit opened. This leads to a better approach (using the number of new units per year) when forecasting preopening expense instead of preopening expense as a percent of sales. In addition, in this case management provides its own targets of typical preopening expense per unit (Bistros $350,000 to $400,000, whereas Pei Wei typically is only $140,000 to $160,000). Our analysis generally confirms management's estimates except for the two new Pei Wei units opened in 2010.

Finally, section D of Table 6-8 analyzes capital expenditures by each restaurant unit. Thanks to the information provided, we can distinguish between capital expenditures for new stores and refurbishing or other items. We see, on average, that a new Bistro requires between $2.4 and $2.9 million of capital expenditures, which is in line with management's guidance. Pei Wei's, except for 2010, require capital expenditure outlays in line with management's guidance of $750,000 to $850,000. The refurbishing capital has trended downward because normal upgrades have been delayed owing to the economic uncertainty of 2008 through 2010.

Based on this information, we can forecast separate operating income statements for the Bistros and Pei Wei. Table 6-9 illustrates the hypothetical assumptions that will lead to the forecasts in Table 6-10. Both tables are discussed together. The assumptions in Table 6-9 are detailed by both brands. The first three lines of each section list the specific assumptions used to estimate future sales. Management needs to estimate:

- The number of new restaurants
- The expected sales per new restaurant
- The sales growth rate for existing units

There are several approaches that we, as outsiders, could take in forecasting sales, including (1) total number of units times average sales per unit, (2) prior year's sales grown by a total growth rate, (3) even more detailed sales projections based on when the restaurant was opened (2002 to 2010 or pre–2002 in total), or (4) other creative ways. There are additional approaches that management could use, including by restaurant brand by region or even by individual restaurants. However, if this were the case, the "strategic" part of the plan might be diminished because the strategic plan would take on the operating characteristics of a tactical annual budget. In this example, the strategic nature could be defeated by the weight of too many details.

As shown in Table 6-9, restaurant-level expenses are extrapolated from panel B of Table 6-8 and improved as management "tasks" expense reductions each year. Each expense line is targeted, with total restaurant expense falling for Bistros by 0.81 percent of sales and for Pei Wei by 0.84 percent of sales from 2010 to 2015. Preopening expense follows the guidance offered by management for each new unit opened.

TABLE 6-9

P. F. Chang's Assumptions
($ millions)

	Actual		Planned			
	2010	2011	2012	2013	2014	2015
Bistro						
New restaurants opened	4	8	12	14	16	18
Sales per new unit ($ millions)	$ 4.62	$ 4.65	$ 4.67	$ 4.72	$ 4.79	$ 4.89
Existing unit sales growth	−2.47%	0.00%	0.50%	1.00%	1.50%	2.00%
Expenses % sales						
Cost of sales	26.01%	25.90%	25.80%	25.70%	25.60%	25.50%
Labor	33.16%	33.05%	32.95%	32.85%	32.75%	32.65%
Operating	16.47%	16.50%	16.50%	16.50%	16.50%	16.50%
Occupancy	5.65%	5.75%	5.75%	5.75%	5.75%	5.75%
Depreciation and amortization	6.07%	6.15%	6.15%	6.15%	6.15%	6.15%
Total restaurant expense	87.36%	87.35%	87.15%	86.95%	86.75%	86.55%
Preopening expense per unit	$ 0.37	$ 0.37	$ 0.38	$ 0.38	$ 0.39	$ 0.40
Pei Wei						
New restaurants opened	2	15	20	25	30	35
Sales per new unit ($ millions)	$ 1.85	$ 1.85	$ 1.87	$ 1.89	$ 1.90	$ 1.90
Existing unit sales growth	−0.35%	1.00%	2.00%	2.50%	2.50%	3.00%
Expenses % sales						
Cost of sales	26.75%	26.65%	26.50%	26.45%	26.40%	26.35%
Labor	32.84%	32.75%	32.70%	32.65%	32.60%	32.55%
Operating	17.80%	17.75%	17.70%	17.65%	17.65%	17.65%
Occupancy	6.84%	6.80%	6.80%	6.75%	6.75%	6.75%
Depreciation and amortization	6.11%	6.20%	6.20%	6.20%	6.20%	6.20%
Total restaurant expense	90.34%	90.15%	89.90%	89.70%	89.60%	89.50%
Preopening expense per unit	$ 0.26	$ 0.16	$ 0.16	$ 0.16	$ 0.16	$ 0.16

The operating income forecast for each restaurant brand as well as consolidated sales and operating income is provided in Table 6-10. On a consolidated basis, it is estimated that sales and operating income will grow each year. However, as a result of opening a total of 68 Bistros and 125 Pei Wei restaurants, preopening expenses have a significant impact on operating margins, which improve only by 0.13 percentage point from 2010 to 2015 in total.

Our calculation of total sales involves a three-step approach. I will discuss 2015 for Bistros using the assumptions from Table 6-9.

1. *Sales of newly opened stores.* We assumed 18 new Bistros opening in 2015 (or time period t) with average annual sales of $4.89 million. Also, an underlying assumption is that all new restaurants are opened an average of six months (some 10 months and some 2 months but on average 6 months) in their first year. Thus there is only a half a year of sales when the stores are first opened. Given this information, the calculation is New stores opened$_t$ × sales per store$_t$ × 0.5 year, which amounts to 18 × $4.89 million × 0.5 = $44.0 million.

2. *Sales of stores opened in previous year.* The 2014 (or time period $t - 1$) sales annualization process takes place on this line to reflect the full-year impact of sales from stores that were opened in the previous year. As such, our calculation is New stores opened$_{(t-1)}$ × sales per store$_{(t-1)}$ = $76.6 million.

3. *Sales of established stores.* For 2015 (period t), this is calculated as 2014 sales from established stores ($1,071.4 million) and 2014 sales from stores opened in the previous year ($66.1 million) grown by the existing unit sales growth rate (2.0 percent), resulting in 2015 sales of existing stores of $1,160.3 million. In other words, after the initial year of opening and the first full operating year, stores opened two years ago become part of the existing store sales base and will grow at only a modest existing store sales growth.

After we estimate sales for the current year, we project the restaurant expenses by multiplying brand sales by the brand expense assumptions (Table 6-9). This provides the restaurant expense projections for both Bistros and Pei Wei. The final expense item is preopening expense, which is estimated as the preopening expense per unit assumption times the number of new units opened in a given year. Restaurant operating income is sales less restaurant expenses and preopening expenses.

This approach illustrates the planning process. It does stop short of a comprehensive strategic plan because this focuses only on the income statement.

Before discussing a hypothetical comprehensive strategic financial plan for The Hershey Company, it is also interesting to review the level of capital expenditure detail provided by PFCB. Table 6-11 provides some necessary hypothetical assumptions and forecasts to estimate total capital expenditures. Once again, management's decision on how many and what brands of restaurants to open drives a large portion of the capital expenditure forecast. To calculate this, take

TABLE 6-10

P. F. Chang's Projected Operating Income
($ millions)

	Actual		Planned			
	2010	2011	2012	2013	2014	2015
Bistro						
Sales, newly open stores	$ 8.0	$ 18.6	$ 28.0	$ 33.0	$ 38.3	$ 44.0
Sales, stores opened in previous year	34.2	18.6	37.2	56.0	66.1	76.6
Sales, established stores	887.0	929.2	952.5	999.6	1,071.4	1,160.3
Total sales	929.2	966.4	1,017.7	1,088.6	1,175.8	1,280.9
Annual total sales growth	0.42%	4.00%	5.31%	6.97%	8.01%	8.94%
Restaurant expenses						
Cost of sales	241.7	250.3	262.6	279.8	301.0	326.6
Labor	308.1	319.4	335.3	357.6	385.1	418.2
Operating	153.1	159.5	167.9	179.6	194.0	211.4
Occupancy	52.5	55.6	58.5	62.6	67.6	73.7
Depreciation and amortization	56.4	59.4	62.6	67.0	72.3	78.8
Total restaurant expense	811.8	844.2	886.9	946.6	1,020.0	1,108.6
Preopening expense	1.5	3.0	4.6	5.3	6.2	7.2
Bistro operating income	$ 115.9	$ 119.3	$ 126.2	$ 136.7	$ 149.6	$ 165.1
Bistro operating margin	12.47%	12.34%	12.40%	12.56%	12.72%	12.89%

Pei Wei						
Sales, newly open stores	$ 2.7	$ 13.9	$ 18.7	$ 23.6	$ 28.5	$ 33.3
Sales, stores opened in previous year	11.9	3.7	27.8	37.4	47.2	57.0
Sales, established stores	295.5	313.2	323.2	359.8	407.1	467.9
Total sales	310.1	330.8	369.7	420.8	482.8	558.2
Annual total sales growth	2.44%	6.68%	11.76%	13.82%	14.73%	15.62%
Restaurant expenses						
Cost of sales	83.0	88.2	98.0	111.3	127.5	147.1
Labor	101.8	108.3	120.9	137.4	157.4	181.7
Operating	55.2	58.7	65.4	74.3	85.2	98.5
Occupancy	21.2	22.5	25.1	28.4	32.6	37.7
Depreciation and amortization	18.9	20.5	22.9	26.1	29.9	34.6
Total restaurant expense	280.1	298.2	332.4	377.5	432.6	499.6
Preopening expense	0.5	2.4	3.2	4.0	4.8	5.6
Pei Wei operating income	$ 29.5	$ 30.2	$ 34.1	$ 39.3	$ 45.4	$ 53.0
Pei Wei operating margin	9.50%	9.12%	9.23%	9.35%	9.41%	9.50%
Consolidated						
Total sales	$ 1,239.3	$ 1,297.2	$ 1,387.4	$ 1,509.4	$ 1,658.6	$ 1,839.1
Annual total sales growth	0.92%	4.67%	6.95%	8.79%	9.88%	10.88%
Total operating income	$ 145.4	$ 149.5	$ 160.4	$ 176.1	$ 195.0	$ 218.1
Operating margin	11.73%	11.52%	11.56%	11.67%	11.75%	11.86%

TABLE 6-11

P. F. Chang's Capital Expenditures
($ millions)

	Actual		Planned			
	2010	2011	2012	2013	2014	2015
New restaurant assumptions						
Bistro						
Number of new restaurants	4	8	12	14	16	18
Capital expenditures per unit	$ 2.86	$ 2.90	$ 2.93	$ 2.95	$ 2.98	$ 3.00
Pei Wei						
Number of new restaurants	2	15	20	25	30	35
Capital expenditures per unit	$ 1.30	$ 0.75	$ 0.78	$ 0.80	$ 0.83	$ 0.85
Total capital expenditures						
Bistro						
New restaurants	$ 11.4	$ 23.2	$ 35.2	$ 41.3	$ 47.7	$ 54.0
Refurbishing and other	14.5	14.0	15.5	17.0	18.5	20.0
Total Bistro capital expenditures	25.9	37.2	50.7	58.3	66.2	74.0
Pei Wei						
New restaurants	2.6	11.3	15.6	20.0	24.9	29.8
Refurbishing and other	5.8	5.8	6.0	6.2	4.8	4.0
Total Bistro capital expenditures	8.4	17.1	21.6	26.2	29.7	33.8
Shared Services capital expenditures	2.8	2.9	3.0	3.1	3.2	3.3
Total capital ependitures	$ 37.1	$ 57.2	$ 75.3	$ 87.6	$ 99.1	$ 111.1

the number of units to be opened in a year and multiple it by the capital requirement per unit. While this is not extremely difficult, it should be highlighted that Bistros cost over three times the capital amount invested in a new Pei Wei. Management needs to search for an optimal combination of units.

A second capital expenditure decision is also very common in any retail company: How much should we spend on refurbishing and other capital items? This is similar for a nonretailing company because decisions are made for investing in capital for new products, cost savings, capacity expansion, and so on. These assumptions are further detailed on Table 6-11, along with the resulting estimates. Some retailers administrate programs that have units on a five- or seven-year cycle, and every five (or seven) years, the unit gets a major face lift. Sometimes companies plan on rolling out a new look and will go through an intense period of spending to convert all units to this new decor. In this example, we just estimate refurbishing as a steady annual increase for Bistros and a slight trailing off of refurbishing capital for Pei Wei. *Shared services* is another term for corporate capital spending. PFCB almost triples its capital expenditures from 2010 given these estimates.

FORECASTING FINANCIAL STATEMENTS

Chapter 2 discussed the basic financial statements (i.e., income statement, balance sheet, and cash flow statement) and numerous accounting issues surrounding those statements. We discussed and considered financial statements for their rear-view mirror qualities. They showed us where we were. We will use the Chapter 2 principles along with the performance metrics of Chapter 3 to develop forward-looking financial statements. We will use these forward-looking financial statements to anticipate the accounting ramifications that result from implementing our strategic plan successfully. These pro-forma financial statements allow us to establish additional financial performance benchmarks by which to measure first the feasibility of our aspirations and second the success of attaining those objectives.

The financial statement forecasting process has five steps that are discussed below:

1. Frame the projection detail and periods.
2. Develop appropriate assumptions.
3. Calculate the financial statement values.
4. Review the projections for reasonableness.
5. Consider the impact of varying assumptions.

Each of these will be presented below.

Establishing the Financial Forecast Framework

We must first decide the level of detail to which we should create the projected financial statements. An annual budget should be extremely detailed, with every *actual* number having a corresponding *budget* value. Within a strategic plan, the level of detail is flexible. As we saw in Tables 6-2 and 6-3, financial statements can be presented at extremely aggregated levels; conversely, they can be presented on a disaggregated level, as we just saw in Table 6-10. However, it is important to provide enough detail, at a precise enough level, to reasonably reflect anticipated performance and provide a managerial road map.

For many organizations, each division or subsidiary prepares a strategic financial plan. That is, each division prepares a strategic plan that includes an income statement, balance sheet, and cash flow statement. Corporate planning consolidates the divisions' plans along with functional corporate administrative area plans and miscellaneous corporate items (e.g., deferred taxes). The final financial statements parallel the statements as reported in the annual report.

For some organizations, partial income statements underlie each divisional plan for the major SBUs and major products sold. The partial income statements include sales projections offset by the cost of goods sold and any direct brand expenses such as advertising, trade promotions, consumer promotions, and so on. Consolidation of these partial income statements occurs at a divisional level and forms the foundation for the division's forecasted income statement. Balance sheet projections generally are not completed at a product or SBU level but instead are completed at a divisional level. Accounts receivable, inventory, and accounts payable policies often do not change by product because the divisional management implements working capital policies for the division and generally not a specific brand. Additionally, often the division's facilities or capital expenditures are aggregated at a division (not SBU) level.

The following sections depart from this divisional consolidation perspective and develop a corporate-level strategic financial plan that includes projections for the total corporation's sales, expenses, assets, liabilities, equity, and cash flows. In this case, a five-year period is considered. Strategic plans generally tend to be anywhere from 3 to 10 years in duration.

The model contains a page of assumptions (Table 6-12), a set of final financial statements (Tables 6-13, 6-14, and 6-15), and a summary page with performance metrics (Table 6-16). The model includes two years of history (2009–2010) as reference points, five years of projections (2011–2015), and an assumptions/comments column. Tables 6-12 through 6-16 lay out the framework of our financial model. Each financial statement has been slightly modified for illustrative purposes and will be discussed below. The next section discusses the assumptions.

Strategic Assumptions, Objectives, and Performance Standards

A financial plan is driven by the organization's strategic objectives and performance standards targeted by senior management. The objectives manifest themselves as a series of plan assumptions. Numerous objectives and performance standards are established for each financial statement. These objectives are all interrelated and directly support the overall mission, goals, and strategies of the organization. While we use the term *assumption*, for example, to describe a projected performance standard such as inventory turnover, the reader must keep in mind that this specific objective is part of the overall objective of the firm to reduce investment while providing high-quality customer service.

The phrase "*garbage in, garbage out* (GIGO)" describes the importance of using reasonable performance standards as assumptions. It's important to remember that financial plans are a series of projections. The strength of a plan revolves around the quality of the assumptions.

The term "*garbage in, gospel out* (GIGO)" also gets mistakenly applied to a plan. A false sense of precision should not be imputed for any plan. Eight-decimal-place accuracy should not be a feature of any plan.

The performance standards, corporate objectives, and ultimately, the assumptions are derived from a number of sources. As depicted in Table 6-12, a strategic plan incorporates information from many external and internal sources. Senior management ultimately assumes responsibility for all assumptions and projections. Some assumptions involve direct objectives set by senior management with the concurrence of the operating managers. The finance area (i.e., treasury, tax, and accounting departments) assumes responsibility for developing minor and/or technical projections.

Table 6-12 depicts the assumptions and their sources used in preparing this hypothetical strategic financial plan.

Income Statement Objectives and Assumptions

The basis for most important assumptions on the income statement come directly from objectives set by senior management. These assumptions come from observing Hershey's past performance, comparisons with the general movement and levels of the industry group, general economic conditions both nationally and internationally, and the tone set by Hershey's management team. The major assumptions, sales growth and margin improvement are even shared publicly. From this I have created a reasonable set of assumptions to drive the hypothetical planning model.

Technical estimates complete the income statement assumptions. Depreciation expense can be estimated in a variety of ways. In its simplest form, depreciation can be estimated as a percent of sales. While this approach is simple, it does not consider alternative levels of projected capital expenditures. Whether you anticipate capital expenditures of $100 million per year or $500 million per year, depreciation expense remains unchanged when expressed simply as a percent of sales.

A very detailed approach to estimating depreciation expense lies at the other extreme of the continuum. Depreciation is the one expense that can be estimated with certainty given the existing asset base, capital expenditures projections, and estimates of equipment or plant disposals. Each existing asset or anticipated new

TABLE 6-12

The Hershey Company Hypothetical Strategic Plan: Assumptions
($ millions)

	Actual		Projected					Assumptions
	2009	2010	2011	2012	2013	2014	2015	
Income statement								
Sales growth	3.2%	7.0%	5.0%	4.5%	4.0%	3.5%	3.0%	Senior management with sales department input
Cost of sales (exc depr), % Sales	57.8%	53.9%	53.5%	53.2%	53.0%	52.8%	52.8%	Senior management with manufacturing input
Depreciation	$ 182.4	$ 197.1	$ 209.6	$ 232.9	$ 247.9	$ 261.6	$ 276.1	See below
S,M, & A, % Sales	22.8%	25.2%	26.0%	26.5%	26.0%	25.5%	25.0%	Senior management with marketing input
Interest income rate	1.5%	1.0%	1.0%	1.5%	1.5%	2.0%	2.0%	Economic forecast, treasury
Interest expense rate	5.5%	5.7%	6.0%	6.0%	6.0%	6.5%	6.5%	Historical & economic forecast, treasury
Tax rate	35.0%	37.0%	37.0%	37.0%	37.0%	37.0%	37.0%	Tax department
Total shares outstanding	228.0	227.0	227.0	227.0	227.0	227.0	227.0	Finance estimate: no change
Balance sheet								
Accounts receivable turnover	12.91	14.54	14.60	14.70	14.80	14.90	15.00	Operational objective
Inventory turnover	6.24	6.10	5.75	5.80	5.85	5.90	6.00	Operational objective
Change in other current assets	$ (58.4)	$ (4.8)	$ 10.0	$ 15.0	$ 20.0	$ 25.0	$ 30.0	Finance estimate: $ amount of change
Change in goodwill	$ 16.9	$ (47.5)	$ –	$ –	$ –	$ –	$ –	Finance estimate: no change
Change in other assets	$ 37.1	$ (7.6)	$ 20.0	$ 25.0	$ 30.0	$ 35.0	$ 40.0	Finance estimate: $ amount of change

								Description
Accounts payable turnover	11.27	7.92	7.40	7.30	7.20	7.10	7.00	Operational objective
Accrued liabilities turnover	5.56	5.40	5.05	5.00	5.00	5.00	5.00	Operational objective
Other long-term liabilities	9.5%	8.7%	8.5%	8.5%	8.5%	8.5%	8.5%	Finance estimate: % of sales
Cash-flow assumptions								
Capital expenditures	$ 126.3	$ 179.5	$ 350.0	$ 215.0	$ 185.0	$ 190.0	$ 200.0	Senior management with engineering
Short-term debt	$ (458.0)	$ 1.2	$ (24.1)	$ –	$ –	$ –	$ –	Debt repayment schedule, treasury
Long-term debt	$ (8.3)	$ 276.7	$ (261.4)	$ (93.7)	$(250.1)	$ (0.1)	$ (250.1)	Debt repayment schedule, treasury
Cash dividends, payout	60.4%	55.6%	55.0%	54.0%	54.0%	53.0%	53.0%	Treasury estimate
Repurchase of stock	$ 9.3	$ 169.1	$ –	$ –	$ –	$ –	$ –	Senior management with treasury
Historical depr. schedule	$ 182.4	$ 197.1	$ 192.1	$ 187.1	$ 182.1	$ 177.1	$ 172.1	Based on 2010 net, PP&E schedule of depreciation
Average life (years) =	10.0							
2011 Capital expended	$ 350.0	n/a	17.5	35.0	35.0	35.0	35.0	Based on 2011 expenditures
2012 Capital expended	$ 215.0	n/a	n/a	10.8	21.5	21.5	21.5	Based on 2012 expenditures
2013 Capital expended	$ 185.0	n/a	n/a	n/a	9.3	18.5	18.5	Based on 2013 expenditures
2014 Capital expended	$ 190.0	n/a	n/a	n/a	n/a	9.5	19.0	Based on 2014 expenditures
2015 Capital expended	$ 200.0	n/a	n/a	n/a	n/a	n/a	10.0	Based on 2015 expenditures
Total depreciation	$ 182.4	$ 197.1	$ 209.6	$ 232.9	$ 247.9	$ 261.6	$ 276.1	Calculation: Sum of all estimated depreciation

asset has its own underlying depreciation schedule. The detailed depreciation schedules of existing and planned assets can be developed and totaled to estimate a projected depreciation expense. Of course, this assumes that all projected capital expenditures will be fully detailed as to the exact property, plant, or equipment that will be acquired. While projecting a general level of capital expenditures is a reasonable exercise, the specific equipment details are usually unavailable.

Numerous estimation techniques exist between these two extremes (percent of sales and asset-by-asset depreciation schedules). We have chosen a reasonable technique that takes into account the projected level of total capital expenditures without detailing project-by-project depreciation schedules. In fact, the depreciation estimation technique used in this model assumes that all projected capital expenditures are spent acquiring assets with average 10-year lives, with a half-year convention in the first year. This assumption can be adjusted to fit the profile for each specific company/industry.

The process (detailed at the bottom of Table 6-12) starts with the historical depreciation schedule that represents the total depreciation on every depreciable asset held by the firm as of December 31, 2010. At the end of 2010, Hershey had property, plant, and equipment net of $1,437.7 million. The historical depreciation schedule line represents the depreciation for the next five years of that amount. As an analyst working for the company (as an employee or consultant), this schedule is readily available from internal sources with penny accuracy. As an external analyst, you know that the schedule is estimated and reflects declining annual depreciation because some historical assets are fully depreciated each year, resulting in reduced historical depreciation year after year.

Added to this base is an estimate of $17.5 million for anticipated 2011 capital expenditures of $350 million (from the cash flow assumptions), that is, straight-line depreciation assuming a 10-year life of the capital expenditure amounts. However, the half-year convention dictates that half the depreciation is taken in the first year and half the eleventh year of the asset's life because, on average, it is assumed that the expenditures occur at midyear. Thus, only $17.5 million ($350 million/10 years × ¹/₂) is added to the 2011 base level to derive 2011's estimated depreciation expense of $209.6 million. As you can see in Table 6-12, the process continues for 2012, when the historical depreciation schedule ($187.1 million) is augmented for a full year of depreciation on the 2011 capital expenditures ($35.0 million) and half year of depreciation ($10.8 million) on the 2012 capital expenditures for a total depreciation of $232.9 million for 2012. The estimated depreciation expense for 2015 is $276.1 million, assuming the projected capital expenditures. If any of the projections change in an alternative scenario, the depreciation expense needs to be recast.

Interest rates and income tax rates are examples of external assumptions from the finance department. The treasurer has responsibilities for providing interest-rate forecasts. Once again, specific interest rates for every existing debt instrument can be detailed, or as in this case, the interest expense rate can reflect a "blended" weighted average of existing debt instruments and anticipated borrowing rates.

Also, this model's approach distinguishes between the borrowing interest expense rates and interest income rates earned on any corporate savings in cash and equivalents. The interest income rate considers the high-quality, high-liquidity short-term nature of marketable securities, which results in a significantly lower interest rate.

The tax rate is an all-inclusive income tax rate that is projected by the tax department. The rate includes the income tax impact from all governments: federal government, foreign taxing authorities, state revenue departments, and local municipalities.

Finally, the year-end shares outstanding represent shares outstanding from the previous year increased (decreased) by the number of shares issued (repurchased).

Balance Sheet Objectives and Assumptions

Balance sheet assumptions come from two sources: operational objectives and finance/accounting estimates. The operational objectives include performance standards for accounts receivable, inventory, accounts payable, and accrued liabilities. The objectives are listed as year-end turnovers, but they also could be expressed as days outstanding by dividing 365 days in a year by the turnover objective. See Chapter 3 for more information about turnovers and days outstanding. In all cases except inventory which experiences a recovery from a 2011 decline, the objectives represent improving efficiency, effectiveness, and performance. That is, the turnover of assets is increasing, which represents relatively less investment in working capital. Lower turnover in liabilities increases the use of suppliers' cash for investments—once again, less investment in working capital. These objectives are often tied to a specific area's compensation objectives (e.g., receivables manager held responsible for receivables turnover, inventory manager for inventory, etc.).

Assumptions related to miscellaneous assets and liabilities complete the balance sheet and generally are less significant. Numerous refinements can be used to estimate the values or year-to-year changes (dollars or percent) in these miscellaneous items. Other long-term liabilities are estimated as a percent of sales. The projected values and the minimal annual changes remain immaterial throughout the planning period.

Cash Flow Objectives and Assumptions

The cash flow statement assumptions consist of capital investment and financing (including dividends) objectives and requirements. These values come directly from senior management or finance.

The capital expenditure plan often begins with engineering, which accumulates anticipated capital expenditures for new products, new plants, other capacity expansion, cost-reduction projects, and so on. The senior management team oversees the capital investment process and may limit the amount of capital investment. This is called *soft rationing* of capital in contrast to *hard capital rationing*, which is imposed by financial markets. In the example, the initial level of estimated capital expenditures includes $190 million (2011) and $65 million

(2012) for a major capital initiative undertaken by Hershey in 2010. In this base scenario, no business acquisitions have been included. If an organization anticipated acquiring or divesting of businesses, the estimated expenditures or proceeds should be captured in this section as well.

Finally, in conjunction with senior management, treasury supplies assumptions about debt issuance or repayment, cash dividends, and any stock repurchases. The debt repayment may include scheduled (or required) debt repayment. Dividends are estimated as a percent of net income (dividend payout). In the base scenario, stock repurchases are assumed to be zero. If there is excess cash or management wants to recapitalize, outstanding shares can be repurchased.

Once the modeling approach is developed (framework and structure) and management objectives are translated into a series of assumptions, the next step is to calculate the financial statements using the framework and objectives, performance standards, and assumptions.

Calculating the Financial Statements

Tables 6-13 through 6-15 present the statements with calculations noted line by line. Discussed below are four basic calculation approaches using the noted assumptions as well as a lengthier discussion about interest expense and income.

Basic Calculations

1. *Growth.* On the income statement, net sales are estimated as the prior year's sales increased by the assumed growth rate. For example,

$$Sales_t = sales_{(t-1)} \times (1 + growth_t)$$

or

$$Sales_{2011} = sales_{2010} \times (1 + growth_{2011})$$
$$= \$5,671.0 \, (1 + 0.050) = \$5,954.6$$

2. *Percent of sales.* Cost of sales (excluding depreciation) and selling, marketing, and administrative expenses, as well as other long-term liabilities, are projected based on sales and the assumed relationship as a percent of sales:

$$COS_t = sales_t \times percent\ of\ sales\ assumption_t$$

or

$$COS_{2011} = Sales_{2011} \times percent\ of\ sales_{2011}$$
$$= \$5,954.6 \times 0.535 = \$3,185.7$$

Likewise, selling, general, and administrative expenses and other long-term liabilities are estimated using their relationship with sales and the projected sales.

T A B L E 6-13

The Hershey Company Hypothetical Strategic Plan: Income Statement
($ millions)

	Actual		Projected					Calculations
	2009	2010	2011	2012	2013	2014	2015	
Net sales	$5,298.7	$5,671.0	$5,954.6	$6,222.6	$6,471.5	$6,698.0	$6,898.9	Prior-year sales × (1 + g)
Cost of sales (exc depr)	3,063.1	3,058.7	3,185.7	3,310.4	3,429.9	3,536.5	3,642.6	Sales × (assumed % COS)
Depreciation (Depr)	182.4	197.1	209.6	232.9	247.9	261.6	276.1	Assumed depreciation schedule
Selling, marketing, & administrative	1,208.7	1,426.5	1,548.2	1,649.0	1,682.6	1,708.0	1,724.7	Sales × (assumed % SMA)
Restructuring and other one-time	82.9	83.4	–	–	–	–	–	Assumed as $0.0 for 2011–2015
Total costs	4,537.1	4,765.7	4,943.5	5,192.3	5,360.4	5,506.1	5,643.4	Sum of all expenses
Earnings before interest and taxes	761.6	905.3	1,011.1	1,030.3	1,111.1	1,191.9	1,255.5	Sales – total costs
Operating margin	14.4%	16.0%	17.0%	16.6%	17.2%	17.8%	18.2%	EBIT/sales
Interest expense, net	90.5	96.4	100.8	81.4	72.6	56.7	49.0	See discussion in this chapter
Pretax income (PTI)	671.1	808.9	910.3	948.9	1,038.5	1,135.2	1,206.5	EBIT – interest
Provision for in. taxes	235.1	299.1	336.8	351.1	384.2	420.0	446.4	Tax rate × PTI
Net income	$ 436.0	$ 509.8	$ 573.5	$ 597.8	$ 654.3	$ 715.2	$ 760.1	PTI – taxes
Net margin	8.2%	9.0%	9.6%	9.6%	10.1%	10.7%	11.0%	Net income/sales
EPS, basic	$ 1.91	$ 2.25	$ 2.53	$ 2.63	$ 2.88	$ 3.15	$ 3.35	Net income/shares outstanding

TABLE 6-14

The Hershey Company Hypothetical Strategic Plan: Balance Sheet
($ millions)

	Actual			Projected				Calculations
	2009	2010	2011	2012	2013	2014	2015	
Current assets								
Cash and cash equivalents	$ 253.6	$ 884.6	$ 741.6	$ 950.7	$ 1,056.2	$ 1,444.0	$ 1,603.5	Beginning balance + change in cash (CF)
Accounts receivable, trade	410.4	390.1	407.8	423.3	437.3	449.5	459.9	Sales/assumed turnover
Inventories	519.7	533.6	590.5	610.9	628.7	643.7	653.1	(COGS + Deprec)* assumed turnover
Other current assets	201.7	196.9	206.9	221.9	241.9	266.9	296.9	Beginning balance + assumed $ increase
Total current assets	1,385.4	2,005.2	1,946.8	2,206.8	2,364.1	2,804.1	3,013.4	Sum of current assets
Plant, property, and equip, net	1,404.8	1,437.7	1,578.1	1,560.2	1,497.3	1,425.7	1,349.6	Begin balance + capital expend − deprec
Intangibles from business acq.	571.6	524.1	524.1	524.1	524.1	524.1	524.1	Assumed constant
Other assets	313.2	305.7	325.7	350.7	380.7	415.7	455.7	Beginning balance + assumed $ increase
Total assets	$ 3,675.0	$ 4,272.7	$ 4,374.7	$ 4,641.8	$ 4,766.2	$ 5,169.6	$ 5,342.8	Sum of assets
Current liabilities								
Accounts payable	$ 287.9	$ 410.6	$ 458.8	$ 485.4	$ 510.8	$ 534.9	$ 559.8	(COGS + Deprec)* assumed turnover
Accrued liabilities	583.4	602.7	672.3	708.7	735.6	759.6	783.7	(COGS + Deprec)* assumed turnover
Short-term debt	24.1	24.1	–	–	–	–	–	Begin balance + ST debt issuance, repayment
Current portion of LT debt (CPLTD)	15.2	261.4	93.7	250.1	0.1	250.1	–	Assumed next year LT debt repayment
Total current liabilities	910.6	1,298.8	1,224.8	1,444.2	1,246.5	1,544.6	1,343.5	Sum of current liabilities
Long-term debt	1,502.8	1,541.8	1,448.1	1,198.0	1,197.9	947.8	947.8	Begin balance + LTD issuance − CPLTD
Other long-term liabilities	501.3	494.5	506.1	528.9	550.1	569.3	586.4	Assumed % of sales
Total liabilities	2,914.7	3,335.1	3,179.0	3,171.1	2,994.5	3,061.7	2,877.7	Sum of liabilities
Stockholders' equity	760.3	937.6	1,195.7	1,470.7	1,771.7	2,107.9	2,465.1	Begin balance + net inc − dividends
Total liabilities and stockholders' equity	$ 3,675.0	$ 4,272.7	$ 4,374.7	$ 4,641.8	$ 4,766.2	$ 5,169.6	$ 5,342.8	Sum of liabilities and stockholders' equity

* For consistency with chapter 3 metrics, depreciation is once again added back to COGS.

The Hershey Company Hypothetical Strategic Plan: Cash Flow Statement
($ millions)

	Actual			Projected				Calculations
	2009	2010	2011	2012	2013	2014	2015	
Net income	$ 436.0	$ 509.8	$ 573.5	$ 597.8	$ 654.3	$ 715.2	$ 760.1	From income statement
Depreciation	182.4	197.1	209.6	232.9	247.9	261.6	276.1	From income statement
Change in:								
Accounts receivable, trade	46.6	20.3	(17.7)	(15.5)	(14.0)	(12.2)	(10.4)	Calculated change from balance sheet
Inventory	74.0	(13.9)	(56.9)	(20.4)	(17.8)	(15.0)	(9.4)	Calculated change from balance sheet
Other current assets	n/a	n/a	(10.0)	(15.0)	(20.0)	(25.0)	(30.0)	Calculated change from balance sheet
Other assets	n/a	n/a	(20.0)	(25.0)	(30.0)	(35.0)	(40.0)	Calculated change from balance sheet
Accounts payable	37.2	90.5	48.2	26.6	25.4	24.1	24.9	Calculated change from balance sheet
Accrued liabilities	n/a	n/a	69.6	36.4	26.9	24.0	24.1	Calculated change from balance sheet
Other long-term liabilities	n/a	n/a	11.6	22.8	21.2	19.2	17.1	Calculated change from balance sheet
Other assets and liabilities	293.3	13.8	n/a	n/a	n/a	n/a	n/a	Used only for the actual financials
Other, net	(3.8)	83.8	n/a	n/a	n/a	n/a	n/a	Used only for the actual financials
Cash from operating activities	1,065.7	901.4	807.9	840.6	893.9	956.9	1,012.5	Sum of operating sources (uses)

(Continued)

TABLE 6-15

The Hershey Company Hypothetical Strategic Plan: Cash Flow Statement (*Continued*)
($ millions)

	Actual		Projected					Calculations
	2009	2010	2011	2012	2013	2014	2015	
Investment activities								
Capital expenditures	(126.3)	(179.5)	(350.0)	(215.0)	(185.0)	(190.0)	(200.0)	Assumption
Other, net	(24.0)	(19.8)	n/a	n/a	n/a	n/a	n/a	Used only for the actual financials
Cash (used for) investing	(150.3)	(199.3)	(350.0)	(215.0)	(185.0)	(190.0)	(200.0)	Sum of investing sources (uses)
Financing activities								
Change in ST borrowings	(458.0)	1.1	(24.1)	–	–	–	–	Assumption
LT Borrowings	(8.3)	276.6	(261.4)	(93.7)	(250.1)	(0.1)	(250.1)	Assumption: Total LT debt including CPLTD
Cash dividends	(263.4)	(283.4)	(315.4)	(322.8)	(353.3)	(379.0)	(402.9)	Net income × assumed payout %
Repurchase of stock	(9.3)	(169.1)	–	–	–	–	–	Assumption
Other	40.1	103.7	n/a	n/a	n/a	n/a	n/a	Used only for the actual financials
Cash (used for) financing	(698.9)	(71.1)	(600.9)	(416.5)	(603.4)	(379.1)	(653.0)	Sum of financing sources (uses)
Change in cash	$ 216.5	$ 631.0	$ (143.0)	$ 209.1	$ 105.5	$ 387.8	$ 159.5	Sum of all cash sources (uses)

3. *Turnovers.* Receivables, inventory, payables, and accrued liabilities are all expressed in management terms as turnovers based on sales (receivables) or cost of sales:

$$\text{Receivables}_t = \text{sales}_t/\text{receivables turnover assumption}_t$$

or

$$\text{Receivables}_{2011} = \text{sales}_{2011}/\text{turnover}_{2011}$$
$$= \$5,954.6/14.60 = \$407.8$$

Inventory, payables, and accruals would be calculated in a similar fashion except that cost of sales plus depreciation would be used in place of sales.

4. *Changes in.* There are two approaches that highlight the integrative nature of the balance sheet and cash flow statement. One approach, such as accounts receivable, projects the balance sheet item and then reflects the change in the balance sheet item on the cash flow statement. A decrease (increase) in an asset (liability) produces a source of cash. A use of cash is just the opposite.

The other approach is based on an assumed change in the balance sheet item such as other current assets (OCA). This assumption is reflected directly on the cash flow statement and then added to the account on the balance sheet:

$$\text{OCA}_t = \text{OCA}_{(t-1)} + \text{change in OCA}_t$$

or

$$\text{OCA}_{2011} = \text{OCA}_{2010} + \text{change in OCA}_{2011}$$
$$= \$196.9 + \$10.0 = \$206.9$$

Either approach works fine as long as it is coordinated between the balance sheet and cash flow.

5. *Accounting relationships.* There are two additional accounting relationships that are important when projecting the balances of (1) plant, property, and equipment, net (PP&E, net) and (2) stockholders' equity, as discussed in Chapter 2:

2011 Projected Plant, Property, and Equipment, Net		2011 Projected Stockholders' Equity	
2010 PP&E, net	$1,437.7	2010 Stockholders' equity	937.6
From the 2011 cash flow statement:		From the 2011 cash- flow statement:	
+ Capital expenditures	350.0	+ Net income	573.5
− Depreciation	(209.6)	− Dividends	(315.4)
		− Repurchases	(0.0)
Equals:		Equals:	
2011 PP&E, net	$1,578.1	2011 Stockholders' equity	$1,195.7

This provides mechanical linkage between the balance sheet and the other financial statements.

6. *Interest expense (income).* For our example, interest expense or income is calculated based on last year's balances of interest-bearing debt and cash:

Interest expense, net$_t$ = interest expense$_t$ – interest income$_t$
= (interest-bearing debt$_{(t-1)}$ × interest expense rate$_t$) –
(Cash and cash equivalents$_{(t-1)}$ × interest income rate$_t$)

Interest expense, net$_{2011}$ =
(interest-bearing debt$_{2010}$ × interest expense rate$_{2011}$) –
(cash and cash equivalents$_{2010}$ × interest income rate$_{2011}$)
= ($\$1{,}827.3$ × 0.060) – ($\$884.6$ × 0.010)
= $\$109.6$ – $\$8.8$ = $\$100.8$

For 2011, net interest expense is estimated to be $100.8 million, that is, $109.6 million of interest expense offset by $8.8 million of interest income.

Notice that the interest is calculated with the interest-rate assumptions for this year times the balances as of the end of last year (or the first day of this year). There are numerous ways to project interest. This approach assumes that all beginning balances are maintained throughout the period. All debt repayment (issuance) and cash flow occur on the last day of the fiscal year and consequently have no impact on the amount of interest expense (income). This is a less than accurate portrayal of actual cash flow. However, more advanced techniques require the use of iterative (or even circular) logic to zero in on a more exacting projection. For my illustrative purposes, this methodology will be appropriate, but it may need to be strengthened in practice to reflect cash flow throughout the year.

The 2010 interest-bearing debt includes:

Interest-Bearing Debt	2010
Short-term debt	$ 24.1
Current portion of long-term debt	261.4
Long-term debt	1,541.8
Total interest-bearing debt	$1,827.3

7. *Other Calculations.* The provision for income taxes is estimated as the amount of pretax income times the assumed tax rate:

Taxes$_t$ = PTI$_t$ × assumed tax rate$_t$

or

Taxes$_{2011}$ = PTI$_{2011}$ × tax rate$_{2011}$ = $\$910.3$ × 0.370 = $\$336.8$

Earnings per share result from dividing net income by the assumption of average number of shares outstanding. In this Hershey example, the complexity of a dual class of stock has been ignored because common shares and class B shares are considered together. For our purposes, this is fine, but in practice, this would need to be further developed.

Margins and the earnings-per-share (EPS) growth rate are calculated as in Chapter 3:

$$\text{Operating margin} = \text{EBIT/net sales}$$

$$\text{Net margin} = \text{net income/net sales}$$

Totals, subtotals, and other calculations are noted on Tables 6-13 through 6-15.

Financial Statement Summary

Tables 6-12 through 6-15 include a lot of numbers. The amount of numbers and information is overwhelming. To make the process more user friendly, a one-page summary is recommended. The summary (Table 6-16) brings together the financial statements, including a margin and annual growth analysis of the income statement. Also, on the far right-hand side of Table 6-16, annual growth rates for 2010 to 2011, as well as the compound annual growth rate (CAGR) for the five-year period from 2010 to 2015, are noted. Table 6-16 continues to analyze the financial statements using DuPont analysis, a review of Hershey's trend in operating and cash cycle, and a quick check of liquidity by examining the current ratio.

A summary should include all the financial data that the organization feels are necessary and important. From the DuPont analysis (see Chapter 3), the pretax margin improved owing to objectives that reduced the cost of sales, selling, general, and administrative expense, and interest expense. Since the income tax rate is projected at a constant 37.0 percent, the net margin is also improving.

The total asset turnover fell as Hershey became less efficient in the use of its assets. That is, despite the challenges of increasing the receivables and inventory turnover, decreasing the payables and accrued liabilities turnover, and implementing minimum capital expenditures, total asset turnover is declining. Just as we saw in Chapter 3, notice that cash and cash equivalents continue to build until they exceed $1.6 billion (that's billion with a *b*) by 2015! Cash started at an elevated level in 2010 as 20.7 percent of total assets, and by 2015, cash will be 30.0 percent of total assets. This increase is weighing down the total asset turnover.

The impact of an increasing net margin is dampened but not overridden by the decreasing turnover, except for 2012. Return on assets increases ever year after 2012, rising to 14.23 percent by 2015.

Once again, owing to the major buildup of cash, combined with modest debt repayment, the financial leverage (assets/equity) fades from a 2010 level of 4.557 (when every dollar of equity supported almost $4.56 of assets) to a 2015 level of 2.167 (when for every dollar of equity, the corporation has almost $2.17 of assets). This depresses the return on equity by more than 23 percentage points from 2010 (54.37 to 30.84 percent).

TABLE 6-16

The Hershey Company Hypothetical Strategic Plan: Summary and Performance Metrics
($ millions)

| | Actual | | Projected | | | | Growth Rates | |
	2009	2010	2011	2012	2013	2014	2015	10–11	10–15
Net sales	$ 5,298.7	$ 5,671.0	$ 5,954.6	$ 6,222.6	$ 6,471.5	$ 6,698.0	$ 6,898.9	5.00%	4.00%
Annual growth	3.20%	7.03%	5.00%	4.50%	4.00%	3.50%	3.00%		
Operating income (EBIT)	$ 761.6	$ 905.3	$ 1,011.1	$ 1,030.3	$ 1,111.1	$ 1,191.9	$ 1,255.5	11.69%	6.76%
Operating margin	14.37%	15.96%	16.98%	16.56%	17.17%	17.79%	18.20%		
Annual growth	–1.31%	18.87%	11.69%	1.90%	7.84%	7.27%	5.34%		
Net income	$ 436.0	$ 509.8	$ 573.5	$ 597.8	$ 654.3	$ 715.2	$ 760.1	12.50%	8.32%
Net margin	8.23%	8.99%	9.63%	9.61%	10.11%	10.68%	11.02%		
Annual growth	–1.34%	16.93%	12.50%	4.24%	9.44%	9.30%	6.29%		
Earnings per share	$ 1.91	$ 2.25	$ 2.53	$ 2.63	$ 2.88	$ 3.15	$ 3.35	12.50%	8.32%
Cash and cash equivalents	$ 253.6	$ 884.6	$ 741.6	$ 950.7	$ 1,056.2	$ 1,444.0	$ 1,603.5	–16.16%	12.63%
Interest-bearing debt (IBD)	1,542.1	1,827.3	1,541.8	1,448.1	1,198.0	1,197.9	947.8	–15.62%	–12.30%
Total liabilities	2,914.7	3,335.1	3,179.0	3,171.1	2,994.5	3,061.7	2,877.7	–4.68%	–2.91%
Stockholders' equity	760.3	937.6	1,195.7	1,470.7	1,771.7	2,107.9	2,465.1	27.53%	21.33%
Total assets	3,675.0	4,272.7	4,374.7	4,641.8	4,766.2	5,169.6	5,342.8	2.39%	4.57%
Cash from operations	$ 1,065.7	$ 901.4	$ 807.9	$ 840.6	$ 893.9	$ 956.9	$ 1,012.5	–10.37%	2.35%
Cash used for investing	(150.3)	(199.3)	(350.0)	(215.0)	(185.0)	(190.0)	(200.0)	75.61%	0.07%
Cash used for financing	(698.9)	(71.1)	(600.9)	(416.5)	(603.4)	(379.1)	(653.0)	–745.15%	–55.81%
Cash flow	$ 216.5	$ 631.0	$ (143.0)	$ 209.1	$ 105.5	$ 387.8	$ 159.5	–122.66%	–24.05%
Dividends	$ 263.4	$ 283.4	$ 315.4	$ 322.8	$ 353.3	$ 379.0	$ 402.9	11.29%	7.29%

Pretax margin	12.67%	14.26%	15.29%	15.25%	16.05%	16.95%	17.49%
(1 – Tax rate)	0.650	0.630	0.630	0.630	0.630	0.630	0.630
Net margin	8.23%	8.99%	9.63%	9.61%	10.11%	10.68%	11.02%
Total asset turnover	1.442	1.327	1.361	1.341	1.358	1.296	1.291
Return on assets	11.86%	11.93%	13.11%	12.88%	13.73%	13.83%	14.23%
Financial leverage	4.834	4.557	3.659	3.156	2.690	2.453	2.167
Return on equity	57.35%	54.37%	47.96%	40.65%	36.93%	33.93%	30.84%
Days outstanding							
Accounts receivable	28.27	25.11	25.00	24.83	24.66	24.49	24.33
Inventory	58.45	59.82	63.48	62.93	62.39	61.86	60.83
Operating cycle	86.72	84.93	88.48	87.76	87.05	86.35	85.16
Accounts payable	32.38	46.03	49.32	50.00	50.69	51.40	52.14
Cash cycle	54.34	38.90	39.16	37.76	36.36	34.95	33.02
Current ratio	1.521	1.544	1.589	1.528	1.897	1.815	2.243

In this hypothetical strategic plan, Hershey institutes operating objectives for meaningful growth, improving margins, and more aggressive working capital management. These heightened objectives lead to improving income and cash flow generation. However, owing to the buildup in cash and stockholders' equity, turnover and financial leverage decline. This dampens return on assets and reduces return on equity.

Fortunately, this is only a plan! Issues such as these can be addressed and adjusted. Plans can be made to seize opportunities for improving Hershey's performance from this base scenario.

Hershey's working capital management continues to show improvement, as measured by decreasing operating and cash cycles after 2012, while maintaining and improving liquidity, as measured by a solid current ratio.

Performance Objectives

Setting company performance objectives that are linked directly to the company's strategic financial plan is one of many different potential uses of this modeling. By linking the two, the company's future is driven by managers of the firm. Often, two levels of performance targets are set. As a total organization, we are a team, so everyone shares in the team's overriding objective, let's say, return on assets (ROA). In this case, the overall performance target is a return on assets of 13.11 percent for 2011. We are a team, we work toward an ROA of 13.11 percent for 2011, and we all celebrate achieving that milestone.

However, a common extension is to make the managers responsible for their direct impact by assigning specific performance objectives to various managers. The assignments become that manager's performance objectives for the year in many cases, and the manager's bonus is often tied directly to achieving those goals as well as the company goals (Table 6-17).

Attaining a sales level of $5,954.6 million is the primary responsibility of marketing and sales. Achieving the expense objectives is a widely held responsibility shared by many, depending on the nature of the expense. Items on the balance sheet also are the responsibilities of the appropriate areas, such as the inventory manager and production jointly sharing the responsibility for limiting investment in inventory to $590.5 million.

SENSITIVITY ANALYSIS

The one thing we know with absolute certainty is that the strategic financial plan is wrong. Various externalities will find a way to interrupt any long-range plan. It is therefore important to know what is the most impactful. Where must management devote its attention and endure sleepless nights? Through sensitivity analysis, one assumption at a time is adjusted and the results are summarized in Table 6-18.

TABLE 6-17

Performance Monitoring: Return on Assets, 2011
($ millions)

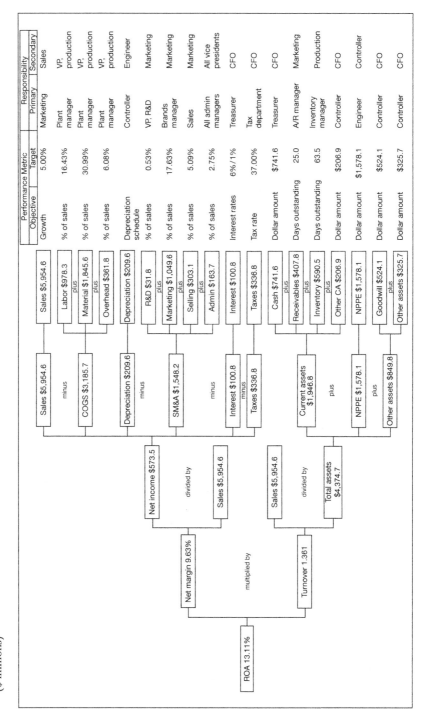

	Performance Metric		Responsibility	
	Objective	Target	Primary	Secondary
Sales $5,954.6	Growth	5.00%	Marketing	Sales
Labor $978.3	% of sales	16.43%	Plant manager	VP, production
Material $1,845.6	% of sales	30.99%	Plant manager	VP, production
Overhead $361.8	% of sales	6.08%	Plant manager	VP, production
Depreciation $209.6	Depreciation schedule		Controller	Engineer
R&D $31.8	% of sales	0.53%	VP, R&D	Marketing
Marketing $1,049.6	% of sales	17.63%	Brands manager	Marketing
Selling $303.1	% of sales	5.09%	Sales	Marketing
Admin $163.7	% of sales	2.75%	All admin managers	All vice presidents
Interest $100.8	Interest rates	6%/1%	Treasurer	CFO
Taxes $336.8	Tax rate	37.00%	Tax department	CFO
Cash $741.6	Dollar amount	$741.6	Treasurer	CFO
Receivables $407.8	Days outstanding	25.0	A/R manager	Marketing
Inventory $590.5	Days outstanding	63.5	Inventory manager	Production
Other CA $206.9	Dollar amount	$206.9	Controller	CFO
NPPE $1,578.1	Dollar amount	$1,578.1	Engineer	Controller
Goodwill $524.1	Dollar amount	$524.1	Controller	CFO
Other assets $325.7	Dollar amount	$325.7	Controller	CFO

Sales $5,954.6 minus COGS $3,185.7 minus Depreciation $209.6 minus SM&A $1,548.2 minus Interest $100.8 minus Taxes $336.8 → Net income $573.5

Net income $573.5 divided by Sales $5,954.6 → Net margin 9.63%

Current assets $1,946.8 plus NPPE $1,578.1 plus Other assets $849.8 → Total assets $4,374.7

Sales $5,954.6 divided by Total assets $4,374.7 → Turnover 1.361

Net margin 9.63% multiplied by Turnover 1.361 → ROA 13.11%

TABLE 6-18

Sensitivity Summary, 2015
($ millions)

Sensitivity Analysis – Adjustments for Each Year

	Base Scenario	+1% Sales Growth	1% COGS Decrease	1% Interest Rate Decrease	1% Tax Rate Decrease	+1 AR Turnover	+1 Inventory Turnover	10% Less Cap Expend.
Sales	$ 6,898.9	$ 7,237.0	$ 6,898.9	$ 6,898.9	$ 6,898.9	$ 6,898.9	$ 6,898.9	$ 6,898.9
Operating income (EBIT)	1,255.5	1,330.5	1,324.5	1,255.5	1,255.5	1,255.5	1,255.5	1,265.8
Net income	760.1	808.2	804.9	758.6	772.4	761.3	761.3	767.6
Cash	1,603.5	1,702.4	1,685.9	1,609.5	1,627.9	1,698.6	1,698.6	1,694.5
Stockholders' equity	2,465.1	2,526.5	2,559.6	2,471.1	2,489.5	2,466.9	2,466.9	2,475.4
Total assets	5,342.8	5,494.1	5,413.7	5,348.8	5,367.2	5,344.6	5,344.6	5,349.6
Net margin	11.02%	11.17%	11.66%	11.00%	11.20%	11.04%	11.04%	11.13%
Asset turnover	1.291	1.317	1.274	1.290	1.285	1.291	1.291	1.290
Return on assets	14.23%	14.71%	14.86%	14.18%	14.39%	14.24%	14.24%	14.35%
Equity multiplier	2.167	2.175	2.115	2.165	2.156	2.167	2.167	2.161
Return on equity	30.84%	31.99%	31.42%	30.70%	31.03%	30.86%	30.86%	31.01%

Changes from Base Scenario

Sensitivity Analysis – Adjustments for Each Year

	Base Scenario	+1% Sales Growth	1% COGS Decrease	1% Interest Rate Decrease	1% Tax Rate Decrease	+1 AR Turnover	+1 Inventory Turnover	10% Less Cap Expend.
Sales	$ 6,898.9	$ 338.1	$ –	$ –	$ –	$ –	$ –	$ –
Operating income (EBIT)	1,255.5	75.0	69.0	–	–	–	–	10.3
Net income	760.1	48.1	44.8	(1.5)	12.3	1.2	1.2	7.5
Cash	1,603.5	98.9	82.4	6.0	24.4	95.1	95.1	91.0
Stockholders' equity	2,465.1	61.4	94.5	6.0	24.4	1.8	1.8	10.3
Total assets	5,342.8	151.3	70.9	6.0	24.4	1.8	1.8	6.8
Net margin	11.02%	0.15%	0.64%	-0.02%	0.18%	0.02%	0.02%	0.11%
Asset turnover	1.291	0.026	(0.017)	(0.001)	(0.006)	–	–	(0.001)
Return on assets	14.23%	0.48%	0.63%	-0.05%	0.16%	0.01%	0.01%	0.12%
Equity multiplier	2.167	0.008	(0.052)	(0.002)	(0.011)	–	–	(0.006)
Return on equity	30.84%	1.15%	0.58%	-0.14%	0.19%	0.02%	0.02%	0.17%

In the table, we examine the effects of changes to seven different assumptions:

- One percentage point increase to sales growth
- One percentage point reduction in cost of sales
- One percentage point interest-rate reduction, interest income, and expense rate
- One percentage point tax-rate reduction from 37 to 36 percent
- One additional accounts receivable turnover
- One additional inventory turnover
- Ten percent reduction in capital expenditures

The assumption adjustments were made individually (one at a time) for all five years, but only 2015 is captured in Table 6-18. The upper portion of the table shows 11 critical financial measures, and the lower portion shows the change from the base scenario.

Growth provides the largest impact, followed closely by cost of sales reduction, at least looking at net income. The change in sales growth is the only factor that affects the level of sales, and only the changes in sales growth, cost reduction, and capital expenditures affect operating income. The adjustments to interest rates, tax rate, and working capital turnovers have little impact on the financial results.

ALTERNATIVE SCENARIOS

From the base strategic financial plan, additional strategies can be explored. Should operations be challenged further? Should sales and marketing be tasked with additional sales growth? Or should the organization consider additional strategies? This analysis is referred to as *scenario analysis* because it identifies the results of multiple assumption changes at one time.

By challenging operations through tasking additional sales growth, improving margins, or enhancing working capital management, the strategic plan will produce additional income and cash flow while improving return on assets and return on equity. By examining alternative "go to business" strategies, management can consider many approaches to accomplish its goals and objectives.

Two often competing scenarios involve a growth scenario (often proposed by the marketing group) and a "cash cow" scenario (often proposed by the CFO). Table 6-19 summarizes the distinctions between the alternative scenario and the cash cow scenario. Notice that the enhanced growth rates found in the growth scenario are facilitated by additional marketing spending. Conversely, within the cash cow scenario, management is willing to live with lower growth rates as long as selling, marketing, and administrative costs are reduced.

TABLE 6-19

Scenario Assumptions: Growth versus Cash Cow

		Projected			
	2011	2012	2013	2014	2015
Sales growth rate					
Base scenario	5.00%	4.50%	4.00%	3.50%	3.00%
Growth scenario	5.50%	6.50%	5.00%	4.00%	3.00%
Incremental	0.50%	2.00%	1.00%	0.50%	0.00%
Cash cow scenario	4.00%	2.50%	3.00%	3.00%	2.50%
Incremental	−1.00%	−2.00%	−1.00%	−0.50%	−0.50%
Selling, marketing, and administrative					
Base scenario	26.00%	26.50%	26.00%	25.50%	25.00%
Growth scenario	27.50%	28.50%	27.00%	25.50%	25.00%
Incremental	1.50%	2.00%	1.00%	0.00%	0.00%
Cash cow scenario	23.50%	24.50%	24.00%	23.50%	23.00%
Incremental	−2.50%	−2.00%	−2.00%	−2.00%	−2.00%

From Table 6-20, both alternative scenarios produce higher projected net income than the base scenario and net income that is similar in each approach. However, the growth scenario develops sales by almost $600 million more than the cash cow. The cash cow gets to 2015 by driving the margin and reaping the rewards of reduced expenses. However, by 2015, there is a sharp contrast in the results of the two business strategies, as reflected in the DuPont analysis. The growth scenario minimally improves both profitability (margins) and effectiveness (turnover). The cash cow starts with a significantly higher margin but not as strong of an asset turnover. Consequently, either scenario leads to approximately the same return on assets. Further, leverage increased (declined) for the growth (cash cow) scenario and caused a return on equity difference of almost 2 percentage points, with the growth scenario showing significant improvement.

The final scenario presented on Table 6-20 considers the impact of a stock-repurchase program. In this case, the base-case assumptions all remain as before except that each year includes a $300 million share repurchase.

A decision for a company to repurchase its outstanding stock is a complicated managerial, business, and economic event. A financial strategic plan assists in understanding the accounting ramifications of a stock-repurchase program. First and foremost, the decision must be a good economic decision.

For our purposes, let's assume that the company developed the base-scenario strategic financial plan discussed earlier. Managers recognized that by the year 2015, they will have over $1.6 billion in cash. If the following are true—(1) operations are stretched, (2) there are no viable substantial acquisition candidates, (3) the current

TABLE 6-20

Scenario Summary 2015
($ millions)

	Base Scenario	Growth Scenario	Cash Cow Scenario	Share Repurchase Scenario
Sales	$ 6,898.9	$ 7,166.7	$ 6,573.7	$ 6,898.9
Operating Income (EBIT)	1,255.5	1,314.9	1,314.7	1,255.5
Net Income	760.1	797.3	798.3	744.8
Cash	1,603.5	1,608.9	1,689.9	87.0
Stockholders' Equity	2,465.1	2,440.7	2,587.6	948.6
Total Assets	5,342.8	5,389.7	5,378.9	3,826.3
Net Margin	11.02%	11.13%	12.14%	10.80%
Asset Turnover	1.291	1.330	1.222	1.803
Return on Assets	14.23%	14.79%	14.84%	19.47%
Equity Multiplier	2.167	2.208	2.079	4.034
Return on Equity	30.84%	32.67%	30.85%	78.52%

	Changes from Base Scenario			
	Base Scenario	Growth Scenario	Cash Cow Scenario	Share Repurchase Scenario
Sales	$ 6,898.9	$ 267.8	$ (325.2)	$ –
Operating Income (EBIT)	1,255.5	59.4	59.2	–
Net Income	760.1	37.2	38.2	(15.3)
Cash	1,603.5	5.4	86.4	(1,516.5)
Stockholders' Equity	2,465.1	(24.4)	122.5	(1,516.5)
Total Assets	5,342.8	46.9	36.1	(1,516.5)
Net Margin	11.02%	0.11%	1.12%	−0.22%
Asset Turnover	1.291	0.039	(0.069)	0.512
Return on Assets	14.23%	0.56%	0.61%	5.24%
Equity Multiplier	2.167	0.041	(0.088)	1.867
Return on Equity	30.84%	1.83%	0.01%	47.68%

stock price is undervalued, and (4) the cash balance is earning only 1.0 percent interest income (0.6 percent after corporate taxes)—the company should consider a share-repurchase program. The economics of the share-repurchase strategy are validated through a self-valuation study found in Chapter 14. The following additional assumptions are made.

With the base scenario in hand, senior management (led by the recommendation of the chief financial officer) can examine a strategy of repurchasing $1.5 billion in shares over this five-year projection period. The results of the repurchase strategy reflect improved performance in the strategic plan. While sales and operating income do not change between the base scenario and the share-repurchase scenario, net income falls owing to "lost" interest income. Cash, stockholders' equity, and total assets all decline by the same $1,516.5 million, which reflects the share-repurchase total of $1,500.0 million and the lost after-tax interest income.

The major impact is once again found via DuPont analysis. While margins are slightly lower (because of the lost interest income), asset turnover is increased significantly and produces a return on assets of almost 19.5 percent (a 5.24 percent improvement over the base scenario). The equity multiplier is significantly stronger as well and results in a return on equity approaching 79 percent (a 47.68 percent improvement over the base scenario).

Working with a strong, supportive, and flexible financial model, analysts can generate multiple scenarios with multiple refinements. The modeling proves a valuable tool enabling senior management to chart the course of the corporation and build the strategies that will support the corporation's objectives, leading to a successful completion of the corporation's mission.

SUMMARY

Figure 6-2 illustrates the annual budgeting process that begins with a direct link to the strategic plan, builds on the identified priorities, and turns the first year of the strategic plan into detailed, actionable budgets used to facilitate and manage implementation and performance monitoring. In addition, most organizations have an integrated forecast or outlook process that updates the anticipated performance of the firm for the remaining portion of the year. This information and actual annual performance serve as a baseline for next year's strategic financial planning.

The value of the strategic planning process:

- Facilitates communication among the senior executives of an organization
- Sets a business direction
- Identifies, clarifies, and prioritizes opportunities and requirements
- Establishes business performance standards and objectives

Today's finance professional and business executive needs to understand the strategic planning process and how a company's objectives are translated into financial plans and performance targets. Whether the company has a long-established track record or is a startup organization in need of financing, an integrated financial business plan that demonstrates the ramifications of implementing objectives and strategies is a requirement.

This chapter provided an overview of the strategic planning process and considered simple models that lead to a strategic financial planning model. The comprehensive strategic financial planning model presented a realistic integrated model and used it to quantify the strategic plan while establishing performance targets. The financial model provided a complete system of financial statements—income statement, balance sheet, and cash flow statement—that functioned as a coordinated management tool.

Also the comprehensive strategic financial planning model is useful to bankers, who ultimately want to know if a company can pay back a loan, how they intend to pay it back, and what happens if the plans do not come to fruition.

THREE

CAPITAL ANALYSIS AND CORPORATE INVESTMENT DECISIONS

THE TIME VALUE OF MONEY

The *time value of money* (TVM) is one of the most fundamental concepts in business and an analytical cornerstone. TVM spans the disciplines of finance, accounting, and economics. The concept is found in the financial analysis of any multiperiod decision. Business decisions such as research and development investment, investment in new products, capital expenditures, lease versus borrow, build versus buy, bond refunding, security valuation, acquisition valuation, financial structure decisions, and the whole concept of the cost of capital are subjects that cannot be understood without knowledge of the TVM, compound interest, and discounted cash flows. The analysis of all multiyear business decisions with any type of financial implication can be handled with only a few basic concepts and the mechanical aspects developed in this chapter.

THE NATURE OF FINANCIAL DECISIONS

This chapter on the time value of money (TVM) is key to the main theme of this book. In earlier chapters we used the concept of compounded annual growth rates (CAGRs) to determine growth of sales, income, assets, and so on over more than one year. Growth is a major source of value, and the analysis of expected future cash flows is the basis of the calculation of value. This theme is implemented throughout the chapters that follow. This chapter discusses the basic mechanics (building blocks) for the analysis of growth and value.

Most of us are already familiar with the concept of TVM. Through personal investments and savings we understand the idea of compound interest or earning interest on the interest. While business decisions may be more involved than our simple personal savings, the fundamentals of TVM are the same.

Many of us also have numerous and various loans outstanding. Whether it's a home mortgage, home equity loan, car loan, school loan, or credit-card loan, the basics of TVM come into play. Many of us are saving for various life events, such as a college education, travel, weddings, or retirement. Each of these savings events requires an understanding of the TVM.

In fact, most decisions we face in our everyday lives, as well as the decisions that confront business firms, involve a comparison of the present with the future, that is, current sacrifices for future benefits. This involves comparing cash flows at different times—present outlays versus future benefits or present consumption versus future payments or forgone future benefits. For example, consider an investment of $1,000 today that pays $1,080 at the end of one year. The return on the investment is 8 percent. If the cost of funds is 10 percent, this is not a good investment because we are not earning the cost of funds. If funds cost 6 percent, we have made a net gain.

Most financial decisions require comparisons of these kinds. Because funds have earning power, $1,000 today is not the same as $1,000 received one year from today. If we have $1,000 today, we can invest it to have more than $1,000 in the future. Financial decisions involve the TVM—decisions across time. Values are determined by the timing of the future cash flows to be received. Funds received next year are worth more than the same amount of funds received in the third or fifth year. This chapter formalizes the concepts of TVM and discounted cash-flow analysis, which represents the fundamental technique for measuring the TVM. Most financial decisions at both the personal and business levels must take into account the TVM. The materials in this chapter therefore are key to this important topic of corporate finance and investment.

TIME VALUE OF MONEY CONCEPTS AND APPLICATIONS

In the following sections, the future value and present values of a single (or lump) sum as well as a stream of periodic cash flows (called an *annuity*) are presented. This leads to a discussion of the case where cash flows change over time as well as extend into perpetuity. We begin with the future value of a single sum and consider five different approaches to solving for the future value of a $1,000 investment. These five approaches include a graphic approach, a mathematical equation, a TVM table, a financial calculator, and Excel (or other spreadsheet). It is recommended that at these early stages the relationships between these approaches all be explored.

Future Value—Single Sum

A person invests $1,000 in a security that pays 8 percent compounded annually. How much will this person have at the end of one year, at the end of two years, and at the end of three years?

Graphs and Equations

Figure 7-1 shows the growth of this $1,000 investment. To treat the matter systematically, let us define the following terms:

P_0 = principal, or beginning amount, at time 0 (i.e., $1,000).

r = rate of return or interest rate (i.e., 8 percent).[1]

$P_0 r$ = total dollar amount of interest earned at r.

$FV_{r,n}$ = future value at end of n periods at r.

---

[1] In this chapter, r represents the rate of return, or interest rate. Later in this chapter, g is used in a similar way to represent growth. In later chapters involving topics such as the cost of capital and valuation, I will use k instead of r. In one sense, k is a particular kind of rate of return or discount factor. In another sense, r and k could be used interchangeably.

FIGURE 7-1

Future value of single sum: graphic.

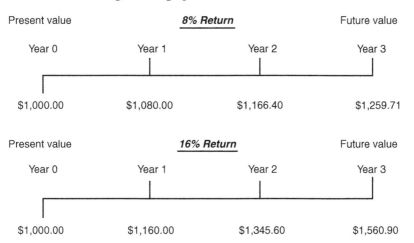

When n equals 1, then $\mathrm{FV}_{r,n}$ can be calculated as shown in Eq. (7.1):

$$\mathrm{FV}_{r,1} = P_0 + P_0 r \tag{7.1}$$
$$= P_0(1 + r)$$

Equation (7.1) shows that the ending amount $\mathrm{FV}_{r,1}$ is equal to the beginning amount P_0 times the factor $1 + r$. In the example, where P_0 is $1,000, r is 8 percent, and n is 1 year, $\mathrm{FV}_{r,n}$ is determined as follows:

$$\mathrm{FV}_{8\ \text{percent, 1 yr}} = \$1,000(1.0 + 0.08) = \$1,000(1.08) = \$1,080$$

The future value is $1,080 at the end of year 1.

An individual leaves $1,000 on deposit for three years; to what amount will it have grown at the end of that period if interest is earned on interest? Equation (7.1) can be used to construct Table 7-1, which shows the answer. Note that $\mathrm{FV}_{r,2}$, the balance at the end of the second year, is found as follows:

$$\mathrm{FV}_{r,2} = \mathrm{FV}_{r,1}(1 + r) = P_0(1 + r)(1 + r) = P_0(1 + r)^2$$
$$= \$1,000(1.08)^2 = \$1,166.40$$

Similarly, $\mathrm{FV}_{r,3}$, the balance after three years, is found as:

$$\mathrm{FV}_{r,3} = \mathrm{FV}_{r,2}(1 + r) = P_0(1 + r)^3$$
$$= \$1,000(1.1)^3 = \$1,259.71$$

In general, $\mathrm{FV}_{r,n}$, the compound amount at the end of any future year n, is found as shown in Eq. (7.2):

$$\mathrm{FV}_{r,n} = P_0(1 + r)^n \tag{7.2}$$

Equation (7.2) is the fundamental equation of compound interest. Equation (7.1) is simply a special case of Equation (7.2) where $n = 1$.

The preceding is straightforward, but some important subtleties need to be spelled out. First, consider simple interest. Under a simple-interest contract, the investor would receive interest of $80 for each of the years. While contracts are sometimes written to provide for simple interest, the powerful logic behind the idea of compound interest is demonstrated by Table 7-1.

If the money is invested for three years and the interest earned each year is left with the financial institution, interest is earned on the interest. As shown by column (2) in Table 7-1, the amount of interest earned under compound interest rises each year. Therefore, the value of the amount at the start of the year on which interest is earned during the year includes the interest earned in previous time periods. In year 2, an additional $6.40 of interest is earned on year 1's interest of $80, and so on. In total, there is $240.00 of interest earned on the original $1,000 over this three-year period, along with $19.71 of *interest on the interest*.

Notice that at an interest rate of 16 percent, the same $1,000 earns a total of $560.90 in interest. Instead of doubling the $259.71 in interest earned at 8 percent to $519.42, at 16 percent, an extra $41.48 is earned ($560.90 less $519.42). As demonstrated in Table 7-1, this is once again from the power of compounding and the fact that more interest is generated initially on which additional interest is earned.

Table 7-1 illustrates how compound interest-rate relationships can be developed on a year-by-year basis. You also could use Eq. (7.2) to calculate what the future value of $1,000 would be at the end of three years, directly, without stepping through each year individually. Any calculator with a y^x function would enable you to quickly calculate the results shown in Table 7-1.

TABLE 7-1

Compound Interest Calculations

Year n	(1) Amount at Start of Year PV	(2) Interest Earned (1) $\times$ r	(3) Amount at End of Year (1) $\times$ (1 + r) $FV_{r,n}$
r = 8% or 0.08			
1	$1,000.00	$ 80.00	$1,080.00
2	1,080.00	86.40	1,166.40
3	1,166.40	93.31	1,259.71
r = 16% or 0.16			
1	$1,000.00	$160.00	$1,160.00
2	1,160.00	185.60	1,345.60
3	1,345.60	215.30	1,560.90

Time Value of Money Tables

Although TVM tables generally are no longer used in practice, they are helpful to illustrate these concepts further and round out this discussion. The same future value of $1,000 at 8 percent interest can be obtained from a TVM table. These tables have been constructed for values of $(1 + r)^n$.

For a given interest rate r and time period n, let the future value interest factor (FVIF) be calculated as shown in Eq. (7.3):

$$\text{FVIF}_{r,n} = (1 + r)^n \tag{7.3}$$

We can rewrite Eq. (7.2) as $\text{FV}_{r,n} = P_0[\text{FVIF}(r, n)]$. It is necessary only to go to an appropriate TVM table to find the proper interest factor. For example, the correct interest factor for the illustration given in Table 7-1 can be found in Table 7-2.

Look down the period column to the three-year row and then across that row to the appropriate number in the 8 percent column to find the interest factor— 1.25971. With this interest factor, the future value of $1,000 after three years is:

$$\text{FV}_{8\text{ percent, 3 yr}} = P_0[\text{FVIF}(8 \text{ percent, 3 yr})] = \$1,000(1.25971) = \$1,259.71$$

This is the same value that was obtained by the other methods.

Equation (7.3) can be used to calculate how the interest factor is related to the interest rate and time, as shown numerically in Table 7-2 and graphically in Figure 7-2.

Figure 7-2 demonstrates the power of compound interest. Notice that the items that are sold at the "dollar store" today will sell for over $2.19 in 20 years if inflation is 4 percent. At 8 percent, the store will need to change its name to the $5 store (actually, $4.66 store). Finally, at 12 percent inflation for 20 years, you will get change back from your $10 bill when you buy an item at the $9.65 store, and you also will get change back from your $20 bill at the $19.46 store with 16% inflation for 20 years. This is the power of compounding!

T A B L E   7-2

Future Value Interest Factors

Period	FVIF$_{r,n}$ = $(1 + r)^n$				
n	0%	4%	8%	12%	16%
1	1.00000	1.04000	1.08000	1.12000	1.16000
2	1.00000	1.08160	1.16640	1.25440	1.34560
3	1.00000	1.12486	1.25971	1.40493	1.56090
4	1.00000	1.16986	1.36049	1.57352	1.81064
5	1.00000	1.21665	1.46933	1.76234	2.10034

FIGURE 7-2

Future value interest factor of $1.

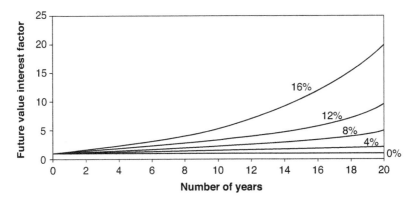

Period			$FVIF_{r,n} = (1 + r)^n$		
n	0%	4%	8%	12%	16%
0	1.0000	1.0000	1.0000	1.0000	1.0000
1	1.0000	1.0400	1.0800	1.1200	1.1600
2	1.0000	1.0816	1.1664	1.2544	1.3456
3	1.0000	1.1249	1.2597	1.4049	1.5609
4	1.0000	1.1699	1.3605	1.5735	1.8106
5	1.0000	1.2167	1.4693	1.7623	2.1003
6	1.0000	1.2653	1.5869	1.9738	2.4364
7	1.0000	1.3159	1.7138	2.2107	2.8262
8	1.0000	1.3686	1.8509	2.4760	3.2784
9	1.0000	1.4233	1.9990	2.7731	3.8030
10	1.0000	1.4802	2.1589	3.1058	4.4114
11	1.0000	1.5395	2.3316	3.4785	5.1173
12	1.0000	1.6010	2.5182	3.8960	5.9360
13	1.0000	1.6651	2.7196	4.3635	6.8858
15	1.0000	1.7317	2.9372	4.8871	7.9875
15	1.0000	1.8009	3.1722	5.4736	9.2655
16	1.0000	1.8730	3.4259	6.1304	10.7480
17	1.0000	1.9479	3.7000	6.8660	12.4677
18	1.0000	2.0258	3.9960	7.6900	14.4625
19	1.0000	2.1068	4.3157	8.6128	16.7765
20	1.0000	2.1911	4.6610	9.6463	19.4608

Notice that at an 8 percent interest rate, the investment doubles in slightly more than about nine years. At 12 percent, it doubles in six years, and at 16 percent, the investment doubles in a little more than four years.

The nature of the compound interest relationships is the basis for the *rule of 72*. While this is labeled a rule, it really is a useful mathematical relationship.

If we divide 72 by the interest rate, we obtain the number of years required for an investment to double. At 8 percent, an investment doubles in approximately nine years; at 4 percent, in about 18 years; at 12 percent, in roughly six years. Or, if we have the number of years, we can use the rule of 72 to calculate the compound interest rate required for an investment to double. If an investment doubles in six years, the interest rate is about 12 percent; in 18 years, roughly 4 percent; in six years, approximately 12 percent. Thus, if we are told that a stock price will double in 10 years, that represents only a 7.2 percent return—relatively modest. If a stock price doubles in three years, that represents a 24 percent rate of return, which is extraordinary. The rule of 72 is a handy rule of thumb.

Using a Financial Calculator
So far we have discussed the concept of future value using graphs, equations and mathematical calculations, and TVM tables. Ultimately, most finance professionals use a financial calculator to answer these questions. A good financial calculator is highly recommended and will help the professional in many ways related to business and personal activities such as loans, investing, and so on. While there are many types of financial calculators, most work in similar ways. The Hewlett Packard 10bIL+ and the Texas Instruments BA II Plus are briefly discussed throughout this chapter. For more information please consult each company's website.

In brief, a financial calculator has five important TVM keys:

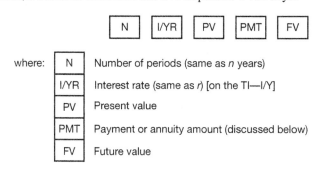

To begin, there are three steps that we must do:

1. *Clear all your calculator's registers.* For the HP, press the second-level button and then the key labeled "Clear All"; for the TI, press the second-level button and then "CLR TVM."

2. *Set the display.* For the HP, push the second-level button (shift key), then the DISP key, and finally the number 4—for four decimal places. For the TI, press the second-level button, then the "FORMAT" key, and "4 ENTER."

3. *Set the number of periods per year to 1.* For the HP, push the second-level button, enter the number 1, and then push the P/YR key. The HP default setting is 12 (months per year), so it is important to change the setting for further discussion throughout this chapter and book. For the TI, the default is 1 period per year. So there is nothing to adjust. However, in the event that the TI calculator does need to be adjusted to 1, press the second-level key, followed by pressing the P/Y key, then press the number 1 and ENTER.

For our purposes of calculating a future value, clear all the calculator's registers by "clearing all," then enter:

3	N
8	I/YR
-1,000	PV

Push 3 and then the N key; push 8 and then the I/YR key; and push -1000 and then the PV key. The present value is entered as a negative number, indicating that it is an outflow.

The final step is to solve for the future value. If you use a TI calculator, you first push the CPT key to tell the calculator to "compute" and then press the FV key. If you use an HP calculator, simply push the FV key. In either case, the calculator displays the answer of $1,259.71.

Excel Functions

Finally, spreadsheet software such as Excel includes functions to calculate the components of the TVM equation. To calculate the future value of a number in Excel, use the "FV" function as "=FV(rate,nper,pmt,PV)". In this example, the entry "=FV(0.08,3,0,-1000)" and the result returns $1,259.71. More will be discussed about annuities or payments below. At this point, "PMT" was set to zero. For more information about the financial functions built into Excel, please refer to Excel, under "Formulas" in the top "ribbon" and then "Financial Functions".

Present Value—Single Sum

The present value concept has numerous applications in finance. Understanding present value provides the *basic foundation* of all investment decisions.

An example will illustrate the relationship between future value, present value, and the basic foundation of investment decisions under certainty. We have the opportunity to invest $1,000 today in an asset that can be sold one year later for $1,100; the applicable market rate of interest is 8 percent. We can analyze the decision using the concepts of future value, present value, and rate of return.

Under future value analysis, we could invest the $1,000 at the market (or financial instrument) interest rate of 8 percent. At the end of the year, we would have:

$$\$1,000(1 + 0.08) = \$1,080$$

But the asset investment under consideration has a year 1 value of $1,100, which is higher than the financial instrument. Thus you should make the investment in the asset. Said differently, that asset investment provides a $100 (or 10 percent) rate of return.

Alternatively, we can use the concept of present value to compare the two investments. Finding present values (or *discounting*) is simply the reverse of compounding, and Eq. (7.2) can readily be transformed into a present value formula by dividing both sides by the discount factor $(1 + r)^n$ and expressing P_0 as $PV_{r,n}$.

Thus, solving for present value, we get:

$$PV_{r,n} = \frac{FV_{r,n}}{(1+r)^n} = FV_{r,n}\left[\frac{1}{(1+r)^n}\right] \tag{7.4}$$

$$= FV_{r,n}\,[(1+r)^{-n}] = FV_{r,n}\,[PVIF\,(r,n)]$$

The subscript zero in the term P_0 indicates the present. Present value quantities can be identified by either P_0 or $PV_{r,n}$ or, more generally, as PV (present value).

For our simple example, the present value of the financial instrument investment is $1,000, whereas the present value of the asset investment is the future value of $1,100 "discounted" at 8% or $1,018.52:
Asset investment:

$$P_0 = \$1,100/1.08 = \$1,018.52 = \$1,100(0.92593)$$

So we should invest in the asset because its present value is $1,018.52, which is greater than our invested amount of $1,000. We can calculate the present value by dividing by 1 plus the interest rate expressed as a decimal or by multiplying the future value by $1/(1 + r) = (1 + r)^{-1}$.

Finally, in this special one-year investment case, we note that the market investment has a rate of return of 8 percent [(FV/PV) -1 = ($1,080/$1,000) $- 1$ = $0.08 = 8$ percent], whereas the asset investment has a return of 10 percent [(FV/PV) $- 1$ = ($1,100/$1,000) $- 1 = 0.10 = 10$ percent]. Later in this chapter, I present more about deriving implied interest rates when the present value and future value are known, but the interest rate is not.

To summarize the three comparisons, we have:

	Market Investment	Asset Investment
Future value	$1,080	$1,100
Present value at market rate	$1,000	$1,019
Rate of return	8%	10%

By all three methods or criteria (i.e., comparison of future values, comparison of present values, and comparison of rates of return), the asset investment is superior to a financial instrument investment at the market rate of 8%. The interrelationship among FV, PV, and r has been illustrated while explaining the basics of present value and its use.

Present Value Equation—Multiple Years

What if the asset investment paid $1,166, but it took two years instead of one. In this case, we are indifferent between a two-year investment that pays $1,166 because it has a present value of $1,000:

$$PV_{r,n} = FV_{r,n}[(1 + r)^{-n}] = \$1166/(1 + 0.08)^2 = \$1,000$$

More generally, to obtain the present value, we divide the future value by $(1 + r)^n$ [or multiply by $(1 + r)^{-n}$].

If the asset did not pay anything for three years and at the end of the three years was worth \$1,200, we would reject the investment because it would only have a present value of \$952.60, today:

$$PV_{r,n} = FV_{r,n}[(1 + r)^{-n}] = \$1200/(1 + 0.08)^3 = \$952.60$$

It would be better to invest our \$1,000 at the market investment rate of 8 percent and have \$1,259.71 at the end of three years.

Present Value Using TVM Tables

Tables have been constructed for the present value interest-rate factors— $(1 + r)^{-n}$ for various rates r and time intervals n. (see Table 7-3.)

For example, to determine the present value of \$1,000 to be received three years from now with a discount factor of 8 percent, look down the 8 percent column in Table 7-3 to the third row. The figure shown there, 0.79383, is the present value interest factor (PVIF) used to determine the present value of \$1,000 payable in three years, discounted at 8 percent.

$$PV_{r,n} = P_0 = FV_{8\text{ percent},3\text{ yr}} [PVIF(8\text{ percent}, 3\text{ yr})]$$
$$= \$1,000(0.79383)$$
$$= \$793.83$$

The present value tells us what a future sum or sums would be worth to us if we had those funds today. It is obtained by discounting the future sum or sums back to the starting point, which is the present. Present value analysis clearly involves discounting projected future cash flows back to the present. It should be understood, however, that the standard practice in finance is to call all compound interest calculations involving present values *discounted cash flow (DCF) analysis*.

T A B L E 7-3

Present Value Interest Factors

Period	PVIF$_{r,n}$ = $(1 + r)^n$				
n	0%	4%	8%	12%	16%
1	1.00000	0.96154	0.92593	0.89286	0.86207
2	1.00000	0.92456	0.85734	0.79719	0.74316
3	1.00000	0.88900	0.79383	0.71178	0.64066
4	1.00000	0.85480	0.73503	0.63552	0.55229
5	1.00000	0.82193	0.68058	0.56743	0.47611

TABLE 7-4

Compound Interest Calculations

Year n	(1) Amount at Start of Year PV	(2) Interest Earned (1) × r	(3) Amount at End of Year (1) × (1 + r) $FV_{r,n}$
r = 8% or 0.08			
1	$ 793.83	$ 63.51	$ 857.34
2	857.34	68.59	925.93
3	925.93	74.07	1,000.00

Said slightly differently, Table 7-4 illustrates further the present value/future value concepts. An initial amount of $793.83 is invested at 8 percent, earning $63.51 the first year and accumulating to $857.34. This amount is reinvested for the second year, earns 8 percent, or $68.59, and grows to $925.93 at the end of year 2. Once again, this amount is reinvested, earns $74.07 (or 8 percent), and becomes $1,000. So you can see that $793.83 today is equivalent to $1,000 in three years if you can earn an 8 percent rate of return.

Present Value Using a Financial Calculator

A financial calculator provides an easy and effective way of calculating a present value. First, clear all the registers, and then enter:

3	N
8	I/Yr
1,000	PV

As a matter of convention, the future value is entered as a positive number, indicating that it is an inflow. The final step is to solve for the present value. If you use a TI calculator, you first push the CPT key to tell the calculator to "compute" and then press the PV key. If you use an HP calculator, simply push the PV key. In either case, the calculator displays the answer of $793.83. (Actually, the display shows −793.83, indicating a $793.83 investment.)

Finally, spreadsheets provide appropriate functions to calculate the present value of a future sum. In this example, the PV works as before. It includes "=PV(rate,nper,pmt,FV)" and would be set as "=PV(0.08,3,0,1000)". This provides an answer of $−793.83 or an investment of that amount.

Annuities

So far I have discussed the concepts of future value and present value for a single (lump sum) outflow or inflow. I next consider annuities.

An *annuity* is defined as a series of same-dollar amounts of payments or receipts for a specified number of periods. The payment or receipt may occur at the end of the year or at the beginning of the year. If it occurs at the end of the year, it is called an *ordinary annuity* (or *annuity paid in arrears* or simply an *annuity*); if the payment or receipt occurs at the beginning of the year, it is called an *annuity due* (or an *annuity paid in advance*). Mortgage payments typically are made at the end of the period; lease payments usually are made at the beginning of the period. For most problems, payments are received at the end of the period, so my emphasis will be on ordinary annuities.

Future Value of an Annuity

One of the best examples of an annuity is an investment that requires the individual (or company) to invest on a periodic (or annual) basis and reap the reward *n* years into the future. Figure 7-3 illustrates a three-year investment in an 8 percent retirement account. Remember, as an annuity, the contract is signed today, but the first deposit does not happen until the end of the year for the next three years. In fact, the first investment of $1,000 grows for the two remaining years at 8 percent, reaching a future value of $1,166.40 at the end of three years. The second-year investment is made at the end of year 2. Consequently, it grows for one year and reaches a value of $1,080.00 at the end of the three-year period. The final cash flow of $1,000 is invested at the end of three years and has no time to accrue interest. The future value of this $1,000 annuity is merely the sum of the future values of the individual annual investments, as illustrated on Figure 7-3, or $3,246.40.

Future Value of an Annuity—Equation
From a conceptual perspective, the future value of an annuity is the sum of the future value of all payments of the annuity, as illustrated in Eq. (7.5):

$$\text{FVA} = \sum_{t}^{N} \text{ANN}(1 + r)^{(N - t)} \tag{7.5}$$

F I G U R E   7-3

Future value of an annuity: graphic.

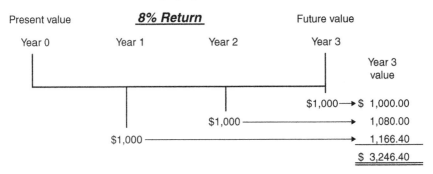

where FV = future value
ANN = annuity = $1,000
r = return = 0.08
N = number of years = 3
t = years = 1, 2, 3

Or

FV = $1,000(1 + 0.08)^2 + $1,000(1 + 0.08)^1 + $1,000(1 + 0.08)^0$

= $1,166.40 + $1,080.00 + $1,000.00 = $3,246.40

Conceptually, Eq. (7.5) is easy to envision and parallels the graphic approach illustrated in Figure 7-3. However, it is awkward in larger calculations. Thus, from a computational perspective and for calculating the future value of an annuity at an interest rate of r and the number of periods reflected in N, denoted by $FVA_{r,N}$, where the rate of geometric growth is $1 + r$, we can write:

$$FVA_{r,N} = ANN\left[\frac{(1+r)^N - 1}{r}\right] \tag{7.6}$$

This can be readily solved with any standard calculator:

$$FVA_{r,N} = \$1,000\left[\frac{(1+0.08)^3 - 1}{0.08}\right] = \$1,000\left(\frac{1.25971 - 1}{0.08}\right) = \$1,000\left(\frac{0.25971}{0.08}\right)$$

$$= \$1,000(3.24640)$$

The resulting value, as we saw before, is $3,246.40.

Future Value of an Annuity—TVM Table

The interest factor in Eq. (7.6) also can be written with an abbreviation in letters, as shown in Eq. (7.6a).

$$FVA_{r,N} = a[FVIFA(r, N)] \tag{7.6a}$$

FVIFA has been given values for various combinations of r and n. To find these, see Table 7-5.

TABLE 7-5

Future Value Interest Factors Annuity

Period	$FVIFA_{r,n} = (1 + r)^N$				
N	0%	4%	8%	12%	16%
1	1.00000	1.00000	1.00000	1.00000	1.00000
2	2.00000	2.04000	2.08000	2.12000	2.16000
3	3.00000	3.12160	3.24640	3.37440	3.50560
4	4.00000	4.24646	4.50611	4.77933	5.06650
5	5.00000	5.41632	5.86660	6.35285	6.87714

To find the answer to the three-year, $1,000 annuity problem, simply refer to Table 7-5. Look down the 8 percent column to the row for the third year, and multiply the annuity amount of $1,000 by this factor of 3.24640, as shown below.

$$FVA_{r,N} = a[FVIFA(r, N)]$$
$$FVA_{8\text{ percent},3\text{ yr}} = \$1,000(3.24640) = \$3,246.40$$

Notice that the FVIFA for the sum of an annuity is always larger than the number of years of the annuity. The reader should verify that the same result can be obtained with a hand calculator using the formula in Eq. (7.6).

Future Value of an Annuity—Financial Calculator

Once again, a financial calculator provides a very effective tool to calculate the future value of an annuity. Before working with TVM keys, it is important to be sure that the calculator is set for annuities occurring at the end of the period and not annuities due at the beginning of the period. Both the HP 10bII+ and the TI BA II Plus come preset that all annuities occur at the end of the period. The "BEGIN" (HP) or "BGN" (TI) annunciator should *not* appear in the display screen. If it does, consult your calculator's user's guide to adjust the setting.

To calculate the future value of an annuity, clear all the calculator's registers, and then enter:

3	N
8	I/YR
-1,000	PMT

Push 3 and then the N key, push 8 and then the I/YR key, and push −1,000 and then the PMT key. The annuity or payment amount is entered as a negative number, indicating that it is an outflow. The final step is to solve for the future value. If you use a TI calculator, you first push the CPT key to tell the calculator to "compute" and then press the FV key. If you use an HP calculator, simply push the FV key. In either case, the calculator displays the answer of $3,246.40. Be sure that you cleared all the registers!

As we saw before, to calculate future value in Excel, use the "FV" function as "=FV(rate,nper,pmt,PV)". In this example, "=FV(0.08,3,−1000,0)" and the result returns $3,246.40. This time, the annuity is entered as "PMT" and PV is zero. In fact, Excel assumes PV is zero. So the PV does not need to be included into the function.

Present Value of an Annuity

Many decisions in finance use the concept of the present value of an annuity. Its basic formulation is used in analyzing investment decisions in capital equipment or financial assets, in valuation calculations, and in many other applications. I start with a simple investment decision. H&N Industries is considering the purchase of a new piece of production equipment for $2,500. The equipment will reduce costs and generate additional cash flows of $1,000 per year for three years. The cash flows are considered available at the end of each year (ordinary annuity); the applicable discount rate is 8 percent. Will H&N gain from the investment? Figure 7-4 demonstrates the investment opportunity.

Clearly, by Figure 7-4, the investment is worth $2,577.10. The analysis is a comparison between the present value of the future cash inflows and the initial investment. The present value of the future cash inflows is $2,577.10. H&N would be willing to pay up to that amount for this new piece of production equipment. The net present value (NPV) of the investment is the present value of benefits less the present value of costs. In our example, the NPV is $2,577.10 − $2,500.00 = $77.10. The investment adds value to the firm, so it should be made. (The NPV concept, which is the basis for value creation, is used throughout this book.)

Present Value of an Annuity—Equation

From a conceptual perspective and as shown in Figure 7-4, the present value of an annuity is the sum of the present values of all annuity payments, as illustrated in Eq. (7.7):

$$\text{PVA} = \sum_{t}^{N} \frac{\text{ANN}}{(1+r)^t} \qquad (7.7)$$

where PV = present value
   ANN = annuity + $1,000
      r = return = 0.08
     N = number of years = 3
     t = years = 1, 2, 3

FIGURE 7-4

Present value of an annuity: graphic.

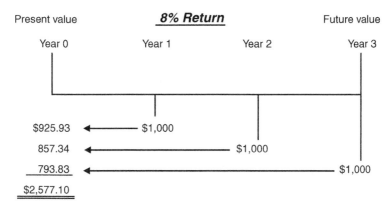

Or

$$PV = \$1{,}000/(1 + 0.08)^1 + \$1{,}000/(1 + 0.08)^2 + \$1{,}000/(1 + 0.08)^3$$
$$= \$925.93 + \$857.34 + \$793.83 = \$2{,}577.10$$

Conceptually, Eq. (7.7) is easy to envision and parallels the graphic approach illustrated in Figure 7-4. However, just as we saw before, when looking at the future value of an annuity, Eq. (7.7) becomes burdensome for longer calculations. Using the background developed in Eq. (7.5) leads to Eq. (7.8), and the present value of an annuity ($PVA_{r,t}$) is expressed as:

$$PVA_{r,N} = ANN\left[\frac{1 - (1 + r)^{-N}}{r}\right] \qquad (7.8)$$

Just as a reminder, the mathematical expression X^y means X times X times X when $y = 3$. The mathematical term X^{-y} means 1 divided by the product of X times X times X when $y = 3$ or simply $1/X^y$. Using PVIFA, the present value of an annuity interest factor, we can write:

$$PVA_{r,N} = aPVIFA_{r,N} \qquad (7.8a)$$

For our simple numerical example, we have:

$$= \$1{,}000\left[\frac{1 - (1.08)^{-3}}{0.08}\right] = \$1{,}000\left[\frac{1 - 0.7938}{0.08}\right] = \$1{,}000\,(2.5771) = \$2{,}577.10$$

Notice that the PVIFA for the present value of an annuity is always less than the number of years of the annuity, whereas the FVIFA for the sum of an annuity is larger than the number of years for which it runs.

Present Value of an Annuity—TVM Table
PVIFA in Eq. (7.8a) has been given values for various combinations of r and t. To find these, see Table 7-6.

TABLE 7-6

Present Value Interest Factors Annuity

Period N	PVIFA$_{r,n}$ = [1 − (1 + r)$^{-N}$]/r				
	0%	4%	8%	12%	16%
1	1.00000	0.96154	0.92593	0.89286	0.86207
2	2.00000	1.88609	1.78326	1.69005	1.60523
3	3.00000	2.77509	2.57710	2.40183	2.24589
4	4.00000	3.62990	3.31213	3.03735	2.79818
5	5.00000	4.45182	3.99271	3.60478	3.27429

To find the answer to the three-year, $1,000 annuity problem, simply refer to Table 7-6. Look down the 8 percent column to the row for the third year, and multiply the factor 2.57710 by $1,000, as shown below.

$$PVA_{r,N} = aPVIFA(r, N)$$

$$PVA_{8 \text{ percent},3 \text{ yr}} = \$100(2.57710) = \$2,577.10$$

As earlier, this same result can be obtained with a hand calculator using the formula in Eq. (7.8).

Present Value of an Annuity—Financial Calculator

A financial calculator can easily assist in the calculation of the present value of an annuity. Remember to check that the "BEGIN" (HP) or "BGN" (TI) annunciator does *not* appear in the display screen. If it does, consult your calculator's user's guide to adjust the setting.

To calculate the present value of an annuity, clear all the calculator's registers, and then enter:

3	N
8	I/YR
1,000	PMT

Push 3 and then the N key, push 8 and then the I/YR key, and push 1,000 and then the PMT key. The final step is to solve for the present value. If you use a TI calculator, push the CPT key to tell the calculator to "compute" and then press the PV key. If you use an HP calculator, simply push the PV key. Either calculator displays the answer of −$2,577.10. The negative value indicates that you should pay $2,577.10 for an investment that returns $1,000 each year for the next three years to earn an 8 percent return.

Finally, to calculate present value in Excel, use the "PV" function as "=PV(rate,nper,pmt,FV)". In this example, "=PV(0.08,3,1000,0)" and the result returns $−2,577.10, indicating that you would pay that much for this investment. Once again, the annuity is entered as "PMT" and FV is zero. Similar to before, Excel assumes that FV is zero, so FV can be ignored.

Any of the fundamental calculation approaches—graphs, equations, tables, financial calculators, or spreadsheets—provides the same result.

ADDITIONAL TVM TOPICS

At this point, the fundamental relationships of TVM have been presented while introducing methods to calculate present values and future values of a single lump sum or of an annuity. The next sections develop additional topics necessary to complete a background in TVM. Topics that will be covered include determining interest rates of lump sums or annuities, valuing unequal annual cash flows, perpetuities or perpetual cash flows, multiple compounding periods within a year, and effective interest rates.

Determining Interest Rates

In many instances, the present values and cash flows associated with a payment stream are known, but the interest rate is not known. Suppose that a bank offers to lend you $1,000 today if you sign a note agreeing to pay the bank $1,259.70 at the end of three years. What rate of interest would you be paying on the loan? To answer this question, you use Eq. (7.2), which I repeat below for easy reference:

$$FV_{r,n} = P_0(1 + r)^n = P_0[FVIF(r, n)]$$

We simply solve for the FVIF and then look up this value in Table 7-2 along the row for the third year:

$$FVIF(r, n) = \frac{FV_{r,3yr}}{P_0} = \frac{\$1,259.71}{\$1,000.00} = 1.25971$$

Using the TVM table (Table 7-2), look across the row for the third year and find the value 1.25971 in the 8 percent column; therefore, the interest rate on the loan is 8 percent.

Precisely the same approach is taken to determine the interest rate implicit in an annuity. For example, suppose that a bank will lend you $2,577.10 if you sign a note in which you agree to pay the bank $1,000 at the end of each of the next three years. What interest rate is the bank charging you? To answer this question, you solve Eq. (7.8a) for PVIFA and then look up the PVIFA in Table 7-6:

$$PVA_{r,t} = aPVIFA_{r,N}$$

$$PVIFA_{r,N} = \frac{PV_{r,3yr}}{a} = \frac{\$2,577.10}{\$1,000.00} = 2.57710$$

Looking across the third-year row of Table 7-6, find the factor 2.57710 under the 8 percent column; therefore, the bank is lending you money at an 8 percent interest rate.

A third illustration of finding "interest rates" involves determining growth rates. One method is the endpoints method. You can calculate growth rates (geometric average) using the future value formula, Eq. (7.2).

For Hershey's revenue stream, the five-year compound annual growth rate (CAGR) from 2005 sales of $4,819.8 million to 2010 sales of $5,671.0 million is 3.31 percent. Substituting these into the formula, we have:

$$\$5,671.0 = \$4,819.8(1 + r)^5$$

$$\left(\frac{\$5,671.0}{\$4,819.8}\right)^{1/5} - 1 = r$$

$$(1.1766)^{(1/5)} - 1 = 1.0331 - 1 = r$$

$$r = 3.31 \text{ percent}$$

This is read as a compound annual growth rate of 3.31 percent or a CAGR of 3.31 percent.

More generally, to calculate the growth rate g or interest rate r, use Eq. (7.9):

$$r = \left(\frac{X_n}{X_0}\right)^{1/n} - 1 = \left(\frac{FV}{PV}\right)^{1/n} - 1 \tag{7.9}$$

where r = CAGR (or geometric average) for the period

X_n = endpoint value = FV

X_0 = beginning value = PV

n = number of periods of growth

A caution must be given when using the endpoints method to determine a CAGR. The CAGR may not reflect the data patterns for the periods between the endpoints.

Using a Financial Calculator to Determine Interest Rates

Building on the earlier discussion and recalling the five TVM keys on a financial calculator, we can easily calculate an unknown interest rate if we know the time period and any two of the three periodic flows (PV, PMT, or FV).

To illustrate the use of a financial calculator, let us review some of the earlier examples:

1. *Bank loan of $1,000 today with a promise to repay $1,259.70 in three years.* To calculate the interest rate when you know the present value, future value, and number of years, begin by clearing all the calculator's registers, and then enter:

3	N
-1,000	PV
1,259.7	FV

The final step is to solve for the interest rate. If you use a TI calculator, first push the CPT key to tell the calculator to "compute," and then press the I/YR key. If you use an HP calculator, simply push the I/YR key. In either case, the calculator displays the answer of 8.00 percent.

Notice that the present value was entered as a negative number. One of the two periodic values must be entered as a negative number to indicate a cash outflow. It is generally customary to assume that the present value amount is entered as the negative value because that's when most investments occur.

2. *Bank loan of $2,577.10 with a three-year annuity repayment of $1,000 per year.* To calculate the interest rate when you know the present value, annuity amount, and number of years, begin by clearing all the calculator's registers, and then enter:

3	N
2,577.1	PV
−1,000	PMT

As with a single sum, the final step is to solve for the interest rate. If you use a TI calculator, first push the CPT key to tell the calculator to "compute," and then press the I/YR key. If you use an HP calculator, simply push the I/YR key. In either case, the calculator displays the answer of 8.00 percent.

Notice, in this case, that the cash flow with the negative sign is the annual payment. The same 8.00 percent could have been obtained if the PV were denoted with a negative sign and the PMT had a positive sign.

3. *Hershey's revenue growth from 2005 ($4,819.8 million) to 2010 ($5,671.0 million).* Begin by clearing all the calculator's registers, and then enter:

5	N
−4819.8	PV
5,671.0	FV

Compute the CAGR by using the I/YR key as earlier. The calculator displays the answer of 3.31 percent. Keep in mind, although this 2005 to 2010 period spans six years, the change is for five years (N): Years 2005 to 2006 = 1 year; years 2006 to 2007 = 2 years; 2007 to 2008 = 3 years; 2008 to 2009 = 4 years; and finally, 2009 to 2010 = 5 years of changes.

Unequal Payments

Thus far I have used constant annual inflows to develop the basic relationships. The concepts can be applied easily to uneven payments by using the simple present value formula. The assumed cash inflows and their present value are shown in Table 7-7. Each inflow is discounted separately and summed eventually.

TABLE 7-7

Present Value of Unequal Inflows

Year n	Cash Inflow	$PVIF_{8\%,n}$	PV of Each Inflow
1	$ 1,000.00	0.92593	$925.93
2	2,000.00	0.85734	1,714.68
3	3,000.00	0.79383	2,381.49
4	4,000.00	0.73503	2,940.12
5	5,000.00	0.68058	3,402.90
Present value of unequal inflows			Σ $11,365.12

This is the same as the process that a financial calculator goes through. The analyst enters each year's cash flow ($0 for year 0) and calculates the present value of those unequal annual cash flows with the touch of a single key, the NPV-key. Please see your calculator's manual for more detailed instructions. Chapter 9 will explore the topic of capital evaluation techniques and specifically net present value (NPV) in much greater detail.

Perpetuities

Some securities carry no maturity date. For example, a company could pay a constant dividend that may continue forever. Or some products, such as Hershey Kisses or Kleenex tissues, seemingly will go on forever. These are *perpetuities*— an annuity that continues forever. The future value of a perpetuity is infinite because the number of periodic payments is infinite. However, the present value of an annuity can be calculated by starting with Eq. (7.10):

$$PVA_{r,t} = a\left[\frac{1-(1+r)^{-n}}{r}\right] \tag{7.10}$$

Notice that the term $(1 + r)^{-n} = 1/(1 + r)^n$ is always less than 1 for positive interest rates. For example, suppose that $r = 8$ percent; then:

$$(1 + r)^{-1} = 0.92593 \quad (1 + r)^{-2} = 0.85734 \quad (1 + r)^{-3} = 0.79383 \quad \cdots$$
$$(1 + r)^{-50} = 0.02132 \quad \cdots \quad (1 + r)^{-100} = 0.00045$$

As the number of years becomes very large (i.e., infinite), the term $(1 + r)^{-n}$ goes to zero. Consequently, if the annuity of constant payments is perpetual, Eq. (7.11) is the final result:

$$PVA_{r,\infty} = a\left(\frac{1}{r}\right) = \frac{a}{r} \tag{7.11}$$

Thus the present value of a perpetuity is the periodic flow a divided by the discount rate. Equation (7.11) is a simple expression with many implications.

This is an easy value to calculate. You do not need a financial calculator to compute this result. However, just to double-check the result using a financial calculator, and because most financial calculators do not have a "perpetuity" key, you can approximate the results by using 1,000 years as N, 8 percent as I/YR, and $1,000 as PMT. The resulting value is almost $12,500. As a perpetuity, though, the value is exactly $12,500.

$$PV = \frac{\$1,000}{0.08} = \$12,500$$

TABLE 7-8

Present Value of an Annuity

Years	Amount Annuity	Interest Rate	PV of Annuity
3	$ 1,000.00	8.0%	$ 2,577.10
10	1,000.00	8.0%	6,710.08
50	1,000.00	8.0%	12,233.48
100	1,000.00	8.0%	12,494.32
200	1,000.00	8.0%	12,500.00*
500	1,000.00	8.0%	12,500.00*
1000	1,000.00	8.0%	12,500.00*
Infinity	1,000.00	8.0%	12,500.00

*PV of an annuity is greater than $12,499.99 but not exactly $12,500.

Table 7-8 demonstrates the present value impact of annuities over various time periods. Notice that at 100 years, the value is approximately the same as the perpetuity value.

If r rises to 10 percent, PV falls to $10,000. If r falls to 6 percent, PV rises to $16,666.67. Accordingly, PV is very sensitive to the size of the discount factor. This is also true for any investment, even if it does not have an infinite life; however, the impact is largest for a perpetuity.

Perpetuity with Growth
A perpetuity that grows over time is a unique type of perpetuity but not an uncommon perpetuity. For example, The Hershey Company paid a dividend of $1.28 per share in 2010. The dividends are expected to grow at 5 percent forever.

The value of a perpetuity with growth can be found using Eq. (7.12):

$$PVA_{r,\infty} = \frac{a_0(1+g)}{(r-g)} \tag{7.12}$$

where a_0 indicates the periodic payment in year 0, and g denotes the underlying growth. Notice that if g is 0, Eqs. (7.11) and (7.12) are equivalent.

Continuing the example, let's have a_0 equal the current dividend D_0 and r (the required rate of return on Hershey stock) equal 8.0 percent. Using Eq. (7.12), we have:

$$PVA_{r,\infty} = \frac{\$1.28(1+0.05)}{(0.08-0.05)} = \frac{\$1.3440}{0.03} = \$44.80$$

Notice that $D_0(1 + g)$ or $\$1.28(1.05)$ which equals $\$1.3440$ or the amount of the expected dividend during the first year, as shown with Eq. (7.13):

$$D_0(1 + g) = D_1 \tag{7.13}$$

Thus, more generally, using a_1 denotes the perpetuity amount at the end of year 1, and Eq. (7.12) can be rewritten simply as Eq. (7.14):

$$PVA_{r,\infty} = \frac{a_1}{(r-g)} \tag{7.14}$$

Using this approach, the value of Hershey's stock should be $44.80, which is a little bit lower but approximates its closing stock price at the end of 2010.

Semiannual and Other Compounding Periods

In all the examples used so far, it has been assumed that returns were received annually. For example, in the section dealing with future values, it was assumed that the funds earned 8 percent a year. However, suppose that the earnings rate had been 8 percent compounded semiannually (i.e., every six months). What would this have meant? Consider the following example.

You invest $1,000 in a security to receive a return of 8 percent compounded semiannually. How much will you have at the end of one year? Since semiannual compounding means that interest is actually paid every six months, this is shown in Table 7-9. Here the annual interest rate is divided by 2, but twice as many compounding periods are used because interest is paid twice a year. Comparing the amount on hand at the end of the second six-month period, $1,081.60, with what would have been on hand under annual compounding, $1,080.00, shows that semiannual compounding is better for the investor. This result occurs because the saver earns interest on interest more frequently. Thus semiannual compounding results in a higher *effective annual rate* (EAR). Notice that at the end of three years (or six semiannual compounding periods), the $1,000 investment would be worth $1,265.32 versus a three-year annual compounded value of $1,259.71.

By market convention, the quoted interest rate is stated as "8 percent with semiannual compounding." The quoted interest rate is also called the *annual percentage rate* (APR). In this example, the APR is 8 percent, but the *effective annual rate* or *yield to maturity* is based on compounding at intervals of six months and, as reflected on Table 7-9, is 8.16 percent.

TABLE 7-9

Future Value with Semiannual Compounding

Year	Period n	(1) Amount at Start of Year PV	(2) Interest Earned (1) $\times r$	(3) Amount at End of Year (1) $\times$ (1 + r) $FV_{r,n}$
	1	$1,000.00	$40.00	$1,040.00
Year 1	2	1,040.00	41.60	1,081.60
	3	1,081.60	43.26	1,124.86
Year 2	4	1,124.86	45.00	1,169.86
	5	1,169.86	46.79	1,216.65
Year 3	6	1,216.65	48.67	1,265.32

Note: The interest rate r is an 8% APR or 4% per period.

Equation (7.15) is a generalization of the procedure for within-the-year compounding, where q is frequency and n is years:

$$FV_{r,n} = P_0 \left(1 + \frac{r}{q}\right)^{nq} \tag{7.15}$$

I extend this simple example for more frequent compounding within the year and illustrate Eq. (7.15). I calculate the future sum for one year for multiple compounding periods within the year for an interest rate of 8 percent and an initial principal of $1,000, as shown in Table 7-10. You can see that daily compounding increases the effective annual interest rate by 0.33 percent.

The prior four TVM tables can be used when compounding occurs more than once a year. Simply divide the APR (or stated nominal) interest rate by the number of times compounding occurs per year, and multiply the years by the number of compounding periods. For example, to find the amount to which $1,000 will grow after two years if semiannual compounding is applied to an 8 percent APR interest rate, divide 8 percent by 2, and multiply the two years by 2. Then look in Table 7-2 under the 4 percent column and in the row for the fourth period, where you will find an interest factor of 1.16986. Multiplying this by the initial $1,000 gives a value of $1,169.86, the amount to which $1,000 will grow in two years at 8 percent compounded semiannually. This compares with $1,166.40 for annual compounding.

The same procedure is applied in all cases covered—compounding, discounting, single payments, and annuities. To illustrate semiannual compounding in calculating the present value of an annuity, for example, consider the case described earlier in the section on the present value of an annuity—$1,000 a year

TABLE 7-10

Effective Annual Rates with Multiple Compounding Periods within the Year

Compounding Period	Calculation	Resulting Value of $1,000	Effective Annual Return	Compounding Periods per Year
Annual	$FV_{r,1} = P_0(1+r)^q$	$1,080.00	8.00%	$(q = 1)$
Semiannual	$= P_0\left(1+\dfrac{r}{2}\right)^2$	1,081.60	8.16%	$(q = 2)$
Quarterly	$= P_0\left(1+\dfrac{r}{4}\right)^4$	1,082.43	8.24%	$(q = 4)$
Monthly	$= P_0\left(1+\dfrac{r}{12}\right)^{12}$	1,083.00	8.30%	$(q = 12)$
Daily	$= P_0\left(1+\dfrac{r}{365}\right)^{365}$	1,083.28	8.33%	$(q = 365)$

for three years discounted at 8 percent. Using a financial calculator, the same logic is applied:

4	I/YR	8% APR / 2 compounding periods
6	N	6 six-month periods in 3 years
–500	PMT	Half the $1,000 annual payment

This results in the same present value of $2,621.07 as calculated earlier.

Continuous Compounding and Discounting

By letting the frequency of compounding q approach infinity, Eq. (7.15) can be modified to the special case of *continuous compounding*. Continuous compounding is extremely useful in theoretical finance but may have limited applications. Thus only a quick mention is appropriate at this time.

When we compound continuously, the result is Eq. (7.16), the equation for continuous compounding:

$$FV_{r,t} = P_0 e^{rt} \qquad (7.16)$$

where e is the constant 2.7183.

As an example, if $t = 3$ years and $r = 8$ percent, the product is 0.24. To use Eq. (7.16) requires a calculator with an e^x key. Both the HP 10bII+ and the TI BA II Plus calculators have an e^x function, so we use Eq. (7.16): Enter 0.24 and push the e^x key to obtain a three-year continuous compounding factor of 1.2712. For annual compounding, the calculation is $(1.08)^3 = 1.2597$. A \$1,000 investment at 8 percent for three years would be worth \$11.50 more with continuous compounding than with annual compounding. For continuous discounting, the terms of Eq. (7.16) need to be rearranged.

Effective Annual Rate

Different types of financial contracts use different compounding periods. Most bonds pay interest semiannually. Some savings accounts pay interest quarterly, but money-market accounts at most financial institutions pay interest daily. Department stores, oil companies, and credit cards also specify a daily rate of interest. In addition, to obtain a home mortgage loan, the lender often uses monthly compounding. To compare the costs of different credit sources, it is necessary to calculate the *effective annual rate* (or the EAR, as it is generally called). The EAR is always compounded once per year.

To calculate EAR, you should recognize that you are simply making another application of Eq. (7.15), where $n = 1$. Remember that r represents the stated interest rate, which is also called the *annual percentage rate* (APR). Equation (7.15) then becomes Eq. (7.17):

$$FV_{r,1} = P_0 \left(1 + \frac{r}{q}\right)^q \qquad (7.17)$$

The effective annual rate (EAR) of interest can be determined as follows:

$$\frac{FV_{r,1}}{P_0} = \left(1 + \frac{r}{q}\right)^q = 1 + EAR$$

Solving for the EAR, you have:

$$EAR = \left(1 + \frac{r}{q}\right)^q - 1 \qquad (7.17a)$$

Revisiting Table 7-10, we have already calculated $1 + EAR$; the EAR in each of the examples was obtained by subtracting 1. For example, with a stated interest rate or APR of 8.00 percent, the EAR rises from 8.16 percent for semiannual compounding to 8.30 percent for monthly compounding.

To help clarify these concepts, most banks offer a menu of savings options such as presented in Table 7-11. The left-hand side shows the stated interest rate

TABLE 7-11

Hypothetical Bank Investment Offerings

Stated Rate (APR)	Investment Instrument	Effective Annual Rate*
0.50%	Statement savings, below $1,000	0.5012%
1.00%	Statement savings, $1,000 to $10,000	1.0050%
1.75%	Statement savings, over $10,000	1.7654%
3.00%	1- to 6-Month certificate of deposit	3.0453%
3.50%	6- to 12-Month certificate of deposit	3.5618%
4.00%	12- to 36-Month certificate of deposit	4.0808%
4.25%	37- to 60-Month certificate of deposit	4.3413%
4.65%	37- to 60-Month certificate of deposit, over $25,000	4.7595%

*The EAR assumes daily compounding: $(1 + APR/365)^{365} - 1$.

or the APR, whereas the right-hand side shows the adjusted interest rate including the compounding, which is the effective annual rate of return. A 4.00 percent APR certificate of deposit yields 4.0808 percent with daily compounding, and so on.

Further, some credit-card companies list their APR as 16.99 percent and then in the fine print and based on daily compounding report the EAR as 18.51 percent. Applying Eq. (7.17a),

$$EAR = \left(1 + \frac{0.1699}{365}\right)^{365} - 1 = 18.51\%$$

In many transactions, and in addition to the highly marketed APR interest rates, government regulations require that the lender provide the borrower with a written statement of the EAR in the transaction. The EAR is the proper rate to compare when reviewing different sources of financing or savings.

SUMMARY

Knowledge of compound interest and present value techniques is essential to an understanding of important aspects of business finance covered in subsequent chapters—capital budgeting, financial structure, security valuation, and other topics. These are also important concepts from a personal perspective—loans, investments, retirement planning, and other topics.

The four basic equations with the notation that will be used throughout this book are repeated below:

$$FV_{r,n} = P_0 FVIF(r, n) = P_0(1 + r)^n \tag{7.2}$$

$$PV_{r,n} = FV_{r,n}PVIF(r, n) = FV_{r,n}(1 + r)^{-n} \tag{7.4}$$

$$FVA_{r,N} = aFVIFA(r, N) = a[(1 + r)^N - 1]/r \tag{7.6}$$

$$PVA_{r,N} = aPVIFA(r, N) = a[1 - (1 + r)^{-N}]/r \tag{7.8}$$

These four equations are fundamental to all TVM analysis and corporate finance.

These TVM formulas can be used for either an even or uneven series of receipts or payments. Some of the many applications of the basic formulas are used to find (1) the annual payments necessary to accumulate a future sum, (2) the annual receipts from a specified annuity, (3) the periodic payments necessary to amortize (pay off) a loan, and (4) the interest rate implicit in a loan contract. These concepts are the foundation for all valuation formulas. The formulas also can be used with more frequent than annual compounding, including semiannual, monthly, daily, and continuous compounding.

The general formula for within-the-year compounding is q frequency, n years:

$$FV_{r,n} = P_0[1 + (r/q)]^{nq} \tag{7.15}$$

The EAR (effective annual rate) is a critical comparative measure for any investment or any borrowing. The EAR is not the same as the stated rate or APR because of the frequency of compounding. The formula for the EAR is given in Eq. (7.17a).

Multiple compounding periods per year result in EARs that are greater than the stated rates (APRs), and the more compounding periods per year, the higher is the EAR.

A perpetuity is a special case of an annuity where the stream of cash flows goes on forever. Their present value is captured by Eq. (7.12), which includes a growth component. A perpetuity with no growth is simply valued as a/r.

As discussed throughout, a financial calculator such as the HP 10bII+ or the TI BA II Plus is a very effective tool to assist in these calculations.

CHAPTER
EIGHT

INTEREST RATES AND VALUATION OF FINANCIAL SECURITIES

This chapter continues to build on the time value of money (TVM) tools developed in Chapter 7 while also providing additional applications centered on valuing bonds (an annuity with a lump-sum maturity) and equity (a perpetuity). Before reaching valuation, additional foundation is offered to better understand the financial system as well as how interest rates (rates of return) are determined.

Within the discussion of fixed-income security valuation (bonds), I will review a loan amortization table and the bond rating process. Within the discussion of the valuation of equity, groundwork is laid for the chapter on the cost of capital (Chapter 11), as well as the strategic valuation found in Chapter 14.

FINANCIAL SYSTEM

The financial system links households and businesses that have cash needs (i.e., investors in physical capital) to the financial sector of the economy, where financial capital is supplied from savers (i.e., other households or businesses with surplus cash; see Figure 8-1). In return, the investors manage the physical asset, generate a cash return, and provide financial returns to the savers. Financial intermediaries, financial markets, and even direct investment play a role in facilitating efficient and effective allocation of financial capital, which ultimately is the goal of the financial system.

Types of Financial Instruments

Savings-surplus units (a *unit* could be a business firm or an individual), whose savings exceed their investment in real assets, own financial assets. Savings-deficit units, whose current savings are less than their investment in real assets, incur financial liabilities.

Although real capital in an economy is represented by things—for example, plants, machinery, and equipment—long-term financial instruments are regarded as ultimately representing claims on the real resources in an economy.

FIGURE 8-1

Overview of the U.S. financial system.

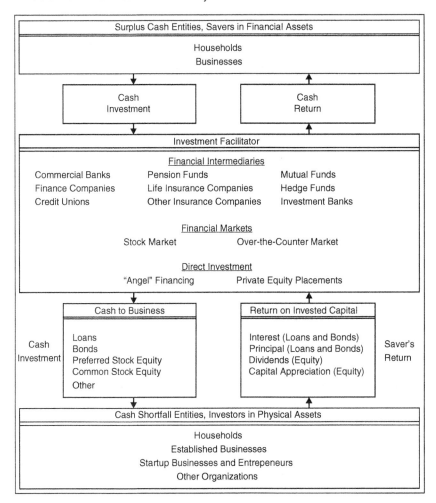

For this reason, the markets in which these instruments are traded are referred to as *capital markets*.

The basic classification of financial instruments involves two major categories: debt and equity claims. Debt or credit instruments represent promises to pay to the creditor specified amounts plus interest at a future date or dates. Different segments of the financial markets are characterized by different maturities. When the financial claims and obligations bought and sold have maturities of less than one year, the transactions constitute *money markets*. If the maturities are more than one year, the markets are referred to as *capital markets*. *Equity* generally means common stock representing the equity or ownership claims on an organization.

The preceding classification covers the two major types of financial instruments. However, variations on these basic types have produced many different kinds of financial instruments proliferating into a complex variety of forms, particularly in recent years with the development of more sophisticated financial modeling, which is referred to as *financial engineering*. Financial engineering has lead to the great variety of financial instruments now observed. These new securities are several different types of building blocks, each of which can have different characteristics and can be combined in many different ways with other securities.

Financial Intermediaries

Financial intermediation brings together, through transactions in the financial markets, the savings-surplus units and the savings-deficit units so that savings can be redistributed into their most productive uses. The specialized business firms whose activities include the creation of financial assets and liabilities are called *financial intermediaries*. Without these intermediaries and the processes of financial intermediation, the allocation of savings into real investment would be limited by whatever the distribution of savings happened to be. With financial intermediation, savings are transferred to economic units that have opportunities for profitable investment. In the process, real resources are allocated more effectively, and real output for the economy as a whole is increased.

The major types of financial intermediaries are listed in Figure 8-1. Commercial banks are defined by their ability to accept demand deposits subject to transfer by depositors' checks (physical and electronic). Commercial banks facilitate many household financial activities—both for savers (e.g., certificates of deposit, savings accounts, etc.) and for investors (e.g.,mortgages, home equity loans, auto loans, school loans, etc.)—as well as small to medium-sized businesses. Finance companies are business firms whose main activity is making loans to other business firms and to individuals. Credit unions are formed by large corporations or other organizations for the benefit of their employees or members. Credit unions provide the financial capital and share the earnings among all members while often providing attractive borrowing rates to their members.

Pension funds collect vast amounts of contributions from employees and/or employers and then disburse those sums as financial resources on a member's retirement. Life insurance companies sell financial protection against the loss of income from premature death or disability. Other insurance companies sell a variety of financial protections for various life events such as home insurance (e.g., financial loss owing to fire), auto insurance (e.g., financial loss owing to an automobile accident), health insurance (e.g., financial loss owing to medical expenses), and so on. In all these cases, the pension fund or insurance company has control over large sums of financial resources for a number of years.

Mutual funds sell shares to investors and use the proceeds to purchase existing financial securities. Often hedge funds are established as private investment partnerships that are open to only a few investors and require large initial minimum investments.

Investment bankers are financial firms that buy new issues of securities from business firms at a guaranteed, agreed-on price and seek immediately to resell the securities to other investors. Related financial firms that function simply as agents linking buyers and sellers are called *investment brokers*. Investment dealers are those who purchase for their own account from sellers and ultimately resell to other buyers. While investment bankers operate in the new issues market, brokers and dealers engage in transactions of securities that have already been issued.

Financial Markets

One basis for classifying securities markets is the distinction between *primary markets*, in which stocks and bonds are sold initially, and *secondary markets*, in which stocks and bonds are traded subsequently. Initial sales of securities are made by investment banking firms that purchase the securities from the issuing firms and sell them through an underwriting syndicate or group. Subsequent transactions take place in organized securities or less formal markets.

Financial markets, such as the New York Stock Exchange (NYSE), the American Stock Exchange (ASE), regional and international stock exchanges, and the over-the-counter (OTC) exchange, were developed to facilitate transactions of seasoned offerings. In this way, liquidity is provided for anyone who holds financial assets.

While the other exchanges started with a physical presence, the OTC exchange was an electronic trading system that is referred to as the National Association of Securities Dealers Automated Quotation (NASDAQ) system. Today, even though most of the exchanges have maintained a physical presence, almost all trading takes place electronically. Certain exchanges still favor their original clientele:

- NYSE (now NYSE Euronext)—large, prestigious companies
- Regional exchanges—an area's regional businesses
- International exchanges—various countries' businesses
- NASDAQ—younger, often smaller, high-tech, pharmaceutical, or research and development (R&D) firms

The exchanges operate as auction markets; the trading process is achieved through agents making transactions at one geographically centralized exchange location. On an exchange, firms known as *specialists* are responsible for matching buy and sell orders and for maintaining an orderly market in a particular security. In contrast, the OTC market is a dealer market; that is, business is conducted across the world by broker-dealers known as *market makers*, who stand ready to buy and sell securities in a manner similar to wholesale suppliers of goods or merchandise. The exchanges are used to match buy and sell orders that come in more or less simultaneously. However, if a stock is traded less frequently (perhaps because it is a new or a small firm), matching buy and sell orders may require an extended period of time. To avoid this problem, some broker-dealer firms maintain an inventory of stocks. They buy when individual investors want to sell and sell when investors want to buy. At one time, these securities were kept in a safe; when they were bought and sold, they literally were passed over the counter.

The *third market* refers to these transactions from dealer accounts in the OTC market. Unlisted stocks will be handled only in the OTC market, but listed stocks also may be involved in these transactions. They also can include trades of large blocks of listed stocks off the floor of the exchange, with a brokerage house acting as intermediary between two institutional investors.

The *fourth market* refers to direct transfers of blocks of stock among institutional investors without an intermediary broker.

Direct Investment

The concept of private capital markets (direct investment) embraces several types of activities. These include private equity firms and hedge funds. They are sometimes referred to as *financial buyers*. Private equity funds generally are organized as limited partnerships, controlled by a small number of general partners. Financing is obtained from pension funds, financial institutions, and wealthy individuals who become passive limited partners in the fund. Private equity funds and other venture-capital sources have been important in raising capital for new firms, which I discuss further in the chapter (chapter 12) on long-term financing sources.

A related financial activity is a hedge fund, generally organized as a partnership similar to private equity. A hedge fund can have a variety of investment strategies, including direct investment in a firm.

In general, *private capital markets* refer to companies and other investments not traded in public markets. Valuation and transactions do not have publicly traded prices to inform them. Business firms (privately owned) with annual sales of less than $250 million are referred to as being in the *middle market*.

Whether funds are secured through an exchange or from a private investor, it is important to appreciate how interest rates are determined.

INTEREST RATES AND MATURITY: TERM-STRUCTURE PATTERNS

Figure 8-2 shows monthly U.S. interest rates from 1954. It compares short-term rates (one-year U.S. Treasury bonds) and long-term rates (10-year U.S. Treasury bonds).

A few points are immediately striking:

- Interest rates have been volatile over the past 57 years. Both rates started low in the 1950s, peaked in the late 1970s and early 1980s, and trended downward since. Of course, even the general trend has been disrupted by volatility.

FIGURE 8-2

Historical interest rates, 1954–2011.

The data are from January 1 of the noted year. *Source*: FRED, Federal Reserve Economic Data, Federal Reserve Bank of St. Louis: *Interest Rates*; http://research.stlouisfed.org/fred2/categories/115; accessed February 22, 2011.

——1-Year US Treasury Bond   ——10-Year US Treasury Bond

- Generally, long-term rates exceeded short-term rates. This is the case in over 80 percent of the 685 months (1954–2011) in Figure 8-2. Long-term rates were 0.89 percent higher than short-term rates. This is also said as 89 basis points higher. The differential ranged from 3.40 to –3.07 percent.

- Additional analysis of the differential is found in Table 8-1, panel A. Most of the observations (264, or 38.55 percent) were found in the differential range of 0.00 to 1.00 percent. However, in 285 months (41.60 percent), long-term rates exceeded short-term rates by a differential of between 1.01 and 3.40 percent.

In addition to the comparison provided by Figure 8-2, additional analysis comparing the 10-year U.S. Treasury bond and the 20-year U.S. Treasury bond is found in Table 8-1, panel B.

- The range of the difference between 20-year long-term rates and 10-year long-term rates is much more narrow: 1.06 to –0.87 percent differential.

- The average differential was only 21 basis points (0.21 percent).

- Over 500 observations (almost 74 percent) fell between 0.00 and 1.00 percent.

TABLE 8-1

Comparison of Short- and Long-Term Interest Rates
(1-Year, 10-Year, and 20-Year Maturities, 1954–2011)

Differential (Longer-term less Shorter-term)	A. 10-Year vs. 1-Year		B. 20-Year vs. 10-Year	
	Number	% of total	Number	% of total
Greater than 3.00%	28	4.09%	0	0.00%
2.00% to 3.00%	81	11.82%	0	0.00%
1.00% to 2.00%	176	25.69%	5	0.73%
0.00% to 1.00%	264	38.55%	506	73.87%
(1.00%) to 0.00%	107	15.62%	174	25.40%
(2.00%) to (1.00%)	25	3.65%	0	0.00%
Less than (2.00%)	4	0.58%	0	0.00%
Total	685	100.00%	685	100.00%

Another view of interest rates is provided at a moment in time across all maturities using a graph that is referred to as the *yield curve*.

Yield Curve

A yield curve demonstrates interest rates over all maturities of U.S. government bonds at a given moment in time. This is also referred to as the *term structure of interest rates* and is illustrated for specific days in 1981, 1985, 1990, 1995, and 2000 in Figure 8-3.

In 1981, the yield curve was "downward sloping," or long-term rates were lower than short-term rates, as we saw in Figure 8-2. Also, as we saw in Figure 8-2, 1981 was a time when interest rates were at their highest level. The 1981 yield curve shows that short-term U.S. Treasury Bills rates were over 15 percent, the five year rates on U.S. Treasury Notes were about 13 percent, and 20 year rates (U.S. Bonds) were just over 12 percent.

But interest rates change over time. By 1985, short-term rates dropped to 8 percent, whereas long-term rates were just under 12 percent. The 1985 yield curve also shows the more common upward-sloping term structure. By 1990, long-term rates fell to the same level as short-term rates at 8 percent. This is referred to as a *flat yield curve*. By 1995, short-term rates fell to 6 percent, whereas long-term rates remained at just under 8 percent. In 2000, short-term rates were under 6 percent, and long-term rates were just shy of 7.00 percent.

Figure 8-4 updates yield curves since 2000, a decade of interest-rate volatility and changes. Notice that by 2004, short-term rates dropped below 1 percent, and long-term rates fell to 5 percent. By 2007, short-term rates increased even to

FIGURE 8-3

Selected yield curves, 1981–2000.

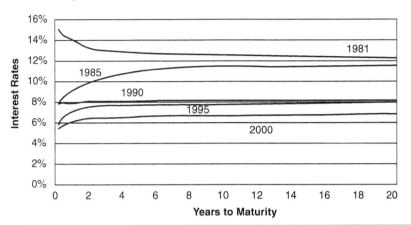

The data are from January 1 of the noted year. *Source:* FRED, Federal Reserve Economic Data, Federal Reserve Bank of St. Louis: *Interest Rates;* http://research.stlouisfed. org/fred2/categories/115; accessed February 22, 2011.

FIGURE 8-4

Selected yield curves, 2000–2011.

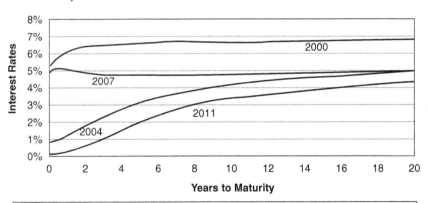

The data are from January 1 of the noted year. *Source:* FRED, Federal Reserve Economic Data, Federal Reserve Bank of St. Louis: *Interest Rates;* http://research.stlouisfed.org/fred2/categories/115; accessed February 22, 2011.

the point where some short-term rates were greater than long-term rates. In fact, the first 18 months of the 2007 yield curve contain a "hump." Finally, in 2011 (and even for months before), short-term rates were less than 50 basis points, whereas long-term rates were just over 4 percent.

HOW THE MARKET DETERMINES INTEREST RATES

Three theories have been advanced to explain the term structure—the relationship between short- and long-term interest rates: the liquidity preference theory, the market segmentation theory, and the expectations theory. We consider each in turn.

Liquidity Preference Theory

The *liquidity preference theory* considers three components of the yield curve: the liquidity preference component itself, expected inflation, and a risk premium. Liquidity preference holds that long-term bonds must yield more than short-term bonds for two reasons. First, in a world of uncertainty, savers will, in general, prefer to hold short-term financial securities because they are more liquid; short-term securities can be converted to cash without losing principal. Savers prefer to be liquid, prefer to hold onto their purchasing power, and therefore will accept lower yields on short-term securities. Second, borrowers (who are also investors in real assets) react exactly the opposite from savers—business borrowers generally prefer long-term debt because short-term debt subjects a firm to greater dangers of having to roll over debt under adverse conditions. Accordingly, firms are willing to pay a higher interest rate, other things held equal, for long-term funds. This satisfies the investor's basic need of a higher return to be in a less liquid position, as illustrated in Figure 8-5.

FIGURE 8-5

Liquidity preference.

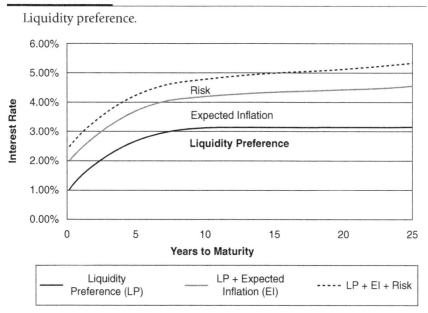

The next component is related to expected inflation. Investors want to maintain their purchasing power and consequently want to be rewarded through a higher return for expected inflation. Returning to the 1981 yield curve in Figure 8-3, inflation was expected to be very high in the early periods, which gave rise to a downward-sloping yield curve. By 1985, short-term expectations of inflation moderated, but in general, there was still a strong degree of expected inflation built through all maturities of the yield curve. Steadily, expectations of future inflation declined to the point of the 2000 yield curve.

The final component of the liquidity preference theory is a level of return commensurate with the underlying risk—the addition of a risk premium. The higher the risk, the larger is the risk premium.

Equation (8.1) shows that interest rates are a function of these three components:

$$\text{Nominal rate of return} = f\,[E(\text{liquidity premium}),$$
$$E(\text{inflation}), E(\text{risk premium})] \qquad (8.1)$$

Note that each term on the right-hand side is preceded by an expectations operator E. For example, $E(\text{inflation})$ is the market's estimate of expected future inflation. Investors try to estimate what inflation will be, and consequently, the market rates of return on securities with different lives will reflect the market's expectation of inflation over the life of the asset.

The expected risk of a corporate bond is assessed by credit rating agencies such as Moody's Investors Service (Moody's), Standard & Poor's Corporation (S&P), and Fitch Ratings. The rating agencies are independent organizations with no ties to commercial banks, investment bankers, or other financial institutions.

Bond Ratings and the Cost of Debt

Bond ratings seek to measure the default risks of bonds. Simply put: The higher the probability of default, the lower is the probable recovery of the principal. And the lower the probable recovery of the principal, the higher is the required yield on a debt instrument. Bond ratings examine a company's financial conditions, its general business conditions, and the overall economic conditions. Based on an agency's perspective of the capacity or vulnerability of the borrower, a bond is rated.

The S&P ratings scale ranges from AAA to D with eight major intermediate categories. Some of those major categories are further refined with a plus (+) or minus (–) to indicate the relative strength within the major rating category. Comparative ratings are shown in Table 8-2.

Another reason why bond ratings are significant is that insurance companies, banks, and other financial institutions are only permitted by law to purchase a limited amount of below-investment-grade bonds. Bonds with a rating at or below BB by S&P do not qualify as investment-grade debt. The inability for a bond issuer to achieve investment grade will reduce the breadth of the available funds market as well as increase the required interest yields.

T A B L E 8-2

Standard & Poor's Ratings

Grade	Rating	Qualities
Investment grade	AAA	Extremely strong capacity to meet financial commitments.
	AA	Very strong capacity to meet financial commitments.
	A	Strong capacity to meet financial commitments, but somewhat susceptible to adverse economic conditions and changes in circumstances
	BBB	Adequate capacity to meet financial commitments, but more subject to adverse economic conditions.
	BBB–	Considered lowest investment grade by market participants.
Speculative grade	BB+	Considered highest speculative grade by market participants.
	BB	Less vulnerable in the near-term but faces major ongoing uncertainities to adverse business, financial, and economic conditions.
	B	Currently vulnerable and dependent on favorable business, financial, and economic conditions to meet financial commitments.
	CCC	More vulnerable to adverse business, financial, and economic conditions but currently has the capacity to meet financial commitments.
	CC	Currently highly vulnerable
	C	A bankruptcy petition has been filed or similar action taken, but payments of financial commitments are continued.
	D	Payments default on financial commitments

Source: Guide To Rating Performance Essentials, Standard & Poor's, "General Summary of the Opinions Reflected by Standard & Poor's," August 12, 2010, p. 10. Reproduced by permission of Standard and Poor's Financial Services.

T A B L E 8-3

Global Corporate Average Cumulative Default Rates, 1981–2009
(% of Total Bonds Rated by Category at the Beginning of Year 1)

Original Rating	Years After Issuance (% Defaulted)									
	1	2	3	4	5	6	7	8	9	10
AAA	0.00	0.03	0.14	0.26	0.39	0.51	0.58	0.68	0.74	0.82
BBB	0.26	0.72	1.23	1.86	2.53	3.20	3.80	4.40	5.00	5.60
CCC to C	27.98	36.95	42.40	45.57	48.05	49.19	50.26	51.09	52.44	53.41

Source: "Guide to Rating Performance," Standard & Poor's, "Global Corporate Average Cumulative Default Rates 1981–2009 (%)", August 12, 2010, p.11. Reproduced by permission of Standard and Poor's Financial Services.

Importance of Bond Ratings

The lower the bond rating, the higher is the possibility of default over time. Table 8-3 reflects the default rate of AAA-, BBB-, and CCC- to C-rated bonds measured as a cumulative percentage of the number of bonds originally rated in that category at the beginning of year 1. This table covers 1981 to 2009.

Notice that the lower the rating, the larger was the default rate. For example, within one year of issuance, there were no defaults recorded for AAA bonds, but for BBB bonds, 0.26 percent defaulted, and over a quarter of the CCC- to C-rated bonds defaulted within their first year. By 10 years after bond issuance and original rating, fewer than 1 percent of the AAA-rated bonds defaulted, whereas over half the CCC- to C-rated bonds defaulted. In keeping with the liquidity preference theory and the risk premium portion of the yield curve, the higher default probability translates into higher interest rates, as seen in Figure 8-6.

From Figure 8-6, for most of the period, AA-rated bonds cost the issuing company between 4 and 6 percent. Also, BB-rated bonds cost the issuer 6 to 8 percent interest. However, when the financial crisis began in the second half of 2008, all interest rates spiked. In particular, AA-rated bonds were issued at 7 percent, whereas BB-rated bonds reached an interest rate of almost 14 percent.

The average yield to maturity for the period 2008–2010 is shown on Figure 8-7.

In general, the higher-rated bonds had lower average cost for the issuer except for the AA– versus A+ bonds. This abnormality was a direct result of when the bonds were issued over this three-year period. There were proportionately more AA– bonds issued during the early part of this time frame when rates were higher.

FIGURE 8-6

Historical corporate bond yields of newly issued bonds.

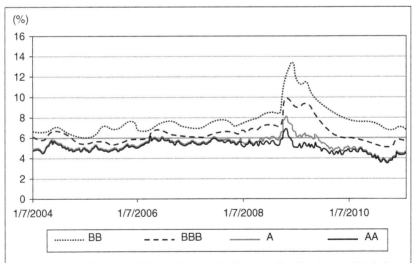

Source: Credit Trends: The Relationship Between Corporate Credit Ratings and Debt Cost Across the Maturity Curve and through Stress Periods:1945–Present Diane Vazza and Cameron Miller, RatingsDirect®, Standard & Poor's Financial Services LLC, February 24, 2011. Reproduced by permission of Standard and Poor's Financial Services.

FIGURE   8-7

Average new corporate bond yields by issue rating, 2008–2010.

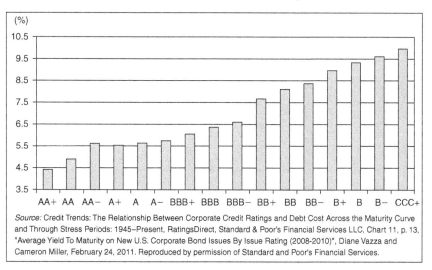

Source: Credit Trends: The Relationship Between Corporate Credit Ratings and Debt Cost Across the Maturity Curve and Through Stress Periods: 1945–Present, RatingsDirect, Standard & Poor's Financial Services LLC, Chart 11, p. 13, "Average Yield To Maturity on New U.S. Corporate Bond Issues By Issue Rating (2008-2010)", Diane Vazza and Cameron Miller, February 24, 2011. Reproduced by permission of Standard and Poor's Financial Services.

Market Segmentation Hypothesis

The liquidity preference theory states that an upward bias exists—the yield curve slopes upward because savers prefer to lend short and borrowers prefer to borrow long. The *market segmentation theory* hones liquidity preference within specific maturities. Some savers prefer short horizons, such as commercial banks to avoid long-term liquidity issues, and others, such as insurance companies and pension funds, prefer long horizons to earn the extra return. On the other hand, borrowers often relate the maturity of their debt to the maturity of their assets, and consequently, borrowers have maturity preferences. Bonds with different maturities are not substitutes for one another because of different demand preferences of both lenders and borrowers.

The 5-year (intermediate) and 20-year (long-term) markets are illustrated in Figure 8-8. Funds are demanded in order to invest them in profitable projects. The demand schedule D is downward-sloping because investors take the most valuable projects first. As a result, the expected rates of return on incremental investments decline. The supply schedule S is upward-sloping because higher and higher rates of return are needed to induce suppliers to lend greater amounts of money. Simply put, when interest rates are high (low), borrowers will demand fewer (more) funds and suppliers will offer more (fewer).

Market segmentation holds that any interest rate is the rate that equates the overall demand for funds with the overall supply given a specific maturity. The real rate of return equates supply and demand, as shown in Figure 8-8. Projects

FIGURE 8-8

Market segmentation.

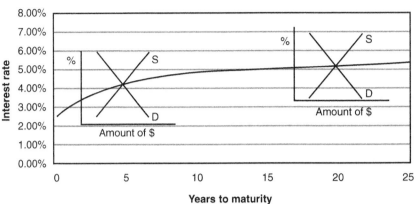

Years to maturity

that earn more than the real rate will be undertaken, and the funds will be acquired to finance them.

Expectations Theory

The *expectations theory* is a different perspective on the yield curve and claims that longer-term interest rates are tied directly to short-term rates and expectations of future interest rates. For example, consider a cash manager who has an opportunity to invest excess cash of $100,000 for two years. Looking at the yield curves of Figures 8-5 and 8-6, the manager focuses on a choice between two short-term investments:

Maturity	Rate
1 Year	2.90%
2 Years	3.33%
3 Years	3.71%
4 Years	4.01%

If the money manager decides to invest the full amount for two years, at the end of the two years, $106,771 [$100,000 $\times$ (1 + 0.0333)^2] would have accumulated.

The other alternative is to invest the money for one year, earn 2.90 percent for one year for a total of $102,900, and "roll over" that amount for the second year at the then-prevailing interest rate. If the cash manager believes that in the second year the one-year interest rate will be 4.00 percent, this rollover is the appropriate strategy because the final accumulated amount would be $107,016 [$102,900 $\times$ (1 + 0.040)]. On the other hand, if the money manager expected that the second year's one-year interest rate were going to be only 3.25 percent, the total accumulation would be only $106,224

[\$102,900 × (1 + 0.0325)], and the two-year investment alternative would be more attractive.

This logic at the heart of the expectations theory is as follows: Longer-term interest rates are tied directly to short-term rates and expectations of future interest rates. The expectations or forward rate is denoted as $_1f_2$, in this example. As we saw with market segmentation, there is an equilibrium point where the market's expectations are embedded in today's two-year interest rate of 3.33 percent. This equilibrium can be found by setting both strategies (two-year investment and rollover) equal to each other and solving for what the market is expecting next year's one-year interest rate ($_1f_2$) to be, as shown in Eq. (8.2):

$$\$100,000(1 + 0.0333)^2 = \$100,000(1 + 0.0290)(1 + {}_1f_2)$$
$$\$106,771 = \$102,900(1 + {}_1f_2)$$
$$\$106,771/\$102,900 = (1 + {}_1f_2)$$
$$3.76\% = {}_1f_2 \tag{8.2}$$

With an expected one-year interest rate one year from now of 3.76 percent, both the two-year investment and the rollover strategy provide the same accumulated return. Consequently, if the money manager expected next year's one-year interest rate to be less (more) than 3.76 percent, a two-year (rollover) investment strategy optimizes the return.

This point, 3.76 percent, reveals the market's expectations for future rates. If the market felt the rate was going to be 4.00 percent, today's interest rates (both the one- and two-year rates) would adjust until they would reflect a 4.00 percent forward rate. Likewise, if the market had an expectation of only a 3.50 percent future rate, today's yields on one- and two-year rates would adjust to reflect a 3.50 percent expectation.

We now can generalize this simple example, building on Eq. (8.2):

$$(1 + {}_0r_N)^N = (1 + {}_0r_P)^P(1 + {}_Pf_N)^{(N-P)} \tag{8.3}$$

Where P stands for the interim period and N stands for the full investment period. This equation can be used to find the implied (forward) two-year interest rate two years from now using the preceding information:

$$(1 + 0.0401)^4 = (1 + 0.0333)^2(1 + {}_2f_4)^{(4-2)}$$
$$4.69\% = {}_2f_4$$

Thus, continuing our example, a money manager could invest for four years at a known rate of 4.01 percent and accumulate \$117,031. Or he or she could invest for two years at 3.33 percent for an accumulated amount of \$106,771 and reinvest that amount for two more years at 4.69 percent (assuming that the actual rate will be the expected rate) and have the same amount of \$117,031. Once again, if the money manager felt that the two-year rate would be higher than 4.76 percent in two years, then a rollover strategy would be optimal.

Empirical studies suggest that there is some validity to each of these theories. Specifically, the evidence indicates that if lenders and borrowers have no reason for expecting a change in the general level of interest rates, the yield curve will be upward-sloping because of liquidity preferences. (Under the expectations theory, the term structure of interest rates would be flat if there were no expectations of a change in the level of short-term rates.) However, it is a fact that during periods of extremely high short-term inflation rates, the yield curve is downward-sloping, and this indicates that liquidity preference theory also operates. At still other times, when supply and demand conditions in particular maturity sectors change, the term structure seems to be modified, reflecting the market segmentation theory.

ISSUES OF DEBT AND DEBT INSTRUMENTS

Most people have had some experience with debt. Almost everyone has a credit card, which involves borrowing for short or longer periods. Many homeowners have borrowed on a mortgage or through a home equity line of credit with their home as security. There are also auto loans, school loans, personal lines of credit, and so on. All of the these are forms of what is called *household debt*.

Other forms of debt are identified by the economic characteristics of the borrowers. The federal debt of the U.S. government is pivotal because of its size. The U.S. Treasury debt generally is regarded to be free of the risk of default at maturity. Treasury bills (T-bills) have a maturity of one year or less. Treasury notes have maturities from one up to 10 years. Treasury bonds (T-bonds) have maturities of 10 or more years. Treasury securities have no default risk but have the risk of interest-rate fluctuations discussed in topics toward the end of this chapter.

Individual states and cities also issue debt referred to as *municipal securities* or *municipals*. Companies that trade in bonds, dealers and brokers, also distinguish between financial and nonfinancial firms (e.g., see www.bondsonline.com). The flow of funds data of the Federal Reserve System also recognizes this distinction. Financial firms have some special characteristics. They are government regulated to some degree, invest mainly in financial assets, and have high ratios of debt to equity.

Nonfinancial debt is issued by corporations, single proprietorships, partnerships, and other forms of business organizations. A distinction usually is made between farm and nonfarm debt. Clearly, a wide range of individuals and institutions are issuers of debt.

Debt issued by foreign governments or foreign corporations is also considered as a distinct category. The main reason is that when denominated in a foreign currency, the special risk of fluctuations of the foreign currency in relation to the U.S. dollar may occur. So foreign debt carries an exchange-rate risk.

LOAN AMORTIZATION TABLES

The time value of money (TVM) concepts (Chapter 7) and the topics of interest rates and debt found in this chapter are very important in business and in personal life. An amortized loan is found with home mortgages, home equity loans, car loans, or other loans that comingle principal and interest payments on a regular basis. An *amortizable loan* is a loan where the periodic payment (monthly in these examples) includes principal repayment along with interest payments.

Recalling from Chapter 7 and using a financial calculator, enter the information that you know, and solve for the annuity (or payments). Therefore, in this example, let's say that we want to know the monthly payments on a 30-year mortgage of $100,000 at a rate of 5.40 percent. Remember to check that the "BEGIN" (Hewlett-Packard [HP]) or "BGN" (Texas Instruments [TI]) annunciator does *not* appear in the display screen. Also, be sure that the calculator is set to one payment per year (P/Y button). If either of these is not set properly, refer to Chapter 7 or your calculator's user's guide to adjust the setting. Clear all the calculator's registers, and then enter:

360	N	Or 30 years × 12 payments per year
0.45	I/YR	Or 5.40 percent APR/12 periods for monthly compounding
100,000	PV	

Push 360 and then the N key, push 0.45 and then the I/YR key, and push 100,000 and then the PV key. The final step is to solve for the payment. If you use a TI calculator, push the CPT key to tell the calculator to "compute," and then press the PMT key. If you use an HP calculator, simply push the PMT key. In either case, the calculator displays the answer of $561.53.

The payment on a four-year, 7.2 percent, $22,500 car loan can be calculated as follows:

48	N	Or 4 years × 12 payments per year
0.60	I/YR	Or 7.2 percent APR/12 periods for monthly compounding
22,500	PV	

The monthly payment is $540.88.

Suppose that you borrow $10,000 (PV) for 4 (*n*) years at 10 percent (*i* percent). As determined earlier, your annual payments would be $3,154.71. A portion of the payment pays for the period's interest, whereas the remaining portion reduces principal. This is shown in Table 8-4.

In the first year, $10,000 is outstanding for the full year at a 10 percent interest rate, for a total interest payment of $1,000. But the payment was $3,154.71! Therefore, the difference between the payment and the interest, or $2,154.71, reduces the outstanding loan balance. At the end of year 1 (or beginning of year 2), the remaining balance on the loan is $7,845.29, which is subject to 10 percent interest for that year. Thus the year 2 interest component is only

TABLE 8-4

Loan Amortization Table
(4 Years, $10,000, 10%)

Year	Beginning Balance	Payment	10.0% Interest	Principal	Ending Balance
1	$10,000.00	$3,154.71	$1,000.00	$2,154.71	$7,845.29
2	7,845.29	$3,154.71	784.53	2,370.18	5,475.11
3	5,475.11	$3,154.71	547.51	2,607.20	2,867.91
4	2,867.91	$3,154.70	286.79	2,867.91	–

$784.53, and a larger portion of the payment reduces the remaining principal amount. This process continues until the loan is paid off in year 4. You also will notice that the fourth year has been adjusted to reflect rounding.

Amortized loans require monthly payments, not annual payments. The approach is exactly the same, except it takes a lot longer with a financial calculator. Excel is an excellent tool to use to create these more realistic monthly loan amortization schedules.

VALUATION OF DEBT INSTRUMENTS

The generally accepted methodology for the valuation of any asset (financial or physical) is the *discounted cash-flow (DCF) procedure*. The value of a bond, common stock, equipment, or buildings is the present value of their expected future cash flows (Eq. 8.4):

$$\text{Value} = \frac{CF_1}{(1+k)} + \frac{CF_2}{(1+k)^2} + \frac{CF_3}{(1+k)^3} + \cdots + \frac{CF_n}{(1+k)^n} \qquad (8.4)$$

where value = value of any asset or financial instrument
CF = future cash flows
k = required yield or discount factor
n = number of periods

While the patterns of future cash flows may vary, the DCF procedure is sufficiently flexible to perform the valuation.

The valuation of a debt instrument such as a bond or note uses the concepts developed in Chapter 7. However, a bond has unique cash-flow patterns; bonds pay periodic interest payments as well as return the face value of the bond at maturity (see Eq. 8.5):

Bond value = present value of an annuity + present value of a future sum:

$$= PVA_{k,t} + PV_{k,n} \qquad (8.5)$$

Equivalent expressions are shown in Eq. (8.6):

$$B_0 = \sum_{t=1}^{n} \frac{c_t}{(1+k_b)^t} + \frac{M}{(1+k_b)^n} \tag{8.6}$$

where B_0 = current value or price of a bond
  c_t = coupon payment = $70
  k_b = required return on the bond reflecting its risk and market condition = 7 percent
  M = maturity value of the bond = $1,000
  t = discounting periods running from 1, 2, 3, ..., n
  n = period at which the final coupon payment is made = 10

We can make Eq. (8.6) more explicit by using an example with the data inputs given with the definitions listed earlier:

$$B_0 = \sum_{t=1}^{8} \frac{\$70}{(1+0.07)^t} + \frac{\$1,000}{(1+0.07)^{10}} = \$1,000 \tag{8.6a}$$

Using the numerical inputs and Eq. (8.6), we determine the bond value to be $1,000. We could have obtained the same result by using TVM tables. Additionally, a financial calculator is also a valuable practical tool for evaluating bonds. From Chapter 7 you will recall that a financial calculator has five important TVM keys:

| N | I/YR | PV | PMT | FV |

where

N	= number of periods (same as n years)
I/YR	= interest rate (same as r)
PV	= present value
PMT	= payment or annuity amount (which is discussed below)
FV	= future value

For our purposes of calculating the value of this bond, clear all the calculator's registers, and then enter:

10	N
7	I/YR
70	PMT
1,000	FV

Push 10 and then the N key (maturity), push 7 and then the I/YR key (required return), push 70 and then the PMT key (coupon interest payment), and push 1,000 (maturity value) and then the FV key. The final step is to solve for the present

value. If you use a TI calculator, you first push the CPT key to tell the calculator
to "compute," and then press the PV key. If you use an HP calculator, simply push
the PV key. In either case, the calculator displays the answer of $–1,000 or sim-
ply $1,000. Recall from chapter 7, the negative sign for the PV indicates the cost
of the bond. We have now established the basic valuation formula for bonds. Now
we can develop some of its implications.

If market conditions change causing the required return on the bond to change,
the bond's value changes. Continuing this example with a drop in interest rates to
6 percent, push 6 and the I/YR key, and then compute the present value as $1,073.60.
If interest rates increased to 8 percent, push 8 and the I/YR key, and then compute the
present value as $932.90. Since the interest and principal repayments are contractual
and set, as the market interest rate changes, so does the price of the bond. In this
example, the 7 percent interest rate was the stated rate of the bond. It was useful to
understand the annual dollar amount of interest, 7 percent × $1,000, or $70 per year.

Table 8-5 captures this volatility for the base case and extends that to include
bonds of varying maturities. Notice that a one-year bond has limited volatility; at
6 percent, the value rises to $1,009.43, or if the interest rate is 8 percent, the value
falls to $990.74. A 30-year bond has significant volatility; in this case, at 6 percent,
the value is $1,137.65, and at 8 percent, the value falls to $887.42.

One final perspective is important—*duration*, which is similar to maturity.
However, duration is a weighted average of each year based on the present value
of that year's cash flow. Table 8-6 illustrates duration for three separate bonds,
each with a different coupon, but each also selling for $1,000.

Looking at the 7 percent bond example, the coupons are $70 each year, with
repayment of the $1,000 maturity value. As you see, the value of the bond is also
$1,000. The year 1 present value of the $70 coupon is $65.42, or 6.54 percent

TABLE 8-5

Impact of Market Rates on Bonds with Different Maturities
(Annual Bond, $70 Coupon, $1,000 Maturity)

Market Rate	Years to Maturity				
	1	5	10	20	30
3.0%	$ 1,038.83	$ 1,183.19	$ 1,341.21	$ 1,595.10	$ 1,784.02
4.0%	1,028.85	1,133.55	1,243.33	1,407.71	1,518.76
5.0%	1,019.05	1,086.59	1,154.43	1,249.24	1,307.45
6.0%	1,009.43	1,042.12	1,073.60	1,114.70	1,137.65
7.0%	1,000.00	1,000.00	1,000.00	1,000.00	1,000.00
8.0%	990.74	960.07	932.90	901.82	887.42
9.0%	981.65	922.21	871.65	817.43	794.53
10.0%	972.73	886.28	815.66	744.59	717.19
11.0%	963.96	852.16	764.43	681.47	652.25

TABLE 8-6

Bond Duration

Year	5% Cash Flow	5% PV of CF	5% Wt. Aver.*	7% Cash Flow	7% PV of CF	7% Wt. Aver.*	9% Cash Flow	9% PV of CF	9% Wt. Aver.*
1	$ 50.00	$ 47.62	0.0476	$ 70.00	$ 65.42	0.0654	$ 90.00	$ 82.57	0.0826
2	50.00	45.35	0.0907	70.00	61.14	0.1223	90.00	75.75	0.1515
3	50.00	43.19	0.1296	70.00	57.14	0.1714	90.00	69.50	0.2085
4	50.00	41.14	0.1645	70.00	53.40	0.2136	90.00	63.76	0.2550
5	50.00	39.18	0.1959	70.00	49.91	0.2495	90.00	58.49	0.2925
6	50.00	37.31	0.2239	70.00	46.64	0.2799	90.00	53.66	0.3220
7	50.00	35.53	0.2487	70.00	43.59	0.3051	90.00	49.23	0.3446
8	50.00	33.84	0.2707	70.00	40.74	0.3259	90.00	45.17	0.3613
9	50.00	32.23	0.2901	70.00	38.08	0.3427	90.00	41.44	0.3729
10	1,050.00	644.61	6.4461	1,070.00	543.93	5.4393	1,090.00	460.43	4.6043
		$1,000.00	8.1078 **		$1,000.00	7.5152 **		$1,000.00	6.9952 **

*The weighted average is calculated as a year's present value of its cash flow divided by the total present value times the year.
**The sum of the weighted averages is call the *duration*. It is a more accurate reflection of the bond's true age.

(0.0654) of the bond's total present value. Multiply this by the number of the year (1) to get a component of the weighted average ("Wt. Aver."). For the second year, the present value of the $70 coupon is $61.14, or 6.11 percent (0.0611) times the number of the year (2) to get a component of the weighted average of 0.1223, and so on. Sum all the weighted-average components to get a duration of 7.5152 for this 7 percent, 10-year bond.

Given the nature of duration, or this weighted average, the relative life of the bond can be determined. Notice that the 5 percent bond selling at $1,000 has a duration of 8.1078 (greater than the 7 percent bond's duration) because more value is realized later in the bond. The 9 percent coupon bond selling for $1,000 has a duration of 6.9952, or the shortest of any of the bonds in Table 8-6.

One final example involves a 10-year, 0 percent coupon bond. This is a bond that pays no interest over its life. It does repay the maturity value of $1,000 at the end of 10 years. This bond sells for $508.35, assuming a 7 percent return. Its duration components are all 0.0000 for the first nine years of its life because there is no coupon payment. However, in year 10, the full value is received (or 100 percent times 10 years) for a duration of 10 years. Thus, while all four bonds have a maturity of 10 years, each bond provides different durations.

Semiannual Coupon Payments

To this point, the coupon payments have been assumed to be made annually. Annual coupon payments represent the general convention for European countries, but the United States uses semiannual payments. Chapter 7 set forth a general procedure for converting annual payments to semiannual and other compounding periods. The nominally stated interest rate is divided by q (the frequency of compounding within the year), and n (the number of years) is multiplied by q *to determine the number of periods*. Using the market convention for semiannual compounding, you can calculate the value of the bond using Eq. (8.6), in which n becomes $2n$ and the discount rate k_b is divided by 2, and get Eq. (8.7):

$$B_0 = \sum_{t=1}^{nq} \frac{c_t/q}{(1+k_b/q)^t} + \frac{M}{(1+k_b/q)^{nq}} \tag{8.7}$$

Using a financial calculator, clear the calculator, and be sure that it is set to one payment per year (P/Yr). Enter the time period as 20 (10 years times two payments per year), the coupon payment (Pmt) as 35 ($70 divided by two half-payments per year), 1,000 as the future value (FV), and finally, the interest rate (I/YR) as 3.5 percent (7 percent current market rate divided by 2), $1000 results.

Bond Yields

When dealing with bonds, the terms of the bond are well known (i.e., maturity, interest payments, frequency of those payments, and maturity value), and often the price of the bond is also known. In this case, the question becomes, "What is the return or yield to maturity (YTM) provided by the bond?" We use annual discounting. We need to solve for k_b to understand the return. Suppose that the price for a 10-year-maturity bond with an annual coupon rate of 7 percent were $1,073.60. The information provided enables us to calculate the YTM value. With a financial calculator, we input 10 for N, –$1,073.60 for PV, $70 for PMT, and $1,000 for FV. We solve by pushing the I/YR key. We obtain 6.0 percent as the required YTM.

Next, we assume semiannual compounding, so we input 20 for N, –$1,073.60 for PV, $35 for PMT, and $1,000 for FV. We solve by pushing the I/YR key. We obtain 3.005 percent as the required half-year YTM. The resulting annual percentage rate is 6.01 percent, or simply 3.005 percent × 2. The reason that this yield is slightly larger than with annual coupons is that the buyer receives his or her funds earlier.

As the market interest rate rises, the bond value falls, and as market rates fall, the bond becomes more valuable. Said differently, if bond prices are up, this implies that interest rates fell. If bond prices dropped, then the market's interest rates increased.

Hence the reported YTM will change as expectations of the future change. This is a general characteristic of the prices and yields of financial and physical assets. The financial models developed to deal with future risks and uncertainties are discussed in later sections of this chapter and throughout this text.

In the discussion of bond prices in the preceding section, we found that when the bond coupon rate equals the required market yield, a bond sells at its face value of $1,000, or it is reported as 100. When the coupon rate is below the market rate, a bond will sell at a discount from its face value and conversely at a premium when the market rate is below the coupon rate. It follows that the YTM on a bond purchased at a discount is the coupon rate plus a capital gain rate. The YTM on a bond selling at a premium is the coupon rate less a capital loss rate. Since bond prices and required yields change continuously, the expected or promised yield to maturity is likely to differ from the actual or realized yields.

Another perspective is the *current yield*, which is simply the annual coupon interest payments divided by the current price of the debt instrument. In the example where the YTM was 6 percent and the price of the bond was $1,073.60, the current yield would be 6.52 percent (or $70 divided by $1,073.60).

Interest-Rate Risk

It has been established that a decline (increase) in the required YTMs in relation to bond coupon rates increases (decreases) bond prices. I generalized these relationships in Table 8-5. Shorter-term bonds exhibit smaller fluctuations in values or prices than longer-term maturities. However, the magnitude of the price increases for required YTMs below coupon rates is larger than for required YTMs above coupon rates.

Nevertheless, interest-rate fluctuations represent significant interest-rate risk. For business firms that raise funds by selling debt instruments, the risk faced is a decline in interest rates. In practical terms, a firm with substantial debt that pays interest rates that are higher than current market rates is at a competitive disadvantage. The firm is paying more for funds than competitors who are raising funds at the prevailing lower rate. Conversely, when a firm has debt outstanding with coupon rates that are lower than prevailing required market rates, its debt instruments have increased in value, and its cost of funds is lower than that of firms currently raising funds.

For savers, the risks are reversed. Financial investors (savers) are hurt if they hold fixed-income securities whose coupons are lower than current required yields. Savers gain if their fixed-income securities have coupons higher than current required yields.

The risk faced by firms raising funds and by investors holding debt securities is not solved by always using short-term securities. When short-term interest rates are high, a firm using short-term financing is at a competitive disadvantage to firms that raise long-term funds at lower rates. Similarly, a saver earning less than 1 percent on short-term funds, as in 2009–2011, could have earned much more had his or her prior investments been made in longer-term securities when interest rates were higher. The risks of interest-rate fluctuations are substantial over the life of a bond, especially the longer-life bonds.

Valuing Equity

The preceding section developed valuation approaches for bonds, which are securities with fixed returns (i.e., interest and principal) that mature over a specified period of time. This section develops simple valuation models for two types of equity securities—preferred stock and common stock.

Preferred stock is a hybrid security that is similar to a bond in that it pays a contractually set amount of cash each year to its holder. Unlike a bond, there is no maturity date for a share of preferred stock, and the instrument is classified as equity not debt.

Common stock is a security that represents ownership in a company. As such, there is no contractual arrangement to return any cash flow to the equity investor, and there is no maturity date. While on the surface no contractual cash flow and no maturity may seem less than attractive, the holder of common stock participates in the growth of the organization through increasing earnings and cash flow. Hence the common stockholder has unbounded upside potential while also having limited (albeit, limited to –100 percent) downside risk.

Valuation of a share of stock is analogous to valuing a perpetual cash flow (or recurring cash flows that will last forever), as discussed in Chapter 7. That chapter introduced two varieties of perpetuities—a zero-growth model and a constant-growth model.

Zero growth: $$V_{0,r,\infty} = \frac{CF}{r} \tag{8.8}$$

Constant growth: $$V_{0,r,\infty} = \frac{CF_1}{(r-g)}$$ (8.9)

where $V_{0,r,\infty}$ = value of firm at time 0 continuing perpetually
        CF_1 = cash flow at the end of year 1[1]
        r = cost of equity
        g = constant growth

These basic models are at the heart of all equity securities. Later chapters will develop valuation models far beyond these conceptual but limited frameworks.

Although Hershey has no preferred stock outstanding, let's assume that it does have a preferred stock share that pays $4 a year in dividends and that the appropriate market rate of required return is 8 percent. Equation (8.8), the value of a perpetuity without growth, provides the proper valuation model:

$$V_{0,r,\infty} = \frac{CF}{r}$$
$$= \$4 / 0.08$$
$$= \$50$$

While the $4 preferred stock dividend is set contractually, the required return is not, and much like interest rates, it fluctuates with general economic conditions. Thus, if the required return drops to 6 percent, the value of the preferred share increases to $66.67; if the required return increases to 10 percent, the price of the preferred share decreases to $40.00.

Valuing Common Stock: Perpetuity with Growth

As a common stockholder, you own a piece of the corporation and its cash flows. Sometimes the cash flows are paid out as dividends, and sometimes cash flows are reinvested into the business, and the business continues to grow and flourish. Regardless of whether the cash flow is paid out or reinvested, a common stockholder owns a piece of the company and its cash flows as well as the growth of the firm and growth of its cash flows.

The Hershey Company generated about $700.0 million of cash flow in 2010 (cash provided from operating activities less capital expenditures and capitalized software additions). If we assume no growth in these operating cash flows and that investors require about an 8.5 percent rate of return (also called the *cost of equity*, which is the topic of Chapter 11), the value of Hershey is $8,235.3 million (or $700.0/0.085) from Eq. (8.6).

However, if we assume that Hershey will continue to grow its cash flow by 2.0 percent per annum owing to sales growth, margin improvement, and other

---

[1]Remember that the cash flow at the end of the year (CF_1) is also the same as growing this year's cash flow and can be written as $CF_1 = CF_0(1 + g)$.

efficiencies, Hershey's value increases to almost $11.0 billion, calculated from Eq. (8.9a):

$$
\begin{aligned}
\mathrm{PVA}_{r,\infty} &= \frac{\mathrm{CF}_{(0)}\,(1+g)}{(r-g)} \\
&= \frac{\$700\,(1+0.020)}{(0.085-0.020)} = \frac{\$714}{0.065} = \$10,985\,\text{million}
\end{aligned}
\tag{8.9a}
$$

Much depends on the assumptions! Is Hershey grossly overvalued or severely undervalued? Table 8-7 provides a sensitivity analysis on the expected growth rate and the required rate of return. The value of $10,985 million (center of the table in bold and at a required rate of return of 8.5 percent and growth rate of 2.0 percent) forms the base-scenario valuation. The assumed growth rate and required rate of return are critical to determining the value of Hershey. Notice that if we assumed a slightly higher growth rate of 2.5 percent while maintaining an 8.5 percent discount rate, the value of Hershey jumps to almost $12 billion! On the other hand, if we overestimated the potential growth rate at 2 percent (base scenario) and a more realistic growth rate is 1.5 percent, then the correct value is $10,150 million, or $835 million lower than the base scenario. Honing the assumptions is critical.

The initial cash flow is also important but generally is a more solid assumption. In this case, for every $25 million (either increase or decrease) of initial cash flow, the value of Hershey fluctuates by $392 million, as shown in Eq. (8.9b):

$$
\begin{aligned}
\mathrm{PVA}_{r,\infty} &= \frac{\mathrm{CF}_{(0)}\,(1+g)}{(r-g)} \\
&= \frac{\$25\,(1+0.020)}{(0.085-0.020)} = \frac{\$25.5}{0.065} = \$392\,\text{million}
\end{aligned}
\tag{8.9b}
$$

TABLE 8-7

Common Stock Valuation Sensitivity
($ millions)

		Growth Rate						
		0.0%	1.0%	1.5%	2.0%	2.5%	3.0%	4.0%
	7.0%	$ 10,000	$ 11,783	$ 12,918	$ 14,280	$ 15,944	$ 18,025	$ 24,267
	7.5%	9,333	10,877	11,842	12,982	14,350	16,022	20,800
Required	8.0%	8,750	10,100	10,931	11,900	13,045	14,420	18,200
Rate of	8.5%	8,235	9,427	10,150	**10,985**	11,958	13,109	16,178
Return	9.0%	7,778	8,838	9,473	10,200	11,038	12,017	14,560
	9.5%	7,368	8,318	8,881	9,520	10,250	11,092	13,236
	10.0%	7,000	7,856	8,359	8,925	9,567	10,300	12,133

Even from this simple model, the managerial implications are evident:

- Grow the operating cash flows of the business
  - Profitable sales growth
  - Cost reductions and margin improvements, including tax rate reduction
  - Effective working capital management
  - Fixed capital investment that adds value
- Reduce the cost of capital (or discount rate)
- Generate more operating cash flow right away

These topics are discussed in much more detail in the upcoming chapters.

SUMMARY

The financial sector of the economy, an important part of the financial manager's environment, is comprised of financial markets, financial institutions, and financial instruments. The goal of the financial system is to efficiently and effectively transfer funds from units with excess cash to units with deficit cash or investors in real assets, such as buildings, equipment, land, working capital, and so on. This transfer of funds creates a financial asset for the surplus unit and a financial liability for the deficit unit. The deficit unit (investor in real assets) manages those assets and provides a financial return to the supplier of the financial capital.

Transfers can be made directly between a surplus and a deficit unit or can involve one of many financial intermediaries. The money markets involve financial assets and liabilities with maturities of less than one year, and the capital markets involve transfers for longer periods. Two major forms of financing are used by business firms—various forms of debt financing and equity financing through preferred and common stock.

The initial sale of stocks and bonds is known as the primary market. Subsequent trading takes place in the secondary market, the organized exchanges. The over-the-counter market, the third market, is a dealer market, where broker-dealers throughout the country act as market makers. Sometimes large blocks of stock are traded directly among institutional investors, constituting the fourth market.

For the past 60 years, interest rates started low, peaked in the late 1970s and early 1980s, and have generally declined since then. A yield curve describes interest rates compared with maturities at any point in time. Most yield curves generally have been upward-sloping owing to liquidity preference of the providers of funds. Also, expected inflation and risk play a role in setting the general level of interest rates. Specific interest rates may be set based on market forces as well as the market's expectation of future interest rates.

The valuation of a bond is a special case of general valuation using discounted future cash flows. The market price or valuation of a bond is determined by the discounted values of its expected future cash flows. The yields of bonds can be calculated given their current prices and expectations with regard to interest payments, maturity dates, and maturity values.

Equity valuation in its simplest form requires the use of a basic foundation from Chapter 7—valuation of a perpetuity. The managerial lessons are clear:

- Increase your cash flow.
- Grow the business.
- Reduce your cost of funds (required return).

Even these simplistic models lead to useful managerial observations. However, much more will be said about value management and valuing-enhancing activities as you continue through this text. For now, though, these models demonstrate value creation.

CAPITAL INVESTMENT DECISIONS

The capital investment decision combines many aspects of business, economics, finance, and accounting, along with the organization's strategy. Chapter 2 introduced financial statements and cash flows, which provide the basic information necessary for financial evaluation. Chapters 3 and 6 discussed financial performance metrics and strategic financial planning, respectively. Chapter 7 provided the fundamental tool, the time value of money (TVM), which is necessary to value future cash flows. Building on these topics, this chapter advances the discussion on evaluating corporate investment decisions by examining the capital investment program and introducing evaluation techniques.

A number of business factors combine to make business investment perhaps the most important financial management decision. All departments of a firm—engineering, production, marketing, logistics, and so on—are vitally affected by investment decisions, so all managers, no matter what their primary responsibility, must be aware of how capital investment decisions are made and how to interact effectively with management in the processes.

Chapter 10 continues the discussion started in this chapter. Another interrelated topic is found in Chapter 11. The cost of capital represents the appropriate discount rate (or required rate of return) for any capital investment analysis.

OVERVIEW OF INVESTMENT ANALYSIS

The broad application of the techniques presented in this chapter make these tools germane to a wide variety of corporate investment decisions. A four-phase capital investment approach, along with a successful implementation, characterizes a successful investment program. Each organization also imposes managerial directives designed to balance evaluation and control with analytical appropriateness, materiality, and flexibility.

Applications of Investment Analysis

The investment analysis techniques presented in this chapter are widely applicable to many business decisions. Each investment begins with identifying a need, clarifying the investment proposal, considering alternatives, and developing cash-flow projections. Table 9-1 lists many types of investment decisions where the application of these techniques is appropriate.

New product introductions require rigorous analysis whether the nature of the decision is a line extension, entering a new line of distribution, or a geographic expansion. New products require investment in equipment and marketing expenses (i.e., advertising and promotions). For a new product, an investment analysis captures the projected sales, related expenses, income, and cash flow to determine the economic viability of that product.

Capital expenditure analysis represents the traditional capital investment analysis (also referred to by some as *capital budgeting*). Capital expenditures include investments in equipment and plants. These expenditures may reduce production costs, reduce working capital investment, speed production, expand production capacity, or enhance product quality. Cash-flow impacts correspond to the investment motive.

T A B L E   9-1

Applications of Investment Analysis

- New production introduction
  - New products
  - Line extension
  - Lines of distribution
  - Geographic expansion
- Capital expenditure
  - Investments in equipment
    - —Cost savings initiatives
    - —Capacity expansion
  - Investments in new production facilities
- Information technology
  - Hardware investments
  - Software investments
- Major operating decisions
  - Research and development
  - Advertising campaigns
  - Outsourcing decisions
- Mergers and acquisitions
  - External acquisitions
    - —Total company
    - —Brand, line, or region
  - Divisional valuation
    - —Using internal strategic plans
  - Divestiture analysis

For example, cash flows related to cost-reduction (or cost-avoidance) projects include savings from a reduction in incremental variable and/or fixed after-tax costs. These reductions form the foundation necessary to evaluate the investment opportunity. In conjunction with reduced costs, some capital expenditures also reduce the amount of working capital (often inventory) invested in the business. The investment analysis should include all cash savings as well as all related expenditures.

Capital expenditures motivated to enhance the speed of production, add required capacity, or improve the product's quality often result in increased sales along with possible cost reductions. Corresponding cash flows include the incremental sales, expenses, income, and cash flow generated by these types of projects.

In the "new economy," many companies invest heavily in information technology (IT). Even nontraditional IT-driven companies are relying more and more on various software systems that require new hardware. Whether it is technology aimed at the Internet and a changing business model or the implementation of an upgraded enterprisewide solution such as an enterprise resource planning (ERP) system, companies are embracing technology and significantly investing in it. Investors and senior managers demand a return on this investment. The traditional investment analysis techniques provide a useful evaluation framework.

Investment analysis is not limited to capital decisions but also can be applied to business investments that are treated as expenses, such as investment in research and development (R&D), advertising campaigns, or many other operating decisions such as the make-versus-buy decision or outsourcing. The pharmaceutical industry, technology-related businesses, and automobile manufacturers are some of the top R&D spenders. Each company that invests heavily in R&D has some form of R&D management that includes capital investment analysis, as illustrated in this chapter and the next, as well as their unique internal management approaches.

While advertising *investment* may be more difficult to analyze, it provides an interesting model to ensure that corporate funds are potentially "invested" in value-enhancing activities.

Finally, the analytical capital investment tools form the basis for financial evaluation of acquisition or divestiture candidates whether that is the business in its entirety or a brand, line of business, division, or regional location. Identification of a business candidate occurs. Development of projected future cash flows leads to an application of the valuation tools introduced in this chapter.

ACCOUNTING RATES OF RETURN

Before discussing the appropriate approach to use when evaluating capital investment, it is helpful to understand how *not* to make the capital investment decision. Chapter 2 reviewed financial information and financial statements. Chapter 3 discussed financial performance metrics, including profitability metrics such as return on assets (ROA) and return on equity (ROE). While the financial performance metrics, in general, and return on assets, specifically, are valuable metrics used to manage the business day to day, set performance standards and objectives, and benchmark against other organizations, these measures are inappropriate for investment decision making.

Accounting-based performance measures (including accounting-based rates of return) differ greatly from economic rates of return. While accounting metrics can result from future financial statement projections, as in Chapter 6, the nature of the accounting returns differs from the economic returns discussed in this chapter.

Table 9-2 compares accounting rates of return (Chapter 3) versus the economic returns developed later in this chapter. The major differences are summarized in the table.

Accounting returns are determined for discrete single time periods (i.e., month, quarter, year, etc.), whereas economic returns consider a continuous time frame over multiple periods both historical and projected. Accounting returns are income-based (accrual accounting), whereas economic returns center on cash flows. Accounting returns can vary widely over the life of an asset as the asset depreciates because accounting returns use historical book values. Asset life affects the accounting returns through depreciation expense as well as the declining level of net investment (or net plant, property, and equipment).

For example, many years ago and as part of a business diversification strategy, Hershey bought Friendly Ice Cream Corporation. Friendly is primarily a domestic Northeastern restaurant chain that specializes in ice cream. A few years after Hershey purchased the company, the chain's growth slowed, and margins stopped improving. Some analysts and the business press looked at Friendly as a drag on Hershey's stock price. One major popular business publication encouraged Hershey to sell Friendly and reinvest the proceeds into the Chocolate Division because, as the publication saw it, the Friendly "return on investment" was only 14 percent, whereas the Chocolate Division's return was 35 percent.

The author of the recommendation used segment data as reported by Hershey and calculated the return on investment as the rate of return on each business segment's identifiable assets using Eq. (9.1):

$$\text{Return on investment} = \frac{\text{operating income}}{\text{identifiable assets}} \qquad (9.1)$$

$$\text{Chocolate Division return on investment} = \frac{\$212.7}{\$611.4} = 34.8\%$$

$$\text{Restaurant operations return on investment} = \frac{\$43.3}{\$310.9} = 13.9\%$$

In this case, the return on assets calculation from Chapter 3 was used to judge the quality of the Friendly investment.

TABLE 9-2

Return Differences

Accounting Returns	Economic Returns
Single time periods	Multiple time periods
Discrete time	Continuous time
Accrual income-based	Cash-flow-based
Historical book values	Market values

At that time, the chocolate and confectionery line of business had limited capital reinvestment because some of its functioning, efficient assets were over 70 years old. In fact, those assets were fully written off long ago and were included in the balance sheet at a zero dollar book value. On the other hand, when Hershey acquired Friendly Ice Cream Corporation, Hershey "wrote up" all of Friendly's assets as part of the acquisition accounting. As a division of Hershey, one of the restaurant's growth strategies included opening additional restaurants, which required additional capital investment. So Friendly's assets tended to be no more than six years old with an average age of approximately three years, whereas the Chocolate Division had assets with an average age of greater than 15 years. Thus the Chocolate Division had more income over a significantly reduced base to produce superior returns. Blind application of accounting-based returns led to the divestment recommendation, but the decision was skewed owing to the average age of the assets.

The recommendation also was shortsighted because it was only reflecting history. Did the world really need another candy bar? Was there an investment that was not already underway at Hershey? So many future business issues go unaddressed when looking solely at historical accounting rates of return.

Eventually, Hershey sold Friendly Ice Cream Corporation, but not as a result of accounting returns. Hershey sold Friendly only after Hershey had an offer to sell the business to a restaurateur that exceeded the economic evaluation of Friendly's strategic plan.

Consider also a new product introduction of a consumer-related product. Often there is an investment in equipment and working capital followed by introduction (and sales) of the new product. However, product introductions usually require marketing support through promotions, advertising, and so on. The first year or two of a new product's life may result in net income losses. No matter how you analyze it, if accounting returns are the focus, new products tend to have negative returns for the first few years of their life. Accounting returns and a one-period focus tend to limit the introduction of new products.

The following sections describe the common economic performance metrics used to evaluate investment decisions, but one final piece of capital investment background is needed—the *four phases of a successful capital program*.

FOUR PHASES OF A SUCCESSFUL CAPITAL PROGRAM

While nothing can guarantee the success of corporate investments, a four-phase approach increases the likelihood of success. The four phases include (1) planning, (2) project or capital evaluation, (3) status reporting, and (4) postcompletion reviews. Of course, successful implementation is paramount to any successful investment.

Capital Expenditure Planning

The planning phase originates with the strategic financial plan. In the strategic financial plan, capital expenditures are estimated in total with limited supporting details, except for "major" projects that may be specifically identified with minor capital expenditures estimated in total. Capacity reviews augmented with facilities reviews and merged with new product ideas identify significant future capital investment needs. Advanced project identification leads to advanced planning, evaluation, and prioritization.

Table 9-3 details the major projected capital expenditures in the five-year (2011–2015) strategic financial plan (see Chapter 6, specifically the strategic financial plan's assumptions, i.e., Table 6-12). Some of these planned expenditures are carryovers from 2009 and 2010. If a project does not have carryover into the planning period, that project's expenditures are combined and reported on the miscellaneous line. Thus, for example, 2009 saw hundreds of capital projects initiated and completed. The "Production line 12 renovation" began in 2009, carried through 2010, and will be completed in early 2011. This project is detailed. However, the other 2009 capital expenditures are accumulated and listed in total. More 2010 projects are detailed because of more carryover.

Notice that capital expenditures are broken into four major categories for planning purposes:

- *Cost savings*. Reduce the costs of production, distribution, etc.
- *Capacity expansion*. Support the corporate growth objective and strategies through increasing production capacity for existing products.
- *New products*. Support the corporate growth objective and strategies through capital investment in new product manufacturing equipment.
- *Miscellaneous*. Provide necessary capital for information technology, regulatory and safety, administration, research and development, etc.

In this hypothetical example, notice that the plan includes Hershey's current major project, "Next Century", and anticipates building a new Orlando production facility starting in 2015.

For cost savings, capacity expansion, and new products, capital project identification and expenditure estimates are determined more easily for the early years of the plan. This does not mean that capital will not be spent in the latter years. It does mean that at this point in time, when the strategic financial plan is

TABLE 9-3

Strategic Plan: Capital Expenditure Summary
($ millions)

	Actual Expenditures		Planned Expenditures					Total	
	2009	2010	2011	2012	2013	2014	2015	Plan Only	Total
Cost savings									
Production line #12 renovation	$ 4.8	$ 15.1	$ 2.0	$ —	$ —	$ —	$ —	$ 2.0	$ 21.9
Production line #14 renovation	—	5.0	17.0	3.0	—	—	—	20.0	25.0
Production line #16 renovation	—	—	6.0	8.0	4.0	—	—	18.0	18.0
Production line #41A renovation	—	6.6	24.0	—	—	—	—	24.0	30.6
Production line #41B renovation	—	—	6.0	12.0	—	—	—	18.0	18.0
Production line #42 renovation	—	—	—	15.0	21.5	—	—	36.5	36.5
Truck fleet replacement	4.0	4.5	4.5	5.0	5.0	5.5	7.5	27.5	36.0
Miscellaneous cost savings	48.1	31.2	16.3	17.4	45.0	50.0	50.0	178.7	258.0
Total cost savings	$ 56.9	$ 62.4	$ 75.8	$ 60.4	$ 75.5	$ 55.5	$ 57.5	$ 324.7	$ 444.0
Capacity expansion									
New milk handling line	$ —	$ 2.3	$ 15.0	$ —	$ —	$ —	$ —	$ 15.0	$ 17.3
Project "Next Century"	—	30.6	190.0	65.0	5.0	—	—	260.0	290.6
Automated warehousing robotics	—	—	9.7	6.1	8.9	—	—	24.7	24.7
Plant: Orlando location	—	—	—	—	—	—	20.0	20.0	20.0
Other capacity	20.7	29.8	10.5	14.0	16.0	20.0	20.0	80.5	131.0
Total capacity	$ 20.7	$ 62.7	$ 225.2	$ 85.1	$ 29.9	$ 20.0	$ 40.0	$ 400.2	$ 483.6

(Continued)

TABLE 9-3

Strategic Plan: Capital Expenditure Summary *(Continued)*
($ millions)

	Actual Expenditures			Planned Expenditures				Total	
	2009	2010	2011	2012	2013	2014	2015	Plan Only	Total
New product									
Sweet Morsels of Chocolate	$ –	$ –	$ 20.0	$ 25.0	$ –	$ –	$ –	$ 45.0	$ 45.0
Love'O'Chocolate	–	–	–	9.7	18.0	25.0	–	52.7	52.7
Joy Bites	–	–	–	–	20.0	45.0	–	65.0	65.0
Miscellaneous new products	26.4	33.6	7.0	7.0	8.6	8.0	62.0	92.6	152.6
Total new products	$ 26.4	$ 33.6	$ 27.0	$ 41.7	$ 46.6	$ 78.0	$ 62.0	$ 255.3	$ 315.3
Miscellaneous									
Information technology	$ 8.5	$ 5.1	$ 6.0	$ 8.0	$ 10.0	$ 10.0	$ 12.0	$ 46.0	$ 59.6
Regulatory and safety	4.0	5.0	5.0	4.0	4.0	5.0	5.0	23.0	32.0
Administrative	3.8	2.2	2.5	3.0	4.0	4.0	4.0	17.5	23.5
Research and development	6.0	8.5	8.5	12.8	15.0	17.5	19.5	73.3	87.8
Total miscellaneous	$ 22.3	$ 20.8	$ 22.0	$ 27.8	$ 33.0	$ 36.5	$ 40.5	$ 159.8	$ 202.9
Total capital expoenditures	$ 126.3	$ 179.5	$ 350.0	$ 215.0	$ 185.0	$ 190.0	$ 200.0	$ 1,140.0	$ 1,445.8

prepared, longer-term capital expenditures have not been detailed. Funds are included in the strategic financial plan without all the necessary specific project details in the outer years. Notice that the amount of miscellaneous expenditures increases throughout the planned years.

This advanced capital planning facilitates communication among the members of senior management and aligns functional areas. For example, engineering and manufacturing may plan to add more production capacity for a product. Marketing, on the other hand, may see declining product sales trends and may be planning to eliminate the product. This needs to be discussed, coordinated, and resolved. A strategic plan provides this opportunity. From the strategic capital plan, more detailed annual capital expenditure budgets can be created.

Good capital planning and budgeting will improve the timing of asset acquisitions and perhaps the quality of assets purchased. This result follows from the nature of capital goods and their producers. Firms often do not order capital goods until sales are beginning to press on capacity. Such occasions occur simultaneously for many firms. When the heavy orders come in, the producers of capital goods go from a situation of idle capacity to one where they cannot meet all the orders that have been placed. Consequently, large backlogs accumulate. Since the production of capital goods involves a relatively long work-in-process period, a year or more of waiting may be involved before the additional equipment is available. Furthermore, the quality of the capital goods, produced on rush order, may deteriorate. These factors have obvious implications for purchasing agents and plant managers.

Another reason for the importance of long-term capital budgeting is that asset expansion typically involves substantial expenditures. Before a firm spends a large amount of money, it must make the proper plans—large amounts of funds may not be available automatically. A firm contemplating a major capital expenditure program may need to plan its financing several years in advance to be sure of having the funds required for the expansion.

Capital Evaluation and Authorization (Phase 2)

In most companies, plan or budget identification of a capital project generally is not authorization to proceed with the project. Authorization (or acceptance) of a project happens during the project evaluation phase. This phase is the primary focus of this chapter and will be discussed in more detail below.

Capital Status Reporting (Phase 3)

After project evaluation and management approval, a project manager is assigned to implement the project on (or below) budget and on (or before) schedule. Status reporting tracks the project investment. This process reports the total budgeted amounts, project spending, and project commitment of funds. A *commitment* of funds represents signed contracts and commitments to pay that have not been billed by the vendor. Without delivery and billing, the expenditure is not recognized.

By using this report, the project manager (as well as senior management) can track the project's investment compared with the authorized approval.

Table 9-4 illustrates a hypothetical capital expenditure status report for the period ended June 30, 2011. The first section details actual expenditures and budget information for the current period (April to June) and for the year to date (January to June). Although this is a quarterly report, it also could be a monthly report if a company preferred. The report includes analysis by specific pieces of equipment within the total project. Continuing this hypothetical case, "Production line #14 renovation" has five specific major pieces of equipment identified along with some miscellaneous funds.

The budget for the second quarter was $3,200.0 thousand, with actual expenditures providing a favorable $115.5 thousand (3.6 percent) variance. The largest "savings" for the quarter came from the "V-belt conveyance" for $150.0 thousand, whereas "Piston A568–93" was over the second quarter budget by $150.0 thousand. For the year to date, actual expenditures totaled $6,850.7 million, with $350.7 thousand (5.4 percent) unfavorable to the budget. The "Piston A568–93" favorable variance for the year to date is $20.0 thousand, which implies that in the first quarter there was a $170.0 thousand favorable variance (perhaps a timing difference). This portion of the status report helps the project manager to track spending against the budget for a specific period of time.

The second section of Table 9-4 considers the full life of the project (October 2010 through March 2012), along with the actual amounts expended over the project's life, the project's total budget, the total commitment (which includes the expenditures), and a revised outlook. The budgeted amount of $25.0 million does not change over the project's life. It represents the amount approved by management and is an unchanging performance benchmark. The revised outlook is similar to a revised budget but reflects the project manager's latest estimate for completing the project. In this example, the outlook portrays a $1.0 million (or 4.0 percent) favorable variance, as mentioned in the footnote. Unfavorable outlook variances need to be addressed by the project manager and the management team. Project overruns and project supplements may need to be requested from management.

The project life "Actual vs. Budget" comparison shows how much of the budgeted funds remain, whereas the "Uncommitted" columns (calculated as outlook less commitment) shows the project manager the amount of uncommitted funds ($9,000.0 thousand) that remain against the latest outlook. Ultimately, if the project manager overcommits funds, a project cost overrun results.

By using a consolidated summary status report, senior management can monitor the implementation progress of all projects.

Postcompletion Reviews (Phase 4)

Postcompletion reviews are an often overlooked phase of capital investment. Even companies that conduct postcompletion reviews often consider this to be their weakest phase of the capital expenditure process. Postcompletion

TABLE 9-4

Hypothetical Capital Expenditure Status Report
($ millions)

Project: Production Line #14 Renovation   June 30, 2011   Manager: MSH

Asset Category	Item	Period: Second Quarter 2011		Actual vs. Budget		2011 Year to Date: Second Quarter 2011		Actual vs. Budget	
		Actual	Budget	$	%	Actual	Budget	$	%
Equipment	Drive shaft #31313	$ 1,134.5	$ 1,250.0	$ 115.5	9.2%	$ 3,650.7	$ 3,000.0	$ (650.7)	−21.7%
Equipment	Drive shaft #45562	–	–	–	0.0%	500.0	500.0	–	0.0%
Equipment	Piston A568–93	650.0	500.0	(150.0)	−30.0%	980.0	1,000.0	20.0	2.0%
Equipment	Stainless steel casing	–	–	–	0.0%	–	–	–	0.0%
Equipment	V-belt conveyance	850.0	1,000.0	150.0	15.0%	850.0	1,000.0	150.0	15.0%
Equipment	Miscellaneous	450.0	450.0	–	0.0%	870.0	1,000.0	130.0	13.0%
	Total	$ 3,084.5	$ 3,200.0	$ 115.5	3.6%	$ 6,850.7	$ 6,500.0	$ (350.7)	−5.4%

Project Life (October 2010–March 2012)

Asset Category	Item	Actual	Budget	Actual vs. Budget		Commitment	Outlook	Uncommitted	
				$	%			$	%
Equipment	Drive shaft #3131	$ 4,725.7	$ 10,000.0	$ 5,274.3	52.7%	$ 7,800.0	$ 9,350.0	$ 1,550.0	16.6%
Equipment	Drive shaft #4556	2,700.0	2,500.0	(200.0)	−8.0%	2,700.0	2,700.0	–	0.0%
Equipment	Piston A567	2,500.0	2,500.0	–	0.0%	2,500.0	2,500.0	–	0.0%
Equipment	Stainless steel casing	–	7,500.0	7,500.0	100.0%	–	7,200.0	7,200.0	100.0%
Equipment	V-belt conveyance	850.0	1,000.0	150.0	15.0%	850.0	850.0	–	0.0%
Equipment	Miscellaneous	1,075.0	1,500.0	425.0	28.3%	1,150.0	1,400.0	250.0	17.9%
	Total	$ 11,850.7	$ 25,000.0	$ 13,149.3	52.6%	$ 15,000.0	$ 24,000.0	$ 9,000.0	37.5%

Note: Project life outlook compared with project life budget represents a total $1,000 (4.0%) project investment favorable cost reduction.

reviews are conducted any time (one year, three years, or whenever) after the project is completed. Depending on the company, multiple postcompletions might be completed.

The review compares the project's original approved cash flows and economic evaluation indicators such as net present value, internal rate of return, and so on, which are discussed later in this chapter, with the cash flows and indicators based on updated operating performance and information. That is, actual project cost or investment is compared with the projected investment estimated when the project was approved. The first year (in the case of a one-year postcompletion review) of actual performance is substituted for the projected first year's performance. In the case of a three-year review, three years of actual performance are substituted for the first three years of projected performance. Finally, the cash flows for the remaining years are reestimated given new information and current performance. Based on this combination of actual investment, current performance, and reforecasted future performance, the economic evaluation indicators are recalculated and improvement or shortfalls addressed.

Postcompletion reviews are excellent learning tools for the organization. However, they are time-consuming, provide little "actionable" direction, and continue to incorporate projections. If a project is not performing up to the standards established in the project approval, performance shortfalls can be eradicated by painting an even rosier picture in the remaining years. Nonetheless, postcompletion reporting remains a valuable learning tool from which judgments can be made about future capital evaluations, requests, and authorizations.

Many organizations provide a supportive atmosphere where postcompletion reports are used to "fix problems" and not "fix blame." Some companies prepare postcompletion audits on all projects over a certain dollar threshold of investment (say, $5 million or $10 million), and other organizations require the three or five largest projects each year to undergo a review. Some companies do the postcompletion one year after the project has been implemented and in this way focus on the actual investment amount versus the projected investment and whether any major projected operating assumptions have changed. Other organizations also may retest a major project three years into the project to compare actual performance over the first few years with the projected performance, as well as compare the assumptions for the remaining time period (now versus the original projections).

At least two benefits occur with postcompletion audits. In the short run, if a project has gone off track, a postcompletion serves as an early-alert mechanism. Corrective action or alternative uses may be employed to right any issue.

In the longer term, corporate senior management can learn lessons over the years from trends in postcompletion reviews and better evaluate predispositions from one operating unit to another. Some operating units may display what is referred to as "sandbagging" predispositions, where their postcompletion reviews may indicate that this unit continually exceeds the evaluation and authorization projections. For example, if the unit's projection of sales is $70 million but a level of $60 million is enough to justify the project, that unit's management group may opt to report this more conservative estimate in the original project proposal. While estimate conservatism generally is a good practice, it then falls on corporate senior management to try to determine how conservative the authorization request is so as not to misallocate capital to another project.

On the other hand, another business unit may be overly optimistic in the evaluation phase with optimistic projections that few postcompletion reviews (e.g., actual performance) live up to. When funding requests come in from this business unit, the project champions should be questioned more rigorously and challenged by corporate senior management.

A postcomplete review is illustrated in Chapter 10. The next section focuses on the second phase of a successful capital investment program—the evaluation and authorization phase.

OVERVIEW OF THE INVESTMENT PROCESS

Table 9-5 summarizes the investment process. The process begins by projecting operating cash flows for a potential investment. The projected cash flows are the basis on which capital investment techniques are applied and the investment efficacy determined. The basics of determining cash flows are covered more fully in Chapter 10.

The major capital investment evaluation techniques include:

Payback period (PBP)

Net present value (NPV)

TABLE 9-5

Overview of Investment Analysis Process

Project future cash flows related to the project
Major capital investment evaluation techniques:
    Payback period (PBP)
    Net present value (NPV)
    Internal rate of return (IRR)
    Modified internal rate of return (MIRR)

Additional capital investment techniques:
    Discounted payback period (DPBP)
    Profitability index (PI)

Retest assumptions
    Sensitivity analysis
    Scenario analysis

Internal rate of return (IRR)

Modified internal rate of return (MIRR) or terminal rate of return (TRR)

Additional techniques covered in this chapter include:

Discounted payback period (DPBP)

Profitability index (PI)

These techniques will be fully developed throughout this chapter.

Finally, after calculating the evaluation criteria, most projects warrant a sensitivity and scenario analysis. This, too, will be covered in Chapter 10.

MAJOR INVESTMENT EVALUATION TECHNIQUES

The following sections illustrate the major investment analysis techniques: payback period, net present value, internal rate of return, and modified internal rate of return (or terminal rate of return). This section details the calculation of each technique along with a review of the strengths and weaknesses of each technique.

The point of capital investment analysis—indeed, the point of all financial analysis—is to make decisions that will maximize the value of the firm. The capital budgeting process is designed to answer three questions: (1) Is a project a worthwhile investment and a worthwhile use of the organizations funds? [in other words, an accept or reject (yes or no) decision], (2) Which investment alternative among mutually exclusive[1] investments should be selected? and (3) How many projects in total should be accepted?

When comparing various capital budgeting criteria, it is useful to establish some guidelines. The optimal decision rule will have four characteristics:

1. It will consider all appropriate (incremental after-tax) cash flows.

2. It will evaluate the cash flows at the appropriate market-determined opportunity cost of capital.

3. It will select a project from a group of mutually exclusive projects that maximizes shareholders' wealth.

4. It will allow managers to consider each project independently from all others. This has come to be known as the *value-additivity principle*.

The value-additivity principle implies that if we know the value of separate projects accepted by management, then simply by adding their values Vj will give us the value of the firm. If there are N projects, then the value of the firm will be as shown in Eq. (9.2):

---

[1] A mutually exclusive investment is a project that is competing directly with another project. The selection of one project makes the other project unnecessary. For example, if Hershey were considering building a new plant in Georgia or Florida, when the decision is made, the other choice is no longer appropriate.

$$V = \sum_{j=1}^{N} V_j \qquad \text{where } j = 1,...,N \qquad (9.2)$$

This is a particularly important point because it means that projects can be considered on their own merit without the necessity of looking at them in an infinite variety of combinations with other projects.

Now I present alternative capital investment analysis techniques. It becomes apparent that only one technique—the net present value method—satisfies all four of the desirable properties for capital budgeting criteria.

Table 9-6 presents the cash flows for two cleverly labeled projects, Projects A and B. They both have the same life, four years, and they require the same investment outlay, $1,000. The projected cash flows are also 100 percent certain and do not fluctuate. However, as you can see, these cash-flow projections have been inverted. Both projects are hypothetical for illustrative purposes only. The sole purpose of projects A and B is to help illustrate the evaluation techniques. These projects and their cash flows will be used to discuss the capital evaluation techniques.

Payback Period

Payback period (PBP) represents the number of years required to return the original investment. As illustrated in Table 9-7, Project A has a 1.60-year payback period, while Project B has a payback period of 3.14 years. Project A costs $1,000, but pays back $700 cash in the first year and $500 cash in the second year. To calculate the payback period, we must include the total cash flow generated in the first year ($700). This leaves $300 outstanding until the project is "paid back." Assuming even cash flows throughout the year, it takes an additional 0.60 year (or the remaining outstanding $300 divided by the project's $500 second-year cash flow). In total, the project pays back in 1.60 years. Project B generates $100 in the first year, $300 in the second year, and $500 in the third year, or a total of only $900 through the first three years. This leaves $100 until Project B is paid back from year 4's cash flow of $700, or 0.14 years ($100/$700), assuming level cash flows throughout the year for a payback period of 3.14 years.

TABLE 9-6

Cash Flows of Illustrative Projects

A	Projects	B
$ (1,000)	Cost (outflow) year 0	($1,000)
700	Cash inflow year 1	100
500	Cash inflow year 2	300
300	Cash inflow year 3	500
100	Cash inflow year 4	700

TABLE 9-7

Payback Period

A	Projects	B
$ (1,000)	Cost (outflow) year 0	($1,000)
700	Cash inflow year 1	100
500	Cash inflow year 2	300
300	Cash inflow year 3	500
100	Cash inflow year 4	700
	Accumulated cash inflow	
$ 700	Year 1	$ 100
1,200	Year 2	400
1,500	Year 3	900
1,600	Year 4	1,600
1.60 years	Payback period	3.14 years

If the projects are mutually exclusive, choose either Project A or Project B (but not both). You should choose Project A because it pays back faster. Said differently, Project A has a shorter time horizon for when the cash investment is exposed.

If the projects are independent (not mutually exclusive), management needs to establish some cutoff criteria for the acceptable length of payback. These criteria should correspond to the underlying business. For example, most domestic manufacturing firms use a rule of thumb payback period of three to five years. In this case, with a payback-period acceptance criterion of four years, both these projects would be acceptable. However, if the cutoff period were only three years, Project B would be rejected and miss the cutoff period by almost two months.

As another example of this cutoff period, a high-tech company used a payback-period acceptance criterion of less than one year for some projects because in its words, "If the project did not pay back in one year, the technology would be obsolete and would not provide a return beyond the one-year period."

Three arguments can be given for use of the payback method. First, it is easy to use. Second, for a company in a tight cash position, it may be of great interest to know how soon it gets back the dollars it has invested. And third, longer-term projections often have more volatility in their estimates and may be less certain. Remember, for our purposes, the cash flows of all of these examples are 100 percent certain!

However, the payback period has significant drawbacks that may result in the wrong investment decision (Table 9-8):

TABLE 9-8

Payback Period: Additional projects

C	Projects	D
$ (1,000)	Cost (outflow) year 0	($1,000)
200	Cash inflow year 1	1,000
300	Cash inflow year 2	-
400	Cash inflow year 3	-
10,000	Cash inflow year 4	-
	Accumulated cash inflow	
$ 200	Year 1	$ 1,000
500	Year 2	1,000
900	Year 3	1,000
10,900	Year 4	1,000
3.01 years	Payback period	1.00 years

1. *The payback period approach does not look beyond the payback period.* As shown in Project C (and remembering that the cash flows are certain), the project has a payback period of more than three years (3.01 years). Strictly using the payback period leads us to continue to accept Project A despite the substantial payoff offered by Project C because of its fourth-year cash flow.

2. *The payback period does not consider the time value of money.* Consequently, Project D has an acceptable one-year payback period and would be the first choice of all four projects. However, it never returns a positive amount on the investment. You simply recover what you put into it! As discussed later, the discounted payback period eliminates this shortcoming.

Nonetheless, while the payback period is not the recommended investment evaluation tool, many decision makers continue to use it as a rule of thumb.

Net Present Value

Net present value (NPV) is the present value of the projected future cash flows discounted at an appropriate cost of capital or hurdle rate less the cost of the investment. Figure 9-1 graphically depicts the net present value of Project A. The projected cash flows are discounted back to today (year 0) by using the TVM tools developed in Chapter 7 and by using Eq. (9.3):

$$\text{Present value} = \sum_{t}^{N} \frac{\text{cash flow}_t}{(1+r)^t} \qquad (9.3)$$

$$\text{Present value of Project A} = \frac{\$700}{(1+0.08)^1} = \$648.15 = PV(CF_1)$$

$$+ \frac{\$500}{(1+0.08)^2} = \$428.67 = PV(CF_2)$$

$$+ \frac{\$300}{(1+0.08)^3} = \$238.15 = PV(CF_3)$$

$$+ \frac{\$100}{(1+0.08)^4} = \$73.50 = PV(CF_4)$$

The first-year cash flow of $700 is discounted for one year at 8 percent for a present value of $648.15, and so on. This project is worth $1,388.47 (the sum of the present values), but the investment requirement is only $1,000. Subtracting the investment from the present value of the cash flows results in a net present value of $388.47.

The discount rate in this example is 8 percent, which approximates the organization's cost of capital. The cost of capital is the after-tax cost of all financing sources, debt and equity. The cost of capital is often referred to as the firm's *hurdle rate, discount rate,* or *required return*. For further definition and description of the cost of capital, please see Chapter 11.

More generally, net present value can be written as shown in Eq. (9.4):

$$
\begin{aligned}
NPV &= \frac{CF_1}{(1+k)^1} + \frac{CF_2}{(1+k)^2} + \cdots + \frac{CF_N}{(1+k)^N} - I_0 \\
&= \sum_{t=1}^{N} \frac{CF_t}{(1+k)^t} - I_0 = \$0
\end{aligned}
\tag{9.4}
$$

where CF_t = cash flow in period t
k = cost of capital
t = time period
N = total number of periods
I_0 = investment in time 0

Table 9-9 compares the net present values for both Project A and Project B. If these projects are independent, management should accept both projects because both have positive net present values and add value to the organization. If the projects are mutually exclusive, rank the projects based on the size of the net present value, and Project A is the investment choice under mutual exclusivity.

The NPV of the project is exactly the same as the increase in shareholders' wealth. This fact makes it the correct decision rule for capital budgeting purposes. The NPV rule also meets the other three general principles required for an optimal capital budgeting criterion. It takes all cash flows into account. All cash flows are discounted at the appropriate market-determined opportunity cost of

FIGURE   9-1

Present value of Project A.

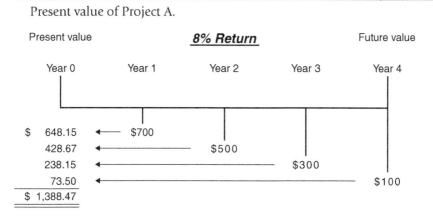

capital in order to determine their present values. Also, the NPV rule obeys the value-additivity principle. Thus each project can be evaluated on its own merits.

If a project has zero NPV, it should be accepted because it can pay off the investment amount, interest, dividends, and capital gains and still provide "extra" to cover the required rate of return. A positive-NPV project earns more than the required rate of return, and equity holders receive all excess cash flows because debt holders have a fixed claim on the firm. As a result, equity holders' wealth increases by exactly the NPV of the project. This is the direct link between shareholders' wealth and the NPV definition and makes the NPV criterion so important in decision making.

For our analysis of Project A, let's further assume that there are 388 shares outstanding. If the benefits and impact of this project could be communicated

TABLE   9-9

Net Present Value

A	Projects	B
$ 648.15	Present value of year 1 cash flow	$ 92.59
428.67	Present value of year 2 cash flow	257.20
238.15	Present value of year 3 cash flow	396.92
73.50	Present value of year 4 cash flow	514.52
$ 1,388.47	Total present value cash flow	$ 1,261.23
1,000.00	Less: Investment (year 0)	1,000.00
$ 388.47	Net present value (8%)	$ 261.23
$ 186.48	Net present value (18%)	$ (34.43)

effectively to the stock market, and if the market would believe that the project could be successfully implemented as presented, then the stock price should reflect an immediate $1 per share increase ($388/388 shares). But these are two very large *ifs*!

Notice in Table 9-9 that at an 18 percent cost of capital, the NPVs of both projects decrease. Project B's NPV turns negative and consequently indicates that Project B is not a good investment. With an 18 percent cost of capital, Project B should be rejected, and only Project A should be accepted regardless of whether these are mutually exclusive projects or independent projects.

Internal Rate of Return

The *internal rate of return* (IRR) is the interest rate that equates the present value of projected future cash flows to the investment expenditure. It is the discount rate where the NPV equals $0, as calculated by Eq. (9.5):

$$NPV = \frac{CF_1}{(1+IRR)^1} + \frac{CF_2}{(1+IRR)^2} + \cdots + \frac{CF_N}{(1+IRR)^N} - I_0$$

$$= \sum_{t=1}^{N} \frac{CF_t}{(1+IRR)^t} - I_0 = \$0$$

(9.5)

Notice that the IRR formula (Eq. 9.5) is simply the NPV formula (Eq. 9.4) solved for that particular value of k that causes the NPV to equal zero. In other words, the same basic equation is used for both methods, but in the NPV method, the discount rate k is specified as the market-determined opportunity cost of capital, whereas in the IRR method, the NPV is set equal to zero, and the value of IRR that forces the NPV to equal zero is found. Figure 9-2 demonstrates the IRR for Project A graphically.

F I G U R E   9-2

Internal rate of return—Project A.

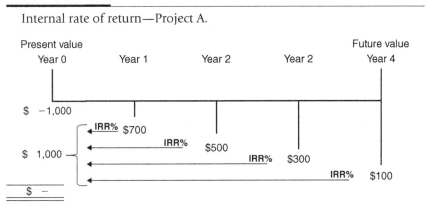

Financial calculators (such as the Hewlett Packard 10bII+ or Texas Instrument BA II Plus) or personal computers with spreadsheet software are discussed briefly in the next section. However, with an ordinary calculator, the internal rate of return can be found by trial and error. First, compute the present value of the cash flows from an investment using an arbitrarily selected interest rate, for example, 8 percent. Then compare the present value with the investment's cost. If the present value is higher than the investment amount (positive NPV), try a higher interest rate, and go through the procedure again. Conversely, if the present value is lower than the cost, lower the interest rate, and repeat the process. Continue until the present value of the flows from the investment is approximately equal to its cost. The interest rate that brings about this equality is defined as the *internal rate of return*.

Table 9-10 shows computations for the IRR of Project A. As mentioned earlier, the computations involve trial and error, guessing discount rates, and using those discount rates to test whether the net present value is zero. From the NPV calculation, we saw that a discount rate of 8 percent yields a positive $388 NPV, and the yield is consequently too low. Likewise, at 16 percent, Project A's NPV is $222, so we try 32 percent with a $(19) NPV. At 24 percent, the NPV is $89, so the IRR must be between 24 and 32 percent. Trying 28 percent, the NPV is $32, 30 percent resulted in an NPV of $6, and 31 percent resulted in an NPV of $(7). So a guess of 30.5 percent yielded approximately a $0 net present value on the eighth try!

In Table 9-11, the IRR for both Projects A and B are presented. Project A has a more precise IRR of 30.46 percent, whereas Project B has an IRR of 16.62 percent. If the projects are independent projects, the IRR should be compared with the cost of capital or a hurdle rate. If the IRR exceeds this risk-adjusted cost of capital, the project should be accepted. If the project's IRR is less than the risk-adjusted cost of capital, the project should be rejected. If the projects are mutually exclusive and exceed the hurdle rate, in general, choose the one with the larger IRR. In this example, choose Project A!

Financial Calculator and Spread-Sheet Calculations

While calculation of the NPV and IRR are easy to understand, most actual calculations can be facilitated easily with a financial calculator or spreadsheet software. Chapter 7 focused on two popular financial calculators, the Hewlett-Packard (HP) 10bII+ and the Texas Instruments (TI) BA II Plus, provides specific instructions on the use of both calculators. In general, both calculators function the same way:

1. Clear the calculator.
2. Be sure that the cash flows are set as one-period per year (push 1, then the second-level key, and the P/YR button).
3. Input the cash-flow values using the appropriate cash-flow keys.
4. Supply the discount rate in the case of the NPV.
5. Calculate NPV and IRR.

TABLE 9-10

Calculating IRR—Project A

| | Project A Cash Flow | | Discounted Cash-Flow Value | | | | | | | |
		Trial 1 8.0%	Trial 2 16.0%	Trial 3 32.0%	Trial 4 24.0%	Trial 5 28.0%	Trial 6 30.0%	Trial 7 31.0%	Trial 8 30.5%
Cash inflows									
Year 1	$ 700	$ 648	$ 603	$ 530	$ 565	$ 547	$ 538	$ 534	$ 536
Year 2	500	429	372	287	325	305	296	291	294
Year 3	300	238	192	130	157	143	137	133	135
Year 4	100	74	55	33	42	37	35	34	34
Total present value		$ 1,388	$ 1,222	$ 981	$ 1,089	$ 1,032	$ 1,006	$ 993	$ 999
Investment		1,000	1,000	1,000	1,000	1,000	1,000	1,000	1,000
Net present value		$ 388	$ 222	$ (19)	$ 89	$ 32	$ 6	$ (7)	$ (1)

IRR ≈ 30.5%

T A B L E   9-11

Internal Rate of Return

A	Projects	B
30.46%	Internal rate of return (IRR)	16.62%
	Present value at IRR	
$ 536.57	Present value of year 1 cash flow	$ 85.75
293.79	Present value of year 2 cash flow	220.58
135.12	Present value of year 3 cash flow	315.24
34.52	Present value of year 4 cash flow	378.43
$ 1,000.00	Total present value cash flow	$ 1,000.00
1,000.00	Less: Investment (year 0)	1,000.00
$ 0.00	Net present value (at IRR%)	$ 0.00

For example, using the HP 10bII+ to calculate the NPV and IRR of Project A:

Enter value	Push key
−1,000	CFj
700	CFj
500	CFj
300	CFj
100	CFj
8	I/YR

Using the CFj key, the cash flows are entered in order (year 0 to year 4) into the calculator, and the annual interest rate (8 percent) is also entered. The following steps complete the calculations:

Push key	Answer
NPV	388.47
IRR/YR	30.46

The TI BA II Plus is also as simple to use by using similar keys. Please see the TI owner's manual for the exact key strokes.

Spreadsheet software such as Excel enable simplified calculations of net present value, internal rate of return, and modified internal rate of return.

Modified Internal Rate of Return

The internal rate of return (IRR) implicitly assumes reinvestment of the intermediate cash flows at the IRR. Although Eq. (9.5) does not explicitly address reinvestment, implicitly, reinvestment at the IRR is assumed. For Projects A and B, what if you cannot reinvest at their IRRs? Management would enjoy having 30.46 percent-returning projects (like project A) just sitting around waiting for funding. What if other 30.46 percent-return opportunities do not exist? What if the best the company can do is reinvest at 8 percent, its cost of capital? The modified internal rate of return explicitly addresses the reinvestment assumption.

Modified internal rate of return (MIRR) or *terminal rate of return* (TRR) is the discount rate that equates the cost of the investment with the accumulated future value of the intermediate cash flows that are assumed to be reinvested at an appropriate risk-adjusted cost of capital.

Figure 9-3 illustrates calculation of the MIRR for Project A. The calculation is a two-step process. The first step explicitly reinvests the intermediate cash flows at 8 percent, the cost of capital. For example, the first-year cash flow is invested for three years between the end of the first and fourth years. The first-year cash flow of $700 accumulates to $881.80 by the end of year 4 [i.e., $700(1 + 0.08)^3$]. The second-year cash flow of $500 grows to $583.20 with reinvestment for

FIGURE 9-3

Modified internal rate of return—Project A.
(Reinvestment at 8% cost of capital)

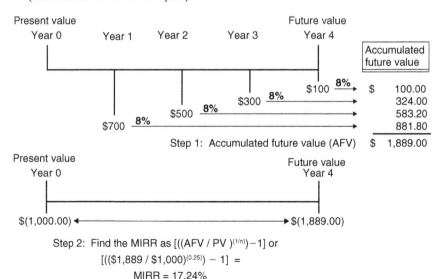

Step 2: Find the MIRR as $[((AFV / PV)^{(1/n)}) - 1]$ or
$[(($1,889 / $1,000)^{(0.25)}) - 1] =$
MIRR = 17.24%

two years at 8 percent (years 3 and 4). The third-year cash flow of $300 grows to $324.00 with reinvestment for one year at 8 percent, and the final year's cash flow of $100 remains $100.00 because it lacks time to grow. In total, the accumulated future value (or terminal value) of the intermediate cash flows that are assumed reinvested at 8 percent, the cost of capital, is $1,889.00.

The second step compares the investment with the accumulated future value of the projected and reinvested cash flows. The lower portion of Figure 9-3 illustrates this final step:

$$MIRR_{Project A} = \left(\frac{\text{accumluated FV}}{\text{investment PV}}\right)^{1/n} - 1 = \left(\frac{\$1,889}{\$1,000}\right)^{1/4} - 1 = 17.24\%$$

This is the same equation used in Chapter 7 to solve for the compound annual growth rate (CAGR) when you have two lump sums, present value and future value. For Project A, the modified internal rate of return is 17.24 percent and reflects the interest rate that equates the cost of the investment ($1,000) with the accumulated future value of $1,889.

Table 9-12 captures the MIRR for both Projects A and B and compares them. Project B has an accumulated future value (assuming 8 percent reinvestment) of $1,715.89 in year 4, which equates to a 14.45 percent TRR.

Although there are arguably a number of reinvestment rates to consider, including marginal or average rates of return, the reinvestment-rate assumption is actually an inaccurate use of terminology for what should be called the *opportunity-cost assumption*. The term *reinvestment rate* is misleading because it causes an unnecessary distraction and debate about whether or not cash flows from the project can be reinvested at the IRR of the project. The real issue is this: Given the risk of the project, at what rate can funds be invested (or reinvested) somewhere else for the same level of risk? All investment projects of equal risk will have the same opportunity cost from the point of view of all investors.

T A B L E 9-12

Terminal Rate of Return at 8 Percent Reinvestment

A	Projects	B
$ 881.80	Future value of year 1 cash flow	$ 125.97
583.20	Future value of year 2 cash flow	349.92
324.00	Future value of year 3 cash flow	540.00
100.00	Future value of year 4 cash flow	700.00
$ 1,889.00	Total accumulated cash flow	$ 1,715.89
$ 1,000.00	Investment (year 0)	$ 1,000.00
17.24%	Modified internal rate of return	14.45%
30.46%	Internal rate of return	16.62%

It is assumed that Projects A and B are equally risky and that all investors require at least an 8 percent rate of return to invest in the projects. The rate of 8 percent is the appropriate opportunity cost of capital for the assumed level of risk of the project. This is why we discount the cash flows at an 8 percent rate when calculating the NPV. When calculating the MIRR, if the reinvestment rate is a risk-adjusted cost of capital (or hurdle rate), the reinvestment rate is neutral to the accept/reject decision. Consequently, the appropriate "reinvestment rate" is the opportunity cost of capital.

If the projects are independent projects, the MIRR should be compared with the reinvestment rate, the risk-adjusted cost of capital. If the MIRR exceeds this opportunity cost, the project should be accepted. If the project's MIRR is less than the risk-adjusted cost of capital, the project should be rejected. If the projects are mutually exclusive and exceed the reinvestment rate, choose the one with the larger MIRR. In this example, again, choose Project A!

Notice the comparison of IRR and MIRR for both projects:

	Project A	Project B
IRR	30.46%	16.62%
MIRR at 8%	17.24%	14.45%

Although Project A is preferred under either criterion, its rate of return more realistically reflects reinvestment at the cost of capital (8 percent). Comparing the IRR and MIRR for Project A, the rates of return drop significantly more with Project A because of the difference in reinvestment-rate assumptions (e.g., a realistic 8 percent versus the implied and unrealistic 30.46 percent IRR) and the timing of the cash flows. The MIRR reflects a more realistic return for management's scrutiny and approval.

Before leaving the MIRR discussion, let's revisit the implicit reinvestment assumption included in the IRR using the TRR framework. That is, the IRR assumes reinvestment at the IRR. Figure 9-4 illustrates this graphically for Project A.

In the figure, the intermediate cash flows are reinvested at 30.46 percent, Project A's IRR. The resulting accumulated future value of the intermediate cash flows is $2,896.65 compared with an investment of $1,000 and yields a modified internal rate of return of 30.46 percent, which is equal to the IRR! The major difficulty with the IRR method is that it makes an inappropriate opportunity-cost assumption—reinvestment at the IRR. There is a substantial difference between the accumulated future value of $1,889.00 (8 percent reinvestment, the cost of capital) and $2,896.65 (30.46 percent reinvestment at the IRR). Table 9-13 details both Projects A and B.

So far I covered the four most often used capital evaluation techniques: payback period, net present value, internal rate of return, and modified internal rate of return. In reality, the MIRR is not a widely used technique, but it is a valuable permutation of IRR.

FIGURE   9-4

Internal rate of return—Project A.
(Reinvestment at 8% cost of capital)

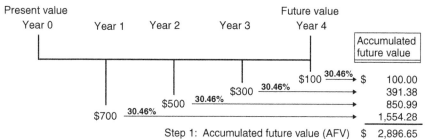

Step 1: Accumulated future value (AFV) $ 2,896.65

Step 2: Find the MIRR as $[((AFV / PV)^{(1/n)}) - 1]$ or
$[(($2,896.65 / $1,000.00)^{(0.25)}) - 1] =$
MIRR = 30.46%

TABLE   9-13

Terminal Rate of Return at the Implicit Project's IRR

A	Projects	B
$ 1,554.28	Future value of year 1 cash flow	$ 158.60
850.99	Future value of year 2 cash flow	408.01
391.38	Future value of year 3 cash flow	583.10
100.00	Future value of year 4 cash flow	700.00
$ 2,896.65	Total accumulated cash flow	$ 1,849.71
$ 1,000.00	Investment (year 0)	$ 1,000.00
30.46%	Explicit reinvestment rate at IRR	16.62%
30.46%	Modified internal rate of return	16.62%
30.46%	Internal rate of return	16.62%

ADDITIONAL INVESTMENT EVALUATION TECHNIQUES

Two additional investment evaluation techniques are discussed briefly below: (1) discounted payback period, which is a variant of payback period, and (2) profitability index (PI), which is a permutation of NPV.

Discounted Payback Period

Discounted payback period is an augmentation of the payback period and reflects the number of years required to return the original investment based on estimated future cash flows, which are discounted at an appropriate cost of capital or hurdle rate. One of the illustrated shortcomings of the payback period technique was that it did not consider the time value of money (TVM). Using discounted cash flows, as illustrated in Table 9-14, eradicates this issue.

The discounted cash flows (at the 8 percent cost of capital) for Projects A and B are found in Table 9-14. In the first year, Project A experiences $648.15 of discounted cash inflows and requires an additional $351.85 to cover the investment of $1,000. The second year provides a discounted cash flow of $428.67. Assuming even cash flow throughout the year, Project A needs 0.82($351.85/$428.67) of the second year's cash flow to repay the investment. Project A's discounted payback period is 1.82 years.

Notice that after three years, Project B has an accumulated present value of each of the first three years' cash flows of only $746.71. In order to "pay back" the original investment of $1,000, a fourth-year requirement of $253.29 is

TABLE 9-14

Discounted Payback Period

A	Projects	B
$ (1,000.00)	Cost (outflow) year 0	$ (1,000.00)
700.00	Cash inflow year 1	100.00
500.00	Cash inflow year 2	300.00
300.00	Cash inflow year 3	500.00
100.00	Cash inflow year 4	700.00
	Cash-flow present value at 8%	
$ 648.15	Year 1	$ 92.59
428.67	Year 2	257.20
238.15	Year 3	396.92
73.50	Year 4	514.52
	Accumulated cash inflow	
$ 648.15	Year 1	$ 92.59
1,076.82	Year 2	349.79
1,314.97	Year 3	746.71
1,388.47	Year 4	1,261.23
1.82 years	Discounted payback period	3.49 years
1 +		3 +
351.85/428.67		253.29/514.52

necessary. This required amount is 0.49 year of year 4's discounted $514.52 amount. Thus the discounted payback for Project B is 3.49 years, or 3 years and $253.29/$514.52 of year 4. Project A remains the preferred project if these projects are mutually exclusive.

This approach improves on the payback period by considering the TVM, but in the process, this technique complicates the calculation of the payback period and reduces its commonsense appeal. To extend the illustration from earlier in the chapter, using the discounted payback period, the company would correctly reject Project D (from Table 9-8):

Year	Cash Flow Project D	Discounted CF at 8 %
Year 0	$(1,000)	$(1,000)
Year 1	1,000	926
Year 2	—	—
Year 3	—	—
Year 4	—	—

Project D never pays back at any discount rate. At 8 percent, from earlier, the project has a negative NPV of ($74) and correctly should be rejected.

However, strict adherence to this technique does not look beyond the payback period. As presented earlier in this chapter (Table 9-8), Project C has a large payoff in year 4.

Year	Cash Flow Project C	Discounted CF at 8%
Year 0	$(1,000)	$(1,000)
Year 1	200	185
Year 2	300	257
Year 3	400	318
Year 4	10,000	7,350

Project C has a discounted payback period of 3.03 years. Project A is still preferred, and the organization continues to miss out on the substantial fourth-year cash flow.

Profitability Index

The *profitability index* (PI) is a variation of net present value. It is calculated as the present value of estimated future cash flows, discounted at an appropriate cost of capital or hurdle rate, and divided by the cost of the investment, as shown in Eq. (9.6):

$$\mathrm{PI} = \sum_{t=1}^{N} \frac{\mathrm{CF}_t}{(1+k)^t} \div I_0 \qquad (9.6)$$

Of course, the NPV subtracts the investment amount from the present value of the cash flow. The PI suggests that for every dollar invested, you receive a present value dollar return equal to the PI.

Table 9-15 demonstrates the PI for Projects A and B. The NPV remains as calculated in Table 9-9, $388.47 for Project A and $261.23 for Project B. Using the PI, once again, Project A is preferred. Every dollar invested in Project A provides a return of $1.388 versus a return of $1.261 for Project B.

So far, all the investment evaluation techniques lead to choosing Project A under terms of mutual exclusivity. Are the techniques always consistent? What if conflicts arise? Which is the best approach? These questions will be addressed in the upcoming section.

Investment Technique—Conflict Resolution

The only apparent structural difference between the NPV and IRR methods lies in the discount rates used in the two equations—all the values in the equations are identical except for IRR and k. Further, we can see that if IRR $> k$, then NPV $>$ \$0. Accordingly, it is correct that the two methods give the same accept/reject decisions for specific projects—if a project is acceptable under the NPV criterion, it is also acceptable if the IRR method is used.

However, the following example illustrates that this statement is incorrect when it comes to mutually exclusive projects. Consider the pattern of cash flows in Table 9-16, which contains information about two mutually exclusive projects, cleverly labeled X and Y. Both projects cost $1,000 and have varying (and inverted) cash flows over a five-year period. Although these numbers were contrived to illustrate a point, this conflict is sometimes evident when evaluating

T A B L E   9-15

Profitability Index

A	Projects	B
$ 648.15	Present value of year 1 cash flow	$ 92.59
428.67	Present value of year 2 cash flow	257.20
238.15	Present value of year 3 cash flow	396.92
73.50	Present value of year 4 cash flow	514.52
$ 1,388.47	Total present value cash flow	$ 1,261.23
1,000.00	Less: Investment (year 0)	1,000.00
$ 388.47	Net present value (8%)	$ 261.23
	Profitability index	
1.388	Present value / investment	1.261
($1,388.47/$1000)		($1,261.23/$1000)

investment opportunities that stretch over 10 to 12 years. These numbers were contrived to fit in a five-year window and to illustrate the points. Another side benefit of Table 9-16 is that readers can confirm their understanding of the calculation mechanics.

For both projects, it is assumed that there is no risk in the cash flows and no life beyond the noted five-year period. Notice that if we simply add the underlying five years of cash flow, Project X (Project Y) generates $2,405 ($1,895) in total cash flow. Just summing the generated cash flows and ignoring the time value of money leads us to accept Project X. Effectively, this is a net present value assuming a 0 percent discount rate!

T A B L E   9-16

Illustrative Recap with Noted Selection Conflict

Project X	Cash Flow and Criteria	Project Y	Project Selection
$ 150	Future value of year 1 cash flow	$ 1,000	
225	Future value of year 2 cash flow	400	
350	Future Value of year 3 cash flow	300	
450	Future value of year 4 cash flow	150	
1,230	Future value of year 5 cash flow	45	
$ 2,405	Total accumulated cash flow	$ 1,895	
$ 1,000	Investment (year 0)	$ 1,000	
$ 1,405	Net present value (0%)	$ 895	Project X
$ 778	Net present value (8%)	$ 648	Project X
546	Net present value (12%)	546	Either one
355	Net present value (16%)	456	Project Y
26.06%	Internal rate of return	46.85%	Project Y
21.17%	Modified internal rate of return (8%)	19.35%	Project X
22.20%	Modified internal rate of return (12%)	22.20%	Either one
23.26%	Modified internal rate of return (16%)	25.05%	Project Y
1.778	Profitability index (8%)	1.648	Project X
1.546	Profitability index (12%)	1.546	Either one
1.355	Profitability index (16%)	1.456	Project Y
3.611	Payback period	1.000	Project Y
4.071	Discounted payback period (8%)	1.216	Project Y
4.217	Discounted payback period (12%)	1.336	Project Y
4.394	Discounted payback period (16%)	1.464	Project Y

In a more traditional application, which project would you prefer at an 8 percent cost of capital when using net present value? The one with the higher net present value, Project X ($778 NPV versus Project Y's NPV of $648) should be accepted. At 12 percent, both projects have the same NPV, so the choice should be made for "strategic" or other reasons. At a 16 percent cost of capital, Project Y is preferred.

But why should investment analysis be so complicated? Project Y's IRR is almost double the IRR of Project X (46.85 versus 26.06 percent). Choose Project Y using the IRR! Yes, that's true—*if* you can reinvest at 46.85 percent. But what if you can't reinvest at 46.85 percent?

Using the modified internal rate of return with an 8 percent "reinvestment rate," choose Project X. With a 12 percent reinvestment rate, strategic rationale and other criteria need to be considered because the MIRRs are identical at 22.20 percent. At a reinvestment rate of 16 percent, choose Project Y. Notice that with the same investment amount for both projects ($1,000), NPV and MIRR give consistent accept/reject decisions and project rankings. Another consideration is that MIRR provides a more realistic view of the rate of return provided by both projects, but especially Project Y.

Notice that the profitability index follows the same accept/reject pattern provided by both NPV and MIRR for each project.

One final observation regarding Table 9-16: The payback period approach always points to selecting Project Y—whether it is a traditional payback period or a discounted payback period. This is a function of the assumed cash flows, which are heavily skewed toward the first year for Project Y and the later years for Project X.

The selection criteria used, along with the appropriate discount rate, can play a role in which project gets accepted and which project gets rejected. Net present value is the criterion of choice that satisfies all the evaluation qualities discussed previously. The appropriate discount rate is the firm's cost of capital, or the opportunity cost of funds could be deployed in cash flows or projects of similar risk, in our case 8 percent. More will be said about the cost of capital in Chapter 11.

From Table 9-16, MIRR and PI also provide the same accept/reject decisions as NPV. But this is for a special case where the investment is exactly the same for both projects. If the investment amounts differ, even NPV, MIRR, and PI can provide different accept/reject results.

Further Comparison of Techniques

A basic shortcoming of IRR, MIRR, and PI is illustrated by a simple example involving two projects with a one-year project life and a significant size differential. Suppose that Project R involves an outlay of $1,000 and returns $1,500 in one year or a present value of $1,389 (at 8 percent discount rate). Its net present value is $389, and its profitability index is 1.389. Another investment requires an outlay of $10,000 and at the end of the year has a return of $12,500 in one year or a present value of $11,574 (at an 8 percent discount rate). Its NPV is $1,574, and its PI is 1.157:

Projects	R	S
Investment (year 0)	$1,000	$10,000
Cash flow (year 1)	1,500	12,500
PV of cash flow (8%)	1,389	11,574
Net present value (NPV)	$ 389	$ 1,574
Profitability index (PI)	1.389	1.157
Internal rate of return (IRR)	50%	25%
Modified IRR	50%	25%

Under the NPV rule, the larger investment with the larger NPV is clearly superior. Under PI, the firm would select the smaller project (with a PI of 1.389) and enhance its value by only $389 (NPV). If the firm can finance all available investments, the PI would not provide a ranking that the firm would want to follow.

Notice, also, in this example with such wide disparity in the size of the two competing projects that the MIRR also breaks down. In this example, the smaller project has a MIRR of 50 percent, whereas the larger project has a MIRR of 25 percent. Strict adherence to the PI or MIRR rules may lead to the wrong decision when comparing two mutually exclusive projects that differ widely in investment size.

In practice, such wide investment disparity in alternative competing projects may be less than common. If you were faced with a personal investment decision that accomplishes exactly the same end, but one alternative requires an investment of $1,000 and the other requires $10,000, what decision would you make? Ask yourself these questions: If this were my investment choice, would I prefer a 50 percent IRR or a 25 percent IRR? If this were my investment choice, would I prefer a 50 percent MIRR or a 25 percent MIRR? If this were my investment choice, would I prefer a PI of 1.389 or a PI of 1.157? Finally, if this were my investment choice, would I prefer to earn my required 8% return and a windfall of $389 or a windfall of $1,574? Quickly, the percentages give way to actual hard-cash preferences—personally (because that's what we spend at the grocery store) and in business. NPV is the preferred investment metric.

Nonetheless, the point is made that owing to size differences, an incorrect selection could take place if the organization centered its decision on IRR, MIRR, or PI. NPV leads to enhanced shareholder value.

Project Profiles

Figure 9-5 graphs the project profiles for both Project X and Project Y. Project X is the dashed line; the *x* axis lists the discount rate, and the *y* axis denotes the net

FIGURE   9-5

Project profiles.

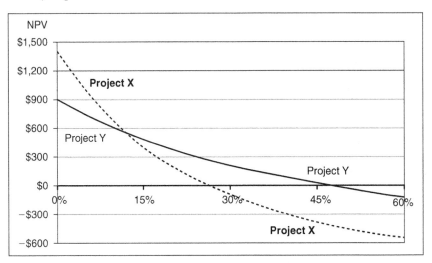

present value. The project profile illustrates the NPV for the cash flows in Table 9-16 at different discount rates.

A few points need to be established in Figure 9-5. At a zero discount rate, that is, no discounting of the cash flows, the net present value is simply the sum of the cash inflows less the investment amount. For Project X, the sum of the cash inflows is $2,405 less the $1,000 investment or an NPV of $1,405 without discounting. Project Y's cash inflows total $1,895 less the $1,000 investment or an NPV of $895 (at 0 percent). These two points are plotted on the y axis of the profile, which corresponds to 0 percent discount rate.

The IRR, by definition, is the interest rate (discount rate) that equates the present value of projected cash flows to the investment amount, or simply, the IRR is the interest rate where the NPV is zero. For Project X, the IRR is 26.06 percent, and for Project Y, the IRR is 46.85 percent. These points are plotted on the x axis representing a zero NPV.

The points in between the x axis and y axis reflect the NPV for a given discount rate. Each of the NPV and discount rate combinations from Table 9-16 is plotted on this profile. The plot includes the 12 percent discount rate calculation, where both projects enjoy a $546 net present value. Notice that with a cost of capital (discount rate) to the left (0 to 12 percent) of this crossover point, Project X provides a higher net present value. With a cost of capital to the right (12 to 46.85 percent), Project Y is preferred. Beyond 46.85 percent, neither project is acceptable because both projects have negative NPVs. If your cost of capital is less (greater) than 12 percent, choose Project X (Y), provided that the NPV is still positive.

Projects with Different Lives

We have established that the NPV rule is the correct economic criterion for ranking investment projects. It avoids the deficiencies of the alternative methods. It discounts cash flows at the appropriate opportunity cost of funds. It allows managers to evaluate projects and decide to accept or reject them separately. Finally, NPV calculations should lead directly to improvements in stock price.

Following the NPV rule maximizes the value of the firm. Indeed, the value of the firm is the sum of the NPVs of the total portfolio of projects represented by the firm's assets. From the basic net present value expression, general and valid valuation measures can be derived. Thus the NPV rule is consistent with fundamental valuation principles.

Although NPV is the preferred investment valuation technique, one application caveat should be pointed out when comparing projects with different lives. So far, using our examples, project lives always have been the same. But what if a company evaluates three alternatives with differing project lives? The projects must be compared using an equivalent annuity approach.

Project J has a six-year life, investment of $1,000, annual cash flows of $300, and a $387 NPV (at an 8 percent discount rate); Project K has only a three-year life, investment of $600, annual cash flows of $320, and a $225 NPV; and Project L has only a two-year life with an investment of $400, annual cash flows of $330, and a $188 NPV. Applying the net present value rule would lead us to accept Project J while rejecting Projects K and L. However, the projects are not comparable because they have different lives.

An approach to apply when considering the "unequal" life problem is a technique called the *equivalent annual annuity technique*. Each project's (J, K, and L) NPV could be thought of as the NPV of an annuity:

- Project J: Six-year annuity with a present value of $387
- Project K: Three-year annuity with a present value of $225
- Project L: Two-year annuity with a present value of $188

Using the Chapter 7 techniques, a $387 six-year project has an equivalent annual annuity ($N = 6$, I/YR $= 8$, PV$=387$) of $83.71. Project K has an equivalent annual annuity of $87.31 ($N = 3$, I/YR $= 8$, PV $= 225$). And Project L's equivalent annual annuity is $105.42 ($N = 2$, I/YR $= 8$, PV $= 188$). Project L is preferred. You also can assume project replication until a "common denominator" life is obtained, but I favor the equivalent annual annuity technique.

ADDITIONAL MANAGERIAL ISSUES

At the beginning of this chapter, I presented some managerial aspects of capital investment analysis. Within these four phases of the capital investment process, each corporation must decide on a number of other issues related to the capital investment process. For example, at planning time, how much detail is necessary to facilitate a capital expenditure strategic plan, and how much detail is necessary within the annual budget for capital projects? During the evaluation process, which technique(s) should be reported, and what happens when there is a conflict? When a project has been approved and is in the implementation phase, what is the correct balance between detailed status reporting (i.e., micromanaging by senior management) and staying informed, and how should allowances for cost overruns be managed? Finally, how and when should an approved and implemented project have a postcompletion audit performed?

The management team needs to determine what approaches work best for their organization and their needs. Additionally, management must decide on other attributes of its capital investment program, as discussed below. The following discusses project categories, budget identification and spending, budget authorization, project evaluation threshold, and authorization levels.

Project Categories

Most companies categorize projects by the nature of their expenditures. In this way, management can broadly monitor where its capital is being invested. The categories relate to the underlying rationale of the expenditure and at times are assessed different required rates of return. For example, Table 9-3 categorized projects by their nature:

- Cost savings
- Capacity expansion
- New products
- Information technology
- Regulatory and safety
- Administrative
- Research and development

These categories are similar to the categories used at Hershey and many other companies. While these are common categories, each company can develop its own group of projects. In a separate survey, one company used 26 different categories, including five varieties of new products.

Budget Identification and Spending

In the strategic planning phase, every organization struggles with the proper level of detail. If the requirements are too detailed, productivity is lost. If the requirements are on a summary level only, then an opportunity to discuss future capital needs is minimized. Each organization must find its own careful balance for detailed requirements during the planning phase.

Within the annual budget, projects that are anticipated for the coming year are specifically identified. Most organizations will spend about 100 percent of the budgeted capital expenditures in total. However, a common reality is that only half is spent on identified projects. The other half is spent on unidentified projects that result during the year from changing priorities, market conditions, and so on. Management must balance the organization's need for flexibility and the stringent demands of a budget.

Budget Authorization

For most companies, the annual capital budget process is separate from expenditure authorization. Just because a project is identified at budget time, this generally does not authorize the project. Each project must undergo its own rigorous evaluation and authorization.

Project Evaluation Threshold

As mentioned previously, the economic evaluation techniques are appropriate for most, if not all, expenditures. However, if a project analysis were required every time that someone needed to purchase a calculator, many person-hours of effort would be wasted. On the other hand, manufacturing should not be given carte blanche for investments in new production facilities costing several hundreds of millions of dollars. A careful balance must be struck to attain a certain comfort level for management and costs incurred to do the analysis.

Until the early 1990s, Hershey had a project evaluation level of $10,000. Management felt that it needed to stay involved with investment decisions. As the management team grew more comfortable, the evaluation level was increased to $100,000. This eliminated the evaluation of over 450 projects each year, which represented less than 10 percent ($15 million) of the total capital spent by Hershey. Increasing the evaluation threshold eliminated person-years of time spent in project development and management review on projects valued at between $10,000 and $100,000. It also focused management's time on more substantial capital project reviews.

Authorization Levels

First, at what dollar threshold must the capital evaluation process take place? If you want to buy a $30 calculator, do you need to go through the process of creating a discounted cash flow (DCF) analysis, or should you just buy the calculator? What about a $2,000 fully loaded laptop? Do you need to perform a DCF analysis on this expenditure level? What dollar threshold is meaningful for the organization and requires a capital investment analysis?

When that threshold is established, the next question that needs to be addressed is how deep into the organization should capital authorization be allowed, and at what dollar level. For example, is a senior engineer allowed to authorize capital expenditures? If he or she is, how much should he or she be allowed to authorize?

As an example, let's say that directors can approve up to $50,000, vice presidents up to $500,000, and so on:

Position	Authorization Amount
Director	$ 50,000
Vice president	500,000
Senior vice president	1 million
President and COO	2.5 million
Chief executive officer	5.0 million
Board of directors	5.0+ million

In this example, the CEO can approve up to $5 million, with any project exceeding an estimated $5 million investment requiring board-level approval. Of course, out of courtesy and career preservation, even though approval authority may rest in your domain, it is always a good decision to seek your boss's concurrence on a project before you authorize the project.

Each corporation must find a structure that provides enough control without hampering operations with needless bureaucracy.

SUMMARY

Capital investment decisions, which involve commitments of large outlays whose benefits (or drawbacks) extend well into the future, are of great significance to firms. Decisions in these areas therefore will have a major impact on the future well-being of a firm. This chapter focused on how capital investment decisions can be made more effective in contributing to the health and growth of a firm while increasing shareholder value. The discussion stressed the development of systematic procedures and rules throughout all four phases of capital investment.

The chapter emphasized that one of the most crucial phases in the process is the evaluation and authorization of a proposal. Four commonly used procedures for ranking investment proposals were discussed in this chapter: payback, net present value, internal rate of return, and modified internal (or terminal) rate of return.

Payback is defined as the number of years required to return the original investment. Although the payback method is used frequently as a simple rule of thumb, it has serious conceptual weaknesses because it ignores the facts that (1) some cash receipts are realized beyond the payback period, and (2) a dollar received today is more valuable than a dollar received in the future (the time value of money).

Net present value is defined as the present value of future cash flow discounted at the cost of capital less the cost of the investment. The NPV method overcomes the conceptual flaws noted in the use of the payback method.

Internal rate of return is defined as the interest rate that equates the present value of future cash flow with the investment outlay. The internal rate of return method, like the NPV method, discounts cash flows while searching for the discount rate. However, the internal rate of return assumes reinvestment at the IRR.

Modified internal rate of return (or *terminal rate of return*) is the interest rate that equates the cost of the investment with the accumulated future value of the intermediate cash flows that are assumed to be reinvested at an appropriate risk-adjusted cost of capital. The MIRR explicitly incorporates an opportunity cost of capital as a reinvestment rate.

In most cases, the discounted cash flow methods give identical answers to these questions: Which of two mutually exclusive projects should be selected? How large should the total capital budget be? However, under certain circumstances, conflicts may arise. Such conflicts are caused primarily by the fact that the IRR method makes different assumptions about the rate at which cash flows may be reinvested, or the opportunity cost of cash flows. The assumption of the NPV and MIRR methods (that the opportunity cost is the cost of capital) is the correct one. While the MIRR is an improvement on the IRR, it may lead to an incorrect choice of mutually exclusive projects if the sizes of the investment are significantly different. Accordingly, my preference is for using the NPV method to make capital investment decisions, and this will be the tool of choice used in the remainder of this book.

DETERMINING CASH FLOWS

Projected cash flows form the foundation for all the investment analysis techniques and applications. Determining projected cash flows is one of the most important steps in the capital investment analysis process. In practice, when evaluating investment proposals, discussions about the derivation of assumptions and the resulting cash flows dominate reports and presentations. Reasonable assumptions that are realized when the project is implemented assure the organization that the project will enhance shareholder value to the level of the projected net present value. Unrealistic, aggressive assumptions make the project look significantly better in the analysis phase. However, when the project is implemented and the projected level of performance is unattained, destruction of shareholder value occurs.

This chapter considers general concepts that support the development of cash flows, defines specific structures to analyze cash flows, and develops cash-flow models for traditional investment evaluation (i.e., new products and cost savings) and nontraditional evaluations (i.e., information technology and administrative projects). Although this chapter concentrates on developing explicit cash flows under conditions of certainty, this chapter also progressively covers the handling of uncertainty.

The final section raises additional managerial issues that a successful organization must address to satisfy its particular needs within its capital investment program.

OVERVIEW OF A CAPITAL AUTHORIZATION REQUEST

Chapter 9 presented the four phases of investment analysis. This chapter centers on developing cash-flow projections for the second phase, *capital project evaluation*, which is also called the *project-approval phase*.

While serving a vitally important financial and economic function, a good investment analysis process possesses similar managerial and organizational qualities as a good strategic planning process. Thorough investment evaluation and managerial authorization:

- Facilitates communication among the senior executives of an organization
- Sets a business direction
- Prioritizes opportunities and requirements
- Establishes business performance standards and objectives

In addition, the investment analysis must be a living, actionable tool. Significant investment analysis may involve many areas within an organization. A new product decision involves research and development, marketing, sales, engineering, production, logistics, finance, human resources, legal, corporate communications, and so on. All areas of the organization need to be involved in the decision process, albeit to varying degrees. Even in a simple equipment-replacement analysis championed by manufacturing and engineering, marketing and sales must be involved to provide consistent product sales projections. Replacing equipment for a product that marketing plans to discontinue may not be feasible financially.

To facilitate the investment analysis process, a *capital authorization request* (CAR) is comprised of many pages of project justification, assumption development, and financial analysis with several supporting sections that may include:

- A summary cover page
- A complete project description and link to the firm's strategy
- Decision case cash-flow assumptions and amounts
- Decision case net present value analysis (or the firm's evaluation metric of choice)
- Sensitivity and/or scenario analysis
- Investment components, potential vendors, and cost basis
- Quarterly capital expenditure budget

The complete request could range from a few pages to more than 100 pages depending on the size of the project and its complexity.

Table 10-1 illustrates a summary cover page. This page supports the collaborative nature of capital investment analysis by providing numerous areas to capture all the appropriate signatures: project originator, project sponsor, analyst/engineer who completes the capital authorization request, and of course, management. Not all the signatures are necessary for every project. The form includes an administrative header and identification information, an abbreviated project description, budget information, anticipated project expenditure summary, numerous financial indicators, and of course, the signatures.

The base case (or decision case) assumptions, cash-flow amounts, and net present value analysis will be more fully developed throughout this chapter, along with sensitivity and scenario analysis.

The complete project description includes a full write-up of the project, its rationale, justification of the key assumptions, alternatives considered and rejected, fit with strategic objectives, details of budget inclusion, and key technical/engineering data, if appropriate. Sensitivity and scenario analysis examine the degree to which changes in key assumptions affect the net present value. A detailed list of equipment components and potential vendors is provided for technical (operational) consideration. The cost basis identifies whether the expenditure estimate is a vendor quote (little volatility) or an estimate with potentially significant volatility. Finally, for a detailed cash flow budget, the last schedule of

T A B L E   10-1

Capital Authorization Request Summary

Division / Department	Cost Center	Date Prepared	Prepared By	Project Number
Project Title		Starting Date	Closing Date	Internal Reference

Project Description [ ] Budgeted ($000's) $____ [ ] Not Budgeted	Summary of Project Expenditures
	($ 000's)
	New Fixed Assets $ -
	Transferred Fixed Assets -
	Capitalized Expense -
	Prior Approvals -
	Total Capital Requested $ -
	Operating Expenses $ -
	Working Capital -
	Other -
	Total Other Requested $ -
	Total Project Amount $ -

Financial Indicators	Project Analysis Signatures
Net Present Value @ _____%	Cost Estimates By
Modified Internal Rate of Return @ _____%	
Internal Rate of Return	Technical Development By
Pay Back Period - Years	
Maximum Cash Exposure	Financial Data By
Project Life - Years	

Management Signatures	
Board of Directors	Chief Executive Officer
Chief Operating Officer	Division President
Chief Financial Officer	Vice President
Vice President	Vice President
Vice President	Vice President
Vice President	Vice President
Request Originator	Project Sponsor

the capital authorization request documents anticipates project expenditures by quarter. In this way, the organization (treasurer) can be sure to have funds available when needed.

Cash-Flow Identification

Identifying the appropriate cash flows is the true challenge of all capital investment analysis. You want to isolate incremental after-tax cash flows that occur solely as a result of the project's implementation. Cash flows for some projects are easy to identify and can be supported with detailed engineering studies. However, for many projects, cash-flow estimation is more difficult and is based on experience and reasonable assumptions.

For a cost savings project, engineering studies can support and validate productivity (labor) savings. The life of the project again can be determined through engineering studies and experience with similar types of equipment. These cash flows may be easier to determine. But what about cash flows from a new product, a new process, or information technology (IT)? What about the cash flows that result from years of research and development (R&D) investment or advertising investment to build brand awareness? These cash flows become more tentative and more difficult to quantify. Nonetheless, a reasonable cash flow or a range of reasonable cash flows must be identified to ensure sound financial management. The next few sections provide added terminology before developing an example.

Funds Availability

On the dimension of funds availability, there are two extremes: unlimited funds and capital rationing. Unlimited funding a financial situation in which a firm is able to accept all independent projects that provide an acceptable rate of return. I know of no such organization. Every organization has funding limitations.

At the other end of the funds availability continuum lies capital rationing. Capital rationing has two forms: hard capital rationing forced on the organization by the financial markets and soft capital rationing, which is imposed by management. Unfortunately, at some point in the lives of some organizations, the financial capital markets say, "Enough is enough—you can have no more capital." This is referred to as *hard capital rationing* and leads to either dramatic turnaround or bankruptcy.

Management may impose *soft capital rationing* (internally imposed) for a variety of reasons. Soft rationing may be due to other impediments that confine the firm's ability to execute all potential projects, such as limitations in the number of employees available to do the implementation, limitations in management's ability to handle a number of major simultaneous projects, facilities physical constraints, concerns over violation of debt covenants, and restrictions imposed by the customer market. Sometimes managers will postpone or delay the amount of capital investment to enhance short-term accounting performance metrics, that is, return on assets.

Capital Decisions

As we saw in Chapter 9, the first issue addressed by capital investment analysis is the accept or reject investment in a project. When two competing, mutually exclusive projects have acceptable net present values (or returns), the decision becomes one of ranking the projects. The capital authorization phase facilitates, first, the accept/reject decision and, second, project ranking.

Cash-Flow Patterns

A conventional capital project has an initial period of project investment (or cash outflows) followed by years of positive cash flow. A nonconventional pattern of cash flows is one that starts with investment, followed by positive cash flows, followed by a period or two of negative cash flows, and then maybe back to positive cash flow. This nonconventional pattern often results when added investment is required to refurbish or overhaul the original investment. Although the refurbishment or overhaul decision can be made at a later time, if it is anticipated and is integral to the project, the refurbishment or overhaul should be considered in the initial project stage.

Sunk Costs

A *sunk cost* is a cost (or cash outlay) that has already been made. There is nothing to do to change the fact that cash was expended during some previous time period. Sunk costs have no relevance to the immediate decision and should not be considered as part of the investment.

As an example, often when Hershey introduced a new product, a year-long test market preceded that introduction. That test market often cost millions of dollars depending on the size and duration of the test. After a successful test, a product's investment was "scaled up" to accommodate the projected sales level suggested by the test. Resulting operating cash flows were projected, and the project's net present value was determined. As in Chapter 9, a positive net present value indicates a solid and acceptable investment. Thus, for example, let's say that after a successful test market ($2.5 million expenditure), engineering determined that a new $40.0 million production line was the proper scale and size for this new product. Furthermore, very simplistically, after-tax cash flows were estimated at $7.2 million each year over the project's eight-year life. At a discount rate (cost of capital) of 8 percent, the project is acceptable with a positive $1.4 million net present value. (To review from Chapter 7 and using a financial calculator set to N = 8, I/Yr = 8, and PMT = 7.2, this results in a present value [PV] of $41.4 million, less the investment, providing an NPV of $1.4 million.)

With a positive NPV, management should accept the project. However, years ago at Hershey, that project might have been rejected. You see that the sunk cost of the test market was imposed in the investment analysis. The investment was considered $42.5 million—the $40 million to purchase the new production line and the $2.5 million spent in the previous year for the test market. In this example, the new product introduction would have been rejected because the

$42.5 million investment would have exceeded the present value of the operating cash flows, resulting in a negative net present value of $(1.1) million.

Identifying a sunk cost is easy when you are not a part of the analysis. However, at that time (and this was changed in the early 1990s), management argued that the $2.5 million test market expense needed to be tracked. Someone or some project needed to be held accountable for that $2.5 million. Unfortunately, this was management's way of controlling, monitoring, and "accounting for" test markets.

A breakthrough came only through contorted logic. Assuming that management was correct to include this sunk cost for test marketing, the question was put to management, "Which would you rather do, (1) accept a project with a negative $1.1 million NPV or (2) lose the full $2.5 million by rejecting the project?" Management made the correct choice and accepted the project with a positive $1.4 million NPV.

Opportunity Costs

Opportunity costs represent cash flows that could be realized from the best alternative use of a surplus asset that will be used in the proposed project. What if a project proposal includes the use of an idle asset that once was used by the business? What value should be attributed to the asset? As in many circumstances, the answer depends on additional information.

If the asset has no alternative use and has no current market value or scrap value, that asset should be included at a zero dollar value in the analysis. On the other hand, if you can sell the asset in the open market, that value should be included as part of the project's investment. If you can sell the idle asset only as scrap, that limited amount should be included in the investment analysis. On the summary page (Table 10-1), this value is included in the project expenditures as a transferred fixed asset.

Determining an alternative use and estimating alternative values often are confounded by the asset's book value. The book value of the idle asset has no role in the investment analysis and should not be considered when arriving at the investment amount, but book value may be necessary when transferring the asset on the accounting books (e.g., fixed asset register) between different business units or divisions of the firm for managerial control and reporting purposes.

Cost Savings versus Cost Avoidance

Cost savings occur whenever a project's implementation reduces expenses from the *current level of expenditures. Cost avoidance* occurs whenever a project's implementation reduces expenses from a *projected level of expenditures*. This is not much of a distinction in a finance professional's mind. However, in the mind of management, there is a huge difference.

Cost savings can be documented. By implementing this capital investment, you can reduce operating expenses by $14 million per year through a reduction in the labor force. You see the 200 employees and can determine that their fully loaded cost is, on average, $70,000 each, including salary and wages, bonuses, benefits, and employment taxes.

On the other hand, a cost avoidance is based more on projection. By implementing this capital investment, you can avoid hiring 200 people (at $70,000 each) and avoid $14 million in added operating expenses per year. Analytically, there is no difference in the designation of the $14 million in annual cash flow. Often, however, management teams treat these two costs as different. From a financial perspective, the difference may lie in the risk surrounding the nature of the expense. In the case of the cost savings, the savings rely on follow-through on current costs. This one-step approach is easy to trace and easy to audit after completion. In the case of the cost avoidance, management first must rely on the projected expense pattern without the capital investment. Management must be convinced that without this expenditure, expenses will escalate immediately by $14 million, and management must be convinced that this capital will avoid the estimated $14 million of projected future expense. The analysis involves a two-step cash-flow determination process that cannot be audited. Management distinguishes more risk and less confidence and consequently sees the cash flows as distinct categories, savings versus avoidance.

BASIC CASH-FLOW STATEMENT

A cash-flow projection includes three interlinked cash-flow sections:

- *Initial investment*—relevant cash outflow (or investment) at the beginning of the investment proposal
- *Operating cash flow*—relevant after-tax incremental cash inflows or outflows from the project throughout its life
- *Terminal cash flow*—after-tax nonoperating cash flow occurring in the final year of the project

Determining operating cash flows will follow discussion of the initial investment and terminal cash flow.

Initial Investment

The initial investment is comprised of three items, as listed on Table 10-2.

The first item reflects what is usually the major cash outflow, the installed cost of any new asset. The installed cost includes the cost of new assets purchased from vendors, the opportunity cost of equipment absorbed by (or transferred to) the project, and all installation costs. The installation costs include fees paid to external consultants, designers, and engineers, along with "capitalized in-house engineering expense" or other noncapitalized operating expenses incurred by the organization. *Capitalized in-house engineering expense* is an accounting requirement that captures the costs of all engineer employees (fully loaded—salary,

T A B L E   10-2

Initial Investment

+ Installed cost of new asset
    Cost of the new asset
    + Value of transferred assets
    + Shipping and destination charges
    + All installation charges

− After-tax proceeds from sale of old equipment (if applicable)
    Proceeds from the sale of old equipment
    ± Taxes recovered (paid)

± Investment (recovery) in net working capital

= Initial investment

bonus, benefits, and employee taxes). Instead of expensing these costs at the time they are incurred, the costs are *capitalized*, or added to the total cost of the project and depreciated over the project's life. The assumption is that if these in-house engineers were not productively employed installing this project, they would be productively engaged on another project or not employed by the firm.

The installed cost of the new asset is offset by any after-tax proceeds from the sale of any equipment that is being replaced if this is a machine replacement project. To calculate the after-tax proceeds, we need the selling price, the current tax book value of the asset, and the marginal tax rate. The current tax book value reflects the installed cost of the replaced asset less its accumulated tax depreciation, as determined using Eq. (10.1):

$$\text{Tax book value} = \text{initial cost of replaced asset} \\ - \text{accumulated tax depreciation} \qquad (10.1)$$

Table 10-3 illustrates the cash flow from the sale of an existing asset for three different selling prices: (1) no gain or loss (selling price = tax book value), (2) a gain (selling price > tax book value), and (3) a loss (selling price < tax book value).

In this example, the asset was purchased a few years ago for $5,000. A total of $4,000 was depreciated since the asset was purchased. This results in a book value of $1,000, which is constant over the three different selling price examples. In the first column, no gain or loss, the asset is sold for exactly its book value of $1,000. There are no tax consequences. There is no taxable gain or loss. Thus the cash flow is equal to the selling price, or $1,000.

In the second column of Table 10-3, the asset is sold for $1,500, resulting in a gain of $500. Assuming a 35 percent tax rate, the organization would pay $175 on the gain. The cash flow is the $1,500 selling price offset by the $175 tax expense, or $1,325.

T A B L E   10-3

Cash Proceeds from Asset Disposal
($ 000s)

	No Gain or Loss	Gain	Loss
Selling price	$ 1,000	$ 1,500	$ 500
Tax book value	1,000	1,000	1,000
Taxable Gain (Loss)	–	500	(500)
Taxes (35%)	–	175	(175)
After-tax gain (loss)	$ –	$ 325	$ (325)
Selling price	$ 1,000	$ 1,500	$ 500
Taxes	–	(175)	175
Cash proceeds	$ 1,000	$ 1,325	$ 675

The final column illustrates a selling price of $500, resulting in a loss of $500. Assuming that the organization can offset other gains immediately with this loss, a $175 tax savings offsets the loss. The cash flow is the $500 selling price and the $175 tax savings for a total cash flow of $675.

The after-tax proceeds of the sale of the old asset offset the cost of a new asset. On a personal basis, this is similar to having a trade-in when you buy a new car. Or more precisely, this is like buying a new car and selling your old car yourself. It's the net incremental cash flow (e.g., investment) that we are interested in.

The final initial investment component is any additional working capital investment. When we introduce a new product, we need to invest in inventory (i.e., raw materials, goods in process, and finished goods). This ensures that we have inventory on hand to fill customers' initial and subsequent orders.

Customers who buy the new products will require us to invest in accounts receivable as they continue their payment habits of 30 or so days until invoices are paid. Offsetting this is spontaneous operating financing that is enjoyed as accounts payable are extended automatically from suppliers. Notice that this definition of net working capital considers only short-term operating assets and liabilities. It does not include cash and short-term debt. Each year of operations may require subsequent net working capital investment. This will be dealt with in the development of operating cash flows, after the discussion of terminal cash flow.

Terminal Cash Flow

The terminal cash flow includes nonoperating cash flows that occur at the end of a project's life. These cash flows are unique and nonrecurring. To figure out the total cash flow for the project's final year, terminal cash flows need to be combined with the final year's operating cash flow. Table 10-4 lists the components of terminal cash flow.

TABLE 10-4

Terminal Investment

+ After-tax proceeds from sale of new equipment
Proceeds from the sale of old equipment
± Taxes recovered (paid)
− After-tax proceeds from sale of old equipment (if applicable)
Proceeds from the sale of old equipment
± Taxes recovered (paid)
± Recovery (investment) in net working capital
= Terminal investment

The terminal cash flow begins by calculating the incremental cash generated from disposing of the new asset versus the opportunity cost of disposing of the replaced asset that many years later. Remember, you are estimating the incremental financial impact of replacing or not replacing a piece of equipment. If you do not replace, there may be some value left in that old piece of equipment at the end of the analytical period. Often, the after-tax proceeds from the sale of the replaced equipment are considered negligible in the final year of the new asset, so most analysts ignore its inclusion.

Once again, the cash flow from the sale of the asset is calculated on an after-tax basis, similar to the calculations in Table 10-3 and discussed earlier.

The terminal cash flow includes the recovery of net working capital. Usually, in the final year, the assumption is that all inventories are sold, all receivables collected, and all accounts payable paid in full. In other words, the full amount invested in working capital, initial investment, and all subsequent operating investment made throughout the intervening years is fully recovered. There are no tax consequences associated with full working capital recovery. However, the full-recovery assumption can be adjusted, if necessary, to indicate only 95 percent (or whatever percentage) inventory recovery owing to obsolescence or shrinkage and only 97 percent (or whatever percentage) accounts receivable collection owing to bad debts of deadbeat customers. In these cases, additional tax savings may result from these losses, and these tax savings need to be part of the terminal cash flows as well.

In rare cases, the incremental working capital could be negative. For example, if computer technology was partially justified on initial operating net working capital savings (an initial positive inflow), the terminal period may reflect a cash outflow that signifies the return to the previous working capital investment level.

Operating Cash Flow

Many considerations of operating cash flows complete this chapter. In Chapter 9, you were asked to take the cash flows as given. Now I explore the derivation of cash flows. The process is similar to the cash-flow statement introduced in Chapter 2 and reconsidered in Chapter 6. As seen previously, the cash-flow projection begins with a projected income statement, adds back any noncash expenses, and considers all additional operating cash-flow expenditures.

Chapter 9 introduced different bases for project implementation and different project categories, such as new products, cost-saving machine replacement, capacity expansion, and so on. Each project category has its own specific investment rationale, and the resulting analysis generally can capture all incremental after-tax operating cash flows in a basic cash-flow statement.

Although the general framework supports the analysis of many different projects, not all line items will be used for all analyses. For example, a cost savings project results only in expense or working capital reduction. The sales level is unaffected by a cost savings project. In an analysis of an advertising campaign and its subsequent incremental sales, depreciation would not be considered unless incremental assets also are included in the project proposal.

CAPITAL EVALUATION: THE NEW PRODUCT DECISION

From this point forward, I will use the net present value (NPV) method for all capital evaluation decisions. The following new product decision is an example of a typical problem and illustrates the use of cash flows for capital evaluation decisions. This illustration emphasizes that all project cash flows must be represented as incremental or as changes in the firm's cash flows. And it demonstrates the NPV method of discounted cash flows.

New product development is a strategy that supports the growth objective embraced by almost all organizations. New products are the lifeblood of an organization and ensure that the firm will renew itself and meet the changing needs, desires, and tastes of its customers and consumers. The following describes the process of evaluating a new product. Although the project is totally hypothetical, it does maintain the Hershey theme and illustrates the necessary evaluation to validate the viability of an investment in a new product faced by every organization. The specifics are different from organization to organization, but the evaluation is the same.

This hypothetical new product capitalizes on Hershey's knowledge of the confectionery market and its strengths in producing, selling, and distributing the product. The new product builds on valuable relationships with customers (such as Walmart, Target, Costco, Kroger, CVS, etc.) and the consumer's favorable impressions of Hershey's quality and value. The hypothetical new product is derived from a new process created by the R&D area for $1 million. The new candy bar is swirled with white chocolate throughout the milk chocolate base with macadamia nut inclusions.

The launch of a new product takes cooperative teamwork that seamlessly unites all functions within the organization. In this example, the product idea is jointly championed by sales, marketing, and R&D. A multifunctional new product task team is quickly assembled to analyze the product's viability, including its financial viability.

Straight-Line Depreciation Example

We are going to analyze this new product decision first using straight-line depreciation and then switch to a modified accelerated cost recovery system (MACRS). The capital investment decision (including new products) calls for five steps: (1) estimate the initial investment attributable to the new investment, (2) determine the incremental operating cash flows, (3) project the terminal cash flows or expected salvage value and add the terminal cash flows to the operating cash flows, (4) find the gross present value of the total incremental cash flows, and (5) determine whether the NPV is positive. These steps are explained further in the following sections.

Step 1: Initial investment. The initial investment is detailed in two ways: (1) capital expenditure for the new equipment, along with (2) the initial working capital investment.

- Engineering and manufacturing understand the equipment necessary to produce this type of new product. They estimate the configuration and number of lines necessary to fulfill the marketing projections. In this example, engineering estimates that the corporation needs to buy only one production line. An engineer, who is a member of this new product task team, speaks to a select group of capital equipment suppliers and writes a *request for proposal* (RFP) that is circulated to all approved equipment suppliers. The successful RFP confirms the technical production feasibility and provides a solid estimate for a total installed expenditure of $20 million.

- Accounting and finance, with the input of the complete team, estimate the initial (year 0) investment in working capital—an investment of 5 percent of sales, or $1,250 thousand, to support the first year's sales.

In total, the investment amount for year 0 is $21,250 thousand.

Step 2: Incremental operating cash flow. Working together, the members of the task team develop the following operating assumptions:

- Marketing develops an initial sales projection along with an annual growth profile through test panels, test marketing, and other marketing research means. The initial assumptions are revisited and revised with every new piece of information.

- Originally, gross product sales were estimated at $27 million for the first year. However, it was estimated that this new product would "cannibalize" or displace approximately $2 million of sales of other Hershey products, such as the more traditional Hershey Bar. These cannibalized sales are relevant and a collateral incremental impact of accepting this project. Consequently, the first year's net sales were estimated at $25 million. In addition, after a sophomore-year reduction in sales of –10 percent, sales of this product would increase at 15, 10, and 5 percent (for the third through fifth years, respectively) before settling into a 3 percent annual growth rate until year 8, when the product would be discontinued. The sophomore-year sales reduction occurs for a number of reasons: Consumer initial trials are heaviest in the first year, the retail inventory pipeline is filled in the first year and only "take away" is replenished, and marketing promotional and advertising expenses are reduced significantly in the second year.

- Marketing and sales also estimate that they will need $12.5 million ($10 million in year 1 and $2.5 million in year 2) for advertising, consumer coupons, and trade promotions to support the initial new product launch. This is in addition to an ongoing expenditure level of 18 percent of sales, which also includes hiring a brand manager and an assistant.

- Manufacturing, with the help of R&D and cost accounting, estimates that it will cost 60.0 percent (for every sales dollar) to produce this product initially. This will pay for the raw materials (i.e., cocoa, sugar, milk, nuts, etc.), direct labor, and overhead, as well as distribution expenses. By the fourth year and again in the seventh year, anticipated efficiencies reduce the production cost to 59.5 percent (years 4 through 6) and 59.0 percent (in years 7 and 8).

- Accounting and finance estimate the incremental tax rate (35 percent) and calculate the straight-line depreciation on the asset. For our purposes, we will assume that the entire $20 million asset investment is depreciated over the eight-year life, resulting in annual depreciation of $2.5 million. Alternatively, we could have assumed that only the investment amount less the residual value was depreciated. The logic will become apparent when MACRS depreciation is illustrated in the next section.

- After estimating the initial investment (year 0) in working capital, accounting and finance, with the input of the complete team, estimate ongoing working capital needs at 5 percent of next year's anticipated sales. Additional investment (or recovery as in year 1) is required to support the projected sales for the next year. Note that for year 2, sales actually are expected to decline, so only $1,125 thousand of net working capital needs to be on hand. Since we already have $1,250 thousand of net working capital, we can recover

$125,000 of working capital. In subsequent years, 5 percent of next year's projected annual incremental sales must be invested until full recovery in year 8. Once again, the working capital investment is made in inventory (to ensure that inventory is on hand to complete sales transactions) and receivables (to finance customers' purchases) offset by spontaneous operating financing provided by suppliers through accounts payable. Notice that all the working capital ($1,633 thousand) is recovered in the final year.

- Finance also determines an appropriate cost of capital for this project at 8 percent.

Step 3: Project the terminal cash flows or expected salvage value and add to the final year's operating cash flow. Nonoperating cash flows directly attributable to this project and above and beyond the day-to-day operations are also estimated:

- Engineering and production estimate that in eight years the assets will have a residual value of $1 million before tax considerations.
- Accounting and finance estimate full recovery of the working capital investment.

The first portion of Table 10-5 documents the key assumptions. The second portion dollarizes the assumptions and evaluates them.

In this analysis, you can see that sales are approaching $33 million in the final year. Also, the after-tax operating income displays a loss for the first two years owing to the additional product launch expenses. After the third-year, the product contributes positive after-tax operating income through the remainder of its life. This project produces positive cash flows starting in the second year. The terminal cash flows include a $650,000 after-tax residual value along with working capital recovery of $1,633 thousand.

Step 4: The accumulated gross present value of the eight years of incremental cash flow can be determined using Eq. (10.2). We get:

$$PV = \sum_{t=1}^{N} \frac{CF_t}{(1+k)^t} \tag{10.2}$$

While this is a general model, the specific case in hand can be solved more straightforwardly using a financial calculator and the net present value function, as described in Chapter 9. The present value of the estimated cash flows is $21,860 thousand.

Step 5: Determine the net present value. The net present value (after subtracting the year 0 investing of $21,250 thousand) is $610,000, and the project should be accepted. The total value of Hershey's stock should rise by $609,000.

TABLE 10-5

New Product Decision
(Straight-Line Depreciation)
($ 000s)

	Initial Investment	Year 1	Year 2	Year 3	Year 4	Year 5	Year 6	Year 7	Year 8
				Key Assumptions					
Purchase price of new equipment	$ 20,000			$ 610					
Working capital (% of incremental sales)	5.0%								
Initial sales		$ 25,000							
Sales growth			-10.0%	15.0%	10.0%	5.0%	3.0%	3.0%	3.0%
Cost of sales (excluding depreciation, % of sales)		60.0%	60.0%	60.0%	59.5%	59.5%	59.5%	59.0%	59.0%
Operating costs (% of sales)		18.0%	18.0%	18.0%	18.0%	18.0%	18.0%	18.0%	18.0%
Additional product launch expense		$ 10,000	$ 2,500	$ —	$ —	$ —	$ —	$ —	$ —
Tax rate		35.0%	35.0%	35.0%	35.0%	35.0%	35.0%	35.0%	35.0%
Residual value									$ 1,000
Cost of capital	8.0%								
				Capital Evaluation					
Purchase price	$ (20,000)								
Initial working capital	(1,250)								

(Continued)

T A B L E 10-5

New Product Decision (*Continued*)
(Straight-Line Depreciation)
($ 000s)

	Initial Investment	Year 1	Year 2	Year 3	Year 4	Year 5	Year 6	Year 7	Year 8
Incremental operating cash flow									
Sales		$ 25,000	$ 22,500	$ 25,875	$ 28,463	$ 29,886	$ 30,783	$ 31,706	$ 32,657
Cost of sales exc. deprec.		(15,000)	(13,500)	(15,525)	(16,935)	(17,782)	(18,316)	(18,707)	(19,268)
Depreciation*		(2,500)	(2,500)	(2,500)	(2,500)	(2,500)	(2,500)	(2,500)	(2,500)
Gross income		7,500	6,500	7,850	9,028	9,604	9,967	10,499	10,889
Operating expenses		(4,500)	(4,050)	(4,658)	(5,123)	(5,379)	(5,541)	(5,707)	(5,878)
Additional product launch expense		(10,000)	(2,500)	—	—	—	—	—	—
Operating income		(7,000)	(50)	3,192	3,905	4,225	4,426	4,792	5,011
Taxes (35%)		2,450	18	(1,117)	(1,367)	(1,479)	(1,549)	(1,677)	(1,754)
After-tax operating income		$ (4,550)	$ (32)	$ 2,075	$ 2,538	$ 2,746	$ 2,877	$ 3,115	$ 3,257
After-tax operating income		$ (4,550)	$ (32)	$ 2,075	$ 2,538	$ 2,746	$ 2,877	$ 3,115	$ 3,257
Depreciation		2,500	2,500	2,500	2,500	2,500	2,500	2,500	2,500
Additional working capital (investment)		125	(169)	(129)	(71)	(45)	(46)	(48)	—
Incremental operating cash flow		(1,925)	2,299	4,446	4,967	5,201	5,331	5,567	5,757
Residual value, after tax*									650
Working capital recovery									1,633
Total cash flow	$ (21,250)	$ (1,925)	$ 2,299	$ 4,446	$ 4,967	$ 5,201	$ 5,331	$ 5,567	$ 8,040
Present value 8.0%	$ (21,250)	$ (1,782)	$ 1,971	$ 3,529	$ 3,651	$ 3,540	$ 5,331	$ 3,248	$ 4,344
		$ 21,860	Gross present value (PV – cash-flow years 1–8)						
Net present value	$ 610								

*Assumed straight-line depreciation to $0 residual value.

Notice that if the previously mentioned R&D sunk cost of $1 million is included in this analysis, the identified investment amount increases, and the project is unacceptable, with a negative net present value [NPV = $(390,000)]. The $1 million R&D costs should not be considered in this analysis. Those costs have long been spent. Accepting or rejecting this project does not change the sunk costs for R&D. By rejecting this project, the organization forgoes $610,000 of value.

One additional consideration to point out is that no financing costs or financing cash flows are included in the cash-flow projection. That is, no interest expense (or income), no debt service, no dividends, and no other financing-related cash flows are considered. Financing costs and cash flows are considered in the discount rate (cost of capital) and are discussed fully in Chapter 11. The discount rate is assumed as a given at this point, and the cash-flow projections are evaluated based solely on operating cash flows.

New Product Analysis with Accelerated Depreciation

Next, the effect of modified accelerated cost recovery system (MACRS) depreciation on the new product decision is considered. MACRS is the Internal Revenue Service (IRS)–designated method of depreciation. It groups equipment into broad classes of assets and provides accelerated (or faster) depreciation in the early years. The analysis of the new product decision using MACRS depreciation is illustrated in Table 10-6.

> *Step 1: Estimate initial cash outlay.* Just as with straight-line depreciation, there is no difference using either straight line or MACRS. The initial cash outflow is anticipated to be $20,000 thousand for the equipment as well as $1,250 thousand for working capital.
>
> *Step 2: Determine annual incremental operating cash flows.* There is no change to any of the operating projections, with the exception of the depreciation. Sales, cost of sales (excluding depreciation), selling, general, and administrative, and product-launch expense do not change. Neither does the tax rate, working capital requirement, or the discount rate. With the change in depreciation, though, all measures of annual income and cash flow do change.

MACRS is discussed more fully in Chapter 4. As it pertains to this analysis, most manufacturing equipment is considered a seven-year class life for tax purposes under MACRS, as seen in Table 10-7. Some equipment in very specific industries, such as semiconductor manufacturing, may be considered to have a different life (i.e., five years). However, for the most part, the exact purpose of the machinery or the industry generally does not matter to the IRS. If the manufacturing equipment is used to make chocolate or cars or televisions, the equipment will have a life of seven years for tax purposes.

TABLE 10-6

New Product Decision

(Modified Accelerated Cost Recovery System [MACRS] Depreciation)
($ 000s)

	Initial Investment	Year 1	Year 2	Year 3	Year 4	Year 5	Year 6	Year 7	Year 8
				Key Assumptions					
Purchase price of new equipment	$ 20,000								
Working capital (% of incremental sales)	5.0%								
Initial sales		$ 25,000							
Sales growth			−10.0%	15.0%	10.0%	5.0%	3.0%	3.0%	3.0%
Cost of sales (excluding depreciation, % of sales)		60.0%	60.0%	60.0%	59.5%	59.5%	59.5%	59.0%	59.0%
Operating costs (% of sales)		18.0%	18.0%	18.0%	18.0%	18.0%	18.0%	18.0%	18.0%
Additional product launch expense		$ 10,000	$ 2,500	$ —	$ —	$ —	$ —	$ —	$ —
Tax rate		35.0%	35.0%	35.0%	35.0%	35.0%	35.0%	35.0%	35.0%
Residual value									$ 1,000
Cost of capital	8.0%								
				Capital Evaluation					
Purchase price	$ (20,000)								
Initial working capital	(1,250)								

Incremental operating cash flow

	Investment	Year 1	Year 2	Year 3	Year 4	Year 5	Year 6	Year 7	Year 8
Sales		$ 25,000	$ 22,500	$ 25,875	$ 28,463	$ 29,886	$ 30,783	$ 31,706	$ 32,657
Cost of sales		(15,000)	(13,500)	(15,525)	(16,935)	(17,782)	(18,316)	(18,707)	(19,268)
Depreciation*		(2,858)	(4,898)	(3,498)	(2,498)	(1,786)	(1,786)	(1,786)	(890)
Gross income		7,142	4,102	6,852	9,030	10,318	10,681	11,213	12,499
Operating expenses		(4,500)	(4,050)	(4,658)	(5,123)	(5,379)	(5,541)	(5,707)	(5,878)
Additional product launch expense		(10,000)	(2,500)	–	–	–	–	–	–
Operating income		(7,358)	(2,448)	2,194	3,907	4,939	5,140	5,506	6,621
Taxes		2,575	857	(768)	(1,367)	(1,729)	(1,799)	(1,927)	(2,317)
After-tax operating income		$ (4,783)	$ (1,591)	$ 1,426	$ 2,540	$ 3,210	$ 3,341	$ 3,579	$ 4,304
After-tax operating income		$ (4,783)	$ (1,591)	$ 1,426	$ 2,540	$ 3,210	$ 3,341	$ 3,579	$ 4,304
Depreciation		2,858	4,898	3,498	2,498	1,786	1,786	1,786	890
Additional working capital (investment)		125	(169)	(129)	(71)	(45)	(46)	(48)	–
Incremental operating cash flow	(1,800)	3,138	4,795	4,967	4,951	5,081	5,317	5,194	
Residual value, after tax									650
Working capital recovery									1,633
Total cash flow	$ (21,250)	$ (1,800)	$ 3,138	$ 4,795	$ 4,967	$ 4,951	$ 5,081	$ 5,317	$ 7,477
Present value 8.0%	$ (21,250)	$ (1,667)	$ 2,690	$ 3,806	$ 3,651	$ 3,370	$ 3,202	$ 3,102	$ 4,040
	$ 22,194		Gross present value (PV – cash flow years 1–8)						
Net present value	$ 944								
*MACRS depreciation rate		14.29%	24.49%	17.49%	12.49%	8.93%	8.93%	8.93%	4.45%

T A B L E   10-7

MACRS Depreciation

Class	Assets Included	
5-Year	Autos, computers, copiers, equipment for semiconductor manufacturing	
7-Year	Most industrial equipment and office furniture and fixtures	

Year	5-Year	7-Year
1	20.00%	14.29%
2	32.00%	24.49%
3	19.20%	17.49%
4	11.52%	12.49%
5	11.52%	8.93%
6	5.76%	8.93%
7		8.93%
8		4.45%
Total	100.00%	100.00%

In Table 10-7 you will notice that seven-year-life MACRS depreciation actually stretches over eight years, assuming a half-year convention in the first and last years. The given percentages are applied directly to the purchase price of the asset without considering any anticipated salvage value. As seen in the table, after four years, 68.76 percent of the asset has been depreciated, or $13,752 thousand, and under straight-line depreciation, after four years, half the asset's purchase price ($10,000 thousand) is depreciated. Of course, over the full eight-year period, the total amount of $20,000 thousand is depreciated using either MACRS or our example of straight-line depreciation.

MACRS is the correct technique to use in capital evaluation. However, it is sometimes needlessly cumbersome when introducing or even discussing capital evaluation. But it is the correct approach for capital evaluation. After this example and the cost savings analysis example that follows, we will revert back to using straight-line for conversation purposes. In keeping with the technique used in MACRS, though, we will assume depreciation to zero and then be pleasantly surprised as the residual value materializes. If the asset has any residual value, the full gain will be realized and taxed. This is consistent with the straight-line depreciation example earlier.

> *Step 3: Project the terminal cash flows or expected salvage value and add to the final year's operating cash flow.* There is no change here from the straight-line depreciation example earlier. Since the asset is fully depreciated, the $1,000 thousand residual value is fully taxed and results in a $650,000 gain and final-year cash flow. Working capital

investment is also fully recovered, resulting in an additional cash flow of $1,633 thousand.

Step 4: Find the present value of the future cash flows. This is illustrated in Table 10-6 and provides a project valuation of $22,194 thousand.

Step 5: Determine the net present value. The project's net present value is found as the sum of the present values of the inflows, or benefits, less the outflows, or costs ($000s), as shown in Eq. (10.3):

Net present value = gross present value of total cash flow − initial investment

$$= \$22,194 - \$21,250$$

$$= \$944 \tag{10.3}$$

As before, the net present value is positive, indicating that the new product should be accepted.

Using MACRS results in a NPV that is $334 thousand higher than straight-line or 1.67 percent higher than the original $20 million capital investment. MACRS provides a small incentive to invest in new assets.

CAPITAL EVALUATION: COST SAVINGS DECISION

This section considers an analysis of a cost savings capital expenditure. Once again, the decision will be considered with an illustration of MACRS, and the section will conclude with analysis based on straight-line depreciation.

Cost Savings—MACRS Depreciation Example

The mass production of chocolate confection is a very interesting process. Hershey's Web site contains actual video as well as a tutorial on the production of Hershey chocolate. Hershey sells many of its different products in a variety different bag sizes. For this hypothetical example, an eight-ounce bag of Hershey Kisses will be considered.

The Hershey Kiss was introduced in 1907 and over the years has undergone a number of changes starting with the insertion of an almond (Kisses with Almonds), white chocolate (Hugs and Hugs with Almonds), and many specialty varieties, including caramel, peanut butter, cherry, and other inclusions and flavor varieties.

The production process is straightforward. After the product is deposited onto a conveyor belt or into a mold, it is cooled, wrapped, bagged, boxed, and distributed.

The vice president of production is concerned that too much product is being given away for free. For example, sell an eight-ounce bag of Kisses that weighs exactly 8 ounces, and the customer is happy. Sell an eight-ounce bag that weighs only 7.90 ounces or even 7.99 ounces, and Hershey is subject to litigation for not delivering what was promised. Sell an eight-ounce bag with 8.5 ounces in it, Hershey is giving away product, and the consumer doesn't even know it, so there is no goodwill being built with the consumer. This is not a "free give-away" promotion that could drive sales volume or sales growth. There is just product given away for free.

Almost any consumer goods company faces this situation on a routine basis if they sell containers (bags or boxes) of their product based on weight rather than the number of pieces inside. To combat this issue, capital equipment manufacturers have addressed this concern with new weighing and bagging processes. The new equipment is design to fit into the production process after the individual pieces of the product have been produced and are fully inspected but before the conventional bagging process.

The machine operates on a total of 24 individual bags at a time. Each bag is filled randomly with approximately 4 ounces of Kisses before the new technology kicks in. It is at this point that the scale weighs each individual piece of candy and distributes the candy to one of the 24 bags. The next piece of candy gets weighed, and it too is distributed systematically to one of the 24 bags of candy. This process is repeated over and over again at a rate approaching 600 units per minute. Individual Kisses are sent to designated bags in an attempt to get to exactly 8 ounces in each bag (or realistically 8.02 to 8.05 ounces or however tightly the tolerances are set).

In the past, random sampling has shown, on average, that an eight-ounce bag of Kisses weighed 8.13 to 8.16 ounces, on average, with a range of 7.98 ounces to 8.23 ounces. In practice, Hershey believes that it can tighten the tolerances to eliminate all underweights and save 0.12 ounces of product given away for free.

The vice president of production is interested in seeing if this new technology could work at Hershey. Therefore, a production engineer and a plant manager are assigned to take on this task. First, a request for proposal (RFP) is circulated to a group of equipment suppliers. This will confirm the feasibility of the approach and provide a solid investment quote. After the two team members confirm the technical feasibility, then marketing, accounting, and finance join the team. Together the team develops the business case along with the following assumptions, as summarized in Table 10.8:

- The equipment, delivery, and installation will cost $10.0 million.
- The equipment will save $1.65 million in product give-away. This value was estimated based on the following:
  - An eight-ounce bag of Kisses sells retails for $2.25, with a wholesale price from Hershey to the retailer of $1.50 on average.
  - The cost of goods sold excluding depreciation and distribution is approximately $0.90 per bag (or $0.1125 per ounce).
  - The team estimates that it should be able to reduce the average cost of a bag by 1.50 percent, which results in a cost savings of $0.0135 per bag.
  - Marketing confirms that sales have held steady at $183.4 million for this product, and they are anticipated to remain at this level in the

TABLE 10-8

Cost Savings Decision—MACRS Depreciation
($ 000s)

	Initial Investment	Year 1	Year 2	Year 3	Year 4	Year 5	Year 6	Year 7	Year 8
Purchase price	$ (10,000)								
Incremental operating cash flow									
Reduction of overweight give-away		$ 1,650	$ 1,650	$ 1,650	$ 1,650	$ 1,650	$ 1,650	$ 1,650	$ 1,650
Elimination (net) of 4 operator positions		240	240	240	240	240	240	240	240
MACRS depreciation*		(1,429)	(2,449)	(1,749)	(1,249)	(893)	(893)	(893)	(445)
Operating Income		461	(559)	141	641	997	997	997	1,445
Taxes (35%)		(161)	196	(49)	(224)	(349)	(349)	(349)	(506)
After-tax operating income		$ 300	$ (363)	$ 92	$ 417	$ 648	$ 648	$ 648	$ 939
After-tax operating income		$ 300	$ (363)	$ 92	$ 417	$ 648	$ 648	$ 648	$ 939
Depreciation		1,429	2,449	1,749	1,249	893	893	893	445
Incremental operating cash flow		1,729	2,086	1,841	1,666	1,541	1,541	1,541	1,384
Terminal cash flow									
Residual value, after tax									650
Total cash flow	$ (10,000)	$ 1,729	$ 2,086	$ 1,841	$ 1,666	$ 1,541	$ 1,541	$ 1,541	$ 2,034
Present value 8.0%	$ (10,000)	$ 1,601	$ 1,788	$ 1,461	$ 1,225	$ 1,049	$ 971	$ 899	$ 1,099
		$ 10,093	Gross present value (PV – cash flow years 1–8)						
Net Present Value	$ 93								
*MACRS depreciation rate		14.29%	24.49%	17.49%	12.49%	8.93%	8.93%	8.93%	4.45%

335

foreseeable future. At an average wholesale price of $1.50, this inevitably translates to 122.27 million eight-ounce bags of Kisses. With a savings of $0.0135 per bag, the total savings are expected to be $1,650 thousand each year.

- The plant manager also believes that the workforce at the plant can be reduced by four inspectors if the new equipment is implemented. Each operator has a total cost (i.e., salary, wages, benefits, and taxes) of $60,000.
- The standard operating procedure (SOP) assumes an eight-year life of the equipment with $1,000 thousand salvage value at the end of the project.
- The tax rate is assumed to be 35 percent, and the cost of capital (the discount rate) is 8 percent.
- There is no working capital impact.

As with the new product example, this decision calls for a five-step analytical approach.

Step 1: Initial investment. The estimated equipment investment was honed with a quote from a potential supplier of $10,000 thousand.

Step 2: Incremental operating cash flow. The savings are from the two sources mentioned earlier: (1) $1,650 thousand from reduced free product give-away, and (2) the reduction in labor estimated at $240,000. But these savings are offset by higher depreciation expense. Of course, for most years, the firm will pay higher taxes because its expenses will be lower and its income higher. Taxes are estimated at 35 percent. No working capital is required.

Step 3: Project the terminal cash flows or expected salvage value and add to the final year's operating cash flow. After tax salvage value is anticipated at $650,000 after eight years, and there is no working capital.

Step 4: Find the present value of the future cash flows. The next step is to determine the present value of the benefit stream. This can be accomplished using Eq. (10.2), a handheld financial calculator, or Excel. The present value of the estimated cash flows is $10,093 thousand.

Step 5: Determine the net present value. The project's net present value is found as the sum of the present values of the inflows, or benefits, less the outflows, or costs ($ thousands) using Eq. (10.3):

New present value = gross present value of total cash flow – initial investment
= $10,093 – $10,000
= $93

Since the NPV is positive, the project should be accepted. While this does not sound like a large amount of money, remember that this project does provide the necessary 8 percent (opportunity cost of capital) and even $93,000 more!

Cost Savings—Straight-Line Depreciation Example

Table 10-9 recasts the cost savings analysis with the only difference that straight-line depreciation is substituted for MACRS depreciation. Remember that MACRS is the correct depreciation technique to use, but for illustrative purposes, I will revert to using straight-line depreciation.

Step 1: Initial investment. The estimated equipment cost remains the same, $10,000 thousand.

Step 2: Incremental operating cash flow. The savings are from the two sources mentioned earlier: (1) $1,650 thousand from reduced free product give-away, and (2) the reduction in labor estimated at $240,000. But these savings are offset with higher depreciation expense. Using straight-line depreciation, the operating cash flows are the same each year ($1,666 thousand).

This amount can be verified by the following ($000s):

Item	Calculation (Tax Rate = 35%)	Cash Flow
Overweight reduction	$1,650 × (1 – tax rate)	$ 1,072.5
Reduction in operators	$240 × (1 – tax rate)	156.0
Additional depreciation	$1,250 × (tax rate)	437.5
	Total cash-flow impact	$ 1,666.0

Both identified savings reduce expense and increase income. Taxes must be paid on this increased income. Since depreciation is a noncash expense, the indirect impact of depreciation is the tax shield that it provides. Again, no working capital is required.

Step 3: Project the terminal cash flows or expected salvage value and add to the final year's operating cash flow. After tax salvage value of $650 thousand is anticipated after eight years, and there is no working capital to recover.

Step 4: Find the present value of the future cash flows. The next step is to determine the present value of the benefit stream. This can be accomplished using Eq. (10.2), a handheld financial calculator, or Excel. The present value of the estimated cash flows is $9,926 thousand.

Step 5: Determine the net present value. The project's net present value is found as the sum of the present values (determined in step 4) less the investment amount ($ thousands), again using Eq. (10.3):

Net present value = gross present value of total cash flow – initial investment

$$= \$9,926 - \$10,000$$

$$= \$(74)$$

TABLE 10-9

Cost Savings Decision—Straight-Line Depreciation
($ 000s)

	Initial Investment	Year 1	Year 2	Year 3	Year 4	Year 5	Year 6	Year 7	Year 8
Purchase price	$ (10,000)								
Incremental operating cash flow									
Reduction of overweight give-away		$ 1,650	$ 1,650	$ 1,650	$ 1,650	$ 1,650	$ 1,650	$ 1,650	$ 1,650
Elimination (net) of 4 operator positions		240	240	240	240	240	240	240	240
MACRS depreciation*		(1,250)	(1,250)	(1,250)	(1,250)	(1,250)	(1,250)	(1,250)	(1,250)
Operating income		640	640	640	640	640	640	640	640
Taxes (35%)		(224)	(224)	(224)	(224)	(224)	(224)	(224)	(224)
After-tax operating income		$ 416	$ 416	$ 416	$ 416	$ 416	$ 416	$ 416	$ 416
After-tax operating income		$ 416	$ 416	$ 416	$ 416	$ 416	$ 416	$ 416	$ 416
Depreciation		1,250	1,250	1,250	1,250	1,250	1,250	1,250	1,250
Incremental operating cash flow		1,666	1,666	1,666	1,666	1,666	1,666	1,666	1,666
Terminal cash flow									
Residual value, no gain (loss)									650
Total cash flow	$ (10,000)	$ 1,666	$ 1,666	$ 1,666	$ 1,666	$ 1,666	$ 1,666	$ 1,666	$ 2,316
Present value 8.0%	$ (10,000)	$ 1,543	$ 1,428	$ 1,323	$ 1,225	$ 1,134	$ 1,050	$ 972	$ 1,251
		$ 9,926	Gross present value (PV – cash flow years 1–8)						
Net present value	$ (74)								

338

Since the NPV is negative, this is a strong indication that the project should not be accepted.

Of course, for the correct decision and project analysis, MACRS should be used, and this project would be accepted. But what if our collective judgment about the assumptions is incorrect? We treated these assumptions as certain. What if these cash flows are not certain? The next sections discuss different techniques to understand the uncertainty underlying assumptions and their valuation impacts.

ASSUMPTION UNCERTAINTY

To help you better understand the impact of uncertainty on a capital evaluation, I will use the new product example with MACRS depreciation from earlier and review:

- Sensitivity analysis
- Scenario analysis
- Excel's data tables
- Probabilistic analysis
- Monte Carlo analysis

Uncertainty underlies any projection. Each organization needs to find the approach that best assists it to understand and deal with uncertainty in capital investment analysis.

Sensitivity Analysis

Sensitivity analysis occurs by varying each assumption individually and observing the resulting change in net present value. Table 10-10 tests the impact on the net present value for a reasonable positive change in each assumption. For example, if the cost of the new asset declines to $18,000 thousand from the original estimate of $20,000 thousand, the net present value increases to $2,408 thousand, or an increase of $1,464 thousand. The table documents the NPV increase that results from each of the changes noted in the table.

Notice that some changes in assumptions have little impact, whereas other changes in assumptions have significant consequences. The working capital support (percent of incremental sales), the tax rate, and residual value have minimal impact. Other assumptions, such as the cost of the equipment, initial sales levels, growth rates, expenses as a percent of sales, product launch expense, and cost of capital, have major impact.

T A B L E   10-10

New Product Sensitivity Analysis
(MACRS Depreciation)
($ 000s)

	Orginal Assumption	Revised Assumption	Revised NPV	Change in NPV
Purchase price of new equipment	$ 20,000	$ 18,000	$ 2,408	$ 1,464
Working capital (% of incremental sales)	5.0%	4.5%	1,008	64
Initial sales	$ 25,000	$ 27,500	3,208	2,264
Additional sales growth	0.0%	1.0%	1,703	759
Additional COS (exc deprec, % of sales)	0.0%	−1.0%	1,982	1,038
Operating costs (% of sales)	18.0%	17.0%	1,982	1,038
Reduction in launch expense, year 1	$ −	$ (1,000)	1,546	602
Tax rate	35.0%	34.0%	1,040	96
Residual value	$ 1,000	$ 1,100	979	35
Cost of capital	8.0%	7.5%	1,508	564

The original Net Present Value for this New Product project was: $ 944

From Table 10-10, clear business imperatives are noted. In order to drive the value of a new product, a capital investment, or an organization, the actions are clear:

• Buy the specific asset at the lowest price.
• Enhance sales and sales growth every year.
• Reduce your costs (including the cost of capital).
• Limit your investment in fixed or working capital.

Delivery on these imperatives with the right amount of product quality balance is the challenge facing all management teams.

Before leaving Table 10-10, a few easy mechanical observations are in order. For example, a $1,000 reduction in the first year's product launch expense results in a $650 after-tax savings and additional cash flow in the first year. In present value terms, this equates to $602 additional NPV. (Recall from Chapter 8, for example, $650/(1.08).] Also, $100 additional residual value is $65 after tax, but in year 8. Thus, in present value terms, the net present value is enhanced by $35(or $65/(1.08)^8). Finally, while it is much more difficult to see the impact of an improvement in expenses (1 percent of sales), it is interesting to notice an identical impact whether it is a cost of sales reduction or an operating cost reduction. The capital evaluation does not distinguish between product expense or operating (selling, general, and administrative) expense.

Scenario Analysis

Scenario analysis examines different business models or different circumstances by combining adjustments to a number of assumptions simultaneously. Table 10-11 illustrates three different scenarios (i.e., business models). The original case is documented, along with a cost-cutting scenario and two growth scenarios:

- The cost-cutting scenario trades off reduced volumes (sales) and growth for reduced investment levels, cost of sales, and marketing expenses. Also, no residual value is assumed for this lower-priced equipment.

- The moderate-growth scenario trades off higher initial sales and sales growth for additional investment in working capital and moderately higher marketing (operating) expense. Since the equipment is used more heavily to produce more product, its residual value is assumed to be zero.

- The aggressive-growth scenario trades off a higher initial sales level and more substantial growth for additional investment, in the new equipment and working capital, production costs, and marketing (operating) expense. Once again, since the equipment is used more heavily to produce more product, its residual value is assumed to be zero.

T A B L E   10-11

New Product Scenario Analysis
($ 000s)

	Orginal Assumptions	Cost Cutting	Moderate Growth	Aggressive Growth
Assumptions				
Investment in new equipment	$ 20,000	$ 18,000	$ 20,000	$ 22,500
Working capital (% of incremental sales)	5.0%	4.5%	5.5%	6.0%
Initial sales	$ 25,000	$ 20,000	28,000	32,000
Additional sales growth (years 2–5)	0.0%	−2.0%	2.0%	5.0%
Additional COS (except deprec, % of sales)	0.0%	−1.0%	0.0%	0.5%
Operating costs (% of sales)	18.0%	15.0%	20.0%	21.0%
Product launch expense, year 1	$ 10,000	$ 7,500	$ 12,000	$ 14,000
Tax rate	35.0%	35.0%	35.0%	35.0%
Residual value	$ 1,000	$ –	–	–
Cost of capital	8.0%	8.0%	8.0%	8.0%
Year 8 selected values				
Sales	$ 32,657	$ 24,175	$ 39,468	$ 50,426
Operating income	6,621	5,726	7,398	8,832
Total cash flow	7,477	5,611	7,870	9,768
Valuation summary				
Gross present value	$ 22,194	$ 20,213	$ 22,478	$ 25,657
Initial investment	21,250	18,900	21,540	24,420
Net present value	944	1,313	938	1,237
Change from original case	n/a	369	(6)	293

Both the cost-cutting scenario and aggressive-growth scenario produce higher NPVs than the original (or base) case, with the cost-cutting scenario showing $369,000 advantage. The moderate-growth scenario provides similar results (actually $6,000 lower) to the base (original) case. Remember in this situation that you have a cleaver and not a scalpel when interpreting the results.

Excel Data Tables

A data what-if analysis tool that is available in Excel are *data tables* found under data and then scenario analysis. Two of the most impactful operating variables are sales growth rate and expenses (as a percent of sales). Data tables assist the analyst in drawing a landscape of the tradeoff between sales growth and expenses.

Table 10-12 shows the results of a data table centered on incremental or decremental sales growth rates and cost of goods sold. Notice that the cell under the 0 percent incremental sales growth column and across the 0 percent incremental cost of sales row is our base-case net present value of $944,000. The table shows the various tradeoffs. Of course, the most advantageous position is to be in the southwest corner (+2 percent added sales growth and −2 percent COS as a percent of sales); the least desirable location is in the northeast corner, where sales growth is 2 percent lower than the base case, and COS is 2 percent of sales higher. While these two corner points are extreme and possibly unattainable, this table does help management to understand business tradeoffs. For example, if costs get out of control and increase by 1.0 percent of sales, sales will need to grow by approximately an additional 1.5 percent to maintain the same net present value. Or another example, if costs can be cut by 1 percent of sales, the sales growth could decline by almost 1.35 percent, and the new product would be more financially viable.

Chapter 14 introduces the mechanics for calculating a data table along with company valuation. For now, appreciate the power of a data table. In this example, 81 scenarios were created in this "9 by 9" table in less than five minutes.

Probabilistic Analysis and Monte Carlo Simulation

Probabilistic analysis and expected values may be an appropriate extension of the basic capital investment analysis, wherein probabilities are assigned to potential outcomes (NPVs) and an expected value is derived. This technique sees only limited application, but it is viable for larger projects.

Another approach that is gaining some usage is Monte Carlo analysis. Monte Carlo simulation is a statistical technique that allows the analyst the opportunity to describe a range of potential values for specific assumptions. For instance, returning to the new product example, you can specify a range of potential values for each of the assumptions that you deem appropriate. Thus, for example, we could

TABLE 10-12

Data Table Illustration
(New Product Example with MACRS Depreciation)
($ 000s)

Net present value

		Incremental (Decremental) Sales Growth							
		2.0%	1.5%	1.0%	0.5%	0.0%	-0.5%	-1.0%	-1.5%	-2.0%
Incremental (decremental) COS % of sales	2.0%	$ 275	$ (87)	$ (443)	$ (791)	$ (1,133)	$ (1,469)	$ (1,798)	$ (2,122)	$ (2,439)
	1.5%	829	458	94	(263)	(614)	(958)	(1,296)	(1,627)	(1,952)
	1.0%	1,383	1,003	630	264	(95)	(447)	(793)	(1,132)	(1,466)
	0.5%	1,938	1,549	1,167	792	425	64	(290)	(638)	(979)
	0.0%	2,492	2,094	1,703	1,320	944	575	212	(143)	(492)
	-0.5%	3,047	2,639	2,240	1,848	1,463	1,086	715	351	(5)
	-1.0%	3,601	3,185	2,777	2,376	1,982	1,596	1,218	846	481
	-1.5%	4,155	3,730	3,313	2,904	2,502	2,107	1,720	1,341	968
	-2.0%	4,710	4,276	3,850	3,431	3,021	2,618	2,223	1,835	1,455

Change in net present value

		Incremental (Decremental) Sales Growth							
		2.0%	1.5%	1.0%	0.5%	0.0%	-0.5%	-1.0%	-1.5%	-2.0%
Incremental (decremental) COS % of sales	2.0%	$ (669)	$ (1,031)	$ (1,387)	$ (1,735)	$ (2,077)	$ (2,413)	$ (2,742)	$ (3,066)	$ (3,383)
	1.5%	(115)	(486)	(850)	(1,207)	(1,558)	(1,902)	(2,240)	(2,571)	(2,896)
	1.0%	439	59	(314)	(680)	(1,039)	(1,391)	(1,737)	(2,076)	(2,410)
	0.5%	994	605	223	(152)	(519)	(880)	(1,234)	(1,582)	(1,923)
	0.0%	1,548	1,150	759	376	–	(369)	(732)	(1,087)	(1,436)
	-0.5%	2,103	1,695	1,296	904	519	142	(229)	(593)	(949)
	-1.0%	2,657	2,241	1,833	1,432	1,038	652	274	(98)	(463)
	-1.5%	3,211	2,786	2,369	1,960	1,558	1,163	776	397	24
	-2.0%	3,766	3,332	2,906	2,487	2,077	1,674	1,279	891	511

include the base case's initial year sales as a range—most likely $25 million, best case $28 million, and worst case $19 million. We also can specify a range for the cost of sales (60 percent with a standard deviation of 1 percent) in the first year and estimate working capital investment between 4 and 6 percent with uniform probabilities. We can continue until we define all the assumptions as a range of potential values.

Monte Carlo simulation is facilitated by simulation software. Using a random-number generator, the software selects assumption values based on the ranges, probabilities, and probability distributions that we outlined. Once the random assumptions have been selected, the spreadsheet is projected, and the net present value is calculated. The simulation software repeats the process hundreds or thousands of times and describes the expected NPV with its accompanying range and statistics.

The @Risk software provided by Palisades Corporation or Crystal Ball software by Oracle are very supportive and flexible Monte Carlo simulators. They are spreadsheet templates that rest on top of Excel or other spreadsheet software. The ease of use ranges from very straightforward and user friendly to extremely technical and intricate, incorporating relationships between variables. In order to best use this approach, management must be comfortable in using statistical analysis to make an informed business decision.

Before considering other applications of investment valuation, it is appropriate to consider a few remaining topics using the new product investment analysis.

ADDITIONAL KEY CONCEPTS

Now that you have seen comprehensive project analysis, this section reviews additional key concepts about cash flow and investment analysis.

Inflation

Should the projected cash flows be based on nominal estimates (including inflation), or should the estimates be based on "real" (excluding inflation) cash-flow estimates? For a number of reasons, the cash flows should be nominal and include reasonable estimates of inflation because:

- Inflation is a fact of life for most organizations.
- Deflation is also a part of life for some industries.
- Inflation affects prices and costs differently.
- Cost of capital includes a market expected general rate of inflation.
- Comparing a nominal (including inflation) cost of capital with real (excluding inflation) cash flows can lead to rejection of otherwise acceptable projects.

- Comparing a real cost of capital with real cash flows may lead to acceptance of an inferior project due to an understatement of working capital investment.

- Nominal cash flow projections provide a comparative basis for postcompletion audits.

A chief financial officer (CFO) who used projections of real cash flows remarked, "Our company is not in the business of forecasting inflation." This is precisely the point! Whenever cash-flow projections are made, there is an implicit assumption about inflation. If we do not address inflation explicitly, implicitly we are saying that inflation is expected to be 0.0 percent, which may be a good or a bad estimate.

Inflation affects sale prices, raw materials costs, labor contracts, overhead, and so on in different ways, which demonstrates another reason to use nominal cash flows. These cost increases may not be able to be passed fully onto the consumer. Also, with inflation, additional working capital investment must be increased because inventory and accounts receivables all increase. By using differentiated estimated inflation rates, additional analysis and tactical decisions can be shaped.

Another benefit of using nominal cash flows is that performance standards are established immediately at the time of project approval. This audit trail promotes postcompletion audits. Yes, circumstances are rare that the underlying inflation rate will match the projected inflation rate, but the difference may be minimal, and lessons can be learned for future applications. If real cash flows are projected, there is little to no chance of comparing actual results with the anticipated cash flow.

Allocated Costs

To repeat from the beginning of the chapter, when determining cash flows, you are interested in only relevant incremental cash flows. This is clearly the case in the preceding two examples, new products and equipment replacement. Considering the new product investment analysis, the administrative costs to hire a brand manager and an assistant were specifically included in the projected operating expenses. We did not allocate the salaries and related expenses of the marketing director, vice president of marketing, the marketing department, the chief operating officer, or the chief executive officer. We did not allocate floor space and related occupancy expenses. The executive salaries, related expenses, and occupancy expenses are not a function of the acceptance or rejection of the new product. They are not incremental, and they are not relevant.

The words *allocate, allocated*, and *allocation* should raise red flags. Any allocated expenses must be reviewed and their incremental nature determined. If the expenses are not incremental, they should not be included in the analysis.

Financial Costs and Financial Servicing

The two preceding projects, new products and equipment replacement, illustrate the operational nature of the investment analysis cash flows. Related interest costs, debt repayment, dividends, stock repurchases, and so on are considered financing-related cash flows and are not considered directly in the investment cash-flow development. Only operating cash flows are projected directly and considered for investment analysis. Financing implications are captured through the discount rate (the cost of capital). Consequently, if financing cash flows are explicitly included in the cash-flow analysis and then discounted by the cost of capital, the financing cash flows would have been double counted.

Accounting Measures and Investment Analysis

Chapter 3 introduced and discussed a number of accounting performance metrics, and Chapter 9 discussed the differences between accounting measures and economic measures. While a hypothetical example, the new product analysis in this chapter is representative of the cash-flow patterns exhibited by new retail (consumer) products. Based on almost any accounting metric, return on assets or return on equity, this project should not be accepted because it does not generate positive returns in its first few years despite increasing shareholder value by $944,000 over its eight-year life.

    While it is important to understand the accounting ramifications of new product introductions through strategic planning (see Chapter 6), economic measures dictate the acceptance or rejection of an investment.

ADDITIONAL APPLICATIONS

Aspects of two additional applications are discussed briefly below: information technology (IT) analysis and employee identification (badge) system.

IT Application

Table 10-13 illustrates a hypothetical software investment. This example assumes the following (headings below correspond to the line items in Table 10-13):

- Total estimated savings:
  - Head-count reduction of 10 human resources support personnel at an average cost (salary, benefits, and taxes) of $35,000—total $350,000, 3 percent inflation
  - Elimination of costs to support the old human resources system— $220,000, 3 percent inflation
  - Management time savings—$1,250,000 annually, no inflation

- Total ongoing expenditures:
    - Consultant fees of $150,000 and $100,000 in the first two years
    - Training fees of $150,000 and $100,000 in the first two years
    - Maintenance contract—$150,000, 10 percent inflation
- Depreciation and amortization: Related expenses for direct investment (five-year MACRS schedule)
- Total direct investment of $1,605,400 (year 0):
    - New human resources software—$800,000
    - Additional expenditures to buy servers and equip employee kiosks—$600,000
    - Consultant expenses, training, travel, and so on—$205,400 as part of the investment
- Other assumptions:
    - Cost of capital—14 percent
    - Tax rate—40 percent

Table 10-13 modifies and expands the typical evaluation format. It begins by listing the savings offset by the added expense to derive operating income through to cash flow. Note, also, a five-year MACRS depreciation approach is taken to determine depreciation and amortization. As presented, this project has a net present value of almost $2.5 million.

Notice that the third benefit (savings) is a managerial time savings. This one assumption dominates the net present value; without this savings, the NPV is a negative $(0.4) million. The question is, "Is this savings a relevant incremental savings?" If the savings are the direct result of enabling an increase in managers' and directors' span of control and result in a head-count reduction of 12 managers, the savings are relevant and incremental and should be considered in the analysis. If the savings are calculated as a half an hour savings per day for all managers, as detailed below, the savings do not represent incremental savings:

Savings per manager per day	½ hour
Days per year	250 days
Savings per manager per year (A)	125 hours
Number of managers (B)	200
Average manager's wage, bonus, etc.	$104,000/year
Hours per year	2,080 hours
Hourly manager's cost (C)	$50/hour
Management time savings (A) × (B) × (C)	$1,250,000/year

In order for this to be an actual savings, all managers must take a $6,250 (125 hours × $50 per hour) pay cut, or there must be a head-count reduction of 12 managers!

TABLE 10-13

Human Resources Software Investment Analysis

($ 000s)

	Year 0	Year 1	Year 2	Year 3	Year 4	Year 5	Year 6
Estimated savings							
Head-count reduction		$ 350.0	$ 360.5	$ 371.3	$ 382.4	$ 393.9	$ 405.7
Ongoing expenses of old system		220.0	226.6	233.4	240.4	247.6	255.0
Management time savings		1,250.0	1,250.0	1,250.0	1,250.0	1,250.0	1,250.0
Total savings		1,820.0	1,837.1	1,854.7	1,872.8	1,891.5	1,910.7
Ongoing expenses							
Consulting fees		150.0	100.0	–	–	–	–
Training fees		150.0	100.0	–	–	–	–
Maintenenace contract		150.0	165.0	181.5	199.7	219.7	241.7
Depreciation and amortization		321.1	513.7	308.2	184.9	184.9	92.5
Total expenses		771.1	878.7	489.7	384.6	404.6	334.2
Operating income		1,048.9	958.4	1,365.0	1,488.2	1,486.9	1,576.5
Taxes (40.0%)		419.6	383.4	546.0	595.3	594.8	630.6
After-tax operating income		$ 629.3	$ 575.0	$ 819.0	$ 892.9	$ 892.1	$ 945.9
After-tax operating income		$ 629.3	$ 575.0	$ 819.0	$ 892.9	$ 892.1	$ 945.9
Depreciation and amortization		321.1	513.7	308.2	184.9	184.9	92.5
Working capital investment		–	–	–	–	–	–
Fixed capital investment	$ (1,605.4)	–	–	–	–	–	–
Cash flow	$ (1,605.4)	$ 950.4	$ 1,088.7	$ 1,127.2	$ 1,077.8	$ 1,077.0	$ 1,038.4
Net present value, 14%	$ 2,497.4						

Determining relevant incremental cash flows is extremely important in the investment analysis and authorization phase.

Employee Identification (Badge) System

Whether you hang them around your neck or hang them from your shirt pocket, employee identification systems or employee ID badges have become popular at most organizations. In evaluating these projects, after-tax cash benefits (or savings) result from a reduced number of security guards, reduced insurance premiums, and enhanced security for employee and corporate safety. The after-tax cash savings for a reduction in the number of security guards and reduced insurance costs can be calculated easily. But what is the cash-flow impact of a breach in security?

At Hershey, I encountered such an investment proposal. I sharpened my pencil and resharpened my pencil to estimate the savings for security guard expenses and insurance premium reductions. Nothing was formally documented or considered as the "cost" of a security breach for legal reasons. No matter how many times I reexamined the cash flows, the NPV always was negative and approximately $(50,000). (Although this is not the actual number, it is representative.) A negative NPV indicates that the project should not be accepted. However, in this case, I argued that this "cost" represented a one-time premium for a 10-year additional insurance policy designed to reduce the risk of security breaches. In other words, I positioned the negative NPV as an administrative cost of $50,000. The project was approved!

SUMMARY

This chapter provides the culmination of my presentation of investment analysis. Using the tools developed in Chapter 9, this chapter promotes the development of cash flows through various examples of investments and the development of their underlying cash flows.

Relevant nominal, incremental, after-tax cash flow development is the backbone of financial investment analysis. However, just as a strong strategic planning process has strong financial considerations, which also enable managerial processes, so too does a strong capital investment process and its evaluation and authorization phase. A strong evaluation and authorization phase:

- Facilitates communication among the senior executives of an organization
- Sets a business direction
- Prioritizes opportunities and requirements
- Establishes business performance standards and objectives

Within this chapter, a consistent but flexible investment analysis framework is developed and applied to a variety of projects. The framework is used successfully to value new products, cost savings (or equipment replacement) projects, investment in information technology, and administrative projects.

After examining investment analysis with static and known cash flows, this chapter considers various alternatives for handling uncertain cash flows. The suggested approaches include:

- Sensitivity analysis
- Scenario analysis
- Probabilistic approaches
- Monte Carlo analysis

Additional considerations for capital investment decisions are presented in Chapter 14 including a valuation of the The Hershey Company via the hypothetical strategic plan developed in chapter 6.

LONG-TERM FINANCING STRATEGIES

COST OF CAPITAL, HURDLE RATES, AND FINANCIAL STRUCTURE

Chapter 9 examined numerous capital investment analysis techniques, and Chapter 10 discussed how to determine cash flows through the use of numerous project examples. Paramount to the investment evaluation is the discount rate— the cost of capital. The cost of capital is the opportunity cost of funds invested in the firm. It represents the minimum acceptable rate of return for corporate investments. In the Chapter 10 new product example, a 0.5 percentage point change in the cost of capital (from 8.0 to 7.5 percent) had a significant impact on the net present value (NPV). The NPV increased by $564 thousand, or 60 percent.

For financial executives, managing the cost of capital is one of their most important responsibilities. Remember the inverse relationship between the discount rate and the value of the project. As the discount rate rises (falls), the value of the project falls (rises). Set the cost of capital (discount rate) too high, and the growth of the firm suffers because projects that otherwise would have a positive NPV could have a negative NPV, and the firm would not invest in a "good" new project. Also, if the cost of capital is set too high, the firm operates at a disadvantage. To attain acceptable higher levels of return, the company raises prices or uses less costly (lower-quality) components. All of this has an impact on the long-term performance of the firm. On the other hand, set the cost of capital (discount rate) too low, and many projects that should be rejected for insufficient returns are implemented because they appear to have a positive NPV.

For the nonfinancial executive, understanding the genesis of the cost of capital is critical to ensure that adequate returns are provided on invested capital. This understanding also facilitates the discussions between finance and operations. Some executives already have asked the question of why they need to earn a return of 8 percent on a project when the company can borrow money at 5 or 6 percent. Understanding that debt is only one source of capital is important for any executive.

This chapter develops an estimation approach for the cost of capital, discusses the concept of financial structure and an optimal capital structure, and introduces the concept of divisional or project hurdle rates.

COST OF CAPITAL

A consolidated Hershey balance sheet for December 31, 2010, is presented on Table 11-1. It includes assets, operating and financial liabilities, and stockholders' equity. Accounts payable, along with deferred taxes and other liabilities, comprise "operating" liabilities, or liabilities that are based directly in the operations of the firm. The cash flows attributable to the rise and fall in operating liabilities are accounted for explicitly when determining cash flows, just as you did in Chapter 10. Consequently, these amounts are not considered financial capital.

Capital consists of financial liabilities and the stockholders' equity. From Table 11-1, the book value of capital can be summarized as ($ millions):

Capital Component	December 2010
Short-term debt	$ 24.1
Current portion of long-term debt	261.4
Long-term debt	1,541.8
Total interest-bearing debt (IBD)	1,827.3
Preferred stock	0.0
Common stock	937.6
Total stockholders' equity	937.6
Total financial capital	$2,764.9

I will consider the short-term debt and current portion of long-term debt to be a component of the permanent capital structure because both have existed historically for well over 10 years, and the likelihood is that Hershey intends to refinance both forms of debt.

Continuing the case study of Hershey, I will show how the cost of capital can be estimated for a firm. Although I will attempt to make the procedures specific and numerically precise, you must recognize that considerable judgment must be exercised. Because of the crucial role of the cost of capital estimation in guiding a firm's

TABLE   11-1

Summarized Balance Sheet, December 31, 2010

Cash and equivalents	$ 884.6	Short-term debt*	$ 285.5
Other current assets	1,120.6	Other current liabilities	1,013.3
Net, plant, prop, & equip	1,437.7	Long-term debt	1,541.8
Goodwill	524.1	Other LT liabilities	494.5
Other assets	305.7	Stockholders' equity	937.6
Total assets	$4,272.7	Total liabilities and equity	$4,272.7

*Short-term debt includes current portion of long-term debt, $261.4.

investment decisions, and because the valuation of a firm is highly sensitive to the applicable cost of capital employed, the judgment must be arrived at with great care. The purpose of this Hershey example is to provide a framework of the main procedures that should be employed when estimating the cost of capital.

The cost of capital represents the weighted-average cost of permanent financing raised by the corporation. It is expressed as shown in Eq. (11.1):

$$K_c = w_d K_d + w_{ps} K_{ps} + w_{cs} K_{cs} \qquad (11.1)$$

where K_c, K_d, K_{ps}, K_{cs} = cost of capital, cost of debt (after-tax), cost of preferred stock, cost of common stock

w_d, w_{ps}, w_{cs} = weight in debt, weight in preferred stock, weight in common stock

The cost of capital and the cost of each of its components reflect the opportunity costs or minimum returns required by investors. Each component is evaluated on an after-tax basis, although this has a meaningful effect only on the cost of debt because only the cost of debt (interest expense) is recognized as a tax-deductible expense. For preferred stock or common stock, the pretax cost and the after-tax cost are identical! An after-tax cost of capital is developed because a project's operating cash flows (used in investment analysis, see Chapter 10) are on an after-tax basis. Table 11-2 demonstrates the concept of Eq. (11.1). As you complete this section, values will be substituted into Table 11-2 to illustrate the cost of capital.

This chapter first explains how to calculate the cost of the individual capital components (i.e., debt, preferred stock, and common stock) and then discusses the proper weights to use to finalize the weighted-average cost of capital (WACC). While the concept may seem straightforward, there are many permutations both in theory and in practice. I will present many of these alternatives as I discuss each topic.

COST OF DEBT

Simply put, the *cost of debt* is interest expense. In the United States, interest expense is tax deductible for corporations, and consequently, the cost of debt is

T A B L E   11-2

Cost of Capital Overview

	Weight	$\times$	Cost	$=$	WACC
Debt	$w_d\%$		$K_d\%$		$w_d K_d$
Preferred stock	$w_{ps}\%$		$K_{ps}\%$		$w_{ps} K_{ps}$
Common stock	$w_{cs}\%$		$K_{cs}\%$		$w_{cs} K_{cs}$
Total	100.0%			Σ	WACC

reduced by the amount of the tax savings and is stated on an after-tax basis by using Eq. (11.2):

$$K_d = i(1 - T) \qquad\qquad (11.2)$$

where K_d = cost of debt (after tax)
       i = interest rate (before tax)
       T = marginal tax rate

To illustrate, in Table 11-3, two companies, A and B, are in the same industry, manufacturing, selling, and delivering the same product. Both companies sell the same amount of goods ($10,000) with the same cost of goods sold ($9,000) and the same $1,000 of operating income or earnings before interest and taxes (EBIT).

The only difference is that the first company has no debt, and the second company has $5,000 of debt in its capital base (or capital structure). The second company pays 6 percent interest on its debt. So the company with debt has

TABLE 11-3

Cost of Debt

After-tax cost of debt	=	before-tax cost of debt	×	(1 – tax rate)
		Financial Structures		
		No Debt		**Debt**
Debt		$ 0		$ 5,000
Interest rate		6.0%		6.0%
Interest		$ 0		$ 300
Sales		$10,000		$ 10,000
Cost of goods sold		9,000		9,000
Operating income		1,000		1,000
Interest expense		0		300
Pretax income		1,000		700
Income taxes (40%)		400		280
Net income		$ 600		$ 420
Pretax cost of debt				$ 300
Aftertax cost of debt				$ 180
After-tax cost of debt	=	6.0%	×	(1 – 40%)
	=	3.6%	or	$180/$5,000

another expense ($300 of interest expense) and reports $300 less in pretax income. Since both companies pay the same 40 percent tax rate, the company with debt has a tax payment of $120 lower because of this lower pretax income. Net after taxes, the $300 of added interest expense results in net income that is lower by only $180 owing to the $120 tax savings.

The cost of debt in this example is calculated as follows:

$$K_d = i(1 - T)$$
$$= 6.0\%(1 - 40\%)$$
$$= 3.6\%$$

Debt holders are the first in line in cases of corporate insolvency. This reduces the debt's risk, leading to a pretax cost of debt that is, in general, the least expensive of all capital pools. As illustrated, debt has another significant cost advantage owing to its tax deductibility. The tax deductibility is a unique characteristic of debt. Preferred and common stock do not share this favorable consideration.

Estimating the Cost of Debt

The applicable cost of debt is the current market interest rate. The current market cost of debt reflects the opportunity cost for the bond investor and, consequently, the cost for the borrower. The current market cost of debt also reflects the rate at which the corporation could refinance its current debt portfolio.

But which cost of debt—the cost of short-term debt or the cost of long-term debt? As I indicated when I described the composition of the yield curve in Chapter 8, long-term interest rates reflect an amalgamation of current and future expectations of interest rates. That is, long-term interest rates include this year's one-year interest rate and the expectation of next year's one-year interest rate and the one-year interest rate expectation for the year after that, and so on. The long-term cost of a short-term rollover strategy (i.e., annual borrowing and refinancing) is captured conceptually in today's long-term interest rate. However, for the purposes of this chapter, I provide a blended current cost of long- and short-term debt.

The recommended technique to calculating the cost of debt is to tax-effect the current market cost of long-term debt. But how do you estimate the corporation's current cost of debt? Three approaches include the following:

- Specific bond evaluation (when bonds are traded)
- General interest rates (market indices)
- Discussions with lenders or investment bankers

These three approaches for estimating the current market cost of debt are discussed below.

Specific Bond Evaluation

If the corporation's debt trades frequently, market interest rates are easily discernible. Chapter 8 developed the concept of bond valuation and a bond's market rate of return. Say, for example, that a 30-year corporate bond was issued 20 years ago. The bond pays an annual 8.8 percent coupon (or stated) interest rate and has a maturity value of $1,000. This is the case of a $100 million debenture (unsecured debt instrument) that Hershey currently has outstanding. Let's say, today this 10-year bond sells for 120.6, or $1,206.00 ($1,000 × 120.6%). The current market rate is 6.00 percent, as depicted on Figure 11-1. Said differently, a person who buys this bond today pays $1,206 for a 10-year bond that pays $88 of *coupon interest* per year and returns the principal of $1,000 (in 10 years).

[When using a financial calculator, PV = −1,206, PMT = 88, FV = 1,000, and N = 10. Compute I/YR.] The bond investor earns 6.00 percent, which is this company's pretax cost of debt. On an after-tax basis, assuming a 37 percent tax rate, the after-tax cost of debt is 3.78 percent [6.00% × (1 − 0.37)].

General Interest Rates

Often, debt is placed privately or does not trade on a routine basis. In such cases, the current market rate can be estimated by using the corporation's credit rating and aggregated or general information from sources such as the online version of the *Wall Street Journal*'s public Market Data Center (http://online.wsj.com/mdc/public/page/2_3022-bondbnchmrk.html) or the St. Louis Federal Reserve site (http://research.stlouisfed.org/fred2/) and its "Federal Reserve Economic Data" (FRED) or its publication, *U.S. Financial Data*.

F I G U R E   11-1

Current market cost of debt.

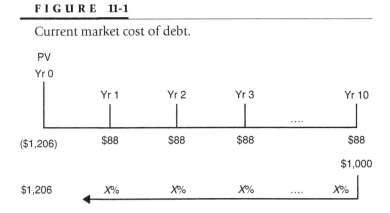

Where: X% = Current or market cost of debt
              = 6.00%

As discussed in Chapter 8, independent rating agencies such as Moody's, Standard & Poor's, and Fitch Investor Services, assess the liquidity risk and default risk of corporations. They also review the contractual provisions of specific indentures. Based on their assessments, bonds are rated. AAA is the highest quality, which commands the lowest interest rate; AA is the next highest quality level, with a slightly higher interest premium; and so on.

According to the January 7, 2011, *U.S. Financial Data*, Aaa long-term bond rates were 5.37 percent, and Baa rates were 6.45 percent as of December 31, 2010. Hershey has been an A-rated company by Standard & Poor's and an A-2-rated company by Moody's for a number of years. Extrapolating between Aaa and Baa, Hershey's borrowing rate was approximately 5.90 percent on a pretax basis or 3.72 percent on a posttax basis, assuming a 37 percent tax rate.

Discussions with Lenders or Investment Bankers

A third approach for estimating the current market cost of debt is to actively engage in talks with potential lenders. This can be done either directly with a lending institution or indirectly with an investment banker. Although this approach can provide the most accurate and committed cost of debt, it may be premature, involve too much time, and put strains on future banking relationships without improving the quality of the estimated cost of debt significantly.

While there may be different approaches to estimating the current (or market) cost of debt, this technique remains my recommendation. An alternative technique, current cost of existing debt, is discussed below.

Alternative Technique: Historical Cost of Debt

The current cost of existing debt looks at the debt that a corporation currently has outstanding and calculates the weighted average cost of that debt. Table 11-4 presents the many debt instruments that were outstanding in December 2010 for Hershey. At that point in time, Hershey's capital structure included $1,827.3 million in debt. The details of the table are found in the footnotes to the financial statements within its 2010 Annual Report (footnote 12, page 78), as discussed in Chapter 2. Hershey has four $250.0 million outstanding notes and one outstanding debenture (unsecured debt) for $250.0 million. Each debt instrument matures at different times ranging from 2011 to 2027. Each of these bonds represents 13.68 percent of Hershey's debt structure, and each of these bonds has a different stated interest rate. As an example, one of these bonds matures in 2016 and carries a pretax interest rate of 5.45 percent.

The next step is to calculate a weighted-average interest rate. Continuing the example, the 2016 note has a weighted interest rate of 0.75 percent (13.68% × 5.45%). The individual weighted interest rates carry little significance. However, when the weighted interest rates are added together, they yield a weighted-average interest rate on Hershey's total $1,827.3 million of outstanding

T A B L E   11-4

Hershey's Cost of Debt: Alternative (Historical) Technique

$ millions	Balance 12/31/10	Weight	Interest Rate	Weighted Cost
Short-term debt	$24.1	1.32%	7.10%	0.09%
Notes				
Due 2011	250.0	13.68%	5.30%	0.73%
Due 2012	92.5	5.06%	6.95%	0.35%
Due 2013	250.0	13.68%	5.00%	0.68%
Due 2015	250.0	13.68%	4.85%	0.66%
Due 2016	250.0	13.68%	5.45%	0.75%
Due 2020	350.0	19.16%	4.13%	0.79%
Debenture				
Due 2021	100.0	5.47%	8.80%	0.48%
Due 2027	250.0	13.68%	7.20%	0.99%
Other	10.7	0.59%	5.60%	0.03%
Total	$1,827.3	100.00%		5.55%
			$\times$ (1 – tax rate)	63.0%
			After-tax cost of debt	3.50%

debt of 5.55 percent. With a normal 2010 tax rate of 37.0 percent (combined all in federal, state, and local income tax rates), the historical cost of Hershey's existing debt is 3.50 percent.

A slight modification to this approach blends the cost of the existing debt with the cost of any anticipated new debt. That is, this modification maintains the framework from Table 11-4 while adding a line to it for new debt to be issued, dollar amount, and estimated interest rate. That new debt is combined with the current debt, weights are recalculated, and a modified cost of debt is calculated. In this way, limited current market conditions are introduced into the calculation.

In summary, the ideal market cost of debt could be observed directly if Hershey's bonds would routinely trade, but they don't. So the recommended current market cost of debt technique estimates Hershey's after-tax cost of debt at 3.72 percent (the previously noted market cost of debt for an A–2-rated borrower). This is 0.22 percent (22 basis points) higher than Hershey's historical cost of debt (calculated in Table 11-4). To reflect the opportunity cost of debt, I remain firm in my recommendation to use the current market cost of debt (3.72 percent).

COST OF PREFERRED STOCK

Preferred stock is a hybrid security (please see Chapter 12 for more details). It is a hybrid in the sense that although it is classified as equity, preferred stockholders do not participate in the successful growth of the corporation like a common stockholder. A preferred stockholder receives a contractually set dividend. This dividend does not change (fixed rate) over time like a debt interest payment. Because the dividend does not change, the cost of preferred stock behaves similarly to the cost of debt. Since preferred stock has no maturity date, the cost also behaves as a perpetual bond or a perpetuity (with no growth in the cash flow).

The cost of preferred stock is calculated using Eq. (11.3):

$$K_{ps} = D_{ps}/P_{ps} \tag{11.3}$$

where K_{ps} = cost of preferred stock
$\quad\quad\ D_{ps}$ = preferred stock dividend
$\quad\quad\ P_{ps}$ = price of preferred stock

For example, if a company has preferred stock with a dividend of $2 and a current price of $25, the cost of the preferred stock is 8.00 percent, as follows:

$$K_{ps} = D_{ps}/P_{ps}$$
$$= \$2/\$25$$
$$= 8.00\%$$

Figure 11-2 illustrates the cash flows to a preferred stockholder. Each year the preferred stockholder receives $2. Although the figure stops at year 100, preferred stock dividends are perpetual. By equating this stream of dividends to the $25 cost of the preferred stock, the resulting return on the investment is 8.00 percent. Said differently, by discounting the perpetual stream of dividends at an investor's required rate of return (i.e., 8.00 percent), that investor would be willing to pay $25 for the preferred stock. Once again, this technique incorporates the

F I G U R E   11-2

Cost of preferred stock.

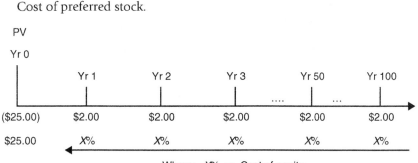

current stock price, resulting in the current opportunity cost of preferred stock. The current market cost is my recommended approach to calculating the cost of preferred stock.

Notice that there are no related tax deductions for the firm that has outstanding preferred stock and pays preferred stock dividends. Since dividends are not tax deductible in the United States, the after-tax cost of preferred stock is the same cost as the pretax cost of preferred stock. Consequently, most manufacturing firms have little to no preferred stock outstanding.

On the other hand, utilities make broad use of preferred stock because it bolsters the equity base of the utility without diluting the common stock ownership. This larger equity base allows a utility to take on additional borrowing. The cost of the preferred stock is passed on to consumers of the utility's services in the rate base. Also, startup companies are another type of company that offers preferred stock so as not to dilute their owner's interest while at the same time raising needed capital.

Cost of Preferred Stock—Alternative Technique

Similar to the historical cost of debt discussed earlier, some firms consider a historical cost of preferred stock. When preferred stock is issued, it is issued with a dividend rate tied to the stated par value of the stock. This rate is the historical cost of preferred stock. In this example, if the preferred stock sold for $20 and had a $20 par value, the resulting historical cost of preferred stock would be 10 percent:

$$K_{ps} = D_{ps}/P_{ps}$$
$$= \$2/\$20$$
$$= 10\%$$

Over time, the market price of the stock fluctuates, and the resulting cost rises or falls in reaction to the underlying preferred stock price movement. By using today's stock price of $25, a more current cost of preferred stock of 8 percent is attained and reflects the opportunity cost of preferred stock funds.

COST OF COMMON EQUITY

Common equity represents a significant component of a corporation's balance sheet. The most common captions from the common equity section of the balance sheet include:

- Common stock at par value
- Additional capital paid in excess of par
- Treasury stock
- Retained earnings
- Numerous accounting adjustments

The first two items, common stock at par and additional capital paid in excess of par, represent the original amounts for which the common stock was issued. Treasury stock reflects amounts paid to repurchase shares of stock that no longer are outstanding but remain available for issuance. Retained earnings include cumulative earnings in the corporation that were retained (i.e., not paid out as dividends) in the corporation. The numerous accounting adjustments include such things as cumulative foreign translation adjustments, certain employee compensation involving shares of stock, and other more recently adopted accounting conventions that recognize the equity impact of certain quasi-income or expense items without requiring those items to be recorded through net income. The cost of equity encompasses all aspects of the common equity section.

Calculating the Cost of Common Equity

When calculating the cost of debt (or the interest), the contractual obligations of interest and the repayment of principal make determining the cost of debt a straightforward and explicit exercise. Common equity has no explicit return obligations. Instead, implicit investor expectations determine stock prices, which, in turn, drive the cost of common equity. The cost of equity represents the opportunity cost of equity capital. To accomplish this estimate, you must attempt to understand what a reasonable investor should expect when making an investment in the equity of a particular firm.

I will present three different approaches to calculating the cost of common equity:

- Dividend growth model (DGM)
- Capital asset pricing model (CAPM)
- Modified CAPM approach

The *dividend growth model* (DGM) is an internally focused company-specific measure. The *capital asset pricing model* (CAPM) and its modified approach are externally focused company-specific measures. The CAPM considers the stock's return relationship to the stock market's return as a whole, whereas the modified approach adjusts for the leverage effects of the industry first and then the specific company. I will discuss the modified CAPM approach when I discuss hurdle rates.

All three techniques are presented and discussed in turn below. Strengths and weaknesses of all three are highlighted. Although carrying its own shortcomings, the CAPM is the recommended approach for estimating the cost of common equity.

Dividend Growth Model

Most corporations have little activity in the common equity market. Their activity is limited to issuing (selling) common stock and repurchasing stock if the corporation has an ongoing share-repurchase program. The stock market's primary purpose is to facilitate secondary trading or trading between individuals (or between financial institutions such as mutual funds, insurance companies, and banks).

If a company chooses to pay dividends (and fewer than 30 percent do pay dividends), those dividends generally are the only ongoing cash-flow contact that a company has with its common equity holders. As a common equity stockholder, the investor also participates in the growth of the corporation into perpetuity. The growth in increased sales, profits, and cash flow is forwarded to the common equity investor through higher dividends, which result in higher share prices.

The DGM (also referred to as the *Gordon dividend growth model* after its originator, Myron Gordon) is an application of the perpetuity notion discussed in Chapter 7, where we solved for the value of a perpetuity with a stream of steadily growing cash flows, as shown in Eq. (11-4):

$$P_{cs} = D_{cs1}/(K_{cs} - g) \qquad\qquad (11.4)$$

where P_{cs} = price of common stock
        D_{cs1} = common stock dividend for year 1
        K_{cs} = cost of common stock
        g = growth rate

Rearranging terms, we get Eq. (11.5):

$$P_{cs}(K_{cs} - g) = D_{cs1}$$
$$(K_{cs} - g) = D_{cs1}/P_{cs} \qquad\qquad (11.5)$$
$$K_{cs} = (D_{cs1}/P_{cs}) + g$$

The DGM approach to estimating the cost of equity combines today's dividend yield using the next year's anticipated dividend over today's stock price, along with the long-term perpetual growth rate. The estimated growth rate is a major component when applying the DGM. As it is illustrated, the estimated growth rate represents the future growth in dividends. However, the future growth in dividends is a function of the underlying growth of the business. That is, the dividend growth rate is tied to the growth exhibited in sales, income, cash flow, and so on.

Determining *g*

There are at least four different approaches to estimating the long-term growth rate g. First, this growth rate can be extrapolated from historical trends. Second, g can be estimated by calculating an internal growth rate. Third, management may have and may share a stated dividend growth objective via the annual report or other public statements. Finally, using information from knowledgeable investment analysts and their company reports can be helpful.

Historical Growth Analysis

By way of extrapolating history, the following table summarizes Hershey's historical growth rates for three distinct periods: annual growth from 2009, a three-year compound annual growth rate (CAGR) from 2007 (see Chapter 7), and a five-year CAGR from 2005. Dividends, of course, are paid out of earnings, which are being driven by sales. Thus we examine all three measures in historical analysis:

	Growth Rates		
	2009–2010	2007–2010	2005–2010
Sales	7.03%	4.66%	3.31%
Normalized income	18.30%	6.99%	0.83%
Total dividends paid	7.60%	3.96%	5.05%

More recently, Hershey's growth rate has been higher than over the five-year period except when comparing the three-year versus five-year dividend growth rate. Nonetheless, looking at history, one could argue that the growth rate is somewhere between 3 and 8 percent.

Internal Growth Rate

The *internal growth rate* is a financial ratio that is an extension of DuPont analysis, which was introduced in Chapter 3, and the return on retained earnings. The return on retained earnings is similar to the return on equity except that the distortive effects of stock issuance and repurchases, as well as the effects of accounting adjustments, have been eliminated. The internal growth rate considers a firm's profitability, tax rate, asset efficiency, capital structure, and dividend policy and assumes that all these underlying relationships remain constant or have minimal fluctuation. The internal growth rate is calculated using Eq. (11.6):

$$g = \text{RORE} \times (1 - \text{DPR}) \tag{11.6}$$

where g = internal growth rate
RORE = return on retained earnings = (normalized income$_t$/retained earnings$_{(t-1)}$)
DPR = dividend payout ratio = (total dividends$_t$/normalized income$_t$)

Return on retained earnings (RORE) is calculated as 2010 normalized income (see Chapter 2) divided by the 2009 retained earnings. The dividend payout ratio (DPR) is calculated as the total amount of 2010 dividends paid per common share divided by 2010 basic normalized earnings per common share.

Equation (11.6) can be rewritten as:

$$
\begin{aligned}
g &= \frac{\text{normalized income}_t}{\text{retained earnings}_{(t-1)}} \times \left(1 - \frac{\text{dividend paid}_t}{\text{normalized income}_t}\right) \\[6pt]
&= \frac{\text{NI}_t}{\text{RE}_{(t-1)}} \times \left(\frac{\text{NI}_t}{\text{NI}_t} - \frac{\text{DP}_t}{\text{NI}_t}\right) \\[6pt]
&= \frac{\text{NI}_t}{\text{RE}_{(t-1)}} \times \frac{(\text{NI}_t - \text{dividend paid}_t)}{\text{NI}_t} \\[6pt]
&= \frac{(\text{normalized income}_t - \text{dividend paid}_t)}{\text{retained earnings}_{(t-1)}}
\end{aligned}
$$

Using the old high school algebra identity trick where 1 is equal to anything dividend by itself, let 1 equal normalized income (NI) divided by NI. Next, combine terms of NI less dividends paid (DP). The NIs cancel each other out, and we are left with g, or internal growth. The internal growth boils down to the change in retained earnings (which, in general terms, are normalized income less dividends) divided by the beginning retained earnings balance or simply the growth in retained earnings. This could have been tacked onto the end of the DuPont analysis in Chapter 3.

In Hershey's case, the 2010 internal growth rate is calculated ($ millions) as follows:

$$g = \text{RORE} \times (1 - \text{DPR})$$
$$= (\$587.7/\$4,148.4) \times [1 - (\$283.4/\$587.7)]$$
$$= 14.17\% \times (1 - 0.4822)$$
$$= 7.34\%$$

Hershey's internal growth rate is 7.34 percent, and this is a viable candidate for g in the DGM.

Management Statements

Beyond number crunching and analysis, comments made by management in annual or quarterly reports, other financial releases, presentations, or elsewhere may be helpful. These comments may include direct comments (targeted growth rate in dividends) or indirect comments such as sales growth, income growth, margin improvement, and so on. However, Hershey's management team has been silent regarding expected dividend growth.

Investment Analysts

A final source to help in determining a growth rate is knowledgeable investment analysts. A company the size of Hershey has approximately 20 investment analysts that follow the company. Larger companies can have even more, whereas smaller companies typically have fewer than 10 analysts.

Value Line is the largest investment advisory service in the United States. It prepares consistently solid investment analysis quarterly reports on 1,700 large, publicly traded companies. Many public libraries subscribe to a hard copy of Value Line.

Value Line estimated a 2011 dividend of $1.38 and a dividend growth rate of 5.00 percent through 2014 (Value Line Investment Service, January 28, 2011, Hershey, p. 1919).

Dividend Growth Model—Hershey Application

Consequently, after considering all the preceding information and applying our best judgment, we use the 5.0 percent Value Line estimate as our dividend growth rate. To apply this to Hershey's specific case, the company is expected to raise its dividend to $1.38 (also from Value Line) for the coming year. The stock price as of December 2010 was $47.32, and our estimated growth rate is 5 percent. Hershey's cost of common equity capital is 7.92 percent, calculated as follows:

$$K_{cs} = (\$1.38/\$47.32) + 5.0\%$$
$$= 2.92\% + 5.00\%$$
$$= 7.92\%$$

The 7.92 percent cost of equity is comprised of a 2.92 percent dividend yield and 5.00 percent expected growth (see below). From the DGM, the cost of equity capital is estimated at 7.92 percent.

Figure 11-3 illustrates the concept behind the DGM. The share of stock pays a $1.38 dividend at the end of year 1. After the assumed 5.0 percent growth, the year 2 dividend is $1.45, and year 3 is $1.52. By year 50, the dividend per share has grown to $15.07, assuming a 5.0 percent growth rate. By year 100, the dividend has grown to over $172.83 per share and is still growing into perpetuity.

The DGM finds the discount rate that equates the future projected dividends (which are projected to infinity) to today's stock price. This process is similar to finding an internal rate of return. Although it sounds as if the mathematics should be more complicated, Eq. (11.5) provides the discount rate.

The DGM approach to estimating the cost of equity has some appeal to management because it directly links the strategic plan, goals, and objectives to the cost of capital, and it is simple to calculate. However, if a company does not pay a dividend or has an erratic growth rate, the DGM becomes less useful in estimating the cost of equity. Alternative approaches must be employed in such cases.

FIGURE 11-3

Interpretation of the dividend growth model.

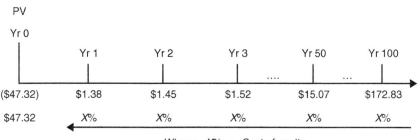

Where: $X\% = $ Cost of equity
                   $= 7.92\%$

Note: Dividends are assumed to grow at 5.0% annually.
          Do *not* buy stock in Hershey based upon this illustrative growth rate.
The stock price in December 2010 was $47.32.

Capital Asset Pricing Model

The capital asset pricing model (CAPM) approach to estimating the cost of equity compares the shareholder return (stock price appreciation plus dividends) with the return of the market (i.e., Standard & Poor's 500 Index). To avoid the issues highlighted by the DGM, CAPM is the recommended approach to estimating the cost of equity.

The cost of common stock K_{cs} or the cost of equity, with the CAPM approach, can be represented as shown in Eq. (11.7):

$$K_{cs} = R_f + \beta(K_m - R_f) \tag{11.7}$$

where R_f = risk-free rate of return
β = beta (a statistical relationship discussed below)
$(K_m - R_f)$ = market's return in excess of the risk-free rate

By using the CAPM, the cost of equity is estimated from a risk-free base level and adjusted for risk relative to the stock market. It provides a relative stock return that is aligned with the overall return of the market.

The market risk premium, as $(K_m - R_f)$ is often called, is the excess return of large company stocks over a risk-free rate, in this case the long-term government bond rate. Equation 11.8 illustrates use of the CAPM for Hershey:

$$K_{cs} = R_f + \beta(K_m - R_f) \tag{11.8}$$

where R_f = 4.65%   (*U.S. Financial Data*, St. Louis Federal
Reserve Bank)

β = 0.65   (Value Line, January 28, 2011)

$(K_m - R_f)$ = 5.00%

K_{cs} = 4.65% + 0.65(5.00%)

K_{cs} = 7.90%

From the CAPM, the cost of equity capital is estimated at 7.90 percent, which coincidentally is approximately the same result as with the DGM.

Issues Related to the CAPM

Estimating the cost of equity via the CAPM has some appeal because it employs an independent statistical relationship between the individual stock and the stock market. CAPM alleviates the need to estimate a long-term growth rate for the firm. Companies can use the CAPM whether or not they have a dividend or a steady, stable growth in that dividend.

However, CAPM has some issues:

- Risk-free rate selection
- Market risk premium
- Beta calculation
- Correlation between one stock and the market
- Conceptual issues

Each one of these issues will be addressed below. Although the CAPM approach remains the recommended estimation technique, anyone employing CAPM should be aware of these issues.

Risk-Free Rate

Many choices are faced when selecting the risk-free rate. Should the rate be based on short-term U.S. Treasury bills, long-term U.S. Treasury bonds, or some other measure of risk-free return? I advocate that the risk-free rate should be measured via the long-term (30-year) U.S. Treasury bonds. As discussed in chapter 8, long-term government bonds incorporate the market's expectations about expected short-term (Treasury bill) interest rates. Also, they are more indicative of a risk-free rate of return with a similar long-term maturity time frame as a share of stock. Consequently, my recommendation is to use the long-term U.S. Treasury bond rate as the risk-free rate.

Market Risk Premium

The *market risk premium* (MRP) measures the excess return as the amount that the market's return exceeds the risk-free rate of return. In the CAPM, it is intended to be a forward-looking measure based on an expected excess return. However, many companies approximate an expected excess return by looking at historical excess returns. Again, it matters whether the risk-free rate is a short-term U.S. Treasury bill, a long-term U.S. Treasury bond, or some other rate. It also matters if the return is the average of annual returns or a compound annual growth rate (CAGR), as calculated in Chapter 7. Finally, it also depends on the time period used to develop historical excess returns.

Numerous academic studies are done each year that examine the market risk premium. These studies employ a variety of the permutations from above and result in a wide range of possibilities: 3.00% to 8.00%. Many studies that use long-term risk free rates as well as point-to-point compound annual growth rates measure the MRP year after year in the 4.5% to 5.5% range. A survey of 5,731 practitioners[1] captures responses from three groups, professors, practitioners, and analysts. The results of this survey indicate that the average risk premium used by the respondents is 5.5 percent, with a standard deviation of 1.7 percent and a range of 1.5 to 15.0 percent. Professors, on average, used 5.7 percent; companies, 5.6 percent; and analysts, 5.0 percent. The survey also indicates that the median of the entire group is 5.0 percent. With all of the evidence and practice from so many sources, my recommendation is 5.0 percent for a market risk premium.

Beta Calculation

Regression analysis is used to determine various statistical properties using the past relationships between a stock's excess return and a broad measure of the

---

[1] "U.S. Market Risk Premium Used in 2011 by Professors, Analysts, and Companies: A Survey with 5,371 Answers," by Pablo Fernandez, Javier Aguirreamalloa, and Luis Corres; available at http://ssrn.com/abstract=1805852.

financial market's excess return. An excess return is calculated as the stock or market's return (capital appreciation and dividends) less the risk-free rate of return. The risk-free rate of choice should have the same basis as the one used in the CAPM equation (Eq. 11.7). From regression analysis, the slope of the line is referred to as the *beta*. More will be said about this below.

Numerous variations in data can be used to calculate the specific returns that underlie the beta calculation. For example, the period of measured return (daily versus weekly versus monthly), the time period of the analysis (180 days versus three years versus five years), the style of return (per period versus annualized), and the market proxy (S&P 500, Wilshire 5000, etc.) all affect the specific value of beta.

Figure 11-4 illustrates regression analysis results using monthly "excess" returns (actual returns less the risk-free rate) of Hershey's stock and monthly "excesss" returns of the S&P 500 for a four-year period (2007–2010). This analysis results in a beta for Hershey of 0.545. This is statistically significantly different from 0, as demonstrated by its *t* statistic of 2.28. (A *t statistic* of 2.00 or greater denotes statistical significance and that the coefficient is statistically different from 0.) The intercept is 0.0002 with a *t* statistic of only 0.02, which indicates that the intercept is equal to 0.

The graphic presentation of the CAPM depicted in Figure 11-4 will help you to visualize the excess returns of Hershey (*y* axis) and the excess return of the market (*x* axis). A straight line was statistically fit through the data using regression analysis. This regression line included the stock's beta, or the slope of this regression line.

In the end, this analysis was illustrative. The many permutations and combinations of underlying assumptions are beyond the scope of this book. My recommendation is to use a consistent approach, which is offered by Value Line,

FIGURE   11-4

Hershey versus the S&P 500.

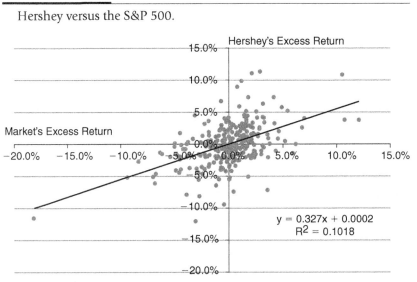

which lists Hershey's (and 1,700 other companies') beta at 0.65. Value Line uses five years (or 260 observations) of annual returns on a weekly basis.

Correlation Between One Stock and the Market

Another statistical relationship is measured by correlation (R) or the goodness of fit between the two variables. The coefficient of determination (or R^2) ranges between 0.00 and 1.00, with a measure of 1.00 indicating an exact relationship between the two variables. A coefficient of determination of 0.00 indicates that the values are random.

From Figure 11-4, clearly, the relationship between Hershey and the S&P 500 is fairly random. Continuing this example, the R^2 is only 24.9 percent. This says that only 24.9 percent of the Hershey stock return is explained by the return of the market (S&P 500). This is not unique to Hershey. Few individual stocks have an R^2 greater than 30 percent. There are other variables that affect a stock's value and returns. The general movement of the stock market is only a portion of that relationship.

The CAPM applied to investments of a well-diversified portfolio (such as a diversified mutual fund) often results in R^2 values greater than 95 percent. In such a case, all but 5 percent of the portfolio's movement is explained by the movement in the marketplace.

The higher the stock's beta, the more sensitive the stock's excess return is to the market's excess return. For example, Figure 11-5 depicts three different stocks: a low-beta stock similar to Hershey, a stock with the same beta as the general marketplace ($\beta = 1$), and a high-beta stock such as a pharmaceutical or Internet company ($\beta = 2$). If the market is up 20 percent, the low-beta stock is up

FIGURE   11-5

Beta relationship—three different stocks.

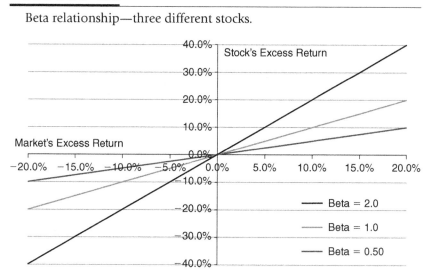

10 percent (0.50β × 20%); the moderate-beta stock with a beta of 1.00 matches the same return, and the high-beta stock (β = 2.00) is expected to have a 40 percent rate of return. On the flip side, if the market is down 20 percent, the defensive stock (β = 0.05) should be down only 10 percent, the stock with the beta of 1.00 should be down 20 percent, and the aggressive stock should be down 40 percent. Beta is a measure of risk between a stock and the marketplace.

Conceptual Issues
The CAPModel remains a conceptually useful framework and an approach that is easy to apply when estimating the cost of equity. However, there are some additional conceptual issues with the CAPM.

The CAPM assumes (1) that all markets are efficient with all investors having access to the same information with the same expectations, (2) that all investors are risk-adverse, rational, and view securities the same way, and (3) that there are no transaction costs or taxes and that there are no restrictions on securities. Numerous studies have called into question the validity of the CAPM. Two issues have been forwarded that from a theoretical view may invalidate the CAPM.

First, for the CAPM to be applicable, the regression line always must pass through the origin. This implies that when the market's excess return is zero, so is the stock's excess return. This is what was found in the example from Figure 11-5. However, some studies have found that the intercept term is significantly different from 0, which invalidates the CAPM.

Second, for the CAPM to be true, no other factors can explain a security's return. Evidence shows that firm size, dividend yield, price-earnings ratios, and seasonality can explain much of the security's return that is unexplained by the CAPM. This also invalidates the CAPM.

COST OF EQUITY: SUMMARY

The cost of debt is an explicit cost (interest expense), whereas the cost of equity is implicit. The preceding sections reviewed two common techniques for estimating the cost of common stock or equity capital. Each technique has certain limitations and interpretations of required assumptions that render each less than perfectly applicable. To summarize:

- *Dividend growth model.* This is most applicable to firms that pay dividends with a steady, stable growth rate underlying those dividends. It is subject to wide variations in expected growth rate assumptions.
- *Capital asset pricing model.* This is subject to wide interpretations and calculation of major components such as the risk-free rate, beta, and the market risk premium.

My recommendation remains: Estimate the cost of equity via the capital asset pricing model (CAPM).

COST OF NEW DEBT AND EQUITY

For new bonds, preferred stock, and common stock, issuance costs must be considered and will increase the cost of each capital source slightly. For debt, new bonds typically are issued close to or at par value, or the maturity value of $1,000. The stated interest rate is the pretax cost of debt. For example, a 10-year bond that is issued at $1,000 and pays $60 in interest each year before returning its $1,000 of principal costs 6 percent before tax and 3.6 percent after tax, assuming a 40 percent tax rate. If there is a 2.5 percent issuance fee, the proceeds are only $975 (instead of $1,000). The cost of debt is recalculated based on this lower initial value, resulting in a pretax cost of debt of 6.35 percent and 3.81 percent after tax, assuming a 40 percent tax rate.

For preferred stock and common stock, the price per share is reduced by the issuance cost per share. Equation (11.3) for preferred stock and Eq. (11.5) for common stock are adjusted to reflect the price of a share of stock less the issuance cost per share.

To illustrate using preferred stock, if a company issues 4 million preferred shares to raise approximately $100 million, the company may pay 2 to 5 percent issuance costs. The final specific issuance fee would be a negotiated point. At a 4 percent issuance cost, this would be $4.0 million of issuance costs, or $1.00 per share. The adjusted cost of the preferred stock would be calculated using Eq. (11.3):

$$K_{ps} = D_{ps}/(P_{ps} - C_{ps})$$
$$= \$2/(\$25 - \$1)$$
$$= 8.33\%$$

This refinement provides a better estimate of newly issued preferred stock and is applicable when the DGM is employed to estimate the cost of common equity.

If CAPM is the preferred approach for measuring the cost of newly issued equity, the issuance cost (as a percent of the proceeds) should be tacked onto just the newly issued equity.

CAPITAL COMPONENT COSTS—SUMMARY

The preceding paragraphs discussed the cost of debt, preferred stock, and common stock. Also discussed were common alternatives used in practice. To summarize my recommendations:

- *Cost of debt*—current market cost of debt, after tax
- *Preferred stock*—cost based on current market value of preferred stock
- *Common stock*—CAPM using the long-term Treasury bond rate as the risk-free rate, a "beta" from Value Line, and a market risk premium of 5.0 percent (which is supported by practice)

The next section discusses the appropriate weights to use to find the weighted-average cost of capital (WACC).

WEIGHTING THE CAPITAL COMPONENTS

At this point, the costs of each capital component—debt, preferred stock, and common stock—were addressed individually. The final step in estimating the cost of capital is to weight each component and calculate the weighted-average cost of capital. There are two customary methods or weighting techniques: (1) book-value weights, and (2) market-value weights.

Book-value weights are based on the capital structure represented by the balance sheet. For Hershey as of December 31, 2010, the balance sheet included debt of $1,827.3 million (short-term debt, current portion of long-term debt, and long-term debt) and equity of $937.6 million for a total capital pool of $2,764.9 million. Hershey has no outstanding preferred stock. Consequently, debt represents 66.1 percent of the historical capital structure, and equity represents 33.9 percent.

Book-value equity is an accounting concept that primarily keeps track of earnings retained in the business over the years, along with the original level of equity capital injected into the firm, net of any stock repurchase and any other comprehensive income or (loss). Most of Hershey's equity capital was injected in the 1920s, with a small issue in 1984. However, from the early 1990s, Hershey bought back over $4 billion of its stock on the open market. The book value of equity is subject to numerous accounting adjustments. In this case, these adjustments significantly decrease the amount of equity on Hershey's books.

The basis for *market-value weights*, the market value of debt and equity, is not subject to the mechanics of accounting. The market value of equity is determined by the total capitalization of the outstanding shares of stock. In this case, Hershey has 227.0 million shares of stock outstanding at $47.32 per share for a market value of $10,741.6 million compared with its book value of $937.6 million. A current stockholder of Hershey demands that Hershey earn the cost of equity (7.90 percent, CAPM) on the current investment value of $47.32, not on the $4.13 book value per share ($937.6 million book value of equity divided by 227.0 million shares outstanding).

The major difference between book- and market-based weights is the value of equity. In the case of Hershey, the following figures hold:

Hershey Foods Capital Structure Weights ($ millions)				
	Book Weights		Market Weights	
	Amount	Percent	Amount	Percent
Debt	$1,827.3	66.1%	$1,827.3	14.5%
Equity	937.6	33.9%	10,741.6	85.5%
Total	$2,764.9	100.0%	$12,568.9	100.0%

In this example, the market value of the debt is similar to the book value of debt. Most of Hershey's debt is privately held. Obtaining current market value of that debt would be almost impossible. The impact of using market or book values for the debt is inconsequential. Therefore, two simplifying approaches may be reasonable and not materially distorting: (1) Extrapolate market-value-to-book-value relationships of traded debt to the privately placed debt or (2) simply assume that the market value of private debt is equal to the book value of the private debt, as I did here. My recommendation remains: Use current market values where available.

Additionally, most corporations have a long-term strategic plan that includes projected financial statements, as advocated in Chapter 6. A corporation also may have as a part of its strategic plan (or separate from it), a long-term financing plan that may include debt issuance, debt repayment, equity issuance, equity repurchase, and so on. A corporation may establish some long-term goals or objectives surrounding its capital structure. This is called a *target capital structure* and should be based on future market values. However, often, when a firm has a targeted capital structure, it is book-based and not market-based. That is, a corporation such as Hershey may set an internal objective of establishing a capital structure of 40 percent debt and 60 percent equity because corporations can better control the book weights. Market weights are always better to consider than book weights. In this regard, current market-based weights are better than current or targeted book weights. However, if a market-based capital structure is a firm's objective and it is diligently working toward that objective, then this target — market-based capital structure — should be used as the appropriate weighting structure. (*Note:* This target capital structure is hypothetical for illustrative purposes and does not reflect an objective that Hershey may or may not have.)

The four potential weighting structures indicate the following capital structures:

	Current		Target	
	Book	**Market**	**Book**	**Market**
Debt	66.1%	14.5%	40.0%	15.0%?
Equity	33.9%	85.5%	60.0%	85.0%?

My ideal recommendation is to use a target capital structure if that target is based on targeted market values. However, since the target capital structure is based on book weights (as most objectives are) or does not exist, my practical recommendation is to use the current market-based capital structure weights including a proxy of book value debt to approximate market value of debt.

Cost of Capital Application

The weighted-average cost of capital (or simply the cost of capital) brings together the individual costs of each capital source. The individual costs are weighted by the capital structure techniques discussed in the preceding section.

Table 11-5 illustrates Hershey's capital structure on a current market weight basis. That is, a total capital structure of $12,568.9 million with 14.54 percent in

T A B L E   11-5

Hershey's Cost of Capital Structure: Market Basis Weights

	Amount ($ millions)	% of Total	After-Tax Cost	Weighted Cost
Debt*	$ 1,827.3	14.54%	3.72%	0.55%
Equity**	$ 10,741.6	85.46%	7.90%	6.75%
Total		100.00%		7.30%

* The market value of the debt is assumed to be the same as the book value of the debt, December 31, 2010.
** The market value of the equity is calculated as $47.32 (price per share, December 31, 2010) times 227.0 million shares outstanding.

debt and 85.46 percent in equity. Hershey's debt on an after-tax basis costs 3.72 percent (current market), whereas equity, using the CAPM, costs 7.90 percent. The resulting cost of capital is 7.30 percent. If Hershey had preferred stock, that would be inserted and considered in a similar fashion.

To summarize and compare other weightings in practice and the resulting cost of capital:

	Current Weights		Target Weights	
	Book	Market	Book	Market
Debt (3.72%)	66.1%	14.5%	40.0%	15.0%?
Equity (7.90%)	33.9%	85.5%	60.0%	85.0%?
Cost of capital	5.1%	7.3%	6.2%	7.3%

Hershey's recommended cost of capital is 7.3 percent. In calculating the cost of capital, it is easy to get carried away with a false sense of precision. Given all the assumptions about the capital structure, future growth rates, beta, the market's excess return, and so on, as well as the ever-changing nature of the precise capital structure and stock price, the degree of precision must be carefully balanced. In the final analysis, we are left with a cleaver and not a scalpel. Once again, judgment must enter into the final recommendation.

FINANCIAL STRUCTURE

This section develops an overview of financial structure. Financial structure indicates the amount of debt and equity used in financing a firm. For any financial structure, debt is always a less expensive form of capital than equity because the cost of debt is tax deductible and in case of bankruptcy, debt holders have priority over equity holders. However, debt also comes with fixed explicit costs. Every dollar of debt increases the risk of the firm and the cost of all financing. With too much debt and wavering business conditions, a firm may be forced into bankruptcy.

Without going into many of the theoretical details underlying financial structure theory, the traditional financial structure is illustrated on Figure 11-6. The x axis shows debt as a percent of the capital (debt + equity) structure—market-based weights. The y axis lists the after-tax cost as a percentage. The graph itself contains three lines—the cost of debt (the lowest line), the cost of equity (the highest line), and the resulting cost of capital (the middle line). Each is discussed in turn.

The cost of debt for a corporation is similar to the cost of personal debt. The more debt you have, the riskier you are, and the higher is the cost of debt. As we saw in Chapter 8, riskier companies had lower debt ratings and required higher rates of return or cost of debt. For an individual, the least expensive form of debt is a mortgage. It is a form of secured debt collateralized by your house, and the interest portion is tax deductible. However, a mortgage can only be used to borrow a limited amount. Personally, it is your least expensive financing source. After your mortgage, the next least expensive debt financing is available through a home equity loan. The home equity loan is collateralized by additional fair market value of equity left in your house beyond the primary mortgage. Once again, a home equity loan has a significant advantage because the interest payments generally are tax deductible. After the home equity loan, educational loans may provide the next least costly form of debt financing. Automobile loans secured by your automobile, unsecured personal loans, and credit-card loans are additional sources of personal borrowing all with increasing costs and no tax deductions. If an individual needs to borrow beyond this level, a visit may be necessary to secondary and tertiary lenders at dramatically higher interest costs.

This same process occurs in concept for a firm and is depicted for a corporation by the cost-of-debt line in Figure 11-6. However, any interest expense generally is tax deductible for a corporation. Up to some point, the cost of debt is relatively flat for a corporation. As it is presented, at somewhere between 25 and 30 percent, debt begins to cost slightly more. As the corporation takes on more debt, its marginal cost continues to increase.

The cost of equity begins with a slight upward trend. The first dollar of debt and each subsequent dollar make the corporation a bit riskier. This added risk is reflected as a higher cost of equity. At some point, as the firm uses more debt, the cost of equity rises more substantially. Notice that for all capital structures, the cost of debt is always less than the cost of equity for any given financial structure.

The cost-of-capital line is a mathematical representation of the individual cost of debt and cost of equity appropriately weighted for the total capital structure. To illustrate the cost-of-capital line, let's review the three financial structures:

> *Financial structure 1.* The first financial structure is for an all-equity firm. This firm uses no debt, and consequently, its cost of capital is equal to the cost of equity, or 9.6 percent. The cost of debt is at its lowest level, but there is no debt outstanding.

FIGURE   11-6

Capital structure theory.

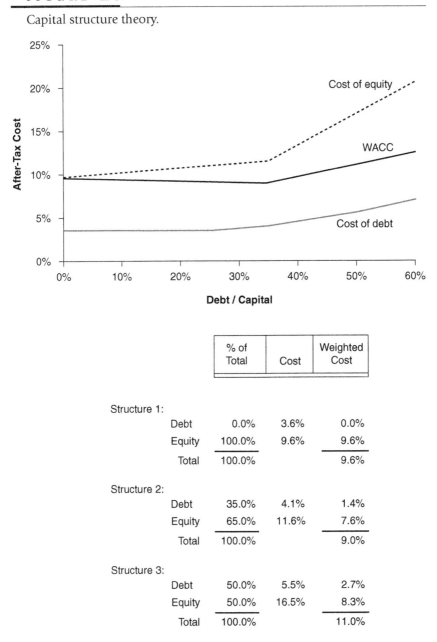

		% of Total	Cost	Weighted Cost
Structure 1:				
	Debt	0.0%	3.6%	0.0%
	Equity	100.0%	9.6%	9.6%
	Total	100.0%		9.6%
Structure 2:				
	Debt	35.0%	4.1%	1.4%
	Equity	65.0%	11.6%	7.6%
	Total	100.0%		9.0%
Structure 3:				
	Debt	50.0%	5.5%	2.7%
	Equity	50.0%	16.5%	8.3%
	Total	100.0%		11.0%

Financial structure 2. At the second financial structure, the firm has
   35 percent debt and 65 percent equity. Notice that the debt and equity
   both cost more under this structure than under the first structure.
   However, by moving to this financial structure from the first financial

structure, the corporation substitutes less expensive debt (4.1 percent—this structure) for more expensive equity (9.6 percent—the first structure). Weighting the individual cost results in a 9.0 percent cost of capital. The second capital structure takes advantage of the less expensive cost of debt and results in a lower cost of capital.

Financial structure 3. At the third financial structure, the firm's financial structure is evenly split 50 percent debt and 50 percent equity. Notice that the debt and equity both cost more under this structure than under the second structure. Unfortunately, owing to the higher cost of both debt and equity, the resulting cost of capital is 11.0 percent, which is higher than either of the preceding structures.

This suggests that there is an optimal financial structure that minimizes the cost of capital, and certainly in this type of illustration, it is easy to see. However, in practice, an optimal mix is very difficult to measure.

In today's cost-reduction environment, businesses are pressed to do more with less. Most organizations have implemented cost-reduction programs. Everyone is striving to wring the costs out of every step in the supply chain and the support functions. Contracts with suppliers are renegotiated to reduce costs. We "beat up" other suppliers and play off relationships to save one-quarter of 1 cent on envelopes or other office supplies. Employees are asked to take lower pay raises or forgo raises or even take pay cuts. The cost of benefit packages and health insurance is now shared with employees, all in the name of cost reduction. While reducing all explicit costs within a firm is important, the most widely used commodity in any organization is capital. The chief financial officer's responsibility is to minimize the cost of capital—by using structure 2 in this case. The impact is major in the valuation of the firm!

Of course, this can change over time. The financial crisis that came to a head in the fall of 2008, as well as the terrorist attacks of September 9, 2001, presented a time when debt was frowned on, and the capital structure curves shifted higher and to the left.

General Theories of Capital Structure

There are two general theories related to capital structure—tradeoff theory and pecking-order theory. The *tradeoff theory* considers the tax deductibility of interest from debt financing to be a strong motivator for increasing leverage. However, the increasing present value of the cost of financial distress (bankruptcy) motivates the manager to limit the amount of debt financing. The tradeoff is what the manager needs to constantly balance. In Figure 11-6, the tradeoff theory leads the manager to carefully balance the tax deductibility of the cost of debt against the likelihood of bankruptcy. In the figure, approximately 35 percent provides an optimal tradeoff.

Additionally, in general, firms with high growth opportunities use less debt because financial distress could destroy the realization of the business potential. Similarly, firms in the pharmaceutical industry have low debt ratios even though their book profit ratios appear to be above average. But risks of unsuccessful efforts at creating new, profitable drugs and risks of law suits resulting from adverse drug effects after years of use are substantial. In general, intangible assets are subject to erosion in financial distress, so debt is avoided by firms with a high ratio of intangible to physical assets.

The *pecking-order theory* says that companies will first use sources of internally generated funds to finance their activities, then net debt financing (net of repayments), and finally new equity financing. The pecking-order theory is strongly supported by historical data on the sources and uses of funds by non-financial corporations in the United States.

My view is that the tradeoff theory and the pecking-order theory both help to explain financial structure decision processes. The pecking-order theory more appropriately may be termed a *dynamic adjustment of capital structures to changing economic conditions and to the changing circumstances of individual firms*. Internal financing accounts for a high percentage of investment needs of firms. Internal financing in growing firms makes sense because investment requirements are high. As equity grows, a basis is established for obtaining debt financing under favorable terms.

General Factors Affecting Financial Structure

The factors influencing capital structure decisions can be grouped under two major categories—economic environments and industry characteristics.

Economic Environments
The state of the economy is a major influence on financing decisions. In an economic expansion, the growth rates of gross domestic product (GDP) are positive and increasing. Corporate profits are also rising. Optimism is high, and the spread between interest rates on low-rated versus higher-rated debt instruments narrows. Firms increase their investment outlays, and rising stock prices provide a favorable environment for merger activity.

The financial environment may perform a counterbalancing role. As noted in Chapter 8, the Federal Reserve System was raising rates to dampen speculative excesses during the economic boom of 2005 through 2007. When the economy turned downwards in 2008, the Fed quickly reversed its course, and a low-interest-rate environment still exists in 2011.

Industry Characteristics
The sales of durable-goods industries are subject to greater volatility than those of nondurable manufacturing industries. Hence one would expect debt ratios for nondurable manufacturing to be higher than for all manufacturing. This is confirmed by the data. The ratio of long-term debt to stockholders' equity is 71.4 percent for nondurable manufacturing; for all manufacturing, the ratio is only 58.8 percent (U.S. Census Bureau, December 15, 2010).

Traditionally, utility industries had high debt ratios. The products they sold were necessities, and as population and income grew, the revenues of utilities could be forecast with a relatively high degree of accuracy.

In addition to the pharmaceutical companies, as mentioned earlier, other industries with low amounts of debt, include electrical equipment, appliances, and components; computer and electronic products; communications equipment; and petroleum and coal products. Their businesses are risky, so the industry as a whole does not want to increase its risk with financial leverage.

INDUSTRY GROUP ANALYSIS
APPLICATION—FOOD INDUSTRY

The food industry is characterized by moderate sales growth, stable cash flows, and balanced investment in current and long-term assets. The industry is viewed favorably by lenders, but these various companies have varying impressions of the amount of leverage that is appropriate. There is a wide dispersion of the use of leverage within the industry. Figure 11-7 presents the market-based capital structure for 11 food companies (part of the industry analysis in Chapter 3) that comprise the food-processing industry. Tootsie Roll and Flower Foods, Inc., use the least amount of leverage, with 0.45 and 4.57 percent of their financial capital (market weights) sourced by interest-bearing debt. Kraft uses the most leverage at 52.95 percent debt. Hershey also has a conservative mind-set because only 14.54 percent of its capital comes from debt. The remaining seven companies average over 20 percent of leverage.

Generally, the food industry as a whole is to the left of the minimum cost of capital and has room to take on some more debt to reduce each company's cost

FIGURE   11-7

Food industry WACC, 2010.

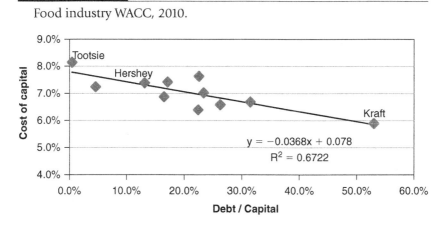

of capital. Perhaps Kraft is at a point which the other members of the industry may not be able to attain. It is difficult to conclude this either way.

However, notice that there is a strong relationship between the amount (percent) of debt in the financial structure and the firm's cost of capital. The R^2 is 67.22 percent. This also indicates that over 30 percent of the firm's cost of capital is due to some other factors, such as other firm-specific factors.

DIVISION OR PROJECT HURDLE RATES

Most corporations are complex entities comprised of numerous divisions or separate businesses. As we saw in Chapters 2 and 6, P. F. Chang's China Bistro, Inc. (PFCB), is comprised of two business units and restaurant formats. The Bistros themselves are casual dining full-service restaurants, and the Pei Wei restaurants are smaller, quicker, and offer limited service. The cost of capital for the company is 9.26 percent, as presented in Table 11-6.

Is it appropriate to use 9.26 percent as the required rate of return for both restaurant formats, or are there differences that underlie both business units that should manifest itself as differences in the required rate of return? Divisional hurdle rates are determined for each division as if it were a stand-alone business. Table 11-7 breaks the restaurant industry into two different segments—casual, full service and quick service.

You will notice that the average segment betas are different between the two groups. The casual-dining segment has an average beta of 1.23 (with a range of 1.05 to 1.50), whereas the quick-service segment is less risky with an average beta of 0.90 (with a range of 0.65 to 1.00). One approach is to adjust only the cost of equity based on the average industry segment betas while continuing to use 4.65 percent as the risk-free rate and 5.00 percent as the market risk premium. This results in a cost of equity of 10.80 percent for the Bistros and 9.15 percent

TABLE   11-6

P. F. Chang's Cost of Capital: Market Basis Weights

	Amount ($ millions)	% of Total	After-Tax Cost	Weighted Cost
Debt*	$ 115.2	9.38%	3.10%	0.29%
Equity**	$ 1,113.0	90.62%	9.90%	8.97%
Total		100.00%		9.26%

* The market value of the debt is assumed to be the same as the book value of the debt, December 31, 2010.
** The market value of the equity is calculated as $48.75 (price per share, December 31, 2010) times 22.83 million shares outstanding.

TABLE   11-7

Restaurant Industry Segment Analysis: Beta

	Beta		Beta
P. F. Chang's China Bistro	1.05	P. F. Chang's China Bistro	1.05
Casual-Dining Restaurant Group		Quick-Service Restaurant Group	
Brinker International	1.25	Chipotle Mexican Grill	1.00
California Pizza Kitchen	1.20	Jack in the Box	0.95
Cheesecake Factory	1.30	McDonald's Corp.	0.65
Cracker Barrel	1.05	Panera Bread Co.	0.95
Darden Restaurants	1.05	Tim Horton's, Inc	0.85
Red Robin Gourmet Burgers	1.25	Wendy's/Arby's Group	0.95
Ruby Tuesday	1.50	Yum! Brands, Inc.	0.95
Average	1.23	Average	0.90

for Pei Wei. Since the two business segments are approximately financed with the same proportion of debt and equity, I will maintain the companywide after-tax cost of debt and capital weighting structures illustrated in Table 11-6. The cost of capital for each business segment follows:

PFCB Industry Segment	Cost of Equity	Cost of Capital
Bistros	10.80%	10.08%
Pei Wei	9.15%	8.58%

Hurdle rates could be established for both business units at 10.1 percent for the Bistros and 8.6 percent for Pei Wei. From Chapters 9 and 10, PFCB should consider two different hurdle rates (required rates of return) for their two restaurant formats when calculating the net present value of opening a new restaurant. Pei Wei should have a lower required rate of return than the Bistros. This means that a new Pei Wei restaurant could be opened, but a Bistro with exactly the same cash flows would be rejected because it would not meet the higher (10.08 percent) hurdle rate, just as a 9.5 percent-returning project might be acceptable in one industry (company) and not another.

Technical Refinement

As seen in the discussion of capital structure in the preceding section, leverage affects the risk of an organization. That risk manifests in the cost of equity through the company's beta. Consequently, there is a technical adjustment that should be done to the segment industry group's betas. This process involves "deleveraging" the betas, or removing the effects of leverage on the betas via Eq. (11.9):

$$\beta_U = \beta_L/\{1 + [(1 - t)(D/E)]\} \qquad (11.9)$$

where β_U = unlevered beta
   β_L = levered beta
   t = tax rate
   D = market value of debt
   E = market value of equity

This refined approach is applied to the restaurant industry group in Table 11-8. It results in refined industry average unlevered betas of 1.07 for the casual-dining segment and 0.81 for the quick-service segment. Additionally, if we

T A B L E   11-8

Restaurant Industry Segment Analysis: Beta

	Beta Levered	D/E	Tax Rate	Beta Unlevered
P. F. Chang's China Bistro	1.05	10.35%	30.0%	0.98
Casual-Dining Restaurant Group				
Brinker International	1.25	26.55%	27.5%	1.05
California Pizza Kitchen	1.20	0.00%	31.0%	1.20
Cheesecake Factory	1.30	0.00%	28.5%	1.30
Cracker Barrel	1.05	49.47%	28.0%	0.77
Darden Restaurants	1.05	23.54%	27.0%	0.90
Red Robin Gourmet Burgers	1.25	28.58%	29.0%	1.04
Ruby Tuesday	1.50	33.22%	25.0%	1.20
Average	1.23	23.05%	28.0%	1.07
Recalculated using the average levered beta, tax rates, and D/E.				1.05
Quick-Service Restaurant Group				
Chipotle Mexican Grill	1.00	0.00%	38.0%	1.00
Jack in the Box	0.95	29.61%	37.5%	0.80
McDonald's Corp.	0.65	14.30%	31.0%	0.59
Panera Bread Co.	0.95	0.00%	38.1%	0.95
Tim Horton's, Inc	0.85	4.90%	32.0%	0.82
Wendy's/Arby's Group	0.95	76.32%	32.0%	0.63
Yum! Brands, Inc.	0.95	15.39%	26.0%	0.85
Average	0.90	20.07%	33.5%	0.81
Recalculated using the average levered beta, tax rates, and D/E.				0.79

would have used the averaged levered beta, the average tax rate, and the average debt-to-equity ratio and recalculated the unlevered industry group beta using those average parameters, the resulting unlevered betas would have been reduced by 0.02. Thus this results in an unlevered beta of 1.05 for the casual-dining segment and 0.79 for the quick-service segment.

The next step is to relever the segment betas using Eq. (11.10):

$$\beta_L = \beta_U\{1 + [(1 - t)(D/E)]\} \tag{11.10}$$

Using the unlevered beta of 1.07 for casual dining and PFCB's 30 percent tax rate and 10.35 percent debt/equity value of capital results in a beta of 1.15, whereas for quick service, the levered beta is 0.87. The final step is to use these refined betas to estimate the cost of equity and the cost of capital for each segment:

PFCB Industry Segment	Cost of Equity	Cost of Capital
Bistros	10.40%	9.71%
Pei Wei	9.00%	8.45%

This more refined approach results in slightly lower hurdle rates for each segment.

Just as a side note: This refined approach is also used by some companies to determine their corporatewide beta, cost of equity, and cost of capital. Some people refer to this as a *modified CAPM approach* when applied at a corporate level. Additionally, this approach is a valid analytical tool to estimate the cost of capital for private companies.

Some companies take the divisional cost-of-capital concept to a deeper level—strategic business unit, project category type, or project cost of capital. Continuing with PFCB, the company opens new restaurants, refurbishes older units, implements administrative projects, and so on. What hurdle rate is appropriate for these types of projects? Although there is limited financial theory that is directly applicable in practice, the conceptual attraction of project hurdle rates is well founded in theory—added risk requires added return. Stepping away from PFCB, other companies usually develop project categories, such as cost reduction, capacity expansion, line extensions, and new products. Often the project categories also include regulatory (or environmental) capital, R&D capital, and administrative capital.

Although a company may not be able to quantify the cost-of-capital requirement exactly for a new product, management recognizes that a new product is riskier than capacity expansion for existing products, which is riskier than investment in a cost savings project. Some companies arbitrarily extend this argument and require higher returns for capacity expansion projects than for cost savings projects and even higher returns for new products than for capacity expansion projects.

SUMMARY

The cost of capital is the opportunity cost of funds that is required to compensate investors for their investment in the organization. Because investors generally dislike risk, the required rate of return is higher on riskier securities. As a class, bonds are less risky than preferred stocks, and preferred stock, in turn, are less risky than common stock. The result is that the required rate of return is lowest for bonds, higher for preferred stock, and highest for common stock. Within each of these security classes, there are variations among the issuing firms' risks; hence required rates of return vary among firms.

The cost of debt is defined as the required yield to maturity on new increments of debt capital K_d multiplied by (1 − tax rate). Financing costs must represent current opportunity costs, so the actual historical financing costs (reflected on the books) are not relevant. The cost of preferred stock with no maturity date is the required yield. It is found as the annual expected preferred dividend divided by the current preferred stock price. The cost of common equity is the return required by a reasonable investor. The cost of common equity may be calculated by two different methods. The recommended approach is the capital asset pricing model (CAPM)—the risk-free rate plus the product of the market risk premium and the firm's beta.

The first step in calculating the weighted cost of capital K is to determine the cost of the individual capital components. The next step is to establish the proper set of weights to be used in the averaging process. The basic issues are whether to use book or market value in calculating the weights of each source of financing and as of what time period, current or targeted (projected). With regard to market or book weights, the theory and practice are quite clear—use market weights. With regard to timing, target is preferred if that target is stated as market-based weights. Most targets are not; most targets are stated as book weights. In such cases, current market weights are preferable to target book weights.

Increasing the leverage ratio in a firm will make the debt and equity riskier because it increases the probability of bankruptcy. If bankruptcy costs are substantial, then with increasing leverage, the cost of capital will fall, reach a minimum, and then rise. The minimum region on this curve indicates an optimal cost of capital and the optimal amount of debt or leverage ratio.

In application within a firm, hurdle rates can be developed if there is a group of publicly traded companies that participates in each separate business segment. However, there are no good industry segment matches or the level of detail is not readily available, such as a cost savings chocolate confectionery project in Germany. In this case, the risk/reward concept may lead management to establish its own set of systematic hurdle rates based on its knowledge of the business.

LONG-TERM FINANCING

This chapter discusses long-term financing—sources, specific forms, and procedures for obtaining long-term financing. The chapter begins with a review of the financing alternatives in the early stage of a firm's existence—private placement of debt and equity through to the initial public offering (IPO) phase, where the organization decides to go public for the first time. The common forms of long-term financing include long-term debt, preferred stock, and common stock. Each is presented, in turn, below.

The chief financial officer (CFO) or treasurer of an organization is responsible for making recommendations to the board of directors and chief executive officer (CEO). These recommendations carefully weigh the advantages and disadvantages of each financial instrument. Once the decision is made, the CFO or treasurer is responsible for obtaining the long-term financing for the organization.

For other executives of the corporation, a basic understanding of the process and available financing alternatives acquaints them with specific terms and concepts, broadens their understanding of financial markets, and enhances their knowledge about why specific financing decisions are made within the organization.

INITIAL SOURCES OF LONG-TERM FINANCING

Through the stages of a firm's development, an organization has available different sources of financing (Table 12-1). During the first phase, the startup, a firm avails itself of financing from personal savings, personal loans, and loans from government agencies such as the Small Business Administration (SBA) or Small Business Investment Corporations (SBIC). The SBA and SBIC are federal agencies. State governments also may have "incubator" funds available to encourage rural or inner-city development or to attract various startup businesses.

During rapid growth, the second phase, a firm finances itself through internal sources or direct financing. The firm can obtain direct financing in the form of a loan from a commercial bank, insurance company, or pension fund. In addition, a firm also can obtain funds from private equity placement with venture capitalists. These sources are discussed in detail below.

The third phase, growth to maturity, is financed by going public and through money and capital markets. An investment bank generally is involved in this process. Investment banking is discussed below, along with the common

TABLE 12-1

Financing Sources Through a Firm's Development

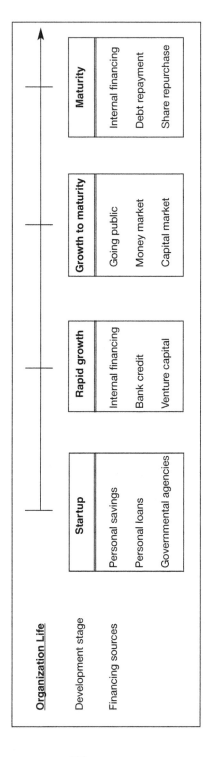

Organization Life

Development stage	Startup	Rapid growth	Growth to maturity	Maturity
Financing sources	Personal savings	Internal financing	Going public	Internal financing
	Personal loans	Bank credit	Money market	Debt repayment
	Governmental agencies	Venture capital	Capital market	Share repurchase

forms of long-term financing—long-term debt (including lease alternatives), preferred stock, and common stock.

During the final phase, maturity and industry decline, a firm finances through internal sources while repaying its debt and/or repurchasing its shares.

Direct Financing: Term Loans and Private Placements

Venture-capital financing is a form of direct financing and is discussed later. This section concentrates on obtaining direct debt financing (loans). Direct long-term financing includes (1) term lending by commercial banks and insurance companies and (2) private placement of securities with insurance companies and pension funds. *Term loans* are direct business loans with a maturity of more than one year but less than 15 years, with provisions for systematic repayment (amortization during the life of the loan). *Private placements* are direct business loans with a maturity of more than 15 years. The distinction is, of course, arbitrary. Private placement differs from the term loan only in its arbitrary maturity length; this distinction becomes even fuzzier when you see that some private placements call for repayment of a substantial portion of the principal within 5 to 10 years. Thus term loans and private placements represent about the same kind of direct financing arrangements.

Evaluation of Direct Financing
From the standpoint of the borrower, the advantages of direct financing are:

1. Much seasonal short-term borrowing can be dispensed with, thereby reducing the danger of nonrenewal of loans or substantially higher interest rates.

2. The borrower avoids the expenses of Securities and Exchange Commission (SEC) registration and investment bankers' distribution.

3. Less time is required for obtaining a loan than is involved in a bond issue.

4. Since only one lender is involved rather than many bondholders, the borrower may have the flexibility to modify the loan agreement (indenture).

The disadvantages to a borrower of direct financing are:

1. The interest rate may be higher on a term loan than on a short-term loan because the lender is tying up money for a longer period and therefore does not have the opportunity to review the borrower's status periodically (as is done whenever short-term loans are renewed).

2. The cash drain is large. Since the loans provide for regular amortization (payment of interest and principal) or sinking-fund payments, the company experiences a continuous cash drain. From this standpoint, direct loans are less advantageous than equity funds (which never have

to be repaid), a preferred stock without maturity, or even a bond issue without a sinking-fund requirement.

3. Since the loan is a long-term commitment, the lender employs high credit standards, insisting that the borrower be in a strong financial position and has a good current ratio, a low debt-to-equity ratio, good activity ratios, and good profitability ratios.

4. The longer-term loan agreement has restrictions that are not found in a 90-day note.

5. Investigation costs may be high. The lender stays with the company for a longer period. Therefore, the longer-term outlook for the company must be reviewed, and the lender makes a more extensive investigation than would be done for a short-term note. For this reason, the lender may set a minimum on any loan (e.g., $50,000) in order to recover the costs of investigating the applicant.

In addition, there are some advantages to the public distribution of securities that are not achieved by term loans or private placement, including:

1. The firm establishes its credit and achieves publicity by having its securities publicly and widely distributed. This initial offering, along with solid financial performance, will enable the firm to engage in future financing at lower rates.

2. The wide distribution of debt or equity may enable its repurchase on favorable terms at some subsequent date if the market price of the securities falls.

Thus direct long-term debt financing has both advantages and limitations. Its use continues through the rapid-growth stage and into the growth-to-maturity stage as a firm assesses and makes tradeoffs with other forms of financing.

Venture Capitalists

Firms that have growth potential face greater risks than almost any other type of business, and their higher risks require special types of financing. This led to the development of private equity placement and specialized venture-capital (VC) financing sources. Some VC companies are organized as partnerships; others are more formal corporations termed *investment development companies*. Some companies are formed for a single investment opportunity, whereas others manage a very active portfolio of properties. Typical sources of VC financing include:

- Many investment banks and commercial banks have established VC subsidiaries.

- VC firms or VC specialists are firms whose owners often have had prior investment banking or commercial banking experience.

- Some VC investment activity is conducted by wealthy individuals. This type of VC financing is categorized as *angel financing*.

- Another long-time source of VC is represented by large, well-established business firms. A number of large corporations, many in the pharmaceutical or computer technology area, have invested both money and various types of know-how to start or to help to develop small business firms. The owner of the small firm is usually a specialist, frequently a technically oriented person who needs both money and help in such administrative services as accounting, finance, production, and marketing. The small firm's owner contributes entrepreneurship, special talents, a taste for risk taking, and a passion to see the successful development and commercialization of his or her idea. Some major corporations have found that there is a mutual advantage for this form of VC investment. In fact, this is how many pharmaceutical companies gain breakthrough compounds and technology.

As you can see, some venture capitalists are purely financial investors. These investors provide capital in the hope of a commensurate rate of return for the risk being undertaken. Other VC investors are strategic investors who also want to earn a commensurate rate of return but who are keenly interested in the company's products or services.

When a new business makes an application for financial assistance from a VC firm, it receives a rigorous examination. Some development companies use their own staffs for this investigation, whereas others depend on a board of advisers acting in a consultative capacity. A high percentage of applications are rejected, but if the application is approved, funds are provided. VC companies generally take an equity position in the firms they finance, but they also may extend debt capital. However, when loans are made, they generally involve convertibility into equity at some point. Often the VC firm will take convertible preferred stock for its investment. This avoids burdening the new capital-hungry firm with a requirement to pay interest on debt or technically be in default. The convertible preferred stock also provides the VC firm with a priority position in liquidation and the opportunity to obtain a substantial equity position if the venture turns out well.

Another technique is the use of a staged capital commitment. In *staged capital commitment* (SCC), the venture capitalist agrees to provide capital in various stages in the venture as opposed to providing all expected capital requirements up front. Also, the venture capitalist typically reserves the option to abandon, revalue, or increase his or her capital commitment to the project at each future round of financing.

SCC reduces the perceived risk to the venture capitalist because the venture capitalist receives a wealth of information about the company (e.g., How has the company performed relative to its initial business plan? Does the management team work well together? Does the market research reveal adequate demand? Has new competition surfaced?) before the next round of financing arrives. This new information reduces the uncertainty of the value of the company and aids in the venture capitalist's decision as to how to proceed.

Also, the knowledge that the company is scheduled to run out of cash is a powerful motivator for management to focus its energies on creating value from its limited resources.

INVESTMENT BANKING

In the U.S. economy, saving is done by one group of persons and investing by another. (Investing is used here in the sense of actually putting money into plant, equipment, and inventory and not in the sense of buying securities.) Savings are placed with financial intermediaries, who, in turn, make the funds available to firms wishing to acquire plants and equipment and to hold inventories.

One of the major institutions performing this channeling role is the investment banking institution. The term *investment banker* is somewhat misleading because investment bankers are neither investors nor bankers. That is, they do not invest their own funds permanently, nor are they repositories for individuals' funds, as are commercial banks or savings banks. What, then, is the nature of investment banking?

The many activities of investment bankers can be described first in general terms and then with respect to specific functions. The traditional function of the investment banker has been to act as the middleman in channeling individuals' savings and funds into the purchase of business securities. The investment banker does this by purchasing and then distributing the new securities of individual companies.

Functions of the Investment Banker

The major functions of the investment banker include underwriting, distribution of securities, and advice and counsel.

Underwriting

Underwriting is the insurance function of bearing the risks of adverse price fluctuations during the period in which a new issue of securities is being distributed. The nature of the investment banker's underwriting function can best be understood by example. A business firm needs $250 million. It selects an investment banker, holds conferences, and decides to issue $250 million in bonds. An underwriting agreement is drawn up. On a specific day, the investment banker presents the company with a check for $250 million (less commission). In return, the investment banker receives bonds in denominations of $1,000 each to sell to the public.

The company receives the $250 million before the investment banker has sold the bonds. Between the time the firm is paid the $250 million and the time the bonds are sold, the investment banker bears all the risk of market price fluctuations in the bonds. Selling bonds conceivably can take the investment banker days, months, or longer. If the bond market deteriorates in the interim, the investment banker carries the risk of loss on the sale of the bonds.

One fundamental economic function of the investment banker, then, is to underwrite the risk of a decline in the market price between the time the money is transmitted to the firm and the time the bonds are placed in the hands of their ultimate buyers. For this reason, investment bankers are often called *underwriters*; they underwrite risk during the distribution period.

Distribution

The second function of the investment banker is marketing new issues of securities. The investment banker is a specialist with a staff and organization to distribute securities and therefore the capacity to perform the physical distribution function more efficiently and more economically than an individual corporation. A single corporation that wants to sell or issue its securities would need to establish a security marketing and selling organization, which would be a very expensive and ineffective method of selling securities. The investment banker has a permanent, trained staff and dealer organization available to distribute securities. In addition, the investment banker's reputation for selecting good companies and pricing securities fairly builds up a broad clientele over time, and this further increases the efficiency with which securities can be sold.

Advice and Counsel

Through experience, the investment banker engaged in the origination and sale of securities becomes an expert adviser about terms and characteristics of securities that will appeal to investors. This advice and guidance are valuable. Furthermore, the firm's reputation as a seller of securities depends on the subsequent performance of the securities. Therefore, investment bankers often sit on the boards of firms whose securities they have sold. In this way, they can provide continuing financial counsel.

Certification Function

A number of factors give rise to the certification function of investment bankers. Information asymmetry exists when the managers know more about a company than the prospective buyers of its securities. Since investment bankers conduct continuing in-depth studies of their companies, they are in a position to reduce information asymmetry. In addition, they are likely to provide monitoring of the company's performance as well. The ability of the underwriter to maintain the confidence of a syndicate of other underwriters, as well as selling firms, depends on its reputation for both knowledge and unquestionable integrity. Thus the reputation of the investment banker depends on being informed and honest. The investment banker has the ability to perform as a guarantor of issue quality and fair pricing.

Investment Banking Operations

Probably the best way to gain a clear understanding of the investment banking function is to trace the history of a new issue of securities. This section describes those steps.

Preunderwriting Conferences

First, the members of the issuing firm and the investment banker hold a pre-underwriting conference, at which they discuss the amount of capital to be raised, the type of security to be issued, and the terms of the agreement.

At some point, the issuer and the investment banker enter an agreement that an *issuance* (or *flotation*) will take place. The investment banker then begins to conduct an underwriting investigation. A public accounting firm is called on to make an audit of the issuing firm's financial situation and also helps to prepare the registration statements in connection with these issues for the SEC.

A firm of lawyers is called in to interpret and judge the legal aspects of the flotation. In addition, the originating underwriter (who is the manager of the subsequent underwriting syndicate) makes an exhaustive investigation of the company's prospects. When the investigations are completed, but before registration with the SEC is done, an underwriting agreement is drawn up by the investment banker. Terms of the tentative agreement may be modified through discussions between the underwriter and the issuing company, but the final agreement will cover all underwriting terms except the price of the securities.

Registration Statement and Prospectus

A registration statement containing all relevant financial and business information on the firm then is filed with the SEC. The statutes set a 20-day waiting period (which, in practice, may be shortened or lengthened by the SEC), during which the SEC staff analyzes the registration statement to determine whether there are any omissions or misrepresentations of fact. During the examination period, the SEC can file exceptions to the registration statement or can ask for additional information from the issuing company or the underwriters. Also during this period, the investment bankers are not permitted to offer the securities for sale, although they can print a preliminary prospectus (known as a *red herring*) with all the customary information except the offering price.

The prospectus summarizes the content of the SEC registration statement for the general public. The document provides an overview of the company, along with historical financial information, and discusses the specific uses of the funds and the underlying business risks. The prospectus also lists the costs of raising the funds. "Road shows" are often scheduled at this time. A road show is a presentation by the company (and often with the investment banker) used to market the stock to potential investors before it is actually available for sale.

A *shelf registration* is a process that quickens the registration process, but it is available only to large firms (over $150 million in assets). This process allows the issuing company to file the general background SEC registration material (company's history and historical financials) well in advance of a potential issue of securities. The shelf registration remains available for a two-year period. Specific use of the funds is often left open for if and when the firm decides to issue new securities. At that time, the company specifies the use of the funds.

Pricing the Securities

The actual price the underwriter pays the issuer is not generally determined until the end of the registration period. There is no universally followed practice, but one common arrangement for a new issue of stock calls for the investment banker to buy the securities at a prescribed number of points below the closing price on the last day of registration. Typically, such agreements have an escape clause that provides for the contract to be voided if the price of the securities falls below some predetermined figure.

The investment banker has an easier job if the issue is priced relatively low, but the issuer of the securities naturally wants as high a price as possible. Some conflict on price therefore arises between the investment banker and the issuer. If the issuer is financially sophisticated and makes comparisons with similar security issues, the investment banker is forced to price close to the market. On seasoned issues with a good historical record of prices, pricing is related to recent patterns. The problem is more difficult on IPOs with no prior public trading.

Underwriting Syndicate

The investment banker with whom the issuing firm has conducted its discussions typically does not handle the purchase and distribution of the issue alone unless the issue is a very small one. If the sums of money involved are large and the risks or price fluctuations are substantial, the investment banker forms a syndicate of investment bankers in an effort to minimize the amount of risk to which any one bank is exposed. A *syndicate* is a temporary association for the purpose of carrying out a specific objective.

The managing underwriter invites other investment bankers to participate in the transaction on the basis of their knowledge of the particular kind of offering to be made and their strength and dealer contacts in selling securities of this type. Each investment banker has business relationships with other investment bankers and dealers and thus has a selling group composed of these people. Each level commits to underwriting certain amounts of the total offering. A dealer purchases securities outright, holds them in inventory, and sells them at whatever price can be obtained. The dealer may benefit from price appreciation or may suffer a loss on declines, as any merchandiser does. A broker, on the other hand, takes orders for purchases and transmits them to the proper exchange; the gain is the commission charged for the service.

GOING PUBLIC AND IPOs

The first portion of this chapter discussed how firms may be aided during the early stages of their growth while still remaining private. This preceding section described the nature of investment banking in bringing seasoned issues of debt and equity to the market. Building on this background, this section discusses going public and IPOs.

Going public represents a fundamental change in lifestyle in at least four respects: (1) The firm moves from informal, personal control to a system of formal controls, (2) information must be reported on a timely basis to the outside investors, even though the founders may continue to have majority control, (3) the firm must have breadth of management in all the business functions to operate its expanded business effectively, and (4) the publicly owned firm typically draws on a board of directors, which should include representatives of the public owners and other external interest groups, to help formulate sound plans and policies.

The timing of the decision to go public is also especially important because small firms are more affected by variations in money-market conditions than larger companies. During periods of tight money and high interest rates, financial institutions, especially commercial banks, raise credit standards and require a stronger balance sheet history and a longer, more stable record of profitability in order to qualify for bank credit. Since financial ratios for small and growing firms tend to be less strong, such firms bear the brunt of credit restraint, as we have experienced in the past few years since 2008.

In a firm-commitment cash offer, the investment banker agrees to underwrite and distribute the issue at an agreed-on price for a specified number of shares to be bought by the underwriters. The issuer still bears some risk with regard to both price and number of shares sold. These are subject to revision by the investment banker between the date a preliminary agreement is signed and the actual issue date after SEC clearance and other procedures have been completed. Typically, a day before the actual issue date in a conference among the investment banker, lawyers, accountants, and the issuer, the number of shares to be sold may be adjusted downward (depending on the strength of the market), and an issue price is set.

A best-efforts offering is subject to the additional risk that if a minimum number of shares is not sold, the investment banker withdraws the offering. Best-efforts offerings generally involve smaller issuers and a smaller size of issue. The investment banker may find it difficult to make a good estimate of the potential market. In a best-efforts offering, the issuer has no assurance that the offer will succeed.

The Decision to Go Public

With all the foregoing as background, what are the pros and cons for a firm in going public? A number of advantages can be stated:

1. Obviously, funds are raised.
2. The disclosure and external monitoring may make it easier to raise additional funds.
3. A public price is established, and its subsequent behavior is a test of the performance of the firm.
4. Public prices are often useful to have for estate and tax purposes.
5. Increased liquidity is provided because of the market that may develop in the stock.

A number of potential disadvantages of going public also must be considered:

1. Some loss of control is involved in sharing ownership.

2. The initial cost of an IPO can be 10 percent or more of the amount of funds raised. There are direct expenses such as the underwriter's fee (or the difference between the proceeds received by the company and the agreed-on price of the securities), attorneys' fees, accountants' fees, and expenses for filing the registration, printing the prospectus, and road show travel. You also have the indirect expense of management's time and the distraction from the business. Finally, other "costs" are involved, such as underpricing, where the securities sell for more than the anticipated price, and the investment banker earns the difference, as well as a "green shoe" option. The green shoe option allows the investment banker to purchase additional securities at the anticipated price. The investment banker enacts such an option only when shares are earning more than the anticipated price. Thus this option "costs" the issuing company lost funds from properly priced initial securities.

3. The activities of the firm now must be more fully disclosed.

4. More formal reporting to public agencies is required, which can be costly.

5. If the firm's shares do not attract a following, the market for them may be relatively inactive, thereby losing the potential benefits of performance evaluation and aligning incentives.

6. Outside investors may push for short-term performance results to an excessive degree.

7. A public firm must publish information that may disclose vital and competitively sensitive information to rival firms.

8. Stockholders' servicing costs and other related expenses also may be a consideration for smaller firms.

9. An advantage of not going public is that major programs do not have to be justified by detailed studies and reports to the board of directors. Action can be taken more speedily, and sometimes getting a new investment program under way early is critical for its success.

Generalization is not possible. The going-public decision depends on the circumstances of the firm and the preferences of its major owners. The advantages and disadvantages of going public may be so closely balanced that the decision may be reversed as time, circumstances, and preferences change.

The following sections discuss concepts about debt, preferred stock, and common stock. Each discussion concludes with advantages/disadvantages to issuers of each form of capital.

LONG-TERM DEBT FINANCING

Chapter 8 developed general background to interest rates and valuation concepts. This section reviews the major characteristics of long-term debt, the advantages and disadvantages of using long-term debt as a source of financing and the advantages to the investor, and concludes with a bond-refinancing analysis and application.

Major Provisions of Long-Term Debt

Table 12-2 lists key long-term debt concepts and provisions.

A mortgage is a form of debt that has underlying property pledged to the debt holder in the case of a default. Similar to the mortgage that an individual might have on his or her house (or car), companies also will borrow against specific property. If a default occurs, the property is transferred to the debt holder or sold on his or her behalf, with the proceeds going to pay the outstanding balance of the loan.

Unsecured debt has no property supporting it, only the general assets and good name of the firm. Subordinated debentures are a junior class of unsecured debt. In the case of a bankruptcy, the subordinated debenture holders are paid only after the debenture holders (nonsubordinated) are fulfilled.

The loan agreement and documentation is referred to as the *indenture*. It contains the covenants to which the bond issuer must adhere. These covenants could include a requirement for the company to maintain a current ratio above a certain level or a debt-to-equity or capitalization ratio below a certain value. Covenants offer the bond investor some formal agreements that the issuer is providing. The purpose of these covenants is to reduce the investor's risk, which

TABLE 12-2

Key Long-Term Debt Concepts and Provisions

Term	Description
Mortgage	Secured debt
Debenture	Unsecured debt
Subordinated debenture	Unsecured debt but junior (second) to other debt instruments
Indenture	Formal bond agreement
Covenants	Protection for bondholders found in the indenture
Call provision	Allows debt to be retired prematurely
Sinking fund	Requires deposits throughout bond's term to fund repayment of the principal
Convertible	Bond can be converted to company's stock.
Indexed	Bond's maturity value or interest payments are indexed to inflation.
Floating rate	Bond's interest rate "adjusts" every period.

should make the purchase of the bonds more attractive while reducing the underlying interest rate.

Two common, major covenants relate to call provisions and sinking funds. A *call provision* allows the bond to be *called*, or repaid, before its term has expired. This offers the borrowing company flexibility in case interest rates drop during the bond's life. Usually, the bond is noncallable for a short period of its life (say, the first five years of a 15-year security). While the bond may become callable after five years, there is a price that the borrower must pay to the debt holder if the company does call the bond. Continuing the 15-year bond example, the sixth year (or the first year that the bond is callable), the bond may be callable with a 5 percent premium (105 percent of the maturity value), the seventh year with a 4 percent premium, the third year callable (or the eighth year of the bond) with a 3 percent premium (103 percent), and so on. Finally, starting in year 11, the bond is callable without a premium.

The *sinking-fund provision* is established for the benefit of the debt holder. After a grace period, the sinking-fund covenant requires the borrower to deposit funds into a separate account so that when the bond matures, there will be proceeds on hand to pay off the principal amount. The sinking-fund provision offers protection to the investor in case the company "sinks."

Other provisions that are used from time to time by some issuers are attempts to "sweeten" the bond issue and thus lower the cost of borrowing (interest rate). Some bonds are offered as *convertibles*, or bonds that can be converted into stock at the bond holder's discretion. A conversion price is established when the bond is sold. This price is higher than the current stock price. However, during the life of the bond, if the stock price exceeds this predetermined price, the bond holder can convert the bond to the company's stock.

A small number of bonds are *indexed* to inflation. The rate on the bond is only for compensation of the general economic liquidity premium and individual company risk. (Please see Chapter 8 for discussion related to liquidity preference.) The interest and/or principal amount is adjusted regularly for the effects of inflation, as agreed to in the bond's covenant.

Finally, *floating-rate* or *adjustable-rate bonds* feature interest rates that will fluctuate based on a set interest-rate barometer. These rates are adjusted annually or every so many years.

Each of these provisions can be agreed to by the borrower and issuer and then written into the indenture agreement.

Evaluation of Debt as a Source of Long-Term Financing

From the viewpoint of long-term debt holders, debt is less risky than preferred or common stock, has limited advantages in regard to income, and is weak in regard to control. To elaborate:

1. Debt is less risky than preferred or common stock because it gives the holder priority both in earnings and in liquidation. Debt also has a definite maturity and is protected by the covenants of the indenture.

2. In the area of income, the bondholder has a fixed return, except in the case of income bonds or floating-rate notes. Interest payments are not contingent on the company's level of earnings or current market rates of interest. However, debt does not participate in any superior earnings of the company and gains are limited in magnitude.

3. In the area of control, the bondholder usually does not have the right to vote. However, if the bonds go into default, then bondholders, in effect, take control of the company.

From the viewpoint of long-term debt issuers, there are several advantages and disadvantages to bonds. The advantages include:

1. The cash cost of debt is limited. Bondholders do not participate in superior profits, if earned.

2. Not only is the cost limited, but the required return is lower than that of equity.

3. The owners of the corporation do not share their control when debt financing is used.

4. The interest payment on debt is deductible as a tax expense.

5. Flexibility in the financial structure of the corporation can be achieved by inserting a call provision (which allows for the early retirement of debt) in the bond indenture.

The disadvantages to the borrower include:

1. Debt has committed charges and nonpayment is considered default.

2. As seen in Chapter 11, higher financial leverage brings higher required rates of return on equity earnings or the cost of equity. Thus, even though leverage may be favorable and may raise earnings per share, the higher required rates attributable to leverage may drive the common stock value down. An indirect cost of using more debt is a higher cost of equity.

3. Debt usually has a fixed maturity date, and the financial officer must make provision for repayment of the debt.

4. Since long-term debt is a commitment for a long period, it involves risk. The expectations and plans on which the debt was issued may change, and the debt may prove to be a burden. For example, if income, employment, the price level, and interest rates all fall greatly, the prior issuance of a large amount of long-term debt may have been an unwise financial policy. In a long-term contractual relationship, the indenture provisions are likely to be much more stringent than they are in a short-term credit agreement. The firm may be subject to much more limiting restrictions than if it had borrowed on a short-term basis or had issued common stock.

5. There is a limit on the extent to which funds can be raised through long-term debt. Generally accepted standards of financial policy dictate that the debt ratio should not exceed certain limits. When debt goes beyond these limits, its cost rises rapidly.

Bond Refinancing

With the fluctuating interest rates that the economy experienced in the past decade, many individuals took advantage of low interest rates and refinanced home mortgages, home equity loans, consumer-credit loans, and so on. Many companies also took advantage of low interest rates and refinanced outstanding debt obligations. Some other companies, after careful review, decided not to refinance or simply were unable to refinance owing to a restriction on quality credit. This section discusses the evaluation process for a refinancing. While this particular discussion is centered on corporate refinancing, the same principles are in place to evaluate a personal refinancing decision.

The analysis of this decision is very similar to the analysis of a capital investment, as discussed in Chapter 9 and Chapter 10. You need to determine the net present value of refinancing by examining the net-of-tax investment and the annual (ongoing) cash savings.

My illustration will revolve around a company that issued a $250 million, 15-year bond five years ago when interest rates were 7.50 percent. The cost of issuing that bond was $6.0 million. A significant decline in interest rates currently allows the company to borrow $250.0 million at 6.00 percent for 10 years (matching the remaining term of the original bond). Once again, the total cost of issuing the bond is estimated to be $6.0 million, assuming no discount. However, the company needed to pay a call premium of 5.0 percent, or $12.5 million, to call the existing bonds from their holders. Intuitively, the question is this: Should the company incur the $18.5 million of cost to reduce its interest expense by $3.75 million each year (1.5% × $250 million)? The analysis can best be framed by comparing the present value of the savings with the present value of the cost. If savings exceed the cost, the original bond should be called and refinanced. However, as with any analysis, important details need to be examined and after-tax cash-flow amounts considered. Let us further assume that this company has a 40 percent tax rate.

Initial Cost

Table 12-3 examines the initial year cost (or benefit) on an after-tax basis. The first item, the $6.0 million cost of issuing (or floating) the new bond, is the same before and after taxes. There are no tax savings in the initial year related to the cost of floating the bond or the bond discounts incurred. Therefore, the full amount is a negative cash outflow in year 0. These floatation costs will be amortized on a straight-line basis and tax shields will be created over the 10-year life of the bond.

The second item represents the $12.5 million of the call premium. This is an immediately recognized expense and fully tax deductible, which results in a net after-tax cash outflow of $7.5 million.

T A B L E 12-3

Bond Refinancing Analysis: Initial Cost
($ 000s)

Initial cost (or benefit), year 0

New or Existing Bond	Item	Pretax Cost (Savings)	Tax Consequence	After-Tax Cost (Savings)	After-Tax Calculation (40%)
			Year 0 Impact		
1. New	Refinancing or floatation cost	$ 6,000.0	Tax savings over bond's life.	$ 6,000.0	No immediate tax impact
2. Existing	Call premium	12,500.0	Immediately tax deductible.	7,500.0	$12,500 (1 – tax rate)
3. Existing	Tax savings on existing bond's original floatation costs:				
	Unamortized portion: $4,000 ($6,000 × 2/3)		Immediate tax savings.	(1,600.0)	$4,000 (tax rate)
	Total after-tax year 0 investment amount			$ 11,900.0	

Finally, we need to consider the impact of the existing bond's unamortized issuance (or floatation) costs. The initial floatation costs and bond discount on the existing bond were $6.0 million. These amounts have been amortized for five of the existing bond's 15 years. If a new bond is issued, the company will be able to immediately deduct the unamortized portion ($4.0 million) of these expenses and receive an immediate tax benefit. These expenses actually were paid for five years ago when the existing bond was issued. Consequently, this is a noncash expense at this time, but it does provide a cash tax savings, which is recognized in Table 12-3.

In total, the initial investment amount is $11.9 million after tax.

Ongoing Benefits

Table 12-4 presents the benefits (or costs) that occur throughout the 10-year life of the new bond.

First, the new bond saves the company just over $3.0 million in interest expense each year. That is, the interest-rate reduction (1.5 percent) on $250.0 million, or $3.75 million offset by the interest on the net initial refinancing cost ($11.9 million). This initial cost of refinancing is rolled into the amount borrowed. Of course, this reduction in interest expense causes the company to pay more taxes. After considering the taxes, the interest-rate reduction will save the company $1,821,600 each year.

Although both the existing bond and the new bond cost $6.0 million to issue, the company amortized the existing bond's cost over a 15-year period ($0.4 million per year). The new bond has a shorter time frame, and hence more amortization occurs each year ($0.6 million). This additional ($0.2 million) noncash expense results in a tax savings of $0.08 million (or $80,000) per year.

In total, the company will have slightly over $1.9 million in after-tax savings each year for the next 10 years if the new bond is issued.

Net Present Value of Refinancing

By comparing the present value of the savings versus the present value of the cost, you can decide to refinance the existing bond or wait for more opportunistic circumstances. Table 12.5 shows this final step.

The present value of the annual after-tax savings for each of the next 10 years is $15.7 million. When compared with the initial after-tax cost of $11.9 million, there is a clear indication to refinance (e.g., a positive net present value of refinancing of over $3.8 million). In this example, the company should complete the refinancing.

Notice that the annual savings were discounted at the after-tax cost of the new debt (3.60 percent) and not at the company's cost of capital. Since you are substituting new debt for an already existing debt issue, you do not consider the cost of equity or the cost of capital. You are looking for the lowest cost of debt, you are comparing similar debt instruments, and therefore, you only use the cost of debt. Since the savings are after tax, it is important to use the after-tax cost of debt.

T A B L E 12-4

Bond Refinancing Analysis: Annual Ongoing Benefits
($ 000s)

Ongoing Benefit (or Cost), Years 1–10

New or Existing Bond	Item		Pretax Cost (Savings)	Tax Consequence	After-Tax Cost (Savings)	After-Tax Calculation (40%)
				Years 1–10 Impact		
1.	Interest payments:					
Existing	7.50% Interest on $250,000.0		$ 18,750.0	Deductible when paid.	$ 11,250.0	$18,750 (1 – tax rate)
New	6.00% Interest on $261,900.0		(15,714.0)	Deductible when paid.	(9,428.4)	$15,714 (1 – tax rate)
	Net savings		$ 3,036.0		1,821.6	
2.	Tax shield from refinancing costs paid in initial year:					
Existing	Amortization of $6,000.0 over 15 years = $400.0/yr				(160.0)	$400 (tax rate)
New	Amortization of $6,000.0 over 10 years = $600.0/yr				240.0	$600 (tax rate)
	Net savings				80.0	
	Total after-tax annual savings, Years 1–10				$ 1,901.6	

T A B L E   12-5

Net Present Value of Bond Refinancing
($ 000s)

Period	After-Tax Impact	Table	Value	Present Value*
Years 1–10	Annual after-tax savings (cash flow)	12.4	$ 1,901.6	$ 15,735.4
Year 0	After-tax investment (cash flow)	12.3	(11,900.0)	(11,900.0)
	Net present value of bond refinancing			$ 3,835.4

*The present value is calculated at the after-tax cost of the new debt, or 3.6% (6.0% × 0.60).

T A B L E   12-6

Net Present Value of Bond Refinancing: Interest-Rate Sensitivity
($ 000s)

Refinancing Interest Rate	NPV Bond Refinancing
5.90%	$ 5,187.3
5.95%	4,510.3
6.00%	3,835.4
6.05%	3,162.6
6.10%	2,491.7
6.15%	1,822.8
6.20%	1,155.9
6.25%	491.0
6.30%	(171.9)
6.35%	(832.8)
6.40%	(1,491.8)
6.45%	(2,148.8)
6.50%	(2,803.8)
7.50%	(15,504.2)

Table 12-6 demonstrates sensitivity analysis centered on the new cost of debt. At 6 percent, it is apparent that the same net present value of the bond refinancing found in Table 12-5 and discussed earlier. As your eyes wander up and down Table 12-6, you will notice that the breakeven point (at which to do the refinancing or not) is slightly above 6.25 percent. Also notice that at a static interest rate of 7.50 percent (the same as the existing financing), the result is $(15.5) million not to do the refinancing. This represents the $11.9 million initial-year expenditure along with the additional ongoing net borrowing costs. Chapter 13 will consider one additional form of debt financing—leasing.

PREFERRED STOCK FINANCING

Preferred stock has claims and rights ahead of common stock but behind all bonds. The preference may be a prior claim on earnings, a prior claim on assets in the event of liquidation, and/or a preferential position with regard to both earnings and assets.

The hybrid nature of preferred stock becomes apparent when you try to classify it in relation to bonds and common stock. The priority feature and the (generally) fixed dividend indicate that preferred stock is similar to bonds. Payments to preferred stockholders are limited in amount, so common stockholders receive the advantages (or disadvantages) of leverage. However, if the preferred dividends are not earned, failure to pay the stipulated dividend does not cause default of the obligation, as does failure to pay bond interest. In this characteristic, preferred stock is similar to common stock.

Major Provisions of Preferred Stock

Preferred stock can be found in many forms. The following sections will look at the main terms and characteristics in each case and examine the possible variations in relation to the circumstances in which they could occur. Key preferred stock concepts and provisions are listed in Table 12-7.

T A B L E   12-7

Key Preferred Stock Concepts and Provisions

Term	Description
Always or almost always	
Priority in earnings	Preferred stockholders are recognized before common stockholders.
Cumulative dividends	Dividends are paid first and any in arrears before common stockholders.
Often	
Convertibility	Preferred stock can be converted to common stock.
Rare	
Voting rights	Right to vote just like a common stockholder.
Participating	Stated dividend plus added dividend from extraordinary earnings.
Sinking fund	Requires deposits throughout term to fund repayment.
Maturity	Maturity date to retire preferred stock.
Call provision	Allows preferred stock to be retired.
Adjustable rate	Preferred stock's dividend "adjusts" every period.
Auction rate	Preferred stock's price or dividend determined at initial auction.

Priority in Assets and Earnings

Many provisions in a preferred stock certificate are designed to reduce the purchaser's risk in relation to the risk carried by the holder of common stock. Preferred stock usually has priority with regard to earnings and assets. Two provisions designed to prevent undermining this priority are often found. The first states that without the consent of the preferred stockholders, there can be no subsequent sale of securities having a prior or equal claim on earnings. The second seeks to keep earnings in the firm. It requires a minimum level of retained earnings before common stock dividends are permitted. In order to ensure the availability of liquid assets, the maintenance of a minimum current ratio may also be required.

Cumulative Dividends

A high percentage of preferred stock issues provide for cumulative dividends—that is, all past preferred dividends must be paid before common stock dividends can be paid. The cumulative feature is a protective device. If the preferred stock were not cumulative, preferred and common stock dividends could be suspended for a number of years. The company could vote a large common stock dividend but only the stipulated payment to preferred stock. Obviously, without the cumulative dividend provision, management could evade the preferred position that the holders of preferred stock have tried to obtain. The cumulative feature prevents such evasion.

Convertibility

A substantial portion of preferred stock issued is convertible into common stock. For example, 100 shares of preferred stock may be convertible into 40 shares of the firm's common stock at the option of the preferred stock shareholder. The convertibility provision remains a "sweetener" that reduces the initial cost of both debt and preferred stock. Note at this point that VC firms frequently use convertible preferred stock. The main reasons are that the VC firm receives income if earned by the firm, has priority in liquidation, and if the firm does well, can convert to an equity position and participate in that position.

Other Provisions

Other provisions encountered in preferred stocks include the following:

1. *Voting rights.* Sometimes preferred stockholders are given the right to vote for directors. When this feature is present, it generally permits the preferred stockholders to elect a minority of the board, say, three of nine directors. The voting privilege becomes operative only if the company has not paid the preferred dividend for a specified period, say, 6, 8, or 10 quarters.

2. *Participating.* A rare type of preferred stock is one that participates with the common stock in sharing the firm's earnings. The following

factors generally relate to participating preferred stocks: (a) the stated preferred dividend is paid first (e.g., $5 a share), (b) next, income is allocated to common stock dividends up to an amount equal to the preferred dividend (in this case, $5), and (c) any remaining income is shared between common and preferred stockholders.

3. *Sinking fund.* Some preferred issues have a sinking-fund requirement, which ordinarily calls for the purchase and retirement of a given percentage of the preferred stock each year.

4. *Maturity.* Preferred stocks almost never have maturity dates on which they must be retired. However, if the issue has a sinking fund, this effectively creates maturity dates. Convertibility also may shorten the life of preferred stock.

5. *Call provision.* A call provision gives the issuing corporation the right to call in the preferred stock for redemption, just like bonds. If it is used, the call provision states that the company must pay an amount greater than the par value of the preferred stock, the additional sum being defined as the *call premium*. For example, a $100 par value preferred stock may be callable at the option of the corporation at $108 a share.

6. *Adjustable-rate preferred stock (ARPS).* Under unexpected inflation, preferred stock with fixed dividend rates becomes undesirable from the investor's point of view because of the risk that the market value of the preferred will fall. In order to share the risk and to make preferred issues more attractive to investors, many companies, particularly utilities, have begun to issue preferred stock with dividends tied to rates on various U.S. government obligations.

7. *Auction-rate preferred stock.* Both ARPS and auction-rate preferred stock have a floating dividend rate and tax advantages. They differ in that while the dividend rate on the ARPS typically is tied to a government obligation, the auction-rate preferred stock is set and reset by Dutch auctions. In the Dutch auction process, the bidder submits to the seller in charge of the auction the number of shares desired and a specified dividend level. The lowest dividend that will allow all the available shares to be completely sold will be the dividend for the next specific period of time until a new auction resets the dividend.

Evaluation of Preferred Stock as a Source of Long-Term Financing

There are both advantages and disadvantages to selling preferred stock. Among the advantages are:

1. In contrast to bonds, the obligation to make committed interest payments is avoided.

2. A firm wishing to expand can obtain higher earnings for the original owners by selling preferred stock with a limited return rather than by selling common stock.

3. By selling preferred stock, the financial manager avoids the provision of equal participation in earnings that the sale of additional common stock would require.

4. Preferred stock also permits a company to avoid sharing control through voting participation. This is the main reason why startup companies often will consider first issuing preferred stock.

5. In contrast to bonds, preferred stock enables the firm to conserve mortgageable assets.

6. Preferred stock is also considered equity. It adds to the equity base (without diluting common stockholders). Consequently, the firm can issue even more debt to meet its future needs. This is why so many utility companies have very intricate and numerous issues of preferred stock outstanding.

7. Since preferred stock typically has no maturity or sinking fund, it is more flexible than a bond.

Among the disadvantages are:

1. Characteristically, preferred stock must be sold on a higher yield basis than bonds.

2. Preferred stock dividends are not deductible as a tax expense, which is a characteristic that makes their after-tax cost differential very great in comparison with bonds.

3. As shown in Chapter 11, the after-tax cost of debt is approximately 60 to 65 percent of the stated coupon rate for profitable firms (implying a 35% to 40% tax rate). The after-tax cost of preferred stock, however, is generally the full percentage amount of the preferred dividend.

In fashioning securities, the financial manager needs to consider the investor's point of view. Frequently, it is asserted that preferred stocks have so many disadvantages to both the issuer and the investor that they should never be issued. Nevertheless, preferred stock provides the following advantages to the investor:

1. It provides reasonably steady income.

2. Preferred stockholders have a preference over common stockholders in earnings and liquidation.

3. Many corporations (e.g., insurance companies) like to hold preferred stocks as investments because 70 or 80 percent of the dividends received on such shares are not taxable.

Preferred stock also has some disadvantages to investors:

1. Although the holders of preferred stock bear a substantial risk, their returns are limited.
2. Price fluctuations in preferred stock may be greater than those in bonds.
3. The stockholders have no legally enforceable right to dividends.
4. Accrued dividend arrearages are seldom settled in cash, comparable with the amount of the obligation that has been incurred.

Basically, preferred stock enables a firm to use leverage without fixed charges. Generally, preferred stocks have been sold mostly by utility companies, for whom the nondeductibility of dividends as an expense for tax purposes is less of a disadvantage because of the nature of the regulatory rate-making process, which essentially treats taxes paid as an expense to be considered in setting allowable rates of return. Most corporations, other than utilities, real estate investment trusts (REITs), and startups, do not use any preferred stock in their capital structure.

COMMON STOCK FINANCING

Two important positive considerations are involved in owning equity—income and control. The right to income carries the risk of loss. Control also involves responsibility and liability.

Through the right to vote, holders of common stock have legal control of the corporation. As a practical matter, members of senior management may also be members of the board or directors. Numerous examples demonstrate that stockholders can reassert their control if they are dissatisfied with the corporation's policies. In recent years, proxy battles with the aim of altering corporate policies have occurred with increasing frequency, and firms whose managers are unresponsive to stockholders' desires are subject to takeover bids by other firms.

Another consideration involved in equity ownership is risk. On liquidation, holders of common stock are last in the priority of claims. Therefore, the portion of capital they contribute provides a cushion for creditors if losses occur on dissolution.

Major Provisions of Common Stock

The rights of holders of common stock in a business corporation are established by the laws of the state in which the corporation is chartered and by the terms of the charter granted by the state. Charters are relatively uniform on many matters, including collective and specific rights. Certain collective rights usually are given to the holders of common stock: (1) the right to amend the charter with the approval of the appropriate officials in the state of incorporation, (2) the right to adopt and amend bylaws, (3) the right to elect the directors of the corporation, (4) the right to authorize the sale of fixed assets, (5) the right to enter into mergers, (6) the right to change the amount of authorized common stock, and (7) the right to issue preferred stock, bonds, and other securities.

Holders of common stock also have specific rights as individual owners: (1) the right to vote in the manner prescribed by the corporate charter, (2) the right to sell their stock certificates (their evidence of ownership) and, in this way, to transfer their ownership interest to other persons, (3) the right to inspect the corporate books, and (4) the right to share residual assets of the corporation on dissolution. (However, the holders of common stock are last among the claimants to the assets of the corporation.)

Nature of Voting Rights and Proxy Contests

For each share of common stock owned, the holder has the right to cast one vote at the annual meeting of stockholders or at special meetings that may be called. Provision is made for the temporary transfer of the right to vote by an instrument known as a *proxy*. The transfer is limited in its duration; typically, it applies only to a specific occasion, such as the annual meeting of stockholders. The SEC supervises the use of the proxy machinery and frequently issues rules and regulations to improve its administration.

A method of voting that has come into increased prominence is *cumulative voting*. While all states allow for cumulative voting for directors, it is required in seven states, including California.

Cumulative voting strengthens the ability of minority shareholders to elect a director by casting multiple votes for a single director. For example, suppose that six directors are to be elected. Without cumulative voting, the owner of 100 shares can cast 100 votes for each of the six openings. When cumulative voting is permitted, the stockholder can accumulate the votes and cast all of them for one director instead of 100 each for six directors. Cumulative voting is designed to enable a minority group of stockholders to obtain some voice in the control of the company by electing at least one director to the board.

Preemptive Right

The preemptive right gives holders of common stock the first option to purchase additional issues of common stock. In some states, the right is made part of every corporate charter; in others, the right must be specifically inserted in the charter.

The purpose of the preemptive right is twofold. First, it protects the power of control for present stockholders. If it were not for this safeguard, the management of a corporation could issue new common stock to new stockholders in an attempt to wrest control from current stockholders.

The second, and by far the more important, protection that the preemptive right affords stockholders concerns the dilution of value. Selling new common stock at below-market value enables new shareholders to buy stock on terms more favorable than those which had been extended to the old shareholders. The preemptive right prevents such occurrences.

Evaluation of Common Stock as a Source of Long-Term Financing

The advantages of financing with common stock include:

1. Common stock does not entail fixed charges. If the company generates the earnings, it can pay common stock dividends. Unlike interest, there is no legal obligation to pay dividends.

2. Common stock carries no fixed maturity date.

3. Since common stock provides a cushion against losses for creditors, the sale of common stock increases the creditworthiness of the firm.

4. Common stock, at times, can be sold more easily than debt. It appeals to certain investor groups because (a) it typically carries a higher expected return than does preferred stock or debt and (b) it provides the investor with a better hedge against inflation than does straight preferred stock or bonds. Ordinarily, common stock increases in value when the value of real assets rises during an inflationary period.

5. Returns from common stock in the form of capital gains may be subject to a lower personal income tax rate on capital gains. The effective personal income tax rates on common stock returns may be lower than the effective tax rates on interest or preferred stock dividends.

6. Employee stock participation programs can be an effective tool used by the company to align the financial interests of its general employee population, its management group, and its owners, the stockholders. Specific employee programs include:

   • Employee purchase plans where the employer encourages the purchase of the company's stock through payroll deductions by absorbing the individual transaction fees or by even allowing the employee to purchase the stock at a slight discount from the current market price

   • Executive and employee stock option plans whose value is tied to the underlying performance of the stock market

   • Employee stock ownership plans (ESOP) that the company establishes to supplement or replace its employee retirement program and then continues to purchase stock on behalf of the ESOP trustee

An additional benefit of using equity as an employee motivator is that a high concentration of stock in employees' hands may limit an unwanted or hostile acquisition. Disadvantages to the issuer of common stock include the following:

1. The sale of common stock may extend voting rights or control to the additional stockowners. For this reason, among others, additional equity financing is often avoided by small and new firms whose owner-managers may be unwilling to share control of their companies with outsiders.

2. The use of debt may enable the firm to use funds at a fixed low cost, whereas common stock gives equal rights to new stockholders to share in the future net profits of the firm.

3. The costs of underwriting and distributing common stock are usually higher than those for underwriting and distributing preferred stock or debt.

4. As you saw in Chapter 11, if the firm has more equity or less debt than is called for in the optimal capital structure, the average cost of capital will be higher than necessary.

5. Common stock dividends are not deductible as an expense for calculating the corporation's income subject to the federal income tax, but bond interest is deductible. The impact of this factor is reflected in the relative cost of equity capital vis-à-vis debt capital.

SUMMARY

This chapter discussed many aspects of long-term financing, including sources of long-term financing, procedures for obtaining that financing, and a review of the unique characteristics and advantages/disadvantages of each form. The chapter also considered financing for the new firm in its initial stages of startup and rapid growth through its seasoned more mature stages.

Three major forms of direct financing are (1) term lending by commercial banks, (2) the private placement of securities with insurance companies and pension funds, and (3) private equity placement, also called *venture capital financing*. Term loans and private placements represent similar financing arrangements. VC financing has taken on increased importance in recent years. Sources of VC financing include commercial banks, investment banks, VC firms, wealthy individuals (also called *angel financing*), and corporate-sponsored venture capitalists. VC firms typically use convertible preferred stock in staged financing as the good performance of the recipient firm is demonstrated.

The investment banker provides middleman services to both the seller and the buyer of new securities, helping plan the issue, underwriting it, and handling the job of selling the issue to the ultimate investor. The investment banker also must look to the interests of the brokerage customers; if these investors are not satisfied with the banker's products, they will deal elsewhere. Thus the investment banker performs a certification role for the issuer.

Going public and IPOs represent a fundamental change in the lifestyle of business firms. Costs of flotation are higher for IPOs than for seasoned issues. Flotation costs are higher for best-efforts offerings than for firm commitments. Best-efforts offerings typically involve smaller firms whose share prices exhibit greater volatility in the after market.

Debt can take many forms, such as secured or unsecured and short or long term. This chapter discussed the appropriate analysis when a company considers refinancing an existing debt instrument.

While the characteristics of preferred stock vary, some patterns persist. Preferred stocks usually have priority over common stocks with respect to earnings and claims on assets in liquidation. Preferred stocks are perpetual (no maturity) but are sometimes callable. They are typically nonparticipating and offer only contingent voting rights. Preferred stock dividends are usually cumulative.

Common stock involves the balancing of risk, income, and control. This chapter analyzed various dimensions of the rights of common stockholders.

LEASING AS A FINANCING AND BUSINESS ALTERNATIVE

No matter the industry or specific business, all firms generally are interested in using buildings and equipment. One way of obtaining their use is to buy them, but an alternative is to lease them. Originally, leasing was most often associated with real estate—land and buildings—but today, virtually any kind of fixed asset can be leased. Leasing is most often a perfect substitute for borrowing. Hence managers should think of the lease/borrow decision rather than the lease/buy decision.

Leasing simultaneously provides for the use of assets and their financing. One advantage over debt is that the *lessor* (owner of the asset) has a better position than a creditor if the user firm (*lessee*) experiences financial difficulties. If the lessee does not meet the lease obligations, the lessor has a stronger legal right to take back the asset because the lessor still legally owns it. A creditor, even a secured creditor, encounters costs and delays in recovering assets that have been financed directly or indirectly. Generally, lessors are less risky than their lessees (renters); as lessees become riskier, there is greater opportunity for the supplier of financing to formulate a leasing arrangement rather than a loan. The relative tax positions of lessors and users of assets also may affect the lease/borrow decision.

This chapter discusses the various types of leases, accounting for leases, and the evaluation of the lease/borrow decision. Generally, the focus is on the lessee's perspective—should you lease or buy the asset and borrow?

TYPES OF LEASES

Leases take several different forms, the most important of which are operating leases, financial leases, and a sale and leaseback. A lease can extend from a day to 30 years or longer.

Before addressing the types of leases, let's clarify the terms *lessor* and *lessee*. The lessor is the party (i.e., individual, corporation, partnership, etc.) that owns the asset. In a building example, we would call the lessor the *landlord*. The lessee is the one who is using the asset. Continuing the building example, the lessee is the *renter* or *tenant*. The lessor is the one selling the use of the property or equipment, whereas the lessee is the one buying the use of the property or equipment. The three major types of leases are described below.

Operating Leases

An *operating lease* is a contractual arrangement wherein the lessor agrees to provide an asset to the lessee for a specified period of time. The lessee agrees to make periodic payments to the lessor for use of the asset. The length of the lease can be a day, a week, a month, a year, or longer but usually less than five years.

Frequently, an operating lease may contain a cancellation clause, giving the lessee the right to cancel the lease and return the asset before expiration of the basic agreement. This cancellation clause usually contains a prenegotiated cancellation penalty that is payable by the lessee. In effect, the cancellation clause is a put option that allows return of the equipment if technological developments render it obsolete or if it simply no longer is needed, which is an important consideration for the lessee.

Another important characteristic of the operating lease is that, frequently, it is not fully amortized. That is, the leasing period is shorter than the useful life of the underlying asset, and the payments required under the lease contract may not be sufficient to recover the full cost of the equipment. Obviously, the lessor expects to recover the cost either in subsequent renewal payments or on disposal of the equipment. In some cases, there may be another option that allows the lessee to renew the operating lease for another period of time or buy the asset at a predetermined price on termination. In any case, at the end of the lease, the asset is returned to the lessor, who can lease the asset again or sell it.

There may be additional clauses within a lease that, among other things, restrict the use of the asset. In a shopping mall, the lessor may try to attract a greeting card store to complement the other stores in the mall. To make this a more attractive location for a greeting card store, the lessor may specifically identify, in leases with the other tenants, that their stores can have only a limited amount of shelf space devoted to greeting cards. Lease agreements for retail space include many different operating considerations, such as security, upkeep, hours of operation, and so forth. Lease payments for retail space often include a fixed portion as well as a variable portion that may be a percent of lessee's sales.

Other examples are found every day in the classified section of the local newspaper. New car dealers often offer attractive leasing rates. You may be able to secure the use of a $22,600 vehicle for $2,000 down and $179 per month for 36 months. The lessee recovers only $8,444 [$2,000 + 36($179)]. Even without considering the time value of money, total payments are far short of the original value of the vehicle. In this case, the lessor is also factoring in the anticipated resale value of the vehicle in three years. To further enhance resalability, the lease limits mileage to 12,000 miles per year before a significant per-mile charge is imposed. The lease also will require the lessee to follow a strict and regular maintenance schedule. The lease even may include a predetermined special buyout provision at termination.

A variation of the operating lease is an operating lease that includes maintenance services in addition to financing. This lease is referred to as an *operating service lease* and often is found on equipment such as office computers and copying machines. Payments on an operating lease are often considered as rent expense by the lessee.

Financial Leases

A strict *financial lease* is one that does not provide for maintenance services, is not cancelable, and is fully amortized (i.e., the lessor contracts for rental payments equal to the full price of the leased equipment). The typical arrangement involves the following steps:

1. The firm that will use the equipment prepares a capital expenditure analysis (see Chapters 9 and 10) that indicates a positive net present value for the project.

2. This firm then selects the specific items it requires and negotiates the price and delivery terms with the manufacturer or distributor. If the specific terms are significantly different from those in the capital evaluation, the net present value must be reexamined and verified.

3. Next, the user firm arranges with a bank or leasing company for it to buy the equipment from the manufacturer or distributor, simultaneously executing an agreement to lease the equipment from the financial institution. The terms call for full amortization of the financial institution's cost plus a return on the lessor's investment. The lessee generally has the option to renew the lease at a reduced rental on expiration of the basic lease but does not have the right to cancel the basic lease without completely paying off the financial institution. Often sellers also have financial institutions that are willing to establish similar leases for lessees.

A special type of the financial lease is a *leveraged lease*. In a leverage lease, the lessor will be an equity partner in the asset. In this case, the lessee will provide, say, 20 percent of the funds to the lessor to purchase the asset.

Sale and Leaseback

Financial leases are almost the same as *sale and leaseback*, the main difference being that the leased equipment is new and the lessor buys it from a manufacturer or a distributor instead of from the user/lessee. A sale and leaseback thus can be thought of as a special type of financial lease. Under a sale and leaseback arrangement, a firm owning land, buildings, or equipment sells the property to a financial institution and simultaneously executes an agreement to lease the property back for a certain period under specific terms.

Note that the seller and now lessee immediately receives the purchase price put up by the buyer and now lessor. At the same time, the seller-lessee retains the use of the property. This parallel is carried over to the lease payment schedule.

Under a mortgage loan arrangement, the financial institution receives a series of equal payments just sufficient to amortize the loan and to provide the lender with a specified rate of return on investment. Under a sale and leaseback arrangement, the lease payments are set up in the same manner. The payments are sufficient to return the full purchase price to the financial institution in addition to providing it with some return on its investment. This return is a point of negotiation.

This type of arrangement is often used to finance new buildings or major pieces of equipment. The initial benefit is that the construction of the facility or equipment is completely the responsibility of the user of the asset. In this way, the lessee designs and builds exactly what it needs. There is no financial intermediary acting as project manager. The project manager is the lessee and the one with expert knowledge about its business needs.

ACCOUNTING FOR LEASES

Consistent reporting of the same economic event is a tenet of U.S. Generally Accepted Accounting Principles (GAAP). Leasing is an area where wide variations in financial performance could be obtained by the lessee if there were no specific rules governing the reporting of leases. I begin with an illustration.

Comparison of Financial Statements

Let us say that at the end of last year, the engineering group at The Spyglass Company (TSC) proposed a cost savings project. A capital authorization request indicated a strong positive net present value, and management approved the project. At the beginning of this year, further analysis was done of the accounting ramifications of three options for acquiring the use of this asset: (1) purchase and borrow, (2) operating lease, and (3) financial (capital) lease.

At the beginning of the year, TSC had the following assets, liabilities, and stockholders' equity:

Assets		Liabilities and Equity	
Current assets	$1,400	Current liabilities	$ 500
		Long-term debt	700
Gross plant, property,		Total liabilities	1,200
and equipment (PP&E)	1,000		
Accumulated depreciation	(400)		
Net PPE	600	Equity	800
Total assets	$2,000	Total liabilities and equity	$2,000

Table 13-1 reflects the projected accounting performance and position under the three alternative financing approaches.

T A B L E   13-1

Accounting Examples, Year 1

Income Statement	Asset Purchase	Operating Lease	Capital Lease
Sales	$ 5,000	$ 5,000	$ 5,000
Expenses:			
Other expenses	4,500	4,500	4,500
New equipment depreciation*	100	180	100
Interest expense	80	n/a	80
Total expense	4,680	4,680	4,680
Pretax income	320	320	320
Taxes (40%)	128	128	128
Net income	$ 192	$ 192	$ 192
Assets			
Current assets	$ 1,703	$ 1,672	$ 1,703
Prior gross plant, prop. & equipment	1,000	1,000	1,000
Prior accumulated depreciation	(480)	(480)	(480)
Prior net PPE	520	520	520
New plant, property & equipment	1,000	n/a	1,000
New accumulated depreciation	(100)	n/a	(100)
New net PPE	900	n/a	900
Total assets	$ 3,123	$ 2,192	$ 3,123
Liabilities & Equity			
Current liabilities	$ 500	$ 500	$ 500
Prior long-term liabilities	700	700	700
New borrowings	931	n/a	931
Total liabilities	2,131	1,200	2,131
Stockholders' equity	992	992	992
Total liability & equity	$ 3,123	$ 2,192	$ 3,123
Financial Metrics			
Net margin	3.8%	3.8%	3.8%
Asset turnover	1.60	2.28	1.60
Return on assets	6.1%	8.8%	6.1%
Financial leverage	3.15	2.21	3.15
Return on equity	19.4%	19.4%	19.4%

* Under the operating lease scenario, the $180 expense represents the operating lease.

Accounting Performance with an Asset Purchase

Let us assume that at the beginning of the current year, TSC enters into an agreement to purchase this asset for $1,000 as well as to finance this asset with long-term debt. The asset is expected to have a life of 10 years and no salvage value at the end of that period. In addition, the asset will be financed with a 10-year amortizable (payments include both interest and principal) loan at 8.0 percent interest and annual loan payments of $149. (Remember from chapter 7: $N = 10$; $I/Yr = 8$; $PV = 1000$ and compute PMT at $149.)

The first column of the table illustrates the financial performance and position of TSC at the end of the year, assuming the purchase of this asset and borrowing of funds. The income statement reflects sales less other operating expenses and $180 of expenses related to the purchasing and borrowing, which leads to a net income of $192. The expense of $180 is comprised of two items: depreciation expense ($100) and interest expense ($80) of the first-year loan payment is considered interest (or $1000 × 8%) and the remaining $69 of the $149 annual payment reduces the long-term debt balance. The balance sheet includes a net amount of $900 for this new asset ($1,000 purchase price, less one year's depreciation) and a net amount of $931 of liabilities for the new loan ($1,000 amount borrowed, less the first-year balance repayment). Stockholders' equity increased by the first year's net income ($192), while current assets (cash) increased by $303. Specifically, net income was a source of $192 cash along with depreciation on the existing net, plant, property, and equipment (a source of $80) and the new equipment's depreciation (a source of $100), offset by the loan repayment portion of the lease payment ($69). Notice the performance metrics at the bottom of the table.

Accounting Performance with an Operating Lease

The second column of Table 13-1 shows what could happen if TSC were to enter into a 10-year operating lease. The terms of the lease agreement require TSC to pay $180 a year, which covers the financing cost, administrative cost (say, $11), and reasonable profit (say, $20) for the lessor.

Reviewing the financial performance, net income continues to be reported as $192 for the projected year because the operating lease payment is equal to the total of depreciation and interest expense in the asset purchase scenario. Consequently, the net margin is the same as in the asset purchase scenario. However, the structural effects of an operating lease are clearly evident on the balance sheet when compared with the asset purchase scenario. Assets and liabilities are underreported. Under U.S. GAAP, the asset *equipment used under operating lease* and the liability *operating lease obligation* are not reported. This is sometimes referred to as *off-balance-sheet financing*. As a result, asset turnover is stronger and financial leverage is stronger than when the asset is purchased. The asset turnover shows greater strength (2.28 versus 1.60) because the new asset is not recorded on the books. Likewise, financial leverage shows a stronger position (2.21 versus 3.15) because the ongoing liability is not recorded on the books either.

While the economics and realities of the situation (a 10-year use of the underlying asset) are the same under either scenario, the reporting and analytical results differ. Under the operating lease scenario as presented on Table 13-1, the company effectively has gained off-balance-sheet financing. This is to say, the company entered into a long-term lease, gained the long-term use of the asset, and never recognized this additional commitment (or liability). The accounting profession recognized this inconsistency and is currently addressing it.

Accounting for Leases—U.S. GAAP

In November 1976, the Financial Accounting Standards Board issued its Statement of Financial Accounting Standards No. 13, Accounting for Leases. FASB Statement No. 13 has implications both for the use of leases and for their accounting treatment. The elements of FASB Statement No. 13 most relevant for financial analysis of leases are summarized below. For some types of leases, this FASB statement requires that the obligation be capitalized on the asset side of the balance sheet with a reduced lease obligation on the liability side. The accounting treatment depends on the type of lease. From the standpoint of the lessee, there are:

1. Capital leases
2. Operating leases (all leases other than capital leases)

From the standpoint of the lessee, if a lease is not a capital lease, it is considered to be an operating lease.

A lease is classified in FASB Statement No. 13 as a capital lease if it meets *one or more* of four Paragraph 7 criteria:

1. The lease transfers ownership of the property to the lessee by the end of its term.

2. The lease gives the lessee the option to purchase the property at a price sufficiently below the expected fair value of the property, and the exercise of the option is highly probable.

3. The lease term is equal to 75 percent or more of the estimated economic life of the property.

4. The present value of the minimum lease payments exceeds 90 percent of the fair value of the property at the inception of the lease. The discount factor to be used in calculating the present value is the implicit rate used by the lessor or the lessee's incremental borrowing rate, whichever is lower. (Note that the lower discount factor represents a higher present value factor and therefore a higher calculated present value for a given pattern of lease payments. It thus increases the likelihood that the 90 percent test will be met and that the lease will be classified as a capital lease.)

The classification of capital lease is more detailed than the two categories of operating and financial leases described earlier for the lessor and includes:

1. Sales-type leases
2. Direct-financing leases
3. Leveraged leases
4. Operating leases (all leases other than the first three)

The first three types are financing leases or capital leases for accounting purposes. Sales-type leases and direct-financing leases meet one or more of the four Paragraph 7 criteria and both of the Paragraph 8 criteria, which are:

1. The collectability of the minimum lease payments is reasonably predictable.
2. No important uncertainties surround the amount of unreimbursable costs yet to be incurred by the lessor under the lease.

Sales-type leases normally arise when manufacturers or dealers use leasing in marketing their products. Direct-financing leases are leases (other than leveraged leases) for which the cost-of-carrying amount is equal to the fair value of the leased property at the inception of the lease, which is the asset value that gets reflected on the balance sheet of the lessee. Leveraged leases are direct-financing leases in which substantial financing is provided by a long-term creditor on a nonrecourse basis with respect to the general credit of the lessor.

Accounting Performance with a Capital Lease
For operating leases, rentals must be charged to expense each accounting period over the lease term. Thus, clearly, a one-week car rental while on a business trip, a three-month rental of additional office space, and a six-month rental of a billboard are examples of operating leases. The associated fees are properly charged to rental expense and handled as in the second column ("Operating lease") in Table 13-1. Footnotes detail future rental obligations for each of the remaining years and in total.

A lease that meets any one of the four criteria just noted is considered a capital lease. For lessees, capital leases are to be capitalized and shown on the balance sheet both as a fixed asset and a noncurrent obligation. This is similar to how the purchase of the asset would be recorded. Capitalization represents the present value of the minimum lease payments minus that portion of lease payments representing executory costs, such as insurance, maintenance, and taxes to be paid by the lessor (including any profit return in such charges). The discount factor is as described in Paragraph 7(4)—the lower of the implicit rates used by the lessor and the incremental borrowing rate of the lessee.

For example, the lease in column two of Table 13-1 would have been classified as a capital lease because it meets at least the third test of Paragraph 7 (lease term is equal to 75 percent or more of the estimated economic life of the property). Recall that the operating lease payment was $180 per year. This payment included $11 of administrative expense and $20 of profit for the lessor. Therefore, the net lease payment was $149 per year. Similar to purchasing the asset, capitalizing this lease payment at an 8 percent incremental borrowing rate for the lessee yields a present value of $1,000 (or the cost of the equipment).

The asset must be amortized in a manner consistent with the lessee's normal depreciation policy for owned assets. During the lease term, each lease payment is to be allocated between a reduction of the obligation and the interest expense to produce a constant rate of interest on the remaining balance of the obligation. Thus, for capital leases, the balance sheet includes the items in the final column of Table 13-1. The accounting for the capital lease is the same as for the purchase and borrow scenario (column one of Table 13-1). Both the asset and liability are recognized on the balance sheet. Off-balance-sheet financing is gone!

For the year, TSC recognizes $100 of depreciation expense and $80 in interest. At the end of the first year, the leased asset has a book value of $900, and the lease obligation has a value of $931. The value of the lease obligation reflects the first year's lease payment of $149, with $80 assigned to interest expense and a $69 principal repayment. The results of a capitalized lease or an outright purchase and borrow are identical. Thus, through FASB Statement No. 13, capitalized leases have eliminated the common distortions between leasing and borrowing.

In addition to the balance sheet capitalization of capital leases, substantial additional footnote disclosures are required for both capital and operating leases. These include a description of leasing arrangements, an analysis of the leased property under capital leases by major classes of property, a schedule by years of future minimum lease payments (with executory and interest costs broken out for capital leases), and contingent rentals for operating leases.

FASB Statement No. 13 sets forth requirements for capitalizing leases and for standardizing disclosures by lessees for both capital leases and operating leases. Capital lease commitments, therefore, do not represent off-balance-sheet financing for capital assets. Standard disclosure requirements provide information about operating leases in the footnotes. Hence the argument that leasing represents a form of off-balance-sheet financing that lenders may not take into account in their analysis of the financial position of firms seeking financing is a weak argument.

Sophisticated lenders may never have been fooled by most off-balance-sheet leasing obligations. However, the capitalization of capital leases and the standard disclosure requirements for operating leases will make it easier for general users of financial reports to obtain additional information on firms' leasing obligations. Hence the requirements of FASB Statement No. 13 are useful. Probably, the extent or use of leasing will remain substantially unaltered because the particular circumstances that have provided a basis for its use in the past are not likely to be greatly affected by the increased disclosure requirements.

International Accounting Standards do not recognize operating leases. Instead, lessees recognize a right-of-use asset along with an obligation to pay rentals liability. As the United States considers adoption of international accounting standards, operating leases may become obsolete.

THE INVESTMENT DECISION

The first step before making the lease or borrow decision is to make the investment decision. Before going any further, you must be sure that the investment should be undertaken in the first place. If the project has a large negative net present value, it will not make any difference how you finance it. Any value added by financing can be easily outweighed by unfavorable operating cash flows from the project itself. Also, remember that strict financial leases are not cancelable, except via bankruptcy.

Owning an asset exposes one to more risk than simply taking a lending or a lease position. Owning and operating a project involves the total risk of its cash flows, not merely the relatively secure risk of a debt position. Let's say, for example, using the tools of Chapter 11, that we estimate that the appropriate cost of capital for this project is 10 percent.

Further, after discussing the potential new product investment with marketing, sales, engineering, production, and logistics, let us accept the assumptions and cash flows as seen in Table 13-2. By the way, this is a good refresher for the topics covered in Chapters 9 and 10.

Under our assumptions, the project generates an incremental cash flow of $140,000 in the first year and grows to $255,000 of cash flow in the fourth and fifth years. For simplicity, straight-line depreciation is used over a five-year period with no estimated salvage value. Also, there are no working capital implications. With a 10 percent cost of capital, these assumptions and resulting cash flow provide a positive net present value (NPV) of $165,000, and the investment should be made. The project is a go!

The question now shifts to how are we going to finance the project? Will we use all equity? Will we use some equity? How large of a role does debt play? These were the issues considered in Chapter 11. If we conclude that we will not issue any additional equity and that we will raise the funds through the debt market, then we need to seek the lowest cost of debt. Leasing is merely an alternative debt form. We are now ready to make the next decision—lease versus borrow.

THE FINANCING DECISION: LEASE VERSUS BORROW

We next consider the framework for the analysis of the cost of owning versus the cost of leasing. We are simply trying to minimize costs and select the lower-cost option—owning and borrowing or leasing.

Cost of Borrowing

We assume that the loan of $625,000 is paid off at a level annual amount that covers annual interest charges plus amortization of the principal. Just as we did in Chapter 8, the loan payments are an annuity that can be determined by the use of a financial calculator (PV = $625,000, I/Yr = 7.5 percent, N = 5) or the present value of an annuity formula, as shown in Eq. (13.1):

$$\$625,000 = \sum_{t=1}^{n} \frac{a_t}{(1+k_b)^t} \tag{13.1}$$

$$a_t = \frac{\$625,000}{(\text{PVIFA})\,(7.5\%, 5 \text{ years})}$$

$$= \frac{625,000}{4.04588} = \$154,478$$

The present value interest factors (PVIF) is from the time value of money tables discussed in Chapter 7. A portion has been replicated in this chapter as Table 13-3. However, Table 13-3 calculates the present value factor by year at

T A B L E   13-2

Capital Project Evaluation
($ 000s)

	Year 0	Year 1	Year 2	Year 3	Year 4	Year 5
Assumptions						
Investment	$ (625)					
First-year sales		$ 1,000				
Sales growth			40.0%	20.0%	10.0%	0.0%
Cost of goods sold		65.0%	64.0%	63.5%	63.5%	63.5%
Selling and marketing		20.0%	20.0%	18.0%	18.0%	18.0%
Depreciation		$ 125	$ 125	$ 125	$ 125	$ 125
Tax rate		40.0%	40.0%	40.0%	40.0%	40.0%
Cost of capital	10.0%					
Capital Investment Analysis						
Sales		$ 1,000	$ 1,400	$ 1,680	$ 1,848	$ 1,848
Cost of goods sold		650	896	1,067	1,173	1,173
Selling and marketing		200	280	302	333	333
Depreciation		125	125	125	125	125
Total expenses		$ 975	$ 1,301	$ 1,494	$ 1,631	$ 1,631
Operating income		25	99	186	217	217
Taxes		10	40	74	87	87
After-tax operating income		$ 15	$ 59	$ 112	$ 130	$ 130
After-tax operating income		$ 15	$ 59	$ 112	$ 130	$ 130
Depreciation		125	125	125	125	125
Investment cash flow	$ (625)	$ 140	$ 184	$ 237	$ 255	$ 255
Net present value	$ 165					

certain discount rates. Only for year 5 at 4.5 and 7.5 percent are the present value interest factor for an annuity (PVIFA) presented. We will use these values later.

Solving Eq. (13.1) for the annual loan payments results in $154,478, which represents the principal plus interest payments listed in column (3) of Table 13-4. Notice that the present value of five years of $154,478 payments at 7.5 percent is $625,000, or the original amount of the investment. The sum of these five annual payments is $772,390, which represents repayment of the principal of $625,000 plus the sum of the annual interest payments. The interest

TABLE   13-3

Time Value of Money: Present Value Interest Factors
(PV of $1)

Year	4.00%	4.50%	5.00%	···	7.00%	7.50%	8.00%
1	0.96154	0.95694	0.95238	···	0.93458	0.93023	0.92593
2	0.92456	0.91573	0.90703	···	0.87344	0.86533	0.85734
3	0.88900	0.87630	0.86384	···	0.81630	0.80496	0.79383
4	0.85480	0.83856	0.82270	···	0.76290	0.74880	0.73503
5	0.82193	0.80245	0.78353	···	0.71299	0.69656	0.68058
Sum		4.38998	PVIFA			4.04588	PVIFA
6	0.79031	0.76790	0.74622	···	0.66634	0.64796	0.63017
7	0.75992	0.73483	0.71068	···	0.62275	0.60275	0.58349
8	0.73069	0.70319	0.67684	···	0.58201	0.56070	0.54027
9	0.70259	0.67290	0.64461	···	0.54393	0.52158	0.50025
10	0.67556	0.64393	0.61391	···	0.50835	0.48519	0.46319

TABLE   13-4

Loan Amortization Table

Year (1)	Beginning Balance (2)	Payment (3)	7.5% Interest (2) × 0.075 (4)	Principal (3) – (4) (5)	Ending Balance (2) – (5) (6)
1	$ 625,000	$ 154,478	$ 46,875	$ 107,603	$ 517,397
2	517,397	154,478	38,805	115,673	401,724
3	401,724	154,478	30,129	124,349	277,375
4	277,375	154,478	20,803	133,675	143,700
5	143,700	154,478	10,778	143,700	-
Total		$ 772,390	$ 147,390	$ 625,000	
PV of the payment =		$625,000			

payments of each year are determined by multiplying column (2), the balance of principal owed at the beginning of the year, by 7.50 percent, the assumed cost of borrowing. The sum of the annual interest payments does in fact equal the total interest of $147,390, obtained by deducting the principal of $625,000 from the total of the five annual payments shown in column (3).

A schedule of cash outflows for the borrow/own (or simply the borrow) alternative then is developed to determine the present value of the after-tax cash flows and, ultimately, the cost of borrowing. This is illustrated in Table 13-5.

The analysis of cash outflows begins with a listing of the loan payments, as shown in column (2). Next, the annual interest payments from Table 13-4 are listed in column (3). Since straight-line depreciation is assumed, the annual depreciation charges are $125,000 per year, as shown in column (4). The tax shelter to the owner of the equipment is the sum of the annual interest plus depreciation multiplied by the tax rate (40.0%). While interest is a tax deductible expense, we are already capturing the cash-flow implications for the interest component within the annual loan payment, as in Table 13-3. Consequently, we only need to explicitly include the tax savings that result from paying interest. Likewise, depreciation is a noncash expense that does provide a tax shelter or tax reduction. The amounts of the total annual tax shield are shown in column (5). Column (6) is cash flow after taxes, obtained by deducting column (5) from column (2).

Since the cost of borrowing is 7.5 percent, its after-tax cost with a 40.0 percent tax rate is 4.5 percent. The present value factors at 4.5 percent are listed in column (7). Once again, these values are found in Table 13-3. These factors are multiplied by the after-tax cash flows to obtain column (8), the present value of the after-tax costs of owning the asset. The total cost of borrowing and owning is $405,500 in present value terms.

Cost of Leasing

Before discussing the cost of leasing from the lessee's (or renter's) perspective, let's explore the lessor's viewpoint to determine the annual lease costs.

Establishing the Lease Payment—Lessor's Viewpoint

The leasing company, or lessor, could be a commercial bank, a subsidiary of a commercial bank, or an independent leasing company. These various types of lessors are considered to be providing financial intermediation services. Each form of financial intermediary is considered to be providing a product, which represents a form of senior debt financing to the company that uses the equipment. Since the product that is being sold by the financial intermediary is a debt instrument, the income to that intermediary is considered to be a return on debt that earns the intermediary's cost of capital. Said differently, a leasing company (or commercial bank) is highly leveraged and typically financed with almost all debt. In this way, the financial intermediary's cost of capital is approximately equal to

TABLE 13-5

Cost of Borrowing

Year (1)	Loan Payment (2)	Interest Expense (Table 13-4) (3)	Depreciation Expense (4)	Tax Shield [(3) + (4)] × 0.40 (5)	After Tax Cash Flow (2)−(5) (6)	0.075 × (1 − 0.40) PVIF 4.5% (7)	Present Value (6) × (7) (8)
1	$ 154,478	$ 46,875	$ 125,000	$ 68,750	$ 85,728	0.95694	$ 82,036
2	154,478	38,805	125,000	65,522	88,956	0.91573	81,460
3	154,478	30,129	125,000	62,052	92,426	0.87630	80,993
4	154,478	20,803	125,000	58,321	96,157	0.83856	80,633
5	154,478	10,778	125,000	54,311	100,167	0.80245	80,378
Total	$ 772,390	$ 147,390	$ 625,000	$ 308,956	$ 463,434	4.38998	$ 405,500

the rate charged on the debt (or equivalent) instruments that comprise its assets (the assets that the lessor will lease).

Given this premise, the lessor is truly a financial intermediary and a conduit for capital to the lessee. Think of the lessor as 100 percent debt at a pretax cost of capital of 7.5 percent and an after-tax weighted cost of capital of 4.5 percent. In other words, the bank or leasing company has to earn at least 4.5 percent after taxes for the lease to have a positive net present value. Note that the after-tax required rate of return is equal to:

$$\text{Lessor's cost of capital} = k_{LOR} = k_b(1 - T) = 0.075(1 - 0.40) = 0.045$$

With these assumptions, the equilibrium lease-rental rate in a competitive market of lessors can be calculated. What has been posed is a standard capital budgeting question: What cash-flow return from the use of an asset will earn the applicable cost of capital? The return is composed of two elements: the cash inflow from the lease-rental and the tax shelter from depreciation. Earlier, we looked at the investment decision for the user of the asset. Does the investment provide enough cash to make it economically viable and yield a positive net present value (NPV)?

The lessor needs to address a similar question before offering to lease the asset: At what minimum lease payment will the lessor be willing to enter into the lease? What lease payment gives the lessor a positive (or $0.0) NPV?

Next, we can compute the minimum competitive lease fee that would be charged by the lessor. Equation (13.2) discounts the lease cash flows at the lessor's after-tax cost of capital (4.5 percent). The cash flows are the after-tax lease payments received plus the depreciation tax shield provided because the lessor owns the asset. The NPV of the lease to the lessor is calculated using Eq. (13.2):

$$
\begin{aligned}
\text{NPV}_{LOR} &= -I_0 + \sum_{t=1}^{n} \frac{L_t\,(1-T)+T\,\text{Dep}_t}{(1+k_{LOR})^t} \qquad\qquad (13.2)\\
&= -I_0 + \text{PVIFA}\,(4.5\%, 5\ \text{years})\,[L_t\,(1-T)+T\,\text{Dep}_t]
\end{aligned}
$$

where Lt = periodic lease payment
T = tax rate
Dep_t = depreciation

Now let's solve for the equilibrium lease-rental rate required by the lessor by using the data inputs we have provided. The NPV of the lease is set equal to zero so that we can compute the minimum lease payment required by the lessor. The minimum fee also will be the competitive fee if the leasing industry is perfectly competitive.

$$
\begin{aligned}
0 &= -\$625{,}000 + 4.38998[0.60L_t + 0.40(\$125{,}000)]\\
&= -\$625{,}000 + 2.63399L_t + \$219{,}500\\
L_t &= \$153{,}949
\end{aligned}
$$

The tax shield on the depreciation provides the lessor with a $219,500 benefit in present value terms. The tax shield reduces the net investment amount and results in a minimum lease payment of $153,949 per year to fully compensate the leasing company and to leave it with a $0 NPV. Another way you could calculate the required lease payment, use a financial calculator [PV = $625,000 (the amount invested); $N = 5$, I/Yr = 4.5 (the after-tax cost of capital)] to get the necessary cash flow of $142,369 each year. The lessor gets a $50,000 tax savings from the depreciation ($125,000 times a 40 percent tax shelter), which leaves $92,369 per year lease requirement after taxes. Adjusting this for taxes yields the previously calculated required lease payment of $153,949 ($92,369/0.60).

Now that we have looked at the transaction from the lessor's perspective, we are ready to resume our analysis of the lease versus borrow decision from the lessee's viewpoint.

Cost of Leasing—Lessee's Perspective

While we developed the logic of how the lessor arrived at the lease payment amount, as a lessee, we simply don't care that much. We just want to know the leasing fee, and obviously, we want to pay less than the original offer. In a similar way, we always would negotiate for a lower price on the equipment or on the lease rate.

The total costs of leasing the asset can be obtained as shown in Table 13-6. Presented with a lease-rental rate of $153,949, the user firm takes the lease fee as an input in making a comparison of the cost of leasing with the cost of borrowing. The annual lease payments are shown in column (2). By multiplying 0.60 (or 1 − tax rate) times the column (2) figures, the after-tax cost of leasing is obtained and shown in column (3). The present value factors (4.5 percent; see Table 13-3) are listed in column (4) and multiplied by the amounts in column (3). Column (5) presents the after-tax costs of leasing by year, which total to $405,500 of net present value cost of leasing.

T A B L E   13-6

Cost of Leasing

Year (1)	Lease Payment (2)	After-Tax Cash Flow (2) × (1 − 0.40) (3)	0.075 × (1 − 0.40) PVIF 4.5% (4)	Present Value (3) × (4) (5)
1	$ 153,949	$ 92,369	0.95694	$ 88,392
2	153,949	92,369	0.91573	84,585
3	153,949	92,369	0.87630	80,943
4	153,949	92,369	0.83856	77,457
5	153,949	92,369	0.80245	74,122
Total	$ 769,745	$ 461,845	4.38998	$ 405,500

Net Advantage of Leasing

From the illustration it can be seen that there is no advantage to leasing. That is, from Table 13.5 the cost of borrowing ($405,500) and from Table 13.6 the cost of leasing ($405,500) are identical in present value or economic (financial) terms. From a financial perspective, the businessperson should be indifferent between (1) borrowing the money, purchasing/owning the assets, and operating the assets and (2) leasing and simply operating the assets.

More formally, this can be presented as Eq. (13.3), the *net advantage of leasing* (NAL):

$$\text{NAL} = \text{cost of leasing} - \text{cost of borrowing} \qquad (13.3)$$

If the NAL is positive, then the asset should be leased. If the NAL is negative, the financial advantage favors borrowing to own the asset. In our case, the NAL is zero!

However, a number of factors could change this result: differences in costs of capital, differences in applicable tax rates or usability of tax subsidies, differences in patterns of payments required under leasing versus owning, and so on. This equality relationship is a helpful starting point and useful to understand and measure the effects of structural factors that may cause differences in the lease versus borrow decision.

Two final points of clarification are in order. First, the modified accelerated cost recovery system (MACRS) and not straight-line depreciation should have been used for any computation involving after-tax depreciation for both the borrower and the lessor. For simplicity in discussing these concepts, straight-line depreciation was presented. Second, this discussion assumed annual lease payments made in arrears, that is, at the end of each year. While this is computationally consistent with the capital investment discussions in Chapters 9 and 10, most actual lease payments occur monthly or quarterly at the beginning of the period and not at the end. In practice, these two adjustments should be made to all actual computations.

The Effect of Taxes

Whenever the lessor (owner of the asset, the leasing company) has a higher tax rate than the lessee (user of the asset), there is a possibility (but not necessity) of a financial advantage of leasing over borrowing in order to finance a project. To illustrate this result, let us assume that the numbers from the lessor's point of view are unchanged. With a 40.0 percent tax rate, the lessor would require a lease fee of $L_t = \$153,949$ in order to earn 4.5 percent after taxes. But suppose that the lessee's tax rate is 0 percent rather than 40.0 percent, as assumed earlier. This may be the case for a corporation with large net operating losses (NOLs), a university, church, or other nonprofit entity. This is one of the major areas where there can be significant structural differences between a lessor and a lessee.

Table 13-7 combines the two analyses, cost of borrowing and cost of leasing, into one schedule that ends with the net advantage of leasing. Just as a reminder, we are trying to minimize the cost.

In this example, the net advantage of leasing is positive because the cost of borrowing is greater than the cost of leasing. The lease has a positive NPV when compared with borrowing. Therefore, from the lessee's point of view, leasing is preferred to borrowing as a means of financing the project. The increased value to the lessee results from the fact that the lessor can take advantage of the tax shelters (depreciation and interest expenses) because of the lessor's higher tax rate.

If an acquirer of an asset has some special tax circumstances [e.g., large net operating losses (NOLs) that will be used to offset any taxable income for the foreseeable future] or the entity is a tax-free entity (e.g., a university), leasing should be considered. While it is impossible to say that leasing always will be more advantageous for an organization with a lower tax rate, it is a sure sign that additional analysis should be conducted.

This example started by assuming equivalent tax rates for the lessor and lessee. Lease payments were established on that premise. The lessor is made whole at lease rates of $153,949 per year. From the tax-free lessor perspective, even if the lease payments rose to $154,200 (an average of the lease payment and the debt payment), there is an advantage to leasing of $1,125. In fact, it is only when annual lease payments reach the same level as annual loan payments ($154,478) that the user of the asset becomes indifferent to leasing. In practice, the actual annual lease payments may be negotiated to somewhere in between $153,949 and $154,478 depending on competitive forces and the negotiating skills of the lessor and lessee.

The analytical framework established in Table 13-7 will be useful as we consider other differences that may arise between lessees and lessors.

ADDITIONAL INFLUENCES ON LEASING VERSUS BORROWING

While a tax rate differential is potentially one important distinctive and advantageous difference in the lessor's and lessee's analysis, a number of other operational ownership factors can influence the user firm's costs of leasing versus owning capital assets. These include:

1. Differences in asset purchase price
2. Differences in maintenance costs
3. Benefits of residual values to the owner of the assets
4. Possibility of reducing obsolescence costs

These four operational differences are discussed below.

TABLE 13-7

Net Advantage of Leasing: Tax-Free Lessee

Cost of Borrowing (similar to Table 13-5)

Year (1)	Loan Payment (2)	Interest Table 13.4 (3)	Depreciation Expense (4)	Tax Shield [(3) + (4)] × 0.00 (5)	After-Tax Cash Flow (2) – (5) (6)	0.075 × (1 – 0.00) PVIF 7.5% (7)	Present Value (6) × (7) (8)
1	$ 154,478	$ 46,875	$ 125,000	$ —	$ 154,478	0.93023	$ 143,700
2	154,478	38,805	125,000	—	154,478	0.86533	133,675
3	154,478	30,129	125,000	—	154,478	0.80496	124,349
4	154,478	20,803	125,000	—	154,478	0.74880	115,673
5	154,478	10,778	125,000	—	154,478	0.69656	107,603
Total	$ 772,390	$ 147,390	$ 625,000	$ —	$ 772,390	4.04588	$ 625,000

Cost of borrowing

Cost of Leasing (similar to Table 13-6)

Year (1)	Lease Payment (2)	After-Tax Cash Flow (2) × (1 – 0.00) (3)	0.075 × (1 – 0.00) PVIF 7.5% (4)	Present Value (3) × (4) (5)
1	$ 153,949	$ 153,949	0.93023	$ 143,208
2	153,949	153,949	0.86533	133,217
3	153,949	153,949	0.80496	123,923
4	153,949	153,949	0.74880	115,277
5	153,949	153,949	0.69656	107,235
Total	$ 769,745	$ 769,745	4.04588	$ 622,860

Cost of leasing $ 622,860

Net advantage of leasing $ 2,140

Differences in Asset Purchase Price

Assuming a competitive economic situation, asset purchase prices generally should be equal for anyone purchasing the same asset. A piece of manufacturing equipment should cost the same amount regardless of whether the lessor or the lessee is purchasing it. This was the assumption earlier when the asset cost was $625,000 for both the lessor and the lessee.

However, there may be situations involving specific assets where the lessor has a distinct purchase-price advantage. For example, some automobile leasing companies get preferential pricing of $1,000 or more below invoice because they are one of the top 10 automobile purchasers in the world. In this case, the leasing company (lessor) can price the lease with this preferential pricing in mind and pass some (or all) of these savings along to the lessee. Another example, with similar circumstances, would be in the technology/computer hardware area.

Land and/or buildings provide another example. It ultimately may be less expensive for a lessor to purchase a 50-acre tract of land than for 10 possible users to purchase ten 5-acre tracts of land. It may be less expensive for the lessor to build one distribution center complex than for 10 different users to build 10 different facilities. If for no other reason than the shared infrastructure (i.e., roadways, permits, initial security installation, etc.), a pricing advantage may be in favor of the lessor and may be passed along in whole (or in part) to the lessee in the form of a reduced lease payment.

Differences in Maintenance Costs

Maintenance costs are included in the lease-rental rate in some cases. For this to be a structural operating advantage, the key question is whether the maintenance can be performed at a lower cost by the lessor or by the lessee.

In the preceding examples, a lessor may or may not be able to provide less expensive maintenance in a timely manner on vehicles or computer hardware. Certainly, such activities would be contracted for by the leasing company, and the question remains: Can the lessor supply the maintenance at a lower price than that for which the user-lessee can contract separately? If the lessor is large, maybe some economies of scale would result that could be passed on as lower lease payments. However, depending on the background (i.e., industry, size, etc.) of the lessee and criticality of the asset to the user, it may be more cost-effective with better, more-timely performance for the lessee to have a separately contracted maintenance department.

In the example of the distribution center, the lessor may be able to provide ongoing building maintenance, area maintenance, security, and so on more efficiently (with less cost) to 10 lessees than each individual lessee could do for themselves on a separate tract of land. On the other hand, for specific manufacturing equipment, the maintenance advantage probably goes to the user-lessee rather than to the financing company.

Residual Values

When a user-lessee leases an asset, the lessor owns the property at the expiration of the lease. The value of the property at the end of the lease is called the *residual value*. On the surface, it would appear that where residual values are large, owning is less expensive than leasing. Once again, these benefits can be passed on to the user-lessee in reduced lease payments that consider an estimated residual value. Or the lessee can be given an opportunity to purchase the asset at the expiration of the lease. Consequently, the existence of a residual value by itself is unlikely to result in materially lower costs of owning.

For the most part, it is difficult to generalize about whether residual value considerations are likely to make the effective cost of leasing higher or lower than the cost of owning. In a limited number of cases, such as vehicles and computer hardware, the lessor once again may have a systematic advantage related to residual or resale value. In the automobile leasing example started earlier, not only does the leasing company have access to vehicles at a lower price, but it also has better access to the resale market and commands a slightly higher residual value. If the lessor chooses, this difference can be passed on in the form of a lower lease payment.

Obsolescence Costs

Another popular notion is that leasing costs will be lower because of the rapid obsolescence of some kinds of equipment. If equipment obsolescence is high, leasing rates also will reflect obsolescence. Thus, in general terms, it can be argued that neither residual values nor obsolescence rates basically can affect the relative cost of owning versus leasing unless the lessor has some operating advantage that increases residual value or reduces the effects of obsolescence.

Certain leasing companies may be well equipped to handle the obsolescence problem. For example, some large equipment manufacturers are also reconditioners of their products and specialists in the tasks that their products perform. Clark Equipment Company has expertise in materials-handling equipment (both new and preowned) and has its own sales organization as well as a system of distributors. This may enable Clark to write favorable leases for equipment. If the equipment becomes obsolete to one user, it may be satisfactory for other users with different materials-handling requirements, and Clark is well situated to locate the other users. The situation is similar in computer leasing.

This illustration indicates how a leasing company, by combining lending with other specialized services, may reduce the costs of obsolescence and increase effective residual values. By such operations, the total cost of obtaining the use of such equipment is reduced. Possibly other institutions that do not combine financing and specialist functions (e.g., manufacturing, reconditioning, servicing, and sales) may, in conjunction with financing institutions, perform the overall functions as efficiently and at as low a cost as do integrated leasing companies. However, this is a factual matter depending on the relative efficiency of the competing firms in different lines of business and with different kinds of equipment.

OTHER CITED INFLUENCES

The following benefits are cited on occasion as reasons to lease or own an asset. I am not convinced that these distinctions exist except in very specific cases over short time periods:

1. *More favorable tax treatment, such as more rapid write-off.* The Internal Revenue Service (IRS) tax code applies equally to lessors and lessees. Of course, MACRS is the IRS depreciation, and I simply considered straight-line depreciation for discussion purposes.

2. *Possible differences in the ability to use tax reduction opportunities, as shown above.*

3. *Different costs of capital for the lessor versus the user firm.* If the lessor has a lower cost of capital than the user, the cost of leasing is likely to be lower than the cost of owning to the user.

4. *Financing costs higher in leasing.* A leasing company generally evaluates its clients just as a financing company would evaluate a loan applicant. Under competitive market conditions, it is unlikely that the disequilibrium conditions implied by the different costs of capital will persist. The supply of lessors either will increase or decrease to restore equilibrium in the benefits to a user lessee firm from leasing versus owning an asset.

5. *Possibility of increased credit availability under leasing.* As we saw before when we compared Table 13-1, asset purchase (column 1) with a capital lease (Table 13-1, column 3), the capital lease requirements of FASB Statement No. 13 has gone a long way to neutralize this point.

The first two items derive their benefit from the tax structure, whereas the last three items are related to financing.

INCLUDING THE ADDITIONAL
INFLUENCES IN THE ANALYSIS

From operations, differences in purchase price, maintenance costs, residual value, and obsolescence costs may provide a large lessor with economies of scale and an opportunity to pass on some of these cost reductions in the form of lower lease payments. As you saw earlier, tax-rate advantages can be claimed by the lessor and passed along to the lessee in the form of lower lease payments.

In the illustration discussed earlier, it was assumed that the lessor and lessee had the same $625,000 purchase price and that the maintenance costs, residual value, and obsolescence costs were the same. Although the illustration was silent as to the last three influences (indicating that their values were zero), we could have assumed that maintenance costs were $10,000 per year for both the lessor and the lessee. With the same tax rate and discount rate, the present value cost is the same for the lease or own-borrow scenarios and consequently does not need to be considered.

To illustrate, let's make the following changes for both the lessor and the lessee:

	Lessor/Lessee
Maintenance costs (per year)	$10,000
Residual (salvage or terminal) value	$50,000

We will assume the same tax rate (40.0 percent) and borrowing rate (7.5 percent pretax, 4.5 percent posttax).

As we did before, let's examine the lessor's view and determine the minimum lease payment under this scenario by employing Eq. (13.2):

$$\text{NPV}_{\text{LOR}} = -I_0 + \sum_{t=1}^{n} \frac{L_t\,(1-T)+T\,\text{Dep}_t}{(1+k_{\text{LOR}})^t}$$
$$= -I_0 + \text{PVIFA}\,(4.5\%, 5\text{ years})\,[L_t\,(1-T)+T\,\text{Dep}_t]$$

We assumed that the asset is completely depreciated. That is, we ignore the residual value when calculating annual straight-line depreciation. We do this in order to better isolate the impact of the residual value assumption. This equation must be expanded to consider the annual maintenance costs and the residual value, as shown by Eq. (13.4):

$$\text{NPV}_{\text{LOR}} = -I_0 + \sum_{t=1}^{n} \frac{L_t\,(1-T)+T\,\text{Dep}_t - M_t\,(1-T)}{(1+k_{\text{LOR}})^t} + \frac{\text{RV}(1-T)}{(1+k_{\text{LOR}})^n} \qquad (13.4)$$
$$= -I_0 + \text{PVIFA}\,(4.5\%, 5\text{ years})\,[L_t\,(1-T)+T\,\text{Dep}_t - M_t\,(1-T)]$$
$$+ \text{PVIF}\,(4.5\%, 5\text{ years})[\text{RV}(1-T)]$$

where M_t = periodic maintenance costs
     RV = residual value—end of the period, year n

As we did before, we can solve this equation for the minimum lease payments or the point where the NPV_{LOR} is equal to zero:

$$\$0 = -\$625,000 + (4.38998)[0.6L_t + 0.4(\$125,000) - \$10,000(0.6)] +$$
$$(0.80245)[\$50,000(0.6)]$$
$$= -\$625,000 + 2.63399L_t + \$219,500 - \$26,340 + \$24,074$$
$$L_t = \$154,810$$

The minimum lease payment is $154,810 (compared with $153,949 from the preceding example). In this scenario and in present value terms, the lessor now has a $24,074 residual value offset by a maintenance expense of $26,340. Compared with the earlier example, this investment costs the lessor $2,266 more than before. These increased costs are passed along to find the slightly higher minimum lease payment of $154,810.

Table 13-8 combines the previous analysis of Tables 13-4, 13-5, and 13-6 into one table. This new table shows the neutral situation where the lessor's operating effects (i.e., maintenance costs and residual value) are the same for the user-lessee as well. Notice that the net advantage of leasing is $0.

What if the lessor enjoys operating advantage over the lessee? Now let's examine the situation when the lessee has purchase price, maintenance cost, and residual value/obsolescence cost advantages as follows:

	Lessor	User-Lessee
Purchase price	$625,000	$650,000
Maintenance costs (per year)	10,000	12,000
Residual value	50,000	40,000

Table 13-9 presents the cost of purchasing and borrowing versus the cost of leasing at the lessor's minimum lease payment. In this case, the leasing option has a $26,302 advantage, and the user should enter into the lease arrangement. Notice that the cost of leasing is still $407,767 (as in Table 13-8), but the cost of ownership has increased.

However, chances are that the lessor would not offer as favorable leasing terms as this and probably would negotiate a higher lease payment. As long as the lease payment is less than $164,796, there is an advantage to leasing!

COST COMPARISON FOR OPERATING LEASES

Under an operating lease, the lessor must bear the risk involved in the use of the asset because the lease is cancelable and therefore may be returned by the lessee. Operating leases are virtually equivalent to having the lessor own the equipment and operate it. In these circumstances, the required rate of return is not the rate on a portfolio of assets of loaned funds. Rather, it is something higher. The operating lease, from the lessor's point of view, has three elements: (1) the cash flows received from the lease contract, (2) the expected market or salvage value of the asset, and (3) the value of an American put option. The put option captures the present value of the lessee's right to cancel the lease and return the asset whenever the value of the economic rent on the asset falls below the lease fee. This may happen if the asset wears out faster than anticipated or if the asset (e.g., a computer) becomes obsolete faster than expected.

Because the lessor is giving up something by allowing the lease to be canceled, it is necessary to charge a higher lease fee. The lessee would be badly

TABLE 13-8

Net Advantage of Leasing: Neutral Operating Benefits

A. Loan Amortization Table (similar to Table 13-4)

Year (1)	Beginning Balance (2)	Loan Payment (3)	7.5% Interest (2) × 0.075 (4)	Principal (3) − (4) (5)	Ending Balance (2) − (5) (6)
1	$ 625,000	$ 154,478	$ 46,875	$ 107,603	$ 517,397
2	517,397	154,478	38,805	115,673	401,724
3	401,724	154,478	30,129	124,349	277,375
4	277,375	154,478	20,803	133,675	143,700
5	143,700	154,478	10,778	143,700	–
Total		$ 772,390	$ 147,390	$ 625,000	

PV of the payment = $ 625,000

B. Cost of Borrowing (similar to Table 13-5)

Year (1)	Loan Payment (2)	Interest Expense (3)	Depreciation Expense (4)	Tax Shield [(3) + (4)] × 0.40 (5)	Maintenance Costs (6)	After-Tax Maintenance (6) × (1 − 0.40) (7)	Residual Value (8)	After-Tax Residual (8) × (1 − 0.40) (9)	After-Tax Cash Flow (2) − (5) + (7) − (9) (10)	0.075 × (1 − 0.40) PVIF 4.5% (11)	Present Value (6) × (7) (12)
1	$ 154,478	$ 46,875	$ 125,000	$ 68,750	$ 10,000	$ 6,000	$ –	$ –	$ 91,728	0.95694	$ 87,778
2	154,478	38,805	125,000	65,522	10,000	6,000	–	–	94,956	0.91573	86,954
3	154,478	30,129	125,000	62,052	10,000	6,000	–	–	98,426	0.87630	86,251
4	154,478	20,803	125,000	58,321	10,000	6,000	–	–	102,157	0.83856	85,665
5	154,478	10,778	125,000	54,311	10,000	6,000	50,000	30,000	76,167	0.80245	61,120
Total	$ 772,390	$ 147,390	$ 625,000	$ 308,956	$ 50,000	$ 30,000	$ 50,000	$ 30,000	$ 463,434	4.38998	$ 407,767

Cost of borrowing

(Continued)

TABLE 13-8

Net Advantage of Leasing: Neutral Operating Benefits *(Continued)*

C. Cost of Leasing (similar to Table 13-6)

Year (1)	Lease Payment (2)	After-Tax Cash Flow $(2) \times (1 - 0.40)$ (3)	$0.075 \times (1 - 0.40)$ PVIF 4.5% (4)	Present Value $(3) \times (4)$ (5)
1	$ 154,810	$ 92,886	0.95694	$ 88,886
2	154,810	92,886	0.91573	85,058
3	154,810	92,886	0.87630	81,396
4	154,810	92,886	0.83856	77,891
5	154,810	92,886	0.80245	74,536
Total	$ 774,050	$ 464,430	4.38998	

Cost of leasing $ 407,767

Net advantage of leasing $ 0

TABLE 13-9

Net Advantage of Leasing: Operating Benefits to Lessor

A. Loan Amortization Table (similar to Table 13–4)

Year (1)	Beginning Balance (2)	Loan Payment (3)	7.5% Interest (2) × 0.075 (4)	Principal (3) − (4) (5)	Ending Balance (2) − (5) (6)
1	$ 650,000	$ 160,657	$ 48,750	$ 111,907	$ 538,093
2	538,093	160,657	40,357	120,300	417,793
3	417,793	160,657	31,334	129,323	288,470
4	288,470	160,657	21,635	139,022	149,449
5	149,449	160,657	11,209	149,448	-
Total		$ 803,285	$ 153,285	$ 650,000	

PV of the payment = $ 650,000

B. Cost of Borrowing (similar to Table 13-5)

Year (1)	Loan Payment (2)	Interest Expense (3)	Depreciation Expense (4)	Tax Shield [(3) + (4)] × 0.40 (5)	Maintenance Costs (6)	After-Tax Maintenance (6) × (1 − 0.40) (7)	Residual Value (8)	After-Tax Residual (8) × (1 − 0.40) (9)	After-Tax Cash Flow (2) − (5) + (7) − (9) (10)	0.075 × (1 − 0.40) PVIF 4.5% (11)	Present Value (6) × (7) (12)
1	$ 160,657	$ 48,750	$ 130,000	$ 71,500	$ 12,000	$ 7,200	$ -	$ -	$ 96,357	0.95694	$ 92,208
2	160,657	40,357	130,000	68,143	12,000	7,200	-	-	99,714	0.91573	91,311
3	160,657	31,334	130,000	64,534	12,000	7,200	-	-	103,323	0.87630	90,542
4	160,657	21,635	130,000	60,654	12,000	7,200	-	-	107,203	0.83856	89,896
5	160,657	11,209	130,000	56,483	12,000	7,200	40,000	24,000	87,374	0.80245	70,113
Total	$ 803,285	$ 153,285	$ 650,000	$ 321,314	$ 60,000	$ 36,000	$ 40,000	$ 24,000	$ 493,971	4.38998	$ 434,069
									Cost of borrowing		$ 434,069

(Continued)

TABLE 13-9

Net Advantage of Leasing: Operating Benefits to Lessor *(Continued)*

C. Cost of Leasing (similar to Table 13-6)

Year (1)	Lease Payment (2)	After-Tax Cash Flow (2) × (1 − 0.40) (3)	0.075 × (1 − 0.40) PVIF 4.5% (4)	Present Value (3) × (4) (5)
1	$ 154,810	$ 92,886	0.95694	$ 88,886
2	154,810	92,886	0.91573	85,058
3	154,810	92,886	0.87630	81,396
4	154,810	92,886	0.83856	77,891
5	154,810	92,886	0.80245	74,536
Total	$ 774,050	$ 464,430	4.38998	
			Cost of leasing	$ 407,767
			Net advantage of leasing	$ 26,302

Primary change from Table 13-8: *Secondary effect of change.*

mistaken to compare the rate required on a cancelable operating lease with the rate required on a straight (noncancelable) financial lease (or comparable debt financing).

SUMMARY

Leasing is available on a wide variety of property and equipment. It may be a viable alternative for acquiring the use of any asset. The lessor leases the asset to a user—the lessee.

The most important forms of lease financing are (1) operating leases, which are often cancelable and call for payments under the lease contract that may not fully recover the cost of the equipment, (2) financial leases, which do not provide for maintenance services, are not cancelable, and do fully amortize the cost of the leased asset during the basic lease contract period, and (3) sale and leaseback, in which a firm owning land, buildings, or equipment sells the property and simultaneously executes an agreement to lease it for a certain period under specific terms similar to a capital lease.

It is important to remember that lease financing is a substitute for debt. There is no such thing as a company that is 100 percent lease financed. Lease financing, like debt financing, requires an equity base. Prior to FASB Statement No. 13, all leases were accounted for as operating leases, which is to say that the financing provided by leasing was off-balance-sheet financing. FASB Statement No. 13 dealt with this issue, provided specific criteria, and resulted in capitalization of financing leases both as an asset and as long-term financing.

The first step in a lease versus buy analysis is the investment decision, which requires the user to discount the cash flows of the project under consideration at the appropriate weighted-average cost of capital. Then, if the project makes investment sense (positive NPV), the second step is to decide how the project will be financed. If it is decided to finance the project with debt, all forms of debt must be examined, including leasing. The net present value of the lease is determined by comparing the cost of borrowing (the investment amount offset by the depreciation tax shield discounted at the after-tax cost of debt) and the cost of leasing (after-tax lease fees discounted at the lessee's after-tax cost of debt). If the net advantage of leasing (i.e., the NPV of the lease) is positive, then leasing is preferred to borrowing as a means of financing the project.

In the absence of major tax advantages and other market imperfections, there should be no advantage to either leasing or owning. A wide range of factors that may influence the indifference result can be introduced. These possible influences include operating differences, tax differences, and financing difference. Whether these other factors actually will give an advantage or disadvantage to leasing depends on the facts and circumstances of each transaction analyzed and the negotiating skills of both the lessor and the lessee.

Hershey is a highly creditworthy corporation whose debt is highly rated. Also, it is a high marginal taxpayer with a very effective purchasing department that vigorously negotiates the best price for its purchases. Consequently, Hershey (or any company in a similar position) is faced with limited structural differences that make leasing advantageous. Two noted areas of opportunity are (1) automobiles and trucks and (2) computer equipment. In these cases, leasing companies have purchasing and disposal advantage they pass on to the lessee (Hershey).

PART FIVE

FINANCE AND CORPORATE STRATEGY

STRATEGY AND VALUATION: CREATING SHAREHOLDER VALUE

At this point, many topics have been presented. While all the topics are interrelated, it may not have always felt that way. This chapter integrates all the previous discussion points and leads to valuing a company, creating shareholder value, and enhancing the value of the firm.

Valuation of a firm begins with a solid understanding of the company's strategic goals and objectives, as well as its day-to-day business practices. To judge the financial success of a firm and to develop a reasonable value for that firm or a share of that firm's stock, it is necessary to know how to read its financial statements (Chapter 2), analyze those statements (Chapter 3), and project the firm's future performance (Chapter 6). It is also important to consider tax ramifications (Chapter 4) as well as the general economic climate (Chapter 8) and to understand the impact that supply chain finance can have on the business operations (Chapter 5).

In Chapter 7, I specifically developed the most fundamental tool of finance — the time value of money (TVM) — and then applied it to financial securities (Chapter 8) and capital investment analysis (Chapters 9 and 10) for new equipment, new products, software, and so on.

Part 4 dealt with financing: cost of capital (Chapter 11), sources of long-term financing (Chapter 12), and leases as an alternative debt source (Chapter 13). This chapter employs all the prior material to arrive at the underlying value for the firm. Firm valuation is similar to a large capital budgeting project, as in Chapter 10:

- Forecast the operating cash flows generated over the life of the project (in this case, the firm), including any terminal value.
- Determine an appropriate rate of return (cost of capital).
- Discount (present value) the annual cash flows to arrive at the value of the firm.
- Adjust that intrinsic valuation of the firm (also called the *value of the operations*) for cash and interest-bearing debt to determine the equity's total value.
- Finally, divide the total equity value by the number of outstanding shares to arrive at a value per share.

I begin by revisiting the concept of perpetuities that was introduced in Chapter 7; then I introduce a comprehensive professional spreadsheet valuation model that is an extension of the strategic financial plan. I illustrate how management can use such a plan to determine alternate value-enhancing strategies. Data tables are presented as an enhanced diagnostic tool for further determining the possibility of cost versus growth considerations.

While I develop the appropriate models and valuation tools, any model is only as strong as its assumptions. As in previous chapters, Hershey will provide an application example. To be clear, this is a hypothetical valuation of Hershey. While the techniques are solid, the assumptions illustrate this application. They are illustrative but hypothetical, similar to the strategic plan presented in Chapter 6. It remains the responsibility of readers to develop reasonable projections for their application of this chapter to their organization.

The chapter ends with a discussion of real options. While the underlying math is beyond the scope of this book, the application concepts are important to consider whenever you analyze significant strategic capital investment.

FUNDAMENTAL PERPETUAL CASH-FLOW VALUATION MODELS

Chapter 7 developed the concept of perpetual cash flows or recurring cash flows that last forever. At that time, I introduced two varieties—a zero-growth model and a constant-growth model. I then placed these models in the context of equity valuation at the end of Chapter 8, as shown by Eqs. (14.1) and (14.2):

$$\text{Zero growth:} \quad V_{0,r,\infty} = \frac{CF_{(t)}}{r} \tag{14.1}$$

$$\text{Constant growth:} \quad V_{0,r,\infty} = \frac{CF_{(t+1)}}{(r-g)} \tag{14.2}$$

where $V_{0,r,\infty}$ = value of firm at time zero continuing perpetually
$CF_{(t+1)}$ = cash flow at the end of year 1
r = cost of capital
g = constant growth

These fundamental models begin our effort at valuing an organization. Remember, the cash flow from year 0 (the last actual year: $CF_{(0)}$ is also the same as growing this year's cash flow and can be written as Eq. (14.3):

$$CF_{(t+1)} = CF_{(0)}(1 + g) \tag{14.3}$$

In order to determine Hershey's operating cash flow in 2010, we begin with Table 14-1 (which is a repeat of Table 2-14), the consolidated statement of cash flow. As you may recall, this statement has three distinct sections: cash flow from operating activities, cash used by investing activities, and cash used for financing. The Hershey Company had $901.4 million in net cash provided by operating activities during 2010.

TABLE 14-1

Consolidated Cash Flow Statement
The Hershey Company
($ millions)

	2010	2009	2008
Cash flow from (used by) operations			
Net income*	$509.8	$436.0	$311.4
Adjustments to reconcile income to cash			
Depreciation and amortization	197.1	182.4	249.5
Stock-based compensation expense, net of tax	30.7	30.4	22.2
Deferred income taxes	(18.7)	(40.6)	(17.1)
Business realignment, net of taxes	77.9	60.8	119.1
Contributions to pension plans	(6.1)	(54.4)	(32.7)
Change in balance sheet items net of acquisitions and divestitures			
Accounts receivable, trade	20.3	46.6	31.7
Inventories	(13.9)	74.0	7.7
Accounts payable	90.5	37.2	26.4
Other assets and liabilities	13.8	293.3	(198.6)
Net cash provided from operating activities*	901.4	1,065.7	519.6
Cash flow from (used by) investing			
Capital expenditures	(179.5)	(126.3)	(262.7)
Capitalized software additions	(22.0)	(19.2)	(20.3)
Proceeds from sale of equipment	2.2	10.4	82.8
Business acquisitions	-	(15.2)	-
Divestitures	-	-	2.0
Net cash (used by) investing activities	(199.3)	(150.3)	(198.2)
Cash flow from (used by) financing			
Net change in short-term borrowing	1.1	(458.0)	(371.4)
Net long-term debt borrowing (repayment)	276.6	(8.3)	242.8
Dividends	(283.4)	(263.4)	(262.9)
Share repurchases	(169.1)	(9.3)	(60.4)
Exercise of stock options, net of taxes	93.5	32.8	38.4
Miscellaneous other stockholders' equity	10.2	7.3	-
Net cash used by financing activities	(71.1)	(698.9)	(413.5)
Increase (decrease) in cash	$631.0	$216.5	$(92.1)

*Includes after tax interest of *$60.7*, $58.8, and $62.0 million, respectively, 2010, 2009, and 2008.

However, as you look more closely, this section begins with net income. Net income included after-tax interest expense of $60.7 million, which is a financing cash flow. Consequently, this amount needs to be added back so that we start with net operating profit after tax (NOPAT) and we remove this financing cash flow from operations. This results in adjusted net cash from operating activities of $962.1 million ($901.4 million + $60.7 million). Next, we eliminate $199.3 million for capital investment from the investing section of the table. Total operating cash flow of $762.8 million ($962.1 million less $199.3) was generated in 2010. To help you to better see the development of operating cash flows, the values were "bolded".

From another perspective, the 2010 increase in total cash was $631.0 million per Table 14-1, but that included a net reduction of $71.1 million for dividends, share repurchases, and additional borrowing, as well as the $60.7 million net income reduction for after-tax interest expense. These three items can be added together to derive the same $762.8 million. To help you to better see the development of operating cash flows from this perspective, the values were "italized and bolded".

We continue to use 7.3 percent as the required return (or cost of capital) for Hershey, as developed in Chapter 11. Further, we assume 2 percent perpetual growth in Hershey. This is sales growth, income growth (assuming constant margins and tax rates), and cash-flow growth (further assuming constant working capital relationships and capital expenditures).

Applying Eq. (14.2) to this set of refined data results in a valuation of Hershey of $14,681.1 million, as shown in Eq. (14.4):

$$PVA_{r,\infty} = \frac{CF_{(0)}\,(1+g)}{(r-g)}$$

$$= \frac{\$762.8\,(1+0.02)}{(0.073-0.020)} = \frac{\$778.1}{0.053} = \$14{,}681.1\ \text{million} \qquad (14.4)$$

These were the same approaches applied in Chapter 8 as a "50,000-foot valuation framework" for valuing equity. My purpose here is to expand these basic equations so that they become more useful management tools.

Expanded Constant-Growth Valuation Model

Equation (14.5) enhances Eq. (14.2) and develops operating cash flows. Cash flows are developed using a percent of sales method and 2010 relationships.

$$V_0 = \frac{R_0\,[m\,(1-T)+d-I_{fg}-I_w\,]\,(1+g)}{(k-g)} \qquad (14.5)$$

where V_0 = value of firm as of today (year 0)

R_0 = revenue (or sales) of firm (last year of actual sales)

m = operating income (EBIT) margin (percent of sales)

T = tax rate

d = depreciation (percent of sales)

I_f = capital expenditures or gross fixed capital invested (percent of sales)

I_w = working capital investment (percent of sales)

g = growth

k = cost of capital (previously called r)

Before continuing on, let's note some relationships by rearranging some terms:

$R_0(1 + g)$ = revenue (or sales) for the next (first) year = R_1

$R_1(m)$ = operating income (EBIT) in year 1

$R_1(m)(1 - T)$ = after-tax operating income in year 1

$R_1(I_f - d)$ = net capital investment

$R_1(I_f - d) + I_w$ = investment in operating assets less operating liabilities (similiar to operating working capital and net, fixed capital)

The complete numerator represents 2010 operating cash flows of $778.1, as in our previous example and equation 14.4:

$$= \$778.1/0.053 = \$14,681.1$$

$$V_0 = \frac{\$5,671.0\,[\,0.1596\,(1 - 0.37) + 0.0348 - 0.0351 + 0.0343\,]\,(1 + 0.02)}{(0.073 - 0.020)} \quad (14.6)$$

To glean more of an business operation sense, equation (14.5) can be rewritten as:

$$V_0 = \frac{R_1\,[m\,(1 - T)] - R_1\,[(I_{fg} + d) + I_w]}{(k - g)} \quad (14.7)$$

or

$$V_0 = \frac{\text{aftere-tax operating income} - \text{net operating investment}}{(k - g)}$$

Assuming an R_1 of $5,784.4 million (2010 sales of $5,671.0 million times 1.020, which represents the 2.0 percent assumed growth rate) and applying Eq. (14.7) ($ millions), we get:

$$V_0 = \frac{\$5,784.4\,[\,0.1596\,(1 - 0.37)] - \$5,784.4\,[(0.0351 - 0.0348) + (0.0343)]}{(0.073 - 0.020)}$$

$$= (\$581.4 - \$1.7 + \$198.4)/0.053 = \$778.1/0.053 = \$14,681.1$$

In this example, Hershey is expected to generate \$778.1 million in operating cash flow, primarily from operating income of \$581.4 million, offset by \$1.7 million net investment in plant property and equipment and increased owing to effective working capital and other long-term operating liabilities management. In fact, in this case, owing to improving working capital management practices and the impact of other noncash expenses such as deferred taxes and other long-term liabilities, Hershey increased its operating cash flows by an additional \$198.4 million per year.

Using the 2010 relationships, it is estimated that Hershey will generate 13.45 cents $[m(1 - T) + d - I_{fg} - I_w]$ or $[(0.1596(1.0000 - 0.3702) + (0.0348 - 0.0351) - (-0.0343)]$ in operating cash flow for every dollar of revenue.

The constant-growth valuation model centers on the critical value drivers of any business and consequently any valuation:

1. Revenue growth
2. Operating profitability
3. Tax rates
4. Net fixed capital investment (capital expenditures less depreciation)
5. Working capital investment, including other long-term operating assets and liabilities
6. Cost of capital

Even in this simple illustration, the way to increase the value of any project or company is to increase growth and profitability while limiting investment. The value of the organization increases because of increased cash flow.

The constant-growth valuation model determines the sources of operating cash flow by allowing the manager, analyst, entrepreneur, or other interested investor to develop each strategic performance objective or assumption appropriately. However, by implication, and owing to the limitations of this equation, this approach infers that these assumptions will remain constant into perpetuity.

What if this is not the case? What if the organization is entering into a high period of growth? Maybe margins are changing? Maybe there is expansion into other lines of business or other countries? Maybe there was an acquisition or a divestiture? Maybe the company has just implemented a new enterprise resource planning (ERP) system? Or maybe it is entering into a high period of investment or starting to reap the rewards of past investments? How should this type of "extraordinary" activity be handled? The next section returns us to considering the strategic financial planning model presented in Chapter 6.

COMPREHENSIVE STRATEGIC FINANCIAL PLANNING VALUATION MODEL

This chapter has been consistent with the other chapters about capital evaluation (Chapters 8, 9, and 10). To determine an asset's value, we discount its expected operating cash flows. Chapter 10 discussed and illustrated the development of those cash flows when purchasing new equipment and introducing a new product.

As you have seen so far, valuation of an organization, a company, division, subsidiary, or brand is no different. We consistently project cash flows and then discount those values using the required rate of return, the firm's cost of capital.

Extension of the Strategic Financial Plan—Explicit Cash Flows

This valuation approach begins with the basic framework set forth in Chapter 6 and is consistent with the organization's strategic financial plan. This requires forecasts of the broader international, national, and industrial economies in which the organization and its competitors operate. The key is in understanding the business economics of the industries and product markets in which the firm operates. This includes an analysis of the competitive forces of the industry along with the industry's historical financial performance. Start with historical data for the firm and its major rivals, just as we did in Chapter 3, to better understand the financial implications of an organization.

Chapter 6 used this historical backdrop, coupled with the current state of the international and domestic economy, the industry, and any trends that could affect the company. From this we developed a detailed set of assumptions for Hershey's projected performance. You may recall that we separately estimated the cost of sales (excluding depreciation), depreciation, and selling, general and administrative expenses. Through a series of reasonable assumptions, we estimated the incremental annual cash invested in all operating assets and liabilities. For example, receivables were estimated on projected sales and a projected receivables turnover. We estimated an increasing inventory turnover owing to implementation of best-demonstrated inventory management practices. We did this with each major operating assumption. As a result, the strategic financial plan in Chapter 6 provided all the necessary information to value Hershey based on five years of explicit operating cash flows and a terminal value.

From the set of assumptions, projected financial statements were prepared. These statements included an income statement, balance sheet, and cash-flow statement.

Table 14-2 combines the projected income statement (Table 6-13) with the projected cash-flow statement (Table 6-15). The forecasted cash flows are identical, with the exception of two items. First, Table 14-2 recasts the income measure to exclude after-tax interest income and interest expense. Second, the valuation cash flow does not consider any financial transactions, such as debt repayment, additional borrowing, equity repurchases, dividends, and so on. The financing cash flows are captured within the cost of capital. Thus we do not want to "double account" for them.

T A B L E   14-2

Valuation
($ millions)

		Projected				
		2011	2012	2013	2014	2015
Net sales		$ 5,954.6	$ 6,222.6	$6,471.5	$ 6,698.0	$ 6,898.9
Cost of sales		3,185.7	3,310.4	3,429.9	3,536.5	3,642.6
Depreciation		209.6	232.9	247.9	261.6	276.1
Selling, marketing, & administrative		1,548.2	1,649.0	1,682.6	1,708.0	1,724.7
Total costs		4,943.5	5,192.3	5,360.4	5,506.1	5,643.4
Operating income (or EBIT)		1,011.1	1,030.3	1,111.1	1,191.9	1,255.5
Operating margin		16.98%	16.56%	17.17%	17.79%	18.20%
Tax expense *		374.1	381.2	411.1	441.0	464.5
Net operating profit after tax (NOPAT)		637.0	649.1	700.0	750.9	791.0
Depreciation		209.6	232.9	247.9	261.6	276.1
Change in						
Accounts receivable, trade		(17.7)	(15.5)	(14.0)	(12.2)	(10.4)
Inventory		(56.9)	(20.4)	(17.8)	(15.0)	(9.4)
Other current assets		(10.0)	(15.0)	(20.0)	(25.0)	(30.0)
Other assets		(20.0)	(25.0)	(30.0)	(35.0)	(40.0)
Accounts payable		48.2	26.6	25.4	24.1	24.9
Accrued liabilities		69.6	36.4	26.9	24.0	24.1
Other long-term liabilities		11.6	22.8	21.2	19.2	17.1
Cash from operating activities	(A)	871.4	891.9	939.6	992.6	1,043.4
Investment activities						
Capital expenditures		(350.0)	(215.0)	(185.0)	(190.0)	(200.0)
Other, net		-	-	-	-	-
Cash (used for) investing	(B)	(350.0)	(215.0)	(185.0)	(190.0)	(200.0)
Free cash flow	(A) + (B)	521.4	676.9	754.6	802.6	843.4
Terminal value		-	-	-	-	16,231.5
Total cash flow		$ 521.4	$ 676.9	$ 754.6	$ 802.6	$17,074.9

Cost of capital	7.3%
PV of explicit cash flows, years 1–5	$ 2,883.1
PV of terminal value	11,412.0
Value of the operations	$14,295.1 PV of Total cash Flow
Add: 2010 Cash and equivalents	884.6
Less: 2010 interest bearing debt	(1,827.3)
Value of equity	$13,352.4
Shares outstanding	227.0
Value per share	$ 58.82

* Tax expense was recalculated based on NOPAT.

Table 14-3 does a side-by-side comparison of the cash-flow statement from the strategic financial plan (Tables 6-13 and 6-15) and the valuation cash-flow statement (Table 14-2). There is $683.9 million more cash flow generated when the interest expense, debt repayment, and dividends are not considered.

TABLE 14-3

2015 Valuation Comparison with SFP*

($ millions)

	SFP* Table 6-13, 6-15	Table 14-2	Valuation Difference
Net sales	$ 6,898.9	$ 6,898.9	$ -
Cost of sales	3,642.6	3,642.6	-
Depreciation	276.1	276.1	-
Selling, marketing, & administrative	1,724.7	1,724.7	-
Total costs	5,643.4	5,643.4	-
Earnings before interest and taxes	1,255.5	1,255.5	-
Operating margin	18.2%	18.2%	0.0%
Interest expense	49.0	-	49.0
PreTax income (PTI)	1,206.5	1,255.5	49.0
Provision for income taxes	446.4	464.5	18.1
Net income (SFP) / NOPAT (valuation)	$ 760.1	$ 791.0	$ 30.9
Net margin	11.0%	11.5%	0.5%
Depreciation	276.1	276.1	-
Change in			
Accounts receivable, trade	(10.4)	(10.4)	-
Inventory	(9.4)	(9.4)	-
Other current assets	(30.0)	(30.0)	-
Other assets	(40.0)	(40.0)	-
Accounts payable	24.9	24.9	-
Accrued liabilities	24.1	24.1	-
Other long-term liabilities	17.1	17.1	-
Cash from operating activities	1,012.5	1,043.4	30.9
Investment activities			
Capital expenditures	(200.0)	(200.0)	-
Financing activities			
Long-term borrowings	(250.1)	-	250.1
Cash dividends	(402.9)	-	402.9
Cash (used for) financing	(653.0)	-	653.0
Change in cash/free cash flow	$ 159.5	$ 843.4	$ 683.9

* SFP stands for Strategic Financial Plan from Chapter 6.

Terminal Value

The five-year plan includes higher growth rates, improving margins, and stronger capital investment management (working and fixed) that results in growing cash flows. These cash flows are referred to as *free cash flows* for this five-year explicit period.

But what about the cash flows beyond those five years? Do they just stop, and Hershey withers away? Or is there continuing value in the business? As of today, does management have clarity and confidence to explicitly project the next five years (years 6 to 10 or even beyond)? As of today, can management estimate that much will change about the foreseeable financial performance of the business, beyond the explicit five-year period? As of today, does management expect unstable value drivers after this five-year explicit time period? If the answer is "Yes" to any one of these questions, management should consider building a model with a longer explicit time frame. Perhaps a 10-year explicit model would better capture management's forecast or strategic vision. But what about the cash flows beyond year 10? So maybe a 15- or 20-year explicit model is in order?

The planning horizon should be long enough to capture the explicit assumption changes. When management starts simply to repeat the assumptions, it needs to consider using that year as the end of the explicit valuation (or planning) horizon.

Our assumption is that after five explicitly derived years of cash flow, Hershey's year 6 and beyond is static in terms of the business value drivers—constant margins, tax rates, and consistent capital management parameters (turnovers). The continuing value is captured in the terminal value.

There are a few different approaches that analysts use when estimating the terminal value of a firm. In principle, most approaches are based on perpetuity models. At this junction, the mechanics behind the calculation of the terminal value and its impact on the estimated value of Hershey should be well understood. The reader should also appreciate the concept that the terminal value captures all the anticipated cash flows from years 6, 7, 8, …, 43, 44, 45, …, 87, 88, 89, …, 174, 175, 176, and so on forever. Three common approaches are:

1. Capitalization using the zero-growth model (Eq. 14.1) where Hershey's cash flows are assumed to remain constant into perpetuity. This is a very conservative view of the business and results in an estimated year 5 (2015) terminal value of Hershey of $11,553.4 million:

$$V_0 = \left(\frac{CF_5}{k}\right) = \left(\frac{\$843.4}{0.073}\right) = \$11,553.4$$

2. Another approach, and the one will be used here, is to use the constant-growth model that capitalizes the year 5 cash flows into perpetuity using an estimated perpetual-growth rate after year 5. This may be a more realistic valuation approach:

$$V_0 = \left[\frac{CF_5\,(1+g)}{(k-g)}\right] = \left[\frac{\$843.4\,(1.02\,)}{(0.073-0.02\,)}\right] = \frac{\$860.3}{0.053} = \$16{,}231.5$$

In this case, we now value Hershey at \$16,231.5 million in year 5, assuming a 2.0 percent terminal growth rate.

3. Some analysts also use a *comparable* (or simply a *"comp"*) basis to estimate the terminal value. A *comp ratio* is established for the base year. The comp could be something such as price-to-sales ratio, price-to-earnings ratio, or price-to-EBITDA ratio, and the list could go on. In Chapter 3, Hershey's 2010 price-to-EBITDA multiple was calculated as 9.74. If we use this comp and assume that it remains constant for the five years, we would take the 2015 operating income plus depreciation (EBITDA) of \$1,531.6 million times the multiple (9.74) and use that value as the terminal value (\$14,917.8 million). If we used the 2010 price-to-sales multiple (1.89) times the projected 2015 sales of \$6,898.9 million, the resulting terminal value would be \$13,038.9 million. As you can see, the comp approach for determining terminal value has little to do with the underlying state of the business but more to do with the choice of the comp measure.

To summarize the results of these techniques:

Technique	Resulting Terminal Value (\$ millions)
Perpetuity, no growth	\$11,553.4
Perpetuity, constant growth (2%)	16,231.5
Comparable, EBITDA multiple	14,917.8
Comparable, price-to-sales multiple	13,038.9

As mentioned, the constant-growth perpetuity (or Gordan Dividend Growth Model) is the preferred approach.

Business Valuation

The first step is complete: Forecast the operating cash flows generated over the life of the project, including the terminal value. The second step involves determining an appropriate discount rate such as the cost of capital (a risk-adjusted required rate of return) developed in Chapter 11. Hershey's cost of capital was estimated at 7.3 percent.

The third step is to discount the cash flows at the cost of capital. As shown on Table 14.2, this leads to a value of almost \$2.9 billion for the explicit five-year period and \$11.4 billion in present value terms for the terminal value. The total of these two or almost \$14.3 billion represents value of the operations (which is also called the *enterprise value* or *intrinsic value of the firm*).

Equity Valuation

As developed earlier, we value the explicit five-year period separately and then value the terminal period. We did that by discounting the projected cash flow at the cost of capital, or 7.3 percent. We arrived at the total value of the corporation (value of the operations) or the enterprise value:

		Present Value ($ millions)
Explicit period		$ 2,883.1
Terminal value		11,412.0
Enterprise value		$ 14,295.1
Value of the operations		$ 14,295.1
Plus	Cash and equivalents (2010)	884.6
Less	Interest-bearing debt (2010)	(1,827.3)
Value of the equity		$ 13,352.4
Shares outstanding		227.0
Value per share		$ 58.82

Up to this point we have valued the entire company. In order to calculate the value of the equity and the value per share, we must (1) add cash, cash equivalents, and marketable securities and (2) subtract all interest-bearing debt (i.e., short-term debt, notes payable, banking borrowings, current portion of long-term debt, and long-term debt). The result is the value of the equity (or $13,352.4 million for Hershey), and dividing this by the number of shares outstanding results in the equity value per share.

This is the value that we are willing to pay for a share of Hershey stock given our set of assumptions. We feel that the stock is worth $58.82 per share. From Chapter 3, Hershey's 2010 year-end stock price was only $47.32. Our estimate indicated that Hershey was undervalued by the stock market. If we were equity analysts, we would issue a buy order. If we were managers at Hershey, this would "green light" our share-repurchase program because we believe that the shares are worth $11.50 more than the current value as of December 31, 2010! (As a side note, the marketplace also became convinced that Hershey was more valuable. From February 2011 to July 2011, Hershey's stock price increased steadily to over $58 per share.)

SENSITIVITY ANALYSIS

Whenever a projection is prepared, it is important to test operating decisions and scenarios. As in Chapter 6, sensitivity analysis tests one item at a time. For example, if sales growth can be increased annually by 1 percent (e.g., 2011 sales growth increases from 5.0 to 6.0 percent) throughout the five-year explicit time period, the value of the operations increases to $15,188.4 million, or an equity value of $62.76 per share. This is an improvement of $3.94 or 6.70 percent from the original value or base scenario. One more thing to consider: Annual operating margin improved owing to a reduction in the cost of goods sold (COGS) of 1 percent of its original (e.g., from the base scenario, the 2015 COGS was 52.8 percent of sales, or $3,642.6 million; with the adjustment, COGS is 51.8 percent, or $3,573.6). This operating margin improvement resulted in an increase in the value per share of $3.23, or 5.49 percent, more than the base scenario.

Table 14-4 considers the value-per-share impact of the improvement in each major assumption, similar to Chapter 6. These adjustments occur, one at a time, for all five years.

This table captures the final year's free cash flow and terminal value. It also displays selected (present) values for the enterprise value and the per-share equity value. The most impactful items are cost of capital and terminal growth rate. While the chief financial officer (CFO) can work to lower the cost of capital, the long-term growth rate underlying the business requires innovation and creativity. Both of these are long-term goals. On a day-to-day basis, sales growth and margin improvements drive value the most. You also can see that investment in working capital and fixed capital influences the company's value, albeit to a smaller degree.

Table 14-5 expands on the analysis of sales growth and expense analysis. The base scenario (no change, or 0.0 percent) is highlighted. As we saw in Table 14-4, if Hershey could increase its annual growth rate by an additional 1 percent (100 basis points) for five years, it would increase its value per share by almost $4.00 to $62.76. On the other hand, if operating margins could be improved by 1 percent, the value per share would increase to $62.05. Incremental sales growth has more impact on the value of Hershey than does margin improvement.

Table 14-6 examines the tradeoffs between growth and margin improvement. Usually, to stimulate growth, you need to advertise, offer promotions, introduce new products, invest in research and development (R&D), lower prices, and so on, resulting in lower margins. In Table 14-6 you'll notice that incremental sales growth crosses over the table, whereas incremental operating margin improvement goes down the page. Obviously, everyone wants to live in the southwest, where sales growth and margins are 2 percent higher than in the base scenario, resulting in a value per share of $73.89. No one wants to be in the northeast corner, where growth has slowed by 2 percent and margins have declined by 2 percent from the base scenario with a value per share of $45.44.

But business is about tradeoffs. If, looking at Table 14-6, marketing at Hershey was convinced that if it could spend more on advertising, it would increase sales growth by 1 percent over the five years, and if it could commit to this by spending only 0.5 percent (of sales) more, then it should proceed, and Hershey's value would rise to $61.09. Actually, if marketing could spend 1 percent (of sales) more and deliver 1 percent more growth, it should be allowed to proceed because the value would be $59.40 and more than the base scenario. However, if marketing needs 1.5 percent (of sales) additional, it needs to explore

TABLE 14-4

Sensitivity Analysis

($ millions, except per share)

| | 2015 | | | | Value per Share | | |
| | | | | | | Share Impact | |
	Free Cash Flow	Terminal Value	Enterprise Value	Value of Equity	$	$	%
Original valuation, base scenario	$ 843.4	$ 16,231.5	$ 14,295.1	$ 13,352.4	$ 58.82	$ -	0.000%
1% Sales growth increase	899.8	17,316.9	15,188.4	14,245.7	62.76	3.94	6.698%
1% Operating margin improvement	886.2	17,055.2	15,027.6	14,084.9	62.05	3.23	5.491%
1% Tax rate decline	855.9	16,472.0	14,509.3	13,566.6	59.76	0.94	1.598%
+1 Accounts receivable turnover	843.9	16,241.1	14,328.2	13,385.5	58.97	0.15	0.255%
+1 Inventory turnover	843.4	16,231.5	14,381.4	13,438.7	59.20	0.38	0.646%
10% Less capital expenditure	859.1	16,533.6	14,591.7	13,649.0	60.13	1.31	2.227%
1% Residual period growth-rate increase	843.4	20,202.4	17,086.9	16,144.0	71.12	12.30	20.911%
1% Cost of capital reduction	843.4	20,006.2	17,707.8	16,765.1	73.86	15.04	25.570%

* A 1% sales growth rate indicates that if the sales growth was 5%, it is now 6%, and so on for all five years.

TABLE 14-5

Data Table Analysis: Separate Incremental Changes to Growth Rates and Margins
($ millions, except per share)

Incremental Growth	2015 FCF	2015 Terminal	Enterprise Value	Equity Value	Per Share
2.0%	$ 959.0	$ 18,456.2	$ 16,123.6	$ 15,180.9	$ 66.88
1.5%	929.2	17,882.7	15,652.8	14,710.1	64.80
1.0%	899.8	17,316.9	15,188.4	14,245.7	62.76
0.5%	871.1	16,764.6	14,734.3	13,791.6	60.76
0.0%	843.4	16,231.5	14,295.1	13,352.4	58.82
−0.5%	815.7	15,698.4	13,856.2	12,913.5	56.89
−1.0%	789.0	15,184.5	13,432.0	12,489.3	55.02
−1.5%	762.6	14,676.5	13,012.5	12,069.8	53.17
−2.0%	737.0	14,183.8	12,604.9	11,662.2	51.38

Incremental Operating Margin	2015 FCF	2015 Terminal	Enterprise Value	Equity Value	Per Share
−2.0%	$ 757.8	$ 14,584.1	$ 12,829.9	$ 11,887.2	$ 52.37
−1.5%	779.2	14,995.9	13,196.0	12,253.3	53.98
−1.0%	800.6	15,407.8	13,562.4	12,619.7	55.59
−0.5%	821.8	15,815.8	13,925.9	12,983.2	57.19
0.0%	843.4	16,231.5	14,295.1	13,352.4	58.82
0.5%	864.8	16,643.3	14,661.3	13,718.6	60.43
1.0%	886.2	17,055.2	15,027.6	14,084.9	62.05
1.5%	907.5	17,465.1	15,392.5	14,449.8	63.66
2.0%	929.0	17,878.9	15,760.2	14,817.5	65.28

another strategy because such a strategy (1 percent incremental growth and a 1.5 percent drop in margin [increase in expenses]) results in a lower value of $57.72. From the CFO's perspective, if margins could improve 2 percent and sales growth only drop by 1.5 percent, the company would see an increased value from the base scenario of $59.23.

Hershey's management has focused on business building, that is, growing the business through "top-line growth" and lowering production costs while financing marketing initiatives. The company had a tremendous opportunity that the management team took advantage of.

The next section discusses a data-analysis tool that is part of Excel: data tables. It is ideal to address the landscape of tradeoffs between growth and margins.

TABLE 14-6

Data Table Analysis: Combined
Incremental Changes to Growth Rates and Operating Margins

					Incremental Sales Growth				
	2.0%	**1.5%**	**1.0%**	**0.5%**	**0.0%**	**−0.5%**	**−1.0%**	**−1.5%**	**−2.0%**
−2.0%	$59.88	$57.94	$56.04	$54.18	$52.37	$50.57	$48.83	$47.11	$45.44
−1.5%	61.63	59.65	57.72	55.83	53.98	52.16	50.38	48.63	46.92
−1.0%	63.38	61.37	59.40	57.48	55.59	53.74	51.93	50.14	48.40
−0.5%	65.12	63.09	61.09	59.13	57.19	55.31	53.47	51.66	49.88
0.0%	66.88	64.80	62.76	60.76	58.82	56.89	55.02	53.17	51.38
0.5%	68.63	66.53	64.45	62.41	60.43	58.47	56.56	54.69	52.86
1.0%	70.39	68.24	66.13	64.06	62.05	60.06	58.11	56.21	54.33
1.5%	72.14	69.96	67.80	65.71	63.66	61.64	59.66	57.72	55.82
2.0%	73.89	71.68	69.49	67.37	65.28	63.22	61.20	59.23	57.31

Incremental Operating Margin (% of sales)

Data Tables

The term *data tables* refers to a built-in Excel analytical tool that facilitates what-if analysis by calculating and listing multiple results as one or two assumptions are changed for a variety of possible outcomes. Data tables help analysts to explore a set of possible outcomes given certain adjustments to the underlying assumptions. It also allows analysts to prepare straightforward reports that focus on just outcome data. Table 14-5 illustrates two data table examples, both involving altering one variable over a range of possible assumptions. Table 14-6 is an example of a two-variable data table.

Data tables are very useful for a wide range of analyses. Throughout this text, data tables could have been used for cash budgets, strategic financial planning, or capital investment analysis. This section describes the process using a very simple projection of a three-year income statement. The income statement is driven from last year's actual sales of $1,000 and sales growth as well as total expenses (as a percent of sales), as seen below:

	A	B	C	D	E
1		Year 1	Year 2	Year 3	Sensitivity
2	Sales growth	10.0%	20.0%	50.0%	0.0%
3	Expenses (% of sales)	90.0%	91.0%	92.0%	0.0%
4					
5	Sales	$1,100	$1,320	$1,980	
6	Expense	990	1,201	1,822	
7	Income	$ 110	$ 119	$ 158	

This is a very simple model! But it is also the first step in demonstrating data tables: build a model.

The second step involves how the assumptions are established. In this case, both assumptions are changing over time. If we want to examine incremental changes, we need to also create sensitivity cells such as E2 for incremental sales growth and E3 for incremental expenses (as a percent of sales). They are set initially at 0.0 percent incremental change.

Third, recast the assumptions to include the sensitivity cell. In this way, when you change the sensitivity cell, each assumption will change. Thus year 1 sales growth is listed as "=0.10+E2," year 2 as "=0.20+E2," and year 3 as "=0.50+E2." Expenses have the same setup: Year 1 is "=0.90+E3," year 2 is "=0.91+E3," and year 3 is "=0.92+E3." Having established the model to accommodate data table analysis, we are ready to build and run data tables.

One-Variable Data Table

To create a one-variable data table centered on sales growth, build a data table with the incremental assumptions in a column such as column A; decide what information is important to display, such as the third year's sales, expense, and income; create (row 9) headers to identify the results (and not a direct part of the data table process); and reference the cell from the model that contains the data results (row 10):

	A	B	C	D	E
8					
9		Year 3 sales	Year 3 expense	Year 3 income	
10		+D5	+D6	+D7	
11	2.0%				
12	0.0%				
13	−2.0%				

Next, highlight the data table area (gray area):

	A	B	C	D	E
8					
9		Year 3 sales	Year 3 expense	Year 3 income	
10		+D5	+D6	+D7	
11	2.0%				
12	0.0%				
13	−2.0%				

From the top "ribbon" in Excel, click on "Data," then on "What If Analysis," and then on "Data Tables" using Excel 2007 or 2010. For Excel 2003, simply click on "Data" then on "Tables." Up pops a box like this:

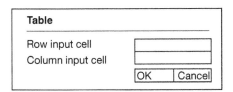

Since our assumptions for sales growth are arranged in a column, enter the sales growth sensitivity cell reference (E2) in the "Column input" box and click on "OK":

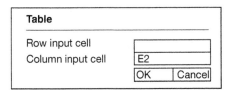

Excel takes 2.0 percent, adds it to the designated sensitivity cell, reruns the model, and lists the data that we requested. Then Excel takes 0.0 percent, puts it in the sensitivity cell, and the process is repeated. Finally, Excel uses –2.0 percent to complete the analysis, and the following data table (one variable) is produced:

	A	B	C	D	E
8					
9	Incremental	Year 3 sales	Year 3 expense	Year 3 income	
10	Sales growth	+D5	+D6	+D7	
11	2.0%	$2,077	$1,911	$166	
12	0.0%	1,980	1,822	158	
13	–2.0%	1,886	1,735	151	

The same steps can be retraced to examine expenses, but this time use "E3" as the column cell input, and the following table is produced:

	A	B	C	D	E
8					
9	Incremental	Year 3 sales	Year 3 expense	Year 3 income	
10	Expenses	+D5	+D6	+D7	
11	2.0%	$1,980	$1,861	$119	
12	0.0%	1,980	1,822	158	
13	–2.0%	1,980	1,782	198	

Notice that sales do not change because we are only adjusting incremental expenses.

Two-Variable Data Table

To create a two-variable data table using sales growth and expenses as the data-assumption variables, build a data table with the first incremental assumptions in a row (sales growth) and the other assumption in a column (expenses); decide what information is the most important to display, such as the third year's income (cell D7); and reference this output data in the upper left-corner cell (A16):

	A	B	C	D	E
14	Incremental				
15	Expenses	Incremental sales growth			
16	+D7	2.0%	0.0%	–2.0%	
17	2.0%				
18	0.0%				
19	–2.0%				

In the case of a two-variable data table, you can only report one model result at a time.

Next, highlight the data table area (gray area):

	A	B	C	D	E
14	Incremental				
15	Expenses	Incremental sales growth			
16	+D7	2.0%	0.0%	−2.0%	
17	2.0%				
18	0.0%				
19	−2.0%				

From the top "ribbon" in Excel, click on "Data," then on "What If Analysis," and then on "Data Tables" using Excel 2007 or 2010. For Excel 2003, simply click on "Data" and then "Tables." Up pops a box just like before:

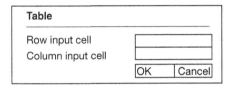

Since our assumptions for sales growth are arranged in a row, enter the sales growth sensitivity cell reference (E2) in the row input cell. Also, since our incremental expense assumption is arranged in a column, enter its sensitivity cell reference (E3) in the column input cell and click "OK":

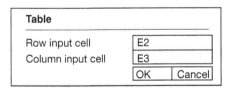

Excel systematically substitutes both incremental variables for all combinations, reruns the model for each pair, and lists the data (year 3 income) that we requested. The following two-variable data table is produced:

	A	B	C	D	E
14	Incremental				
15	Expenses	Incremental sales growth			
16	+D7	2.0%	0.0%	−2.0%	
17	2.0%	$125	$119	$113	
18	0.0%	166	158	151	
19	−2.0%	208	198	189	

While the ability to prepare data tables does not add value to an organization, it does provide a landscape analysis that may help management to chart a course.

STRATEGY FORMULATION AND VALUATION

Within the context of the strategic financial plan (Chapter 6), we observed many financial performance metrics as we tried to summarize the base-scenario plan. We centered our attention on income statement values, balance sheet amounts, cash-flow levels, and financial performance metrics for the first and last years of our analysis. There were many performance indicators to balance when evaluating the quality of the plan and when comparing differing scenarios.

With valuation analysis, the focus is clear—the value of Hershey's business. When finance professionals use the term *adding value*, they are referring to enhancing shareholder value and the share price. So far we developed a valuation model and considered the impact of changing one variable at a time through sensitivity analysis, which provided a general overview of the major (and minor) impacts on the base scenario.

By examining alternative go-to business strategies, management can consider many approaches. As in Chapter 6, two competing scenarios involve a growth scenario (often proposed by the marketing group) and a "cash cow" scenario (often proposed by the CFO). Table 14-7 summarizes the distinctions between the growth scenario and the cash-cow scenario and is identical to the two scenarios defined in Chapter 6 (Tables 6-19 and 6-20). Notice that the enhanced growth rates found in the growth scenario are facilitated by additional marketing spending. Conversely, within the cash-cow scenario, management is willing to live with lower growth rates as long as selling, marketing, and administrative costs are reduced.

Additionally, the growth scenario required more investment in working capital and fixed assets, whereas the cash-cow scenario required less investment. From a "base" scenario value of $58.82, the growth scenario created a value of $60.99 per share, whereas the cash-cow scenario enhanced the value even more to $61.57. The cash-cow scenario should be strongly considered and discussed by the management team.

In Chapter 6 we also considered the impact of a stock-repurchase program on the base-scenario strategic financial plan. That event had dramatic impact on components of the balance sheet and the financial performance metrics. However, the repurchase program does not affect the value of the company or stock today! It is a financing decision, not an operating decision. Since we determined that the value of a share of Hershey stock exceeded Hershey's stock price, Hershey's management should (and does) consider a share-repurchase program.

As evidenced earlier, the value of an organization (whether it is a corporation or division or whether it is publicly traded or privately held) can be derived from the organization's strategic financial plan. It can be discussed, debated, and reassessed while being directly related to the firm's strategic plan.

T A B L E   14-7

Scenario Assumptions:
Growth versus Cash Cow

	Projected				
	2011	2012	2013	2014	2015
Sales growth rate					
Base scenario	5.00%	4.50%	4.00%	3.50%	3.00%
Growth scenario	5.50%	6.50%	5.00%	4.00%	3.00%
Incremental	0.50%	2.00%	1.00%	0.50%	0.00%
Cash-cow scenario	4.00%	2.50%	3.00%	3.00%	2.50%
Incremental	−1.00%	−2.00%	−1.00%	−0.50%	−0.50%
Selling, marketing, and administrative					
Base scenario	26.00%	26.50%	26.00%	25.50%	25.00%
Growth scenario	27.50%	28.50%	27.00%	25.50%	25.00%
Incremental	1.50%	2.00%	1.00%	0.00%	0.00%
Cash cow scenario	23.50%	24.50%	24.00%	23.50%	23.00%
Incremental	−2.50%	−2.00%	−2.00%	−2.00%	−2.00%

However, a more direct valuation approach without considering the strategic plan also can be used. This direct-valuation model follows the next topic on cost management.

MANAGING COSTS WITH FUTURES AND OPTIONS

Adding value is a common phrase that is used in many aspects of business. In the context of our valuation, it means growing the business faster than planned, reducing costs, eliminating working capital investment, and managing investment in fixed assets. While we strive to spend less and enhance value, we also try to avoid increasing costs that destroy value. So we all "work smarter" and "do more with less."

The medium-sized company referenced in Chapter 6 projected its transportation costs at 7.00 percent of sales in 2011. However, its actual expenditure was only 5.85 percent of sales despite heavier volume and gasoline prices above the anticipated level. This had a significant impact on the company's valuation.

When asked about this performance, the senior vice president said that the company had reengineered some of its logistics processes. For example, instead of free overnight delivery of a case or two of product, it started to share the cost of overnight delivery with its customers as well as continuing its free shipping, but only on three-day shipping. For large-order customers that were serviced directly, the company started to "cube out" its delivery trucks. That is, instead of sending a truck that was only a third full, a new ordering/logistics system required trucks to be 90 percent full with regional deliveries to multiple customers. Thus, despite the spike in gas prices and increased sales levels, the company was able to decrease its overall costs, saving the over $1 million and enhancing shareholder value!

How a company goes to business is critical! How a division, function, or department accomplishes its area's objectives is crucial and provides another opportunity to enhance value. Continuous improvement, restructuring, and reengineering always must be considered, well thought out, and implemented effectively.

Adding value also means managing any risk that otherwise would disrupt the value drivers. Futures, forwards, and options are viable derivative tools that companies use to manage their costs.

A *futures contract* is an agreement, made today between a buyer and a seller, to buy or sell a particular commodity at a predetermined price some time in the future. Futures contracts are traded on a futures exchange between anonymous parties (buyers and sellers). Futures often settle on the third Friday of a trading month and may require physical delivery of the asset, whereas others contracts are settled in cash. Of course, if you buy a futures contract today, you also can sell that same contract before it matures, and delivery is negated. Most futures contracts are settled in this way. Finally, each contract is standardized and details the quality and quantity of the underlying asset. This feature facilitates trading on a futures exchange.

The types of commodities futures that are traded include:

- Metals and petroleum
- Agricultural products
- Interest rates
- Currency
- Stock indexes

Of course, there are many different subcategories of each commodity traded. In some cases, multiple exchanges trade the same commodity. For example, wheat is traded on commodity futures exchanges in Chicago, Minneapolis, and Kansas City.

Table 14-8 provides excerpted listings from the *Wall Street Journal* on July 1, 2011. Gold and crude oil (light sweet) are listed because of their high volumes and general interest, whereas cocoa and sugar are listed owing to their importance to Hershey. The table lists the opening price per unit, the high, the low, and the settle (or closing) price, as well as the number of contracts outstanding. The months listed are the contract months for delivery on the third Friday of that specific month. In the case of gold (which is traded in dollars per troy ounce on the Chicago Mercantile Exchange) and crude oil, light (which is traded in dollars per barrel on the New York Mercantile Exchange), the August 2011-dated contracts for both commodities have over 300,000 outstanding "open" contracts each. Cocoa and sugar futures contracts are traded on the International Commodity Exchange in New York City. Neither commodity is as deeply traded as gold or crude oil. Futures contracts are limited by the length of the contract. Some commodities trade only a year or so out, whereas others trade up to 30 months out (for instance, crude oil).

Closely aligned with a futures contract is a forward contract. A *forward contract* is made between two parties to buy and sell a specific commodity quantity some time in the future at a set price without a clearinghouse exchange involved. A forward contract allows for many more delivery-date options as well as a variety of more commodities.

T A B L E   14-8

Selected Commodity Future Contracts
(Listings as of June 30, 2011)

	Open	High	Low	Settle	Open Interest
Gold (CMX) – 100 troy ounces; $ per troy ounce					
July	1511.50	1514.00	1498.80	1502.30	159
August	1512.30	1514.80	1499.10	1502.80	315,635
October	1513.30	1515.40	1501.30	1503.80	12,987
December	1513.80	1516.40	1501.70	1505.00	81,734
June '12	1514.00	1517.30	1506.00	1509.60	13,333
December	1523.30	1523.30	1515.00	1516.40	10,774
Crude oil, light sweet (NYM) – 1,000 barrels; $ per barrel					
August	95.08	95.85	93.85	95.42	311,066
September	95.47	96.32	94.34	95.96	189,646
October	96.03	96.80	95.01	96.50	73,826
December	97.21	97.78	95.95	97.53	185,617
December '12	100.28	101.54	99.30	100.86	146,665
December '13	100.00	101.16	99.82	101.15	72,564
Cocoa (ICE-US), 10 metric tons, $ per ton					
July	3,146	3,176	3,146	3,170	34
September	3,119	3,161	3,104	3,151	68,099
Sugar-Domestic (ICE-US) – 112,000 pounds, cents per pound					
September	35.35	35.45	35.35	35.38	2,116
January '12	36.25	36.35	36.25	36.28	2,491

Excerpted from the *Wall Street Journal*, 7/1/11, p. C12.

While more detailed commodity futures trading is beyond the scope of this book, the concept behind commodity trading is simple. Futures trading originated over 150 years ago. Wheat farmers would borrow money from banks, plant their crop in the spring, work their fields, and harvest their crops in the late summer. Millers would buy the farmers' wheat to mill and turn into intermediary (flour) or other products. All parties would be subject to the whims of the actual (or spot) marketplace. If the cash price fell, millers were happy, but the farmers were not, and the banks worried about repayment of the loans. If cash prices rose, then the millers would be negatively affected, whereas the farmer would make "abnormal profits," and the bankers would be repaid easily.

So producers (farmers) and customers (millers), sellers and buyers, got together and negotiated future prices that would satisfy both their needs. In this way, price risk and cost risk were removed for both parties as well as for the banks. Today's futures market works in much the same way.

In the 1970s, Hershey did not hedge its cocoa costs. The price of cocoa beans fluctuated wildly in that decade. Without the protection of a futures contract, Hershey suffered a loss and actually had a dividend payout of greater than 100 percent for 1 year. During the 1980s, the company began trading cocoa and sugar. Generally, Hershey has prepurchased the next 18 to 24 months of its commodity needs. Besides trading cocoa and sugar futures, Hershey also trades milk futures and diesel fuel futures, as well as various nut (e.g., peanuts, almonds, etc.) forward contracts.

The concept is simple. Hypothetically, the Hershey strategic plan (Chapter 6 and the valuation earlier in this chapter) included direct material expense of $1,845.6 million as part of the cost of goods sold (in Table 6-13 and Table 14-2) for 2011. Further, let's say that cocoa represented $900.0 million of direct materials, assuming a cost of $3,200 per ton (for 281.25 million tons). As seen on Table 14-9, panel A, if Hershey did not hedge its cocoa cost and prices rose by 10 percent (5 percent) to $3,520 ($3,360) next year, this would reduce Hershey's income by $90.0 ($45.0) million. However, if the spot price fell next year by 10 percent or by 5 percent, Hershey would be able to make "gains" from the plan of $90.0 or $45.0, respectively.

Rather than being exposed to the risk of fluctuating commodity prices, Hershey could buy future contracts today to lock in the price of $3,200 per ton and avoid any deviation from plan. Table 14-9, panel B, starts with the same actual commodity market impact. You can see that the operating gains and losses are identical to panel A. However, owing to the futures contract, if the price rises to $3,520, Hershey effectively gains $90 million from the futures transaction while "losing" $90.0 in the cash market. Hershey is perfectly hedged and locked in at $3,200 per ton, and no net loss is incurred.

But look what happens if the price falls by 10 percent to $2,880. Operating costs would have been lower by $90.0 million and Hershey would have realized a gain of $90 million. However, the futures contract lost $90.0 million. If only we would have known then what we know now, we would not have hedged! We

T A B L E   14-9

Cocoa Hedging Results
($ millions, except cost per ton)

	Price −10%	Price −5%	Plan Price	Price 5%	Price 10%
Panel A: No Futures Contracts: Buy at "spot" current market prices					
Required tonnage	281.25	281.25	281.25	281.25	281.25
Spot cost per ton	2,880	3,040	3,200	3,360	3,520
Total cocoa expense ($ mm)	810.0	855.0	900.0	945.0	990.0
Better (worse) than plan	90.0	45.0	–	(45.0)	(90.0)
Panel B: Futures Contract: Buy in 2010 at $3,200 per ton					
1. Spot or cash market operations					
Required tonnage	281.25	281.25	281.25	281.25	281.25
Price per ton	2,880	3,040	3,200	3,360	3,520
Total cocoa expense ($ mm)	810.0	855.0	900.0	945.0	990.0
Operations better (worse) than plan	90.0	45.0	–	(45.0)	(90.0)
2. Futures market					
Tonnage purchased forward	281.25	281.25	281.25	281.25	281.25
Price per ton	3,200	3,200	3,200	3,200	3,200
Total cocoa expense ($ mm)	900.0	900.0	900.0	900.0	900.0
Futures better (worse) than spot	(90.0)	(45.0)	–	45.0	90.0
3. Combined effect					
Combined better (worse) than plan	$ –	$ –	$ –	$ –	$ –

would have made $90.0 million more from operations. But the point of hedging is to remove the underlying risk—in either direction.

Any manager who uses futures or forwards to hedge must realize that hedging reduces risk and locks in prices, as we saw here. It does not provide one-sided coverage only when spot prices rise.

Options on futures contracts do provide such one-sided coverage. An *option* gives the buyer the right (but not the obligation) to buy a commodity futures contract at a specified price and for a specific delivery month. Commodity options are expensive. This is in sharp contrast to a future or forward contract, where only a "good faith" margin of 25 percent or less needs to be posted.

Since this is only a "50,000-foot level discussion," please see more involved commodity futures oriented texts for additional uses and opportunities.

DIRECT VALUATION MODEL

Table 14-10 steps away from the strategic financial plan and recasts the five-year explicit valuation cash flows (from Table 14-2) as a percent of sales. Within an organization, it is appropriate to work at a detailed level that can be supported by various estimates and projections. Detail can be down to a division, business unit, product line, or even a product. However, as outsiders, we obviously do not have that same level of detail. As we prepare to value an organization, we must remind ourselves that we have a cleaver and not a scalpel!

Table 14-11 is derived from Table 14-10, which, of course, stems directly from the hypothetical strategic plan for Hershey (Table 14-2). Both Tables (14-11 and 14-2) result in the same outcomes. However, the comprehensive valuation model (CVM) completes the analysis in one "simple" model. We do not need to forecast accounts receivable, inventory, accounts payable, and so on. We forecast only the impact of working capital.

TABLE 14-10

Valuation Cash Flows as a Percent of Sales
($ millions)

	Projected				
	2011	2012	2013	2014	2015
Net sales	100.00%	100.00%	100.00%	100.00%	100.00%
Cost of sales	53.50%	53.20%	53.00%	52.80%	52.80%
Depreciation	3.52%	3.74%	3.83%	3.91%	4.00%
Selling, general, & administrative	26.00%	26.50%	26.00%	25.50%	25.00%
Total costs	83.02%	83.44%	82.83%	82.21%	81.80%
Operating income (or EBIT)	16.98%	16.56%	17.17%	17.79%	18.20%
Tax expense	6.28%	6.13%	6.35%	6.58%	6.73%
After-tax operating income	10.70%	10.43%	10.82%	11.21%	11.47%
Depreciation	3.52%	3.74%	3.83%	3.91%	4.00%
Change in					
Accounts receivable, trade	−0.30%	−0.25%	−0.22%	−0.18%	−0.15%
Inventory	−0.96%	−0.33%	−0.28%	−0.22%	−0.14%
Accounts payable	0.81%	0.43%	0.39%	0.36%	0.36%
Prepaid expenses	−0.17%	−0.24%	−0.31%	−0.37%	−0.43%
Other assets	−0.34%	−0.40%	−0.46%	−0.52%	−0.58%
Accrued liabilities	1.17%	0.58%	0.42%	0.36%	0.35%
Other long-term liabilities	0.19%	0.37%	0.33%	0.29%	0.25%
Working capital investment, total	0.42%	0.16%	−0.13%	−0.30%	−0.34%
Cash from operating activities	14.63%	14.33%	14.52%	14.82%	15.12%
Investment activities					
Capital expenditures	−5.88%	−3.46%	−2.86%	−2.84%	−2.90%
Cash (used for) investing	−5.88%	−3.46%	−2.86%	−2.84%	−2.90%
Free cash flow, % of Sales	8.76%	10.88%	11.66%	11.98%	12.22%

TABLE 14-11

Comprehensive Valuation Model
($ millions)

		Year 1 2011	Year 2 2012	Year 3 2013	Year 4 2014	Year 5 2015
Panel A: Valuation Assumptions						
Year 0 (2010) Revenue	$ 5,671.0					
Revenue growth		5.00%	4.50%	4.00%	3.50%	3.00%
Percent of Sales						
Cost of sales (excluding depreciation)		53.50%	53.20%	53.00%	52.80%	52.80%
Depreciation (% of sales)		3.52%	3.74%	3.83%	3.91%	4.00%
Selling, marketing, and administrative		26.00%	26.50%	26.00%	25.50%	25.00%
Total operating expense		83.02%	83.44%	82.83%	82.21%	81.80%
Operating margin		16.98%	16.56%	17.17%	17.79%	18.20%
Tax rate		37.00%	37.00%	37.00%	37.00%	37.00%
Fixed capital investment		5.88%	3.46%	2.86%	2.84%	2.90%
Working capital (dis) investment		0.42%	0.16%	−0.13%	−0.30%	−0.34%
Terminal growth rate	2.00%					
Cost of capital	7.30%					
Panel B: Projected Free Cash Flow and Valuation						
Net Revenue		$ 5,954.6	$ 6,222.6	$ 6,471.5	$ 6,698.0	$ 6,898.9
Cost of sales (excluding depreciation)		3,185.7	3,310.4	3,429.9	3,536.5	3,642.6
Depreciation		209.6	232.9	247.9	261.6	276.1
Selling, marketing, and administrative		1,548.2	1,649.0	1,682.6	1,708.0	1,724.7
Operating Income		1,011.1	1,030.3	1,111.1	1,191.9	1,255.5
Taxes		374.1	381.2	411.1	441.0	464.5
After-tax operating income		637.0	649.1	700.0	750.9	791.0
Percent of Sales		10.7%	10.4%	10.8%	11.2%	11.5%
Depreciation		209.6	232.9	247.9	261.6	276.1
Working capital investment		24.8	9.9	(8.3)	(19.9)	(23.7)
Capital expenditures		(350.0)	(215.0)	(185.0)	(190.0)	(200.0)
Free cash flow		$ 521.4	$ 676.9	$ 754.6	$ 802.6	$ 843.4
Terminal value						16,231.5
Total cash flow		$ 521.4	$ 676.9	$ 754.6	$ 802.6	$ 17,074.9
PV of explicit cash flows	$ 2,883.1					
Terminal value	11,412.0					
Value of the operations	$ 14,295.1					

To estimate sales, we need the initial (year 0) sales level and estimated growth. Next, we estimate after-tax operating income by subtracting the three expenses [cost of sales (COS), depreciation expense, and selling, general, and administrative (SG&A)]. COS and SG&A have been projected separately as a percent of sales and show annual improvement over this five-year period. The vice president of manufacturing has been tasked to reduce the COS, whereas the vice presidents of sales, marketing, and the other functional areas have been asked to lead cost reductions in their areas. Depreciation is a mechanical calculation detailed in Chapter 6 but simplified here as a percent of sales. These assumptions lead to a 2015 projected operating income of $1,255.5 million before taxes and $791.0 million after taxes.

Add back in the depreciation (because it is a noncash expense), consider the working capital and other operating assets and liabilities investment (use of cash in 2013 to 2015) or disinvestment (source of cash in 2011 and 2012), and subtract capital expenditures. These last two items also have been estimated as a percent of sales. This results in $843.4 million of cash flow in 2015.

This model is less cumbersome and more directly focused (on valuation) than the complete strategic financial plan (in Chapter 6) and extended earlier in this chapter. However, this model does allow specific assignment of performance objectives and does facilitate discussions with management.

After deriving the annual cash flows, the terminal value, enterprise value, and value per share are calculated as discussed earlier and result in a value per share of $58.82.

REAL OPTIONS

Chapter 10 discussed capital investment analysis and various techniques such as sensitivity analysis, scenario analysis, and even an advanced statistical technique called *Monte Carlo analysis*. Many investment decisions allow a company the ability to modify the project if its performance is not going according to plan. These options on physical assets and investments are called *real options*. To be a growth company, a firm must continuously develop positive net present value— new investment opportunities. These are complex decisions involving considerable uncertainties. These are strategic decisions requiring long-term perspectives. Decision makers can benefit from sequential learning. As more information is developed, the investment programs can be expanded, modified, or abandoned. This is the subject matter of real options.

A firm may acquire real options by the learning developed from embarking on new areas of activity. In the process, a firm may acquire real options through technological advances and increased understanding of new products and markets. A firm may acquire real options through intellectual property rights such as patents and licenses. The organizational capabilities of the firm may be strengthened. Strategic alliances and joint ventures may be used to enhance the firm's market position.

The benefits of a real-options approach to investment decisions can be substantial. A real-options analysis helps to systematize the decision process. The analytical frameworks developed in a real-options analysis can uncover new dimensions and provide deeper insights. It also provides a common language for communication among different managerial functions (e.g., strategy, research, production, marketing, etc.). Real-options analysis may provide insights and intuitions that sometimes may challenge conventional thinking. For example, the higher the volatility of outcomes, the greater may be the value of the investment program.

The actual computational aspects for real options is quite advanced and well beyond this particular text. The concepts are practical in their applications. In fact, at Hershey, we discussed the optionality of projects even before the term *real options* gained acceptance. When considering entry into the refrigerated puddings business, the project did not reach its hurdle rate. But the project's champion argued that if the puddings business were successful, then Hershey could launch other refrigerated desserts. This was a form of real option.

Options on Assets

Option-pricing approaches to valuation are the best way to think about pricing flexibility in the modeling process. Ordinary net present value (NPV) analysis tends to understate a project's value because it fails to capture adequately the benefits of operating flexibility and other strategic factors, such as follow-on investment. Real options and their implications for NPV analysis and investment decisions are summarized below. Real options include the following:

- *Abandonment option.* The option to abandon (or sell) a project is equivalent to a put option. At numerous points in a project's life, management can decide to exit the project and realize proceeds from the sale of that project. If Hershey wanted to enter another line of business, such as the restaurant business, there is an embedded option in that decision. If the industry investment was not living up to expectations, the business could be sold. This represents an abandonment option. Of course, when the original project evaluation is submitted for approval, rarely does this approval include a full discussion about abandoning the project at some point.

- *Option to expand or grow.* The option to expand the scale of a project's operation is equivalent to a call option. Hershey's puddings provided a real option to expand Hershey's refrigerated business into other new products if the puddings were successful. The puddings were not successful, and the call option never exercised.

- *Option to shrink.* The option to shrink the scale of a project's operations is equivalent to a put option. As an example, after an engineer teams up with an accountant, cost estimates are created for building a distribution center. The initial decision could encompass the decision to build a 100,000-, 500,000-, or 1-million-square-foot facility. The cost of building the largest facility may be fractions per square foot of building the other-sized facilities. In this case, management is confident of the need for the larger facility, which gets accepted and built. If the actual performance does not reach the original levels anticipated, the company has an option to shrink by subdividing the building and selling or leasing out that unused portion of the building.

- *Option to defer development.* The option to defer an investment outlay to develop a property or product is equivalent to a call option. Because the deferrable investment gives management the right, but not the obligation, to make the investment to develop a property or product, a project that can be deferred is worth more than the same project without the flexibility to defer development. For a retail company or a restaurant, an investment in a piece of land in a developing area without incurring the construction costs of that restaurant until the site proves more attractive is an example of the option to defer development.

- *Switching option.* This is a general name applied to a few similar types of decisions. Restarting or shutting down options pertain to (as their name suggests) restarting or shutting down plant/line operations. The switching option also relates to flexible manufacturing equipment, which may cost more initially but can produce more than one product. Manufacturing flexibility has value that is captured within a switching option. Extending this thought, in an evaluation of a new product, there always is concern that marketing projections will not be realized. An option is provided if the production line can be easily retrofitted to support the production of other products.

While the exact computational steps for real options are beyond the scope of this text, the recognition of a project's managerial flexibility leads to the consideration of multiple cash-flow scenarios and analyses that span and evaluate the possible alternatives. Applying probabilities to the scenario analyses may aid the management decision-making process.

SUMMARY

The topic of strategic valuation is central to the concept of this text, but more important, it is central to business as well. The valuation process that I advocate is as follows:

- Historical financial analysis (Chapters 2, 3, 4, and 5)
- Review of general economic conditions (Chapter 8)
- Forecasts of future performance (Chapter 6)
- Valuation of projected cash flows (Chapters 7, 9, 10, and 11)

This chapter completes the valuation process. The tools presented here are useful to management and serve different purposes, such as valuing an acquisition candidate or determining the asking price of a divestiture property. Valuation also provides a tool for management to objectively complete the company's self-valuation. The majority of companies prepare a strategic plan such as we saw in Chapter 6. This process is a final step to value that business plan.

The most widely accepted valuation method is the discounted cash flow (DCF) method. The DCF methodology introduced in this chapter begins with the strategic financial plan of Chapter 6. It centers only on operating cash flows.

Using a perpetuity with growth approach, a terminal value of the firm is estimated. The cash flows including the terminal value are discounted, and an enterprise value, as well as the total value of the equity and value per share, is derived.

Valuation is inherently a judgment. It combines science and art. The art of completing valuations is to make an initial estimate based on rational, best-judgment estimates of the determinants (also called *drivers*) of value. Then, based on a sensitivity analysis, data tables, and alternative scenarios, the process can improve understanding of the firm's competitive position and lead to value enhancements.

The mantra in corporate America has been to *enhance shareholder value*. This is the underlying model and a very appropriate technique that is used widely. This approach gives you an opportunity to see directly how you can add value to the organization. Whether it's selling more product, reducing costs, or reducing the investment in both fixed and working capital, we all can create shareholder value.

Futures and options can help a company to hedge its expenses and stabilize its valuation. More broadly, real options and the company's alternatives add to the underlying value of the organization. Additional benefits may be generated from using real-options analysis. The analytical frameworks developed in a real-options analysis can uncover new dimensions and provide deeper insights. It also provides a common language for communication among different managerial functions.

MERGERS AND ACQUISITIONS

In January 1979, The Hershey Company ventured into the restaurant business. For the sum of $165 million, Hershey bought the Friendly Ice Cream (FIC) Corporation, a chain of family restaurants primarily in the Northeast and Florida. As the name implies, one of the Friendly featured items is ice cream. At the time, Hershey paid a 40 percent premium to FIC stockholders. The rationale was simple: diversification. During the 1970s, the price of cocoa whipsawed, and Hershey management felt that it was time to diversify. "After all, people have to eat, and if they don't eat at home, they'll eat out!"

If diversification was the driving motive, and as a Hershey stockholder, I was concerned about the "evil" cocoa bean, why couldn't I just sell some of my Hershey stock and buy FIC stock at the current market price? Why did Hershey need to do this on my behalf and pay a 40 percent premium? These are fair questions to ask. Similar questions should be asked at the start of any potential acquisition.

In 1988, Friendly was sold for approximately $365 million. A postcompletion audit showed that Hershey just attained a slightly positive return that exceeded the cost of capital.

This chapter discusses the major motives for acquisitions and reviews some other alternatives for external growth, followed by an examination of the acquisition process used inside many Fortune 1000 companies. Before looking at accounting for an acquisition or valuing an acquisition, some important general valuation considerations are discussed. The chapter concludes with some useful considerations that may enhance the likelihood of a successful acquisition.

Before we start, here are some important background statistics to carry with you through this chapter. First, 90 percent of all acquisitions are private. That is, one company buys a private company or a division, a business unit, or even a brand. A publicly traded company buying another publicly traded company does not happen that often. This is why when it does, it is often big news. Second, 70 to 80 percent of acquisitions are failures measured in a variety of ways. Finally, there is usually a 40 percent premium paid when a publicly traded company is acquired. That is, a 40 percent premium above the stock price before there was a bid placed on the company.

CHANGE DYNAMICS

Merger and acquisition (M&A) activity in recent years has been driven in part by strong change forces brought about by inexpensive and reliable technology, communications, and transportation throughout the world economy. These change forces reduced the cost of doing business and created global markets. Not only have traditional sources of competition increased, but new forms of businesses and industries also have added competition. On top of it, deregulation has taken place in most industries, and international trade barriers have fallen. With the rise of personal and business wealth, the commoditization of many goods became common, and the search was on for new and improved products. Today, competition is more intense than ever.

Extending Capabilities

The economic theory of mergers is that they help firms to adjust to the many change forces confronting business, including increased competitive pressures. The business rationale for acquiring a new company may be positive net present values. Figure 15-1 demonstrates. Mergers increase value when the value of the combined firm is greater than adding the premerger values of the independent entities together.

F I G U R E   15-1

Synergy: The driving M&A source.

From the figure, if a portfolio manager owns stock in both the target company and the buyer company, his or her portfolio is worth $100. There is no interaction between the two companies, and portfolio managers merely keep track of their investment.

On the other hand, if one company (the buyer) buys, owns, and manages the other company (the target), there is an opportunity to generate additional value between the two. Of course, this needs to be prudently thought through by the buyer because often a premium of 40 percent or more is paid. In the example in Figure 15-1, that premium is $8.

We can formalize these generalizations in the relationship shown in Eq. (15.1):

$$V_{BT} > (V_B + V_T + P) \qquad (15.1)$$

where V_{BT} = value of firms combined
V_B = value of bidder alone
V_T = value of target alone
P = Premium paid by the buyer

When the value of the combined entity V_{BT} exceeds the sum of the premerger value of the buyer, the premerger value of the target, and the premium paid, this is a value-enhancing acquisition. The value of the combined entity is greater than the value of the two organizations separately.

Continuing the example from Figure 15-1, the buyer offers $28 for the target company. The stockholders of the target company accept the offer, and the two companies become one organization. However, in order for this to be a positive net present value acquisition, management at the buyer company needs to generate additional value over and above the $8 premium that was paid for the target. In this regard, the acquisition will be a positive value-adding acquisition if and only if the buyer is able to raise the current and prospective outlook of the company by more than $8.

Enhancing Current Capabilities

Economies of scale provide one of the quickest forms of immediate postacquisition savings as production facilities, distribution centers, retail outlets, and other physical assets are combined into one system and rationalized or streamlined. The same is often true for employees from the executive office through staff levels down to the production floor. Sales forces, marketing staffs, research and development (R&D) personnel, customer-service representatives, and professionals in human resources, legal, finance, accounting, and all departments are subject to review. Workloads sometimes are shifted and positions rationalized.

Technological advances and capabilities may be extended through an acquisition, and greater leverage of those capabilities can be realized. Keep in mind that synergies are not just found in the target company. Synergies create additional value for the new combined company whether they are ascribed to the target or result for the buyer.

Geographic expansion also has been an area of enhancement. From regional expansion, to national and international growth, to becoming a global company, the value of an acquisition often can be enhanced through geographic expansion.

Adding capabilities and new managerial skills can take many forms, including the adoption of best demonstrated practices as one group applies the best of another group.

In some industries, consolidations occur throughout the supply chain as the functions of the organization expand or contract. Manufacturers buy suppliers to source a key ingredient. Food producers buy farms to raise and control their raw materials. While this is more of an operational consolidation, there are strategic (and often more significant) consolidations.

Industry consolidation across the economy also lays the framework to develop synergies. While there are many examples of this in technology, pharmaceuticals, media, and so on, this also was true of Disney, as we saw in Chapter 2. Disney looked beyond theme parks and an occasional film while combining related and strategic industries (e.g., media networks, parks and resorts, studio entertainment, consumer products, and interactive media). All units support and promote the other units and, of course, the "mouse."

Concentration of any U.S. industry is also carefully monitored by the U.S. Department of Justice (DOJ). If the DOJ feels that an acquisition provides monopolist powers, it will block an acquisition from occurring. In some cases, the DOJ may find small pockets of expected monopolistic power in the United States, say, in Pennsylvania. In such circumstances, the DOJ will not allow the acquiring firm to run the new property and the old property in Pennsylvania. The acquirer will need to sell off, close, or carve out that property (effectively, not buy the portion in question).

The DOJ measures industry concentration using the Herfindahl-Hirschman index (HHI), which is measured using Eq. (15.2):

$$HHI = \sum_{j=1}^{N} (S_j)^2 \qquad (15.2)$$

For an industry, square and sum the market share (S_j) for each company $(j = 1$ through N, or the total number of companies). Thus, if there were 100 companies in a competitive industry and each had a 1 percent market share, the HHI would be 100 $\left[\text{or} \sum_{j=1}^{100} (1)^2 \right]$.

If there were five companies in another industry and each had a 20 percent market share, the HHI would be 2,000:

$$
\begin{aligned}
HHI &= (S_1)^2 + (S_2)^2 + (S_3)^2 + (S_4)^2 + (S_5)^2 \\
&= (20)^2 + (20)^2 + (20)^2 + (20)^2 + (20)^2 \\
&= 400 + 400 + 400 + 400 + 400 \\
&= 2,000
\end{aligned}
$$

In this case, HHI measures 2,000, which would be considered a concentrated industry. If company 1 bought company 5, there would only be four companies in the industry—three with a 20 percent market share and one with a 40 percent market share. Under these conditions, the HHI would be 2,800:

$$HHI = (S_1)^2 + (S_2)^2 + (S_3)^2 + (S_4)^2$$
$$= (40)^2 + (20)^2 + (20)^2 + (20)^2$$
$$= 1,600 + 400 + 400 + 400$$
$$= 2,800$$

This is an increase of 800 points. In this case, the DOJ would step in and analyze the monopolistic power of company 1 more thoroughly.

In general, a market with an HHI of less than 1,000 is considered a competitive marketplace, an HHI of 1,000 to 1,800 is looked at as a moderately concentrated marketplace, and a value greater than 1,800 is a highly concentrated marketplace. If an acquisition increases the index by more than 100 points in concentrated markets, the DOJ will raise antitrust concerns.

In summary, the theory of strategic mergers emphasizes adjustments to change forces and broadening capabilities to improve performance without infringing upon the competitive nature of the marketplace. This theory emphasizes market forces that cause firms to use multiple methods of growth. These include internal expansion, licensing, alliances, joint ventures, minority investments, mergers, and acquisitions.

ALTERNATIVE METHODS FOR EXTERNAL GROWTH

Chapter 14 showed how important growth is in driving the value of a company. Companies concurrently pursue multiple growth strategies—internally and externally. Internally, companies support existing products while at the same time developing line extensions and new products. R&D is invested in by corporate America as it searches for the next generation of new products. Companies continue to provide goods and services in existing locations while also developing new regional areas and even new distribution channels. Companies follow many different paths and multiple methods for growth. M&As are only one form.

Table 15-1 summarizes alternative methods for external growth. The table is arranged such that at the top are less formal alternatives that involve little or no corporate control issues. As you work down the table, the formality and complexity, as well as the transfer of ownership, increase.

Licensing is similar to renting to others your proprietary technology, brand name, or trademarks. For example, General Mills (among others) buys Hershey chocolate to put in its cereal Cocoa Puffs. General Mills could be any other "industrial" customer and simply stop there. However, the company feels that the Hershey chocolate is a quality ingredient that will enhance the growth of its cereal. So General Mills would like to tell the world that it includes Hershey

TABLE   15-1

Alternative Methods for External Growth

1. Licensing – Renting to others proprietary technology, brand name, or trademarks.
2. Alliances – Informal inter-business relations.
3. Joint ventures – Two or more businesses get together for a specific purpose to accomplish a specific task over a limited duration.
4. Minority investments – A small fraction, usually less than 5 percent, of the equity of the target is acquired.
5. Mergers – Any transaction that forms one new company from the combination of two or more previous companies.
6. Acquisition – One company buys all (or most) of another company's ownership stakes in order to assume control of the target firm.

chocolate in its cereal. Hershey licenses to General Mills the Hershey name for just that purpose. Licensing is almost a new outlet (and product) that can increase markets and returns on investments already made.

Alliances provide an opportunity for two companies to work together. They are generally informal agreements. The relative size of participants may be highly unequal. Partner firms pool resources, expertise, and ideas so that the partners will have a continuing need for one another. Evolving relationships require adaptability and change over time. The alliance may involve multiple partners. Since the relationships are less legalistic, mutual trust is required. The speed of change in relationships may be rapid. Firms may modify and move to other alliances as attractive possibilities emerge. Some creative people do not wish to be in the environment of large firms, but large firms may increase their access to creative people by alliances with smaller firms.

Alliances may have some advantages over mergers or joint ventures. They are more informal and provide flexibility. They may provide a firm with access to new markets and technologies with relatively small investments. Alliances provide the ability to create and disband projects with minimal formality. Working with partners possessing multiple skills can create major synergies.

A joint venture is a separate business entity that usually involves only a fraction of the activities of the participating organizations. The participants in a joint venture continue as separate firms but create a new corporation, partnership, or other business form. Joint ventures are limited in scope and duration.

Several objectives may be achieved by a joint venture. Working with other firms reduces the investment costs of entering potentially risky new areas. Even though investment requirements are less than solely internal operations, the joint venture still may enjoy the benefits of economies of scale, critical mass, and the learning curve. Also, joint ventures allow firms the opportunity to gain knowledge. Firms may share or exchange technology to accomplish what one firm could not do alone. There is a potential for sharing managerial skills in organization, planning, and control.

Joint ventures have proven to be particularly advantageous in the international setting. In some situations, local governments may not allow an acquisition. A joint venture presents an opportunity to combine some assets without violating such a regulation. International joint ventures usually reduce business and political risks of firms operating in foreign countries. In addition, joint ventures have been used as a means of circumventing certain international trade barriers.

When a firm buys a segment divested by another firm, it may have a high uncertainty about its future performance under the buyer's management. This uncertainty may make it difficult for the parties to agree on a price. Joint ventures can serve a useful function as an interim step. A common pattern is for the acquirer to pay cash for 40 to 45 percent of the divested segment it is buying as its contribution to the formation of the joint venture. The joint venture may be used as a device for the selling firm to convey knowledge of manufacturing and/or distribution. The motivations and the incentives are all in the right directions. The better the selling firm does in teaching the acquirer the potentials of the segment, the more the segment will be worth in the future. As a consequence, after a year or two, the buyer may complete the purchase of the percentage of the joint venture it does not own. Typically, the price paid for the second segment is substantially higher than that for the first segment because the acquirer better understands the potentials of the business. Value is created by minimizing employee turnover and avoiding the impairment of supplier and distribution networks.

Minority investments represent a significant but not controlling interest in another company. For example, the minority investor (similar to a buyer) would buy a stake in a target company. The buyer can learn about new, attractive areas and is positioned to take advantage of the success of the target firm and even to acquire the entire firm at a later date.

M&As result in a full transfer of ownership from the target company. In a merger, both the target and buyer firms join together to form a new organization. In an acquisition, one company buys the other (target) and assumes complete control immediately. Both can add capabilities and markets in a relatively short period of time.

Firms take part in multiple forms of growth and expansion. They are activities that cross many years and the life of the firm.

THE M&A PROCESS

This section reviews the typical acquisition process within many Fortune 1000 companies. It begins with a sound strategic plan that may identify the need for development of the necessary capabilities and infrastructure to integrate any acquired firm.

From there, perhaps a vice president of corporate development, with the consent of management, may develop a three-pronged approach to pursuing acquisitions. This could include a "hit list" or group of companies that are reviewed on a regular basis in case one of them gets put "in play." The second approach is that of a suitor that will court a company for an extended period of time. Finally, and by far the most common, is the sealed-bid offer.

Under the sealed-bid approach, a potential bidder receives an initial contact from the seller's investment bank to see if there would be any interest in reviewing an offering document on this "unnamed" seller. If there is, a confidentiality agreement is signed, and the potential bidder receives the offering document. Approximately six weeks later, the bidder needs to provide a *preliminary non-binding indication of value* to the seller's attorney or investment bank. What could this be worth to you, the buyer, with this partial glimpse inside the organization? If you are one of the top three to five preliminary bidders, you move on to the second round.

The initial offering document is a 40- to 70-page document that provides an overview of the seller along with the seller's:

- History
- Business, including major products, markets, customers, and suppliers
- Management team profile
- List of production facilities, including locations, usage, utilization, and union status
- Limited historical financial information for the past two to five years

The offering document is just the first piece of information. Sometimes the offering document provides an overly optimistic cash-flow forecast that is routinely ignored by a potential bidder.

In the second round, plant visits are scheduled, discussions with the management team are held, and access is provided to the "data room" to further hone valuation assumptions. Finally, approximately four weeks later, final binding, sealed bids are delivered to and opened by the seller. Usually, the highest bid wins unless other conditions are attached.

Prior to submitting the binding sealed bid, there are presentations to senior management and the board of directors. Focus is on strategic rationale and financial valuation. It is a joint presentation between operating managers, who present, review, and discuss the business assumptions, and finance people, who review the base-case valuation with sensitivity, scenario, and data table analysis as well as financing. A bid of "up to $x" is agreed to and submitted.

EMPIRICAL REVIEW OF ACQUISITION RESULTS

Many studies have calculated the stock price impact days before an acquisition announcement and days immediately after the acquisition. These approaches are called *event studies*. This analysis is based on one publicly traded company buying another publicly traded company because those are the only available stock prices for this type of study. These studies also use a measure called a "cumulative abnormal return". This represents the stock's daily returns (less the return of the overall market). These daily abnormal returns are then accumulated over the period of time.

In summary, the returns to target firms begin to rise about 2–3 weeks before the acquisition announcement date even though there is a high degree of secrecy. Rumors abound and a slight price increase results before the announcement date. However, on the announcement date the target firm's stock price increases about 25 to 35 percent (commensurate with the bid) during that one day. In a multiple-bidder contest, the returns to target firms continue to rise after the announcement date as subsequent bids take place. Within one to three months after the announcement date, the returns to the target firms level off at about 40 to 50 percent if there are multiple bidders.

On the other hand, the returns for acquiring firms that are single bidders rise slightly on the announcement date and then drift down towards zero. For acquiring firms that are competing in multiple-bidder contests, the event returns are also slightly positive on the announcement date. Shortly after the announcement date, though, as new bidders come onto the scene, the event returns drop to slightly negative levels for the acquiring firm. In reality, neither the multibidder nor the single bidder experiences returns that are statistically significantly different from zero!

Lessons learned from this overview:

- The target firm (and its shareholders) always win! While the acquiring (or even bidding) companies tend to have limited effects on their stock price.

- Market efficiency takes hold. When there is an announcement of an acquisition and a potential price, the target's stock price jumps immediately.

- A buyer hopes to remain the only bidder and not to get into a prolonged "bidding war". While a target company, would like to see many bidders once the company is "put into play".

The preceding summary has been reflective of a short-term focus on the stock prices of both the target and the buyer. It is difficult to measure the effect of a single acquisition on a firm's stock price over an extended period of time. General economic conditions change, management teams change, and other acquisitions occur.

ACCOUNTING FOR ACQUISITIONS

The Financial Accounting Standards Board (FASB) issued two statements in June 2001 that made fundamental changes in accounting for M&As. The Statement of Financial Accounting Standards No. 141 on Business Combinations requires that all business combinations be accounted for by a single method—the purchase method. Statement of Financial Accounting Standards No. 142 on Goodwill and Other Intangible Assets set forth procedures for accounting for acquired goodwill and other intangible assets as well as for their impairment.

The basic procedures for purchase accounting have a logic to them. A simple example will illustrate. Usually the purchase price will be greater than the book value of shareholders' equity of the target. For example, in 1988, Hershey bought the Dietrich Corporation,[1] located in Reading, PA. The approximate purchase price was $100 million. For its $100 million, Hershey got $65 million in assets such as accounts receivable, inventory, land, buildings, equipment, and so on. Hershey also assumed $25 million of liabilities (i.e., accounts payable, debt, etc.). In total, for the $100 million purchase price, Hershey received net assets of $40 million. The $60 million difference is what is termed *goodwill* or the *extra value* paid for the ongoing business and established products of the Dietrich Corporation. Goodwill is more formally referred to on the balance sheet as *intangibles resulting from business acquisitions*.

Before 2002, this $60 million of goodwill would be amortized over 40 years. Every year, $1.5 million would be expensed as amortization expense. Now Hershey revisits the valuation each year. If the fair value falls below $100 million to, say, $80 million, then $20 million of asset impairment must be recognized and expensed immediately. On the other hand, if the fair value were $120 million, there would be no accounting statement recognition requirement.

ACQUISITION VALUATION

Chapter 14 discussed and examined a valuation model for The Hershey Company. In those models (Tables 14-2 and 14-11), we saw that Hershey was fairly valued at about $58.82 per share. The model is repeated here as Table 15-2. If a buyer wanted to acquire Hershey, a "usual" premium of 40 percent indicates that the amount offered would be about $82.35 per share, or $18,693.5 million (227.0 million shares at $82.35 per share). After adjusting for the cash received ($884.6 million) and the debt incurred ($1,827.3 million) the buyer would need to justify an enterprise value of $19,636.2 million.

The daunting (maybe impossible) task is illustrated on Table 15-3. This is a data table (see chapter 14) that examines the value per share for Hershey in relation to incremental sales growth and incremental margin improvement. Notice that the current value of Hershey is listed in the upper left-hand corner at $58.82. In the far right-hand, lower corner you can see that if an acquirer were able to increase Hershey's growth rate by 8 percent for the five explicit years (2011 to 2015) and improve operating margins by 8 percent, then the value of Hershey would approach $122 per share (or over a 100 percent premium).

---

[1]The Dietrich Corporation sold The Fifth Avenue Bar, Luden's Cough Drops, and a variety of other products.

T A B L E 15-2

Comprehensive Valuation Model
($ millions)

		Year 1 2011	Year 2 2012	Year 3 2013	Year 4 2014	Year 5 2015
Panel A – Valuation Assumptions						
Year 0 (2010) revenue	$ 5,671.0					
Revenue growth		5.00%	4.50%	4.00%	3.50%	3.00%
Percent of sales						
Cost of sales (excluding depreciation)		53.50%	53.20%	53.00%	52.80%	52.80%
Depreciation (% of sales)		3.52%	3.74%	3.83%	3.91%	4.00%
Selling, marketing, and administrative		26.00%	26.50%	26.00%	25.50%	25.00%
Total operating expense		83.02%	83.44%	82.83%	82.21%	81.80%
Operating margin		16.98%	16.56%	17.17%	17.79%	18.20%
Tax rate		37.00%	37.00%	37.00%	37.00%	37.00%
Fixed capital investment		5.88%	3.46%	2.86%	2.84%	2.90%
Working capital (dis) investment		0.42%	0.16%	-0.13%	-0.30%	-0.34%
Terminal growth rate	2.00%					
Cost of capital	7.30%					

(Continued)

TABLE 15-2

Comprehensive Valuation Model *(Continued)*

($ millions)

	Year 1 2011	Year 2 2012	Year 3 2013	Year 4 2014	Year 5 2015
Panel B – Projected Free Cash Flow and Valuation					
Net Revenue	$ 5,954.6	$ 6,222.6	$ 6,471.5	$ 6,698.0	$ 6,898.9
Cost of sales (excluding depreciation)	3,185.7	3,310.4	3,429.9	3,536.5	3,642.6
Depreciation	209.6	232.9	247.9	261.6	276.1
Selling, marketing, and administrative	1,548.2	1,649.0	1,682.6	1,708.0	1,724.7
Operating income	1,011.1	1,030.3	1,111.1	1,191.9	1,255.5
Taxes	374.1	381.2	411.1	441.0	464.5
After-tax operating income	637.0	649.1	700.0	750.9	791.0
Percent of sales	10.7%	10.4%	10.8%	11.2%	11.5%
Depreciation	209.6	232.9	247.9	261.6	276.1
Working capital investment	24.8	9.9	(8.3)	(19.9)	(23.7)
Capital expenditures	(350.0)	(215.0)	(185.0)	(190.0)	(200.0)
Free cash flow	$ 521.4	$ 676.9	$ 754.6	$ 802.6	$ 843.4
Terminal value					16,231.5
Total cash flow	$ 521.4	$ 676.9	$ 754.6	$ 802.6	$ 17,074.9

	Net cash adjustment		$ (942.7)
	Equity value		$ 13,352.4
	Value per share		$ 58.82

PV of explicit cash flows	$ 2,883.1
Terminal value	11,412.0
Enterprise value	$ 14,295.1

TABLE 15-3

Hershey Acquisition Valuation
Incremental Growth Rates and Operating Margins

Value per share			Additional Sales Growth							
		0%	1%	2%	3%	4%	5%	6%	7%	8%
	0%	$ 58.82	$ 61.66	$ 64.61	$ 67.67	$ 70.84	$ 74.13	$ 77.53	$ 81.04	$ 84.69
	1%	62.13	65.12	68.22	71.44	74.78	78.23	81.82	85.52	89.35
	2%	65.45	68.58	71.84	75.22	78.72	82.34	86.10	89.98	94.01
Operating	3%	68.76	72.05	75.45	79.00	82.66	86.45	90.38	94.46	98.67
Margin	4%	72.08	75.51	79.07	82.77	86.59	90.56	94.67	98.92	103.33
Improvement	5%	75.39	78.97	82.69	86.54	90.53	94.67	98.96	103.39	107.98
	6%	78.71	82.43	86.30	90.31	94.47	98.78	103.24	107.85	112.64
	7%	82.02	85.90	89.92	94.09	98.41	102.89	107.53	112.33	117.30
	8%	85.34	89.36	93.53	97.87	102.35	107.00	111.81	116.79	121.95

30% Premium: $76.47
40% Premium: $82.35
50% Premium: $88.23

The values in Table 15-3 differ from corresponding values on Tables 14-5 and 14-6. In this case, depreciation, working capital, and fixed capital investment all adjust to support the impact of sales changes. In chapter 14, these were assumed as fixed values from the strategic plan.

491

The highlighted areas of the table represent approximate valuations of:

Premium Amount	Table 15-3 Recognition
30 percent premium: $76.47	Light-gray shading
40 percent premium: $82.35	Portion between light and dark shading
50 percent Premium: $88.23	Dark-gray shading

Thus a 4 percent additional sales growth coupled with a 3 percent operating margin improvement generates a value of $82.66. A 5 percent operating margin improvement (along with 4 percent incremental sales growth) results in a value of $90.53 and easily higher than the 50 percent premium level. Both values are shown in bold italics on Table 15-3.

Table 15-3 considers only incremental changes to sales growth and operating margins. By virtue of the sales impact, all other values (expenses and investment) adjust to support sales. It is a sensitivity analysis that lies at the heart of almost all acquisition analysis, but it does not anticipate the dynamic and far-reaching aspects of a complete acquisition plan.

The acquiring company would consider many alternative scenarios in order to achieve value at an $82.35 acquisition price per share (40 percent premium). These scenarios would consider the benefits from addressing all business value drivers.

1. Increase revenue growth.
2. Increase operating profitability.
3. Reduce tax rates.
4. Limit fixed capital investment and use of underutilized assets.
5. Reduce working capital investment.
6. Reduce the cost of capital.

An acquiring company would need to review and perhaps streamline all of Hershey's operations in light of the acquiring company's operations. That is, what types of synergies exist when the two entities are combined throughout the "new" supply chain? Can Hershey's growth be stimulated by its products outside North America? In the combined entity, are there underutilized fixed assets that should be shared, considered for future expansion, or eliminated through plant and facility rationalization? Can working capital needs be combined and shared? Are there purchasing synergies to be shared? Can best demonstrated practices be implemented? And the list goes on and on. Eventually, every facet of an acquisition valuation is tested, retested, and accepted by management.

Continuing the Hershey example, another scenario that also gets to a value per share above the 40 percent premium is:

1. Increase sales growth in the first five years as follows:

Sales Growth	2011	2012	2013	2014	2015
Original	5.0%	4.5%	4.0%	3.5%	3.0%
Revised	8.0%	12.5%	9.0%	5.5%	4.0%

2. Reduce expenses leading to the improved operating margins.

Operating Margin	2011	2012	2013	2014	2015
Original	16.98%	16.56%	17.17%	17.79%	18.20%
Revised	17.98%	17.56%	18.67%	19.79%	20.20%

3. Reduce the cost of capital to 7.0 percent from 7.3 percent.

While these objectives don't seem out of reach, a get deal of care must be exhibited to realize these objectives. Table 15-4 captures this scenario and resulting value of slightly more than a 40% premium at $82.89.

COMPARABLE TRANSACTIONS VALUATION

In the comparable transactions valuation approach, key relationships are calculated for a group of similar transactions that were just consummated and closed. This group serves as a basis for the valuation of companies involved in a merger or takeover. For example, some "comps" can be derived as a multiple of income, EBITDA, cash flow, etc. You simply derive the "comp" on recent transactions and apply them to your valuation target. This approach is used as an approximation valuation technique by investment bankers and in legal cases. The method is not complicated. Marketplace transactions are used. It is a commonsense approach that says that similar companies should sell for similar prices. This straightforward approach appeals to businesspeople, to their financial advisors, and to the judges in courts of law called on to give decisions on the relative values of companies in litigation.

While this approach is easy to apply, it does not incorporate the anticipated performance of the target company. This technique also can be used after the discounted cash flow (DCF) approach of valuation is completed. The resulting "comps" derived from the DCF valuation and based on the same standard or income, EBITDA, cash flow, etc. can provide a reasonableness test for the DCF valuation.

GENERAL OBSERVATIONS OF M&A PRICING

As stated earlier, it is generally well accepted that 70 to 80 percent of all acquisitions are failures. With all the analysis leading up to an acquisition, how could things go wrong?

In general terms, there are many theories about why acquisitions fail. Three fundamental issues are:

- *Hubris*. Excessive self-confidence (owing to pride or arrogance). Without any basis of knowledge or experience, management believes that it knows best how to run an acquired business and that anticipated synergies will be readily available.
- *Winner's curse*. In a competitive-bidding situation, "Congratulations, you just won the bid." Now what? Even if there were synergies, the actual or potential competition of other bidders may have caused the winning bidder to pay too much.

TABLE 15-4

Comprehensive Valuation Model – 40% Premium
($ millions)

		Year 1 2011	Year 2 2012	Year 3 2013	Year 4 2014	Year 5 2015
Panel A – Valuation Assumptions						
Year 0 (2010) Revenue	$ 5,671.0					
Revenue growth		8.00%	12.50%	9.00%	5.50%	4.00%
Percent of sales						
Cost of sales (excluding depreciation)		52.50%	52.20%	51.50%	50.80%	50.80%
Depreciation (% of sales)		3.52%	3.74%	3.83%	3.91%	4.00%
Selling, marketing, and administrative		26.00%	26.50%	26.00%	25.50%	25.00%
Total operating expense		82.02%	82.44%	81.33%	80.21%	79.80%
Operating margin		17.98%	17.56%	18.67%	19.79%	20.20%
Tax rate		37.00%	37.00%	37.00%	37.00%	37.00%
Fixed capital investment		5.88%	3.46%	2.86%	2.84%	2.90%
Working capital (dis) investment		0.42%	0.16%	-0.13%	-0.30%	-0.34%
Terminal growth rate	2.00%					
Cost of capital	7.00%					

Panel B – Projected Free Cash Flow and Valuation

Net Revenue	$ 6,124.7	$ 6,890.3	$ 7,510.4	$ 7,923.5	$ 8,240.4
Cost of sales (excluding depreciation)	3,215.5	3,596.7	3,867.9	4,025.1	4,186.1
Depreciation	215.6	257.9	287.7	309.5	329.8
Selling, marketing, and administrative	1,592.4	1,825.9	1,952.7	2,020.5	2,060.1
Operating income	1,101.2	1,209.8	1,402.2	1,568.4	1,664.4
Taxes	407.4	447.6	518.8	580.3	615.8
After-Tax operating income	693.8	762.2	883.4	988.1	1,048.6
Percent of sales	11.3%	11.1%	11.8%	12.5%	12.7%
Depreciation	215.6	257.9	287.7	309.5	329.8
Working capital investment	25.5	11.0	(9.6)	(23.5)	(28.3)
Capital expenditures	(360.0)	(238.1)	(214.7)	(224.8)	(238.9)
Free cash flow	$ 574.9	$ 793.0	$ 946.7	$ 1,049.3	$ 1,111.2
Terminal value					22,668.5
Total cash flow	$ 574.9	$ 793.0	$ 946.7	$ 1,049.3	$ 23,779.7

PV of explicit cash flows	$ 3,595.5		Net cash adjustment	$ (942.7)
Terminal value	16,162.4		Equity value	$ 18,815.1
Enterprise value	$ 19,757.8		Value per share	$ 82.89

- *Agency issue*. Since managers own only a fraction of the ownership shares of a firm, managers may use mergers and acquisitions to increase firm size to increase their own salaries, bonuses, and perks.

These theories regard M&As as departures from rational decision making.

Sound Strategies for M&As

Empirical studies suggest that many mergers represent adjustments to industry shocks. If management responses are not made, the firms increasingly would have serious problems. Extending capabilities on a continuing basis is required by change forces. This judgment is supported by data on the use of multiple growth methods by companies and repeated use of many kinds of M&A activity year after year.

A framework for sound strategic M&A decisions includes a number of broad management principles:

1. Successful M&As must take place within the framework of a firm's strategic planning processes. M&As alone cannot create a strong firm. The acquiring firm must have strength in markets in which its core capabilities give it a competitive advantage.

2. To achieve higher returns to shareholders than its competitor firms requires an effective organization and the development of a strong multidimensional growth portfolio. The combination of internal programs and M&As is required for continued leadership.

3. Alternative growth techniques—internal (new products, geographical expansion, and support for existing products) and external (i.e., alliances, joint ventures, etc.)—should be considered along with M&As. Further, multiple growth initiatives (including multiple M&As) can take place simultaneously.

4. All segments of the firm must recognize the multiple strategies and make contributions to overall corporate results based on boundary-less interactions. A broadly administered executive compensation system should support all positive contributions.

5. The firm must have a group of officers that develops experience in all areas of the business and in different forms of M&As. These officers should be looked to for guidance.

6. The chairman and/or CEO needs to interact continuously to provide inspiration and executive development.

The moral of all of this is that M&As alone cannot do the job. But M&As can perform a critical role in developing an organization that delivers superior returns to shareholders. Firms that have completed the most M&A deals achieved the highest annual excess returns. Integration challenges increase exponentially with the size of targets. Finally, some observations have been made and are related directly to the M&A process.

Before placing a bid:

1. There needs to be business and economic logic to the deal. The logic should be easily articulated.

2. You need to understand what you are buying and the industry into which you are buying.

3. Establish the highest price that you are willing to pay. Unless new information is discovered, do not overbid. And if new but negative information is learned, reduce your maximum bid.

4. Challenge the overoptimism that exists in your valuation model, including the quickness with which the integration moves ahead and added costs that were not anticipated.

5. You do not want to start off with a value that is too high. You cannot negotiate down.

6. "Dress rehearse" the negotiations. Think about the key decision-makers needs throughout the process. Anticipate the target's resistance, and prepare to address and alleviate it.

7. Line up financing, and consider the full effects of taking on the burden of debt. Revisit the strategic financial plan (as in Chapter 6), and verify that you can handle the debt-service requirements. Do not take on too much short-term debt.

After the initial bid:

1. Do not let your CEO or chairperson enter the negotiations. It takes away a negotiating tactic of needing to "ask permission" from corporate to bid higher.

2. Check emotions at the door. Multiple bidders cause overpayment.

3. Before the deal is consummated, there needs to be a clear and specific integration plan with a detailed timeline. The first 100 days are critical to the success of the deal.

4. The plan needs to consider all stakeholders. Remember that everyone wants to know exactly how the acquisition will affect them. Employee productivity drops until this question is addressed.

After the deal is consummated:

1. Immediately begin work on executing your integration plan. Speed is of the essence.

2. Identify and work toward eliminating power struggles, culture clashes, or the attitude that "our way is better."

3. Communicate with all stakeholders. Communicated openly, truthfully, and often.

The bottom line: As you are considering buying a company, plan, execute, and communicate. Even if you adhere to all these suggestions, there are many unknowns and other variables that will challenge the successful implementation.

Day-to-Day Applications

While this chapter deals with lofty and strategic issues of M&As, it is important for all employees to understand the functioning of the M&A process. Everyone will be involved in an acquisition at some point in their career. It may not be at the prebid phase or negotiating table, but it will be in the integration phase. Everyone will be involved with and touched by an acquisition.

If you have an entrepreneurial inclination, you may find yourself sitting at a negotiating table one day. This is the same process that you would follow.

A former Hershey colleague left Hershey to buy a Hallmark card store. Before he put in a bid, he and I used a five-year DCF model based on assumptions derived from the store's past five years of tax returns. He estimated 5 percent growth, a 16 percent cost of capital, and no terminal value. He arrived at a value of $450,000.

He went off to negotiate. His opening bid was $200,000. The seller was offended and left the table. But the seller came back two weeks later, and my friend bought the business for $225,000, or half of what it was worth!

On top of it, he said that he was short of cash, so the seller financed the entire purchase at 4 percent (after tax). Over the five-year period, my friend never experienced less than a 10-percent increase over the same month from the prior year.

In short, he unraveled the secret to creating shareholder value in three steps:

1. Buy the business at a discount.
2. Finance it for less than your cost of capital.
3. Execute above and beyond your plan.

In his one foray directly into the M&A world with no competitive bidding, my friend provided a shining example of a successful acquisition.

SUMMARY

This chapter views business finance decisions in the dynamic framework of M&A activities. It describes the major change dynamics behind the worldwide growth in M&A activities. Growth opportunities can be enhanced by both internal and external strategies. Multiple growth strategies include licensing, alliances, joint ventures, minority investments, mergers, and acquisitions.

Large companies affected by external change factors often require large acquisitions to offset substantial declines in their core businesses. But combining two large firms involves difficult problems of cultural and organizational integration. Empirical evidence demonstrates that performance is superior when firms engage in a large number of relatively small acquisitions.

Merger activities reflect increasingly competitive pressures. In response to such pressures, firms seek to adjust to their changing environments by programs to augment their capabilities and resources. Regardless of whether a high percentage of M&A activities succeeds or fails, economic forces will continue to result in these forms of external investments. In addition, in such turbulent and changing economic and financial environments, numerous opportunities may present themselves.

M&As alone cannot create a superior firm from a weak one. M&As conducted over long periods effectively related to long-range qualitative and strategic financial plans based on strong core capabilities can help managers to achieve superior returns for shareholders.

Valuation uses the target's historical data as a starting point and ultimately includes forecasts. These forecasts include synergies that are expected to come about through the acquisition. Synergies accrue to both the target and the buyer and must be considered in total. The reliability of the forecasts depends heavily on a thorough analysis of the industry — on how it is affected by evolving changes in the economies of the world as well as by competitive strategies and tactics. Valuation requires a thorough understanding of the business economics and financial characteristics of the industry.

Precision is not possible, nor is it required. Recognizing that forecasts are subject to revision has positive aspects as well as challenges. It can be a valuable planning framework for guiding the firm to sound strategies and improved efficiencies. Valuation depends on identifying the critical factors that influence the levels of the value drivers. The DCF valuation approach provides a solid framework to help identify what is really important to the future value of the firm.

Sensitivity analysis identifies the critical factors for future success. Such an analysis helps to develop a business model for the firm with expectations of continuous reviews based on an effective information feedback system in the organization. It supports a flexible long-range planning process as a basis for short- and medium-term budgets. It requires in-depth understanding of the industry, its environment, and its competitors to guide strategies, policies, and decisions.

INDEX

ABOUT THE AUTHOR

Samuel C. Weaver earned a Ph.D. in Finance and Economics from Lehigh University in 1985. He joined the full-time faculty at Lehigh in January 1998 and was appointed Director MBA and Professional Education in 2003 through 2005. Prior to 1998, Dr. Weaver was the Lauer Adjunct Professor of Finance at Lehigh University (1986–1997) and the Director, Financial Planning and Analysis at Hershey Foods Corporation for almost 20 years. That position combined the theoretical with the pragmatic and involved the analysis of many different facets of finance including: mergers and acquisitions, divestiture assessment, strategic planning, performance measurement, operational plans, industry group comparisons, alternative financing evaluations, dividend policy, capital expenditure analysis, and cost of capital and divisional hurdle rates.

Dr. Weaver teaches Corporate Finance at the graduate and undergraduate levels at Lehigh University and has been honored as the outstanding MBA professor of the year on three occasions including 2011. He is a regular in Lehigh's Executive Education programs. His consulting practice includes both large (Fortune 200) and small clients from a variety of industries on numerous topics as well as customized educational workshops for companies, associations, and general audiences.

His research revolves around areas of corporate finance, valuation and investment analysis, financial performance measurement, and supply chain (working capital) management. In addition to *The Essentials of Financial Analysis*, Dr. Weaver is the coauthor of four other books. He, also, has published in numerous professional and academic journals, most recently, the *Journal of Applied Finance*, *Management Accounting Quarterly* winning the Lybrand award for distinguished paper, *The Handbook of Technology Management*, *Corporate Finance Review*, and *Careers in Finance*. He is an Associate Editor for five journals and has been featured in numerous textbooks discussing applications of financial concepts.

His work has been presented at numerous professional conferences including the Financial Management Association's (FMA) Annual Conference (1985–2011), Institute of Management Accountants Annual Conference (2010, 2011), the NACVA/IBA Consultants' Annual Conference (2011), and with many other professional and academic groups.

After serving the FMA in various capacities (Board of Directors and Board of Trustees), currently he represents the FMA in its association with the Institute of Management Accountants and serves as a member of the Board of Regents for the Certified Management Accounting designation.

Additionally, he is a Certified Management Accountant (CMA) and Certified Financial Manager (CFM).

CPSIA information can be obtained at www.ICGtesting.com
Printed in the USA
BVOW06*2347120116

432671BV00007B/146/P